Fold on dotted lines.

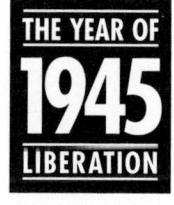

THE YEAR OF
1945
LIBERATION

SOURCEBOOK

UNITED STATES HOLOCAUST MEMORIAL MUSEUM SHOP

THE YEAR OF 1945 LIBERATION

SOURCEBOOK

Please take a moment to answer these questions.

1) ARE YOU A

Teacher of ❏ Middle School ❏ High School ❏ College/University

Student in ❏ Middle School ❏ High School ❏ College/University

Other *(Please explain)* _____

_____

2) HOW DID YOU LEARN OF THIS PUBLICATION?

❏ From the Museum Shop

    ❏ Promotional Mailing ❏ Catalog ❏ In-Shop Display

❏ From the Museum Newsletter

❏ From an Educational Conference

❏ From another Holocaust Organization *(Please identify)* _____

❏ From another Source *(Please identify)* _____

3) HOW WOULD YOU DESCRIBE THE LENGTH OF THIS BOOK?

❏ Too short ❏ Correct length ❏ Too long

4) IS THIS BOOK USEFUL TO YOU IN ITS PRESENT FORM?

❏ Yes ❏ No (Please elaborate below)

5) WHAT MATERIAL(S) WOULD YOU ADD TO OR DELETE FROM FUTURE EDITIONS?

_____

_____

_____

_____

6) IF YOU ARE A TEACHER, HOW WILL YOU USE THIS BOOK? _____

_____

_____

_____

COMMENTS _____

_____

_____

_____

_____

UNITED
STATES
HOLOCAUST
MEMORIAL
MUSEUM
SHOP

Please fold in thirds, tape closed, and mail.
Please do not use staples.

1945: THE YEAR OF LIBERATION

THE YEAR OF
1945
LIBERATION

UNITED STATES HOLOCAUST MEMORIAL MUSEUM
WASHINGTON, DC

A PROJECT OF THE UNITED STATES HOLOCAUST MEMORIAL COUNCIL

©1995 United States Holocaust Memorial Council

Library of Congress Catalog Card Number: 95-60761

ISBN: 0-89604-700-8

Project Director: Stephen Goodell

General Editor: Kevin Mahoney

Historian: Dr. Sybil Milton

Editorial Assistants: Patricia Heberer and Neal Guthrie

Research Assistants: Satu Haase-Webb, Earnest Latham III,
    Wendy Lower, and Claude Zullo

Photo Research: Anthony Sheehan

Copy Editor: Dr. Edward Phillips

Design: Marc Zaref Design, New York

Printing: Collins Lithographing, Inc.

Cover: Former prisoners at Dachau celebrate on April 30, 1945,
the day after the camp's liberation. (NARA)

Frontispiece: Simon Trampetter of Amsterdam cuts from the
coat of his Belgian friend Joseph Keller the Star of David badge
the Nazis ordered all Jews to wear to distinguish them from
the non-Jewish population. Kerkrade, The Netherlands, January
27, 1945. (NARA)

TABLE OF CONTENTS

MESSAGE FROM THE COUNCIL

The United States Holocaust Memorial Museum serves as this country's memorial to the millions of people murdered during the Holocaust, the state-sponsored, systematic persecution and annihilation of European Jews by Nazi Germany and its collaborators between 1933 and 1945. Chartered by a unanimous Act of Congress in 1980 and situated adjacent to the national Mall in Washington, D.C., the Museum strives to broaden public understanding of the history of the Holocaust and related issues, including those of contemporary significance, through exhibitions; research and publications; the collection and preservation of material evidence, art, and artifacts relating to the Holocaust; the distribution of educational materials and teacher resources; and a variety of public programming.

Congress mandated the United States Holocaust Memorial Museum to lead the nation in annual civic commemorations of the victims of the Holocaust, called Days of Remembrance. Jews were the Holocaust's primary victims —six million were murdered. Gypsies, the handicapped, and Poles were also targeted for destruction or decimation for racial, ethnic, or national reasons. Millions more, including homosexuals, Jehovah's Witnesses, Soviet prisoners of war, and political dissidents, also suffered grievous oppression and death under Nazi tyranny.

This year, the 50th anniversary of the end of World War II and the Holocaust, we recall 1945: when the collapsing Nazi regime sought to hide its atrocities by "death march" evacuations of concentration camps and the murder of those too weak to travel; when Allied Forces liberated the concentration camps and began the difficult revival of the survivors' lives; when justice was first applied against the perpetrators of the "Final Solution."

The Days of Remembrance give us all an opportunity to advance the Museum's primary mission to inform Americans about this unprecedented tragedy, to commemorate those who suffered, and to inspire visitors to contemplate the moral implications of their civic responsibilities.

United States Holocaust Memorial Council

Miles Lerman, *Chairman*
Ruth B. Mandel, *Vice Chair*

Days of Remembrance Committee

Benjamin Meed, *Chair*

ACKNOWLEDGMENTS

Compilation of materials for a book of this nature requires a wide range of expert skills and many institutional resources.

We thank Professor Henry Friedlander, Professor of History of the Department of Judaic Studies at Brooklyn College of the City University of New York, whose comprehensive introductory essay brings order and understanding to the disparate events of 1945.

We express our appreciation to the outside academic reviewers: Professor Richard Breitman, American University; Professor Leonard Dinnerstein, University of Arizona; Professor James Harris, University of Maryland, College Park; and Professor Gerhard Weinberg, University of North Carolina at Chapel Hill.

We thank Dr. Michael Berenbaum, Director, U.S. Holocaust Research Institute, as well as Genya Markon, Director, Photo Archives, and her staff; the USHMM Library staff, especially William Connelly, Steven Vitto, Holly Vorhies, and Sherry Schiebel; and Dr. Brewster Chamberlin, Director of Archives, and his staff, especially Dr. Robert Kesting and Jerry Simmons.

We appreciate the contributions of Robin Cookson of the Center for Captured German Records at the National Archives and David Haight of the Dwight D. Eisenhower Library.

We graciously thank the authors, publishers, and photographers who have granted permission to use their materials. Any requests for reproduction of these materials should be directed to the publishers.

Buchenwald 1945. Margaret Bourke-White,
Life Magazine, ©Time, Inc.

DARKNESS AND DAWN IN 1945:
THE NAZIS, THE ALLIES, AND THE SURVIVORS

by Henry Friedlander

On January 17, 1945, after the last evening roll call, the SS commandant ordered the evacuation of the giant Auschwitz-Birkenau concentration camp complex. At that time, there were still about 65,000 prisoners in the camp complex, including the Auschwitz central camp, the Birkenau extermination camp, and the Monowitz (Buna) camp with its satellite labor camps. Throughout January 18, large columns of prisoners were marched toward the west, guarded by heavily armed SS troops. They were forced to march through the snow and ice of the bitter winter weather, without winter clothing, blankets, or sufficient food. Some marched all the way to a camp that would receive them; others only to distant railroad junctions, where they were loaded into freight cars for a long westward trip without heat or provisions. And everywhere the SS guards shot those unable to continue the march, following Commandant Richard Baer's order to leave no prisoner behind. At 1:00 A.M. on January 19, the last large transport left Auschwitz. Only the seriously ill remained in the evacuated camp.[1] Thus started the final phase of the Nazi concentration camp universe, which ended only with the total defeat of Germany four months later.

Background

The year 1944 had marked the defeat, but not yet the collapse or surrender, of Nazi Germany. In the summer of 1944, the Red Army had driven the Germans from Soviet territory, most of the territory of the Baltic states, and the easternmost parts of Poland, while the western Allies had opened the "second front." On June 6 the Allies had crossed the British Channel to land on the coast of Normandy, and on August 15 they had also landed in France along the Mediterranean coast; Paris was liberated on August 25 and Brussels on September 3. By the end of the year, the Soviets had penetrated German territory, and the eastern front stretched along the Oder-Neisse rivers with a precarious German toehold along the Baltic from Königsberg to Danzig and Stettin. From the west, the Anglo-American forces had liberated France and the low countries, blocked the German counteroffensive in the Battle of the Bulge, and breached the territory of the German Reich.[2]

But defeat did not slow German genocide, and the Holocaust continued unabated. Under the cover of war, the Nazi regime had embarked on the physical extermination of human beings because they belonged to a biologically defined group; heredity had determined the selection of the victims. Mass murder began in late 1939, almost immediately after the start of World War II, with the killing of the handicapped. Determined to "cleanse the gene pool" of the German Volk, Adolf Hitler had ordered the murder of disabled Germans, euphemistically designated as "euthanasia," and had assigned the task to his private chancellery, who directed the killings through various front organizations located in Berlin at Tiergarten Street No. 4; this so-called euthanasia was thus known as the T4 killing operation. On the eastern fringes of Germany and in the incorporated areas of western Poland the handicapped were shot in mass executions. But in most of the German Reich, T4 developed a more sophisticated and technological method to select and kill the handicapped. In six killing centers equipped with gas chambers—Brandenburg, Grafeneck, Hartheim, Bernburg, Sonnenstein, and Hadamar—T4 perfected the assembly-line industrial production of mass murder. In August 1941, after at least 70,000 German nationals as well as several thousand handicapped Jews had been killed, public opinion forced Hitler to order a stop to the gassing. Nevertheless, decentralized killings of the handicapped continued by other means.[3]

The German invasion of the Soviet Union on June 22, 1941, provided the cover to expand the killing operation. The new targets for a so-called final solution were two groups of human beings the Nazis considered racial enemies: Jews and Gypsies. At first mass shooting was the killing method used, as mobile units of the German security police and SS security service, the so-called *Einsatzgruppen*, backed by units of the uniformed German police and the Waffen SS, turned the Baltic states and the occupied Soviet Union into a vast killing field.[4] But soon the Germans rationalized the killings, replacing mass shooting with the T4 technique in specially constructed killing centers.[5] The first one, opened in December 1941, was the Chelmno killing center in western Poland. Designed for the murder of Jews and Gypsies in the incorporated Wartheland, Chelmno was staffed by a police commando that in 1940 had killed the handicapped in local state hospitals.[6] In 1942 three much larger killing centers opened in eastern Poland at Belzec, Sobibor, and Treblinka. There, in an enterprise known as Operation Reinhard, German T4 operatives in SS uniform, aided by Ukrainian auxiliaries, murdered the Jews of Poland as well as Jews and Gypsies sent there from Germany, western Europe, and the Soviet Union.[7]

During 1942 and 1943, the Germans had succeeded in killing most of the Jews in Poland, the Baltic states, and the occupied Soviet Union; in addition, large numbers of Jews deported from Germany and the countries of the West had also been killed. Chelmno had ceased operation in 1943 and reopened much later for only the month of July 1944. By the end of 1943, the three killing centers of Operation Reinhard had definitely closed, two of them—Sobibor and Treblinka—after revolts by Jewish prisoners. Most ghettos in the east had been eradicated—the one in Warsaw after a spectacular rebellion—and their inhabitants had been murdered in the killing centers. In the fall of 1943, Jews held in forced labor camps had also been killed; those in the camps of eastern Poland were shot in a few days of November during an operation the SS called "harvest festival." Most of the remaining ghettos and labor camps had been transformed into concentration camps.[8]

After Chelmno, Belzec, Sobibor, and Treblinka had closed in late 1943, only the killing centers operating in the concentration camps of Majdanek and Auschwitz continued to function. While the Majdanek killing operation remained relatively small, the one in Auschwitz—located in Birkenau, also known as Auschwitz II—assumed giant proportions. Situated in Upper Silesia with good railroad connections, Auschwitz-Birkenau served as the final destination of most Jews and Gypsies deported to the East from central, western, and southern Europe.[9]

By 1944, however, the killings of the previous years had substantially reduced the pool from which victims could be selected. Transports from Polish ghettos and camps as well as various European countries continued to arrive in 1944, but the number of Jews in those places was small and shrinking; in some countries, such as France, the speed of deportations depended on cooperation from local authorities. But large numbers of Jews within easy reach of German power could be found in two places: Hungary and the Lodz ghetto. The large Hungarian Jewish community, numbering hundreds of thousands, had survived throughout the war and was therefore an enticing target; the Lodz ghetto, which had been decimated during 1942, nevertheless still housed about 70,000 Jews.[10]

In May 1944, transports of Hungarian Jews arrived in Auschwitz, and most of them were immediately killed in the Birkenau gas chambers. By the time Hungarian transports stopped in early July 1944, almost half a million human beings had been murdered. Early in July, the SS dissolved the so-called family camp in Birkenau, established in September 1943 for German, Austrian, and Czech Jews deported from Theresienstadt, killing all those who had survived previous selections for the gas chambers and had not been sent for labor to other camps.[11] On August 2, 1944, the SS gassed all Gypsies still held in Auschwitz; those who had survived the earlier deportations and killings had been sent to Auschwitz from Germany, Austria, and

other countries, and, except for those transferred to other camps, had been concentrated in the so-called Gypsy camp at Birkenau.[12] During August and early September 1944, the SS deported the remaining Jews of the Lodz ghetto to Auschwitz; most of them perished in the Birkenau gas chambers.[13] And throughout the summer and fall of 1944, occasional transports with Jews arrived from various European countries, including France, Belgium, the Netherlands, Greece, and Italy; thus, on September 5, 1944, more than one thousand Jews arrived from the Dutch transit camp Westerbork, including the family of Anne Frank.[14]

During September 1944, the number of transports arriving in Auschwitz decreased, and the SS readied itself to kill the members of the Jewish *Sonderkommando* working in the four Birkenau crematoria buildings that contained the gas chambers. On October 7, 1944, the *Sonderkommando* revolted and destroyed one of the crematoria before their uprising was suppressed.[15] Still, the remaining crematoria continued to operate and the SS continued to kill thousands of Jews and hundreds of Gypsies selected from the camp population and from arriving transports.[16] On November 2, 1944, the gassings stopped, and shortly thereafter the SS, anxious to destroy the most conspicuous evidence of their crimes, started to dismantle the remaining crematoria; the transport of more than 2,000 Jews that arrived on October 30 from Theresienstadt was apparently the last one murdered in the Birkenau gas chambers.[17]

The German concentration camp system had been drastically transformed during the year 1944.[18] Although war and conquest since 1940 had dramatically increased the number of camps and prisoners, transformed all prisoners into slave laborers, and enriched the SS, much of this expansion had taken place outside the concentration camp system. During 1942 and 1943, vast numbers of Jews were used by the SS in eastern Europe as slave laborers in ghettos and in so-called forced labor camps totally outside the concentration camp system.[19] In 1942, as part of the drive to make the German Reich *judenfrei*, the SS had even transferred to the east almost all Jews held in concentration camps on German soil. This changed radically in 1944.

The few remaining labor camps had been absorbed into the concentration camp system; some became central camps as, for example, Plaszow near Cracow and Kaiserwald in Riga, while others were attached as satellites to existing central camps as, for example, Radom to Majdanek.[20] A growing number of Jews were thus absorbed into the camp system in the east, filling the camps and satellites, especially the string of labor camps together known as Auschwitz III. At the same time, the German war economy's need for labor increased enormously, a need the importation of slave labor from occupied countries, both east and west, no longer fully satisfied. The SS increased enormously the number of concentration camp prisoners it supplied to German factories, reaping profits for both SS and industry. Wherever factories needed workers, the SS set up satellite camps attached to one of the main concentration camps. At the end of 1944, these satellites covered the German Reich; hundreds of such camps—varying in size from a few hundred to thousands of prisoners—were attached to each central camp.[21]

The growing need for workers, as well as the advance of the Red Army in the east, forced the SS to reverse its 1942 policy that neither Jews nor Gypsies should remain on German soil or even in camps located on German soil. In May 1944, Hitler ordered that even Jewish prisoners should be used as labor in underground aircraft factories.[22] Starting in the summer of 1944, Jewish prisoners from the satellite camps in the east were transferred to satellite camps inside Germany. And when transports of Jews arrived in Auschwitz from Hungary, Lodz, and elsewhere, those not immediately sent to the gas chambers were kept in Birkenau—without registration and without receiving numbers—as so-called "Jews on deposit," for later transfer as slave labor to satellite camps inside Germany.[23] Eventually, Jews made up almost one-third of all concentration camp prisoners within the shrinking borders of the German Reich; they were the overwhelming majority of prisoners in the satellite camps, but only one minority among prisoners in the central camps.

The Final Phase

The evacuation of Auschwitz in early January 1945 was only the first of many such evacuations. These evacuations were usually carried out with the utmost brutality and in total disregard of the welfare of prisoners and inevitably led to overcrowding in all remaining camps. In the concentration camp system, prisoners were therefore "living in conditions which at best were ceasing to be tolerable and at worst were those of charnel houses of the living dead."[24]

The command decision that governed the last phase of the camp system was based on events in the summer of 1944. At that time, the Red Army occupied eastern Poland and on July 24, 1944, liberated the Lublin concentration camp known as Majdanek. Although the SS attempted to evacuate all prisoners, the rapid advance of Soviet troops made total evacuation impossible, thus preventing the SS from destroying the camp, killing all prisoners, and escaping in time.

The worldwide publicity about the German crimes committed at Majdanek and the desire to preclude any future revelations undoubtedly led to Hitler's and Himmler's determination to prevent the liberation of intact camps and living prisoners. On July 21, 1944, the Commander (*Befehlshaber*) of the Security Police and SS Security Service in the General Government of Poland thus ordered that "the liberation of prisoners and Jews by the enemy, be it the Polish underground or the Red Army, must be avoided," adding that "under no circumstances must they fall into the enemy's hands alive."[25]

In October or November 1944, the exact date is not certain, Himmler ordered a stop to the automatic mass murder of Jews and Gypsies in the giant gassing facilities of the eastern camps. Mass death thereafter took a different form.[26] On January 15, 1945, just before Auschwitz was evacuated, the concentration camps held 714,211 prisoners: 511,537 men and 202,674 women. At least one-third of these prisoners died during the four months that remained before the liberation of all camps.[27]

Even after fifty years of research, it is virtually impossible to reconstruct the exact fate of prisoners during those last months. As the Allied armies advanced and the territory of the German Reich continued to shrink, the chaos that overwhelmed Germany also engulfed the concentration camp system. Railroad lines and highways were filled with retreating German troops, relocating foreign workers, as well as vast numbers of German civilians fleeing from the advancing Soviet troops. Allied control of the air over Germany added to the chaos, as American and British planes not only continued their saturation bombing of German cities but also strafed trains, trucks, and marching columns at will.

Evacuated concentration camp prisoners had to compete with this massive population transfer. Trains were difficult to obtain; even closed freight cars were hard to find, and most prisoners traveled in open cars through snow and rain. As these trains had the lowest priority, they moved slowly, were repeatedly diverted, and often left standing until all other rail traffic had passed. Those forced to march could not use the main highways, which were crowded with military and civilian traffic, but had to use secondary roads, following a circuitous course. At night the prisoners were squeezed into barns or even forced to make camp on an open field. Without adequate food or water, the prisoners, who obviously had not been in good physical health at the start, died in large numbers during these evacuations, and the trains often arrived at their destination with a majority of prisoners either dead or dying. Among the marching columns, prisoners unable to keep up the fast pace set by their SS guards simply fell and died. Unwilling to leave the dying behind, the SS shot every prisoner unable to continue, and dead bodies marked the path of those death marches.

The chaotic conditions of the final months taxed the camp administrative system beyond endurance, and vaunted German organization and efficiency collapsed. From the first experimental gassing of handicapped Germans in Brandenburg during the winter of 1939–40 to the massive gassings of Jews and Gypsies in Birkenau during the summer and fall of 1944, German organization functioned smoothly, and the Nazi killers devised and followed schedules that selected, transported, and murdered their victims with virtually no glitches. But in the winter of 1944–45, there was no master plan for the evacuation of camps, trains no longer ran on time, and the command structure no longer functioned.

The absence of a master plan did not mean that Himmler and his SS associates did not issue directives on what to do about the concentration camps. But directives outlining policy goals had always depended on a functioning chain of command and on enthusiastic initiatives from mid-level administrators. That is how the killings of the war years

Prisoners on a forced evacuation from Dachau concentration camp, secretly photographed by a German civilian, pass through a Bavarian village in late April 1945.
(Dachau Memorial Museum)

had worked. In 1945, however, the chain of command disintegrated as Germany became a combat zone. The Reich Leader SS, Heinrich Himmler, and the SS central offices, Ernst Kaltenbrunner's Central Office for Reich Security (RSHA) and Oswald Pohl's Central Office for Economy and Administration (WVHA), in part lost their absolute oversight as the advancing fronts forced them to move their staffs and seek safety for themselves. This communication breakdown involved also Department D of the WVHA, the Inspectorate of the Concentration Camps. Although general directives continued to reach them, the concentration camps were left to shift for themselves concerning implementation. At the end, they were subject to orders not only from distant central offices, but also from local SS and Nazi party functionaries.

At the start of 1945, there still remained eleven central concentration camps on territory controlled by Germany: Auschwitz, Bergen-Belsen, Buchenwald, Dachau, Dora-Mittelbau, Flossenbürg, Gross-Rosen, Neuengamme, Ravensbrück, Sachsenhausen, and Stutthof. The fate of their prisoners rested largely in the hands of each camp commandant, who was torn between orders from his superiors, expectations of his subordinates, and his own self-interest. Each of these camps except Bergen-Belsen, also oversaw numerous satellite camps, holding vast numbers of mostly Jewish prisoners. The commandant of each satellite, usually a non-commissioned or junior officer, was often also left on his own and thus equally torn between competing demands. At the end, many of these satellite camps were evacuated to the central camp. But other satellite camps, especially those located some distance from the central camp, followed their own evacuation routes to other central

or satellite camps. The rank and file SS soldiers, who guarded the evacuated prisoners and did the killing, were no longer the disciplined ideological soldiers of the prewar years. They included older men drafted into the SS in the final months, seasoned killers from the extermination camps, and a motley crew of ethnic Germans. They no longer believed in final victory and were torn between following orders and saving their own skin.[28]

As the territory of the German Reich continued to contract, evacuation trains and marches moved from east to west to escape the Red Army, while other evacuations moved from west to east to escape American and British armies. Most had to follow circuitous routes toward the north or the south. Often trains and marches crossed each other or reversed direction, sometimes moving in a giant circle.

The camps located some distance from the borders of the German Reich were evacuated first. Camps in occupied Poland, including Lublin-Majdanek, and in the Baltic, including Riga-Kaiserwald, had already been evacuated in late 1944; prisoners from Polish camps were evacuated to Auschwitz and those from Baltic camps to Stutthof. Late in 1944, the westernmost camp, Natzweiler (Struthof) in Alsace, also had to be evacuated. As 1944 ended, the camps located outside the borders of the Reich had been abandoned. In January and February 1945, the three central camps on Germany's eastern border—Auschwitz in Upper Silesia, Gross-Rosen in Lower Silesia, and Stutthof near Danzig—and their various satellite camps were themselves evacuated.

The evacuation of Auschwitz and the two other eastern camps illustrates the confusion and the failure to implement directives. Orders to evacuate were issued too late to assure an orderly retreat. At Auschwitz, the SS was unable totally to destroy the evidence of its crimes. Moreover, contrary to Himmler's orders, prisoners physically unable to undertake the march west were left behind. Although in some places the SS killed all sick prisoners and burned the camp before departing, in most camps this was not done. Still, the overwhelming majority of prisoners were forced to join the evacuation trains or forced marches. Large numbers were murdered on the way; the rest reached new camps totally exhausted. A small number was liberated by Soviet troops because their evacuation march did not move fast enough. An even smaller number of prisoners was able to escape.[29] The accounts of two young Jewish women can serve as an example.

Gertrude Schneider, later an administrator at the City University of New York, was deported as a teenager from Vienna to Latvia and was first incarcerated in the Riga ghetto and then in the Riga-Kaiserwald camp. In August 1944, she was evacuated from Riga by sea to the Stutthof concentration camp. That camp had become a collection point not only for Jewish women from the Baltic but also for Hungarian Jewish women from Auschwitz. The weak died at Stutthof or were killed in its small gas chamber. The stronger, and the luckier, were selected for labor in one of the Stutthof satellite camps. Together with her mother and sister, Schneider was assigned to Sophienwalde, a satellite not far from the central camp, where the women were to build a military road.

On February 10, 1945, as Soviet troops approached from the east, the Sophienwalde satellite camp was evacuated. Those able to walk—approximately 400 women—were marched away, while the weak who remained behind were murdered. No one was shot on the march, but those unable to march were left behind to die. On February 17, after covering about 50 miles, 347 women arrived at a small camp in Gotentov, which served as a collection point for various transports evacuated from Stutthof. The camp was overcrowded, had no sanitary facilities, and was virtually without food. On March 9, this camp was also evacuated. Those unable to walk were left behind but not shot; those unable to keep up were shot on the road. After marching for a day and a night, the women were put into a barn, where they were liberated by the Red Army. Schneider and about 250 women from Sophienwalde had thus been liberated.[30]

Ruth Klüger, later a professor at the University of California, also was deported from Vienna, first to the Theresienstadt ghetto and then to Auschwitz.[31] Selected for labor from the Theresienstadt family camp at Birkenau, she and her mother were sent to Christianstadt, a satellite of the Gross-Rosen concentration camp, where Jewish women did heavy manual labor with little food during the winter of 1944–45. In early January 1945, the women could hear the thunder of the Soviet guns. All work stopped at the satellite camp, and supply of food became constantly smaller; at roll call, an SS officer taunted the prisoners by shouting: "Roosevelt can't help you now (*Der Roosevelt, der kann euch gar nicht helfen*)."[32] Soon marching prisoners from

other Gross-Rosen satellite camps arrived, stayed for the night, and then continued to the west.

Eventually, the Christianstadt satellite was also evacuated. Klüger remembered that "these were the early February days of 1945. It was still very cold, and we dragged ourselves along country roads and through villages, slowly and always on the edge of total exhaustion."[33] At night they were squeezed into barns. On the second evening, during the chaos that accompanied the end of the daily march, Klüger with her mother and a teenage friend simply walked away. They submerged in the flood of German civilian refugees fleeing toward the west. Eventually, they obtained fraudulent refugee papers from a sympathetic Protestant minister and simply boarded an evacuation train to Bavaria, where they remained, masquerading as German civilian refugees until their liberation by American troops.[34] This unusual escape required audacity, luck, and the linguistic ability to pass as German. But this escape route was open only for women, because male prisoners posing as Germans would have been considered deserters.

Those prisoners who survived evacuation from the eastern camps were dumped into vastly overcrowded camps inside the Reich. In these camps, most newcomers were crowded into the least desirable sections of the receiving camps; usually they were the first to be again evacuated. For example, this was the case in Buchenwald, where the arriving prisoners—mostly Jews—were put into the so-called Little Camp, a section of the camp with its own barbed wire forming a camp within the camp. In 1945 the Little Camp—just like the first such camp established in 1938 to hold the Jews rounded up after the *Kristallnacht* pogrom—was totally overcrowded, lacked adequate sanitary facilities, and received only a minimum of food.[35]

Bergen-Belsen was the most notorious receiving camp.[36] Originally established in spring 1943, it served as a detention camp for selected groups of Jews who might be used in an exchange for Germans interned by the Allies, as well as for Jews selected because they were considered prominent. The first group consisted of several thousand Polish Jews holding immigration papers from some Latin American country. The next group consisted of more than 400 Jews from Salonika and about 200 from Athens, a few functionaries but mostly persons considered Spanish or Portuguese nationals. The third and largest group arrived in late 1943 and the first nine months of 1944 and consisted of several thousand Jews from the Netherlands who held dual citizenship, had a place on immigration lists for Palestine, possessed immigration papers for Latin America, or were prominent persons with connections in enemy countries. Finally, during 1944 smaller groups holding foreign passports arrived, including Jews from France, Yugoslavia, Albania, North Africa, France, Hungary, and Theresienstadt.[37]

The camp's purpose and prison population resembled the so-called model ghetto of Theresienstadt. But Bergen-Belsen, which had previously been a camp for Soviet prisoners of war, did not have the infrastructure to support large numbers of prisoners. Barracks were poorly constructed, roads were unfinished, and sanitary facilities were virtually non-existent. Almost none of the so-called exchange Jews was ever exchanged. The overwhelming majority of the Polish Jews were deported to Auschwitz and killed; most of the others remained in the camp until April 1945, when they were evacuated toward Theresienstadt. But only a few reached foreign countries—Spain, Turkey, Palestine, and Switzerland—as part of an exchange or later as part of Himmler's attempt to ingratiate himself with the Allies.[38]

The character of Bergen-Belsen changed radically in late 1944. Because this camp for Jews destined for exchange had been placed under the authority of the WVHA, it was soon also used for small groups of concentration camp prisoners. The first group of such prisoners—one thousand from Dora-Mittelbau suffering from tuberculosis—arrived in March 1944, and they were housed in an area separate from the exchange Jews. Soon a regular concentration camp existed side by side with the detention camp at Bergen-Belsen. During 1944, further transports of tubercular and other so-called invalid prisoners arrived from Dora and other concentration camps. Bergen-Belsen, which had no satellite camps or factories, was thus an ideal place to dump prisoners who were not expected to do labor. The facilities, however, were not designed to cure those prisoners, and the use of the term "convalescence camp" by WVHA was an example of total SS cynicism. Harsh treatment, absence of physicians and medicines, inadequate housing and clothing, and poor food ensured that most of them would perish.

As the camps in the east, especially Auschwitz, were evacuated, the number of transports arriving in Bergen-Belsen increased dramatically. Although officially those evacuated to the Bergen-Belsen camp were designated as prisoners too ill to work, their selection had followed the arbitrary manner usual in the camps; in composition and condition these prisoners did not differ from those evacuated to other camps. Whatever their condition prior to evacuation, however, the ordeal of the transport and the severity of the camp soon reduced them to skeletons. Overcrowding, inadequate housing, insufficient food, limited drinking water, and few latrines produced epidemics that took a terrible toll. Although tens of thousands died during spring 1945, about 55,000 prisoners filled this overcrowded camp at the time of its liberation, with about one-half requiring intensive hospital care.

The SS administration took no steps to improve those terrible conditions. In December 1944, the WVHA appointed SS Captain (Hauptsturmführer) Josef Kramer as commandant of Bergen-Belsen. Kramer, the last commandant of the Birkenau extermination camp, brought with him SS physicians, administrators, male and female guards who had served with him in Birkenau and were also posted to the west as Auschwitz was evacuated. Obviously, these men and women, trained to regard prisoners—especially Jews, Gypsies, and others considered racially inferior—as un-

worthy of any consideration or even life, did nothing to prevent mass death at Bergen-Belsen. Although conditions were marginal, the central SS offices demanded the admission of more prisoners without providing any help; enough supplies were available to save thousands if the SS had wanted to do so.[39]

Rescue Attempts

As the Allied armies advanced into Germany and chaos began to engulf the Third Reich, the men who ran the concentration camp system had to decide how to dispose of camps and prisoners. At the top stood the Reich Leader SS Heinrich Himmler, but below him the responsibility rested with a variety of Nazi leaders occupying different offices and holding different powers. One group included SS General Oswald Pohl, the chief of the WVHA, and his associates, especially the Inspectorate of the Concentration Camps, headed by SS General Richard Glücks. Another group included SS General Ernst Kaltenbrunner, the chief of the RSHA, and his associates, especially SS General Heinrich Müller, chief of the Gestapo, and SS Lieutenant Colonel (Obersturmbannführer) Adolf Eichmann, head of the Gestapo's Jewish office. A third group included local SS and Police Leaders, responsible for all SS and police units as well as the concentration camps in a war zone, and often also the local Nazi party leaders. Theoretically, each group acted in concert under Himmler's orders, but in reality they often pursued contradictory policies as the command structure began to dissolve.

Himmler and other SS functionaries knew that the Allies considered them war criminals for their direction of mass murder and, as the Third Reich began to collapse, they looked for ways to evade retribution. Because they controlled the fate of hundreds of thousands of prisoners, especially Jews, they deluded themselves that they could trade Jewish lives and the lives of other prisoners for their own rehabilitation. Himmler and his henchmen apparently believed that trading human beings might make them acceptable as postwar German leaders. They wanted to negotiate with the Allies, especially the Americans, and they searched for intermediaries to arrange such deals. Misled by their own propaganda, they turned to Jewish agencies because they believed that the Jews of the world had the power to open the door to negotiations. This was never true; the Jews in Allied countries did not possess such influence. Moreover, Jewish organizations would never have agreed to political concessions for SS killers. Still, Jewish representatives did agree to talk and were perfectly willing to promise what they knew would never be delivered.

Himmler's attempt to bargain started during the deportation of the Hungarian Jews in spring 1944. The negotiations, approved by Himmler, involved SS Colonel (Standartenführer) Kurt Becher, Himmler's economic representative in Hungary, as well as Eichmann and his people, and included proposals to trade Jews for trucks, supplies, or foreign currency, resulting in the failed Joel Brand mission.[40] After the first failure, Becher continued to pursue negotiations, and did so with Himmler's approval. Becher's new contacts were Saly Mayer, a leader of the Swiss Jewish community who represented the American Jewish Joint Distribution Committee (AJJDC), and Roswell D. McClelland, the representative of the War Refugee Board in Switzerland. Discussions during fall and winter 1944 covered various aspects of a supposed trade of Jews for foreign currency, and Himmler did permit 1,684 Hungarian "exchange" Jews from Bergen-Belsen to leave for Switzerland. In addition, Himmler ordered a stop to the gassings at Auschwitz.

At the same time, Himmler pursued different talks with other negotiators through SS General Walter Schellenberg, who headed foreign intelligence for the SS as chief of Office VI in the RSHA. In open competition with Becher, Schellenberg dealt with Jean-Marie Musy, a former president of the Swiss Federal Council who had been sympathetic to the Nazis. Musy fronted for Isaac and Recha Sternbuch, who headed an orthodox Jewish relief organization tied to the Va'ad ha-Hatzalah, the rescue committee created by the Union of Orthodox Rabbis of the United States and Canada. Musy knew Himmler and met with him several times. In a deal similar to the one concluded with Mayer, Himmler permitted twelve hundred Jews from Theresienstadt to enter Switzerland. Himmler received favorable publicity in the Swiss press, which had been one of the conditions of the exchange. But Hitler was informed about the trade and ordered Himmler to stop all further deals. For the moment Himmler obeyed.[41]

The deals with Mayer and Musy produced few results. Himmler had obtained foreign currency and some goods, but no opening to the Allies. In turn, Himmler had released several thousand Jews from Theresienstadt and Bergen-Belsen and had also ordered a stop to the gassing. But he had only released relatively presentable Jews who could not report about Auschwitz on the basis of personal experience; Jews actually in the concentration camps had not been freed. And the stop to the gassing was only a gesture; the approach of the Red Army and the shrinking borders of the Reich had made continued large-scale gassing virtually impossible. But even if the negotiations had yielded no immediate major results, they set the stage for further talks. And those talks would center on the central issue: the deliverance of all concentration camp prisoners.

The approach came from two separate directions.[42] Professor Karl Burckhardt, president of the International Red Cross, in late January approached the German Foreign Ministry with a plan to provide aid to the prisoners in the concentration camps but at first was unable to accomplish anything. The other approach came from Sweden in February. Count Folke Bernadotte, representing the Swedish Red Cross with the tacit approval of the Swedish government, presented to Himmler a proposal to aid Scandinavian concentration camp prisoners.[43] Himmler received this proposal with some interest, as his positive view of Scandin-avians predisposed him to accept Bernadotte's approach. Of course, Himmler also believed that cooperation with the Swedes would provide an opening to the West. In March, Ernst Kaltenbrunner, who had been excluded from the negotiations with Bernadotte, decided to forge his own link to the West by dealing with Burckhardt, thus granting the Swiss Red Cross access to some camps and some prisoners.[44]

Neither Bernadotte nor Burckhardt accomplished much, even after Himmler and Kaltenbrunner started to tolerate their activities. Rapidly deteriorating conditions made all relief difficult, while the dissolving command structure left local authorities to act on their own. The Red Cross representatives, both Swiss and Swedish, had to finance and organize their own relief transport, and they also had to engage in lengthy negotiations with local satraps. Both distributed Red Cross packages, and some of these did reach the prisoners. Both rescued a limited number of prisoners, mostly from Scandinavia and western Europe, but very few Jews. And both attempted to persuade the SS to stop evacuations and to hand over the camps to the Allies. After all, this was the most important issue. We cannot know how many lives their intervention saved, but it appears that their efforts met with only limited success.

These deals made by Himmler and Kaltenbrunner with representatives of the Swiss and Swedish Red Cross superseded but did not totally end negotiations with Jewish representatives. With his Swedish masseur, Felix Kersten, serving as intermediary, Himmler also opened talks with Hillel Storch, representative of the World Jewish Congress in Stockholm. In April, Himmler issued an invitation to a meeting inside Germany. As a Jewish refugee from Latvia, Storch decided not to make the journey and instead sent his associate, Norbert Masur, a native-born Swede. The meeting between Himmler and Masur at Kersten's German farm on April 21 was probably the most bizarre encounter of World War II. Storch and Masur had hoped to gain freedom, or at least protection, for all Jewish concentration camp prisoners, while Himmler, still vacillating between obedience to Hitler and self-preservation, promised only to include Jewish women when releasing non-Jewish women from Ravensbrück.[45]

In the end, however, the survival of prisoners depended mostly on the caprice of the SS on the scene and, of course, on the arrival of Allied troops. The survivors owed their lives to German chaos and Allied victory. On the other side, Himmler and Kaltenbrunner gained little. Obviously, the Allies never accepted them as negotiating partners, and their pathetic last-minute gestures did not help them escape retribution.

Liberation

In the spring of 1945, Allied forces penetrated deep into Germany. On April 25, American and Soviet troops met at the Elbe river. On April 30, Adolf Hitler committed suicide in his Berlin underground hideout, after marrying Eva Braun and naming Admiral Karl Dönitz as his successor. Finally, on May 7 General Alfred Jodl signed Germany's unconditional surrender at Reims; the surrender ceremony was repeated two days later in Berlin. On May 8, the Allied nations celebrated V-E Day; Europe had been liberated.[46]

For the prisoners in the Nazi camps, liberation did not occur in one place or at one time. And for many it did not come at all. The evacuation of the Auschwitz camp complex, including Auschwitz, Birkenau, and Monowitz, had been completed in the early-morning hours of January 19, but thousands of prisoners unable to walk had been left behind. For eight days the remaining Auschwitz prisoners had to shift for themselves, abandoned but not yet liberated. Without food and medicine in unheated barracks, large numbers of incapacitated prisoners died before liberation. Those still able to move foraged for supplies needed for survival—food, blankets, wood—in the desolate winter landscape.[47]

The Germans did not completely abandon the Auschwitz complex. German troops defended the area against attacking Soviet forces, and small groups of SS continued to enter the camp. On January 19, the local SS leader in Breslau issued orders to kill the incapacitated prisoners who had been left behind. But the remaining SS units did not carry out these orders because they no longer had the personnel, organization, and resolve to do so. Fearful of capture by Soviet forces, they found their own escape more important than the killing of prisoners.[48] Still, marauding SS units continued to kill. On January 20, an SS unit dynamited the already demolished crematoria two and three and also found time to shoot about 200 Jewish women in Birkenau.[49] But on January 25, when one SS unit collected about 350 Jewish prisoners in Birkenau and started to shoot them, another arriving group of SS men persuaded them to leave the camp, and most of the prisoners returned to their barracks.[50] Finally, on January 29, the Red Army liberated Auschwitz. They found about seven thousand ill prisoners: 1,200 in Auschwitz, 5,800 in Birkenau, and 600 in Monowitz.[51]

In the following months, evacuations continued regardless of any promises made to neutrals by Himmler and his associates; there is some evidence that Himmler's vacillation and his fear of offending Hitler led the Reich Leader SS to issue conflicting orders, and that one of those was an order to let no living prisoners fall into Allied hands.[52] As the Allied armies advanced into Germany, prisoners were evacuated from virtually every camp and every satellite, away from enemy forces approaching from the east and from the west, and "soon cattle cars and marching columns crisscrossed the shrinking territory of the Third Reich."[53] These evacuations cost tens of thousands of prisoners their lives from exhaustion, exposure, starvation, and disease. In addition, the SS physically murdered thousands of prisoners.

Prisoners were killed during all evacuations, whether in trains both covered and open or on forced marches. The evacuations on foot have generally been described as "death marches," although evacuations by train also resulted in mass death. On trains prisoners died mostly from exposure, dehydration, and starvation, but some also from attacks by Allied planes. Some were murdered by their SS guards. One small example can serve as an illustration. Women prisoners were evacuated by train from Porta Westfalica, a satellite camp of Neuengamme; as the train meandered through northern and eastern Germany, it took three weeks to cover the short distance to Hamburg. Each boxcar had between 150 and 190 female prisoners as well as one SS female guard. There was a severe shortage of food, and space was so limited that some women had to stand so that the others could sit. During one air attack, one of the prisoners screamed in panic and, when her fellow prisoners could not quiet her, the SS female guard killed her.[54]

Forced marches claimed many victims. Some of these marches took weeks, as the SS evaded Allied troops by forcing prisoners to drag themselves mile after mile toward an elusive destination. For example, between three and four hundred prisoners from Sonneberg, a Thuringian satellite of Buchenwald, were evacuated on April 2 and marched toward the Sudetenland. Over circuitous roads, the march covered between nine and twelve miles per day. Finally, on May 7, American troops liberated the marching columns.[55] Prisoners unable to continue were commonly shot and left alongside the road, usually in an arbitrary manner. A bureaucratic procedure employed on one march of one thousand prisoners was somewhat unusual: on a march to Bergen-Belsen of prisoners from Hanover-Stöcken, a satellite of Neuengamme, prisoners were shot only after the accompanying SS physician had certified inability to continue walking.[56]

It is impossible to reconstruct every evacuation from every satellite camp, and thus this account can only sketch the course of these deadly evacuations from major camps, focusing on camps that were almost completely emptied: Ravensbrück, Sachsenhausen, Dora-Mittelbau, and Flossenbürg.

The evacuation of female prisoners started at Ravensbrück in early March, when about 2,000 women were transferred to Mauthausen by train. Overcrowding, little food, and the shortage of water claimed many lives during the seven-day journey. At the same time, thousands of women evacuated from the satellites arrived at Ravensbrück, creating congestion and chaos in the central camp. Although the Bernadotte mission moved Scandinavian and French women prisoners from Ravensbrück to Sweden under the agreement reached with Himmler, evacuations continued during April, until the entire camp was cleared on April 27–28. About 15,000 women were driven on foot toward the west until they were overtaken by Soviet troops. Several thousand ill female prisoners were left in Ravensbrück to be liberated on April 30 by the Red Army.[57]

The evacuation of prisoners started in Sachsenhausen on April 20 on orders of SS General Glücks, whose Inspectorate was located just outside the camp. Plans to load the

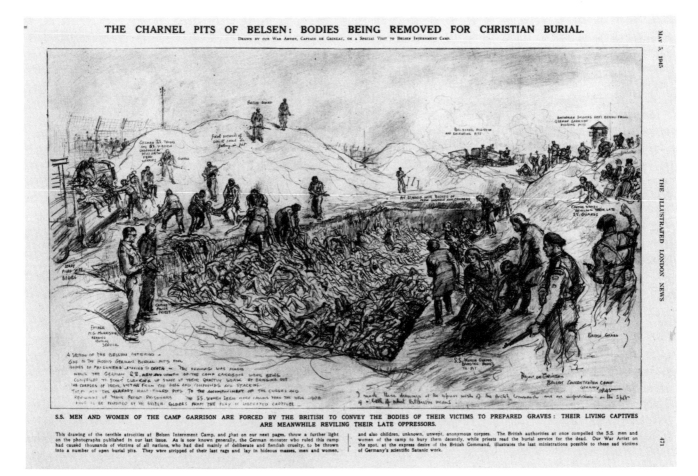

A scene from the liberation of Bergen-Belsen concentration camp that appeared in the May 5, 1945, issue of the *Illustrated London News.* (Illustrated London News)

prisoners on barges and to drown them at sea could not be carried out, and thus over 40,000 prisoners were driven northward through Mecklenburg in large marching columns. Two days later, on April 22, the Red Army liberated Sachsenhausen and the few thousand ill prisoners who had been left behind. The evacuated prisoners were marched with virtually no food, many subsisted on a few raw potatoes scrounged along the way. By April 26 the marching columns reached the Below forest, where they remained until April 29. Thousands of prisoners camped in the open, surrounded by SS guards, with virtually no food and absolutely no shelter. The death toll in the Below forest was enormous; messages carved into the trees are to this day testimony of that Sachsenhausen death march. Members of the International Red Cross, who had been unable to prevent the evacuation, followed the march in several trucks and were able to give some aid to those in the forest. On April 29, the SS resumed the forced march, but the columns disintegrated. Between May 1 and 3, the surviving Sachsenhausen prisoners were liberated piecemeal by Soviet forces.[58]

The evacuation of Dora-Mittelbau began in early April, "but a large camp like Dora, with ca. 17,000 inmates and more than 1,000 SS guards, could not be evacuated on one day or with one transport."[59] Dora, near Nordhausen in Thuringia, had been established in August 1943 as a satellite camp of Buchenwald. There the newly created Mittelwerk concern was to use cheap concentration camp labor to produce V-2 rockets in subterranean caves. With total disregard of the prisoners' health and safety, the engineers and managers of the Mittelwerk company demanded the rapid completion of the factory, and the SS complied, finishing the job in half a year at the cost of thousands of lives. In spring 1944, rocket production started and the work continued at a killing pace. Life below ground was abysmal for the concentration camp prisoners: working conditions were primitive; food, water, and sanitation was minimal; and the regimen enforced by the SS was brutal. In October 1944, as large numbers of new prisoners from the east entered the camp, Dora became an independent concentration camp with the name Mittelbau, and with satellite camps in Ellrich and Harzungen and several subsidiary labor commandos.[60]

The evacuation of Dora-Mittelbau commenced in early April with the departure of the first transport on the evening of April 3.[61] As the Dora prisoners embarked on their death marches, 500 senior German engineers and managers, who had been responsible for much of their suffering, departed Nordhausen by special train; on April 5, Wernher von Braun and his colleagues arrived in Bavaria to wait for the Americans.[62] Braun and many of his associates eventually reached security, comfort, and influence in the American space and rocket program. Only one of them, Arthur L. H. Rudolph, lived long enough to be expelled from the United States. In 1983, the United States Department of Justice moved against Rudolph, charging that "as chief operations director for V-2 missile production at the Mittelwerk underground rocket factory in central Germany, Rudolph had participated in the persecution of forced laborers, including inmates from the Dora-Nordhausen concentration camp, who were employed there under inhumane conditions"; in 1984, following a plea bargain, Rudolph permanently left the United States and renounced his American citizenship.[63]

On April 11, United States troops reached the Dora-Mittelbau concentration camp and liberated about 700 prisoners who had been too ill to evacuate.[64] The overwhelming majority of Dora prisoners were no longer there. They had been evacuated and many of them were no longer alive. For example, of the 1,700 prisoners evacuated on April 3 from the Ellrich satellite camp, only 350 survived until liberation. One of the last evacuation transports, first by train and then on foot, included about 4,000 prisoners. After a three-day train ride, the prisoners were unloaded at Osterode in the Harz mountains, and there started their long march. But before they did so, the SS selected and murdered all prisoners deemed unable to walk.[65] Even more terrible was the fate of an April 5 transport of prisoners from Dora and its satellites. The march stopped near Gardelegen, and the SS drove the prisoners into a barn. They then burned down the barn, shooting all those prisoners trying to escape the inferno.[66] Troops of the U.S. 9th Army found the charred remains and only a few survivors.

The evacuations from the Flossenbürg satellite camps started in the middle of March and were not completed until the end of April. Evacuations from Flossenbürg itself started on April 16 with a rail transport of about 1,800 Jewish prisoners. Pressed into forty boxcars without food, many prisoners died from exposure, starvation, and shootings. On April 19, after the locomotive had been demolished by an Allied air attack which also claimed the lives of prisoners, the remaining prisoners were forced to march for an additional three days; those unable to continue were shot by their SS guards. Finally, American tanks overtook the transport and liberated the survivors.

Transports left Flossenbürg daily after April 16, and the last prisoners were evacuated on April 20. Columns of prisoners moved away from Flossenbürg in various directions until overtaken by American troops. But on these marches at least every tenth prisoner died from exposure and exhaustion or was shot by the SS. The death of 7,000 is the lowest estimate for prisoners killed during the death march-

es from Flossenbürg and its satellites.[67]

Not all major concentration camps were evacuated. Three central camps—Dachau, Buchenwald, and Mauthausen—were liberated by the Allies before too many prisoners were sent on deadly transports. And then there was Bergen-Belsen, whose liberation had the greatest impact on the Allied world.

Conditions at Bergen-Belsen had steadily deteriorated during the months preceding liberation. If the food supply during January had been meager, it got even smaller as more prisoners were crowded into the camp. During March, prisoners "received soup on three nights a week and a little margarine or jam on the other four nights," while bread distribution became a rarity, and there was "no bread at all during April."[68] Soon various epidemics, especially typhus with its high mortality rate, spread through the camp.[69]

Unlike all other camps, Bergen-Belsen was not evacuated, but instead surrendered to the British. As we have seen, Himmler was attempting negotiations with Jewish organizations and apparently thought that a gesture of good faith would lead to an opening to the West. On April 10 Kurt Becher inspected Bergen-Belsen and reported to Himmler, who agreed to surrender the camp without evacuating the inmates.[70] Of course, considering the conditions at the camp, even the SS could not consider evacuation a viable option. Few of the prisoners would have been able to walk at all, and the spread of epidemics to the German population and the SS would have followed any march across the countryside. On April 12, the German military signed an agreement with the British that created a neutral zone around the Bergen-Belsen camps, and the first British soldiers arrived there on the afternoon of April 15.[71]

Unbelievable scenes confronted the arriving British. The stench and squalor of the camp was indescribable, and the emaciated inmates looked like the walking dead. One general officer, Brigadier R. B. T. Daniell, remembered his first impression:

> Inside [one of the huts] a sight revealed itself that daunted even a battle-experienced man like myself. Inside there were tiers of bunks containing one and sometimes even three completely naked human beings, the stench was appalling. It was a truly terrible sight, quite obviously they had received no food or medical attention for some time, yet outside were lusty young SS soldiers, fit and well, milling around. I had had enough. Never will I forget what I had seen that day and never will I forgive the race that produced men capable of [causing] such cold blooded misery and death to the thousands who were driven into Belsen Camp.[72]

Another general officer, Brigadier J. Melvin, the Deputy Director of Medical Services for VIII Corps, recorded his impression with a few laconic words: "Death rate 17,000 in March. Thousands of corpses lying unburied. Inmates starving to death every day. Water and food finished. No light or sanitation. Hundreds dying."[73] These first impressions were no exaggeration. The British had found 55,000 prisoners, 15,000 men and 40,000 women, as well as 10,000 unburied corpses, who had to be bulldozed into mass graves. About

25,000 liberated inmates required immediate medical treatment, and 13,000 of them died in the days and weeks that followed.[74] Pictures and reports from Belsen circulated the globe; they were a grim reminder of Nazi criminality.

While Himmler agreed to turn Bergen-Belsen over to the British, he simultaneously ordered the total evacuation of Buchenwald.[75] In early April, Buchenwald held about 48,000 prisoners, many of them newly transferred Jewish prisoners in the Little Camp, and it seemed probable that as in Ravensbrück, Sachsenhausen, and Flossenbürg this inmate population would be transported and decimated. But in Buchenwald political prisoners occupied more positions of authority than in any other concentration camp and were thus able to exercise some influence over events.

On April 4, the SS ordered all Jews to report for evacuation, but no one reported, something previously considered inconceivable in a Nazi camp. The next day, the SS brutally and arbitrarily selected Jewish prisoners for evacuation, but because many inmate functionaries refused to aid the SS, many of those selected were able to disappear. The SS leaders no longer fully controlled the camp, and without the aid of inmate functionaries could only enforce their will with brute force. The commandant, Hermann Pister, knew the end was near and vacillated between obedience to orders and desire to survive. Of course, he could break prisoner resistance, but he was no longer willing to cause a bloodbath inside the camp. Still, during the following days, thousands of prisoners were selected and evacuated on death marches, but the delaying tactics of the political prisoners had so slowed the evacuations that they could not be completed. On April 11, the SS began to withdraw as the Americans approached. In the afternoon, political prisoners seized control of the camp, while troops of the U.S. Third Army occupied the area. Buchenwald had been liberated.[76] Of the 48,000 Buchenwald prisoners, about 27,000 had been evacuated between April 5 and 10, and about 21,000 had remained to be liberated.[77]

The evacuation of Dachau proved impossible. At the end of April, Dachau still remained in a German enclave, and transports from other camps continued to arrive and swell the inmate population of over 30,000 prisoners. On April 23 labor brigades no longer left the camp for work; the SS moved to evacuate Dachau on Himmler's orders, but time was running out. Still, several thousand prisoners, most of them Jews, were selected and evacuated by train and on foot between April 24 and 27. But at the same time, transports from Flossenbürg and Buchenwald arrived in Dachau, making the job of total evacuation impossible. Finally, on April 29 the SS fled, leaving behind over 30,000 prisoners. American soldiers entered the camp shortly thereafter, and, as in Buchenwald and elsewhere, were confronted by incredible sights of disease and starvation. Even before they entered the camp, the Americans saw railroad cars filled with the dead bodies of evacuated prisoners.[78]

By the end of April, Allied advances had made it almost impossible to evacuate an entire concentration camp.

A former concentration camp inmate is sprayed with DDT as part of the delousing procedure followed at all liberated concentration camps in the spring of 1945. (NARA)

Of course, thousands of prisoners could still be marched away, but the SS knew that there was virtually no chance of reaching a camp still in German hands. And as the Allies approached, SS leaders no longer had the courage to murder the tens of thousands of prisoners held in major camps. This did not mean, however, that the SS could not commit frightful massacres; the fate of the Neuengamme prisoners demonstrated that they were still able and willing to do so.

At the end of March, the Neuengamme central camp held 12,536 male prisoners; together with its satellites it counted 40,393 men and 12,103 women inmates.[79] Located near Hamburg, Neuengamme was one of the last camps to be evacuated, but its satellites, located south and east of the central camp, had to be evacuated early in April. Some went to the central camp, some went to Bergen-Belsen, and many went east, usually ending up in the satellite Wöbbelin near Ludwigslust in the Schwerin district east of the Elbe river.[80] On April 15, a transport left Neuengamme for Bergen-Belsen but, because that camp had already been liberated, was diverted to Wöbbelin. On that day, the last Scandinavian prisoners assembled at Neuengamme under the agreement between Himmler and Bernadotte were moved to Denmark in Swedish buses. Finally, on that day the commandant ordered the total evacuation of the camp.[81]

Between April 19 and 26, the remaining prisoners of Neuengamme, about 6,000, were evacuated toward Lübeck, where they were joined by prisoners from various Neuengamme satellite camps. The SS planned to put more than 10,000 prisoners on ships, thus trying a scheme that had failed to work at Sachsenhausen. Three ships were available to take this human cargo: the *Cap Arcona*, a luxury passenger ship of the Hamburg South American line with a capacity of 380 crew and 1,325 passengers; the *Thielbeck*, a freighter with a crew of 18; and the *Athen*, a smaller freighter. Although the ship captains at first refused to accept prisoners, pressure from the Hamburg Nazi party leader, Gauleiter Karl Kaufmann, changed their minds. On April 30, the day Hitler killed himself, all prisoners had been loaded on the three ships; the crowded conditions below deck were unbearable. For two days the prison ships sat in the Bay of Lübeck near Neustadt, while the city of Lübeck itself was occupied by British troops. Still, on May 2 more prisoners arrived in Neustadt. A transport from Dora was placed on the ships, and three newly arrived barges with prisoners from Stutthof were attached to the ships.[82]

On the afternoon of May 3, British planes attacked the three ships. They had not been identified as holding concentration camp prisoners. The prisoners of the *Athen*, docked at Neustadt, were able to escape, as were the prisoners on the Stutthof barges. German sailors on land tried to prevent their escape, and some prisoners were shot, while the majority was able to find refuge on land. In the bay, the *Thielbeck* sank rapidly and most prisoners drowned. The *Cap Arcona*, the largest of the ships, burned and sank, and most of the prisoners burned or drowned. Both SS and sailors shot at prisoners trying to escape the doomed *Cap Arcona*. More than 7,000 prisoners perished. Later on the afternoon of May 3, British troops captured Neustadt and liberated approximately 3,000 surviving prisoners.[83]

In early May, only one major camp—Mauthausen—had not yet been liberated. Mauthausen had always been a camp primarily for political prisoners and had held few Jews or Gypsies before the evacuation of the eastern camps. In April 1943, there had been only sixteen Jews at Mauthausen, but this had changed during 1944. At the end of March 1945, Mauthausen and its satellites held 78,547 prisoners, including 13,636 Jews, 200 Gypsies, and 2,187 Spanish Republicans.[84] During early April, many of the Mauthausen satellite camps were evacuated. Those unable to march were immediately killed, and those falling behind on the road were also shot. In addition to prisoners from the satellites, Mauthausen also received transports from Dachau, Buchenwald, Dora-Mittelbau, Gross-Rosen, Ravensbrück, and Flossenbürg, overcrowding the central camp and the remaining satellites, especially Gusen and Ebensee.[85]

During April the Swiss Red Cross collected just over one thousand male and female prisoners, most from west European countries (but also one American, one British, and two Arab citizens), and took them to Switzerland. But at the same time, the SS continued to kill other prisoners,

shooting some and killing others in the Mauthausen gas chamber.[86] On April 29, the SS dismantled the gas chamber, and thereafter burned all incriminating documents, completing the job by May 2. On May 3, Mauthausen underwent its last roll call, and shortly thereafter the SS vacated the camp. Thereafter it was guarded by officers of the Vienna fire department, who did not hesitate to use their guns. Finally, at noon on May 5, American troops reached the camp; Gusen was liberated a few hours earlier, but Ebensee not until next morning.[87]

On May 7, 1945, General Jodl signed Germany's unconditional surrender, and next day the world celebrated V-E Day. On that day, only the ghetto of Theresienstadt (Terezin), located in Czechoslovakia, had not yet been liberated by Allied forces. This so-called model ghetto, a "Potemkin village" to fool the outside world, had served as transit camp for Czech Jews as well as for elderly, privileged, and intermarried Jews from Germany, Austria, and the Netherlands. Most of them, however, had either died in the ghetto or had been sent to their death in the killing centers of the east. During spring 1945, the ghetto had received numerous transports of prisoners evacuated from various concentration camps. On May 5 Paul Dunant of the Swiss Red Cross negotiated the departure of the SS, and thereafter the ghetto stood under the protection of the Red Cross. On May 8 German and Soviet troops fought in the area around the ghetto; on the morning of May 9, the Red Army liberated Theresienstadt.[88]

Allied victory had liberated the survivors in the concentration camps. But not everyone had been liberated. The handicapped—in 1940 and 1941 the first victims of Nazi mass murder in gas chambers—continued to remain in confinement in state hospitals that had until the last moment served as places of mass death. The most notorious—for example, Meseritz-Obrawalde in the east—had been investigated by Allied troops, who dug up bodies and arrested culprits. But some hospitals continued business as usual. The Bavarian state hospital at Kaufbeuren, headed by Dr. Valentin Faltlhauser, was one of those places.[89] Late in April 1945, American troops occupied Kaufbeuren but, placing the state hospital "Off Limits," did not interfere with its operation. For two months the institution was able to function without change "less than half a mile from the Military Government, C.I.C., and M.P. Headquarters in this idyllic Swabian town." Only on July 2, 1945, after rumors had reached military offices in Munich, did American soldiers enter the hospital and discover "a wholesale extermination plant." The American investigators were shocked by the sight that confronted them: "Scabies, lice, and other vermin were encountered throughout, linens were dirty and quarantine measures non-existent upon investigators' arrival."[90] On May 29, 1945, "fully thirty-three days after American troops had occupied Kaufbeuren," the staff killed a child in the children's ward for the last time, and at 1:10 p.m. Faltlhauser recorded the death of four-year-old Richard Jenne from "typhus."[91]

The Survivors

Nazi genocide had taken the lives of millions, and Allied victory had been able to save only about a half million of the intended victims. They were the survivors. Of course, the word "survivor" had not yet become the generally accepted term. The Germans had called them "prisoners (*Häftlinge*)," and the Allies referred to them as "internees." We can see this from one of the earliest internal communications of the American Jewish Joint Distribution Committee (AJJDC), the largest Jewish relief agency, as it was poised to enter occupied Germany and Austria. On April 14, 1945, Moses A. Leavitt, the AJJDC Secretary in New York, cabled Joseph J. Schwartz, Chairman of AJJDC's European Executive Council in Paris: "Intense interest here in fate Jewish internees concentration camps Germany." But soon the term "survivor" appeared as well. For example, on May 16, 1945, S. Levine of the Canadian Jewish Congress in Montreal cabled AJJDC in New York: "Would appreciate your wiring what the Joint Distribution Committee doing for survivors in Belsen and other camps in Germany after liberation."[92]

Although all survivors liberated by the Allies celebrated their deliverance and rejoiced in their newly found freedom, their immediate experiences differed from camp to camp and from person to person. Only in major camps where prisoners had not been evacuated—Bergen-Belsen, Buchenwald, Dachau, Mauthausen, and large satellites like Ebensee—did survivors for a time transform the camp into a common liberated community. For survivors liberated in smaller satellite camps or on evacuation transports, there was an immediate break as they moved as a group to completely new shelters, usually assembly centers run by the Allies. Still other survivors immediately struck out for themselves, either alone or in small groups.

A sizable minority still had sufficient strength to liberate themselves from confinement. This minority not only included those who escaped from or were liberated during evacuation transports, but also those who decided to leave the liberated camps immediately after the arrival of Allied troops. Although some of these later entered assembly centers, many found their own quarters among the civilian German population and, with support from local Allied government, continued to reside in regular housing in small groups. But many of these survivors simply traveled, returning to their distant homes to search for relatives. In Theresienstadt, for example, the Red Army liberated about 30,000 persons, of whom 3,000 departed on their own during the first four days. After that the Soviets imposed a quarantine over the liberated ghetto to prevent the spread of a typhus epidemic. Still, three hundred survivors managed to evade the quarantine and depart.[93]

Survivors unwilling or unable to take to the road continued for the time being in the liberated camps or in assembly centers provided by Allied forces. There the Allies had to impose a relatively strict regimen to contain disease, fight malnutrition, and provide for sanitation, habitation, food, and clothing. To do this job, Allied officers usually transferred authority for the implementation of their orders to camp committees composed of prisoners representing different nationalities.

The provision of emergency medical care was the first and most important job facing Allied liberators.[94] Bergen-Belsen is the best example. There 13,000 prisoners died after liberation. British medical teams worked feverishly to save as many lives as possible but were unable to make an immediate impact. Medical staffs had to be assembled, hospital space had to be created, medicines and implements had to be brought in, patients had to be disinfected and moved. The job was immense. Eventually everyone was moved, the barracks of the camp were burned; finally, the death rate dropped dramatically.[95]

As soon as the survivors were restored to health, the Allies moved to repatriate them. This immediately divided the survivors into national groups. Over the next several months, but mostly during May and June, most liberated prisoners were repatriated. The schedule depended on the health of the survivors, availability of transportation, and conditions in the home country. The small number of British and American citizens went first, soon followed by those from western Europe. During the summer, prisoners also returned home to Poland, Czechoslovakia, Yugoslavia, the Soviet Union, and other east, central, and south European countries.

Not every liberated prisoner could be repatriated. This obviously applied to those persecuted on racial and eugenic and not political grounds. Foremost, this applied to the handicapped in German state hospitals, who were saved by Allied victory from death through starvation, neglect, and lethal injections. In 1940 and 1941, their fate had become a matter of public concern both inside Germany and in Allied countries, but after the war, there was no public recognition of their suffering, and certainly no attempt at restitution.[96]

This also applied to Roma and Sinti, the so-called Gypsies, who had been excluded, despoiled, deported, and murdered alongside Jews for racial reasons. They received no rehabilitation or compensation, and often persecution by local German authorities continued even after liberation.[97] There were several reasons for this slight. Although the persecution of Roma and Sinti had been based on race—and this had been clearly enunciated in laws, decrees, and public speeches—the German bureaucracy had labeled them as criminal and anti-social elements, and they had often been forced to wear green or black triangles in the camps. They were therefore not recognized as victims of racial persecution. This no doubt explains why prejudice against Gypsies did not become unfashionable and thus did not diminish. In addition, the surviving Sinti and Roma were German or Austrian citizens, and the Allies did not grant them the special status accorded citizens of Allied nations. Since they did not have defenders in Allied countries, they were unable to convince the Allies to change

A former inmate of Wöbbelin concentration camp lies dead by the roadside as survivors of the camp pass by on their trek homeward in early May 1945. (NARA)

their victim classification. Roma and Sinti did organize, forming for example the Committee of German Gypsies in Munich, which published a journal and submitted evidence at Nuremberg, but were unsuccessful in attempts to influence the Allies or gain concessions from the Germans.[98]

Of course, German and Austrian political prisoners were also considered enemy nationals by the victorious Allies, but their postwar status was not seriously affected by this classification. Their persecution was recognized and rewarded by local German and Austrian authorities, and many served, at least during the immediate postwar year, in responsible positions to assure a democratic and anti-Nazi reconstruction of their countries.

The Jewish survivors formed the largest group of liberated prisoners that could not be repatriated. Of course, we do not know the exact number of Jewish survivors liberated from the concentration camps. If there were about 715,000 prisoners in the camps at the start of 1945, and at least one-third—that is, about 238,000—perished during spring 1945, we can assume that at most 475,000 prisoners survived. As Jews had been systematically murdered, and only those chosen for labor—in Auschwitz about 15 percent—had even had a chance to survive, we must assume that Jews made up no more than 20 percent of the concentration camp population. We can thus estimate that the number of Jewish survivors numbered no more than 100,000.

Although all Jews had shared a common fate, national origin also determined, at least in part, the postwar situation of Jewish survivors. Most of those deported from west and south European countries returned to their homelands as soon as possible.[99] Fewer Jewish survivors returned to their homes in eastern Europe, but even here there were national differences. The largest number of survivors returned to Czechoslovakia and Hungary, although most emigrated later when the communists consolidated their power over those countries in the late 1940s. Some survivors even returned to Poland. But while a few Jews remained to rebuild their lives in postwar Poland, an overwhelming majority returned to occupied Germany and Austria after finding that virtually no Jews had survived while antisemitism continued to flourish. Far fewer Jewish survivors returned to the territory of the Soviet Union, including the Baltic states. The Jewish survivors from Germany and Austria occupied a somewhat unique position, because they had been liberated on the territory of their countries of origin. But they rarely returned to their cities of origin for anything but a brief visit. Some remained in camps or assembly centers. Most settled among the German civilian population but viewed this as an interim stop.

The American Liberators

The sight, sound, and smell of the concentration camps confronted the liberating troops of the United States suddenly and without warning. Regardless of what they had previously heard about German frightfulness, Americans were not prepared for the scenes of carnage thrust upon them. The impact of this encounter upon the liberators has often been described, and photographs of the camps, the survivors, and the liberating soldiers abound. The reaction of one such liberating soldier can serve as a typical example. On April 15, Captain James B. Ficklen, an army chaplain, wrote in a letter to his wife in New York:

> I've seen so many things that are strange and hard to tell about that I hardly know where to begin. On Friday I visited a camp where the Germans kept their slave-laborers. This is the worst thing I've ever seen. The Germans starved their slave-labor till they were living skeletons, and when they became too ill or weak to work they killed them, stacking their bodies in a neat-looking little hut till they got around to hauling them about a mile further up the hill and arranging them on piles of rails (wooden), then putting on steel rails, then a layer of bodies and another layer of wooden rails. Then the whole pile was set on fire and the bodies burned. What was left was thrown into a common grave on the edge of the woods just beyond the fire pile. At the labor camp there were numbers of emaciated bodies shot thru the head and lying in the yard when I arrived. They were just skin and bones. They had on striped housecoats and old clothes. I took pictures of this unbelievable scene to make it clear to people at home that the accounts of German oppression and murder in concentration and labor camps is all too true. I saw dozens of skeleton-like bodies in the process of burial by German civilians whom our army forced to dig graves, take the lime-covered bodies, wrap them in white cloth, provided by the American army, and bury them. I also took photographic evidence of the charred bodies still on the pile of wood at the top of the hill. I went thru the so-called barracks in which these prisoners existed. I saw some men who were still alive. One man was eating an apple—it must have been the first fresh fruit he had had in many a long month. Usually they got bread and water once a day. I saw one man lying in bed dead. He appeared to have died from hunger. Above his bed was the picture of a girl. Most of the men slept on filthy bags stuffed with straw that lay on the floor. This man was in the lower part of a double-decker bed made of wooden slats. I saw other things that will hardly do to write about. That was a hell on earth if there ever was one. This is the sort of oppression that is being ended by Allied victory in Europe.[100]

Not only officers and soldiers reacted in this fashion, but the confrontation with the liberated camps also had their impact on American commanders. They reported their findings to Washington, describing, as did the soldiers they commanded, how savagely the Germans—it was not yet common practice to speak only of "Nazis"—had maltreated their prisoners. One cable sent from Germany to Washington can serve as an example:

> We continue to uncover German concentration camps for political prisoners in which conditions of indescribable horror prevail. *From Eisenhower to General Marshall for eyes only.* I have visited one of these myself and I assure you that whatever has been printed on them to date has been understatement. If you would see any advantage in asking about a dozen prominent editors to make short visit to this theater in a couple of C-54s, I will arrange to have them conducted to one of these places where the evidence of bestiality and cruelty is so overpowering as to leave no doubt in their minds about the normal practices of the Germans in these camps.[101]

George C. Marshall seemed to have agreed with Eisenhower, and soon prominent Americans toured the liberated camps. Buchenwald, Dora-Mittelbau at Nordhausen, and Dachau were visited by a bipartisan congressional delegation composed of Democratic senators Alben W. Barkley of Kentucky, Walter F. George of Georgia, Elbert D. Thomas of Utah, Republican senators C. Wayland Brooks of Illinois, Leverett Saltonstall of Massachusetts, Kenneth S. Wherry of Nebraska, Democratic representatives Ed V. Izac of California, James P. Richards of South Carolina, R. Ewing Thomason of Texas, and Republican representatives James W. Mott of Oregon, Dewey Short of Missouri, John M. Vorys of Ohio. Their findings were reported in the *New York Times*.[102] Individual members of Congress also visited the camps and reported on what they had seen. Republican Representative Clare Booth Luce of Connecticut, for example, on April 21 addressed the House about conditions she had observed at Buchenwald.[103] Even more important for publicizing what the Allies had found, Eisenhower arranged a tour by eighteen influential American publishers and editors, including Julius Ochs Adler, Norman Chandler, John Randolph Hearst, and Joseph Pulitzer, who afterwards reported about the camps in their newspapers and magazines.[104] At the same time, from Britain eight members of the House of Commons and two members of the House of Lords accepted Eisenhower's invitation to visit the camps.[105]

Displaced Persons

The need to care for the survivors of the concentration camps was only one of many problems confronting the victorious Allied armies. In addition to those tasks that military necessity and the needs of their own troops imposed upon them, they also had to administer occupied Germany and Austria, collect and hold German prisoners of war, repatriate Allied POWs and slave laborers, catch and prosecute war criminals, and begin the task of reconstructing devastated Europe. As the war ended, the United States was committed to a harsh policy for defeated Germany. Although the Morgenthau Plan, which called for the deindustrialization of Germany, did not become official policy, Joint Chiefs of Staff Document 1067, which did become policy, reflected the Morgenthau approach and imposed draconian measures on the defeated foe.[106] But President Franklin Delano Roosevelt had died on April 12, 1945, and Harry S Truman, who succeeded him as the 33d President of the United States, did not approve of Henry Morgenthau's ideas about the future of Germany.[107] Although JCS 1067 remained policy, it was not fully implemented.[108] Still, American troops entered Germany with a folded pocket-size card outlining "Special Orders for American-German Relations." These order included the following prohibition:

> American soldiers must not associate with Germans. Specifically it is not permissible to shake hands with them, to visit their homes, to exchange gifts with them, to engage in games or sports with them, to attend their dances or social events, to accompany them on the streets or elsewhere. . . .[109]

Four Allied powers ruled Germany: Great Britain, France, the Soviet Union, and the United States. At the

Potsdam Conference of July 1945, the Big Three—Harry S Truman, Joseph Stalin, and Winston Churchill (replaced during the conference by Clement Attlee)—defined the future of Germany, confirming borders and deciding on reparations. Germany was divided into four zones of occupation, while Berlin, located inside the Soviet zone, was divided into four separate sectors. An Allied Control Council, representing the four occupying powers and sitting in Berlin, was to promulgate laws and coordinate policy for the entire country. But while the Control Council did issue a limited number of laws, each occupying power exercised almost unlimited independent control in its zone. The same applied to Austria, which was also divided into zones, and where Vienna, inside the Soviet zone, was governed by all powers. As each occupying army thus governed according to its own rules and regulations, it is not surprising that attitudes toward the German population and toward the survivors differed from zone to zone.

Millions of uprooted civilians flooded the territories occupied by the western Allies, creating a vast population movement that included prisoners of war formerly held by the Germans, slave laborers who had been conscripted by the Germans, ethnic Germans expelled from eastern Europe, east European collaborators who had fled to the west, and the survivors of the concentration camps. The Allies designated those uprooted by German conquest as displaced persons (DPs), excluding however ethnic Germans and their collaborators from this designation. The survivors thus became displaced persons if they could or would not be repatriated.[110]

The United Nations Relief and Rehabilitation Administration (UNRRA), which was later replaced by the International Refugee Organization (IRO), were the agencies responsible for displaced persons, and they decided which groups of people could receive the status of displaced persons. The great majority were east European refugees—mostly from the Baltic states and the Ukraine. Some had been recruited by the Germans for labor in the Reich, and others had fled from the advancing Red Army. They were nationalists and anti-communists who did not want to return to their Soviet dominated homelands. Undoubtedly that group included those who had collaborated with the Germans, and some had even committed war crimes by participating in the mass killings of Jews and Gypsies.[111] Such individuals were of course excluded from DP status, and the IRO statute did exclude "(1) War criminals, quislings and traitors; (2) Any other person who can be shown: (a) to have assisted the enemy in persecuting civil populations of countries, members of the United Nations; or (b) to have voluntarily assisted the enemy forces since the outbreak of the second world war in their operations against the United Nations."[112] Still, it was often impossible to pick such collaborators from the mass of their fellow east European refugees, and some were later able to enter the United States and other overseas countries as legal DP immigrants.[113]

As we have seen, liberated Jews from central and eastern Europe made up the overwhelming majority of concentration camp survivors classified as displaced persons, because most non-Jewish survivors were eventually repatriated.[114] Until such repatriation, however, they received the same benefits and faced the same restrictions as all other survivors. Allied liberators provided needed medical services, food, and clothing. They also provided official recognition that they had been the victims of Nazi persecution, thus granting them a higher status than that accorded to the German civilian population. But at the same time, the Allies, especially the American and British liberators, attempted to keep the survivors inside the liberated camps or in newly established assembly centers. Although conditions had totally changed, the survivors found themselves still inside a camp, surrounded by barbed wire, and guarded by soldiers. They had to stand in lines, follow camp regulations, accept procedures on health and sanitation, and have passes to leave the camp.[115]

Such compulsory regulations were in part imposed for the good of the survivors, as, for example, the requirement that every survivor must be covered from head to toe with DDT.[116] They were also imposed as a convenience for Allied administration because confinement assured easy delivery of services and prevented potential clashes between survivors and German civilians. Although the survivors at first accepted confinement as necessary, they soon began to view continued regimentation as onerous, particularly in comparison to the treatment of the German population. After all, Germans were able to move freely, and thus view the survivors from outside the barbed wire. Although German civilians had to struggle amidst the ruins of their destroyed cities, large numbers still occupied undamaged houses, especially in the small towns and villages near camps and assembly centers, and still owned good clothing, linens, utensils, and furniture, while the survivors, who had lost everything, had to accept the crude facilities the military provided.

Jewish survivors faced problems as displaced persons not experienced by other groups.[117] They had been persecuted for racial reasons because they were Jews. Their homes had been confiscated or destroyed, their communities eradicated, and their families murdered. The Jewish survivors, especially those from eastern Europe, did not see themselves as citizens of their former homelands and did not want to share quarters with non-Jewish nationals from those countries, especially as some of the latter had collaborated and others still displayed antisemitic tendencies. The Allies, however, refused to recognize Jews as a separate ethnic group, arguing that acceptance of a classification based on religion would perpetuate Nazi policies. Although in the British zone this decision was in part motivated by political considerations concerning the future of Palestine, the Allies, especially the Americans, based this refusal on a tradition that granted international recognition only to nations and not to ethnic groups. For this reason, German Jewish survivors were initially not recognized as displaced persons.[118]

As British and American forces entered Germany and Austria, Jewish relief agencies stood ready to aid all Jews who might have survived. The military, however, did not at first admit any private, non-governmental agencies. Only UNRRA and the International Red Cross were permitted to send representatives into occupied Germany. But the Red Cross did not attempt major relief efforts, while UNRRA was understaffed and inexperienced.[119] The AJJDC made every effort—even before the end of the war—to gain entrance to occupied Germany, but "met resistance all along the line to the idea that a civilian voluntary agency should be granted this opportunity."[120]

AJJDC representatives were not admitted to the camps until late June, and it took even longer to get permission to establish fully staffed offices. By the end of the year representatives of the Hebrew Sheltering and Immigrant Aid Society (HIAS) had also established offices alongside AJJDC in Germany and Austria.[121] But even then the Jewish agencies were supposedly only "to assist military and civil authorities in an advisory and consultative capacity," and were to leave "functional relief activities" to UNRRA and the military.[122]

Until the arrival of AJJDC and HIAS, the Jewish communities received only second-hand information about Jewish survivors forwarded to them by Jewish soldiers and neutral relief agencies.[123] The Jewish survivors, in turn, had to depend on the support of Jewish soldiers. More important, Jewish chaplains in the United States Army worked hard to facilitate contact between survivors and their relatives, intercede with military authorities, and provide material and spiritual assistance.[124]

Jewish survivors did need assistance and support. In many small camps and assembly centers assigned to Jewish survivors, facilities and supplies were primitive. In Neustadt, for example, where thousands of concentration camp prisoners had perished at sea and on land just before British troops arrived, a Jewish dentist working for UNRRA reported that Jewish survivors had to share facilities with German prisoners of war and east European refugees who had fought alongside the Germans. Everything was in short supply—food, clothing, medicine—but the German prisoners were housed in better buildings, received better medical service, and proudly wore their uniforms and medals.[125]

As the soldiers who had liberated the camps were replaced by fresh troops who had not seen the atrocities, attitudes toward Jewish survivors changed. American and British soldiers fraternized with German civilian families and absorbed some of their attitudes toward displaced persons. The military compared Jewish displaced persons to those from the Baltic and the Ukraine; the latter, who had not experienced the same terror or suffered the same losses, appeared healthier, cleaner, more polite, and friendlier. The Jews, by contrast, were seen as argumentative, seemed to lack discipline, and appeared to make no effort to improve their surroundings. American and British soldiers were un-

able to bridge the chasm that separated their own outlook from the experiences of the survivors, and antisemitic stereotypes undoubtedly also helped to channel their frustration with the Jewish displaced persons they deemed difficult. The military also believed that Jews were disproportionately represented in the black market; as everyone, including Allied soldiers, traded on the black market, Jewish participation should have been no surprise, but searches, arrests, and sentences imposed on Jews were disproportionately severe. Of course, much depended on the attitude of the commanders, and conditions for Jewish displaced persons were far better in the region of the American zone occupied by the Seventh Army under the command of General Alexander Patch than in the area of General George S. Patton's Third Army.[126] But even sympathetic American officers were at first appalled at conditions in camps and assembly centers and complained about the attitude of the survivors and their failure to work hard to create a sanitary and wholesome camp environment.[127]

Conditions would have been far worse if the Jewish survivors had not created their own organizations. The large DP camp of Belsen in the British zone, located more or less on the grounds of the infamous concentration camp, can serve as an example of how well Jewish survivors could and did respond to post-liberation adversity. Soon after liberation, the Bergen-Belsen survivors organized the Central Jewish Committee under the leadership of Josef Rosensaft, whose charisma made him a natural leader.[128] One AJJDC representative described his personality and his work as follows:

> "The Chairman Joseph Rosensaft, a veritable Jewish Lincoln, is a national leader but is always incurring the wrath of the Army officials here. He is always threatened with arrest. Rosensaft had been a labor organizer in Poland, and has a tremendous following here. He thinks nothing of flaunting military regulations repeatedly and has made my task of interpreting the committee to the military an exceedingly difficult one."[129]

Indeed, the committee operated without official sanction, because the British did not recognize Jews as a separate national group. Still, the committee ran the camp, assured that all Jews who arrived at Belsen were registered, obtained supplies from abroad, and organized the camp's cultural, educational, and leisure activities.[130]

Of course, organizational work also created friction. The Belsen committee was dominated by Jews from Poland, and the minority of Hungarian and Romanian Jews felt excluded. The British attempted to use their dissatisfaction to split the Jewish group and discredit the committee, but this strategy did not work.[131] Eventually, the committee created the Central Committee of the Liberated Jews in the British Zone to represent all Jewish displaced persons. Norbert Wollheim, who as a young man had served until his deportation to Auschwitz as an official of the Reich Association of German Jews, represented the German Jews on the Committee.[132]

Organization was not as easy in the American zone due to the far larger number of Jewish displaced persons, the existence of many different camps and centers, and possibly also the absence of charismatic leadership. Unlike the British zone, where the Belsen DP camp served as the center for all liberated Jews, there were several large DP camps in the American zone. In addition, liberated Jewish survivors could be found in small numbers in most towns in Bavaria, the area of Third Army, and in Hesse and Württemberg, the area of Seventh Army.[133] At first there was no central organization, as small groups in various camps and towns created ad hoc committees to organize life and appeal to the outside world.[134] The first committee with wide influence was formed in Bavaria by Dr. Zalman Grinberg, a Jewish survivor from Kovno in Lithuania who worked closely with one of the American military chaplains, Rabbi Abraham J. Klausner. Early in July, representatives from various DP camps met at the Feldafing camp and, headed by Grinberg, organized a Jewish central committee for the state of Bavaria, the region occupied by Third Army and holding the largest number of Jewish displaced persons. Only in January 1946 did this committee expand into one that included the entire American zone. Headed by Grinberg, David Treger, and Dr. Samuel Gringauz, this committee was known as the Central Committee of the Liberated Jews in the United States Zone.[135]

No major Jewish organizations emerged in other areas. In the Soviet zone, displaced persons as such were not recognized, and Jewish survivors, who received no special recognition, generally moved into the western occupation zones. The French zone held only small numbers of Jewish survivors, who did not live in camps but had established themselves in various towns "as tenants in private houses"; they were represented by local committees.[136] In Austria, also divided into zones, the number of Jewish displaced persons had shrunk by August, and only a relatively small number continued in DP camps. However, Austria was soon to serve as the transit route for Jews escaping from eastern Europe and for those entering Italy for the illegal journey to Palestine.[137]

Outside the DP camps, German Jews started to reconstitute local Jewish communities—at least for the moment. At the end of the war, the number of surviving German Jews certainly did not exceed 25,000. The majority were those who had survived legally because they were of mixed ancestry or lived in mixed marriages. A minority numbering about 7,000 had survived illegally by evading capture. The number of deported German Jews who lived to be liberated from the camps was also extremely small. Slowly the German Jews, and also those in Austria, reestablished community offices, opened temporary synagogues, and attempted to provide a variety of social services. East European Jewish survivors living outside the DP camps eventually joined these communities, and the German Jewish communities would thereafter always include a mixture of German and east European Jews. Although there was obvi-

ously a certain amount of friction between German Jews and those from eastern Europe, Jewish camp survivors among the German Jews—Norbert Wollheim in the British zone, Philipp Auerbach in the American zone, and Heinz Galinski in Berlin—provided leadership that bridged the gap between German and east European Jews.[138]

After satisfying the requirement of survival—medical services, food, clothing, and housing—the Jewish committees and the Jewish relief agencies moved to provide Jewish substance for the lives of the survivors. They published newspapers; for example, *Undzer Weg* in the Landsberg DP camp in the American zone and *Undzer Shtime* in the Belsen DP camp in the British zone. They assembled Yiddish and Hebrew books and instituted educational programs. They started religious services, imported religious ritual objects, and founded religious schools.[139]

The establishment of contact with Jews in the west was equally important for survivors. At first this was difficult, especially as the military did not usually permit mail to the outside world, but after a few months letters moved smoothly across borders, and a steady stream of "visiting firemen" entered the German and Austrian camps. Jewish organizations in the west, especially in the United States, started to apply political pressure on Allied governments to improve the condition of the Jewish displaced persons. This pressure led to the so-called Harrison report, which has been credited in most postwar accounts with the dramatic improvement of conditions in the Jewish DP camps.[140] But conditions were already improving before the report was issued, and it is at least possible that Jewish displaced persons would have made the same advances even without the report.

On June 22, 1945, President Truman appointed Earl G. Harrison, dean of the University of Pennsylvania Law School, to investigate the "the condition and needs of those among the displaced persons in the liberated countries of Western Europe and in the SHAEF area of Germany—with particular reference to the Jewish refugees—who may possibly be stateless or non-repatriable."[141] Harrison had served in the Roosevelt administration as director of Alien Registration at the Department of Justice, special assistant to the Attorney General, and from 1942 to 1944 as Commissioner of Immigration and Naturalization. In 1945 and 1946, he served as chairman of the nonsectarian National Committee for Postwar Immigration Policy, a creation of the American Council of Voluntary Agencies for Foreign Services, which had been organized by the American Jewish Congress, American Jewish Committee, and HIAS. He was thus closely associated with Jewish organizations and had been appointed by Truman at the recommendation of Henry Morgenthau. On his trip to Europe in July and August, Harrison was accompanied by Joseph J. Schwartz, the European director of AJJDC, Herbert Katzki of the War Refugee Board, also a senior AJJDC officer, and Patrick M. Malin of the Intergovernmental Committee on Refugees.

Harrison reported to the President late in August. In his

Jewish DPs bake matzo in a bakery at the displaced persons camp in Zeilsheim, Germany, 1945.
(Alice Robinson Lev Collection, USHMM)

summary, he correctly pointed out that Jewish displaced persons remained in guarded camps behind barbed wires without meaningful activities, and that they suffered from an insufficiently balanced diet, poor clothing, and substandard housing. He appropriately recommended the establishment of DP camps reserved only for Jews or, even better, the placement of Jewish displaced persons in housing confiscated from Germans. He also recommended that the military not employ German civilians in Jewish DP camps.

Harrison's criticism of the military for mishandling Jewish survivors was at least in part unfair, because he did not recognize difficulties overcome and improvements initiated. And he certainly made an inexcusable comparison when he wrote, "As matters now stand, we appear to be treating the Jews as the Nazis treated them except that we do not exterminate them."

The majority of his recommendations, however, dealt with emigration. He correctly argued that almost all survivors shared a universal desire to leave Germany and Austria, and that few wanted to return to their countries of origin. He further argued that emigration to "Palestine is definitely and pre-eminently the first choice" of almost all survivors, and that they "want to be evacuated to Palestine now, just as other national groups are being repatriated to their homes." Harrison, whose argument undoubtedly reflected the information he received in the camps and from the accompanying Jewish leaders, therefore recommended that Britain revise its 1939 White Paper and immediately issue 100,000 certificates for Palestine.

Harrison was less generous toward those survivors who might want to emigrate to the United States. Conceding that some Jewish survivors did want to go to America, he assured Truman that "the number is not large." He therefore recommended only that "reasonable numbers," mostly those with family ties, be admitted under "existing emigration laws." But his information was inaccurate. AJJDC reports indicated that a much larger number of survivors wanted to enter the United States. Thus at the Landsberg DP camp, just over 62 percent wanted to go to Palestine, almost 18 percent wanted to enter the United States, about 14 percent picked other destinations, while 5.5 percent were undecided.[142] The Landsberg figures were far closer than those of Harrison to the eventual geographic distribution of Jewish survivors.

Whatever the merit of Harrison's criticisms and recommendations, the military moved rapidly to improve conditions and accept the recommendations. Guards were removed from the camps; displaced persons received better housing, clothing, and food; Jews were no longer forced to share camps with other ethnic groups; and Eisenhower appointed a Jewish adviser (first Rabbi Judah P. Nadich and later Judge Simon Rifkind).[143]

The Great Migration

The number of Jewish displaced persons in Germany and Austria increased during the second half of 1945. During that period thousands of Jews from eastern Europe entered the zones occupied by the western Allies in Germany and Austria. Most of the refugees came from Poland, and included survivors who had returned from the west to find relatives, Jews who had survived in hiding or with false papers, and Jewish soldiers who returned with the Polish army from the Soviet Union. After finding that no member of their family had survived and noting that traditional Polish antisemitism had not declined, most decided to cross the border into the West. Early in 1946, almost 200,000 Jews started to return from the Soviet Union under an agreement between the Soviet and Polish governments. They, too, discovered how vicious Polish antisemitism could be. Attacks on Jews had already claimed a few hundred lives in 1945, but Polish violence escalated in 1946. This accelerated the exodus of Jews from Poland, reaching its high point after the July 1946 pogrom in Kielce.[144]

Emigration was the obvious answer to the problem posed by Jewish displaced persons. From the beginning, representatives of the Jewish Agency for Palestine had started to recruit and train Jews in the DP camps for emigration to Palestine. They "infiltrated" a steady stream of Jews to Italy for the sea voyage to the coast of Palestine, where they landed illegally. The British government of Clement Attlee and Ernest Bevin was determined to uphold the White Paper and keep the doors of Palestine closed to Jewish immigration. British troops often intercepted immigrant ships; at first the British sent the displaced persons back to Germany but, after obvious public revulsion, kept them in camps on the island of Cyprus. Nevertheless, illegal immigration to Palestine continued. After the Anglo-American Committee on Palestine, established in late 1945, failed to open the country to immigration, the conflict between the Jewish underground and the British became violent.[145] International public opinion and continued conflict led Britain to return the Mandate to the United Nations, which voted to partition Palestine; this led, in turn, to the creation of the state of Israel in 1948.

The United States also moved to do something about the plight of displaced persons unable to leave the DP camps and emigrate overseas. On December 22, 1945, President Truman issued a directive to ease immigration to the United States. Retaining the rigid quota system based on country of origin, which was generous to persons born in Germany but was extremely small for those born in Poland, he eliminated many of the other onerous requirements that had prevented large-scale immigration. Concentrating on areas occupied by the U.S. Army, he ordered the rapid establishment of consular offices in the American zone of Germany, speedy processing of visas with preferential consideration to orphans, and for the first time permitted welfare agencies to guarantee that immigrants would not become public charges, a requirement of the immigration law that relatives and friends of potential immigrants had previously been forced to meet.[146]

President Truman's directive admitted only a small trickle of displaced persons. The United States did not widely open the gates for immigrants until the congressional enactment of the Displaced Person Act of 1948, revised in 1950, admitted large numbers of non-Jewish, and also Jewish, displaced persons and ended the European refugee crisis. Still, Truman's directive did at least begin to admit displaced persons; in the first seven months, until early August 1946, some 3,452 persons entered the United States. The largest number—1,310—used the Polish quota, while Germany came second with 966 quota immigrants, followed by Austria with 125, Czechoslovakia with 119, and Hungary with 105. Although immigrants of all faiths entered the United States under the Truman directive, 2,477 Jewish displaced persons made up the largest number of those entering in the first seven months.[147]

War Crimes

The Allies had pledged to punish the Nazi war criminals long before the end of the war. In November 1943, at the meeting of foreign ministers of the Big Three in Moscow, the United States, the United Kingdom, and the Soviet Union issued the "Moscow Declaration." In it the Allies pledged to bring to justice the "Hitlerite Huns" for their "atrocities, massacres and cold-blooded mass executions." Retaining the right to try the major Axis leaders, they promised to extradite all other war criminals.[148] Most trials did take place in countries formerly occupied by Germany, where national courts tried war criminals caught on their territory or extradited by the victorious Allies. Eventually Belgium tried 75 criminals, Denmark 80, Luxembourg 68, the Netherlands 204, and Norway 80. More than 5,000 Germans were tried in Poland, including Rudolf Höss, Arthur Greiser, and Juergen Stroop; the exact number of those tried in Yugoslavia and Czechoslovakia, though large, is not known.[149]

On August 8, 1945, representatives of the United States, France, Great Britain, and the Soviet Union signed the London Agreement. "Acting in the interests of all the United Nations," the signatories established the International Military Tribunal (IMT) "for the trial of war criminals whose offenses have no particular geographic location."[150] The laws under which the major war criminals were to be tried were listed in the Charter of the IMT as crimes against peace, war crimes, and crimes against humanity.[151] Both the nature of the crimes charged, especially the charge of conspiring to wage aggressive war, and procedures followed had been proposed by the United States and had been developed by a team of lawyers in the U.S. War Department.[152] The trial opened on October 18, 1945, in Berlin, but then moved to the Palace of Justice in the city of Nuremberg, located in the American zone. Although the IMT was composed of all four powers, the job of staffing, guarding, and supplying the tribunal fell to the United States. U.S. personnel also assembled, duplicated, and made available the vast documentation needed to conduct the trial.

Responsibility for the management of the trial rested with the American prosecution staff, and to a lesser degree with the prosecution of the other three powers. The American prosecution was headed by Justice Robert H. Jackson, who had signed the London Agreement for the

United States. An attorney from upstate New York with good political connections in the Roosevelt administration, Jackson had served as Solicitor General and Attorney General and had joined the Supreme Court in 1942. He took a leave of absence from the Court to accept appointment by Truman to head the prosecution, a job he considered a "grave responsibility."[153] Secretary of War Henry L. Stimson would later assure Jackson that the trial had been worth all his efforts: "Not only will it make a lasting record of the evils which America has fought to suppress, but it will lift the world a long step nearer to the rule of justice and righteousness."[154]

Judges from the four powers presided over the International Military Tribunal, with Lord Justice Sir Geoffrey Lawrence of Britain as president. Each of the powers provided one member and one alternate for the tribunal; on September 24, 1945, President Truman appointed as member "Francis Biddle of Pennsylvania," a former Attorney General, and as alternate "John J. Parker of North Carolina."[155] After the trial, Truman accepted Parker's resignation with a letter of thanks, commenting that Parker had discharged his duties with distinction: "You have served faithfully and well the cause of civilization and of world peace and can safely leave the results of your labors at Nuremberg to the verdict of history."[156]

The IMT tried 21 defendants. It also tried Martin Bormann *in absentia*, although he was probably already dead. The defendants were selected as representatives of the major branches of the Nazi regime (the proposed defendant Krupp was too ill to stand trial; the German industrialists were thus not represented). The IMT convicted eighteen (without Bormann) and did not convict three. Of the eighteen, eleven were sentenced to death, three to life in prison, and four to long prison terms. The IMT also tried seven organizations: the Reich cabinet, the leadership corps of the Nazi party, the general staff and high command of the Wehrmacht, the SA, SS, SD, and Gestapo. It convicted the leadership corps, the SS, SD, and Gestapo.[157]

The trial of the major war criminals before the International Military Tribunal at Nuremberg focused world opinion on the crimes of the German state and the Nazi regime and assembled for posterity a portion of the evidence historians would later use to document these crimes. In his opening before the IMT, Justice Jackson clearly outlined the reasons, still valid today, for the trial of the Nazi war criminals:

> The privilege of opening the first trial in history for crimes against the peace of the world imposes a grave responsibility. The wrongs which we seek to condemn and punish have been so calculated, so malignant, and so devastating, that civilization cannot tolerate their being ignored, because it cannot survive their being repeated. That four great nations, flushed with victory and stung with injury, stay the hand of vengeance and voluntarily submit their captive enemies to the judgment of the law is one of the most significant tributes that Power has ever paid to reason.[158]

Even before the IMT started its deliberations, Allied military courts tried and sentenced Germans guilty of killing Allied soldiers.[159] But these military courts did not restrict themselves to such cases; eventually they would try not only the Malmedy SS killers, who had murdered American POWs during the Battle of the Bulge, but also the administrators and guards of the concentration camps. One of the earliest such trials in the American zone took place in fall 1945 in Wiesbaden before a military commission of the

The defendants at the International Military Tribunal rise as the judges enter the courtroom. Front row, left to right Göring, von Ribbentrop, Keitel, Kaltenbrunner, Rosenberg, Frank, Frick, Streicher, Funk, and Schacht; rear row Dönitz, Raeder, von Schirach, Sauckel (behind Kaltenbrunner), Jodl, von Papen, Seyss-Inquart, Speer, von Neurath, and Fritzsche. (NARA)

U.S. Seventh Army; the commissions were traditional American military courts with a history dating back to the period before the United States Civil War. The defendants were administrators, physicians, and nurses of the Hadamar euthanasia killing center, who in addition to murdering German civilians—a crime that did not fall under the jurisdiction of the commission—had in winter 1944–45 killed ill Polish and Russian forced laborers; as these were citizens of one of the United Nations, the commission assumed jurisdiction. The prosecutor as judge advocate was a Texas attorney, Colonel Leon Jaworski, who was in the 1970s to be the second Watergate prosecutor. Seven Hadamar defendants were convicted; three were executed, one received a life term, and three long prison sentences.[160]

Such trials also took place before military courts in all other zones. Most noteworthy was the trial in fall 1945 before a British military court in Lüneburg of the administrators and guards of the Bergen-Belsen concentration camp, who had earlier also served at Auschwitz and Birkenau. It was the first trial where crimes committed in the concentration camps as well as the mass murder of the Jews was adjudicated. Eleven defendants, including the commandant of Birkenau and Bergen-Belsen Josef Kramer, were sentenced to death.[161] Trials in all four zones involved thousands of defendants, resulted in a high percentage of convictions, and led to a large number of death sentences. More than 500 war criminals were eventually executed by the three western Allies alone.[162]

In December 1945, the Allied Control Council for Germany promulgated Control Council Law No. 10 to provide a "uniform legal basis in Germany for the prosecution of war criminals and other similar offenders."[163] Law No. 10, incorporating the crimes defined for the IMT in the London Agreement, replaced the customary laws of war and international law as the legal basis for trials before Allied military courts.[164] As the Allies permitted the Germans to reconstitute their judicial system, they also permitted them to apply Law No. 10 in cases where war crimes had been committed against German nationals. In 1946, the German courts began proceedings against the euthanasia killers, thus starting the German war crimes trials that would continue for another fifty years.[165]

Most prominent and widely publicized were the trials held under Law No. 10 at Nuremberg. There, United States military tribunals judged German cabinet and sub-cabinet leaders in twelve trials between October 1946 and April 1949. Known as the subsequent Nuremberg proceedings, these trials modeled their procedures on those of the IMT, using American civilian judges and observing strict rules of evidence. The prosecution was led by Brigadier General Telford Taylor, who had served on Jackson's staff at the earlier Nuremberg trial. These subsequent trials focused on crimes against humanity. Most of these trials, including those against government ministers and state secretaries (the Ministries Case), industrialists (the Krupp, Flick, and I. G. Farben Cases), physicians (the Medical Case), and

lawyers (the Justice Case), involved the crimes of the Holocaust. This was particularly true in the trials of administrators of the concentration camp system (the Pohl Case) and of the commanders of the *Einsatzgruppen* (the Ohlendorf Case). The evidence gathered (including the Wannsee protocol) for these subsequent trials forms, together with the evidence from the International Military Tribunal, the Nuremberg documentation. For over forty years, this documentation has been an essential source of knowledge not only about Nazi Germany, but also about the Holocaust.

Postscript

The year 1945 was not only the last year of war but also the first year of peace. In May 1945 the Nazi regime, totally defeated by Allied arms, collapsed as it had started in a paroxysm of unbelievable violence. Those who survived entered the dawn of the postwar world with a great deal of hope; they believed that the lessons mankind had learned would produce a better world, peaceful and just. As the war ended in the Pacific in August 1945, the splitting of the atom also ushered in a new age of technological sophistication; jet airplanes and computers transformed travel and communication. The Marshall Plan helped to rebuild Europe; the end of colonialism created newly independent states, including the state of Israel. And during the following half century of the Cold War the world avoided a third world war.

But the hopes of 1945 have not been fully justified. Hunger, deprivation, and homeless refugees still stalk the earth. Dictatorships, massacres, and terrorism continue to claim human lives. As the Cold War ended, old demons long thought vanquished reappeared. Racism and antisemitism have again become acceptable; scientists and politicians are again pointing to human inequality as justification for an inhuman policy. Nazis and neo-Nazis march again. Fifty years after 1945, the world is still an insecure and dangerous place where eternal vigilance continues to be the price of liberty.

Henry Friedlander is Professor of History in the Department of Judaic Studies at Brooklyn College of the City University of New York. Born in Berlin in 1930, he was deported in 1941 to the Lodz ghetto, Auschwitz and various other camps and was liberated at Wöbbelin on May 2, 1945. His research has focused on the history of Nazi Germany, the Holocaust, war crimes trials, and his study The Origins of Nazi Genocide: From Euthanasia to the Final Solution *will be published by the University of North Carolina Press in 1995.*

Notes

1. *Kalendarium der Ereignisse im Konzentrationslager Auschwitz-Birkenau, 1939–1945*, ed. Danuta Czech (Reinbek bei Hamburg, 1989), 965–75.

2. For a comprehensive treatment of the war, see Gerhard L. Weinberg, *A World at Arms: A Global History of World War II* (New York and Cambridge, 1994).

3. See Ernst Klee, *"Euthanasie" im NS-Staat: Die "Vernichtung lebensunwerten Lebens"* (Frankfurt, 1983).

4. See Helmut Krausnick and Hans-Heinrich Wilhelm, *Die Truppe des Weltanschauungskrieges: Die Einsatzgruppen der Sicherheitspolizei und des SD, 1938–1942* (Stuttgart, 1981).

5. On the connection between T4 and the final solution, see Henry Friedlander, "Euthanasia and the Final Solution," in *The Final Solution: Origins and Implementation,* ed. David Cesarani (London and New York, 1994), 51–61.

6. See *Justiz und NS-Verbrechen: Sammlung deutscher Strafurteile wegen nationalsozialistischer Tötungsverbrechen,* ed. Adelheid L. Rüter-Ehlermann and C. F. Rüter, 22 vols. (Amsterdam, 1968–81) [hereafter cited as JuNSV], vol. 21, no. 594: LG Bonn, Urteil 8 Ks 3/62, March 30, 1963, and July 23, 1965.

7. See Adalbert Rückerl, *NS-Vernichtungslager im Spiegel deutscher Straf-prozesse* (Munich, 1977).

8. See Raul Hilberg, *The Destruction of the European Jews* (Chicago, 1961), chaps. 7–9; Ino Arndt and Wolfgang Scheffler, "Organisierter Massenmord an Juden in nationalsozialistischen Vernichtungslagern," *Vierteljahrshefte für Zeitgeschichte* 24 (1976): 105–35; H. G. Adler, *Der verwaltete Mensch: Studien zur Deportation der Juden aus Deutschland* (Tübingen, 1974); Henry Friedlander, "The Deportation of the German Jews," *Leo Baeck Institute Yearbook* 29 (1984): 201–26; and Wolfgang Scheffler, "The Forgotten Part of the 'Final Solution': The Liquidation of the Ghettos," *Simon Wiesenthal Center Annual* 2 (1985): 31–51.

9. On Majdanek, see Elizabeth B. White, "Majdanek: Himmler's Terror Outpost in the East," *Simon Wiesenthal Center Annual* 7 (1990): 3–21; on Auschwitz, see Hermann Langbein, *Menschen in Auschwitz* (Frankfurt, 1980).

10. On Hungary, see Randolph L. Braham, *The Politics of Genocide: The Holocaust in Hungary,* 2 vols. (New York, 1981); on the Lodz ghetto, see *The Chronicle of the Lodz Ghetto, 1941–1944,* ed. Lucjan Dobroszycki (New Haven, 1984); and Josef Wulf, *Lodz: Das letzte Ghetto auf polnischem Boden* (Bonn, 1962).

11. H. G. Adler, *Theresienstadt, 1941–1945: Das Antlitz einer Zwangsgemeinschaft,* 2d rev. ed. (Tübingen, 1960), 56–59. While Adler gives gives both July 7 (p. 59) and July 12, 1944 (p. 699) as the date for the destruction of the family camp, *Kalendarium Auschwitz-Birkenau,* p. 820, gives the date as July 11.

12. *Kalendarium Auschwitz-Birkenau,* 838. See also Michael Zimmermann, "Von der Diskriminierung zum 'Familienlager' Auschwitz: Die nationalsozialistische Zigeunerverfolgung," *Dachauer Hefte* 5 (1989): 87–114; and *Memorial Book: The Gypsies in Auschwitz-Birkenau,* ed. State Museum of Auschwitz-Birkenau and Documentary and Cultural Center of German Sinti and Roma, 2 vols. (Munich, 1993).

13. *Chronicle of the Lodz Ghetto,* lxiv–lxv.

14. *Kalendarium Auschwitz-Birkenau,* 868–69.

15. Ibid., 897–900.

16. See, for example, ibid., 903–4.

17. Ibid., 920–21.

18. On the concentration camp system, see Martin Broszat, "Nationalsozialistische Konzentrationslager, 1933–1945," in Hans Buchheim and others, *Anatomie des SS-Staates,* 2 vols. (Munich, 1967), 2:11–133; and Henry Friedlander, "The Nazi Concentration Camps," in *Human Responses to the Holocaust,* ed. Michael Ryan (New York and Toronto, 1981), 33–69.

19. Friedlander, "Concentration Camps," 43–44.

20. Ibid., 47.

21. See Comité International de la Croix-Rouge, International Tracing Service, *Vorläufiges Verzeichnis der Konzentrationslager und deren Außenkommandos sowie anderer Haftstätten unter dem Reichsführer-SS in Deutschland und deutsch besetzten Gebieten, 1933–1945* (Arolsen, 1969).

22. Broszat, "Konzentrationslager," 131; Gerald Reitlinger, *The Final Solution: The Attempt to Exterminate the Jews of Europe, 1939–1945* (New York, 1961 [original publ. 1953]), 448.

23. See *Kalendarium Auschwitz-Birkenau,* note on 821.

24. Reitlinger, *Final Solution,* 461.

25. Nuremberg Doc. L-053, cited ibid., 300.

26. Reitlinger, *Final Solution,* 455–56; Nuremberg Doc. PS-3762: Affidavit Kurt Becher, March 8, 1946. For a detailed analysis of the circumstances surrounding the date Himmler issued his order, see

Richard Breitman and Shlomo Aronson, "The End of the 'Final Solution'? Nazi Plans to Ransom Jews in 1944," *Central European History* 25 (1992): 177–203.

27. Broszat, "Konzentrationslager," 132–33.

28. See Eugen Kogon, *Der SS-Staat: Das System der deutschen Konzentrationslager* (Munich, 1974 [1946]), 351–52; Benedikt Kautsky, *Teufel und Verdammte: Erfahrungen und Erkenntnisse aus sieben Jahren in deutschen Konzentrationslagern* (Zurich, 1946), 100–101.

29. See, for example, the account in Leni Yahil, *The Holocaust: The Fate of European Jewry,* trans. from the Hebrew (New York, 1990), 539–42.

30. Gertrude Schneider, "The Unfinished Road," in *The Unfinished Road: Jewish Survivors of Latvia Look Back,* ed. Gertrude Schneider (Westport, CT, 1991), 1–25.

31. See Ruth Klüger, *Weiter Leben: Eine Jugend* (Göttingen, 1992).

32. Ibid., 161.

33. Ibid., 164.

34. Ibid., 169–89.

35. See Kogon, *SS-Staat,* 229ff.

36. For the history of Bergen-Belsen, see Eberhard Kolb, *Bergen-Belsen: Geschichte des "Aufenthaltslagers," 1943–1945* (Hanover, 1962); idem, *Bergen-Belsen: From "Detention Camp" to Concentration Camp, 1943–1945,* trans. from the German (Göttingen, 1985).

37. See the chronology in Julius H. Krizsan, *Bergen-Belsen: Menschen und ihre Schicksale* (Celle, 1985), 4–6.

38. Ibid., 7–8.

39. Kolb, *Bergen-Belsen* (English ed.), 31–50; Krizsan, *Bergen-Belsen,* 4–6, 15–17, 24.

40. See Ronald Smelser, "Introductory Essay: The 'Final Solution' and the War in 1944," in United States Holocaust Memorial Museum, *Fifty Years Ago: Darkness before Dawn* (Washington, 1994), 17.

41. See documents in John Mendelsohn, ed. *The Holocaust: Selected Documents,* 18 vols. (New York, 1982), vols. 15 and 16 (with introduction by Sybil Milton); Paul Lawrence Rose, ed., *Hecht Archive, University of Haifa,* vol. 12 of *Archives of the Holocaust,* ed. Henry Friedlander and Sybil Milton (New York, 1990); Jonathan Helfand, ed., *Yeshiva University, New York,* vol. 18 of *Archives of the Holocaust* (New York, 1991). See also Breitman and Aronson, "The End of the 'Final Solution'?"; Yehuda Bauer, *Jews for Sale? Nazi-Jewish Negotiations, 1933–1945* (New Haven, 1994); idem, *American Jewry and the Holocaust: The American Jewish Joint Distribution Committee, 1939–1945* (Detroit, 1981), chap. 18; and Heinz Höhne, *The Order of the Death's Head: The Story of Hitler's SS,* trans. from the German (New York, 1971), 634–42.

42. On these negotiations, see Reitlinger, *Final Solution,* 461–76.

43. See Count Folke Bernadotte, *The Curtain Falls: The Last Days of the Third Reich* (New York, 1945).

44. Peter R. Black, *Ernst Kaltenbrunner: Ideological Soldier of the Third Reich* (Princeton, 1984), 239–42.

45. Bauer, *Jews for Sale?,* 244–48. See also Felix Kersten, *The Kersten Memoirs, 1940–1945,* trans. from the German (New York, 1957), 284–90.

46. Weinberg, *World at Arms,* 810–27.

47. See, for example, the account in Primo Levi, *If This is a Man,* trans. from the Italian (New York, 1959); paperback ed. as *Survival in Auschwitz: The Nazi Assault on Humanity* (New York, 1961).

48. *Kalendarium Auschwitz-Birkenau,* 979 and note on 990.

49. Ibid., 281.

50. Ibid., 989–90.

51. Ibid., 995.

52. Nuremberg Doc. D-681: Affidavit George Henning von Bassewitz-Behr (Higher SS and Police Leader for North Sea region), February 14, 1946.

53. Friedlander, "Concentration Camps," 57–58.

54. *JuNSV,* vol. 19, no. 549: LG Hamburg, (50) 8/51, October 3, 1951, and (50) 8/52, June 5, 1952.

55. Ibid., vol. 8, no. 281: LG Hanover, 2 Ks 2/50, May 29, 1951.

56. Ibid., vol. 19, no. 549: LG Hanover, 2 Ks 2/63, April 10, 1963.

57. See Komitee der Antifaschistischen Widerstandskämpfer der Deutschen Demokratischen Republik, *Frauen-KZ Ravensbrück* (Berlin, 1986), 177–82.

58. See Barbara Kühle, *Die Todesmärsche der Häftlinge des KZ Sachsenhausen* (Oranienburg, 1985); and Komitee der Antifaschistischen Widerstandskämpfer der Deutschen Demokratischen Republik, *Sachsenhausen: Dokumente, Aussagen, Forschungsergebnisse und Erlebnisberichte über das ehemalige Konzentrationslager Sachsenhausen* (Berlin, 1977), 113–26.

59. Joachim Neander, *Die letzten von Dora im Gebiet von Osterode: Zur Geschichte eines KZ-Evakuierungsmarsches im April 1945* (Berlin and Boon, 1994), 6.

60. See Angela Fiedermann, Torsten Heß, and Markus Jaeger, *Das Konzentrationslager Mittelbau Dora: Ein historischer Abriß* (Berlin and Bonn, 1993).

61. See chart in Neander, *Die letzten von Dora,* 5.

62. Fiedermann, Heß, and Jaeger, *Konzentrationslager Mittelbau Dora,* 56.

63. United States Department of Justice, press release, October 17, 1984. Rudolph conceded that his "U.S. citizenship was illegally procured," and admitted that he was deportable as someone who had mistreated concentration camp prisoners. Office of Special Investigations, Criminal Division, Department of Justice, "Agreement between Arthur Louis Hugo Rudolph and the United States Department of Justice," November 28, 1983.

64. Fiedermann, Heß, and Jaeger, *Konzentrationslager Mittelbau Dora,* 63.

65. Neander, *Die letzten von Dora,* 10–16.

66. Fiedermann, Heß, and Jaeger, *Konzentrationslager Mittelbau Dora,* 58–62.

67. See Peter Heigl, *Konzentrationslager Flossenbürg in Geschichte und Gegenwart* (Regensburg, 1989), 27–54.

68. P. L. Mollison, "Observations on Cases of Starvation at Belsen," *British Medical Journal* (January 5, 1946), 4–5.

69. See Paul Kemp, "The Liberation of Bergen-Belsen Concentration Camp in April 1945: The Testimony of Those Involved," *Imperial War Museum Review* 5 (1990): 40.

70. See Jon Bridgman, *The End of the Holocaust: The Liberation of the Camps* (Portland, 1990), 47–48.

71. Imperial War Museum, *The Relief of Belsen, April 1945: Eyewitness Accounts* (London, 1991), 6–7.

72. Cited ibid., 9.

73. Cited ibid.

74. Krizsan, *Bergen-Belsen,* 24.

75. SS Oberführer Hermann Pister, Kommandant Buchenwald, to WVHA, Amtsgruppe D, April 6, 1945, facsimile in Nationale Mahn- und Gedenkstätte Buchenwald, *Konzentrationslager Buchenwald Post Weimar/Thür.: Katalog zu der Ausstellung aus der Deutschen Demokratischen Republik im Martin-Gropius-Bau Berlin (West), April–June 1990* (n.p., n.d.), 155.

76. Ibid., 152–60; Kogon, *SS-Staat,* 354–62; Kautsky, *Teufel und Verdammte,* 287–97.

77. Kautsky, *Teufel und Verdammte,* 57.

78. See *Dachauer Hefte,* vol. 1, no. 1 (December 1985), special issue "Die Befreiung," 3–11, 192–93; Marcus J. Smith, *The Harrowing of Hell: Dachau* (Albuquerque, 1972), 79–95.

79. Rudi Goguel, *Cap Arcona: Report über den Untergang der Häftlingsflotte in der Lübecker Bucht am 3. Mai 1945,* 2nd ed. (Frankfurt, 1982), 15.

80. See Bogdan Suchowiak, *Mai 1945: Die Tragödie der Häftlinge von Neuengamme,* trans. from the Polish (Reinbek bei Hamburg, 1985), 93–121.

81. Goguel, *Cap Arcona,* 21.

82. Ibid., 23–30, 46–49.

83. Ibid., 54–79.

84. Hans Marsalek, *Die Geschichte des Konzentrationslagers Mauthausen,* 2d ed. (Vienna, 1980), 131–39, 281–84.

85. Ibid., 285–93, 318.

86. Ibid., 322–25.

87. Ibid., 325–31; Hans Marsalek, *Konzentrationslager Gusen: Ein Nebenlager des KZ Mauthausen,* 2d ed. (Vienna, 1987), 43.

88. See Adler, *Theresienstadt,* 198–220.

89. See the documents in Nuremberg Doc. PS-1696.

90. Ibid.: report from Detachment F1F3, July 2, 1945.

91. Ibid.: death certificate and medical record of Richard Jenne.

92. AJJDC Archive (New York), AR4564/393: Cable from War Refugee Board to American Embassy Paris, transmitting Leavitt message, April 14, 1945; cable S. Levine to AJJDC, May 16, 1945.

93. Adler, *Theresienstadt,* 218.

94. See, for example, Smith, *Dachau,* 101–5 and passim.

95. See Kemp, "Liberation of Bergen-Belsen," 28–41.

96. This was first pointed out by Klaus Dörner, "Nationalsozialismus und Lebensvernichtung," *Vierteljahrshefte für Zeitgeschichte* 15 (1967): 121.

97. See, for example, Ludwig Eiber, *"Ich wußte, es wird schlimm": Die Verfolgung der Sinti und Roma in München, 1933–1945* (Munich, 1993).

98. Ibid., 128–29.

99. See, for example, the efforts of one Italian Jew liberated in Auschwitz to return to his home. Primo Levi, *The Reawakening,* trans. from the Italian (Boston, 1965).

100. United States Holocaust Memorial Museum, Collections, 1986 031.24a.

101. Dwight D. Eisenhower Presidential Library, Eisenhower Pre-Presidential Papers, box 134: cable of April 19, 1945.

102. See AJJDC Archive, AR4564/393: Paul Baerwald to Leverett Saltonstall, May 14, 1945.

103. Library of Congress, Clare Booth Luce Papers, box 678, folders 8–9.

104. For the composition of the delegation, see below, Chronology, entry for April 23–May 8.

105. *Buchenwald Camp: The Report of a Parliamentary Delegation* (London, 1945).

106. Edward N. Peterson, *The American Occupation of Germany: Retreat to Victory* (Detroit, 1977), 37–44, 59–70.

107. Harry S. Truman, *Memoirs,* vol. 1: *Year of Decision* (Garden City, NY, 1955), 235.

108. Peterson, *American Occupation,* 59–61.

109. Cited in Smith, *Dachau,* 23.

110. See Leonard Dinnerstein, *America and the Survivors of the Holocaust* (New York, 1982), chap. 1.

111. See, for example, the case of Feodor Fedorenko, a Treblinka guard who entered the United States under the Displaced Persons Act, became a citizen, but was later denaturalized and deported. Fedorenko v. United States, 449 U.S. 490 (1981).

112. Cited in Henry Friedlander and Earlean McCarrick, "Nazi Criminals in the United States: The Fedorenko Case," *Simon Wiesenthal Center Annual* 2 (1985): 73.

113. See U.S. Congress, House Committee on the Judiciary, Subcommittee on Immigration, Citizenship, and International Law, 95th Congress, 1st and 2nd Sessions, *Alleged Nazi War Criminals,* August 3, 1977, and July 19–21, 1978 (Washington, 1978–79).

114. See AJJDC Archive, AR4564/393: Moses A. Leavitt, Secretary, AJJDC, to James Brunot, Executive Director, President's War Relief Control Board, May 15, 1945.

115. See, for example, Smith, *Dachau,* 193–94.

116. Ibid., 63–64.

117. On Jewish DPs, see Angelika Königseder and Juliane Wetzel, *Lebensmut im Wartesaal: Die jüdischen DPs (displaced persons) im Nachkriegsdeutschland* (Frankfurt, 1994). See also the impressionistic account by Leo W. Schwarz, *The Redeemers: A Saga of the Years 1945–1952* (New York, 1953).

118. Dinnerstein, *America and the Survivors,* 13, 28; Königseder

and Wetzel, *Lebensmut im Wartesaal,* 19–21.

119. Dinnerstein, *America and the Survivors,* 12.

120. AJJDC Archive, AR4564/392: confidential memo from Rabbi Jonah B. Wise, August 24, 1945.

121. Ibid., AR4564/393: AJJDC press release "Relief Teams Prepared to Enter Concentration Camps to Aid Surviving Jews," June 21, 1945; HIAS, *Rescue: Bulletin of Information* (December 1945), 6.

122. AJJDC Archive, AR4564/393: James Brunot, Executive Director, President's War Relief Control Board, to Moses A. Leavitt, Secretary, AJJDC, July 3, 1945.

123. See, for example, ibid., AR4564/392: Comité International de la Croix-Rouge, Geneva, to Saly Mayer, St. Gall, August 13, 1945, transmitting information from Norbert Wollheim in Lübeck.

124. Königseder and Wetzel, *Lebensmut im Wartesaal,* 21–23. On the chaplains, see also Alex Grobman, *Rekindling the Flame: American Jewish Chaplains and the Survivors of European Jewry, 1944–1948* (Detroit, 1993).

125. AJJDC Archive, AR4564/392: letter from Dr. Revel, UNRRA Team 268, August 9, 1945.

126. Dinnerstein, *America and the Survivors,* 46–56; Königseder and Wetzel, *Lebensmut im Wartesaal,* 24–31.

127. See American Jewish Archives, *Among the Survivors of the Holocaust—1945: The Landsberg DP Camp Letters of Major Irving Heymont, United States Army* (Cincinnati, 1982), 8–12.

128. Rosensaft organized the committee with the help of nine other survivors, including Hadassa Bimko, Rosensaft's future wife. Königseder and Wetzel, *Lebensmut im Wartesaal,* 81.

129. AJJDC Archive, AR4564/395: report by Maurice Eigen, August 7, 1945.

130. See, for example, ibid.: Josef Rosensaft to Edward Warburg, November 17, 1945.

131. Ibid.: report by Maurice Eigen, September 9, 1945.

132. Ibid., AR4564/391: Josef Rosensaft and Norbert Wollheim to AJJDC, September 18, 1945.

133. See ibid., AR4564/392: AJJDC report by Saul S. Elgart, November 23, 1945; American Jewish Conference report by Hans Lamm, Decem-ber 21, 1945; report by Rabbi Judah Nadich, Major of the Chaplain Corps and Special Consultant on Jewish Affairs, September 16, 1945.

134. See, for example, ibid., AR4564/161: International Jewish Committee, Camp Mauthausen, to Verband der jüdischen Gemeinden in der Schweiz, June 19, 1945; ibid., AR4564/393: letter from "group of Jewish youth" in Straubing, Bavaria, to "the world-over committee of the 'Joint,' New York," June 18, 1945, with cover letter from World Jewish Congress to AJJDC, July 20, 1945.

135. Königseder and Wetzel, *Lebensmut im Wartesaal,* 81–85. See also Grobman, *Rekindling the Flame,* 55–61.

136. On the French zone, see Abraham J. Peck, ed., *American Jewish Archives, Cincinnati: The Papers of the World Jewish Congress, 1945–1950,* vol. 9 of *Archives of the Holocaust* (New York, 1990), doc. 14: report by Zorach Warhaftig, September 28, 1945.

137. See AJJDC Archive, AR4564/161: reports by James P. Rice, October 4 and 14, 1945; Thomas Albrich, *Exodus durch Österreich: Die jüdischen Flüchtlinge, 1945–1948* (Innsbruck, 1987), 18–26.

138. AJJDC Archive, AR4564/392: report by J. M. Shapiro, [Novem-ber 1945]; Leo Baeck Institute, New York, manuscript collection: Bernhard Kolb, "Die Juden in Nürnberg"; Ursula Büttner, "Not nach der Befreiung: Die Situation der deutschen Juden in der britischen Besatzungs-zone, 1945–1948," in *Das Unrechtsregime,* ed. Ursula Büttner with Werner Johe and Angelika Voß, 2 vols. (Hamburg, 1986), 2:373–406; Abraham J. Peck, "Zu den Anfängen jüdischen Lebens nach 1945," in *Aufbau nach dem Untergang: Deutsch-jüdische Geschichte nach 1945,* ed. Andreas Nachama and Julius H. Schoeps (Berlin, 1992), 225–38; Hermann Simon, "Die jüdische Gemeinde Nordwest: Eine Episode aus der Zeit des Neubeginns jüdischen Lebens in Berlin nach 1945," ibid., 274–84; Königseder and Wetzel, *Lebensmut im Wartesaal,* 89.

139. AJJDC Archive, AR4564/406: reports by Koppel S. Pinson, October 31 and December 24, 1945; report by M. J. Joslow, [January 1946]; Judith Tydor Baumel, "The Politics of Spiritual Rehabilitation in the DP Camps," *Simon Wiesenthal Center Annual* 6 (1989): 57–79.

140. Dinnerstein, *America and the Survivors,* chap. 2.

141. "Report of Earl G. Harrison." All references are to the copy of the report in the Eisenhower Library, Pre-Presidential Papers, box 116.

142. AJJDC Archive, AR4564/392: "Summary of recent reports from JDC representatives in Germany," December 18, 1945.

143. Eisenhower Library, Pre-Presidential Papers, box 116: Eisenhower to Truman, September 18 and October 8, 1945. See also Dinnerstein, *America and the Survivors,* chap. 2.

144. AJJDC Archive, AR4564/390: Leo W. Schwartz, "Report on Influx of Jews into U.S. Zone of Occupation in Germany in August 1946." See also Königseder and Wetzel, *Lebensmut im Wartesaal,* 47–57; Dinnerstein, *America and the Survivors,* 107–12.

145. See Yehuda Bauer, *Flight and Rescue: Brichah* (New York, 1970).

146. Public Papers of the Presidents of the United States, *Harry S Truman: Containing the Public Messages, Speeches, and Statements of the President, April 12 to December 31, 1945* (Washington, 1961), 572–78.

147. Harry S Truman Presidential Library, Papers of Harry S Truman, Official File 127: report from T. B. Shoemaker, Acting Commissioner, Immigration and Naturalization Service, to President Truman, August 7, 1946.

148. Moscow Declaration, November 1, 1943. Text in *Trials of War Criminals before the Nuremberg Military Tribunals under Control Council Law No. 10,* 14 vols. [hereafter cited as *TWC*] (Washington, 1950–1952), 1:viii.

149. Adalbert Rückerl, *The Investigation of Nazi Crimes, 1945–1978* (Heidelberg and Karlsruhe, 1979), 31.

150. London Agreement, August 8, 1945. Text in *Trial of the Major War Criminals before the International Military Tribunal,* 42 vols. [hereafter cited as *TMWC*] (Nuremberg, 1947–1949), 1:8–9.

151. *TMWC,* 1:10–18.

152. See Bradley F. Smith, *The Road to Nuremberg* (New York, 1981).

153. Truman Library, Papers of Harry S Truman, Official File 325-A: Robert H. Jackson, "Memorandum for the President," April 29, 1945.

154. Ibid.: Henry L. Stimson to Robert H. Jackson, May 13, 1946.

155. Ibid.: executive order, September 24, 1945.

156. Ibid.: Harry S Truman to John J. Parker, October 12, 1946.

157. For the sentences, see *TMWC* 1:365–67; for the convicted organizations, see *TMWC* 1:255–73.

158. Cited in Telford Taylor, *The Anatomy of the Nuremberg Trials: A Personal Memoir* (New York, 1992), 167.

159. Earl F. Ziemke, *The U.S. Army in the Occupation of Germany, 1944–1946* (Washington, 1975), 390–91.

160. National Archives and Records Administration (NARA), Suitland Branch, RG 338, Records of U.S. Army Commands, 1942–, United States v. Alfons Klein et al., (Case File 12-449), October 8–15, 1945, box 4, file 24: record of trial, February 18, 1946.

161. See Raymond Phillips, ed., *Trial of Josef Kramer and Forty-Four Others (The Belsen Trial)* (London, Edinburgh, and Glasgow, 1949). See also NARA Suitland, RG 338, Records of U.S. Army Com-mands, 1942–, United States v. Alfons Klein, box 2, file 9: report of American observer, Lieutenant Colonel Meade F. Griffin, at Lüneburg, "Auschwitz-Belsen Concentration Camp Trial."

162. Rückerl, *The Investigation of Nazi Crimes,* 28–29.

163. Control Council Law No. 10 (December 20, 1945). Text in *TWC* 1:xvi–xix.

164. See Taylor, *Anatomy of the Nuremberg Trials,* chap. 1; Willard B. Cowles, "University of Jurisdiction over War Crimes," *California Law Review* 33 (1945): 177–218.

165. See Henry Friedlander, "The Judiciary and Nazi Crimes in Post-war Germany," *Simon Wiesenthal Center Annual* 1 (1984): 27–44.

CONCENTRATION CAMPS JANUARY 1945

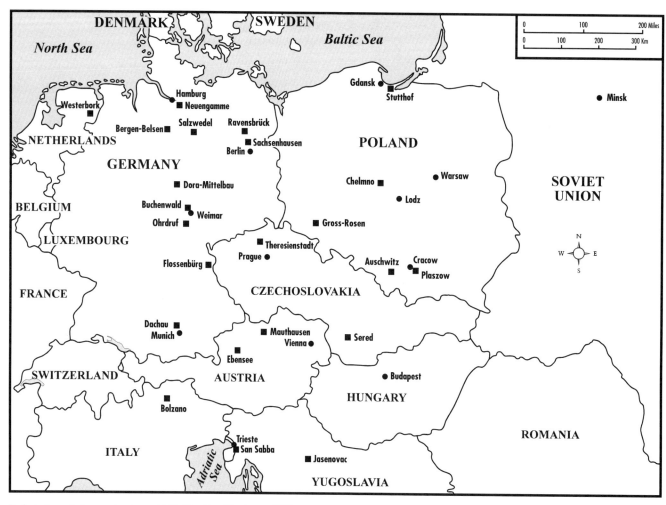

Defacto boundaries as of autumn 1945. The Free Territory of Trieste
was under joint American, British, and Yugoslav administration.

Key:

■ Concentration camps

● Cities

NOTE TO THE READER

The following notes briefly explain the editorial conventions used in this volume:

Glossary entries: Names and terms highlighted by SMALL CAPITALS in the selection introductions and elsewhere are more fully explained in the Glossary, pages 302–315.

Spelling: All selections contain the originally published spellings except where noted. As a result, German language terminology may vary, and German vowels with an umlaut are often transliterated by the addition of an "e": for example, *Führer* becomes Fuehrer.

Photo credits: Photo credits are abbreviated as

USHMM: United States Holocaust Memorial Museum Photo Archive, Washington, D.C.

NARA: Still Picture Branch, National Archives and Records Administration, College Park, Maryland.

THE HOLOCAUST

- The advent of 1945 witnessed the German military retreat from every front. Yet even as Allied armies penetrated the Reich's territory at its eastern and western frontiers, the Nazis continued to carry out their genocidal policies at the cost of tens of thousands of lives.

- At the beginning of 1945, eleven central concentration camps still remained in operation: Auschwitz-Birkenau, Bergen-Belsen, Buchenwald, Dachau, Dora-Mittelbau, Flossenbürg, Gross-Rosen, Neuengamme, Ravensbrück, Sachsenhausen, and Stutthof. With the exception of Bergen-Belsen, each of these camps administered numerous satellite camps holding large numbers of mostly Jewish prisoners.

- In the final months of war, the German economy's growing need for labor and the advance of the Red Army into German-held territory spurred the SS to transfer prisoners from the eastern camps to concentration and satellite camps inside Germany. This mobilization fulfilled Hitler's May 1944 order that even Jewish slave labor should be utilized at various facilities vital to the German war effort within the borders of the Reich proper.

- As Germany's borders continued to contract, evacuation trains and marches moved from east to west before the advancing Red Army while other evacuations moved west to east in order to escape British and American forces.

- The eastern camps like Auschwitz were often evacuated in the most disorderly fashion and with absolutely no concern for the prisoners. Orders were issued too late to ensure an orderly retreat and rarely allowed SS officials sufficient time to obliterate physical traces of their crimes.

- All but the most physically incapacitated prisoners were forced to participate in the evacuation marches. Thousands were shot to death en route and thousands more succumbed to hunger, cold, and exhaustion as their SS guards strove to move their prisoners further and further into the German interior.

- At least 250,000 concentration camp inmates died in forced marches from the summer of 1944 to war's end.

The crematorium ovens at Mauthausen concentration camp as they appeared after the camp was liberated. (USHMM)

20,000 MET DEATH IN NAZI HORROR ASYLUM

by Andy Rooney

Originally a psychiatric institution, the HADAMAR State Psychiatric Hospital and Sanitarium was used by the Nazis as a "EUTHANASIA" facility after 1941. During the war more than eleven thousand people were murdered there. In 1944–45 ill Polish and Soviet concentration camp inmates were killed at Hadamar as well. After the Allies entered Germany, Andy Rooney, then a correspondent for the U.S. Army newspaper Stars and Stripes *and currently a commentator for the television program "60 Minutes," reported on the liberation of this euthanasia facility.*

WITH THE FIRST ARMY, Germany, April 14 — A German mass murder factory hidden in the German insane asylum at Hadamar, four miles from Limburg, has been uncovered by First Army authorities. It is estimated that 20,000 political prisoners, Jews and foreign slave laborers were put to death in the asylum chambers.

German civil authorities said that 10,000 men and women were gassed and cremated, another 5,000 were put to death with drugs and poisons and buried in one grave near the 14-foot walls around the asylum. Still another 5,000 victims were put out of the way by a new German regime in the deathhouse by a needle injection which was pushed through the ribs to the heart. The hypodermic method killed victims in about 20 minutes.

The Nazis said they were too old or hopelessly sick to go on living.

The deathhouse in the pseudo insane asylumn has been operated by the Nazis since 1941 and details of the authenticity of the murder factory appeared beyond question. Confessions have been obtained from two of an unholy threesome of alleged psychiatrists who were running the place.

The asylum sits on a hill overlooking the village of Hadamar. The bodies were hidden behind a wall on the asylum grounds and American officers counted 481 graves. The caretaker admitted, however, that there were 5,000 bodies buried there. Most of the dead, he admitted, were tumbled into graves naked, 20 at a time.

Fifteen thousand others were killed before the present regime took over. The new regime, presided over by a 70-year-old psychiatrist, favored hypodermic injections as a method of killing.

The gas chamber, which was operated by SS officers from Berlin, was discontinued after protests from villagers and the Bishop of Munster.

Three Germans in charge of the deathhouse were all huge men—over six feet tall, according to 1-Lt. W. R. Johnson of Loveland, Colo. Johnson, who took part in the investigation, said that the place gave him the shivers just to walk through it. He wandered through dark underground tunnels dripping with water and was brushed by the whirring wings of bats.

In the upper rooms, the officers found 300 babbling, mad patients. These 300 were "front men" for the visitors and show-window cases used as justification for euthanasia.

Capt. Brinkley Hamilton, former British detective credited with uncovering the murder asylum first visited the place with Maj. Harvey Coverly after Capt. Alton H. Jung, of San Antonio, Tex., reported that the prisoners kept insisting that thousands of people had been murdered in the asylum.

On March 29 when the investigators began to unfold the story they found that the last murder had taken place only eight days before they got there.

The most gruesome touch of all was the drunken orgy which was reported to have taken place in celebration of the 10,000th death at the murder factory. Hamilton said that information was supplied voluntarily by the local magistrate.

"He told us these sadistic SS men who were running the asylum started a wild party with the guests from Berlin," Hamilton said. "The SS men actually drank wine from the preserved skulls of some of their victims."

The citizens of the town of Hadamar knew what was going on in the death factory, according to Hamilton, but were afraid to talk for fear of reprisals. The local magistrate said he learned much about the institution because many of the papers which were supposed to be forwarded to Berlin through secret channels passed through his hands.

—From The Stars and Stripes, *April 15, 1945, German edition.*

CONCENTRATION CAMPS

Auschwitz

SOVIET REPORT ON AUSCHWITZ

During World War II the Soviet government organized so-called "Extraordinary State Committees" to investigate war crimes committed by the Germans and their partners. In May 1945 the committee to investigate AUSCHWITZ, including the KILLING CENTER at BIRKENAU, issued its report, which was published in the weekly English language newsletter issued by the Soviet Embassy during World War II. The total number of victims mentioned in the report has subsequently been revised to a total of approximately 1.1 million people.

On the basis of interrogation and medical examination of 2,819 prisoners of Oswiecim camp who were saved by the Red Army, a study of German documents discovered in the camp, the remains of the crematorium and gas chambers blown up by the Germans as they retreated, bodies found on the territory of the camp, and belongings and documents found in camp warehouses and barracks of the people from various countries of Europe who were killed by the Germans, it has been established that:

One: By execution, starvation, poisoning, and monstrous tortures, the Germans annihilated in Oswiecim camp more than four million citizens of the Soviet Union, Poland, France, Belgium, Holland, Czechoslovakia, Yugoslavia, Rumania, Hungary, and other countries.

Two: German professors and doctors conducted in the camp so-called "medical" experiments on living men, women and children.

Three: In the degree of premeditation, technical organization, and mass scale and cruelty of murder, the Oswiecim camp leaves far behind all German death camps known hitherto.

The Oswiecim camp had gas chambers, a crematorium, surgical departments and laboratories—all intended for the monstrous annihilation of people. The Germans called the gas chambers "special purpose baths." On the entrance to the "bath" was written "For Disinfection," and at the exit "Entrance to Bath." People earmarked for annihilation thus unsuspectingly entered the premises for disinfection, undressed and from there were herded into the special purpose bath—that is, into the gas chamber where they were wiped out by cyclone poison.

Special hospitals, surgical wings, histological laboratories and other institutions were established at the camp, but they existed not to treat people, but to kill them. German professors and doctors carried out wholesale experiments on perfectly healthy men, women and children in these institutions. They conducted experiments in sterilizing women and castrating men and boys, in infecting large numbers of people with cancer, typhus and malaria, conducting observations upon them; they tested the action of poisons on living persons.

The Oswiecim camp was built in 1939 on orders from SS Reichsfuehrer Himmler, especially for the destruction of enslaved citizens of the occupied countries of Europe. The camp occupied a huge area around the city of Oswiecim and consisted of a whole chain of camps: Auschwitz, Birkenau, Monowice [Monowitz], Golesau, Jawisowic, Neidachs, Blechamer [Blechammer], and others. The chief ones—Auschwitz and Birkenau—covered an area of 467.5 hectares and had more than 620 barracks and service buildings. From 180,000 to 250,000 prisoners were always confined in the camps at Oswiecim. All the camps were surrounded by deep moats and belted by a thick barbed wire fence through which a high-voltage current ran.

In 1941, the first crematorium with three furnaces was built in Auschwitz camp to burn the bodies of people put to death. At the crematorium there was the so-called "special purpose bath," that is, a gas chamber for asphyxiating people. The first crematorium functioned until the middle of 1943. In the summer of 1942, SS Reichsfuehrer Himmler inspected the Oswiecim camp and ordered it to be extended to gigantic size and technically perfected.

The construction of large, new crematoriums was commissioned to the German firm of Topf and Sons of Erfurt, which at once began to build four large crematoriums and gas chambers in Birkenau. Berlin, impatient, demanded acceleration of construction and completion of all work by the beginning of 1943. Voluminous correspondence of the camp management with the firm of Topf and Sons was found among the Auschwitz camp office papers. Among them were the following letters:

I.

I. A. Topf and Sons
Erfurt

February 12, 1943

Central Construction SS and Police
Auschwitz (Oswiecim)
Re: Crematoriums Two and Three of camp for war prisoners

We confirm receipt of your telegram of February 10 of the following content: We again confirm receipt of your order for five triple muffle furnaces, including two electric lifts for hoisting corpses and one temporary lift for corpses. Also ordered are a practical device for feeding coal, and a device for transporting ashes. You have to deliver complete installation for crematorium No. 3. We expect you to take all steps for immediate shipment of all machines and parts. Installation must absolutely begin functioning on April 10, 1943.

I. A. Topf and Sons

II

No. 12115/42/er/na.2

With respect to the installation of two triple muffle furnaces; one each for the "special purpose baths," engineer Pruefer has proposed taking them from furnaces prepared for shipment to Mogilev. The head of the Service Section in the SS Economic Administration of the Central Department in Berlin was immediately notified of this and requested to issue further instructions.

SS Untersturmfuehrer (S)
Oswiecim, August 21, 1942

Four new crematoriums contained 12 furnaces with 46 retorts; each retort could accommodate from three to five bodies, which were cremated in about 20 to 30 minutes. "Special purpose baths"—lethal gas chambers—were constructed in the cellars of the crematoriums or in special wings. Besides, the camp had two separate baths, the bodies from which were burned on special pyres. Persons scheduled for execution were herded into the baths with blows from sticks and rifle butts and by dogs. The chambers had hermetically-sealing doors and the people inside were asphyxiated with cyclone [ZYKLON B]. Death ensued in three to five minutes; 20 to 30 minutes later the bodies were taken out and sent to the cremation furnaces. Before the bodies were cremated, dentists pulled out any gold teeth or crowns.

The "productivity" of the baths, or gas chambers, considerably exceeded the capacity of the cremation furnaces, and hence the Germans in addition used huge pyres to burn bodies. Pits 25 to 30 meters long, four to six meters wide, and two meters deep were dug for these pyres. At the bottom ran ditches for ash pits. The bodies were brought up to the pyres on a narrow-gauge line, placed in the pits in layers alternating with logs, and drenched with petroleum. The ashes were thrown into large pits or into the Sola or Vistula Rivers.

To utilize the unburned bones, beginning with 1943 the Germans crushed them and sold them to the Strem Company for the manufacture of superphosphate. Found in the camp were shipping papers addressed to the Strem Company for 112 tons, 600 kilograms of crushed human bones. The Germans also used for industrial purposes the hair shorn from women about to be annihilated.

In the Oswiecim camp the Germans daily executed and burned from 10,000 to 12,000 persons, of whom 8,000 to 10,000 were new arrivals and 2,000 to 3,000 prisoners of the camp.

When interrogated as witnesses, ex-prisoners Shloma Dragon, resident of a small town of Zirovnin, Warsaw Voyevodstvo; and Henry Tauber of the city of Kczanow, Poland, who had worked in a special crew servicing the gas chambers and crematoriums, testified as follows:

"... When the camp first began functioning, the Germans had two gas chambers situated three kilometers apart. They each had two wooden barracks. New arrivals were led into the barracks, undressed and then led into the gas chamber ... from 1,500 to 1,700 at a time were driven into the chambers, and then SS men in gas masks threw cyclone [Zyklon B] inside through trap doors. The gassing lasted from 15 to 20 minutes after which the bodies were taken out and

carted on wagonettes to pits where they were burned. ... Later four crematoriums functioned on the territory of the camp in Birkenau and each had a gas chamber. Crematoriums Nos. 2 and 3 were of similar design and had 15 furnaces each, while crematoriums Nos. 4 and 5 were of different design, less convenient as regards size and technical perfection, and had eight furnaces each. In the course of a day and night these furnaces burned from 10,000 to 12,000 bodies."

Medical Experiments On Living People

In Oswiecim camp the German-fascist professors and doctors widely practiced medical experiments on living persons, displaying monstrous inventiveness.

Among the prisoners saved by the Red Army, Doctors Steinberg of Paris, Gordon of Vilnius, Professor Grossman of Yugoslavia, Erwin Valentin of Berlin, Anna Keppich of Hungary, Edward Devind of Holland, and Albert Flechner of Paris, stated that they had been eyewitnesses to a vast number of medical experiments on camp prisoners by German-fascist professors and doctors.

Surgical operations were performed at the caprice of the German doctors to practice operation technique. Koenig, a young German doctor, selected prisoners with inflammatory processes in the extremities and practised amputation. The German doctors Tillo and Fischer assembled large numbers of prisoners, and with no cause performed hernia operations on them. At the slightest complaint of a stomach pain, Enders, head doctor of the hospital, practiced operating on an ulcer of the stomach.

Experiments on women were conducted in the hospital wards of the Auschwitz camp. Up to 400 women prisoners were confined in the tenth wing of the camp where experiments were carried out on sterilization by X-ray and subsequent removal of ovaries; on transplanting cancer to the cervix of the uterus; on forced childbirth, and on testing substances for roentgenography of the uterus.

In wing No. 28, experiments on inflicting skin injuries with kerosene, various salts, pastes and powders were performed on prisoners. Here also akrichine was used with the purpose of studying invoked jaundice. These experiments were performed by Doctor Emil Koschub.

In wing No. 21, wholesale experiments were performed in castrating men with the purpose of studying the possibility of sterilization by X-ray. Castration was carried out at a definite interval after the rays had been employed. Professor Schuman and Doctor Dering engaged in such experiments with X-rays and castration. Not infrequently the operations consisted in removing one or both testicles for study after the person had been X-rayed.

All these facts are confirmed as well by ex-prisoners of the camp: Judith Klein, Klara Ausen, Mina Garbman, Nona Sonders, Jakob Skurnik, David Sures, and many others upon whom the German doctors carried out one or another experiment.

On orders from Enders, chief German doctor, between

1941 and 1944 prisoners in the camp hospital were put to death by injections of phenol into the heart. The first injections were made by the doctor and later ones by orderlies. The German Kler, a former shoemaker, particularly distinguished himself in this field by killing thousands of victims. A Polish prisoner by the name of Panszczik did 12,000 persons to death by phenol injections (subsequently he was killed by Polish prisoners themselves). Stess, a German, murdered 10,000 persons by such injections.

The facts of the inhuman experiments on prisoners are also confirmed by a number of documents found in the camp office. A report of the surgical department of the camp hospital records that in three months between October and December, 1943, surgeons of the department carried out, among other operations, the following: 89 testicle amputations (castration), 5 sterilizations, 5 removals of ovaries.

In telegram No. 2678, dated April 28, 1943, Colonel Sommer, SS Obersturmfuehrer, instructed the office of the camp commandant to list 128 women under the heading "prisoners for experiments." In a discovered "statistical review by the camp commandant of the number of women prisoners and their distribution in various categories," signed by Sell, assistant camp commandant, there is a permanent heading, "Prisoners intended for various experiments." Recorded under this heading are 400 "women under experiment," on May 15, 1944; 413 on June 5, 1944; 348 on June 19, 1944; 349 on July 30, 1944, etc.

German doctors played a leading role in selecting the prisoners for gassing and cremation. They conducted the selection everywhere: near crematoriums, in hospitals, and in barracks. The weak, sick, and disabled were dispatched to the gas chambers by the German doctors. The following German doctors engaged in selecting prisoners for annihilation: Wirtz, Mengele, Rode, Fischer, Tillo, Kitt, Koenig, Klein, and many others.

On orders from Wirtz, head German doctor of the Oswiecim chain of camps, during the typhus fever epidemics, inmates of entire barracks were put to death by means of gas asphyxiation. The Medico-Legal Commission has established that German doctors in Oswiecim carried out the following experiments on living persons:

1) Mass resection of tissue of cervix of the uterus, or even complete removal of the latter.

2) The testing of a number of unknown substances for roentgenography of the uterus and fallopian tubes. With special instruments these substances were injected under pressure into the cavity of the uterus, which frequently entailed excruciating pain for the victims upon whom the experiments were performed.

3) Sterilization of women by X-raying the pelvic region, with subsequent opening up of the abdomen and removal of the ovaries. These experiments were carried out chiefly on young women.

4) A study of the action of various chemical preparations, by orders of German firms. Doctor Erwin Valentin, a German, testified that there was a case when Glauber, a gynecologist from Koenigshuette, and Gebel, a chemist, representatives of the chemical industry of Germany, bought 150 women from the camp management for such experiments.

5) Sterilization of men by X-rays.

6) Experiments on men involving the application of irritants to the skin or shin to evoke ulcers and phlegmon.

7) A number of other experiments, such as infection with malaria, artificial insemination and the like.

A great many of the experiments ended in a rapid and torturous death for the prisoners. After the prisoners had been fully utilized for experiments, they were killed and cremated. By this means the Germans strove to remove witnesses to their inhuman experiments.

Ex-prisoner Samuel Abramovich Stern, a resident of the city of Bucharest, who was interrogated as a witness, testified: ". . . I worked in Auschwitz camp as a male nurse. On orders from Oberfeldvebel [Senior Sergeant] Koschub I made injections and did other things to prisoners. I know for a fact that kerosene was injected under the skin of the shin on many patients . . . A second method of experimentation was chemical irritation of the skin. Used for this purpose was an 80 per cent solution of aluminum acetate. After this, a whole layer of skin was removed and sent for analysis. In cases of deep irritation of the skin, part of the flesh was cut out together with the skin and sent for analysis. Koschub also invoked jaundice and performed transfusion operations with the blood of malaria patients."

M. Valigura, who was subjected to experiments, stated ". . . Several days after I had been brought to Birkenau—it seems to me it was in the beginning of December, 1942—all young men between the ages of 18 and 30 were sterilized by subjecting the scrotum to X-rays. I was among those sterilized. Eleven months after I had been sterilized, that is, November 1, 1943, I was subjected to castration . . . 200 other persons were subjected to sterilization on the same day as I . . ."

Witness David Sures of the city of Salonika, Greece, gave the following testimony. ". . . About July, 1943, I and 10 other Greeks were registered in some sort of a list and sent to Birkenau. There we were stripped and subjected to sterilization by X-rays. A month after sterilization we were summoned to the central section of the camp, where all who had been sterilized were subjected to a castration operation. . . ."

Ex-prisoner M. Hauser (Nine, Cite Milton, Paris) stated ". . . In Auschwitz we were placed in the tenth wing. We did not know why we had been taken there. This wing contained the hospital section and we were all perfectly healthy women . . . At first in the tenth wing they took a blood sample from me; for what purpose I don't know. At the end of August, 1943, I was taken to the operating room and anesthetized, and an operation was performed on my genital organs. The operation was performed by Doctor Samuel, a prisoner, under the supervision and on the instructions of the German doctor Wirtz. After this operation, I lay ill for 11 months in the tenth wing. Among those who were sterilized was a Jewess from Greece named Bela. I don't know her last name. After X-rays her abdomen was cut open lengthwise. After the operation she recovered and the wound on the abdomen healed. The German doctor Schuman came to the tenth wing and as a control case took Bela to the twenty-eighth wing and then cut open her abdomen crosswise. I myself saw the crosswise cut on her abdomen. Several days later, Bela died."

It has been established by investigation that from three to five trains, each carrying between 1,500 and 3,000 people destined to be done to death, arrived every day in Oswiecim. The victims were brought from all countries of Europe. Among the 2,819 prisoners released from the Oswiecim camp and subjected to examination by the Medico-Legal Commission were 745 from Poland, 542 from Hungary, 346 from France, 315 from Czechoslovakia, 180 from the USSR, 159 from Holland, 143 from Yugoslavia, 91 from Italy, 76 from Greece, 52 from Rumania, and 41 from Belgium.

Between 200 and 500 of the more able-bodied were chosen from each trainload for various work in the camp; the rest were sent straight to the gas chambers and crematoriums.

Stanek Francziszec, traffic dispatcher at Oswiecim station, testified: "Trainloads of prisoners came in 1942, 1943, and 1944 from Czechoslovakia, Belgium, France, Holland, Norway, Greece, Poland, and other countries."

Witness Eduard de Vind testified: "After the Germans occupied Holland a purge was made in November, 1940, of the state apparatus, institutions and educational establishments of Holland. Three of us university assistants were removed. I moved to Amsterdam. A Dutch fascist was found murdered in one of the districts of Amsterdam. In reprisal, the Germans arrested 400 hostages, including myself. I was picked up on the street and brought here to this camp."

Witness Jacob Gordon of Vilnius testified: "I was brought to Oswiecim camp January 22, 1943. There were altogether 3,650 persons in our train; only 265 men and about 80 women were left in the camp; the rest were immediately sent to the crematorium where they were gassed and cremated, among them my wife Mathilda, a doctor by profession, my son aged four and a half, my father aged 73 and my mother aged 64."

Witness Emilie Dessanti, Italian by nationality, testified: "On September 1944, the Hitlerites shipped us out of Italy and brought us to the Oswiecim camp. There were altogether 500 of us Italians; only 30 have survived, the rest were brutally tortured to death and murdered in the camp."

Witness David Sures testified: "I arrived at Oswiecim by train from Greece April 3, 1943. There were more than 2,500 in the train, including my mother, aged 53, my sister with her child, and myself. Of the 2,500, about 300 were sent to the camp; the rest, including my mother and sister with her five-year-old child, were taken straight from the train to the crematorium to be burned."

Witness Georg Kitman from Rumania testified: "At the end of June, 1944, I and my parents together with 3,000 other men, women and children were brought by train to Oswiecim camp. When we alighted from the train all the old people and mothers with small children were separated and sent to the crematorium to be burned. Among them was my father, aged 52, and my mother, aged 48. Of the 3,000 people, no more than 350 were sent to the camp."

Witness Ziska Speter testified: "In February, 1943, I arrived from France with 1,100 other prisoners. On the day of arrival, 205 of the able-bodied were selected and sent to barracks; the remaining 895, old people, women and children, were taken to a gas chamber to be murdered."

Anna Keppich, a former inmate of the camp, a Hungarian from the city of Cluj, testified: "I arrived in Oswiecim camp in June, 1944, among 3,000 Hungarian prisoners. On arrival at the camp, 500 able-bodied people were left for work in the camp, while the other 2,500 were sent the gas chambers to be killed."

Professor Berthold Epstein, a doctor of medicine from Prague University, made the following statement to the Commission: "Selected groups of prisoners were sent to the gas chambers to be put to death. For several months we saw long processions of people going to their death; the biggest groups were exterminated in May, June and July, 1944. In that period the crematoriums were busy day and night, as could be seen from the flames issuing from the smokestacks. We could often smell burning flesh, hair or nails. At that time, besides the fire from the chimneys of the crematoriums, we saw two large bonfires. From the camp came the barking of SS watchdogs. Since the crematoriums were overloaded, the unfortunate victims were led up in groups, and at the sight of the bonfires guessed what was in store for them. I knew that my relatives had suffered the same fate and that I myself would not escape it. Approximately every two weeks the camp doctor Mengele selected new victims. One day 500 children were murdered. Heart-rending scenes took place when these children were sent off, since everyone knew by then where they were going. The SS men and their assistants outdid themselves in brutality. When we arrived in Oswiecim my wife and I were separated and I never saw her again. Later on I learned that she had not been accepted in the camp. There is no doubt that my wife was murdered in the usual way. In March, 1944, the SS also murdered my sister-in-law with her two children, and my niece, aged 38. In July, 1944, my sister was also done to death."

As has been established by the investigation, besides the persons used for the purposes of experiments, some 200,000 prisoners were kept permanently in the Oswiecim camps for exploitation in all kinds of hard labor. Persons thus occupied were driven to a state of extreme exhaustion after which, being unfit for work, they were done away with. Every week the German doctors made "selections" among the prisoners, with the result that all those who were sick and unable to work were done to death in the gas chambers. Their number was constantly replenished by persons selected from new trainloads. This was part of the organized monstrous death-conveyor system: prisoners were done to death and others were put in their places; when ruthless exploitation played havoc with their health, these in turn were sent to the gas chambers.

In 1941 the Germans launched the construction of a large chemical plant of I. G. Farbenindustrie not far from Oswiecim, as well as a war plant for the manufacture of detonators and charges for bombs and shells. Construction was carried out by the Krupp firm and later by the Union and other firms. The labor of tens of thousands of Oswiecim prisoners of various nationalities—Russians, Ukrainians, Byelorussians, Poles, French, Czechs, Yugoslavs, Greeks, Belgians, Hollanders, and Italians—was brutally exploited on this construction work, as well as on the draining of marshes, work in mines, and on road building jobs.

The distance from the barracks of the concentration camps to work was seven or eight kilometers. SS men lined up the prisoners by the thousands and marched them to work under guard, surrounded by jailers with sticks and dogs. During work, the SS men, supervisors and foremen brutally beat up the prisoners for trying to straighten their backs, for not digging deep enough, for working too slowly, and to force them to run while hauling heavy wheelbarrows of earth. "The firm is paying four marks for you," the foremen would say, as they urged the workers on. "You have to work like horses."

Those who fell from exhaustion were shot on the spot. The work site was at the same time the scene of wholesale slaughter of prisoners. Murder was encouraged in every way by the management. Obersturmbannfuehrer Liebenhenschel issued an order to pay the SS men 60 marks for every prisoner they killed "for attempting to escape." In order to get this bonus, guards killed prisoners right and left.

Maurice Stasman, a Belgian and former inmate of Oswiecim, made the following statement about the murder of prisoners on the construction sites:

"In August, 1943, I worked on the construction site of the I. G. Farbenindustrie plant. One day SS men brought 400 prisoners to the site, among whom were Yugoslavs, Greeks, French, and Belgians, led them to a newly-dug ditch and commenced to bury them alive. The doomed men begged for mercy in their respective languages, and the SS men turned to us, saying, 'Work better or the same thing will happen to you.' Two weeks later we were sent to prepare the foundation for one of the buildings at the Auschwitz camp. SS Losman and a group of other SS men selected 30 from our group, led them over to a ditch and buried them up to their shoulders. Then they mounted horses and galloped over the field, trampling 30 helpless victims to death."

A huge area of the Oswiecim swamps became the grave of many thousands of people of various nationalities. More than 300 brigades of from 50 to 1,200 each worked here. As a result of inhuman conditions in the swamps, where the people were forced to labor at all times of the year, the constant beatings, violence and murder, no one lasted more than two or three months on this job. People were done to death in the swamps when they became unfit for work; they were either given injections of phenol in the heart or sent to the gas chambers.

Jacob Koenig, a 60-year-old land-reclamation engineer from Hungary who had worked in the swamps as an ordinary navvy, testified: "I was one of a brigade of 400 prisoners working on draining the swamps. The German criminals who acted as supervisors beat the prisoners with sticks and spades until they lost consciousness. Men and women of all ages worked in our brigade. Many of them were intellectuals, doctors, teachers and professors. There were 14 engineers from Yugoslavia alone working as common laborers."

Simon Maiselier, a Belgian, formerly imprisoned in Oswiecim, stated: "During three months of 1944, between 100 and 200 corpses were brought in daily from a job on which a brigade of 1,200 of us were engaged; new victims were supplied to take their place."

The German executioners were especially savage in their treatment of Soviet prisoners; as a rule the latter were killed immediately upon arrival at the camp, and only in rare cases were the more able-bodied kept alive for work.

The following order regarding Soviet citizens was found in the camp office:

Oranienburg, 15 November, 1941

Confidential
Reichsfuehrer of SS
Inspector of Concentration Camps
Police (Oswiecim: 14 F 14 L)
Re: Execution of Russian War Prisoners
To the Commandants of Concentration Camps: Copy to camp doctors, camp fuehrers of prisoners under surveillance, managements.

The SS Reichsfuehrer and Chief of the German Police has given his consent in principle to the postponement of the execution of those of the total number of Russian war prisoners sent to concentration camps for execution (especially commissars), provided they are physically fit for work in the stone quarries. For this purpose it is necessary to obtain the consent of the Chief of Security Police and the SD police. I therefore order: Upon the arrival of the trains in camp with prisoners to be executed, the Russians physically fit for work in stone quarries are to be selected by the chief of the camp (E) and the chief camp doctor. A list of Russians (in two copies) must be sent to us. On this list the camp doctor must state that there are no objections from the medical standpoint to these people being used for work.

After receiving the consent of the Chief of Security Police and the SD police, shipment of the respective Russians to the stone quarries will be arranged by an order from here.

(Signed)
Glueks, Fuehrer SS Brigade and Major General

On the basis of this order part of the Soviet prisoners of war were retained for the heaviest work, receiving the most brutal and inhuman treatment of all from SS men and supervisors. Marian Gandzlik, a resident of the town of Oswiecim, testified: "For two weeks during the winter of 1941, when the frost was 35 degrees below zero Centigrade, Russian war prisoners were driven with whips and sticks like cattle along the road from Oswiecim camp to Babitse village. Many of them were hatless and dressed only in tunics and underwear, with torn boots on their feet. In the evenings several carts full of corpses of these Russian war prisoners would come from the direction of Babitse village. On top of the cart would sit two or three prisoners with frost-bitten faces, hands and legs, and in a state of complete exhaustion."

The Hitlerites were forever insisting on more and more murders from their subordinates. On February 14, 1944, Obersturmbannfuehrer Liebenhenschel, chief of the Oswiecim garrison, issued an order which read in part as follows: "From prolonged personal observation I have established that too many prisoners whose labor is not utilized are employed on all jobs except war plants. They loaf on the job. We know that in order to heighten labor productivity of prisoners, it is necessary to intensify control by the junior commanding personnel of the SS, but we also know that we have none too many of the latter, since they are either at the front or doing service on other important sectors. We shall have to help ourselves. It is clear that swift action is essential and I hope that each man will do what is required."

As a result of this order, frightful processions of bloody, tormented prisoners surrounded by SS men and supervisors with huge packs of dogs, and carrying the bodies of their comrades on wooden stretchers, were seen coming every evening from all corners of the Oswiecim camps, from factories, swamps and mines, to the barracks. During evening rollcall, the prisoners were lined up with the bodies of the day's dead piled up in front of them, while the supervisors reported to their chiefs on the fulfillment of Liebenhenschel's order. The chiefs thanked those whose brigades had brought back the largest number of corpses. Those of the prisoners who had been found guilty of some misdemeanor during the day were flogged then and there.

Added to the frightful conditions of slave labor were the appalling living conditions prevailing in the barracks. Premises intended for 400 to 500 persons were made to accommodate 1,000 to 1,500 persons. The hunger, disease, torture and unhygienic conditions were all part of a deliberate plan to exterminate the prisoners as quickly as possible.

The Medico-Legal Commission which examined 2,819 Oswiecim prisoners rescued by the Red Army established that 2,189, or 91 per cent, were suffering from extreme physical exhaustion, while 223 had tuberculosis of the lungs. It was likewise established that the Germans had subjected the prisoners to physical torture, as a result of which the Commission found the people suffering from broken ribs, limbs, spines and facial bones, also various wounds, ulcers, and frozen hands and feet. Very many of the released prisoners are suffering from serious nervous and psychiatric ailments.

The Medico-Legal Commission performed autopsies on 536 bodies of prisoners found in various parts of the territory of the camps. It has been established that in 474 cases (88.3 per cent) death resulted from exhaustion.

Hundreds of thousands of children, from infants to 16-year-olds, were slaughtered by the Hitlerites in Oswiecim camp. As a rule, children who arrived by train were immediately sent to the gas chambers. Only a few healthy juveniles were retained for work in the camps.

Investigation has established that children between the ages of 8 and 16 were forced to perform hard physical labor along with adults. Heavy labor, torture and beatings soon reduced the children to a state of complete collapse, whereupon they were murdered.

Doctor Jacob Gordon, a former prisoner from Vilnius, testified: "In the beginning of 1943, 164 boys were selected in the Birkenau camp and taken to a hospital, where they were done to death by injections of carbolic acid into the heart."

Bakash Weldtraut from Dusseldorf, Germany, a former prisoner, testified: "In 1943, when we were building a fence around Crematorium No. 5, I myself saw SS men hurl living children into the flaming pyres."

Testimony of Child Prisoners

Here is what children rescued by the the Red Army have to say about the torments to which they were subjected by the fascist beasts.

Sami Mudianov, aged 15, from Italy, said: "We children were forced to work in groups of 15 or 20, hauling carts of all kinds of freight, but mostly dead bodies, which we brought to a special wing where they were piled up for cremation. We worked from four in the morning until evening. At the end of October, 1944, the Germans who inspected our work ordered us to be punished because the wing was not clean enough. One hundred and fifty of us were lined up on the street and taken to a swimming pool. They made us strip and poured cold water on us and then led us back naked down to the street. Many of the children got sick after that."

Andreas Lerinciakos, a nine-year-old boy from Cles, Hungary, testified: "When we were taken to Wing No. 22 in the camp we were beaten by German women who were put in charge of us. They beat us with sticks. While I was in the camp, Dector Mengele took my blood many times. In November, 1944, all the children were transferred to camp A, the 'gypsy' camp. When they counted us, one was found missing, so Branden, manageress of the women's camp, and her assistant, Mendel, drove us out into the street at one o'clock in the morning and made us stand there in the frost until noon the next day."

Children born in camp were taken from their mothers by the SS and put to death. Pregnant women among new arrivals were immediately sent to a special barrack where premature birth was induced. Women who resisted were sent at once to the gas chamber.

Sofya Isakovna Flax, an ex-prisoner from Cracow, testified: "Many of the women who arrived in August, 1944, had children aged between five and 12. All of them, together with their mothers, were sent to the crematoriums. I was in the seventh month of pregnancy when I arrived. SS Doctor

Koenig, who examined me, sent me to barracks V-3, Birkenau. There were 65 women there in a similar condition. Three days later I was given an injection in the hip to induce premature birth. The injections were made four days in succession. On the fifth day I gave birth and my child was taken away. There were 14 similar cases while I was in the barracks. No one knew where the infants were taken."

Among the prisoners released from Oswiecim and examined by physicians were 180 children, including 52 aged eight, and 128 between the ages of 8 and 15. All of them arrived in camp in the second half of 1944, which means that they spent from three to six months in the camp. A medical examination of these children established that 72 of 180 are suffering from lung and glandular tuberculosis, 49 from alimentary dystrophy, 31 from frostbite, etc.

In the Oswiecim camp the Germans exterminated tens of thousands of prominent scientists and representatives of the intelligentsia of different countries.

Andre Foudrie, from the town of Samot Dipuen, told the Commission the following: "Most of the 600 Frenchmen with whom I arrived in the camp perished within a few months. Among them were Emil Bureau, economist; Professor Joan of the Lyceum of Compiegne; Philippe Geronne, deputy from the Department of Lot; Lebigoux, Mayor of the town of Villevit; Godeau and Broux, schoolteachers Molyneux, architectural engineer, etc."

Professor Henri Limousin of Clairmont Ferrand University, stated: "In November, 1944, I was taken from Dachau camp and sent to Oswiecim as a specialist on pathology. I spent about a month here in the quarantine block, where I was made to clean lavatories, wash floors and carry food to prisoners in jail."

Among those murdered in the Oswiecim camp were Professor Freyda, well known Dutch economist; Doctor Lawoslaw; engineer Kimar; Doctor Endoklyan, an engineer from Yugoslavia; Wisnievski, a Polish engineer; Teichert, a pharmacist from Warsaw; Polish professors Geszcikiewicz and Rubarski; Czechoslavak professors Otto Sitik, neuropathologist, Leo Tausik, psychiatrist, Jan Levit, surgeon; Kraus, a famous lawyer from Vienna; Doctor Jaube, a French army doctor with the rank of general, and many, many others. They were all tortured to death by hard labor, or else suffocated in gas chambers.

Appeal of Liberated Prisoners

The Extraordinary State Committee has received an "Appeal to the Public of the World," written in three languages, German, Hungarian and French, and signed by 27 ex-prisoners from Oswiecim—professors, doctors engineers, lawyers, students and other intellectuals from various countries. The appeal reads as follows:

> We the undersigned, liberated by the great Red Army from bloody Nazi domination, before the whole world accuse the German government under Adolf Hitler of carrying out wholesale murder, brutality and enslavement to an extent

unknown in human history....

We appeal to world public opinion to ascertain the fate of millions of people of all nationalities who have disappeared, and to do everything possible to save millions of prisoners of all nations still languishing in Hitlerite Germany. We were saved by a miracle when the Nazis retreated from Oswiecim camp. Although the Hitlerites left in panic, they took some 58,000 prisoners with them from the Oswiecim camp and its branches. These people, worn out from starvation, were forced to walk, but few of them could have survived more than a few kilometers. We assume that as the front moves farther into the interior of Germany, the same fate awaits all those who are still in the power of the sanguinary Nazis. We, the undersigned, appeal to world public opinion of combatant and neutral countries, and to their governments, in the name of humanity, to do everything possible to prevent a repetition of the atrocities and crimes of the Nazis in the future, so that the blood of millions of innocent victims shall not have been shed in vain.

We and some 10,000 other rescued prisoners of all nationalities ask that the crimes and incredible brutalities perpetrated by the Hitlerites should not go unpunished.

The rescued prisoners owe their lives to the valorous Red Army and they ask the world public and their governments to take this into account and express thanks on our behalf.

At Oswiecim camp the Hitlerites exposed themselves before the whole world not only as bloody killers of defenseless people, but also as rapacious plunderers of their victims. Millions of people shipped from different countries to the Oswiecim concentration camp were methodically picked clean during the first hour after their arrival. All their belongings, suitcases, clothes, bedding, down to underwear and shoes were taken away by the SS men and put into specially designed and equipped warehouses to be shipped to Germany.

Those of the able-bodied victims who were left for hard labor were given striped prison clothes instead of their own. On the territory of the Oswiecim camp there were 35 special-warehouses where clothing and other belongings were sorted out and packed for shipment. The Germans burned down 29 of these with all their contents before retreating under pressure of the Red Army. In the remaining six warehouse premises the following was found: 1) Men's clothing, including underwear, 348,820 outfits; 2) Women's, 836,255 outfits; 3) Women's shoes, 5,525 pairs; 4) Men's shoes, 38,000 pairs; 5) Rugs, 13,964.

A large quantity of tooth brushes, shaving brushes, spectacles, an enormous number of dentures, and all kinds of utensils which the prisoners used, were also found in the warehouses. A large quantity of children's wear, shirts, panties, overcoats and caps were also found there. With bloody hands the Hitlerite child-killers kept a careful account of all these possessions of the children they murdered, and shipped them to Germany.

The Commission established, by inspecting the things found in the warehouse, that they had all belonged to people of diverse nationalities who had been killed outright or tortured to death: French, Belgian, Hungarian, Dutch, Yugoslav, Czechoslovak and other trademarks were found on clothing, shoes and other belongings. Labels of hotels in various European cities were still to be found on the suitcases.

The Commission found on the camp grounds seven carloads of clothing and bedding which the Germans had loaded for shipment to Germany. A statement signed by SS Oberscharfuehrer Reichenbach, found in the camp papers, shows that during 47 days, from December 1, 1944, till January 15, 1945, alone, the following was put in readiness in the camp for shipment to Germany: 1) Children's clothing, including underwear, 99,922 outfits; 2) Women's, 192,652 outfits; 3) Men's clothing, including underwear, 222,269 outfits—a total of 514,843 outfits.

At the tannery in Oswiecim camp the Commission found on March 7, 1945, 293 bales of women's hair, totaling 7,000 kilograms in weight. The commission of experts established that the hair was sheared off the heads of some 140,000 women.

Carefully obliterating traces of their monstrous crimes in Oswiecim, the Germans, before their retreat, took great pains to destroy all papers that might have revealed to the world the exact number of people they had wiped out in the Oswiecim camp. However, the high capacity machinery for murder which the Germans had set up in the camp, the testimony of the Oswiecim prisoners freed by the Red Army, the testimony of 200 witnesses questioned to date, isolated papers that have been found, and other material evidence, are sufficient to expose the German hangmen as having wiped out in Oswiecim millons of people by poisoning and burning. In five crematoriums (52 retorts) alone, the Germans could wipe out during the period they functioned the following numbers of people:

Crematorium No. 1 functioned 24 months, burned 9,000 corpses per month, and during the entire period burned 216,000 corpses. No. 2 functioned 19 months, burned 90,000 corpses per month, and during the entire period burned 1,710,000 corpses. No. 3 functioned 18 months, burned 90,000 corpses per month, and during the entire period burned 1,620,000 corpses. No. 4 functioned 17 months, burned 45,000 corpses per month, and during the entire period burned 765,000 corpses. No. 5 functioned 18 months burned 45,000 corpses per month, and during the entire period burned 810,000 corpses. The total capacity for burning corpses per month was 279,000, and the total capacity for burning corpses during the entire period was 5,121,000. In view of the fact that the Germans widely practiced burning bodies on pyres, the total capacity of the murder installations of Oswiecim must be estimated at a considerably higher figure.

Making allowances for possible undercapacity operation of the crematoriums and stoppages, however, the Commission of technical experts established that during the existence of the Oswiecim camp the German executioners killed in it no less than four million citizens of the USSR, Poland, France, Yugoslavia, Czechoslovakia, Rumania, Hungary, Bulgaria, Holland, Belgium and other countries.

The monstrous crimes committed by the Germans in the concentration camps of Oswiecim were perpetrated in keeping with the directives issued by the Hitlerite government and were under the leadership of hangman Himmler, Reichsfuehrer of the SS and Police. . . .

All . . . who personally participated in the murder and torture of the prisoners at Oswiecim, must be brought before the court of nations and pay the severe penalty they merit.

— From Embassy of the Union of Soviet Socialist Republics (Washington, D.C.) Information Bulletin *54 (May 29, 1945): 1–8.*

Bergen-Belsen

INSIDE BELSEN

Hanna Levy-Haas was born into a Jewish family in Sarajevo, Yugoslavia. After studying in France, she returned home to work as a teacher in Montenegro and became a member of the Communist resistance following the German invasion in 1941. During the occupation, her mother and sister were deported to AUSCHWITZ and killed there; her brother was killed by men of Croatia's USTACHI militia. In 1943, when the Germans took over Italian-controlled Montenegro, she was arrested and held at the GESTAPO prison in Cetinje, Yugoslavia. She began to keep a diary there, continuing it after her deportation to BERGEN-BELSEN in August 1944. She was liberated by the Red Army during a forced march to evacuate the camp in spring 1945. After the war she became active in Israeli feminist and left-wing politics, moving later to Great Britain and France.

Belsen January 1945. I have managed to speak to a few of the women transported here from Auschwitz. Most of them are Jews from Poland, Greece and Hungary. They told us what they had gone through in Auschwitz. In the time they were there, from 1943 to 1944, hundreds of thousands had been wiped out, while they themselves were among the few who had miraculously survived. "Words cannot describe what we have been through," they said. They tell us of the mass murders, of the 99 per cent who have been massacred in the gas chambers, of the obscenities to which they were subjected. And as they talk about these things, their eyes seem to be asking, silently, whether we believe them: sometimes, they say, they themselves even begin to doubt whether they are speaking the truth. They fear nobody will believe them and will put their stories down as the tales of lunatics. Of all the women sent to Auschwitz, only a few hundred have survived. The men and the children were gassed at the very beginning, together with the elderly and the weak. A Jewish woman from Greece told me that only 300 women were still alive out of the 70,000 Greek Jews who had been interned with her in Auschwitz, and that she herself had been made to watch her parents and her whole family burn to death.

Remarkably enough, these women, fugitives from hell, who had worked in the kitchens, in the stores and—believe it or not—in the orchestra, all look healthy and comparatively well. It is strange to compare their physical condition with ours. But they told us that in Auschwitz the prisoners had had sufficient to eat, and that by helping each other, they had managed to get all they needed. In general, they said, they had not gone hungry but the fear of death hung over all of them: each one saw himself the victim of a remorseless, irreversible fate, waiting to be swallowed up by the flames of the inferno.

The death factory, the women told us, worked at full stretch every day. Row upon row of men and women, sometimes hundreds, sometimes one or two thousand, stood in line every day outside the big shower room until it was their turn to be gassed. The smoke poured out of the crematorium, and as they watched, they knew what it meant. It told them that there was the furnace where the bodies of their relatives had been burnt and where their own lives too would soon end.

But in their camp, said our fellow-sufferers from Auschwitz—who were astonished to hear about the systematic starvation to which we were subjected—no one went hungry. The end is the same—only the means are different. In Auschwitz it is a quick, ruthless procedure, mass murder in the gas chambers; in Belsen it is a sadistic, long-drawn-out process of starvation, of violence, of terror, of the deliberate spreading of infection and disease. . . .

Our bodies have adapted themselves to the hunger. Sometimes a man may feel so wracked with hunger that he can no longer stand it and devours his entire supply of bread—three or four days' ration—in one go. At other times people exchange the greater part of their clothes for one or two rations of soup which the pilferers offer them. After bolting down such unaccustomed quantities of foul food, they are overcome by nausea and feel worse than ever. Their digestion cannot cope with the food; they throw up, and are as hungry as before.

Meals are coming more and more irregularly. The soup meant for midday does not arrive until five or six, and supper, which consists of a few drops of boiled water or a tiny piece of processed cheese, has been cut out altogether and arrives either the following morning or not at all. So sometimes sixteen or twenty hours can elapse without a thing to eat. When the food does arrive, the starving prisoners make a rush for the soup pots, and a few hours later comes the inevitable consequence—the whole place reeks of diarrhoea. . . .

Belsen January 1945. Death has now finally settled among us, our most faithful companion, ever present. As a result of their brutal treatment people are dying in masses from malnutrition, from beatings, from dysentery, from the bugs. They simply collapse and fall down—more and more of them. Many of my friends have already come to the end of their days. One, two, three, four—and then one begins to

mistake the dead for the living. Not that there is much difference. We are skeletons that can still move, whereas they are skeletons that cannot. But there is a third category—those who lie stretched out on their bunks, still breathing slightly but unable to move. It is just a question of waiting for them to die and make room for others. Small wonder that when we count our numbers, we confuse them with the dead. . . .

Belsen February 1945. Typhoid fever has begun to dominate the scene. The diagnosis is said to be very involved. At the moment it is chiefly the children who are affected, but they can also die from other causes, and we do not know which. One fine day, as the expression has it, two little girls died in a bed close by, quietly, one after the other. Their mother, a simple, very attractive woman, watched over them as a wolf guards her cubs. When she realised they were dead, she burst into piercing shrieks of agony. Then she began to chant dirges, making up the words with incredible skill as she went along and whispering gently to the tiny bodies. But now she shuffles about with her hair unkempt, does not bother to take off her rags, totally neglects herself and has a glint of madness in her eyes. Life has lost all meaning for her. . . .

All we know or see is the slow plod of endless columns of miserable figures filing past, thousands and thousands of prisoners from all the camps that the Germans have had to evacuate. It is clear that the Germans are in retreat and are dragging their victims with them. This is where they are assembling them. But there is a rumour that we are going to be taken away from here as well: the Allies are said to be close by, so that the Germans would have to evacuate the whole area and send us somewhere else. Rumours like these, the air of uncertainty, with the possibility that we may all in the end be wiped out—the fact that Kramer is here makes this all the more likely—is a form of mental torture that has driven us more than once to the brink of madness.

And the whole time row upon row of pitiful figures, walking skeletons, shuffle past along the road. From the other side of the barbed wire we watch them file by and wonder who they are. What is going to happen to them—or to us? How will they end up—or we end up? What shall we be made to do? What are they waiting for? And the English—what do they intend to do? What plans are they thinking up? They have the situation in their control—are they going to use us all in order to preserve the position that suits them best? They could have finished Germany off long ago. What do they care about human life, about the sufferings of the oppressed, about their death and their rotting corpses? Nothing. Freedom? A confidence trick, which they play as long as it suits them. They exploit smaller countries, abusing their privileged position in the hierarchy of nations. That's why the situation is as it is. The only thing that counts is the policy of the Soviet Union and faith in the triumph of the new society. Otherwise what meaning can it all have? Is war rooted in human nature? If there is no real victory, and the whole world does not become socialist, what is the point of our life? So that we can start all over again, with fresh massacres and new depravities? I am beginning to despair of humankind.

We wish for so many things, have an avid desire for everything. Are we really approaching our end? What about the Jewish question? Where and how is this diabolical comedy going to finish? And our Jewish homeland—where? — why? — how? — in what form? Perhaps our agony will never end. I have never before been so tormented by such thoughts, never asked myself such questions. And now, at this moment, I feel that the problem will go on for ever, like a wound that never heals. Our precious Slav homeland, the land we love—will you still want us? Shall we have become strangers to you too? Or have I gone mad to ask such ridiculous questions! . . .

Belsen March 1945. Death has become an everyday event and leaves us completely indifferent. We have given up thinking about being rescued and have stopped counting the days as we used to. There is no point in knowing when the Allies will arrive, though it seems certain that they are only a few dozen kilometres away. For the present our closest and most loyal ally is death. And if we do begin to count the days again, then it is not with an eye to the moment of our liberation but in order to see how long the one or the other of us can still survive. There is a kind of medical curiosity in us, a strange obsession. There was a time when I was convinced I would only live another month or two. Now, having somehow miraculously got over the bout of typhoid fever, which taxed my power of endurance to the limit, I give myself only ten or fifteen days at the most.

This brief semi-existence that is left to me I spend in the company of other ghosts, some living, some dead. The corpses are still here, lying in our beds. There is no one to take them away and nowhere to put them in the crowded hut. In the yard outside they lie piled on top of each other in great heaps that grow higher every day. The crematorium is not capable of burning them all. . . .

Belsen April 1945. One needs only to observe what has been going on here to reach the inescapable conclusion that Belsen was not built as a temporary camp for civilian or military prisoners, men and women detained on political or security grounds until the end of hostilities. Nothing of the kind. Belsen was deliberately established and equipped in order to exterminate thousands of human beings methodically and with scientific thoroughness. And even if the situation lasts only for another month, it is unlikely that a single one of us will survive.

> —*From Hanna Levy-Haas,* Inside Belsen, *trans. Ronald Taylor (Totowa, NJ: Barnes and Noble, 1982), 51–53, 55–56, 61–63, 67, and 69.*

Gross-Rosen

BETWEEN DESPAIR AND HOPE

Sara Zyskind grew up in Lodz, Poland, and was eleven years old when the German Army invaded Poland on September 1, 1939. She experienced GHETTO life and AUSCHWITZ before she was transferred to the Mittelstein Labor Camp, a subcamp of GROSS-ROSEN. Here she describes the living conditions in Mittelstein as liberation neared.

I had started working night shift again and, as usual, the long week ahead filled me with great trepidation. During the first night, however, something happened that gave all of us a feeling of indescribable elation. At about 3 a.m. the air-raid siren went off for the first time in the camp. In their consternation the *Meisters* and *Aufseherins* [supervisors] scuttled about like poisoned rats. But our happiness knew no bounds. Let them bomb the plant! Even if we got killed, all the Germans would go down with us. Only now did I understand the real significance of Samson's prayer, "Let me die with the Philistines!"

All the people in the plant—the Germans, the POWs, and even we slave workers—were rushed into the air-raid shelter. We kept our faces blank so that the Germans could not see the joy we felt. Fifteen minutes later, the all-clear sounded. Nothing had happened. We went back to our jobs, yet things were no longer the same. It was obvious that the front line was moving closer. There were bound to be changes, and perhaps—we hardly dared to think of it— they would be for the better. . . .

One Sunday, we were assembled in the big square, and the *Kommandoführerin* [work party leader] entered with her Alsatian. She was accompanied by another woman in the uniform of a high army officer, who was introduced to us as our new commandant. In her final address, our former *Kommandoführerin* couldn't refrain from telling us once again that we were nothing but a "nation of shit and *Schweinehund*" and that if we still harbored any illusions about leaving the Mittelstein camp alive, we had better forget them. We scarcely paid attention to what she was saying, being much too happy at the prospect of finally seeing the last of her. We had no doubt that the commandant who was succeeding her couldn't possibly be as wicked as this woman. But we quickly learned that any evil can be replaced by another that is even more vicious.

The day that our former *Kommandoführerin* left the camp remains engraved upon my memory. The roll call began in pitch darkness and during a bone-chilling frost. Soon the first sun rays seeped through the low hanging clouds to settle upon the snowbound mountains and the dark pines shrouded in purest white. The sight of this beauty brought me close to tears. I wanted it to last so I could forget my sorrow as long as possible.

We had been standing at attention for a long time when our former *Kommandoführerin* appeared, out of uniform and wrapped in a heavy fur cape. She emerged from the officers' mess and stepped into a horse drawn sled. The driver's whip set the sled in motion, and before long it vanished among the trees, coming into view again intermittently. We could hear clearly the merry jingle of the bells on the horse's neck.

The sight of the elegant, fur-clad woman gliding away through the sparkling landscape reminded me of the fairy tales I used to love reading in my childhood. So captivated was I by the scene that I paid no attention to the speech made by our new *Kommandoführerin*. My thoughts lingered on that beautiful and savage woman who had flogged more than one wretched prisoner to death. Why was she like a devil in human form? What was lacking in her own life that made her loathe us so unreasonably? Hadn't she unlimited freedom, health, and beauty? What was it that had unleashed such malicious instincts in her?

Our new *Kommandoführerin* was much older than her predecessor and had none of the other's good looks. We hoped that, being older, she would be a little more humane, but we were greatly mistaken. This woman was an alcoholic who became dangerously violent when she was drunk. During inspection lineups she would run amok, dragging women out of the ranks by their hair, assaulting them with drunken fury, and often torturing them to death while we watched. . . .

The coming of spring finally brought some variety to our daily lives. The snow on the mountains melted, and patches of green began to take its place. Now we stood at attention for hours with the sweeping rains of March lashing our faces, and we marched to work through quagmires of sleet and slush. Except for the changing weather, things were just as before: the same routine, the same savagery, the same calculated Germanic precision. We still received smiles and signs of encouragement from the POWs and "forgotten" slices of bread from the *Meisters*. But the hope inspired by these events was soon blotted out by a recurring sense of depression and despair as we listened day after day to the drunken ravings of the *Kommandoführerin*.

Eventually the driving rains stopped. The mud hardened, and the wind had a caressing warmth to it. The glory of spring was all around us, but it did not touch our souls. Full of envy, I looked at the green fields on both sides of the road. The sprouting leaves on the trees were reaching out for the sun, for freedom; the birds were flying high in the sky, chirping and trilling. I, too, would have burst into song had I been as free as they. . . .

A Flickering Hope

It was not long before we were aware of great changes taking place around us. The POWs no longer contented themselves with making the "V" sign or the throat-slitting gesture; instead they would pass close by us, whispering "Don't lose hope now. The war's about to end. The Huns are getting licked and are on the run everywhere." Where the Germans were running to and where from we didn't know, nor were we concerned with the particulars. What mattered were the messages of encouragement that fanned our flickering hopes.

Around this time, I caught a glimpse of the headlines of a newspaper my *Meister* happened to open up near my bench. "Red Army advances in Poland. . ." I managed to read this much before he noticed me, whacked me on the back, and snarled an order that I stick to my work or else. The bit of news that I had glimpsed gave me a thrill of joy. Poland was being liberated! Then thoughts of regret began to assail me. If Salek and I had hidden away in the ghetto, mightn't we have been liberated by now? And the same would be true of Genia and Rishia, provided they had been allowed to stay behind. Perhaps they had already rejoined Rishia's father, brother, and sister. No, the ghetto had been liquidated—there would have been no place they could have hidden.

My thoughts kept chasing one another and finally I decided that only at the end of the war, when I would see my relatives again, would I find out how everyone had fared. But I might not survive that long if the *Kommandoführerin* carried out her threat to finish us off before the end came. Even that, I mused, wouldn't matter so long as the Germans went down with us. To know that their own bitter end was near was my greatest consolation.

Soon there were more signs of the changing situation. One day, my *Meister* failed to turn up for work, and my *Aufseherin* kept leaving her post to go outside, scarcely bothering to keep an eye on us. That day I turned out countless burst discs. I looked around me and talked in sign language with Bronka. During the lunchbreak we heard from the kitchen staff, who had gotten it from the POWs, that several managers and *Meisters* had fled, that the Red Army was approaching. I was quivering with excitement. . . .

At roll calls the *Kommandoführerin* dinned into our ears her intention of killing us all off before the very end. We wouldn't be around to welcome the Russian liberators, she said. The very last German bullets were being kept in readiness to kill every dirty *Schweinehund* in the camp. Ironically, she was unaware of how her drunken ranting rekindled our hopes, for it revealed how close the Red Army was. While she spoke, we took great care not to show any emotion. She would scrutinize our faces closely and virtually foam with fury if she seemed to detect the slightest change of expression. She'd drag the unfortunate prisoner out of the ranks and flog her mercilessly in front of us, shave off her hair, and deprive her of a day's food ration. We dared not twitch an eyelid and almost ceased breathing in her presence.

We lived in a constant state of anticipation, but the days and weeks passed, and still nothing happened. Nothing—except that our hard labor brought us to the verge of death from exhaustion. Many prisoners fell ill, and the infirmary was filled beyond capacity. Our exhaustion deprived us of all ability to think. Order in the camp became a thing of the past, filth and neglect were everywhere, and the stench around us was unbearable. Though the days were getting warmer, I often found myself sleeping in boots and overcoat, too weary to remove them before turning in.

I felt I was coming to the end of my own endurance. The same urgency to get out that had assailed me during my last days in the ghetto took hold of me again. This time I knew that any change might be for the worse, but I no longer cared. All I wanted was to get away! . . .

Mauthausen

GASSINGS AT MAUTHAUSEN

Professor V. Busek, a Czech prisoner who was the secretary for the camp infirmary at Mauthausen, describes here the killings in the camp's gas chamber that occurred in April 1945 as the Allies approached the camp.

In the second half of April 1945 the medical chief, SS Dr. Wolter, ordered the selection of 3,000 sick and ordered them sent to Lager 3 [Camp 3]. We understood immediately the meaning of the order; we assumed that it was the prelude to the evacuation of the revier [sick bay]. . . . During these days, one spoke also of a second order concerning our liquidation, all of us; doctors and workers understood. The first day we formed a group of eight hundred sick whom we escorted to Lager 3. While we were in the camp, an SS man, I don't know his name—told us that he needed 20 strong people to carry the soup, but this was simply a pretext: in fact he chose the last twenty in the column who were the sickest and did not conduct them to the kitchen but through the courtyard of the crematory toward the gas chamber. . . . Out of 1,200 selected in the first day, 120 were gassed during the night. The second day, we again selected the sick. I accompanied those suffering the most; it was a terrible procession. . . . At the door of the entrance, I met the man Trum who gave me the order to place the entire group against the wall, facing the laundry. Trum said to me: "Here are the first whom it is necessary to take to the bath" . . . indicating those who had fallen on the ground. I followed Trum and these men to the entry into the courtyard of the crematorium bunker. . . . I then told the other sick standing before me to follow me to Lager 3. But already Trum had returned from the crematorium. He ordered me to stop and asked me why I didn't leave the group in front of the wall waiting for the shower like he had ordered me.

He then struck me brutally, causing my ear to bleed, and told me to select ninety-six other sick and take them to the crematory. Indicating those selected, Trum said to me again: "Pay attention: if only one is missing I will include you instead." None of the other sick left the revier: We, the deportees, doctors, and workers were all agreed to refuse to make the selection. . . . Our refusal blocked the operation and the last 1,000 were saved, while the gassings continued. Of the 1,819 deportees transferred to Lager 3 during these days, 1,441 were gassed. During this time a column of the Red Cross arrived to take the French, Belgians, and Dutch [prisoners out of the camp]. We profited on this occasion by making fifty deportees of other nationalities pass as French. . . . After the departure of the Red Cross column the extermination was suspended. . . . The physical condition in which we found the survivors of Lager 3 was tragic; during the last week they had received practically nothing to eat.

Entrance to the gas chamber at Mauthausen, where many were killed in the last weeks of the war. This photo was taken in July 1945. (USHMM)

REPORT ON MAUTHAUSEN

Lieutenant J.H. "Jack" Taylor, USNR, was a member of an Office of Strategic Services intelligence mission code-named the "Dupont Mission." Captured by the Germans in November 1944, he was convicted of espionage and sentenced to death. Taylor was transferred to Mauthausen concentration camp, where he remained until the camp's liberation in May 1945. In January 1945 twelve other OSS men, who had been captured in Slovakia after the abortive revolt there

in Fall 1944, were shot at Mauthausen.

In the report on his mission for the OSS, he described the camp and its conditions, part of which is reproduced here. The photographs were taken after the camp was liberated.

—From the Dupont Mission Report, Part III, Record Group 226, box 4, folder 86, entry 110, National Archives and Records Administration.

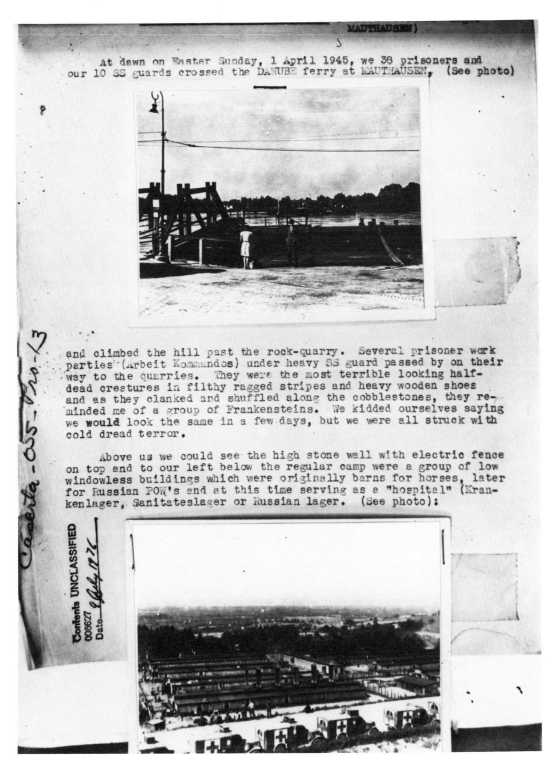

MAUTHAUSEN)

At dawn on Easter Sunday, 1 April 1945, we 38 prisoners and our 10 SS guards crossed the DANUBE ferry at MAUTHAUSEN. (See photo)

and climbed the hill past the rock-quarry. Several prisoner work parties (Arbeit Kommandos) under heavy SS guard passed by on their way to the quarries. They were the most terrible looking half-dead creatures in filthy ragged stripes and heavy wooden shoes and as they clanked and shuffled along the cobblestones, they reminded me of a group of Frankensteins. We kidded ourselves saying we would look the same in a few days, but we were all struck with cold dread terror.

Above us we could see the high stone wall with electric fence on top and to our left below the regular camp were a group of low windowless buildings which were originally barns for horses, later for Russian POW's and at this time serving as a "hospital" (Krankenlager, Sanitateslager or Russian lager. (See photo):

Contents UNCLASSIFIED
006627
Date

We arrived at a group of buildings just outside the main entrance and were turned over to the MAUTHAUSEN SS who didn't waste any time intimidating us. SS Unterscharfuhrer HANS PRELLBERG was particularly brutal as he slapped, punched, kicked and beat most of us over the head with a cane belonging to a crippled Slovak in our group. Two young Russians and a Hungarian were unmercifully beaten because they did not understand German. All commands were given in German and I had to keep extremely alert to save myself similar beatings. We were told certain rules and regulations, the penalty being instant death on all except one which was merely hanging the victim by his wrists chained behind his back. This slight penalty was for failure to stand at attention and remove one's cap whenever an SS man, regardless of rank, passed or when speaking to an SS man. When the next group of new prisoners, following us, were having the same rules and regulations announced to them, the speaker said: "and if you attempt to escape and are recaptured, you will be shot immediately, like this", and simultaneously pulled his pistol and shot an old prisoner standing near, who had just been recaptured after an attempted escape.

We were marched through the main gate (See photo) and lined

up outside the shower room where we were individually questioned, slapped, slugged, and beaten with a stick by three SS men in relays for approximately three hours; in addition, some were spat upon. The worst to me was SS Unterscharfuhrer HANS BRUCKNER who screamed "you American swine" every time he struck me. He also beat unmercifully a Lt. GLAUBER, an ISLD agent (Viennese-born, British citizen) mainly because he was a Jew. I had not seen GLAUBER since the night he was captured in February when I was

- 2 -

called to Kriminalrat SANITZER's office and introduced to him. We were told to talk to each other which we did without saying "anything". Now, he had lost much weight and remarked the same about me.

We were marched to the bath, stripped, and all our belongings confiscated, except three wrist-watches and a wedding ring which we were able to slip to a Polish Kapo. (Kapos were head prisoners of a work detail). All hair was shaved from our bodies, lice inspected, etc., and after a hot shower we were given only an old suit of ragged underwear. We never saw our clothes again and were led out into the cold barefooted where we stood at attention and shivered for over an hour before being marched to our barracks, Block 13. This S.O.P. was not changed even during the most severe part of the winter when men stood barefooted in the snow. Lt. GLAUBER and three others, who were badly in need of medical treatment, went to the hospital. GLAUBER told me that when the Czech doctor found out that he was a British officer, he winked at him and said he would put him in the hospital for a couple of months where he would not have to work. GLAUBER was very happy and we said goodbye warmly. One of the other three was a small Sudetan German who was a mass of bruises from head to foot and also had several festering sores from Gestapo cigarette butt burns.

We received our first food in 48 hours and later were assigned our prison numbers, two of which were stamped on cloth with the appropriate colored triangle indicating political or criminal prisoner and citizenship and one stamped in metal for a wrist bracelet. The cloth numbers were sewn on the left breast of the coat and the outer side of the left trouser half way to the knee. All three numbers had to check before food would be issued. In addition, if the prisoner was not wearing stripes, he had a rectangular hole cut in the middle of the back of his coat and also just below the number on his trouser leg; these spaces were filled in with a rectangular piece of "stripes" so that if an escaped prisoner cut off his stripes, he still had the tell-tale rectangular holes. (See photo):

- 3 -

I worked for three weeks collecting testimony, documents, liaison to Colonel SEIBEL and running down SS men hiding in the area. In the first two weeks I gained over 30 pounds.

One of the most important documents was a collection of 13 Death books (Totenbuch) giving names of "official"deaths for 6 years. These books are labeled "MAUTHAUSEN", "GUSEN" and "Executions", and were witheld at the risk of their lives by ULBRECHT and MARTIN the prisoner secretaries assigned to this registration. These approximately 3,600 pages have been microfilmed and the books are in the custody of OSS, SALZBURG. ULBRECHT and MARTIN by means of tiny secret hyroglyphics were able to put down in many cases the true cause of death (gas, injection, etc.) at the same time as the official (false) death cause, i.e., in the '40 '42 book, all those from number 229 on with "spr" means "injection death" (injection of foreign material into the heart) and those with "COIC" means violent exercise to death. In the '42-43 book, all numbers after 3725 with a dot after the place of birth were by injection. Other small notes in relation to the "official" death cause can be decyphered by MARTIN and ULBRECHT. After 18 April 1945, all prisoners who have in the 4th column the remark "Zellenbau" (prison bldg.) were gassed. On 26 April 1945, 1167 prisoners died at MAUTHAUSEN through starvation, gas, shooting, and clubbing. MARTIN and ULBRECHT's addresses are as follows:

ERNST MARTIN
c/o Hofrat Ing. Leo Sarlay
Innsbruck, Maxmilianstrasse 31

        and

JOSEF ULBRECHT
Zivnobanka
Benesov, Prague

After the Americans had liberated us, I discovered that I should have been executed on 28 April 1945 along with 27 other prisoners from Block 13. A friendly Czech, MYLOS, who worked in the political department had, unknown to me, removed my paper and destroyed it so that I was not included with the 27. A statement explaining this is enclosed.

J. H. Taylor

J. H. TAYLOR
Lt., USNR
178727

Ravensbrück

MY STORY

Gemma LaGuardia Gluck was born in New York City and was the sister of Fiorello LaGuardia, New York's colorful mayor during the 1940s. Returning to Italy early in this century, she married a Hungarian Jew, Herman Gluck, settled in Budapest, and raised a family of two daughters. Following the German occupation of Hungary in March 1944, she was arrested for use as a hostage and, in part, in retaliation for her brother's anti-Nazi activities; her husband was arrested for being a Jew. At first the Glucks were sent to Mauthausen, then Gemma was separated from her husband and transferred to Ravensbrück concentration camp, where she worked in the mess hall (though she was not required to do so because of her status as a special prisoner/ hostage). Her daughter and grandson were deported later and joined her there in August after their arrest. Transferred from the camp to Berlin in April 1945, all three were liberated by the Red Army in May.

On April 7, 1945, a week before I was sent away from Ravensbruck, thousands of big packages came from Canada to our camp. For the first time they were to be distributed among the Jewish women, too. As there were so many Jewish women in the camp, the commander said a trustworthy person must be appointed to be a witness and to hand out these packages, for which each individual was to sign her name. I was the person selected.

I began to give out these packages at 4 p.m., when there were a thousand hungry women standing in line. At 9 p.m. I was still handing out packages. I can't describe what a good feeling it was for me to be present at that scene, which I never want to forget. Some looked at me with such loving and grateful eyes, as if they couldn't believe what they saw. I tried to smile at each of them, as it wasn't permitted to speak to them, and with my smile I wished to encourage each one of them to be brave and patient. At times I thought my heart would burst within me to see these women in such condition, ill, thin, dressed in rags, some were like walking skeletons, some the shadows of beautiful women, some so weak that when I handed them the five-pound packages they fell to the ground.

For the first time since I was in Ravensbruck I forgot myself, but thank God, I was not punished. In my Block 2 there was a woman prisoner who also sat at my table. She wore the Jewish sign on her arm but she insisted that she was a Christian and that she had to wear this sign on account of her husband. She went from one office to another telling them that she was a Christian and in this manner she got rid of the sign. I also had the yellow stripe on top of my political sign, as my husband was a Jew. She once came to me, saying: "Why do you wear this disgusting sign? Go

and get rid of it as I have done." I answered her: "I'm wearing this yellow stripe because of my husband, and as I have been married for thirty-six years to such a good Jewish husband, I am proud to wear this sign."

The argument was finished, and nobody would have mentioned it again, but how great was my surprise when, as I was distributing the packages, I saw this woman standing in line among the Jewish women, waiting for a package. By my side stood the chief superintendent, Frau Binz. On my other side was the chief camp officer of custody, and before me was another women prisoner from Vienna, who had been appointed chief of the camp police. Nevertheless, I forgot myself when I saw this woman coming forward to get a package.

In a nervous voice I shouted: "You impertinent woman. You say you are not Jewish, then what do you want here? If you say you are a Christian, then why will you cheat one of these poor Jewish women by taking a package away from her?" The superintendent heard me and said: "What has happened here?" in her shrill voice. I stood at attention at once and asked to be forgiven but continued: "Even if I am in a camp, I can't bear to see this unjust thing."

The superintendent was kind toward me and told me to explain what the matter was. Then I explained it all to her. The superintendent then said to me: "44,139, I'm glad you told me of this. I will attend to the matter." I became fearful at once of what would happen. But the officer merely called the woman into her office, looked up her records, and verified the fact of her being married to a Jew. She gave her one of the packages, but from then on the prisoner wore the yellow sign again. . . .

One afternoon we received the order that the whole camp was to turn out for an inspection. We couldn't understand what this meant, as we had already stood four hours for roll call that morning. This was about the 2d or 3d of April. Then a second order came that all prisoners must be barefooted. There was great excitement immediately. Each prisoner had a different opinion and there were agitated arguments as more than 50,000 of us women went out to stand barefooted. We then heard that many doctors had come from Berlin to examine the prisoners to see who were sick, weak, or unable to walk.

As the Allies were approaching and the Nazis had to be ready to move quickly, only those prisoners who were strong and could walk would be selected for the march; those who wouldn't be able to walk in the long tramp, forty kilometers a day, would be shot down on the road. So one by one we had to walk in a line before those doctors, who watched our steps.

By this time I was looking very poorly, thin and pale. Besides, I was sixty-four years old. I was put aside with many others for the gas chamber. I can't describe my feelings in this sad moment. All from my block bowed their heads. I knew I was condemned to die, but I didn't care anymore for myself, being so disheartened by everything. But when I thought of my dear ones, especially my baby grandchild, then oh, yes, I did want to live. My feeling at the first moment was as if I were going to choke, but of course I couldn't say anything. When we were dismissed and entered our respective blocks, I got a crying spell, my nerves broke down, and I began to scream like a little child, "I don't want to go through the crematory chimney."

The overseer of our block went at once to speak with Suhren, the commander of the camp, reminding him who I was. Because I was the sister of La Guardia, I was saved, but the others of my poor comrades were killed. The camp personnel director told me afterward that I was kept from the gas chamber because they were fearful that some harm would come to the Germans in New York in reprisal.

— From Gemma LaGuardia Gluck, My Story *(New York: David McKay Company, 1961), 61–63, 73–74, © by the author and S.L. Schneiderman. Reprinted by permission of David McKay Company, a division of Random House, Inc.*

Sachsenhausen

FROM DAY TO DAY

Odd Nansen, son of famed Norwegian arctic explorer Fridtjof Nansen, was a member of the Norwegian resistance. Arrested in January 1942, he was confined to several camps in Norway until his transfer to SACHSENHAUSEN *concentration camp near Berlin in October 1943. During his time in prison he kept a diary, written on thin drawing paper and successfully concealed from the Germans. The diary was originally published in Norwegian under the title* Fra dag til dag *(1946).*

January 25. It's out of laziness that I'm not writing just now. For there's enough to write about. But the life out here at *Herz As* invites to laziness, in spite of all that is happening. One can actually do just as much as one chooses, and no more, and without any risk. There are no SS here, only a few civilians who are not dangerous.

But the situation in general has more and more the stamp of panic and dissolution. One transport of prisoners after another is arriving from other camps that have to be evacuated. Yesterday there arrived at Sachsenhausen or Oranienburg station several trainloads of prisoners. Most of them were dead, frozen to death in open cars in which they had spent up to three days in frightful cold, the temperature right down to zero.

When I hear of this, and that they're dying by hundreds just now of cold and hunger in this camp alone, without anyone being really affected, indeed without anyone even regarding it as unusual, then it occurs to me that no one will believe this when we come to describe it. You exaggerate, they'll say. It's impossible. After all the Germans are a civil-

ized nation. It's as though a stupefying nightmare were passing over us, and I see it with horror as a mere beginning of what's to come. For it is not only prisoners who are freezing to death. It's not only the lives of prisoners that have ceased to count. The German civil population is going the same way. The eastern towns are being compulsorily evacuated, and by degrees their people will be streaming in on us like a tidal wave.

January 26. The accounts of what the evacuated thousands have to suffer are terrible. *Évacués* from the east are constantly streaming toward Berlin.

They arrive on foot or by train. The cars are opened, and stiffened corpses roll out. Mothers, children, old people frozen to death as they sit with their heads in their hands or hunched up in the corners. Undergrounds and cellars in Berlin are crowded with refugees, and their condition is appalling. And still the Russians are drawing nearer.

No evacuation plans for this camp seem to be in existence as yet, we hear from SS quarters. God knows what will happen. We can hardly just sit and wait to be liberated by the Russians. A prison transport of twenty-eight thousand, moving west from Auschwitz on foot, was caught up by Russian panzer spearheads. The SS were immediately overpowered and the prisoners released. The Russians just told them that they were free, but must look after themselves, unfortunately they couldn't take charge of them. Perhaps a doubtful freedom; but still! We should always manage, no doubt. But then our qualifications are exceptional, well nourished as we are, and with good warm clothes. And again one thinks of all the others. Day and night these thoughts torment one. Good God, the things one sees—if one will see, and hear—if one will hear! By the side of one man freezing to death stands another in two pairs of drawers, a ski suit, two pairs of trousers, jerseys, shirts, coats, thick mittens, and first-rate boots. He feels chilly and curses at the frost. The man next to him dies without a word. "Well, poor chap; he wouldn't have come through anyhow. Have you anything to smoke? Damn!"

January 29. Yesterday morning a transport of half-dead men left the camp. Thirteen hundred sick people, all of them the wretchedest and feeblest musselmen [prisoner slang for those prisoners who had lost the will to live] that could be exhibited, chosen from the *Revier* [infirmary], the *Schonungsblocken* ["reprieve" barracks], and the Tub. Many died at the gate of the *Revier*, where they had to line up in frost and snow, half naked, to be called over. They dropped where they stood, or lay down in the snow and died. "In heaps," said Erik, who was watching. "It was dreadful beyond all description." All of them were nearly dead in advance. Most had been taken straight out of their beds, where at least they might have died in peace and comparative warmth.

Wherever one turns, the destruction of guiltless people going on like clockwork! With unalterably certain, devilish calculation the camp is gradually being purged of those who in any case are bound to die. Bound to die? Yes, all who look at those poor wretches know at once that they can never be men again. It's a miracle that they can even hold themselves up. They are literally nothing but bones, skin, and sinews. All have the same expression on their faces, that is if one can talk of expressions and faces, for they are nothing but skulls, death's-heads, like those that are painted on the death placards along the electric (death) fence round the camp. And death's-heads all look much the same. What an abyss of resignation and suffering stares out on you, without a word, without a sound. How is one ever to be rid of those staring eyes? With horror and repugnance one has to realize that one is gradually getting blunted, and that it's an ineluctable necessity, a kind of self-defense. And in this dance of death criminals are playing their game, swindlers, thugs, bank robbers, pickpockets, cheats. Most of them, raised to positions of authority in camp, have a free hand within this community. They steal the food out of starving mouths, the clothes off bodies that are freezing to death.

February 2. Yesterday, after we got back to camp at night, was indescribable. It was almost as though we were already free. All were in smiling spirits, rubbing their hands and breathing deeply. At last! Now it was only a question of hours. The Russians were just yonder in the cutting. Several wouldn't go to bed, at least not to sleep. The Russians might be there at any moment. One must pack and have everything ready. There weren't many who didn't bring back from the squad everything they kept there—clothes, food, and tobacco. They would never be going out there again! Even the pessimists agreed. That kind of mass psychosis, or hypnosis, always makes me a bit skeptical, but on the whole I believed with the majority that the Russians might arrive any time.

I think the same at this moment, though I'm out here on the squad as usual, writing again. For we did go out today as well. But it's quite plain that the end is near. Yesterday two *Selbstschutz* ["self defense"] companies were set up in camp, one German and one Polish, each, I think, of two hundred men. It's said these companies, which consist of prisoners, have already been given arms. Such a drastic step as that of equipping four hundred prisoners with arms and police authority can surely have but one meaning—that the SS intend to run away when the air gets too thick and leave the camp to itself and/or these four hundred.

And what are they, these four hundred? The two hundred Germans are to be led by a major bandit called Jacob, *Blockältester* [block elder] in Thirteen and the "personality" who takes the punishment gymnastics, or took them, for they seem to be over now. His men and brothers-in-arms are mostly BV-ers, a gang of brutes who stop at nothing. And then the Poles! The quality of the Poles in camp is sufficiently well known. Among them are to be found the worst *Vorarbeiters* [foremen] next to the Germans, the

biggest bullies, the worst informers, the scurviest "comrades." Who is to be their leader we don't yet know, but one can easily imagine the sort of man it will be. There are enough to choose from. The C.O. of this whole bandit regime, it's said, is to be the *Luftschutzgeneral* [air defense general], Manske, the German maniac I've already mentioned, who bullies condemned men. Yes, we may have a merry time. But one must say that it's a conclusion to this nightmare in complete harmony with all that has gone before. The felons in the high places!

This morning, as we paraded in working squads, we were met by the unpleasant news that Leo, our "chief" here in the drawing office, had been "called for" at midnight and has not returned. His fate is unknown, but there is reason to fear the worst, as a number of other men were "called for" at the same time, among them a lot of Russian officers and "intellectuals," who are said to have been shot. The BV-er who told us about this and who thinks they've all been "settled," also thinks this is only the beginning of a purge of everything like prominence and intelligence in the camp. Perhaps not among the Norwegians, Danes, and Dutchmen, he adds. . . .

February 6. Yesterday 225 Jews went into the gas chamber. It was a transport from Liberose. All were so wretched and worn out that for most of them death was simply a deliverer. I fear that Strauss has been taken and that the whole "transport" he was to be sent with has gone that way. It's predicted that all the Jews are to be gradually extirpated. The crematory is busy day and night. The crematory gang, twenty-five Jews, are on shift work. The previous gang has been "liquidated"; of course they knew too much. These Jews will doubtless go the same way, when they have done their job.

The evacuation continues. Today it's reported that six thousand are going off. It is still the sick and men unfit for work who are being sent. Later, the report is, all Russians, Ukrainians, Frenchmen, Belgians, and Poles are to go. An "elite" of twelve thousand Germans, Norwegians, Danes, and possibly Dutchmen are to remain in the camp.

We are living in hell, and it's strange to find that even in such a place people can adapt themselves. If one doesn't leave the Norwegian blocks, and if one shuts one's eyes and ears to all that is going on, and that in the immediate neighborhood (which there is nothing to prevent one's doing, and which many do), why, one may even get a kind of impression that hell is a snug, cozy sort of place, with a lot of fun and comfort, though a bit of a squeeze. The alerts have ceased to be noticed as an interruption. The windows are blacked out, and life inside goes on unaffected by the death and destruction pouring down over fellow creatures a few miles away. Indeed many actually don't know there's an alert, they are so absorbed in their novel, their food, or whatever. At night they sleep, sleep, and snore and let the world go as it will. Their only thought is: Shall I escape being evacuated? How much longer will it be before I can go home? Will the food run out before then? Will the parcels stop—and the cigarettes and tobacco? We're all like that at bottom, and let no one cast the first stone. Would it be any better if we sat in tears and despair? Besides there are quite a lot who help; I know of more than I used to. It's only certain people who hoard, and whom it takes all one's self-control not to go for. I know one who has *three* Swedish boxes crammed with food, on which he mounts guard like a dragon. Does he know that hundreds of people are dying of hunger in the camp every day? Yes, he's heard of it. I've told him. But his face betrayed no reaction of any kind. What is it to him? Is he a Jew or a Ukrainian, a Russian, or a Pole? I'm afraid he thinks he's a Norwegian hero!

April 18. The front is drawing nearer. This morning we had some planes over, and we're always hearing guns and machine-gun bursts. The planes set fire to a cargo boat at a wharf a couple of kilometers from here. Really it isn't war now, in the usual sense; it's more an occupation we're witnessing.

Huge transports of prisoners are leaving here every day. Whither no one knows. We merely suspect the very worst. The smoke from the crematory chimney, which on certain days rolls out black and thick and settles with a loathsome stench over the camp, is a reminder that the "harvest" here is still in full swing, while at the same time columns of musselmen are being lined up on the square and marched through the gateway, to the railway cars south of the camp, where they are stowed away and left—often for days and nights before they roll off. Where?

We are hoping to evade the occupation, or things may well be protracted. The next transport leaves tomorrow morning. If one only knew that now one was off to Sweden!

I've heard an unpleasant rumor that everything we take with us and all the clothes we have on, *everything* without exception, is burned when we arrive. Whether in Denmark or Sweden I don't know, but that's the vital point. If it's in Sweden, I shall always manage to save my little odds and ends from the flames. If in Denmark, it may be worse. For it may be the Gestapo's last form of *Filzing*. It would be provoking to lose this diary after I've kept it going so assiduously. I'll have to seduce a Swedish Lotta into taking it. But then Frode took a breadboard with him. I wonder if that escaped? *But now Frode is in Sweden!*

— From Odd Nansen, From Day to Day, *trans. Katherine John (New York: Putnam, 1949), 427–31, 434–35 and 475–76.*

FALKENSEE SONG

The author of these song lyrics, Zbigniew Koczanowicz, was a Polish prisoner who had been arrested in the fall of 1942, deported to Auschwitz that November, and by 1945 was transferred to Falkensee, a subcamp of Sachsenhausen opened in early 1943 to utilize slave labor in armaments production. These and other lyrics were saved by another prisoner, Aleksander Kulisiewicz, a Polish musicologist.

Separated from the world by barbed wire,
We've been rounded up from everywhere . . .

You with the striped rag on your back,
Could you forget who you are—and where?
They stitched a number to your breast,
A red triangle, and the letter "P."

And your shaved head serves to remind you
Of the burden of your unknown sins,
And you yearn for the day,
When your will and your purpose return.

Neither stars nor sun bring you happiness,
Neither night nor day yield pleasure . . .
And you wait, dressed in stripes and shaved bare,
With thousands of men like yourself.

The words of this song are stained with our blood,
Within them are sorrow and grief,
Yet your camp song will carry beyond these barbed wires,
To a distant place unknown to you.

— From Aleksander Kulisiewicz Collection, Record Group 55.003*03, United States Holocaust Memorial Museum Archives. Translated from Polish by Barbara Milewski.

Theresienstadt

THERESIENSTADT RELEASE

At the initiation of the orthodox Jewish relief and rescue agency Va'ad Ha-Hatsala, in the fall of 1944 Jean Louis Musy, a Swiss Catholic conservative politician who had been president of the Federal Council, began negotiations with Heinrich HIMMLER, Reich SS Leader, and Walter Schellenberg, head of foreign intelligence for the SS, for the release of Jewish prisoners from THERESIENSTADT. The deal was finalized in January 1945 and the released Jews were sent to Switzerland the following month.

The exchange received some coverage in the American press. The list of those released reproduced here appeared in PM Daily, *a well-known daily newspaper printed in New York City from 1940 to 1948 that had featured Holocaust-related stories more than any other major newspaper in the country.*

— From "First List of Refugees Freed From Nazi Camp," PM Daily, *February 23, 1945.*

---

8 ★★ PM, FRIDAY, FEBRUARY 23, 1945

First List of Refugees Freed From Nazi Camp

The Vaad Hahatzala Emergency Committee announces the names of 1200 men, women and children released from concentration camps in Theresienstadt, Czechoslovakia, and now safe in Switzerland.

The Vaad Hahatzala was able to arrange for the rescue with the co-operation of President von Steiger, and Federal Counsellor Musy of Switzerland.

The refugees in this transport, the third since last July, arrived in good condition. Vaad Hahatzala is informed that additional transports may now be expected weekly.

Previous transports were from Belensbergen camp, also in Czechoslovakia. Last July, 350 were rescued and last December, 1355.

The Vaad Hahatzala Emergency Committee is supported by orthodox Jewry, the Union of Orthodox Rabbis, the Young Israel Movement, Mizrachi, Agudath Israel and the various Teshivas. Its headquarters are at 132 Nassau St., New York City.

Among its activities of rescue and relief is the support of a refugee college at Shanghai where there are 500 students. This is carried on with the co-operation of the State Dept. Another project is the support of some 4000 persons in Siberia with the co-operation of the Russian Relief.

A list of 298 rescued refugees follows.

A

Ardel, Joseph, 60
Ansbacher, Annaeli'beth, 70
Aronstein, Klara, 67
Atlas, Eva, 22
Adler, Siegfried, 70
Afkan, Karoline, 67
Adler, Doris, 82
Abraham, Joseph, 68
Arendt, Rosalie, 76
Asch, Jenny, 22
Artmann, Ferdinand, 19

Artman, Rosi, 44
Artmann, Beatefriendriko, 7
Aigner, Hermino, 70
Allina, Petergeorg, 8
Allina, Wally, 33
Allina, Hans, 37
Adler, Doris, 82
Abraham, Joseph, 68
Alsi, Cohen Lodemijk, 50
Abt, Julius, 74
Anholt, Emanuel, 26
Anhalt, Schmerla Thea, 26

B

Berliner, Nanaie, 70
Bondi, Bertha, 44
Blumenthal, Toni, 68
Baron, Hugo, 71
Brill, Emmi, 71
Broslauer, Regina, 67
Bohme, Pauline, 76
Beck, Martha, 72
Bamberger, Henriette, 82
Berger, Hedwig, 81
Bing, Sofie, 71
Bettlheim, Bertha, 68

Battner, Paula, 76
Buchsbaim, Franz, 60
Binger, Juliette Aleida, 60
Baumann, Olga, 79
Berg, V.D. G. L. Gratia, 44
Bergmann, L. R. Helena, 47
Bergmann, Ernteduard, 60
Barmat, Dwinter Rosa, 59
Blumenthal, Margarete, 73
Böckmann, Johanna, 71
Beil, Ludwig, 68
Baum, Auguste, 66
Baum, Markus, 72

Bergruen, Hedwig, 68
Baschwitz, Rike, 71
Baschwitz, Adolf, 72
Bierig, David, 69
Bach, Hermann, 71
Brod, Johanna, 6
Broessler, Marta, 40
Broessler, Heinrich, 11
Broessler, Ruth Vera, 16
Bendix, Regine, 68
Bendix, Jacob, 72
Birkenholz, Osias, 70
Bohn, Erna, 49
Baymor, Emilie, 73
Bloch, Ella, 66
Bach, Fanny, 75
Baumann, Olga, 79
Bloemendahl, Alice, 71
Bandmann, Rosa, 79
Bagalnski, Joachim, 8
Bagalnski, Ernaminie, 11
Block, Simon, 63
Baganski, Margarethe, 50
Bilewski, Suse, 64
Brummer, Meta, 62
Bock, Ottilie, 67

Bundsel, Laura, 69
Bien, Eva, 20
Bien, Hilda, 50
Behrendt, Theodor, 67
Buschke, Erna, 68
Bischofsheimer, Fanny, 81
Barcharach, Hermann, 75
Birnbaum, Jettchen, 73
Bacher, Bertha, 82
Buckwitz, Eugenie, 70
Berlin, Nattika, 77
Bernstein, Selma, 72
Beatryr, Emma, 68
Belinfantes, Dora, 38
Broessler, Heinrich, 11
Broessler, Ruthvera, 16
Berlin, Nattika, 77
Bornstein, Selma, 72
Bischofsheimer, Fanny, 81
Bader, Arthur, 60
Bader, Sofie, 67
Blau, Fanny, 83
Blum, David, 70
Blum, Amilie, 59
Bett, Frieda, 74
Baron, Friederike, 43

Brodziak, Emilie, 74
Benesch, Regine, 78
Blumenriech, Else, 68
Bittner, Salo, 77
Bibo, Jakob, 77
Bacharach, Bethie, 70
Baymer, Emilie, 73
Blok, Davida Anny, 42
Bromet, Sinon, 64

C

Cohn, Marta, 67
Cohn, Benno, 69
Cassel, Hulda, 67
Cohn, Helene, 78
Cohn, Emilie, 68
Caro, Klara, 59
Czarnikauer, Laura, 76
Cohen, Aron, 72
Cardozo, Nunes Abra., 71
Cotent, Josina, 56
Cohn, Hulda, 69
Cronheim, Meta, 68
Chaskel, Retter, 64
Cohn, Bertha, 72
Cohnhoff, Gertrud, 67
Cohn, Lucie, 75
Cohen, Henriette, 80
Cohn, Klara, 75
Connard, Anna, 68
Cambitzky, Hulda, 79
Cats, Hilleaum Hanna, 52
Celdenrust, Saartje, 77
Cohen, Tervaert Aleida, 56
Cohen, Tervaert I. M., 81
Cleef, V. V. Praag Alice, 31
Cleef, V. Eduard, 15

Cohen, Bernhard, 63
Cohen, Venderhaan E., 50
Cleef, Polak Elisazeth, 68
Cardozo, Simetje, 49
Cardozo, Nunes, 70
Cambitsky, Hulda, 79
Cohn, Elisabeth, 69
Cohn, Max, 38
Cohn, Horst, 14
Cohn, Gertrud, 37
Cohen, Vanemden E., 70
Cohen, Joels Sphia, 42
Cohen, Leviy, 46
Cohen, Crete, 19
Cohen, VanLeeuwen E., 68
Cardezo, Jeshurun I. N., 67
Cohen, Amalie, 67
Cohen, Joseph, 66
Cohen, Hiewig Serline, 60
Cohen, Jakooba Sofia, 57
Cats, Suse, 18
Cats, Aldred, 50
Cardoso, Nunes Vilente, 70
Cohen, Poluk Marianne, 44
Cohen, Arnold, 45

D

Dorbin, Moritz, 73
David, Jakob, 76
Dults, Annie, 32
Devries, Belia, 57
Drilama, Krant Helene, 32
Drilama, Abraham, 35
Degorter, Amer. V. V., 60
Deutsch, Rudolfine, 69
Dodal, Irene, 45
Davidsburg, Auguste, 76
Deutsch, Bella, 74
Devrics, Elisabeth, 53
David, Sidor, 72
Dublin, Lina, 53
Delbanco, Selina, 81

Deutsch, Amelia, 81
Doellenfeld, Jettchen, 81
Devries, Tuifkaijer E., 51
Dejong, Mijer Esther, 66
Denskamp, Japp, 5
Dejong, Moses, 72
Denekamp, Saul, 6
Denekamp, Vreedbg. A., 37
Deitelzweig, Senior E., 38
Delfans, Herman, 73
Duches, Helene, 60
Delleuw, Vanstraaten M., 30
Deleeuw, Arend, 29
Delime, Martha, 22
Dela Bella, V. Z., 60

Dentz, Elsa, 62
Drielama, Maximab'ham, 43
Drielama, Hess Betzy, 35
Drielama, Aldred Ben., 7
Drielama, Listteklara, 3
Deleeuw, Lucie, 39

Dwinger, Praag Wilh., 30
Dormitz, Wolf, 48
Dormitz, Walljo M., 61
Dormitz, Alice, 18
Dormitz, Helmit, 10
Degoed, 64

E

Ehrlich, Rosa, 83
Elsas, Morgelstein Sarah, 63
Eck, Marieanna, 67
Enthoven, Vanlier Henr., 70
Erb, Anneliese, 12
Erb, Esther, 57
Eichenberg, Gertrud, 78
Epstein, Emma, 71
Einhorn, Martha, 45
Einhorn, Emma, 48
Eschelbacher, Max, 70
Elkan, Doktor Julius, 67
Elkan, Nellie, 64

Elkan, Ludwig, 71
Einhorn, Esther, 75
Ehrlich, Jette, 73
Eldod, Betha, 71
Edernheim, Vand. Hub., 60
Elsner, Gertrudmarie, 53
Elsas, Hermann Lehm., 67
Enthoven Neijmann A., 72
Eisfeld, Lause, 67
Elias, Papernek Luise, 40
Elias, Ven Den Matilde, 67
Elias, Mortizalbert, 40

F

Fialla, Mathilde, 78
Fantel, Ida, 68
Fischel, Else, 54
Fuchs, Erna, 40
Fischer, Hermine, 48
Fleischmann, Klara, 77
Freund, Edith, 46
Fuerth, Olga, 38
Fialla, Katarina, 37
Fialla, Renate, 13
Fliass, Bertha, 58
Frank, Julius, 78
Frankenstein, Recha Reb, 69
Fischer, Kathie, 79
Fried, Leontine, 79
Frankenstein, Dan, 71
Friedland, Arthur, 73
Feiner, Joelabba, 42
Feiner, Johanna, 45
Feiner, Emil, 46
Fackenheim, Anna, 69
Friedmann, Bernhard, 70
Frei, Rosa, 84
Fuchs, Johanna, 83
Falkenberg, Berta, 60
Frankenburger, Cilli, 41
Frankenberg, Pauline, 73
Fischer, Minna, 73

Fleischmann, Berthold, 67
Frenkel, Alexander, 55
Frenkel, Debora, 18
Frenkel, Rosemarie, 13
Frenkel, Doktor Herm., 54
Frankel, Goldschmidt E., 46
Fuldauer, Robert, 61
Francs, Mendes Henri, 58
Francs, Mendes Beaselsa, 56
Frenkel, Mitje, 59
Frenkel, Loepuit Elisa, 56
Frenkel, Karoline, 17
Frenkel, Ely, 14
Frenkel, Hans, 26
Frenkel, Lion, 57
Frenkel, Wiener Karo., 83
Frenkel, Luise, 11
Frenkel, Maria, 15
Frenkel, Hermine, 57
Frenkel, Rosalie, 61
Frenkel, Robert, 8
Frenkel, Betsie, 21
Frenkel, Simon, 13
Fekel, Alida, 45
Frank, Snijders Nuifje, 62
Frommer, Breindel, 67
Fleischmann, Berthold, 67

(More names will be published in the Week-End Edition of PM.)

FORCED EVACUATIONS

Auschwitz

AN SS MEMOIR

Long a trusted SS administrator at the DACHAU and SACHSENHAUSEN concentration camps, RUDOLF HÖSS became commandant of AUSCHWITZ upon its creation in May of 1940. It was Höss who introduced killing with ZYKLON B to AUSCHWITZ-BIRKENAU; gassing, he maintained, was "more hygienic" than the mass shootings of Jews that had taken place in the German-occupied East. In December 1943, Höss was relieved of his duties as commandant and transferred to Office D (concentration camp administration) of the SS CENTRAL OFFICE FOR ECONOMY AND ADMINISTRATION (WVHA). In June 1944, however, he returned to Auschwitz to organize the extermination of 400,000 Hungarian Jews.

This description of the EVACUATION of the camp in January 1945 is taken from Höss's autobiography, which he wrote in prison while awaiting trial for war crimes. On April 2, 1947, Höss was condemned to death by a Polish court and shortly thereafter hanged outside his former residence at Auschwitz.

I have referred on many occasions to the mad evacuation of the concentration camps.

The scenes I saw, and which resulted from the evacuation order, made such an impression on me that I shall never forget them.

When Pohl [Oswald Pohl, head of the SS Central Office for Economy and Administration] received no further reports from Baer during the evacuation of Auschwitz, he sent me post-haste to Silesia to put matters in order. I first found Baer at Gross-Rosen, where he was making preparations for the reception of the prisoners. He had no idea where his camp might be wandering. The original plan had had to be scrapped because of the Russian push to the south. I immediately drove on, in the hope of reaching Auschwitz in time to make sure that the order for the destruction of everything important had been properly carried out. But I was only able to get as far as the Oder, near Ratibor, for the Russian armoured spearheads were already fanning out on the far side of that river.

On all the roads and tracks in Upper Silesia west of the Oder I now met columns of prisoners, struggling through the deep snow. They had no food. Most of the non-commissioned officers in charge of these stumbling columns of corpses had no idea where they were supposed to be going. They only knew that their final destination was Gross-Rosen. But how to get there was a mystery. On their own authority they requisitioned food from the villages through which they passed, rested for a few hours, then trudged on again. There was no question of spending the night in barns or schools, since these were all crammed with refugees. The route taken by these miserable columns was easy to follow, since every few hundred yards lay the bodies of prisoners who had collapsed or been shot. I directed all the columns I could reach to go westwards, into the Sudetenland, so as to avoid the incredibly chaotic bottleneck near Neisse. I gave strict orders to the men in charge of all these columns that they were not to shoot prisoners incapable of further marching. They were to hand them over in the villages to the *Volkssturm* [home guard]. During the first night, on the road near Leobschütz, I constantly came upon the bodies of prisoners who had just been shot, and which were therefore still bleeding. On one occasion, as I stopped my car by a dead body, I heard revolver shots quite near. I ran towards the sound, and saw a soldier in the act of stopping his motorcycle and shooting a prisoner leaning against a tree. I shouted at him, asking him what he thought he was doing, and what harm the prisoner had done him. He laughed impertinently in my face, and asked me what I proposed to do about it. I drew my pistol and shot him forthwith. He was a sergeant-major in the Air Force.

Every now and then I also met officers from Auschwitz who had managed somehow or other to get hold of a vehicle. I posted them at crossroads, to collect these wandering columns of prisoners, and move them westwards, eventually perhaps by train. I saw open coal trucks, loaded with frozen corpses, whole trainloads of prisoners who had been shunted onto open sidings and left there without food or shelter. Then again there were groups of prisoners, often without guards, who had escaped or whose guards had simply vanished. They too were making their way peacefully westwards. I also met unaccompanied British prisoners of war doing the same: they were determined on no account to fall into the hands of the Russians. I saw SS-men and prisoners huddled together on the refugees' vehicles. I came upon columns of building workers and agricultural labourers. No one knew where he was trying to go. Gross-Rosen was the final destination of them all. There was deep snow at the time and it was very cold. The roads were blocked by Army and Air Force columns, and by the crowds of refugees. The slippery surface caused innumerable car accidents.

Beside the roads were not only dead prisoners, but also refugees, women and children. Outside one village I saw a woman sitting on a tree stump, and singing to her child as she rocked it in her arms. The child had been dead for a long time and the woman was mad. Many women struggled through the snow pushing perambulators stacked high with their belongings. They had only one aim, to get away and not to fall into the hands of the Russians.

Gross-Rosen was crammed to overflowing. Schmauser had already arranged for it to be evacuated. I travelled to Breslau to tell him what was happening and to urge him to stop the evacuation. He showed me the wireless message from the Reichsführer SS which made him responsible for seeing that not a single healthy prisoner remained in any camp under his authority.

At the railway station in Gross-Rosen the transports coming in were immediately sent on. Only the smallest ones could be fed. Gross-Rosen itself had no more food.

Dead SS-men lay peacefully in the open cars between dead prisoners. Those still alive sat on top of them, chewing their piece of bread. Terrible scenes, best not described.

— *From Rudolf Höss,* Commandant of Auschwitz: The Autobiography of Rudolf Hoess, *trans. Constantine Fitzgibbon (London: Pan Books Ltd, 1959), 190–192.*

A SURVIVOR'S TALE

Lucie Adelsberger, a Jewish doctor, resided outside of Germany but frequently travelled to Berlin, the city where she grew up, to visit her mother. In 1941, Adelsberger returned to Berlin to take care of her mother who had suffered a stroke. Refusing to abandon her mother, Adelsberger missed her last chance to leave Germany and was later deported. Here she describes the forced march in early 1945 from AUSCHWITZ-BIRKENAU as the Red Army approached.

I will remember the 18th of January 1945, a Thursday, for the rest of my life, even if I live to be a thousand years old. I will never forget that night in which we vacillated back and forth between the prospect of being extinguished now at the end after we had survived all the years in the camp and between the hope of being placed on a transport and getting out of Auschwitz alive. We improvised back packs and bags out of old rags, found our last remaining belongings and packed and unpacked with nervous purposelessness. In between, we, who were also juggling with our own lives, had to calm the patients who were strapped in their beds and overcome with panic. And then someone dear to me was lying there, very sick in his barracks. He was unable to take part in the evacuation. Should I go or stay if the others leave? To leave him in the lurch in certain danger seemed like treason to me. But did one have the right, after surviving two years in Auschwitz, to risk his life out of affection for another even if he could be of no help? Did I not have the duty to disregard all personal considerations and just go? All of this spun around together in my mind during that night.

The official order in the morning stated: "Transport." All sick prisoners were to be taken along, as long as they were capable, to Auschwitz, a three kilometer trek. That was at first. Later the talk was of a fifteen kilometer march. No selection in all the years was more disturbing than the selection of patients for the march, which we prisoners had to make ourselves. Now that the path lay open, we were supposed to leave people behind, people we loved, sick people whom we had looked after and took great pains to keep alive. We were still under the effects of the nocturnal intermezzo. Through the thin laboratory wall, Polish women had accidently overheard the camp doctor talking with his assistants if provisions had been made for handling thousands of dead. For us the destiny of the last remaining in Birkenau was sealed.

The patients were tested again and again if they could walk, sent back to their beds, gotten out of them again and tested again. Whoever did not fall over and wanted to go along was supplied with clothes and shoes, often only wooden shoes. Many returned back to the barracks after the first few steps on the camp street, disappointed and in despair. We wanted to take along a colleague of ours on a stretcher. She was suffering from abdominal typhus. The camp doctor forbade it, and she had to be brought back. Even long afterwards our farewell pained me, how she, awaiting certain death, looked sadly back at us.

We were assembled to roll call and prepared for evacuation many many times, many times in vain. That day we never had a chance to sit or to eat. Finally at five o'clock in the afternoon—the stars were already beginning to shine—our group departed. It was no dream. We, who had never thought it possible to get out of Auschwitz, left Birkenau alive.

Many months later we learned that in retreat the Germans had moved out of Auschwitz and Birkenau leaving the camps behind almost unscathed. The prisoners we had so desperately left behind were liberated by the Russians on 27 January 1945, much earlier than all of us.

Wandering through the Snow

A wise woman once said: "Every wish will be come true but not necessarily at the right time." I had always wanted to have a moonlight party through a wintery landscape, but I would have liked it under different circumstances, and this hiking party was different than I had imagined it.

After the gates of Birkenau had closed behind us, we went toward Auschwitz. It took us almost an hour to walk the three kilometers. We were so heavily weighed down by our blankets that we had wrapped around us, with bread we had quickly amassed and taken out of the storeroom, and by our necessary belongings which weighed more on our backs than when they were being used. Many of us who had been transferred to Birkenau immediately after arrival or those who were deported directly to Birkenau saw Auschwitz for the first time. It seems ironic that this place, whose name today still sends chills down my spine, lives in my memory like a fascinating backdrop on a stage. Perhaps it was the feeling that, despite the unfavorable odds, we had

Prisoners from Dachau on a forced evacuation march on approximately April 27, 1945. Such marches of concentration camp prisoners were commonplace at war's end as the Germans tried to keep the prisoners from the liberating Allies. (Dachau Memorial Museum)

gotten out of the concentration camp alive and would leave the area forever. Perhaps it was the new seed of hope of liberation that sharpened our last impression, or perhaps that night Auschwitz really was stunningly beautiful. The moon cast its glistening light upon everything. The tall stone houses, which appeared enormous to us in comparison to the flat barracks, loomed up powerfully toward the sky, cutting through the horizon with the sharp edges of their roofs, powerfully lifting themselves up from the great snow-covered scene which glittered magically in the light of the moon. Underneath in the shadows, the narrow path snaked along between the bluish walls of the houses, bordered on both sides by barbed wire no longer meant for us. The ghost-like guards, stalking up and down the fence, no longer paid attention to us. They looked like unreal figures, a part of a picture. In between the river of thousands of people slowly surged through the turns and bends, not like before toward the gas chambers but away from them, an endless train of people coming and going like movie extras appearing again and again as if on a revolving stage. It lasted more than two hours until the human mass, about 10,000,

had squeezed through the narrow path and had received their canned meat, two cans per person, which the SS was now kindly handing out. Then we began our journey on the country road. Only now, after being neither loaded into hearses nor shot in Auschwitz, our secret fears left us, and we were finally able to breathe a sigh of relief.

It really was a moonlight party in the snow. The clear, star-filled sky shone above us, the full moon casting its beams, the snow nestled over the fields and meadows like a large velvet carpet, the forest glimmered a blinding white, and on the branches the ice crystals glittered like pieces of filigree work. The snow lay deep on our path crunching under our footsteps. We marched through the entire night and at first relished the hike out in the open with the delight known only by those freed after many years of imprisonment. Those who had overestimated their strength and were tired sat down in the snow to rest and catch up with us later, or leisurely to return back to Auschwitz. Only the many guards on our side, one on each side every ten rows, spoiled our feeling of freedom.

In the morning, the sun rose up behind the Beskids

mountains, and we were still trekking through the snow, no longer as happy as before. We were tired, hungry, hoping for a rest. But we continued onward uphill, downhill, and, as we could see from the position of the sun, south, west, north, through the deep soft snow without a rest, a break or an end—nothing but the snowy landscape and now and then dead bodies. They lay on the side of the road, with bleeding head wounds, in the peaks and valleys of snow drifts. Men and women, in civilian clothing, in blue and white striped prisoner's uniforms, with their bags and bundles, and each one with a number. The first few startled us. We wondered what had happened to them, but then there were more and more of them, and eventually they lined the road only a few yards apart. Gradually the longer we trotted and the heavier our tired limbs became, we realized that these people were from Auschwitz, our trailblazers whose strength had left them and who were now lying here. Our own ranks were already beginning to thin out, and here and there the fatal shot rang out. Whoever could go no further was shot. Once it was a girl whose twin sister, despite all efforts, was unable to help her go on. Another time it was a mother shot before her daughter's very eyes. So this was the end. For this we had suffered through so many years in Auschwitz. And yet we continued to trod along through the snow, which was now speckled red with blood.

Back and forth the path went around in a circle. We had already gone more than 50 kilometers when on 19 January we passed Pless, where long rows of train cars stood with piles of goods, cattle, and hay. The people had quickly left the area. We went by the Prince Pless Park, famous for its natural monuments. We hardly had a chance to glance through the gates as we marched on to an open field behind the city where we stopped for a short rest. Before we could even swallow a mouthful of bread and a handful of snow for our parched throats, the relentless SS pushed us to leave and quickly drove us ahead, mercilessly shooting down those lagging behind. After twenty-six hours of continuous marching, we stopped in a small hamlet where the thousands of us were crammed into two barns. There was nothing edible because the most of us had been so exhausted on the march, we had thrown down everything we were carrying. (When I am evacuated from the next concentration camp, I will only take with me, if I have them, cigarettes and sugar, a tooth brush, and a comb.)

The next morning we started out early. Tired, exhausted, hungry, frozen through—it was between five and minus five degrees Fahrenheit—we marched on, straight ahead, back, in no specific direction. For an entire, never-ending day we walked for our very lives. Around seven o'clock we reached Loslau, summoning all our strength for the last ten kilometers which we ran. We had gone about 100 kilometers with the emaciated individuals from Auschwitz, with the many sick, with 70 children, through valleys and over hills, wading through deep snow—a race against death.

And we still had not arrived at our destination. After a night of far too many people fighting for a place to sit or to get warm in the straw, the next morning, the twenty-first of January, we were led to a train station and were loaded into open coal cars. We were squeezed into them in masses, more and more people being crammed in. The doors were locked shut. There were 120-130 people crammed in together in each car so tightly we could not stand, let alone sit. It was freezing. The cold tore at our skin, ate away at our fingers and toes, and through the freezing air, bored its way into our lungs and insides. Hunger gnawed at our hearts. We barely survived these days with the last remaining scraps we found in our packs and quenching our thirst with the snow that we scraped together off of the dirty wheels of the cars. Whenever the train stopped on an open stretch, a couple of dexterous young girls would quickly climb out over the sides of the car, fetch some snow, and bring it back up into the car. Every handful was bitterly fought for and not just snow but also for the smallest amount of space in the train. It may be that our being packed together so tightly prevented us from freezing to death, but after the hardship of the march, our constant self-defense not to be crushed to death used up our last bit of energy. One of the SS guards in our car was carried out unconscious after two days, and in one single car six people had been trampled to death. The journey went on for six days and six nights without an end in sight. We did not know how long it would last nor where we were going. We followed the individual stations with great agitation. We went by Breslau, Frankfurt on the Oder, where the people were camped out at the train station in masses, the trains leaving jam-packed for the West. We passed Sagan, through the eastern suburbs of Berlin. Then we went to Oranienburg and Furstenberg and to Ravensbrück. There, in one of the infamously worst concentration camps, where since 1933 hecatombs of prisoners perished miserably, we were unloaded from our journey which had begun with so much hope.

For an entire day we lay in the filthy snow and on the embankments of the camp streets—still without a bite to eat or a drop of water for our parched throats. (A gold chain, a watch was offered for a glass of water.) In the evening the 8,000 people were forced into a machine hangar where, for those who were good with their elbows, there was some camp soup and a couple of potatoes.

I don't think that on the women's march more than 15%-20% were lost. That is a terrible number and yet still small enough when one remembers the condition of those who left Auschwitz. Next to experienced, well-trained prisoners there were many starving, emaciated bodies, sick, and children who, by some miracle, had survived. . . .

Disgust

After a sleepless night in the turmoil of the machine hangar the newly arrived prisoners were dispersed among the barracks. A small group was placed in camp barracks, many were housed in tents at five degrees Fahrenheit where the only protection from freezing to death was cramming together as tightly as possible. We, about 800 people, were placed in the penal barracks in Ravensbrück. There, in a room for 500 at the very most, 645 ethnic German convicts were housed. Together with them we brought the number to a record high of 1,445.

The types of people who were herded together in the penal barracks in Ravensbrück were horrifying, with one exception: the Jehovah's Witnesses. The Nazis had sent the Jehovah's Witnesses to the concentration camps. Those we came across in the penal barracks in Ravensbrück already had six to eight years under their belts. Nevertheless, they remained unbroken, their enthusiasm for their belief shone in their eyes. Even in the camp they continued to preach their beliefs and distribute leaflets. For this they were sent to the penal barracks, which the guards and camp police kept cut off from the rest of the camp. The other prisoners were asocials: previously convicted prostitutes, convicts, and criminals of every kind. They fulfilled their sadistic desires on us who, during the January day, shivered from the cold, standing in the courtyard for hours not being able to find a place to sit, not even at night. If we made any attempt to wash or relieve ourselves, we were beaten half to death.

The absolute worst part was during food distribution. First the "ethnic Germans" were fed and ate their fill at our expense. Then we received our soup in the same unwashed bowls from which typhus sufferers and ragged, filthy, infested prisoners had eaten, bowls into which they had spit the remains of their turnips. Again and again the one hundred bowls made their rounds, unwashed and filthy, with the garbage from the previous user into which the portion of one-half ladle was poured. And we, worn down and overpowered by hunger, greedily gulped the soup down.

Why am I telling this disgusting story? Not so that others can also be nauseated by it, but rather as an indication as to how deep we had sunk. During a reeling dance with death one forgets how to act. All inhibitions are gone. There are still other things the memory of which fills me with disgust, things which I find much more difficult to forgive myself for. During our march through the snow there was a girl among us whom I liked very much. She had just recovered from an illness, and the march was too much for her in her weakened condition. She carried herself forward arduously, trying to hang onto my back pack. Myself completely exhausted and hardly able to stand straight, I refused to drag her along. This girl who managed to make it through the train ride and arrived in Ravensbrück with severe famine edema and a festering oral infection would have died anyway, and yet. . . . If it had been my sister or my lover, would I have helped?

— From Lucie Adelsberger, Auschwitz. Ein Tatsachenbericht *(Berlin: Lettner Publishing, 1960), 147–63. Translated from the German by Neal Guthrie.*

Flossenbürg

FLOSSENBÜRG EVACUATION

Benno Fischer, born in Poland in 1914, was a Jewish prisoner at FLOSSENBÜRG concentration camp when it was evacuated by the Germans on April 14, 1945. In this selection he describes highlights of the EVACUATION.

Monday, April 16, 1945. Thank heavens it's morning. The Barracks Leader comes in and in his shrieking voice tells us that it is 5 o'clock, we had enough sleep, and the stinking Jews should get the hell out of here, starts beating people over their heads, backs and any place his stick can reach. There are always a few unfortunates who were not fast enough in leaving the Barracks. We congregate in front of our Barracks, worn out, half sleepy, dazed and hungry. The morning is very, very cold and the chill goes through our skin and thin layer of muscles into our bones, into our spines and head. Everyone is shivering and the teeth rattle incessantly. It is the cold, the hunger or most likely the fear for the unknown, that makes us shiver. The barracks leader counts this wretched motley group in front of him. The secretary recounts, and then another count and the arithmetic seems to be in order. As I mentioned before our barracks is on the highest plateau and we have a bird's eye view on the entire compound. We can see that similar operations are taking place in front of other barracks. Our group walks down the steps and slowly is being pushed into the roll call field. Here we see our comrades assembled already and people from other barracks joining the group. We look around to see how the others look and we think that we must look as miserable as they. To the side we see a group of people from the "hospital." To look at them is really the most depressing experience. At least we have enough strength to stand up, but these poor wretched creatures must hold on to each other, otherwise they would collapse. I do not know if selfishness is the right expression of my feelings at that moment. I was glad that I was not sick and can stand on my two feet without assistance. But I could not but feel sorry for these people in utter misery. Is it possible that there is still a spark of humanity, empathy, compassion left in me? I will be killed in an upright position and they lying down on the ground. What difference does it make? I do not know, but I still feel sorry for them.

We did not mention the Red Cross, their trucks, etc. We do ask ourselves, where are we being driven? Will it be a forest, a cemetery, or just any empty field for our execution? An armed group of S.S.-men is coming towards us, each of them carrying two breads, one package of margarine, one can of preserves, and cigarettes. It is clear that these S.S.-men with guns and provisions will be our guardians. They order us in files, five abreast, 20 rows making 100 people to a column. We are counted again and the number

A train carrying approximately 2500 concentration camp inmates, mostly Jews liberated by the U.S. 30th Infantry Division on April 14, 1945 near Farsleben, Germany. Many of the "passengers" had already died; most of the others were ill or starving. (NARA)

is approximately 2600, i.e., 26 columns. Each column has two S.S.-men in front, four at each side and four in the rear. They are equipped with machine guns. We started marching in the direction of the railroad station in Flossenbürg. From the Camp to the station is about 6 km. We arrived at the station and the freight trains are already waiting for us. We board them, 60 per car with six S.S.-men as our guards. The train had also 10 open wagons. We started moving. No sooner had we made about three or four km, the train stops and we hear planes flying towards our train. We can see through the open doors that the planes, American or English, come down very low and start shooting up the locomotive and, of course, some of the wagons got also hit. The S.S.-men jump from the train and we follow them running in different directions, hiding behind houses and in ditches to avoid the deadly bullets which come down pouring from heaven. The planes swoop down to spray the wagons with

bullets, get up and in a sweeping circle come back again. Some of the people do not pay any attention to the flying bullets and start robbing the S.S. food packs, taking bread, margarine, cigarettes, and what have you. Some started digging in the fields and finding potatoes, turnips, etc. I am very hungry, but have no guts to rob the rucksacks, or look for potatoes. The S.S. order us to get back to the wagons, firing shots into the air, scream, and finally let their dogs free in order to gather up the scattered people. On the way back to the wagons we see some of the inmates lying in agony, shot by the planes and some of the S.S.-men who could not find cover and were also hit. We finally boarded our wagon, but our number is only 50. Some of the people got killed and maybe some ran away and were hiding in the adjacent forest. The S.S. is checking their rucksacks and luckily nothing is missing. Despite this situation they go with a delegation to the Commandant of the transport and tell him that their bread, margarine, and cigarettes were stolen. The Commandant listens to their complaints, comes to our wagon, and starts screaming and cursing us: "How could we, the stinking Jews, knowing that we will be exterminated anyhow, rob the property of a German?" There were, of course, no protests, and the verdict was to take away half of our bread portion. The epilogue is more tragic than the bread we have lost. They kill the wounded ones and a few others by whom they found some extra food, a potato or turnip. It is 10 o'clock and we eat up quickly our bread in order not to part with it in case of another verdict. It is 5 P.M. by now and we get a slice of bread and a piece of cheese. We swallow it immediately and our hunger instead of being stilled is stimulated. Or maybe the stomachs which were irritated by this piece of bread, require more food, or maybe the thought of another fast heightens our hunger. Finally a new locomotive is being attached to our wagons and some sort of a childish joy permeates our bodies. Maybe these are the memories of our past years when we, as children, went on a trip and were overjoyed when the train started to move and the landscape changed. Yes, the train started moving and we on our way. We are going, but where? Nobody knows, but at least we will leave this place which devoured about 60 people. We come to a station called Weiden, which is about 30 km. from Flossenbürg. The train stopped and we are getting ready for our night's sleep, and dreams, or nightmares. . . . *[The locomotive was attacked by Allied aircraft the next day. However, it returned the train to Weiden that evening, where the prisoners remained until Thursday morning.]*

Thursday, April 19, 1945. A new locomotive came on our line and is being connected to the wagons and with a typical screech is pulling away from the station. Thank heavens we are going to Schwarzenfeld (black field); an appropriate name for our destiny. The English or American planes must have spotted us and started flying quite low. The S.S.-men opened the door and started jumping off the train. The pilots must have noticed them and thought this is probably a military transport. They started showering the train with machine guns; the locomotive was, of course, the first victim and then they raked the train from beginning to end at each side of the wagons, from the front and rear. The bullets killed many people and this picture will show what happened in my wagon.

People started jumping off the train and we can see some without hands, with one leg, the skull shattered and the brain oozing out. Some are asking the S.S.-men to finish off their suffering, but the merciful gangsters do not want to waste their bullets; no mercy is shown even in this tragic moment. I was destined to survive this massacre and so can describe these horrible scenes which I had witnessed. I mentioned destiny, because I escaped death. The bullets killed three people on my side and six people on the other half. The fellow next to me was hit by a bullet which tore off half of his behind. I have seen a flash in front of

my face and the bullet killed a fellow on the other side. At this moment I thought or maybe I said: *"Shma Isroel, Adonei alohenu, Adonei echod."* I opened the eyes and saw pieces of flesh and ribs glued on to the boards of the wagon. The people died, of course.

This was one of the miracles which kept me from crossing the Hades and is an answer to the question being asked: "How did you survive the war?" There were 18 wounded and 43 dead. We forgot food and hunger. But some of the boys could not resist the hunger and went into the fields which I shall describe later. The following scene, I witnessed, confirms the known saying that hunger can lead a person to frantic (crazy) deeds. I hear about hunger, read some books covering this subject, but my fantasy was too limited to grasp a picture of hunger, a condition of hunger plaguing a man for many years. Being in camp, I had the possibility to observe this condition on my own skin, as well as see others suffering hunger. I was maybe too frightened or maybe too cowardly to follow other inmates. They ran into the fields while the planes were covering the area with a hail of bullets. The were indifferent to the barking of the S.S. dogs, the S.S.-men shooting left and right, to the groaning of their dying comrades. They do not see the people with shattered skulls, bleeding bellies or arms. The only goal they have is to dig up a few potatoes and eat them. Unfortunately their daring did not pay off. The S.S.-men check everyone and start searching everybody. The moment they found a piece of potato or saw earth-covered hands they killed the victim. I remember seeing one boy shot five times, but he was still screaming *"Ich möchte am Leben bleiben"* (I want to live). Finally another S.S.-man came and shot him in the head and the poor fellow collapsed with a piece of potato in his mouth. The S.S.-men went wild and started shooting people whom they suspected of stealing potatoes. Maybe they swallowed them already; thus freeing themselves from the first verdict. This was a tragic encounter with hunger in its ugliest form. What difference does it make now? Some got killed by the Allies: why cannot they, our guardians, get rid of some and have less trouble with the transport. The fewer people they will have, the easier it will be to keep an eye on them. They leave the dead, wounded, sick, and select the so-called healthy and strong. What a wonderful feeling to be part of this elite which will undertake a march into the unknown. We receive 14 oz. of bread and are being told that this should last for two days. The day which has passed and we did not get anything to eat, but this does not count, because it has passed already. It is 6 P.M. It starts getting dark and we are being put into columns and being hit with the guns to make nice, clean, perfect lines. They select a few people to pull their wagons with their belongings. Hiding behind my own shadow I took off my glasses; thus I was spared the privilege of pulling the S.S. rucksacks, sleeping mats and what have you. Each time they tried to select some people for a certain job, I quickly took off my glasses. The logic is simple: The Jews with glasses belong to the intelligentsia, a Jewish intellectual is not fit for work, he cannot produce for the Fatherland. The food he is getting is just wasted on him and the logical step is a bullet in his head.

Leaving the rhetoric behind I follow the marchers. We pass a village and ask the people along the road for some water, but a brown-clad local militia man chases away the kids, women, and elderly people who try to get closer to us and give us some water. We are marching on and by now it must be past midnight. We get off the road and come to a meadow surrounded by a young fir forest. We are being told to lie down and go to sleep. The moon is looking down on us, the grass is fresh and green; we are surrounded by the dogs and the armed S.S.-men. Where in the world could we have a better protection? We do not know the terrain and maybe there are bad wolves lurking in the forest. Now free from fear we can sleep peacefully, free from danger and planes. The bedding is nice and soft because the meadows in springtime are saturated with moisture which normally evaporates during the hot summers. If we do not catch pneumonia it is another miracle. When one believes in miracles and I do belong to this group, one must admit, that to survive this march is a miracle in itself. It is moist, but at least we can breathe fresh air. It is a good change from the stuffy wagons. . . .

— From "Survivor Testimony," Record Group 02.039, United States Holocaust Memorial Museum Archives, 11–14, 18–21.

Gardelegen

GARDELEGEN MASSACRE

As the Allies advanced into Germany, they continually encountered evidence of Nazi atrocities perpetrated against concentration camp inmates and slave laborers. Near the town of Gardelegen a column of camp prisoners evacuated in the face of the Allied advance were burned alive by their SS guards. A survivor described the massacre to GIs of the 102nd Infantry Division "the Ozark troops," who discovered the site and included the following description in their Division's history.

One of these [survivors], a Hungarian musician named Bondo Gaza, told his story on a beautiful spring morning as the citizens of Gardelegen buried the bodies of his former comrades.

Gaza said that the group originally had a strength of over two thousand. They had been making airplane parts in a factory in eastern Germany. When the Russians approached from the east they were jammed into a train and shunted around the country for seven days. They had nothing but bread to eat. The train eventually reached Mieste, some

twelve kilometers from Gardelegen. There the group began their death march, but only 1,200 reached Gardelegen. The lame and halt were more fortunate. They were shot as they fell by the wayside. For a day the 1,200 were housed in and around a hospital. There three hundred of them, German political prisoners, were drilled and placed as guards over their former comrades. For their services they were promised freedom. Next day the group marched to the barn on a little hill outside town. Again some fell out and were shot.

It was Friday evening, April 13, when they were herded into the barn, a large empty structure measuring roughly a hundred by fifty feet. The prisoners were ordered to sit down. If they did not realize their fate at first they most certainly must have feared the worst when they saw the gasoline-soaked straw scattered knee-deep on the floor. At the last moment, after machine guns had been emplaced, the three hundred guards were also forced into the building, They had only five minutes to contemplate their fate before an SS corporal opened a door and laughingly struck a match to the straw. He was all of sixteen years of age. Fifty or sixty prisoners rushed to the opposite side of the building. A door gave way. There was a dash for freedom—a short dash ended by machine-gun fire. Meanwhile others managed to beat out the flaming straw with bare hands.

Once again SS troops ignited the floor, this time keeping the prisoners away from the fire by throwing hand grenades into the frantic masses. Exploding grenades spread the flames. At one door where stubborn prisoners beat out the fire several times a burp gun ripped into the struggling groups and signal flares reignited the straw. When the SS guards were finally satisfied that the flames were out of control the big doors were closed and barricaded.

Gaza, huddled in a corner, was digging a hole under a door. Others tried to do the same. One man managed to get his head through the opening before he died. But Gaza was lucky. He, his comrade, and a Pole dug for an hour before they had a tunnel big enough. The Pole went out first. It was then about 2100 hours and getting dark. If they could reach the corner they might escape by crawling through the grain fields to the north. Just as the Pole reached the corner, a dog came sniffing by. The Pole tried to control his quaking limbs and feign death, but the dog howled and a guard came running. A bullet denied the Pole his freedom. Behind him lay Gaza grimly awaiting his turn. Again he was lucky. Dog and master returned to the opposite side of the barn. Gaza and his comrade then crawled two miles to a damaged farmhouse.

Another man, a Frenchman, managed to remain alive in the burning barn. Sheltered by a mass of charred bodies he somehow escaped suffocation. He later said that SS men returned in the morning, calling that they were ready to give medical aid to anyone who had survived the night. When several survivors indicated they were alive they were shot on the spot.

Local slave laborers were rounded up Saturday morning to dig great trenches around the barn, bury the remains, and otherwise clean up the evidence. Over seven hundred bodies were thus concealed before this work was interrupted by the surrender of the town. Freshly dug common graves in the nearby field mutely emphasized the haste with which all signs of this atrocity were being concealed. If Gardelegen had held out another day no visible evidence of the incident would have remained.

No trace could be found of the SS troops who participated in this massacre, apparently at the request of the *Kreisleiter* (county supervisor) of Gardelegen. Nor was the *Kreisleiter,* a man named Gerhardt Thiele, ever found although his wife was apprehended and later despairingly hanged herself in the city jail. Several other implicated persons also committed suicide. These included the commanding officer of the local *Volkssturm* company and one of his men, both of whom admitted shooting at the prisoners when they tried to escape from the pyre.

The Division Commander directed that every available male citizen in Gardelegen be marched to see the ghastly sight. Accordingly, under the supervision of Ozark troops, they together with the *Bürgermeisters* from all neighboring towns, were conducted to the barn where they viewed the still smoldering victims of their Nazi regime. There they were formally charged with the responsibility of telling their communities the sordid tale. Later the citizens of Gardelegen established a memorial cemetery near the building.

While soldiers of the 327th Engineer Combat Battalion stood by with fixed bayonets to enforce the order, every able-bodied German civilian in the neighborhood was required to contribute to the tasks necessary to disinter and give the victims a decent burial. A final resting place was laid out to specifications of American military cemeteries. The citizens of Gardelegen dug the graves, interred the bodies, erected a cross or a Star of David over each, and finally surrounded the entire site with a white fence. Every family in the city was impressed with the responsibility of forever caring for one of these nameless graves; and in order that these instructions will be followed in later years, records were left with the city officials. At the mass funeral of these pitiful remnants of humanity, the Division Chief of Staff, Col. George P. Lynch, aptly stated the feelings of the Division when he told the assembled townspeople of Gardelegen, "You have lost the respect of the civilized world."

— *From Major Allan Mick,* With the 102nd Infantry Division Through Germany *(Washington: Infantry Journal Press, 1947), 212–16.*

CONFRONTING THE HORROR

The forced evacuations from the concentration camps were ordered by the SS lest the prisoners be rescued by the Allies. Thousands perished from illness, starvation, the cruelty of the guards, exposure, and privation. Their SS captors, fearing retribution, also often simply murdered the surviving prisoners when Allied troops drew near.

A typical instance took place at Gardelegen, Germany, on April 13, 1945. More than 1,000 inmates, evacuated from several concentration camps, were herded into a hay-barn by SS and German Army guards, who then lit the gasoline-drenched straw and, using hand grenades to drive back desperate prisoners trying to smother the flames, closed the barn's doors after shooting the last defiant few. The next day the SS made slave-laborers dig large trenches to bury the bodies, a final and futile attempt to hide evidence of their barbarity. Only a few prisoners survived.

The commander of the U.S. 102d Infantry Division ordered the townspeople to view the hellish scene in the barn. Later that month, the citizens were made to disinter the hastily buried corpses, dig new graves for the slain prisoners, bury them properly, and attend a funeral ceremony under the supervision of U.S. soldiers.

The presence of U.S. Army photographers, who took most of these photos, as well as American correspondents led to widespread publicity of this atrocity in Life *magazine and the American press.*

A heavily guarded forced evacuation from
Dachau concentration camp, photographed by an
unknown German photographer, passes through
a Bavarian village in late April 1945. The march
of the Gardelegen prisoners was similar.
(Dachau Memorial Museum)

The south side of the barn on the Isenchibbe estate at Gardelegen where more than 1,000 prisoners were burned to death on April 13, 1945. The severity of the fire can be seen from the charred areas around the doors. (NARA)

A hideously blackened victim at Gardelegen photographed on April 16, 1945, several days after the discovery of the atrocity site. (NARA)

Corpses of prisoners who died while attempting to escape the inferno by crawling under the barn door. (NARA)

Over a six-day period, U.S. troops marched all the citizens of Gardelegen to view the victims at the barn. (NARA)

German civilians placing victims' bodies in rows of individual graves. (USHMM)

A formation of Gardelegen's civilians carrying the shovels and U.S. Army-issue grave markers for the re-burial of the victims. (NARA)

Flanked by a cluster of grave markers, local German civilians dig graves for the victims of the massacre. (NARA)

Germans erecting markers over the graves
they dug for the victims of this massacre.
(USHMM)

Grünberg

ALL BUT MY LIFE

Gerda Weiss Klein, born in Poland, was fifteen years old when the war started. Her elder brother was drafted for forced labor in autumn 1939; she and her parents were forced into a GHETTO in their hometown of Bielitz in April 1942. When the ghetto was liquidated soon thereafter, she was separated from her parents and sent first to Sosnowiec concentration camp, then, in July 1942, to work as a slave laborer at a mill in Bolkenhein. In August 1943 she was transferred to Marzdorf and then to another mill at Landshut. In May 1944, she was again transferred, this time to Grünberg, a subcamp of GROSS-ROSEN, where she remained until the camp was evacuated in January 1945.

Yet another day we marched on in a westward direction. It was the last day that we had bread. We were no longer counted. They could not keep track of how many were shot or died during the night. I was cold and hungry but for the time being I minded the cold more. At night I felt Ilse's hand in mine. I took off my shoes and curled myself over them, for fear that someone might steal them. There was muffled crying all around me. I did not cry, but there, in those barns, I stopped praying. Through all the years I had prayed to God ardently and with hope. Now I prayed no more. I did not consciously know why, for I was closer to my Maker than ever. One short shot away . . . I wanted to be at peace with God, but I could not pray. . . .

On the fourth day of our march we heard artillery fire. It was rumored that the Russians were moving forward rapidly. Once I think we were almost overrun by them. We heard two SS men discussing the destruction of the railroad, and thus we learned that we were to have been shipped by rail to the death camp. Now we would have to go all that way on foot.

On the fifth morning a number of SS women were missing. Apparently they had no mind to march on. Perhaps they wanted to return to their homes.

The war was coming to an end, we thought, but so was our strength. We had now gone four days without food. It was over a week since we had left Grünberg. It was an icy day. A sharp wind bit at our faces. We marched longer than usual before the midday break, and when we took it, we were anxious to get moving again.

That afternoon, as we were marching through a thicket, we heard shots. A moment later one of the SS men pointed a gun at me. "Come along!" he shouted.

I stepped out of line. The SS pulled out three more girls. I heard the column marching on. I no longer felt the snow whip my face. I felt no rebellion, no wild pounding of my heart. I just felt at peace. Oddly enough, I thought of a winter's day at home, and Schmutzi, my cat, bringing her

newborn kittens into the kitchen to warm them by the stove. I tried desperately to remember what we had named the kittens, but I couldn't. After a few steps—I had been daydreaming for only a moment—we came to a clearing. There were two bodies in the snow.

"Take them to the woods," the SS man commanded.

My arms felt unequal to it.

"Take her head," snapped the girl nearest me.

I looked at the dead girl's face. I did not know her. Her eyes were open. I lifted her head. The snow beneath was red. The two of us were too weak to lift her, so we took her by the arms and dragged her into the trees. When we left her, she looked alive. I scooped up snow to wash her blood off my hands. We did not see the other girls.

The SS man stood smoking a cigarette. I thought our turn was next, but he made us hurry to join the column. Ilse looked relieved when I returned. We held hands silently. I was in a state of shock.

We walked for a long, long time that evening, passing through tiny villages. Here and there a light showed. Smoke came from chimneys. We could see women preparing supper. How snug and warm everybody looked!

We entered another town. It was dark now. Nobody was in the streets. The wind was howling as we were led to a low hill where a church stood. The SS women and the favorites were lodged in town. The three SS guards who accompanied us told us to lie on the frozen earth in front of the church. The wind swept the snow over us. After a few minutes we were covered. Ilse and I cuddled close, trying with our bodies to warm each other.

Towering over us, the church stood silent, not even with its bell ringing the hours of our misery. The bells had probably been melted to make bullets.

"I am so cold," Ilse chattered.

We pressed our cold cheeks together. The snow did not even melt on our faces.

I thought of the girl I had dragged into the forest. By now the snow had given her its decent burial.

"Ilse," I said.

She didn't seem to hear me. I remembered a lamp burning softly under the yellow shade in my nursery, Niania reading to me the story of the Little Match Girl. I could hear Niania's warm tones: "And the little match girl smiled, she did not feel the cold any more. . . ."

"Ilse!" I shook her.

"Leave me alone!" she protested.

"Ilse!" I shouted. "Wake up. You are not going to sleep!"

She was awake now. I rubbed her face, her stiff hands. I called to Suse and Liesel. They responded. We passed the word around not to sleep. The SS men were stamping and blowing on their hands. Here and there a girl stood up.

"Lie down!" the SS men would shout.

We did everything we could think of to keep each other awake and encouraged. Finally, dawn broke and the wind stopped. In the gray morning light, we could see the miserable faces, the deep, hungry eyes. Those of us who had the strength brushed the drifts from silent mounds: there were a number of Little Match Girls.

"How foolish we are!" Suse exclaimed. "We should have all gone to sleep."

The frost broke. The air felt warmer. We were thirsty and started to eat snow.

Late that afternoon we came to Camp Christianstadt. We waited before its gates a long time. Then we were admitted, put into one huge room, and given something warm to eat. I don't know what it was, but no meal was ever more welcome.

We dried our clothes, and most of us in the warm room began to itch. The lice had already started on us. The taste of food and the warm camp made most of us optimistic again. We did not have to stand roll call. They just left us as we were, gave us something to eat twice a day, and we were happy. We knew the war was almost over.

When we had been in Christianstadt three days we heard that we were to move again. Ilse was beside herself. I had never seen her like that. Before, I had had the power to make her moods change—her belief in me was so strong that it embarrassed me at times—but I failed to help her now.

We marched west again, and that first evening the streets and roads were full of people, all moving in the same direction. They were fleeing before the Russian advance—horses and buggies, children in their parents' arms. We could hear the steady firing of artillery behind us.

I was elated. It is coming! This is the end! The circle is drawing to a close! The Germans are beginning to pay the penalty for their crimes.

The sight of refugees fired my imagination with new hope. That first night after we left Christianstadt we slept in another barn. A few more girls did not rise with us in the morning.

The next day we saw more refugees. From their speech we knew that they were from Silesia.

We began toying with the idea of escape. Several girls had already slipped away under cover of darkness when we marched at night. From various sources we learned that some survived and were taken in by peasants but that others were found and shot.

Our column got smaller and smaller. Probably only half the girls who had left Grünberg remained. We would not be able to stand much more. . . .

A week passed, two, perhaps three. We lost count of time. About every second day there would be warm soup, if one were lucky enough to be among the first in line, cold soup when one was among the last. At times there wasn't enough to go around.

We usually slept in barns. One night we rested in a bombed-out church listening to artillery fire both from the East and farther away from the West. We felt ourselves lucky if we found a few grains of wheat or oats in the barns.

Everywhere we left some dead. Some we buried, others we simply left. Hundreds of girls had frozen feet, bloody and full of pus. I saw one girl break off her toes as

though they were brittle wood.

Waking one night in a barn, I felt the girl next to me leaning too heavily on my legs. I protested. She did not move. My legs ached, I felt crushed under the weight. I tried to push her—and found she was dead. I remembered her from Bolkenhain. She had worked at the loom next to mine. I don't remember her name, but I do remember the way she stooped over the loom to repair a thread—the way she smiled when our eyes met.

One girl spotted a milk can leaning against a tree. She ran out of line to see if there were any milk in it. An SS man grabbed her by the neck, forced her to her knees. I saw her turn, petrified, when he took the rifle from his shoulder.

"Mercy! Mercy!" she pleaded.

She threw her arms up as he fired. Was it in prayer or desperation? And as he turned to go, the SS man kicked her aside.

I watched it all in horror and wished that I were dead.

There were planes roaring above us; we heard machine guns in the distance. The front lines were not far, yet they weren't close enough. How fortunate the soldiers were, to be able to carry guns! I had dreams about stealing a gun from an SS man during the night and shooting them all. But those were only dreams—I didn't even know how to fire a gun.

Why did we march? Why did we let them slaughter us? Why did we not try to fight back? What difference would it have made if they had killed some of us? We were dying anyway, and they would kill the survivors sooner or later in any case.

Our group shrank to a quarter of its original size. Why should I hope? I thought. Why should I be free, and the others dead? Why should I think that I would be a privileged one? But these thoughts were dangerous. I had to hope. I had to go on to the end. If Papa, Mama, and Arthur survive, they will wait for me, hoping and praying. I must not disappoint them.

"Be strong," Arthur had whispered, almost six years before.

"Be strong," Mama had called over the mass of voices as I left Bielitz.

The snow melted and it became mild. It could almost have been spring. For miles and miles now we saw road signs pointing to Dresden. A big, beautiful city—I remembered it from my history books. We must have marched about two hundred and fifty kilometers since Grünberg. The SS evidently wanted to reach the city before nightfall. It was getting dark, and big trucks were constantly coming toward us, forcing us off the road, and slowing our march.

As we approached the outskirts of Dresden we heard air-raid sirens blowing warnings, and soon hundreds of planes roared through the skies.

We stood on a bridge over the Elbe as the SS watched us from the banks. They probably felt the bridge was a likely target and this would be an easy way to get rid of us.

It was as if the world were coming to an end. Giant bombers roared over us. Heaven and earth shook. Houses collapsed like dominoes. People screamed and some jumped in flames into the icy river. Germany was being destroyed.

I was not afraid for my life, I felt triumphant watching Dresden being destroyed. And yet I had a painful feeling of detachment and utter loneliness. I don't remember how long the attack lasted, how we finally got off the bridge. I only remember the triumph and the loneliness.

And so passed another night.

The mild weather held for a few days, and we marched on. One afternoon as we passed through Freiberg the windows of a pretty house were open, and someone inside was playing the piano. Soft music floated in the air. As we came closer, our steps drowned out the music; only after we passed the house did I begin to hear it again.

In my mind I wrote a story to go with the music. It was about someone who tended a plant all his life, and it never blossomed. Only after the person died did the flower bloom.

I looked at Ilse. She was crying without a sound—the way Mama cried when we took Papa to the station for the last time.

— From Gerda Klein, All But My Life *(New York: Hill and Wang, 1957), 185, 186–89, 191–93. Copyright © 1957 and renewed © 1985 by Gerda Weissman Klein. Reprinted by permission of Hill and Wang, a division of Farrar, Straus & Giroux, Inc.*

Neuengamme

CAP ARCONA DISASTER

Paul Weissmann, German prisoner number 9794, was held under protective custody in the hospital of a satellite camp of Neuengamme *concentration camp. Here he remembers the last days before liberation and the* evacuation *of the Neuengamme inmates on ships sent into Lübeck Bay.*

20 April 1945. Early in the morning on the roll call ground, the prisoners are put into groups. With small bundles in hand and without any lists or formalities, they are led to the train station to be loaded into cars, fifty people in each. A new order empties the sick barracks, too.

We, as well as the sick, are taken to the train cars by truck. Around midnight our train leaves.

21 April 1945. By morning we are outside of Hamburg. . . . Around evening we pass Lübeck and stop at a harbor behind warehouses. Across from us are two grain silos. Two freighters are docked next to each other at the pier. The *Elmenhorst* and the *Thielbek.* The first train cars are unloaded, and the prisoners march up the ladder and disappear into the ship through the hatchway. In the meantime the dead are removed from the cars. About 100. We wait until it is our turn. But it stops.

22 April 1945. We're going now, too. On the ship's ladder, I turn around and see Heinz, my best friend from the camp, standing in a train car waving at me. Something

compels me to go through the *Elmenhorst* and onto the *Thielbek.* I am barely on the cargo room ladder when I hear, "Paul! Paul!" Ehler, a Spanish Republican from the camp, is standing at the front of the ladder pointing me towards my friends. Franz Richter, Valentin Eckert, and Georg, all three Spanish Republicans, take me into their group. . . .

In each of the two, two-story cargo rooms (bow and stern) . . . there are between two to three thousand people packed together. In the lower cargo room are all the nameless people, especially the sick and weak: primarily Russians, French, and Dutch if they have no friends among the leading Germans—primarily convicts. Food, excrement, washing, everything is a problem there. . . .

23 April 1945. The first night is over. In the morning a third ship arrives. The *Athen.* On board are the four hundred of the first commando, picked up by special order. Will we also be transferred? It's said we will be put onto the *Cap Arcona.* She is somewhere on the Lübeck Bay. The *Athen* left the other morning. Every day after the murderous pushing and shoving, we still get a thin slice of bread and a half of a liter of bad, often inedible soup. Yet our provisions from our Red Cross packages help us through. For the moment, we even have enough to smoke.

Every day the dead are pulled out from the lower cargo rooms. If you look down between the planks, you're seized by the horror. One emaciated body packed in next to the other. There isn't a handsbreadth of floor space to be seen. The way to the "latrines" leads over the bodies of the others. Many do not even have the strength to try. If someone with a Red Cross package goes down below, an inhuman scream breaks out. One minute later, he has been completely plundered.

25 April 1945. The *Athen* has returned to port. We learn from a cabin boy that the prisoners have been transferred to the *Cap Arcona* on the Bay of Neustadt, also where the rest will be transported. Two thousand prisoners are transferred from our ship. Then it steams off again with us who have stayed behind, about 150 men. However, we now have a lot to do. We have to sweep up the dirt and trash from the ship and dump it overboard. Then we look for a nice spot for ourselves. The prisoners from the *Elmenhorst* are coming over to our ship. We political prisoners, about thirty of us who all know each other, stay together. . . .

On 2 May 1945 we are still at port. A tug boat has already tied on to our ship. In the early afternoon, the tug boat had its steam up and off it went. We were not allowed on deck. Up there were the guard troops from Neuengamme as well as their canine units bedded on wood shavings. The police dogs and blood hounds that had found many escaped prisoners and had torn them apart. During the voyage, we experience a few air attacks. Some machine gun salvos pelter the upper deck, and the four-barreled machine guns mounted on the bow and stern return fire. . . .

3 May 1945. What? They say that one hour after our departure the English entered Lübeck without resistance.

Why did they drag us out here? They say the *Cap Arcona* is not even seaworthy. Are we supposed to wait for the end of the war in these floating coffins, or do they want to kill us?

Around noon English planes fly over the ship. The ship's artillery barks out after them a few times. It is almost three o'clock. The noise from airplane motors again forces its way into our iron hide-out. A few people climb up on the deck and keep watch. Shots whip out, detonations shake the ship. From the deck we hear that the *Cap Arcona* is on fire. Airplanes dive, shooting at our decks. Aircraft canons roar. Our deck is on fire. The wood shavings for the dogs have caught on fire. Everywhere there is panic. . . . Clusters of people are hanging on the ship's ladders and beating and kicking, trying to work their way upward. They grab the rungs, the legs of others, use the shoulders and bodies of others as support eventually just to fall off. I am standing there and cannot comprehend the whole of it. Why so much excitement? Because of a little bit of burning wood shavings? I try to calm them down, but they had scattered. I'm almost the only one standing against the wall of the cargo room. Just to be safe, I untie my shoes.

When I look up, I see some of my comrades running about undressed. They are desperately trying to get up above. What for? I look out of the port hole and see the ocean sparkling. The ship is listing and is beginning to tilt more and more to one side. I undress almost mechanically, completely. An almost unnatural peace overcomes me. Stop, I think, this means I will have to swim. . . . People, both dressed and undressed, are running crazily around the deck. Only a few have the courage to jump overboard. Boards, panels, everything that floats, is thrown overboard. In the water below, the drowning people scuffle for it. A few resort to their own strength and swim away from the ship toward the nearest bank of the bay. I would estimate the distance at two thousand to three thousand meters. On the deck I recognize almost no one. Where are my comrades? The ship continues to lean more and more to one side. When will it sink? I turn around again and see the black silhouette of the *Cap Arcona* surrounded by smoke and flames. Screams a thousand fold are carried over here. You can see the heads of people who are drifting and swimming around the gigantic body of the ship. None of the lifeboats can be lowered down. I decide to jump into the water. . . . Going between the whimpering dogs—who would have thought to untie them—and through pools of blood and over dead bodies, I head for the hatchway, right next to the ship's bridge. Over a mountain of potatoes and turnips, I slide down toward the hull of the ship. As swift as an arrow, I slide down into the water on a rope and the water crashes together over my head. I shudder from the cold, however I immediately begin to swim. The screaming on board sounds muffled to me now between the sharp bang of gun shots.

Is the SS shooting at the prisoners, is there a battle for the lifeboats, rafts, or driftwood? It doesn't affect me. Quietly I swim away from the ship. I look back two of three times. The *Cap Arcona* is still burning. The *Thielbek* is hardly still afloat. Having looked around, I've lost my sense of direction. I look for some mark. There is a capsized boat between the now sunken *Thielbek* and the coast. I will try to reach it, rest there a while, and then go on. My strength will last, however, the cold in my feet continues to rise further and further up my legs. Will I make it to shore?

To the right and left of me, I see individual swimmers. About four or five. Finally I climb onto the overturned boat and try to catch my breath. Suddenly I feel myself weakening. Shortly before me, two prisoners had left the boat. I can hear an engine. Two coast guard boats are coming this way from the coast heading for the *Cap Arcona*. I can estimate that they will pass about 100 meters from my boat. I pull myself together, jump off, and swim over to intercept them. I almost reach the first one, but the rope ladder hanging overboard slips through my hands. I try to turn around to reach the second boat, but a noose is thrown over my head. Only with great effort am I able to get my arms through it, then it's over. I'm pulled up like a sack. I can't even climb over the railing. Eventually, I find myself lying on the deck and can only whimper. Who is going to worry about me; everyone has enough to worry about himself. The sailors try to rescue others. A sailor nudges me and asks me go up into the galley. Wrapped in a blanket, I slowly begin to come to, only my feet seem to have died off. I don't notice as the boat reaches the *Cap Arcona*, as it turns away to leave.

As my strength begins to return, so do my thoughts. I've been saved!. . . What now? I dream of a bed, of hot coffee or even some alcohol. Then the boat stops. "Out! Out! Everybody out! We want to go back." Shaking, I climb up the stairs and jump onto the pier. We run along the pier toward shore, looking around, where some young sailors are standing pointing machine guns at us. They group us together and force us to lie down. There are about one hundred of us. Eventually, we are allowed to go into a garage and stand on the cold cement floor. After an hour, the guard changes. A truck arrives. We are told we are going to Neustadt. We, completely undressed, climb into the closed truck. After driving for fifteen minutes, we stop. A soldier in a steel helmet looks inside and says, "Gentlemen, you are free!" Shouting with joy, we fall into each others' arms. Rescued and free!—The English officer orders us to go to the hospital to get medical treatment.

5 May 1945. Having first been taken to a school, I'm given some clothing in a barracks of the former U-boat school. Here we are cared for to a certain extent. I have met up with a lot of friends except for one whom I had hoped to find. Out of the group with the Spanish Republicans, I am the only survivor.

Every day I run from one barracks to the other. I go into the city, look through the quarters there, the hospitals. All in vain! There were about 100 political comrades on the *Thielbek*, and so far I have not been able to find one of them. On the *Cap Arcona* there were over four thousand prisoners. About 150 reached shore drifting on rafts or swimming. A number of them drifted around the vicinity of the ship until it rolled over onto its side and just continued to float that way. The prisoners climbed onto the burning hot ship paying no attention to the burns they received. They were not picked up off of the boat until around nine o' clock that evening: 310 of them. More than 3,500 prisoners drowned, burned to death, or were shot from the lifeboats. Not even one hundred people of the 2,000 prisoners on board the *Thielbek* were saved. The *Athen* with 2,000 prisoners followed the request of the English and was the only ship to reach land. Almost all the prisoners were rescued.

Numerous shallops were strewn out across the bay. For the most part they were carrying prisoners from Stutthof, women, children, Jews. Some of them drifted onto shore. The SS, trying to inhibit any rescue attempt, shot in between them with machine guns. The beach was covered with dead bodies. At one place 108, at another 200 were counted. Mostly women and children.

> —*From Christoph Ernst and Ulrike Jensen,* Als letztes starb die Hoffnung *(Hamburg, Germany: Rasch and Röhring Verlag, 1989), 118–24. Translated from the German by Neal Guthrie.*

Ravensbrück

THE EVACUATION OF SCHÖNEFELD

Schönefeld, where aircraft parts were made, was a sub-camp of RAVENSBRÜCK *concentration camp near Berlin. As the Soviet Army approached Berlin in April 1945, the camp was evacuated. The author of this selection is an anonymous young French woman who had been arrested by the* GESTAPO *in January 1944 while working for the French Resistance. She was deported first to Ravensbrück and later to Schönefeld.*

It was at this period that my health showed signs of breaking. Work in the open proved even worse for me than on the factory detail; I developed a violent and uninterrupted fever, started coughing and finally spit blood without ceasing. Then I became so weak that I could not work any more and in the Concentration Camps not to work meant: Death.

Consequently, after several days they sent me away from my Kommando to the Oranienburg camp to undergo a so-called medical examination. We all knew what this meant—as a rule these "examinations" led directly to the crematory ovens.

On March 13th, five of us bound for the same place left under guard of an *Aufseherin* [supervisor].

By great good luck the camp doctor at Oranienburg happened to be a Frenchman; he saved my life by saying that I was not sick at all and that my refusal to work was due to pure laziness. But he added softly in French that my left lung was affected and that after liberation I should have to take great care of myself.

In spite of my frightful thinness and blood sputum the SS believed him.

But this unforgettable day was marked by other incidents. At Schönefeld we lived in a huge aviation factory and next to an aviation camp without having been bombed; but at Oranienburg on March 15th, I ran into one of the worst air-raids that Germany had ever suffered. It is true that the camp was near a munitions factory and an important railroad junction.

At 2 P.M. we were in one of the Blocks when suddenly we heard the characteristic sound of diving planes and a terrible deflagration took place. Without understanding what had happened I was thrown to the ground. I got up at once; the whole block was shattered and the women around me lay lifeless, covered with blood. I was not hurt, the blast had only ripped off my shoes. (I never understood why.)

I ran barefoot through the debris and broken glass without even cutting myself (God protects you in moments like this) but it was impossible to leave the camp—which was surrounded by electrified barbed wire. I lay down and waited; hundreds did the same thing.

For two solid hours, without a let up, tons of bombs burst around us. All the Blocks were in flames; the heat was so intense that it scorched my hair and skin. Bombs fell endlessly. Hardly had one wave of planes passed over us than another took its place. I was not afraid, I knew that this was not "it" and that my time had not come; around me women screamed and died. I counted 17 waves of bombers.

When it was over we got up—about a dozen survivors in the midst of a field of corpses. That is all that remained of a camp of approximately 8000 women. We could see charred corpses in the burning Blocks more than half consumed. I can assure you that we did not bless the Americans that day; nevertheless we did pick up the pamphlets they had dropped giving us the exact position of the Allied Armies. The Russians were so near—why did they not come?

Then we crossed the barbed wire, for the current was dead, and hid in the woods. All my comrades, who had come with me from Schönefeld were dead, so were the *Aufseherins*. It was then that I noticed that my leg was covered with blood. Washing myself in the river I discovered that I had quite a deep gash on my right leg; I had not felt it at all and it did not hurt in the least.

With the others I went into the woods—almost all were Russians. There were also 2 Yugoslavs and a little French girl "Denise," whom I had not known before.

We walked for a long time to get away from the delayed action bombs. We were free, but we were used up by hunger and exhaustion and now my leg began to hurt me greatly. The Russians proved to be very nice, for they helped me to walk and toward the end they even carried me.

We camped in the forest and started a fire, for it was very cold. We did not know what to do next; we had no money, nothing to eat, and we wore prison garb. We could not hope to escape. So it was not difficult for the SS to catch up with us; by nightfall our fire gave us away. They did not ill treat us. Being themselves much afraid of air-raids, they had acquired a sort of respect for people who had just come through strafing.

They gave us bread and took us to the Sachsenhausen camp near by (there were camps all over Germany)—it was a man's camp; there we were given soup and a bed.

I stayed in this camp for three days. We were not ill treated and were better fed than at Schönefeld. But what a state the poor men were in! We seemed to have gone back to New Bremen.

In three days time an *Aufseherin* from Schönefeld, whom we had christened the "Adder," came to fetch me back to my Kommando. She was particularly malevolent and had no mercy on my wounded leg, forcing me to walk very fast. In point of fact she had not left her *schlague* [cudgel] behind.

We walked for about 20 kilometers without finding any transport in working order. During this trek I had the opportunity of admiring the excellent work the Americans had done during the air-raid; 20 kilometers of ruined houses, no more roads, destruction everywhere. At last in Berlin we took the subway. My leg felt as heavy as lead and bled a great deal. We came back to Schönefeld by train. I was greeted with tears by my comrades—for they thought that I was dead.

From this time on my health got worse and worse. I continued to spit blood and then I developed dysentery. As a rule this disease killed its victims in a few days, and it is a wonder that I escaped. Intestinal hemorrhages (from which I am not yet cured) aggravated the dysentery and a very dangerous and horribly painful fissure of the anus further complicated matters.

I felt then that I was about to die; I had come to the end of the road. During my stay at Oranienburg I had managed to lose several more pounds and I was now a walking skeleton with whitened hair (fortunately the colour came back later)—I looked fifty or so.

The only thing that kept us going was the feeling that the war was nearing its end. On our way to work we saw the roads clogged with files of panic-stricken people escaping with children, carriages, piles of linen, etc.

The Russian front, quiescent for two months, had waked up and the noise of the Red artillery was terrific and never stopped.

Prisoners evacuated from Dachau concentration camp are marched through the German town of Grünwald in late April 1945. This photo was apparently taken by a German civilian. (Dachau Memorial Museum)

At last, one Saturday at noon, our comrades (detailed to dig trenches on the Berlin highway) came back before the appointed time; armed soldiers had taken over the trenches—the Russians were close by!

That same Saturday, at four o'clock, the Commandant blew his whistle and started dividing us into groups. We were supposed to leave at once to try and escape the Russians. I must tell you that the Germans had an insane fear of the Red Army and their one idea was to put themselves in American hands—believing that thus they would be less roughly handled.

Fortunately for me I was in the Commandant's own detachment; we started down the road and walked and walked. All those who fell, or could not keep up, were mercilessly machine-gunned by the SS. We headed west, crossing Berlin at dead of night. A defeated Berlin, silhouetted on three sides by a crimson sky. I shall never forget that sinister city, full of roadblocks, teeming with crazed soldiery, and plunged into the deepest night. What a scene; it gave us courage!

We walked all that night and all the next day. Many fell and died by the wayside. Ill as I was, I kept walking—drawing strength from what I saw. Everywhere—abandoned arms, tanks, distracted soldiers, a mix-up of all the services, men in trucks, in horse-drawn vehicles, on bicycles, all headed west—to escape the Russians.

Finally toward nightfall, after numberless marches and countermarches (the Commandant wanted to take us to Sachsenhausen, but the Russians were already there) we reached Nauen, 50 kilometers or so from Berlin.

The Commandant parked us in a field under SS guard; it was cold and windy. We were so tired that, in spite of this, we fell asleep, little realizing that these were to be the last hours of slavery.

Toward 10 o'clock the Commandant returned to tell us that the Russians were only 5 kilometers away, would reach here by morning, and that we must leave at once.

Our legs would not carry us any further, so we Frenchwomen announced that we did not want to move on. For a minute the Commandant hesitated, wondering whether he would order us all killed; the SS guards armed with tommy-guns stood ready—but, as a man, he did not quite dare order the assassination of an entire group of women, so he turned and went off with his SS and those prisoners willing to follow him.

Luck was with us, for the "Adder" ordered the entire group under her wiped out—before they could be liberated. She was nineteen. Judge what German women are!

— *From "Montluc-Ravensbrück: A Record of Imprisonment," Survivor Testimony, Record Group 02.038, United States Holocaust Memorial Museum Archives, 14–18.*

Stutthof

THE UNFINISHED ROAD

Gertrude Schneider, deported from Vienna, was imprisoned in the Riga GHETTO and later in the Riga-Kaiserwald camp. In August 1944 she was relocated with her mother and sister to Stutthof concentration camp near Danzig. Later that month they were transferred to Sophienwalde, a subcamp of STUTTHOF. Dr. Schneider became a historian and lectured on the Holocaust at several U.S. universities.

On February 1, Schultz [a guard] called all of us together—we were now 480, including eighty-two who could no longer get up from their sickbeds—and told us that we would be taken back to Stutthof. Since there were no trains available, however, we would have to walk a distance of 130 kilometers. In a reasonable manner he indicated that such a feat would not be possible for everyone and that the two physicians would therefore have to decide who could and who could not walk that far. He also added that he was told to bring back no more than about 250 of us.

Following his speech, he left the building. In the meantime, in small groups the women entered the physicians' large new examination room. When she saw the three of us come in, the Slovakian doctor did not waste words. She said that in view of my mother's recent illness and our general physical condition, she could not permit us to go along. Our pleas fell on deaf ears. She was adamant. At one point, Dr. Stein suggested timidly, "Perhaps just one of them?" "Absolutely not!" was the firm reply and with that she sent us out.

We were devastated. We knew what it meant to stay behind. We had come so far, and now this! Rumors ebbed back and forth; we saw some of the women smiling, others were crying, and during the next few days, when we no longer went to work, there was a constant stream of women going in and out of the doctors' office. Leah Granierer, who was my mother's age, told us that she, too, had been put on the "bad" list. However, she had gone back and had given the Slovak doctor a 20 rubel gold coin—not her own, but the last piece of value from beautiful, redheaded Mariasha Gershonowitz from Vilno, her son's girlfriend in Kaiserwald. Dr. Loewy pocketed the coin and put Leah Granierer on the "good" list.

Although we had nothing to buy our lives with, I decided to go back and appeal to the doctors once more, without mentioning what I knew about the gold coin. Nothing helped. Dr. Stein remained silent and Dr. Loewy said that we would be a burden to the other walkers, herself and Dr. Stein included, and "that's the way it is!" I realized then that there was no hope for us and that she meant to let us die. Yet, I could do nothing except curse her—a thing that I had never done before nor have I done since. In a mixture of Romany and Hungarian learned from the gypsies in Stutthof, I wished her the worst death possible! At least I had the satisfaction to see her face lose its smug expression. She turned white; being from Koshice, she understood only too well what I had said. Dr. Stein was mystified, but I said nothing to her. I saw that she had no power to help us. Walking out, I knew that my mother, my sister, and I were doomed.

On February 9, the day before the departure of the "lucky" ones, the order was given that all those who were staying behind had to give up their shoes to those who would be leaving. We panicked even more if that was possible and so did others. I used the general confusion to play out my last card. First, I handed my good shoes to my mother who hid them inside her dress, which had gotten very big on her. Then, unnoticed by anyone, in stockinged feet, I ran upstairs to where the SS women spent their time. My luck held. Erika was on duty. She came out after I knocked and pointing at my feet, said "Are you crazy?" In my very best manner and holding back tears, I told her about the lists and the shoes and our wish to leave . . . after all, I could not tell her that I knew we were to be murdered; she was an SS woman and not to be trusted, even then. Still, I begged her, for the sake of both of our mothers, to save us! When she said, "I'll do what I can," the same wild hope surged through me as on the day I left Stutthof.

She handed me the key to a small room at the bottom of the stairs where cleaning utensils were kept and told me to get my mother and sister there. "Don't let anyone in until you hear my voice and don't give up your shoes just yet," she said, and I ran down and managed to get Mama and Rita to come to the little room. People were so busy with their own problems, the exchange of shoes, a few fights, and much unhappiness, that no one paid attention when we slipped out, one by one.

It could not have been more than an hour, although it seemed much longer, when Erika knocked and we opened the door. She smiled, and calling my mother "Mutti," told us to go back up and join the others. "There'll be an announcement in ten minutes," she said. "Don't worry about anything!"

We had hardly reached the teeming hall, when the *Kommandant*, accompanied by *Unterm sturmführer* [SS second lieutenant], the *"Standortarzt,"* that is, a physician, arrived. Schultz was smiling and Roppert addressed us gruffly, saying, "Everyone who believes he can walk all the way back to Stutthof, should be ready by next morning." Schultz added, "The women who are in the hospital will remain in Sophienwalde; they will be tended by two nurses."

It turned out that the nurses, the sisters Lucy and Edith Trampler from Vienna, had volunteered to stay behind. Also staying were two young girls from Kovno; the older one was in her ninth month of pregnancy, and her fifteen-year-old sister did not want to leave without her. Among the sick was Margit Reckler, who had been married in the ghetto to Percy Brandt, the famous Latvian violinist. This beautiful woman was only a shadow of her former self. Her equally beautiful daughter Eva could have walked, but she preferred to stay with her mother. Thus, a total of eighty-six women were left behind. Did we grieve for them? Did their fate upset us? I am sure we felt terribly sorry, but we were so caught up in making preparations for the journey, that we did not think of them. At least not just then.

People re-exchanged shoes, some cut up their blankets to make pants that would guard against the cold and did not have to be carried, the lucky ones baked potatoes, and there was a coming and going in the building; everyone was excited. Women such as us, who had faced certain death, were relieved and euphoric.

Three hundred ninety-four of us left on the morning of February 10, accompanied by the three SS women and fourteen guards. The two slim, blond Trampler sisters stood and waved to us, and they smiled.

They were dead only about three hours later. According to eyewitnesses interviewed by me in Dziemiany, all eighty-six had been put into two vans, and were taken to the forest at Lesno. A Latvian detachment had shot them there, leaving their bodies to be buried by the inhabitants of the village. Supervising the operation were *Sturmscharführer* [SS master sergeant] Schultz, our *Kommandant, Untersturmführer* Roppert, the SS physician, and the *Unterscharführer* [SS senior corporal] of the guards, Nikolaus Knapp. Schultz and Knapp reached our straggling column on their bicycles several hours after we had left Sophienwalde.

While the *Unterscharführer* behaved exactly as he had always done, screaming at us and at his men, it seemed that Schultz was no longer the same. He had aged in these few hours and never said a word to the marchers, nor did he joke, as was his custom. We were too busy putting one foot in front of the other to think much about this, nor could anyone among us believe that he had been party to murder. All we knew was that he had always been decent to us and had tried to alleviate our suffering.

After a short conversation with the three SS women, Schultz went on ahead, still on his bike, and arranged for a barn where we would spend the night.

We never got much rest. Unaccustomed to marching, many women had picked up snow from the side of the road to slake their thirst. Since there were no toilets, they now went behind the barn to relieve themselves and this went on all night. When morning came, a disgusted Schultz asked for ten volunteers to clean up the mess. He promised each a small jar of beet marmalade. My mother immediately volunteered. She needed the sweet stuff for Rita, who was clearly jaundiced. An old folk remedy for yellow jaundice is sugar, and Rita was not only yellow, but ran a fever as well. We tried to keep her sickness a secret and when several stragglers were permitted to ride on a wagon drawn by a horse, which Schultz had requisitioned from a farmer, my mother, distrustful and cautious, did not let my sister ride on it.

As we walked on that second day, I remember that some of the smarter women among us were puzzled by the direction we took. We were walking west, yet Stutthof was situated to the northeast of Sophienwalde.

A clandestine photo by an unknown German photographer of prisoners evacuated from Dachau passing through Heberthausen, Germany on April 27, 1945. The prisoners were evacuated from the camp in the face of the lightning advance of U.S. troops.
(Dachau Memorial Museum)

While no one had been shot so far, even though Knapp was heard to say that he would shoot anyone who stopped walking, several women had not survived the first night and it did not look good for many others. Schultz ordered the two physicians to do their best, even though they, too, were affected by the march. As we stopped next to a barn where we would spend the second night, each of us received a slice of bread. We had walked only twenty-five kilometers in these two days, and already our strength was taxed to its limits. Again there were several deaths during the night. The bodies were left one on top of the other next to the barn.

We did not walk much on the third day. It was only February 12, but the day was unusually warm. The snow was melting and the ground under our feet turned into a morass. Since the majority of the women wore wooden clogs, they frequently fell. Whenever this happened, the *Unterscharführer* prodded them with his rifle and made them get up and walk. He raved and ranted, but he did not shoot them. We believed that he must have had such orders from Schultz, who was still not quite his usual jolly self.

After we had walked ten kilometers that day, we arrived at the outskirts of Bütow, now Bytow, where Schultz found a very good, spacious barn for us and announced that we would rest there all of the next day. In addition, he sent Bertl Schwartz and her helpers to cook a potato soup for us at the nearby farmhouse.

Indescribably happy, Rita and I settled down. Our mother saw another large barn across the road and with her usual audacity went to investigate. Inside it was not a barn at all, but a barracks for American prisoners of war! Neither their guards nor our guards interfered when several other women followed my mother and went for a "visit." The Americans were shocked at the way we looked. Among

them were two Jews from Brooklyn, New York. I was one of those who spoke a little English, and we told them some of what had happened to us in the last few years. They did not have much food either, but in a lovely gesture, they literally gave us the undershirts off their backs. I still have mine! Rita got a piece of soap with a swan on it.

The two doctors were quite busy the next day. Several women had died during the night; all of them had suffered from spotted typhoid fever. Whenever the doctors looked at my mother, my sister, or at me, they averted their eyes. We never said a word to them and they never said a word to us. I could not forgive them, even though I was busy worrying about Rita. Although the beet marmalade, mixed with snow, had helped her, mother and I realized that it took all her willpower to march again on the next day of our journey.

Now we were marching north. After thirteen kilometers, the commandant ordered us into another barn. It was awful. It stank and it was filthy; when we found several corpses behind the barn, we realized that Jewish male prisoners had used it the night before. Schultz left to look for another barn but soon returned saying that he could not find anything.

When Resi Goldstein counted us the next morning, she at first believed that one woman had escaped. Her corpse, however, was soon found on top of the male corpses. The mystery of why she went outside to die in this way was never solved.

Weary in body and in spirit, we started marching once again. It snowed all day—big, wet flakes. At one point, while walking through a small town, several boys who had just come out of school, started pelting us with snowballs. Our obvious discomfort only increased their fervor. They called us vile names and their aim was quite good. Suddenly, out of the whirling snow an enormous *Schupo* (policeman) appeared and roared, "You miserable kids . . . stop it . . . stop it right now! Don't ever let me catch you again throwing snowballs at those unfortunate people . . . haven't they suffered enough?" The boys did stop and scattered, while he just stood there and looked at us, shaking his big head.

I remember the bitter tears I cried as I continued walking. His unexpected kindness and his recklessness in taking our part touched me to the core. I never cried when treated badly, but this show of sympathy for our plight made me fall apart.

After we had walked twelve kilometers, we were ordered to go into yet another barn. While it was better than the last one, there was very little straw and its roof and walls were dilapidated. In an attempt to make a joke, Rita said that she would be between Mama and myself and she would keep us warm since she still ran a high fever.

The next morning, February 16, we were each given a slice of freshly baked bread and Schultz looked very pleased with himself. This was a time when very few bakeries still operated and he seemed glad to have found one. Resi Goldstein came to us and gave Rita an additional piece of bread. We were stunned—it meant so much. As we stood lined up in front of the barn for the inevitable roll call, she said that eleven women had died during the night and that we numbered 365.

That day the weather was very good, the road was smooth, and we managed to walk thirteen kilometers. (The distances between the villages were clearly marked and I wrote everything down whenever we rested. My little stub of a pencil was my greatest treasure. I wanted to keep a record because I had promised my father that I would do so and because I wanted to read all this to him when the war would be over and when we would finally be together again. I never got that chance. But I did check the signs when I went back to that part of Poland and there were no mistakes. Only now, the signs have Polish instead of German place names.)

We continued walking, north by northeast. Our poor feet were like automatons. Step by step. Hoping not to fall behind and be prodded by a guard. Relieving ourselves at the edge of the road, oblivious to what anyone would think. Almost inhuman. But so were our conditions. Inhuman.

Another road, another barn, more dead. In between, it seemed that Schultz was in touch with Stutthof via telephone. A rumor had it that he talked about new orders to the women in front, and it must have been true, for on Saturday, February 17, around noon, our march came to an end. After having walked eighty-three kilometers, we had arrived at the village of Gotentov, now Godetowo. There were 347 of us who had made it! Schultz told us that we were to stay here for a few days and that we would be joined by other prisoners, also on their way to the main camp.

Gotentov had a small camp, consisting of two parts. Half of the barracks were at the bottom of a hill next to a lake, and the other half were at the top of the hill. We could get water from the lake, but there was very little food for us. We received half a liter of soup each day; it was really only lukewarm, colored water. Every second day, we received a slice of bread.

After the arrival of other prisoners, the women who had come from Sophienwalde ended up in what was the worst barracks. It stood at right angles to the others and was very dilapidated. Before we came, all of the barracks had been home to forced laborers. They left only dirt behind; we found nothing that could be of use.

Among the arrivals over the next few days, we met the last remnants of Jews who had come from Riga to Stutthof on October 1, 1944. We could hardly recognize each other. The death toll in the coming weeks was very high. Conditions in Gotentov were the worst so far. People slept wherever they could find space, healthy and sick next to each other, some on bunks, some on the floor, and some on benches.

The barracks at the top of the hill housed the various SS personnel and all the commandants from the various camps who had walked. There was also a detachment of female German soldiers. They marched and sang while right below them we died *en masse* and grew weaker by the hour.

Our two physicians were given a room at the top as well. There were some other doctors who had been with the later arrivals and they, too, were quartered at the top. There was not much they could do for the many sick in the camp, since very little in the way of medication was available.

My sister had recovered from jaundice, but on March 6 I started to feel dizzy and passed out. Typhoid fever had caught up with me and the next three days are a blur. I was permitted to remain inside the barracks during roll call.

On Friday afternoon, March 9, Schultz came in while the others were being counted outside. He addressed me as "little roofer" and then said in a rather serious manner: "Listen well! You must pull yourself together. We are leaving here within the next few hours and you cannot and must not stay behind! I order you to come along! You cannot stay here!"

In the state I was in just then, his speech seemed like a dream. I told my mother what he had said, and it did not take long for orders to be given to line up and start marching once more. Mother went to look for Erika, who was by now in her seventh month of pregnancy and quite huge. Erika urged her to make me walk, no matter what; she gave my mother a large piece of bread for the journey. I could not swallow solid food, but I did drink the soup we were given and then, supported by my mother and sister, I walked out of the camp.

Our two physicians stayed in Gotentov. We found out later that their room caught fire that same night, while they slept, and both of them perished in the flames. Of the other prisoners who stayed behind, only a handful were alive when the Russians came in late afternoon on the very next day. But contrary to what Schultz evidently believed, not one of them was killed.

I remember only snatches of this long, horrible night. I know that there were other prisoners, besides those from Sophienwalde. I remember seeing many soldiers, and hearing shots, both near and far away. Many times I begged my mother and sister to just let me lie down, to let go of me, to let me have peace, to let me die. They would not hear of it. Mother consoled me by saying that we would soon be allowed to rest, just like on our earlier march. Whenever someone fell behind, he or she was shot. Among the many other SS officers who accompanied this long, unwieldy column, Schultz was of no account, since his rank was comparatively low. He, Martha, Lotte, and bulky Erika walked at our side. "His" women were at the end of the column. According to my mother's estimate, there were no more than about 250 of us left.

Among the soldiers who passed us, walking toward what was evidently the frontline, were Austrians; their dialect made it obvious. My mother asked one of them for soup, and I heard her. For the rest of her life, she never forgot that I, delirious and surely at the end of my strength, said with all the arrogance I could muster, *"Mama, man bettelt nicht!"* (Mama, one does not beg!) She told the story many, many times and always added that the young Viennese soldier gave her a tin of soup for me, smiling as he did so, and obviously amused by what I had said.

There was the noise of fighting and it was not too far away. Schultz remarked to the women within hearing distance, "I am leading you to freedom!" My mother, unaware of his part in the murder of the women who had been left behind, or perhaps oblivious to it, advised him to get out of his uniform; she promised to get him home to his wife and children. He thought about it for a while and then declined, telling her that he could not do so because, as he said, "Someone is sure to betray me. But I thank you!"

After having walked all night, about fifteen kilometers, we reached the little town of Chinov, now Chynowie. An enormous barn, larger than most others, next to a grassy slope, was to be ours for the day. On that slope were many wagons, loaded high with household goods. Their owners were trying to escape from the Russians. The barn contained several live horses, a few dead ones, and hundreds of dead and hunger-crazed Jewish men and women who had arrived a few days earlier. Some of them were cutting pieces from the dead horses and were intent on chewing the raw meat.

My mother put me into a fodder trough between two horses and told my sister to stand right next to me so that I should not fall out. Meanwhile she stood at the barn's entrance, observant and alert. Suddenly, in a changed voice, she said, *"Kinder, da kommen Russische Panzer!"* (Children, Russian tanks are approaching!) Rita turned to me and said, *"Um Gottes Willen, die arme Mama hat den Verstand verloren!"* (For God's sake, poor Mama has lost her mind!) But my mother was right . . . the Russians had taken that obscure road, and freedom had come for us.

Despite my weakened state and my illness, I wanted to savor this long awaited moment. In my delirium, I found a truck full of sugar, but eventually my mother coaxed me to come down. Then, together with her and my sister and some other women, we stood on the square in front of the barn and watched as the Russians brought out all the SS men they could find in the houses behind the barn. Among us were women who understood and spoke Russian and it was they who first realized that the SS men would be shot at the edge of the road, where the forest began, only a few meters from where we were standing.

When the Russians brought out Willie Schultz, pushing him to go faster, it was one of "his" women, Mrs. Klara Schwab of Libau, who tried to intercede for him. She, too, had no idea about what he had done in Sophienwalde. The Russian officer in charge, to whom she spoke in flawless Russian, accused her of being a German spy—she was a blonde woman and good looking even then—and he threatened to kill her, too, if she continued to ask that Schultz's life be spared. She came over to where we had gathered, and silently we stood by and watched as one by one, the guards and the officers were shot, among them *Unterscharfuehrer* Knapp and our commandant. Martha was nowhere to be seen, but Lotte and Erika were taken along on separate tanks.

The civilians of the town, as well as those who were on the slope, were ordered by the remaining Russians to put the dead SS men on a pile and then to do the same with the dead Jews who had expired in the barn. This was done. All those corpses, intermingled as they were . . . and there were no more differences. In death they were all equal.

For us, the living, freedom had come, with all its glories, with all its disappointments and the pain of finding out the extent of the Jewish people's destruction, with all its responsibilities, and with all of life's uncertainties.

There was one thing, however, we could be sure of: We would never, ever finish that road in Sophienwalde!

— From Gertrude Schneider, ed. and comp., The Unfinished Road: Jewish Survivors of Latvia Look Back *(New York: Praeger Publishers, 1991), 16–25. Reprinted with permission of Greenwood Publishing Group, Inc. Westport, CT.*

Bullenhuser Damm Murders

AN ASSASSINATION OF CHILDREN

In November 1944 twenty children were transported from AUSCHWITZ *to* NEUENGAMME *concentration camp to serve as subjects for German doctor Kurt Heissmeyer's experiments based on his already discredited theory for curing tuberculosis. The experiments began in December; by Christmas, the children were all bedridden.*

As the Allies approached in April 1945, the camp administration was ordered to eliminate all traces of the experiment: Kill the children. On April 20 the children were taken to Bullenhuser Damm, the ruins of a school in Hamburg which had recently served as a subcamp of Neuengamme. SS Dr. Trezbinski prepared the children for their deaths; he testified about the event, excerpted here, at his postwar trial. A British court sentenced him to death in May 1946, and he was hanged that October. Dr. Heissmeyer was only arrested in 1963 and sentenced to life imprisonment in 1966. SS Obersturmführer (first lieutenant) Arnold Strippel, commandant of Bullenhuser Damm, was sentenced to life in 1949 for crimes committed earlier at BUCHENWALD *concentration camp. The sentence was later commuted to time served, and he received compensation from the West German government for his prison term. He was never successfully tried for the murder of the children.*

I asked Strippel to come with me into a separate room. I said, "They've gone completely mad in Berlin. Now they've sent an order that the Heissmeyer Section has to disappear, and Pauly has thought up the pretty task for me to poison the children." I said I couldn't do that, and anyway I had no poison with me. Strippel said, "If Pauly ordered you to do it, you simply have to do it." I said, "I want to tell you something. I purposely didn't bring any poison along." That got

Strippel angry, and he said, "So you think I'll let myself be put against the wall by Pauly if things happen here that don't suit him?" I said it was madness to kill the children. But Strippel said, "They know what they're doing in Berlin, and why. And if we get an order, we have to carry it out." We continued to talk about the poison that wasn't there. Finally he said, "If you're such a coward, I'll have to take matters into my own hands." Then he drove his car to Bullenhuser Damm. We followed him and arrived there about ten minutes later. . . .

When we arrived and got out of the truck, Strippel, Jauch, and Frahm were just coming out the door. Strippel went right to his waiting car and said in passing that everything was in order. I took that to mean that he arranged things in such a way as to carry out the order from Berlin. Now the occupants of the truck got out—first the Russians, then the orderlies, and then the children. The Russians were led into the boiler room; then the orderlies and the children were brought in. The orderlies were put in a room across from the children, the children themselves in an air-raid shelter. I forgot to mention that before the children and the orderlies were brought in, I had a chance to speak with Jauch. In fact, I asked him: "Have you received any information?" He said: "Yes, I know what's what." I stayed with the children, for by now they had been separated from the orderlies. So I stayed with the frightened children. They had all their things with them—some food, some toys they had made themselves, etc. They sat down on the benches and were happy that they had gotten out. They didn't suspect a thing. They were between five and twelve years old—half of them boys, the other half girls. They all spoke a broken German with a Polish accent. . . .

After a while Frahm came in and said the children should get undressed. I saw that the children were somewhat taken aback, so I told them: "You have to get undressed because you'll be vaccinated against typhus." I now took Frahm aside and asked him softly, so the children would not hear anything, "What's to happen with the children?" Frahm was also quite pale and said, "I'm supposed to hang the children." I could tell stories and make myself out to be a hero, or say that I threatened him with a gun and so on, but that wouldn't be the truth. We did not discuss this any further because in my opinion the children could no longer be saved. If I had acted as a hero the children might have died a little later, but their fate could no longer be averted. I now knew what horrible end awaited them, and I at least wanted to ease their final hours. I had morphine with me in a 1 percent solution. So that I could administer the proper dosage, I diluted this bottle further with 100 grams of distilled water. Thus, depending on their ages, I could give each child the correct dosage. I went up to the door of the room where there was a stool for the syringes and another stool next to it. I called in the children one by one. They lay down over the one stool, and I gave them the shots in the buttocks, where it would be the least painful. Each child then went back into the room where they had gotten un-

dressed, and another one came in. Frahm said the children were lying down, but that wasn't so. They lay down only afterwards, when they became tired. To make the children think that they were really being vaccinated, I used a new needle every time. According to their age and size I injected them with anywhere from 2 to 6 cubic centimeters. Out of the 120 cc about 20 cc were left over. The purpose of the individual dosages was to make the children sleepy. In the meantime they had gotten dressed again, thinking the vaccinations were over. But Frahm now told them they had to take their clothes off once more so they could be bathed. A person who has already taken part in many executions says almost automatically that the people should get undressed. And Frahm, who was rather simpleminded anyway, imagined that only people without clothes on could be hanged. I could have prevented it, but in my confusion I no longer placed any value on these things. The children started to get tired, and we laid them on the ground and covered them with their clothes. Every so often Frahm would leave the room, and I had the impression that he also took part in the execution of the men.

I must say that in general the children's condition was very good, except for one twelve-year-old boy who was in bad shape. He therefore fell asleep very quickly. Six or eight of the children were still awake—the others were already sleeping. Now this is so terrible that it's hard for me to speak about it. But I suppose I must. Frahm lifted up the twelve-year-old boy and said to the others that he was taking him to bed. He took him to a room that was maybe six or eight yards away, and there I saw a rope already attached to a hook. Frahm put the sleeping boy into the noose and with all his weight pulled down on the body of the boy so that the noose would tighten. I had seen a lot of human suffering during my days at the camps and, in a sense, had become indifferent to it; but children being hanged—that I had never seen before. I felt sick and left the building and walked around the block a couple of times.

—*From Gunther Schwarberg,* The Murders at Bullenhuser Damm: The SS Doctor and the Children *(Bloomington, IN: Indiana University Press, 1984), 37–41. Published in German as* Der SS-Arzt und die Kinder, *Copyright © 1980 by Stern Bücher im Verlag Gruner & Jahr AG & Co.*

THE APPLICATION OF GENOCIDE CONTINUES

Deportations

STUTTGART TRANSPORT

At the beginning of World War II, there were in Stuttgart approximately 2,000 Jews identified as being in privileged mixed marriages or as MISCHLINGE *(part-Jews). As* DEPORTATIONS *east continued through 1944, fewer than 200 remained. Initially the Nazi regime did not implement radical measures against such part-Jews, since they feared opposition from* ARYAN *relatives in the German population. By autumn 1944, however, Heinrich* HIMMLER *ordered that all male* Mischlinge *and Germans married to them be assigned to forced labor deportations by* ORGANIZATION TODT. *Female*

Mischlinge *were assigned to forced labor in the localities where they resided, and minor children under 16 were exempted from deportation and labor. They were assigned to clean air-raid rubble, to build the German defenses west of the Rhine, the West Wall, and to build and repair roads. By early February 1945, many Stuttgart* Mischlinge *and those in mixed marriages were ordered to report for deportation to* THERESIENSTADT.

Secret Police
Stuttgart Headquarters
No. IV 4b - 30/45   Stuttgart 27, January 1945

(14) S t u t t g a r t. - Bad Cannstatt
    Emser St. 14

You are to report to the Transit Camp Bietigheim (Ludwigsburg County) on Monday 12 February 1945 for assignment to an external work commando.
    You must bring with you
        rations for 5-day march
        1 suitcase or backpack with the following equipment:
        1 pair of work shoes, 2 pairs of socks
        2 shirts, 2 pairs of underwear
        1 set of work clothes
        2 wool blankets, 2 sets of bed linen
            (bed linen with blankets)
        1 bowl, 1 cup, 1 spoon
You must report your departure as well as relinquish any food ration cards to the police by 10 February 1945. Children under the age of 16 are to be placed in the care of relatives.

— *From Marlene P. Hiller, ed.,* Stuttgart im Zweiten Weltkrieg *(Gerlingen: Bleicher Verlag, 1989), 181. Translated by Sybil Milton.*

Geheime Staatspolizei
Staatspolizeileitstelle Stuttgart   Stuttgart,den 27.1.1945
Nr. IV 4 b - 30/45.

(14) S t u t t g a r t. - Bad Cannstatt
    Emserstr. 14

    Sie haben sich zu einem auswärtigen Arbeitseinsatz am Montag,den 12.Februar 1945 im Durchgangslager Bietigheim, Krs.Ludwigsburg einzufinden.
Mitzunehmen sind
            Marschverpflegung für 5 Tage,
            1 Koffer oder Rucksack mit folgenden
              Ausrüstungsgegenständen :
            1 Paar Arbeitsschuhe,2 Paar Strümpfe,
            2 Hemden,2 Schlüpfer,bezw. Unterhosen,
            1 Arbeitsanzug,bezw. Arbeitskleid,
            2 Wolldecken, 2 Garnituren Bettzeug,
              (Bettbezüge mit Laken),
            1 Eßnapf, 1 Trinkbecher,1 Löffel.
    Lebensmittelkarten sowie polizeiliche Abmeldung hat auf 1c.2.1945 zu erfolgen.
Vorhandene Kinder unter 16 Jahren sind Verwandten in Pflege zu geben.

                            Im Auftrag:

Euthanasia

THE KILLING CONTINUES AFTER LIBERATION

At a mental institution near the Bavarian town of Kauf-beuren, the Germans established a EUTHANASIA facility as part of their "14F13" (an extension of OPERATION T-4) extermination program. The activities of the institution continued for a short time after the Allies occupied the area.

The resulting scandal appeared in the U.S. press in early July. It was widely reported but soon faded from the headlines as the case against war criminals became the major story about the Holocaust.

— From PM Daily, *July 5, 1945.*

NEWS YOU CAN'T GET ELSEWHERE

PM Daily
FIVE CENTS
(Copyright, 1945, by The Newspaper PM, Inc.)
VOL. VI — No. 16
Thursday, July 5, 1945
Partly Cloudy; Warm

COMPLETE EDITION

By Victor H. Bernstein:

Nazis Kept Up Euthanasia
Killings 30 Days *Page 3*
After We Moved In

Tokyo Reports:

U. S. Warships Shell Sakhalin *Page 6*

Philippines Freed; Balikpapan Falls *Page 7*

Newspaper Strike Still On
Page 10

Jobs Wanted for Veterans
TEXTILE Technician; design, analysis, construction, testing, research laboratory; Phila. Q.M. Depot; personal work, army; licensed teach. textiles, N. Y. C. high schools. I. L. 138-30 Coolidge Ave., Jamaica 2, N. Y.
—And Others on Back Page

Truman May Act In FEPC Jam
Page 8

PM TELLS YOU MORE NEWS IN LESS TIME

THE WORLD

Euthanasia After U. S. Moved In

By VICTOR H. BERNSTEIN
Staff Correspondent
(Copyright, 1945, by The Newspaper PM, Inc.)

MUNICH, July 5.—German personnel of the Kaufbeuren Sanitorium and Insane Asylum, about 30 miles south of here, were still killing children by injections a full month after the Americans had occupied this town, it was revealed today.

The institution is within rifle shot of the Military Government headquarters and the offices of the CIC—Counter-Intelligence Corps—of the local area, yet no steps were taken to stop these killings.

What makes the situation worse is that there is indisputable proof that certain American military authorities were apprised of what was happening in the asylum as long ago as June 19, and again nothing was done except to arrest certain asylum officials on purely political grounds—because these particular officials happened to be Nazi Party officers of a rank subjecting them to automatic apprehension.

One reason for the lack of action was that there was no doctor attached to the local military government.

It was not until Maj. Marvin Linick, of New York, chief health officer for the Munich Military Government, and his assistant, Capt. Loyal W. Murphy, Memphis, Tenn., moved into the picture a few days ago that the full story of what has been happening at the asylum was made known and steps were taken to arrest the guilty—whether they were party members or not.

Maj. Linick's investigators found that the last child was killed by injections at Kaufbeuren on May 29—21 days after VE Day and 31 days after American forces moved into the town. Moreover, Maj. Linick's investigators found in the non-refrigerated morgue of the hospital the bodies of nine adult inmates who had died from starvation not more than two or three days before. The lightest of these corpses weighed 54 pounds; the heaviest weighed 66 pounds.

(According to a BBC broadcast, picked up by NBC, officials of the murder factory insisted that they continued their "experiments" after the armistice and American occupation on order of "certain German civil authorities" whose names they would not specify. They protested that they were performing "experiments "for the improvement of the race." Many cripples and deformed children were among the murdered inmates.)

Records Also Cremated

The Kaufbeuren asylum belongs to the same network of "mercy killings" institutions as the asylum at Haar-Egelfing which I described in these columns on June 30. Like Haar-Egelfing, it operated under the general direction of the Reichs Committee for Serious Hereditary Diseases and Malformations in Berlin.

And again, like Haar-Egelfing, children and adults were killed both by drug injections and starvation.

Nurse Woerle, an employe at Kaufbeuren, has confessed to Capt. Murphy that she killed at least "211 minors" in the last two years—and that she got 35 reichsmarks—about $14 at normal exchange rates—a month bonus for her work.

Nurse Woerle closed her verbal testimony by asking plaintively, "Will anybody do anything to me?"

It is impossible to estimate how many have been killed by drugs and starvation at Kaufbeuren since the murder routine started in 1940. Many records were destroyed, but on a basis of partial records which have been recovered, there are definitive entries showing that 26 inmates were drugged to death this year up to May 29; 75 in 1944 and more than 60 in 1943.

There are no adequate records to show how many inmates were starved to death. The bodies were cremated on the grounds and apparently at the same time the telltale records were shoved in with the bodies.

Records available do show that the death rate at the asylum, which had a total capacity of about 300 inmates, rose from 4.6 per cent in 1939 to 25.6 per cent in 1944.

Moreover, the killings at the hospital were apparently well known to the inhabitants of the town of Kaufbeuren, which is the capital of the Swabian District and has a population of about 13,000.

One child on the streets of the town, chosen at random, was asked about the asylum buildings and he said, "Oh, that's where they kill them." And a nurse at the asylum, commenting on records which showed that many inmates were shifted from Kaufbeuren to Haar-Egelfing, Linz, Gunzburg and other towns where similar institutions were located, said to the American investigators:

"Some of the people in town objected to the smell of burned bodies in our crematorium. So we sent some of our inmates elsewhere to be destroyed."

Since I wrote the Haar-Egelfing story and learned about Kaufbeuren, I have been asking Germans in Munich whether they knew that inmates of German asylums were being killed as a regular matter. Most say they knew. But they insist they didn't know that many were killed by slow, torturous starvation.

Letters Prove Brutality

All to whom I talked insisted they thought only that "hopeless cases" were killed and then only by quick humane means.

But the letters found at Kaufbeuren, on official stationery, dispel forever such a fantastic notion. One example is a letter written in the office of the Swabian State Welfare Assn. to the Director of the Kaufbeuren institution, which reads in part:

"I have the honor to inform you that all patients transferred from your institution on Aug. 11, 1940, have died in the month of January at the institutions of Grafeneck, Bernberg, Sonnestein and Hartheim."

Another revealing letter, this one from the Bavarian minister of health to the chief of the institution at Gunzburg:

"In your letter dated Nov. 13, 1942, you have requested the dispatch to you of suitable epileptics for the further carrying through of your research work. I have had the opportunity to discuss this matter with Dr. Faltelhauser, chief of the Kaufbeuren asylum, and Dr. Pfannmuller, chief of Haar-Egelfing.

"Both are most agreeable to turning over to you suitable stock. For various reasons, primarily patients of Kaufbeuren are to be selected. If that institution does not have suitable material, I am satisfied if patients from Haar-Egelfing are transferred to Gunzburg for your research purpose (*forschungs Zwecke*)."

This letter was signed by Dr. Gaum, deputy in the Bavarian health ministry.

The Sinister Dr. Conti

The Kaufbeuren records also revealed to me for the first time in an official form the role played by a man of whom I have been hearing for several months but whose identity I never could exactly place.

He is Dr. Leonardo Conti, whose long list of titles include that of SS Obergruppenfuehrer, Prussian State Councillor, Reich Public Health Chief, Chief of the Reich Medical Assn. and Leader of National Socialist Headquarters for Public Health.

The Kaufbeuren records now show that Dr. Conti was the sinister designer of the "mercy killing" program throughout the Reich and the Reichs Committee—known as RA for *Reichsauschuss*—whose stamp always appears on death warrants for children, was his principal instrument.

It goes without saying that all personnel of Kaufbeuren involved directly or indirectly in the killing are now under arrest—and steps are being taken to discover why local American authorities of the town failed to move against those murderers in the personnel who didn't happen to hold Nazi Party cards.

KAUFBEUREN REPORT

Even after unit F1F3 of the Civil Affairs Branch of the US Army had set up operations in occupied Kaufbeuren to administer the area in April 1945, the killings at the Kaufbeuren EUTHANASIA facility continued. Once the killings became known, the Public Relations Office, or PRO, of the *Civil Affairs detachment issued a statement on the matter, reproduced here.*

— From "Report on Kaufbeuren," European Civil Affairs Division 1944–45, Record Group 492, Detachment F1F3, box 54, Miscellaneous Detachments, National Archives and Records Administration.

1

"Special Statement of Fact"

KAUFBEUREN, BAVARIA, July 2 (sic)

A wholesale extermination plant functioned to this date* within less than half a mile from the Military Government, C.I.C. and M.P. Headquarters* in this idyllic Swabian town and virtually every inhabitant was fully aware of the fact that human beings were both used as guinea pigs and were systematically butchered. The perpetrators or passive collaborators involved were in no way conscious of their crimes, they were Germans and not Nazis. Among them were Catholic sisters. The chief nurse, who had confessed without coercion, that she had murdered "approximately" 210 children in the course of two years by intramuscular injection, asked simply "will anything happen to me?"

The large complex of the lunatic asylum has a maximum capacity of 3000, lies on the open road, in size is the most outstanding landmark of the sleepy village and received its orders from such Government authorities as the Reich and Bavarian Ministries of the Interior. The experiments were made for the improvement of the race; the SS or "bad Germans" were hardly involved. Bodies which had been living beings less than 12 hours before investigators came, weighing 27 Kgs (60 pounds approx.) were found in the morgues. A twelve year old urchin selected at random in Kaufbeuren when asked what kind of a sanatorium the large complex of buildings on the hill might be, answered casually, "Oh that's where they kill them (das ist wo sie's umbringen)."

* Not released to press

OFF LIMIT posters and signs reading "Lunatic
Asylum" in the English language were in considerable
number distributed around the premises. Although
Staff Members of the institutions had been arrested
"For political reasons" local American authorities
were obviously completely unaware of what happened
to this day -- within MI rifle range of their
respective Headquarters.

When asked to see the second doctor in charge
investigators were nonchalantly informed that he
had hanged himslef the night before. No one seemed
to be aroused or emotionally upset at his violent
end. Such was the callous attitude the doctors and
nurses had for violent death. Observers found, in
an uncooled morgue stinking bodies of men and women
who had died 12 hours to 3 days before. Their weight
was between 26 and 33 kilos. Among the children still
living was a 10 year old boy whose weight was less
than 10 Kilos and whose legs at the calf had a diameter of $2\frac{1}{2}$ inches. Informant stated that tuberculosis and other diseases are rampant. Scabies,
lice and other vermin were encountered throughout,
linen was dirty and quarantine measures non-existant
upon investigators' arrival.

Freemasons, Homosexuals, and Jehovah's Witnesses

SURVEILLANCE OF FREEMASONS

This circular was issued on January 2, 1945, by the GESTAPO Office Koblenz to order the increased surveillance of all German Freemasons for potential subversive activities.

Gestapo Office Koblenz   Altwied, 2 January 1945
IV 4b - 314/44
a) to the
    Police President,
    Koblenz
b) to the
    Security Service Koblenz,
    located at Strassenhaus
c) to the
    District Administrators in
    Koblenz and Trier
d) to the
    District Branch Offices at
    Trier, Betzdorf, Koblenz, and Bad Kreuznach

Re: Activities of International Freemasons
Prior File: None
Enclosures: 2 copies for District Branch Offices

Special circumstances necessitate increased surveillance of all former German Freemasons. International Freemasonry is once again attempting to gain a foothold in Germany.

I therefore order that all persons known as Freemasons receive special attention. Special notice should be given to links between Freemasons and foreign conscript labor on Reich territory. All means must be employed promptly to identify and eliminate all subversive activities by Freemasons.

Reports are requested by 1 April 1945.

Appended for the District Branch Offices.
Copies of decrees from the Central Office for Reich Security (RSHA).

> *— From the Records of Deputy Judge Advocate General, Record Group 338 T2, case # 66-658, box 405, National Archives. Translated from the German by Sybil Milton.*

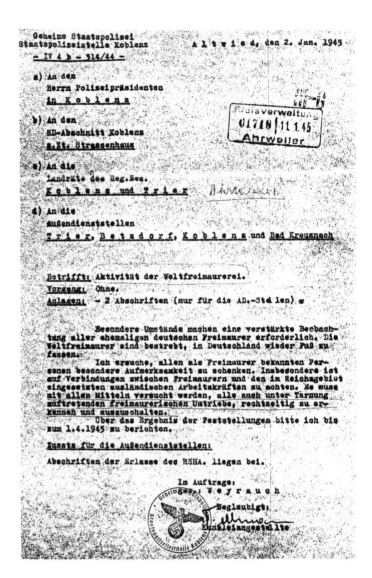

MEDICAL EXPERIMENTS ON HOMOSEXUALS

The persecution of homosexuals began in Nazi Germany in 1933 and led to the prosecution, arrest, and the systematic registration of homosexuals in 1936 by the police and the Subsidiary Reich Central Office for Combating Homosexuality and Abortion. During the war years, the criminalization of homosexuality (which began during the 1920s) and the physical terror for homosexuals in concentration camps increased. Homosexual prisoners were subjected to medical experiments, castration, and even death.

The following document is a note from the files of SS Captain Dr. Gerhard Schiedlausky, the Waffen SS Chief Garrison Physician in Weimar sent to SS Major Dr. Carl Vaernet. Vaernet was attempting to change the sexual orientation of his subjects with artificial hormones.

Weimar-Buchenwald, 3 January 1945

Garrison Physician of the Waffen-SS
Weimar

To
Captain Dr. med. Vaernet
Prague IX
Petergasse 10

Enclosed are the records of prisoners on which operations have been performed (13 in total). *[Archive records at the State Archive in Buchenwald indicate only 12 homosexuals and castrated individuals were involved in this experiment.]*

Those on whom operations were performed bear the following numbers: *[The names of the experimental subjects were deleted for privacy in the postwar period.]*

_____(21926) No. 1   _____(20998) No. 3
_____(31462) No. 4   _____(21957) No. 6
_____(9576) No. 5. _____(6169) No. 5a
_____(not legible) No. 5b

Prisoner No. 20998 (3) died on 21 December 1944 at 8:00 a.m. from heart failure due to infected intestines and to general physical debilitation. No notations of any kind were made regarding this prisoner.

The collected urine samples are ready for transport.

Garrison Physician of the Waffen-SS, Weimar
Signed by proxy *[for Gerhard Schiedlausky]*
[signature illegible]
SS Captain

— *From Wolfgang Röll,* Homosexuelle Häftlinge im Konzentrationslager Buchenwald *(Weimar: Weimardruck GmbH, 1991), 38. Translated from the German by Patricia Heberer.*

EXODUS FROM ORANIENBURG

Wilhelm Coenraad Laros, born in 1902 in Delft, The Netherlands, became a Jehovah's Witness in April 1937, after the death of his infant daughter. He was arrested by the Nazis on February 10, 1941, for his religious beliefs, and was incarcerated in several concentration camps, the last being SACHSENHAUSEN. *Here he recounts his experiences during a forced* EVACUATION.

In the course of 19 and 20 April 1945, the camp had to be evacuated due to the threat of Russian occupation. Everything went toward the North in rows of 500 prisoners, fleeing from the Russians. We as Jehovah's Witnesses, without any food and under armed escort, were almost the last to leave the place where we had endured such trials with the help of the Lord. All together there were 213 brothers and 17 sisters. The Himmler order shortly before 19 April stated that no prisoners were to fall into the hands of the Russians, Americans, or English alive. With us there were also several sick brothers and one sick sister, whom we carried along in a cart. We had to continue marching through the night and the following day until eight o'clock in the evening, during which time we covered 51 kilometers. We segregated ourselves from the rest of the group, sleeping that night in a barn.

The following morning, after receiving two or three potatoes each, we marched on, singing and hoping for the help of Jehovah. All along the side of the road were the dead bodies of prisoners who, completely undernourished, could go no further and were finished off with a bullet in the nape of the neck by the SS. The first stop for our march was in Witstok, 120-130 kilometers from Oranienburg. Here we had to spend three days out under the open sky. We had to be reformed into new groups because the mass murdering along the way had reduced several groups down to 270-300 people. Only the Jehovah's Witnesses did not have to leave anyone behind. Here, after five days, we once again received something to eat through the Red Cross. The Red Cross officer warned the head of the SS men to stop the murder of the prisoners. If he did not, the Red Cross officer would let all the world know.

On 28 April, we began the march again. Along the streets were endless streams of cars and motorcycles with fleeing soldiers, horses and wagons with fleeing civilians, and in between endless rows of prisoners. Above all of this were Russian and American planes bombing in front of and behind us, burning and burned cars, dead horses, women, men, and children shot to death, everywhere puddles of blood as we were continually being driven forward, a scene never to be forgotten. But every day we continually saw the protection of Jehovah anew. On 1 May, when we were just five kilometers outside Schwerin, we heard a rumor, one SS man telling it to another, their faces distorted from fear, that "The Americans were in Schwerin and the Russians were just behind us." Then we had to go into a forest along the road. One by one SS men, "the heroes," disappeared without a sound. At that time, with liberation only hours away, we made a resolution with overfilled, grateful hearts to our great God and His Justifier/Vindicator Who had so wonderfully protected, led, and blessed us.

— *From "The Papers of Wilhelm Conrad Laros," RG 32.011.01, Jehovah's Witnesses, United States Holocaust Memorial Museum. Translated from the Dutch by Neal Guthrie.*

Last Directives

HIMMLER'S ORDER

With the Allies well within the borders of Germany, Hitler still had the "FINAL SOLUTION" very much in mind. He ordered that no concentration camp prisoners should fall into Allied hands. In 1946, the following deposition about a telegram concerning this order was taken by British officials from Georg Henning, Count von Bassewitz-Behr, at the War Criminals Holding Center in Minden.

Bassewitz-Behr was a member of the Nazi Party and SS since 1931. By 1943, he had become a HIGHER SS AND POLICE LEADER after service in Russia. The British tried him in 1947 for killing foreign civilian workers and concentration camp inmates. In 1949, he was extradicted to Russia, where he subsequently died.

> *— From Testimony of George Henning, February 14, 1946, Record Group 238, document D-681, National Archives and Records Administration.*

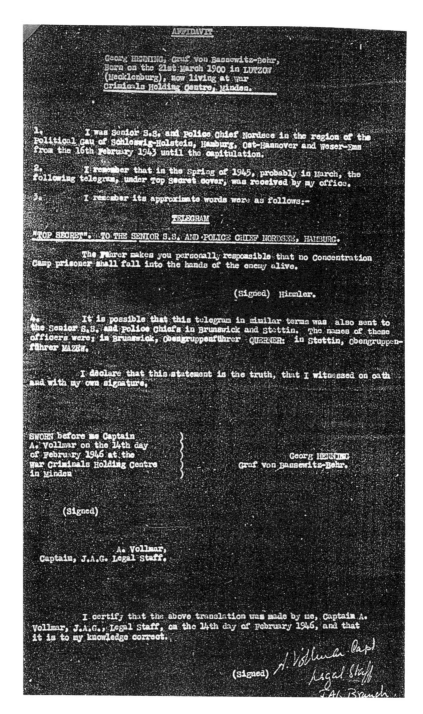

RESCUE EFFORTS AND RESISTANCE

Under Occupation

QUIET HEROES

Parts of the Netherlands were still occupied by the Germans in 1945, and the hunt for Jews continued unabated. Lidia Feenstra lived with her husband and daughter in the town of Groningen in northern Holland. By early 1945 three Jews were hidden in their home; in addition, an elderly Dutch refugee couple had been billeted with the Feenstras by the Germans. Toward the end of January, this elderly couple denounced the family to the German police, who then raided the home. Lidia and her daughter escaped; her husband was killed. After the war the case against this couple was dropped for lack of evidence. Mrs. Feenstra eventually emigrated to Canada.

We could have avoided most hardships caused by the occupation other than the humiliation of being vanquished. Neither one of us could remain insensitive, however, to the anti-Jewish measures that pushed our friends towards an ominous fate.

"They are no longer permitted in restaurants, parks, libraries, laundries, or grocery stores," I lamented, wringing my hands—a sure sign of my agitation. (By the way, to this day I have never lost this habit.) "Now they are branded like cattle. How long can this go on?"

"There's worse, Lidia; they have been taking them to Germany and Poland. They claim that the Jews are being used in constructive labour—hard, but they're being fairly remunerated. But we know the truth. Over four hundred Jews were taken to the quarries of Mauthausen after the February Strike in 1941. Not one of them is alive. Since then more and more of them disappear. Reprisals for sabotage activities, the bastards claim, with a cynical shrug of their shoulders." Willem was outraged over the fate of our Jewish compatriots.

"We have to do something, Willem. I don't know what, but we can't just watch them disappear in those camps. How can I remain uninvolved and live at peace with myself? 'What can one person do, anyway?' Emma van Wijk asked me yesterday when I proposed that we do something to help the Jews. 'Nothing except get caught and be taken to Westerbork with the Jews or get shot in the back.' 'No, absolutely not,' I disagreed with her. 'If we all saved just one Jew, the Germans wouldn't find a soul to deport. Even they can't wipe out a whole nation of sixteen million.'". . .

[After the Jews had been hidden for a time] ... we were informed that, like most people in the north, we had to take in evacuees. How could we object? As far as the authorities knew, only three people inhabited that huge house.

The Takens arrived with the new year, 1945, our fifth year of German occupation. They were in their late sixties, both of fragile construction, both embittered by five years of nomadic existence at the twilight of their lives. They had lost their home, all of their belongings, and their ability to generate an income on which to subsist. While they were not rabid anti-Semites, they resented the Jews and blamed their ill-fate on their existence.

The presence of the three young [Jewish] men upstairs had to be explained to them somehow, so we passed them off as Dutch Christian students who didn't want to serve under the Germans. The Takens shook their heads disapprovingly when they heard their story. "It's not our business, of course, but if all the young men hid rather than collaborating with our government, the Germans would completely dominate us. Besides, it's just not natural for healthy young men to hide in attics, eating up the meagre reserves the country still possesses, depriving those who have no means to provide for themselves." Inga Takens had one constant preoccupation: was there going to be enough food.

"The Takens have made some alarming contacts," Willem whispered to Lexie and me in the kitchen, a few weeks later. "One of my workers saw them leaving Police Headquarters in the company of an SD man. Philip said they seemed pretty chummy. We've got to do something."

"I'll speak to the boys tonight," an unusually pensive Lexie replied.

The next morning, Dolph informed us that he and Sammy were leaving that night. He thanked us for everything and he explained the reasons for their hasty departure.

"I can't tell you not to go, boys." Willem looked unusually nervous. "I'm not entirely sure that I share your concern. Only you two know what risks you are able to live with and what is beyond your means. Dolph, let me check on your contact today, just to make sure you have a place to go. If you don't, I'll try to arrange something for you. And you, Lexie, you can stay, of course, as long as you feel like it. You are like family now."

That night Dolph and Sammy left our dark house after we had seen the Takens retire. A man took them away in a horse-drawn wagon full of junk.

Saturday, January 20, Willem came home a little later than usual. He had a shapeless package, wrapped in newspaper and tied with coarse string, under his arm.

"Rejoice, one and all, the farmers' thirst for wine has paid dividends again. What you see under your very eyes is an appetizing hunk of pork. Need I say, illegally slaughtered, which should make it more flavourful and, I'm afraid to say, more dangerous.

"We'll eat with our mouths closed," Lexie proposed, "so no one can catch us salivating suspiciously."

"Not to worry, by tomorrow night it will be transformed into a delicious soup. We'll just have to keep the lid on." I winked at my two boys.

"We'll have to invite the Takens, of course, if for no other reason than to shut their mouths, so to speak." Willem couldn't chase from his mind the warning about the ominous meeting between our billets and the SD man. "They wouldn't want to squeal on the pig that yields the bacon."

"Old lady Takens would sell her soul for a piece of meat," I agreed. "But what do I tell them if they ask where it came from? After all, famine is ravaging the country. Where could we be procuring meat without doing something illegal?"

"Silent meat tells no story," Lexie philosophized. "I would keep them mystified. When it comes down to the crunch, they would prefer to have their stomachs satisfied rather than their curiosity."

Sunday morning, after I had finished tidying up with Lexie's assistance, we put on the soup. Lexie was sitting next to the stove, reading a book as if he were guarding our treasure from some unexpected thief. Willem took Lizzie for a sleigh ride. Around eleven o'clock Lexie heard Mrs. Takens clunking down from upstairs. She was on her way to the only toilet in the house, located right next to the kitchen. Minutes later, the kitchen door opened a crack and through it appeared the old woman's sniffing nose.

"Something smells mighty good in here. This old nose hasn't been tickled by such a delicious aroma for years. It reminds me of the good old days." By then she was in the kitchen, inching her way closer to the stove. The pot was a powerful magnet whose attraction she wasn't about to resist. "Some people manage to get everything even in these days of national starvation. I wonder how. Let's just see what's in there that smells so criminally delicious." With that she lifted the lid, inhaling the steam of the contraband soup through all the pores of her face.

"It's not lady-like to peek into somebody else's soup pot," Lexie commented nonchalantly. He couldn't care less about etiquette of that sort, but this nosy old buzzard rubbed him the wrong way. My heart stopped beating when I heard Lexie's arrogant comment.

"And is it gentlemanly to be cheeky with someone who could easily be your grandmother, you good-for-nothing coward!" She slammed the kitchen door behind her, storming upstairs with the grace of an offended queen.

My forehead was instantly covered with beads of cold sweat. "You shouldn't have said that to her, Lexie, you shouldn't have. She's going to bring sorrow on this house. I can feel it in my bones. She is spiteful and mean. This might be the occasion she's been waiting for to lash out at us. I don't know what, but we've got to do something."

"Me and my big mouth, now I've brought fear into your home. You've been better to me than anyone else ever has, and look how I pay you back. If it helped, I would vanish this instant, but it's just as criminal to have an illegally slaughtered pig in your house as it is to have a Jew."

When Willem and Lizzie came back, I sent her to play while I related to my husband what had just happened. "Let's just pretend that we attach no importance to the incident," Willy suggested after a few moments of reflection. He sounded in control of his emotions but he was far from being calm. "Why don't you knock on their door and invite them for lunch? That may just do the trick of appeasing the hungry beast."

No one noticed that the Takens had snuck out without a word. When I went up to knock on their door I found it locked.

"I knew it, they went out instead of sticking around for lunch. They always loiter about on Sundays in anticipation of lunch. They must have gone to look for their SD friend. Oh, my God, this pork will kill us all." Willem didn't like it, either. It was bitterly cold outside, it was snowing, and the sidewalks were slippery. Hardly a day for two brittle elderly people to go on a pleasure promenade, especially at lunchtime. We all lost our appetites, except for Lizzie. We sat around the kitchen table without a word. That Sunday, in our home on the Hereweg, the shadow of death was floating in my golden soup.

Around six o'clock, the doorbell rang downstairs. "Lidia, you run up to warn Lexie. I'll go to open the door." There was a quiver in Willy's voice. Four jack-booted SS men in their ominous black uniforms pushed past him. Two of them were holding Dobermann pinschers on short leashes.

Wo ist der Jüdische Spion? One of them cut right to the point. Willy had nothing to say. "We know for a fact that you're hiding three Jewish spies in your house"—one of the Germans confronted Willem in almost flawless Dutch—"Lexie, Dolph, and Sammy. Where are the Jews?" His voice was calm but threatening. "You can tell me now or you can tell me later, but you will tell me where you keep the Jews hidden." Willy just stood there, defiantly speechless.

They let the dogs run free. In a flash, the killer beasts were ripping at Willy's flesh. Three mangled, bloody fingers dangled lifelessly from Willy's right hand—he had used it to protect his face. The dogs were ordered to follow their masters upstairs. Lizzie was screaming in horror. She wanted to run to her father but one of the SS men stopped her with the butt of his pistol. He didn't hurt her—he just froze her with terror. From the third floor we heard the dogs' guttural bark. I stood there, petrified, unable to say a word. The chopped cough of gunshots ripped through the house. One of the SS men ran down the stairs. With a solid yank he grabbed Willy and dragged him upstairs. Now they were all on the third floor, except me and my screaming child who was calling for her daddy. Two more shots. That was all I needed to snap out of my shock and grab my daughter. I ran down the steps with Lizzie in my arms and flew out the open door into the street.

"My God, they are killing us. Please save my child. Don't let them kill us," I was muttering, amid streams of tears. In slippers and housecoat, I ran, stupefied, with my child pressed to my chest across the wide street. A few minutes later, I was banging on Willy's mother's door.

"They've got Lexie and Willy. The house is crawling with SS. Willy is badly hurt, maybe worse. . . . Mother, take care of Lizzie. I've got to go under. . . ." Witless and numb with horror, I roamed the back streets of my neighbourhood. Not one person's face emerged from the mist of my memory. After an hour of this trance the fog began to lift from my mind. "The milk tanker man! Of course!" He was Willy's contact man and he didn't live far from us.

Minutes later, I was sitting in Jan Nijkamp's kitchen, wearing his wife's housecoat, while my feet soaked in a basin of hot water. I was clutching on to a mug of tea as if my life depended on it.

"Oh, my God, it all went terribly wrong at our house; my husband and Lexie may be dead by now, I don't know what happened; I just heard the shots from upstairs. I didn't see anything after the dogs tore off Willy's fingers. Thank God, Lizzie's safe . . . but my poor man, who knows if he's alive." I kept repeating my story like a broken record. The Nijkamps didn't interrupt my ravings. Exhausted, I droned myself into a troubled sleep with my feet in the wash basin.

"I can't stay here, I've got to disappear, they'll be looking for me, without a doubt. I'll need some clothes to go under."

Nijkamp set the network in motion to spirit me out of Groningen where every cobble-stone meant danger and death for me. It was impossible to get any specific information about what had happened in my home on that macabre January evening. Broken threads of murky rumour reached the resistance outposts about a Jew being shot, possibly killed, but no one was speaking with the authority of known fact.

I spent most of the next two days floating between delirium and oblivion. I couldn't even begin to tell you about the sinister dreams I had, even though I remember them as if all this had happened yesterday. Torturers larger than life looming over my brittle body, shapeless monsters with thousands of teeth ripping at Lizzie's flesh, mocking SD men forcing me to watch my husband being shredded with a chainsaw. . . .

— *From Andre Stein,* Quiet Heroes *(New York: New York University Press, 1988), 102–03, 117–22.*

Red Cross

DELEGATION TO RAVENSBRÜCK

Charlotte Müller, born in 1901, became a member of the Communist Party in 1928. In November 1941, she and many of her comrades were tried for high treason against the THIRD REICH. Because there was insufficient evidence against her, she was sentenced to only fifteen months in prison minus time spent in custody during investigation. On April 28, 1942, just as she had feared, she was placed in "protective custody" as a political "red triangle" prisoner in the women's concentration camp at Ravensbrück. Here Charlotte Müller talks about the official visit made by the Swedish Red Cross to RAVENSBRÜCK camp as part of their rescue efforts under COUNT FOLKE BERNADOTTE in spring 1945, and how the leaders of the camp attempted to fool the delegation into believing that living conditions within the camp were quite good.

The inhuman conditions in the concentration camp had been brought to the world's attention, and nations furiously protested against the barbaric torture and exploitations of fascism.

This worldwide protest of nations did not fit into the political concepts of the fascist rulers. In order to show that even opponents of the Regime were treated justly, they expressed their willingness to permit a delegation of the Swedish Red Cross with its president, Prince Bernadotte, to inspect a few concentration camps, even Ravensbrück.

Of course the delegation would be allowed to see nothing of the catastrophic conditions in the overcrowded camp, none of the misery in which the prisoners had to live and work. One should be of the opinion that the concentration camps were actually "protective-custody" camps. Therefore, the camp leadership decided to let only barracks 1 and 2, as well as two infirmaries be inspected. These were made ready in great haste.

Everything that could give offense had to be avoided. No transports were sent. No prisoners were allowed on the camp streets. Only the bread-fetchers went to the bread pantry. A comedy was being staged.

Barracks 1, the kitchen barracks, had always had bed linen which was changed often out of fear of pestilence. Now this barracks received white table cloths and small vases with branches of evergreen. It was strange and ridiculous: we had to hang curtains in the windows of our barracks, the administrative barracks. The prisoners in barracks 1 had previously always made "paper curtains" out of white paper. The Polish women could cut out the most beautiful paper patterns which they glued to the windows. We in barracks 2 were given paper curtains which we attached with drawing pins. However, the curtains had to be given back after the Red Cross inspection. In addition, we received fresh bed linen for the first time in a long while: white blankets and blue and white checkered sheets. We scrubbed the floor boards with sand and soap powder which they normally never gave us. Everything was to be in order the evening before the unusual visit. For that reason we had to remove our clogs or shoes before we entered the barracks to keep from tracking in any dirt.

The next morning we were allowed to use only the first sinks in the washroom because it would have taken too long to clean up all the sinks again and make them shine. We had to scrub the cabinets inside and out, and hand towels hung in each. Our personal belongings were stowed away in boxes under our beds or straw sacks. Those on cleaning duty did not have to go out for roll call. They were responsible for all the beds which had to be lined up straight and square. Even the dumpsters were scrubbed clean, standing in the sun, their galvanized coating against rust scratched off.

It was all a big exciting to-do. After the morning roll call, the SS barracks leader appeared and checked everything down to the tiniest detail. What was striking was that her treatment of us was almost polite. Yet at the same time she did not forget to give us strict instructions that no one was permitted to speak to the Red Cross delegates, even if one were spoken to. Only the SS was to share any information with the gentlemen of the Red Cross.

Early in the morning the delegation finally appeared in our area and was led first to the kitchen barracks. Afterwards they entered our barracks. There were about ten delegates in flawless Red Cross uniforms accompanied by the camp leadership.

There were very few of my fellow prisoners in the barracks. Most of them had been led off to work as usual. With the order "Attention!" we lined up against the wall across from the entrance. The SS barracks leader stepped forward, and the block leader reported.

First the sleeping quarters were shown. When the delegation was inspecting the washroom, an SS-man had the nerve to state: "Here in the foot basins there is hot water after four in the afternoon." There was never hot water in the barracks! In both summer and winter we had to wash ourselves and our laundry in cold water.

In the day room the closets were opened and inspected. A fellow prisoner was asked how long she had been here. As ordered, she gave no answer. That was an embarrassing mistake. Camp Commandant Suhren winked at her: "Well, answer the man, please!" We thought, "My God, he said please. Normally he just screams at us." Then the prisoner gave her answer.

Another prisoner was asked what her nationality was, and she also answered, although reluctantly. The barracks leader whispered to the barracks elder. She ran and got the barracks book out of which Suhren read the numbers of each nationality represented in the barracks.

Afterward we were asked how we liked it in the camp. The barracks leader answered quickly for us. "Here all the women have order, cleanliness, and regular meals." She had not finished speaking when one of the delegates added,

"The women here must have it better than criminal prisoners because they are not convicts." "Yes, that is true," answered Suhren humbly. "They have it better here. They are in protective custody and are being re-educated. When we have ascertained that they have improved, they will be released. Afterwards I will show you how many have already been released."

We stood there like stone; not a single muscle moved. Our faces did not show what we felt about this exchange. We had been trained against that. Everything we had to say we tried to express with our eyes. We simply looked at the delegates, and I believe they understood us.

Since the visitors did not speak German, one member of their group interpreted. The conversation was visibly unpleasant for the camp leadership, and they invited the delegates now to visit the sick-barracks. The inspection of other barracks would be of little interest since they were all the same.

In the infirmary several small rooms had been prepared for inspection in which selected patients had been placed. The delegation was split up and the prisoners now had the opportunity to approach the delegates. Anette Eekman, a young Dutch woman, was able to whisper to the last delegate in English. "Every day countless women die in the camp. Typhus is raging. The sick never receive any medicine. In the Uckermark camp women no longer able to work are killed with rat poison. In all the other barracks the conditions are inhuman." The delegate nodded to her imperceptibly as a sign that he had understood her.

A short while after their visit, the Swedish Red Cross sent serum for typhus. We now knew that the delegation had understood our Dutch inmate and wanted quickly to help us. However, the first to be inoculated were the members of the SS who came in contact with prisoners. Only then did the prisoners themselves become inoculated. Of course there was not enough serum for everybody, and the camp leadership decided who would receive it. . . .

Only liberation by the Red Army put an end to our misery. Yet how many of us did not survive to experience that day? In the last three months ca. 4,000 women and girls died from typhus alone.

—From Charlotte Müller, Die Klempnerkolonne in Ravensbrück (Berlin: Dieter Verlag, 1981), 188–93. Translated from the German by Neal Guthrie.

THE RED CROSS MISSION TO MAUTHAUSEN

Louis Haefliger was an employee in a bank in Zürich in 1945 when he was selected by the INTERNATIONAL COMMITTEE OF THE RED CROSS to join the rescue mission being organized to repatriate French prisoners from Mauthausen. He entered MAUTHAUSEN in the lead vehicle of the nineteen-truck convoy that arrived at the camp after the rescue mission of April 20, apparently at the end of the month.

The following morning, the column drove towards Mauthausen. Lieutenant Hoppler waited for us in the middle of the road and received the commander of the column. At the entrance to the camp, it was necessary to unload the parcels [brought to the camp for the prisoners as part of an agreement between the IRC and Germans the previous month]; at this time we got to see the commandant of the camp, Ziereis, who had the rank of *Standartenführer* [colonel]. This is a forty-year-old man, with an energetic but worried appearance; the corners of his mouth tremble. SS officers appear. We explain to them the terms of the agreement between the president of the Red Cross and Kaltenbrunner, the head of the concentration camps. A representative of the Red Cross must be able to enter the camp and distribute these parcels. It is necessary that he stay in the camp until its final liquidation. Ziereis pretends that he does not know about this agreement. He declares that my presence in the camp is undesirable. He complains about the lack of trust by the Red Cross concerning the distribution of provisions under the camp's direction. Seeing the impossibility of fulfilling my mission, the head of the column is of the opinion that I should return to Switzerland. I refuse this in the most categorical fashion, deciding to fulfill my duty at any price and enter the camp. I insist that they let me enter and that I be allowed to stay in the camp. Ziereis declares that he is ready to send a telegram to Kaltenbrunner whose tone will be the following:

"The Red Cross, whose representative is here, demands that a Swiss representative be able to enter the camp to distribute parcels. The presence of this representative, demanded by the Red Cross, is not essential. Answer by telegram if the representative is authorized to enter the camp or not. Signed, Ziereis."

This telegram furnished me with a pretext to stay in the vicinity of the camp and I expressed to Ziereis my firm intention: I would come to learn of the answer to the telegram, even if I must walk each day the six kilometers which separate Saint-Georgen from Mauthausen. My mistrust in regard to the SS was only increased.

[*Haefliger stayed at Saint-Georgen for three days while the column returned to Switzerland.*] On the third day, carrying all my belongings, I made my way by car to the camp where, entering without permission, I was immediately ushered in to Ziereis. I asked him firmly that, not counting any more on Kaltenbrunner's response, I required authorization for entry. Ziereis then assigned me to part of *Obersturmführer* [1st Lt.] Reiner's room which I would share with him: the representative of the Red Cross would sleep next to an SS man on whose cap was adorned the death's head! For the prisoners whose terror I felt around me, I accepted such torture.

In the following days, I had conversations with Ziereis about the precise circumstances that prevailed in the camp: lack of bread, clothes, shoes, the horrible shortage of linen. The Mauthausen camp was overcrowded, those in Gusen I and II filled to bursting. The sick lay by fives in the narrow beds of the camp. There were 60,000 human beings—men, women, children. . . The chimneys of the crematoriums smoked day and night. For a few days, the prisoners received no bread. The sanitary conditions fell to the lowest. They [the prisoners] died from hunger. Ziereis himself pretends to be moved. He affects pity, this man with whom I must take my meals, this monster who, one day, had a truck filled with bodies drive by the window of his wife so he could boast of his work.

I propose to go to Linz to Gauleiter Eigruber to try to get flour without delay. . . . [*Haefliger did go but Eigruber refused the request for flour. However he did allow Haefliger to take some wheat from a nearby ferry to Mauthausen. Haefliger also telegramed Geneva in the hope of having supplies sent to the camp.*] On my return to Mauthausen I discuss with the surgeon Podlaha the gravity of the situation. He describes to me his impotence in running of the camp. He does not give me any way to assure humane treatment for the prisoners; for several weeks they have not been washed nor disinfected. They roam, clothed in unspeakable rags. I succeed in organizing a conference between the surgeon Podlaha, Ziereis, and myself. Upon my proposal, Ziereis orders that the prisoners take a bath and be disinfected immediately; during this time, the clothes which they wear will be washed.

I also ask Ziereis to place at my disposal forty horse carts to fetch potatoes, many damaged, to the camp, but which will allow the prisoners to put a little something between their teeth.

I vehemently object to Ziereis about the manner in which the unloaded parcels had been distributed before my entry into the camp. One part only was distributed to the prisoners and many parcels had been emptied of their most precious contents: condensed milk, chocolate, biscuits, butter. . . .

—*From Christian Bernadac,* Les 186 Marches *(Paris: Editions France-Empire, 1974), 356–59. Translated from the French by Kevin Mahoney.*

War Refugee Board

RESCUE STATISTICS

Established by executive order of President ROOSEVELT *in January 1944, the* WAR REFUGEE BOARD *aided European Jews escaping from occupied Europe during the latter stages of the war. An estimate of the numbers of people rescued by the Board, dating from February 1945, is included here.*

—*"McCormick to Executive Director," February 14, 1945, War Refugee Board, Box 28, File: War Refugee Board, Volume 3, Franklin D. Roosevelt Library, Hyde Park, NY.*

EXECUTIVE OFFICE OF THE PRESIDENT
WAR REFUGEE BOARD

INTER-OFFICE COMMUNICATION

DATE February 19, 1945

TO : The Executive Director

FROM : P. J. McCormack

Re : Number of Persons Rescued Since the Establishment of the War Refugee Board.

I. Movements to Neutral and Allied Areas

Roumania	to	Turkey	6,527	
Bulgaria	to	Turkey	448	
	To	North Africa	906	(Fedhala)
			400	(Phillipville)
	To	Middle East	45,000	
	To	Palestine	10,000	
Italy	to	United States	965	(Ft. Ontario)
Within Yugoslavia			4,840	
	To	Switzerland	9,172	plus several thousand in early 1944
Hungary	to	Roumania	2,000	
Occupied	to	liberated Slovakia	250	
Greece via Turkey to Middle East			900	
Transnistria to Roumania			48,000	
Spain to Portugal			1,532	
France to Spain			2,638	
Norway, Finland, and Baltic Areas to Sweden			4,770	
Yugoslavia to Italy			11,229	
Protective Documents in Hungary			14,000	
Latin American Passport Recognition			1,000	
Spanish Sephardic Recognition			555	
Portuguese Sephardic Recognition			400	
Restoration Turkish Citizenship certain Jews			700	
Exchange (actual and/or lot improved)			1,000	
United States Visas			4,350	
			126,604	

II. Situation in Liberated Areas

(See Attachments 1, 2, and 3.)

The Haven at Fort Ontario

THE ONTARIO CHRONICLE

The refugees at the FORT ONTARIO Refugee Center began to print their own newspaper soon after their arrival in August 1944. The last issue of the paper appeared on September 6, 1945.

— Ontario Chronicle, *6 Sept 1945, reproduced courtesy of the Leo Baeck Institute, New York.*

Vol. 1 No. 42   Fort Ontario, Oswego, N.Y.   September 6, 1945

SCHOOL LIFE STARTED AGAIN

School life started again on Tuesday, September 4th with exception of St. Paul's and Campus School on the State Teacher's College.

St. Paul's started on Wednesday, September 5th, while Campus School will reopen on Monday, September 10th. At the same date Teacher's College reopens.

The Rochester Business Institute at Oswego which will be attended by seven students of the Shelter, held registration on Tuesday, September 4th.

Having spent vacations at the Shelter, with many and various activities, such as sports, music, arts and crafts, creative writing, American short hand, etc.-most directed by the American Friends- our children returned to school in excellent physical and moral conditions.

It may be added that twelve new pupils of six years age attend now normal schools at Oswego.

To all our children and students we wish happiness and success for their new term.

THE FUNERAL OF NATHAN ZINDWER

The funeral of Dr. Na-than Zindwer who died last Friday at the Shelter hospital, took place Sunday, September 2th. Many residents of the Shelter and his two sons and daughter accompanied Nathan Zindwer on his last way. He was buried on the Jewish cemetery of Oswego where-helas-are also other graves of Shelter residents in a considerable number.

The religious ceremony was performed by Rabbi Moses Tzechoval who in to heart goind words praised the high qualities of Dr. Zindwer. Mendel Gottlieb, Wilhelm Loew and Sally Schnaymann delivered then moving fare-well speeches in the name of the Shelter community. Many residents were in tears, expressed their sympathies to the children of the deceased and left the cemetery in an impressive silence.

PRAYER SERVICES IN SYNAGOGUE (BLDG. 101)

The following schedule for prayers during Rosh-Hashana 5706 is fixed for Synagogue, (Bldg101): Friday,Sept.7th: 6:00 and 6:55 p.m.; Saturday,Sept. 8th: 6:30 a.m.,3:30,5:30 and 8:10 p.m.; Sunday, Sept. 9th: 6:30 and 9:30 a.m.,and 5:30 and 8:05 p.m.

A MESSAGE FOR ROSH-HASHANA

During the days of Rosh-Hashana, those holy days when the blessed God, Ruler of the World, sits upon his heavenly throne to judge the world with justice and mercy, I appeal to you, dear brethren, and call upon you to repentance. Assemble in the houses of worship and unite your thouhts in holy prayer, give thanks to the Almighty God for the past, and pray to our Heavenly Father for complete forgiveness, good life, peace and true redemption for yourselves, your families and relatives, for the noble American nation, her President and Government and for the whole humanity.

May you have a happy and prosperous New Year, the year of freedom!

Rabbi Moses Tzechoval

The Post-Office of the Shelter will be closed on Saturday,Sept. 8th and Monday,Sept. 17th for the Jewish Holidays.

PRESIDENT TRUMAN'S STATEMENT

At the end of 1945, the status of the FORT ONTARIO refugees was settled by a directive from President HARRY S TRUMAN. The immigration of displaced persons, including Jewish survivors, from occupied Germany and Austria to the U.S. was simplified and given priority. However, because the FORT ONTARIO refugees were already in the United States, they could not immigrate under this new policy. An adjustment in their status allowing them to stay was made by the president with this directive of December 22, 1945.

The war has brought in its wake an appalling dislocation of populations in Europe. Many humanitarian organizations, including the United Nations Relief and Rehabilitation Administration, are doing their utmost to solve the multitude of problems arising in connection with this dislocation of hundreds of thousands of persons. Every effort is being made to return the displaced persons and refugees in the various countries of Europe to their former homes. The great difficulty is that so many of these persons have no homes to which they may return. The immensity of the problem of displaced persons and refugees is almost beyond comprehension.

A number of countries in Europe, including Switzerland, Sweden, France, and England, are working toward its solution. The United States shares the responsibility to relieve the suffering. To the extent that our present immigration laws permit, everything possible should be done at once to facilitate the entrance of some of these displaced persons and refugees into the United States.

In this way we may do something to relieve human misery, and set an example to the other countries of the world which are able to receive some of these war sufferers. I feel that it is essential that we do this ourselves to show our good faith in requesting other nations to open their doors for this purpose.

Most of these persons are natives of Central and Eastern Europe and the Balkans. The immigration quotas for all these countries for one year total approximately 39,000, two-thirds of which are allotted to Germany. Under the law, in any single month the number of visas issued cannot exceed ten per cent of the annual quota. This means that from now on only about 3900 visas can be issued each month to persons who are natives of these countries.

Very few persons from Europe have migrated to the United States during the war years. In the fiscal year 1942, only ten per cent of the immigration quotas was used; in 1943, five per cent; in 1944, six per cent; and in 1945, seven per cent. As of November 30, 1945, the end of the fifth month of the present fiscal year, only about ten per cent of the quotas for the European countries has been used. These unused quotas however do not accumulate through the years, and I do not intend to ask the Congress to change this rule.

The factors chiefly responsible for these low immigration figures were restraints imposed by the enemy, transportation difficulties, and the absence of consular facilities. Most of those Europeans who have been admitted to the United States during the last five years were persons who left Europe prior to the war, and thereafter entered here from non-European countries.

I consider that common decency and the fundamental comradeship of all human beings require us to do what lies within our power to see that our established immigration quotas are used in order to reduce human suffering. I am taking the necessary steps to see that this is done as quickly as possible.

Of the displaced persons and refugees whose entrance into the United States we will permit under this plan, it is hoped that the majority will be orphaned children. The provisions of law prohibiting the entry of persons likely to become public charges will be strictly observed. Responsible welfare organizations now at work in this field will guarantee that these children will not become public charges. Similar guarantees have or will be made on behalf of adult persons. The record of these welfare organizations throughout the past years has been excellent, and I am informed that no persons admitted under their sponsorship have ever become charges on their communities. Moreover, many of the immigrants will have close family ties in the United States and will receive the assistance of their relatives until they are in a position to provide it for themselves.

These relatives or organizations will also advance the necessary visa fees and travel fare. Where the necessary funds for travel fare and visa fees have not been advanced by a welfare organization or relative, the individual applicant must meet these costs. In this way the transportation of these immigrants across the Atlantic will not cost the American taxpayer a single dollar.

In order to enter the United States it is necessary to obtain a visa from a consular officer of the Department of State. As everyone knows, a great many of our consular establishments all over the world were disrupted and their operations suspended when the war came. It is physically impossible to reopen and to restaff all of them overnight. Consequently it is necessary to choose the area in which to concentrate our immediate efforts. This is a painful necessity because it requires us to make an almost impossible choice among degrees of misery. But if we refrain from making a choice because it will necessarily be arbitrary, no choice will ever be made and we shall end by helping no one.

The decision has been made, therefore, to concentrate our immediate efforts in the American zones of occupation in Europe. This is not intended however entirely to exclude issuance of visas in other parts of the world.

In our zones in Europe there are citizens of every major European country. Visas issued to displaced persons and refugees will be charged, according to law, to the countries of their origin. They will be distributed fairly among persons of all faiths, creeds and nationality.

It is intended that, as soon as practicable, regular consular facilities will be reestablished in every part of the world, and the usual, orderly methods of registering and reviewing visa applications will be resumed. The pressing need, however, is to act now in a way that will produce immediate and tangible results. I hope that by early spring adequate consular facilities will be in operation in our zones in Europe, so that immigration can begin immediately upon the availability of ships.

I am informed that there are various measures now pending before the Congress which would either prohibit or severely reduce further immigration. I hope that such legislation will not be passed. This period of unspeakable human distress is not the time for us to close or to narrow our gates. I wish to emphasize, however, that any effort to bring relief to these displaced persons and refugees must and will be strictly within the limits of the present quotas as imposed by law.

There is one particular matter involving a relatively small number of aliens. President Roosevelt, in an endeavor to assist in handling displaced persons and refugees during the war and upon the recommendation of the War Refugee Board, directed that a group of about 1000 displaced persons be removed from refugee camps in Italy and settled temporarily in a War Relocation Camp near Oswego, New York. Shortly thereafter, President Roosevelt informed the Congress that these persons would be returned to their homelands after the war.

Upon the basis of a careful survey by the Department of State and the Immigration and Naturalization Service, it has been determined that if these persons were now applying for admission to the United States most of them would be admissible under the immigration laws. In the circumstances it would be inhumane and wasteful to require these people to go all the way back to Europe merely for the purpose of applying there for immigration visas and returning to the United States. Many of them have close relatives including sons and daughters who are citizens of the United States and who have served and are serving honorably in the armed forces of our county. I am therefore directing the Secretary of State and the Attorney General to adjust the immigration status of the members of this group who may wish to remain here, in strict accordance with existing laws and regulations.

The number of persons at the Oswego camp is, however, comparatively small. Our major task is to facilitate the entry into the United States of displaced persons and refugees still in Europe. To meet this larger problem, I am directing the Secretary of State, the Attorney General, the Secretary of War, the War Shipping Administrator and the Surgeon General of the Public Health Service to proceed at once to take all appropriate steps to expedite the quota immigration of displaced persons and refugees from Europe to the United States. Representatives of these officials will depart for Europe very soon to prepare detailed plans for the prompt execution of this project.

—From "Statement and Directive by the President on Immigration to the United States of Certain Displaced Persons and Refugees in Europe, December 22, 1945," Public Papers of the Presidents of the United States: Harry S. Truman, April 12 to December 31, 1945 (Washington D.C.: Government Printing Office, 1961), 572–75.

Jewish Soldiers

JEWISH SOLDIERS IN A POLISH ARMY

Following the German invasion of Russia in 1941, Polish exiles in the Soviet Union formed military units under the command of General Berling. These units fought with the Soviet Army on the eastern front during the last years of the war.

This selection was written by an anonymous German Jewish woman who had been deported to the Riga GHETTO in occupied Latvia in 1942. In August 1944, she was evacuated to Stutthof concentration camp and from there transferred to Sophienwalde, a subcamp of Stutthof, where she was liberated in March 1945. Shortly thereafter, she was picked up by a medical unit of the Polish 2nd Army, one of the armies formed by Polish exiles.

This Jewish officer was in command of a Sanitary Battalion in the Polish 2nd Army. He took me in as a nurse. I was given a military coat, a warm wadded cap, a pair of great Russian boots, and a Red Cross case containing cotton, wool, iodine, ointment, and a pair of scissors. There I stood—a complete military nursing Sister.

On our journcy, there were several clashes with as yet unconquered groups of German soldiers. We had to retire to deserted villages, where we would spend a few days doing laundry work, over-haul ambulances, and prepare food. At last, on a gray, rainy day, early in the morning, we reached Deutsch Krone, a little Pomeranian town not far from the former Polish border. . . .

The young Jew from Lodz was a good fellow. I should not have expected such a wan-looking youth to be so full of energy and pugnaciousness. In every clash, in every emergency, he was the first to volunteer for a dangerous post. I spoke about him to the captain and he explained,

"Man is a good-natured animal, and we Jews are especially so. You can compare human nature with water. Water tends always to flow downward, but if you boil it, up and up it springs; and if you steam it and force it through pipes, it can rise to a mountain top. Is that its nature? No! An alien power has taken possession of it and made it do these things. It's the same with a man. You can bring him to such a pitch that he will do what is far, far away from being what is natural to him."

Artillerymen of the Jewish Brigade in action during the crossing of the Senio River in Italy, April 1945. Jewish volunteers from Palestine composed the Jewish Brigade and fought during the last months of the war. (NARA)

The Lodz youth told me many interesting facts that I did not know. For instance, he told me about the Jewish Generals in the Russian Army, the Jewish Brigade in the British Army, Maidanek, Babi-Yar, Treblinka, the Lodz Ghetto, and Herr Hans Bibov, [Biebow] the "Reich's Representative" and executioner of the Jewry of Lodz.

Hans Bibov was the one who "set the water on to boil" and made of a good-natured, generous and lovable boy, a youth who now lived for one thing only, and that was revenge; revenge to be taken on Hans Bibov. The Lodz youth had never come across Bibov, but he kept looking for him on German soil. He could see Bibov's murderous face in every German that he met. To him, every German village represented Bibov's home. For every German, he had only one greeting, one speech; namely, hate and a click of his trigger.

Melancholy days.

Outside, the rain fell without a break. We were encamped in a village near Zlatow. I was on night-duty in the ambulatorium.

The instruments had been boiled and placed in the sterilizer. I had no more duties to peform, so I sat and made notes in my journal. The captain sat on his camp-bed, read a front line newspaper, and smoked. The Lodz lad came in from his post. His coat was soaked through and through. He grumbled,

"A damned country and a damned climate. It does nothing but pour."

The captain asked,

"Perhaps you would like to warm yourself with a drink?"

"Thanks, captain, I do not drink brandy, but I would like a cup of tea."

I put away my pages and started making tea. The captain and I had become very fond of the boy from Lodz. Indeed, his simplicity, honesty, and modest behavior had made him a general favorite among the men; and his courage, his promptness, and quickness of mind in any attack or clash had won him the respect and admiration of his Christian fellow-soldiers. I had learned, besides all this, that he wrote verses.

The Lodz youth said, "I had never in my life written anything, but lately I felt an inner urge to write."

Thus he excused himself for his writing, as any shy child might.

The captain laid his newspaper aside and turned to the Lodz boy and said,

"While the tea-kettle is boiling, tell us something about yourself and your life."

The boy did not need to be asked twice. He pulled off his wet boots, sat down by the stove, took his rifle in his hand, cleaned it bit by bit, and related the following:

"My name is Jacob Mandelbaum. I was born in Lodz where I went to Cheider [Elementary Hebrew School] and the Yeshiva. Later in life, I became a weaver. I worked and studied, attended classes, borrowed books, made acquaintance with Jewish and general literature, associated with others of my age, and had a good time until 1939.

"When the Germans entered Lodz, I went to Bialystock. After this, I travelled toward Russia. My parents and my young sister remained in the Lodz Ghetto. Up to 1941, I worked in a coal-seam in the Don Basin, and after that I was in Central Asia on the banks of the Darya. By day, I was scorched by the sun; and by night, I shivered with malaria, the scorpion's bite. My hands were swollen from plucking 'Djugara,' 'Chlopok,' (cotton) and rice. After that, I served in the Soviet Army on the Leningrad front. I received distinction, awards, medals, and a wound. I then returned to the front again, but this time I served in the Polish Army. As a Polish soldier, I took part in the marches from Lublin to Lodz. All this toughened and strengthened me. I had looked death in the face many times, but the longing for home, the love for my parents and my only sister, and the hope of seeing them again, gave me the courage to carry on through every hardship. Five long years I held fast to the hope that I still had a home, and that I still had a little sister, father, and mother.

"I was among the first to break in and take possession of my home-town. The moment I was given a few hours leave, I headed for the Ghetto. Upon arriving there, I realized that I had become an orphan. I stood still and gazed at the narrow street in which I was born and raised. The ruins gazed back at me like tomb-stones. The wire enclosing the Ghetto twisted itself around my neck like a serpent and choked back my tears. I roamed the once familiar streets looking for a trace of my homelife, something that was still mine, the faintest reminder of what had been 'I' of the former days; but the work of Bibov's executioners had been done with German precision and thoroughness. The Ghetto had been destroyed and Lodz Jewry had been dispatched to Radoqoshtsh, Chelmna, Treblinka, Buchenwald, and Auschwitz.

"With a heart turned to stone, I left what had been my home, and I vowed as I took my last look at the ruined Ghetto, that I would have revenge on the Bibovs, and that I would repay them for the Ghetto Tax, for the Yellow Badge, and for the 'Children Liquidation Campaign.' With shot and shell from the Russian automatic guns, I would repay them with interest."

At this point, his tale came to an end. His weapon, which he was cleaning as he spoke, was now clean and bright. He carefully put it away in a corner as though it were a precious treasure. He then took his filled cup of tea and drank it. After this, he took a faded photograph out of the pocket of his blouse. Attached to the photograph were decorations and medals which were held in a scrap of newspaper. On the photograph was a Jew with a sparse beard and a skullcap, and beside him was a woman wearing a silken shawl and a "Shield of David" brooch on her breast.

"Sir, captain, these are my parents," the youth stated.

"He resembles my own father of blessed memory," sighed the captain.

"And she," I whispered to myself, "is like my mother."

Who could have foreseen that this was to be my last talk with the boy from Lodz?

We made our way through a wooded district. The main roads were crowded with mechanized armored divisions hurrying day and night in the direction of Berlin. Horse and cart transport had to detour through woods and scattered villages.

Late evening—the rain pelted down monotonously. We were surrounded by woods. The signpost indicated that the next village was three kilometers distant, that is, twenty-one kilometers from Deutsch Krone.

Suddenly—shooting. There was a hailstorm of shots over our heads.

The boy from Lodz jumped down from his cart, and was followed by a few more soldiers. They opened fire on the woods, but the shooting went on. Stray bullets hit a comrade here and there, and among those hit was the boy from Lodz. In the noise and commotion around us, his last groan was not heard. With all haste, they dug his grave by the roadside. By the light of a flashlight, they wrote on a board:

Jacob Mandelbaum-Sheregovi (Private)
Born 1922 in Lodz
Fallen-March 26, 1945
Honor his memory

—*From Herman and Suzanne Taube,* Remember, *trans. Helena Frank (Baltimore: N. A. Gossmann Publishing Co., 1951), 82–83, 85–93.*

CONCERN OVER THE HOLOCAUST

ACCOMPLICES TO MURDER

Dorothy Parker, the author of this selection, was an American author, poet, and journalist best known for her biting wit. She was prominent in the anti-fascist movement in the U.S. before and during the war. In 1945 she spoke about the Nazi atrocities in Europe at a function honoring Senator Guy Gillette of Iowa, a well-known supporter of a Jewish state in PALESTINE.

Her comments were published in Answer, *a magazine edited by an associate of Peter Bergson, the driving force behind the Emergency Committee to Save the Jews of Europe, a Jewish activist organization striving to increase rescue efforts.*

I believe what we are doing here tonight is technically known as honoring Senator Gillette, but I think the truth of the case is that it is Senator Gillette who brings honor to the whole human race.

He realized that the day of words was over long ago, and the day of action is already at its noon.

There have been so many statesmen, and they have said so many words. They have said them beautifully, and they were lovely words that do credit to the hearts of those who have said and felt them; only their day is done. Maybe they never had a day; maybe they never were of any use. If, on your path you find a desperately wounded man, it really does very little good to turn away from him and run back home and write him a letter of sympathy, even though you get your most attractive friends to sign it.

Senator Gillette is not a member of the condolent school. He believes in saving lives while there are still lives to be saved. He introduced one resolution after another to our Congress. He dogged all the departments of the Government until a beginning was made towards the saving of human beings. One man was responsible for that beginning. It takes more than one to keep on from there. It takes all of us.

For a while, just a little way back, it looked as if we would not have to work, as if everything had been done for us. When our armies went tearing magnificently through the violated countries, liberating their people, it seemed that everything would be all right, and there would be justice and decency and life itself for everyone in the world. But it did not turn out like that. People are being liberated, I suppose, though in slow and strange ways; not all people, and certainly not the Jews.

Even in their frantic fighting, the Germans take time out to murder Jews, and in the liberated countries, the Germans left behind them the fear and hatred of Jews that is like poison left in wells. Fascism crawls in, God knows, through many openings, but its first entrance is by the door marked "Anti-Semitism."

It seems so little, what the Jews of Europe want; only a shelter; not a charity orphanage, but a haven, which is their right; a place in which to be safe to work and to hope. And yet there are those over here—and the awful thing is that there are Jews among them—who are annoyed that they ask even that. They do not want to be reminded of horror or death. It irritates them.

I met a man the other night, a nice, comfortable man, filled with a nice, comfortable dinner, sitting in a nice, comfortable room, who was pretty badly bored with the Jews in Europe. He said, "Why don't these Jews keep quiet? Why do they want to draw attention to themselves? They have only brought it on them if they are all killed."

He was a lot bigger than I am, and, besides, the room was full of pleasant people, and somebody got the subject changed almost in time; but, when I was leaving, the nice, comfortable gentleman said to me, "Look, I feel sorry for those poor devils, too, but I don't go around getting worked up about them. I just take it easy."

I can only say this time behind his back that I hope to God I never take it easy while traitors to their race and accomplices to murders are still at large.

There are the innocent who have been driven and tortured and killed; there are the monsters who have murdered them; and then there are other people. There are the people who read and hear and know of hideous human suffering, and let it go on. Their hearts are heavy, they would say, with sorrow, but it is guilt that wears them down. Their doorsteps are shining clean. You cannot see the blood on them, but it is there.

There is no time for hopeful waiting; there is no time to stay elegantly apart. What happens to even one human being anywhere is the business of every human being everywhere.

The bell that tolls for the Jews of Europe tolls for you and me. While there are slaves, no one of us is free; while they die by murder, no one of us is truly alive.

—From "Accomplices to Murder," Answer Magazine, *February 1945, 16.*

A few of the thousands of wedding rings the Germans
removed from their victims in order to salvage the gold.
Buchenwald, Germany, May 1945. (NARA)

LIBERATION

- As Allied armies fought their way through German-held territory, they encountered the last grisly remnants of the Nazi concentration camp system. Often by accident Soviet, American, British and Canadian forces uncovered the thinly guarded Nazi camps, filled to overflowing with prisoners of every nationality, category, and confession. Malnourished and disease-ridden, these survivors clung to life amid conditions of the most unspeakable horror.

- In the east, the Red Army had already confronted horrifying scenes before liberating Auschwitz on January 27, 1945: since late July 1944 they had liberated the Majdanek death camp and located the camouflaged sites of other Nazi extermination centers in Poland. More secretive than the Western Allies, Soviet authorities did not always reveal to the outside world all that they had uncovered.

- In the west, British and American soldiers were unprepared for the startling sights they encountered as they liberated the major concentration camp sites in Germany's interior. Shock, shame, and anger spurred American and British military authorities to expose Nazi crimes to the full glare of publicity.

- Even after liberation, the Holocaust still claimed victims. Tens of thousands of liberated concentration camp prisoners continued to die as a result of maltreatment, malnutrition, and disease weeks after Allied soldiers liberated Nazi camps.

- While widespread goodwill between survivors and their liberators marked the first days following liberation, patience quickly eroded as former prisoners (mainly Jews) incapable of repatriation compounded an already complex refugee crisis.

American troops and prisoners at
Buchenwald concentration camp soon after
the camp's liberation in April 1945.
(Collection of the Center for Holocaust Studies,
Museum of Jewish Heritage)

113

BROADCAST FROM BUCHENWALD

by Edward R. Murrow

Edward R. Murrow, the preeminent American radio and television broadcaster of the 1940s and 1950s, reported on the war in Europe from its beginning for the CBS network. In April 1945, he reached Buchenwald soon after the liberation and broadcast to the United States on April 15 the following report on what he saw there.

But this is no time to talk of the surface of Germany. Permit me to tell you what you would have seen, and heard, had you been with me on Thursday. It will not be pleasant listening. If you are at lunch, or if you have no appetite to hear what Germans have done, now is a good time to switch off the radio, for I propose to tell you of Buchenwald. It is on a small hill about four miles outside Weimar, and it was one of the largest concentration camps in Germany, and it was built to last. As we approached it, we saw about a hundred men in civilian clothes with rifles advancing in open order across the fields. There were a few shops; we stopped to inquire. We were told that some of the prisoners had a couple of SS men cornered in there. We drove on, reached the main gate. The prisoners crowded up behind the wire. We entered.

And now, let me tell this in the first person, for I was the least important person there, as you shall hear. There surged around me an evil-smelling horde. Men and boys reached out to touch me; they were in rags and the remnants of uniform. Death had already marked many of them, but they were smiling with their eyes. I looked out over that mass of men to the green fields beyond where well-fed Germans were ploughing.

A German, Fritz Kersheimer, came up and said, "May I show you round the camp? I've been here ten years." An Englishman stood to attention, saying, "May I introduce myself, delighted to see you, and can you tell me when some of our blokes will be along?" I told him soon and asked to see one of the barracks. It happened to be occupied by Czechoslovakians. When I entered, men crowded around, tried to lift me to their shoulders. They were too weak. Many of them could not get out of bed. I was told that this building had once stabled eighty horses. There were twelve hundred men in it, five to a bunk. The stink was beyond all description.

When I reached the center of the barracks, a man came up and said, "You remember me. I'm Peter Zenkl, one-time mayor of Prague." I remembered him, but did not recognize him. He asked about Benes and Jan Masaryk. I asked how many men had died in that building during the last month. They called the doctor; we inspected his records. There were only names in the little black book, nothing more—nothing of who these men were, what they had done, or hoped. Behind the names of those who had died there was a cross. I counted them. They totalled 242. Two hundred and forty-two out of twelve hundred in one month.

As I walked down to the end of the barracks, there was applause from the men too weak to get out of bed. It sounded like the hand clapping of babies; they were so weak. The doctor's name was Paul Heller. He had been there since 1938.

As we walked out into the courtyard, a man fell dead. Two others—they must have been over sixty—were crawling toward the latrine. I saw it but will not describe it.

In another part of the camp they showed me the children, hundreds of them. Some were only six. One rolled up his sleeve, showed me his number. It was tattooed on his arm. D-6030, it was. The others showed me their numbers; they will carry them till they die.

An elderly man standing beside me said, "The children, enemies of the state." I could see their ribs through their thin shirts. The old man said, "I am Professor Charles Richer of the Sorbonne." The children clung to my hands and stared. We crossed to the courtyard. Men kept coming up to speak to me and to touch me, professors from Poland, doctors from Vienna, men from all Europe. Men from the countries that made America.

We went to the hospital; it was full. The doctor told me that two hundred had died the day before. I asked the cause of death; he shrugged and said, "Tuberculosis, starvation, fatigue, and there are many who have no desire to live. It is very difficult." Dr. Heller pulled back the blankets from a man's feet to show me how swollen they were. The man was dead. Most of the patients could not move.

As we left the hospital I drew out a leather billfold, hoping that I had some money which would help those who lived to get home. Professor Richer from the Sorbonne said, "I should be careful of my wallet if I were you. You know there are criminals in this camp, too." A small man tottered up, saying, "May I feel the leather, please? You see, I used to make good things of leather in Vienna." Another man said, "My name is Walter Roeder. For many years I lived in Joliet. Came back to Germany for a visit and Hitler grabbed me."

I asked to see the kitchen; it was clean. The German in charge had been a Communist, had been at Buchenwald for nine years, had a picture of his daughter in Hamburg. He hadn't seen her for almost twelve years, and if I got to Hamburg, would I look her up? He showed me the daily ration—one piece of brown bread about as thick as your thumb, on top of it a piece of margarine as big as three sticks of chewing gum. That, and a little stew, was what they received every twenty-four hours. He had a chart on the wall; very complicated it was. There were little red tabs scattered through it. He said that was to indicate each ten men who died. He had to account for the rations, and he added, "We're very efficient here."

We went again into the courtyard, and as we walked we talked. The two doctors, the Frenchman and the Czech, agreed that about six thousand had died during March. Kersheimer, the German, added that back in the winter of 1939, when the Poles began to arrive without winter clothing, they died at the rate of approximately nine hundred a day. Five different men asserted that Buchenwald was the best concentration camp in Germany; they had had some experience of the others.

Dr. Heller, the Czech, asked if I would care to see the crematorium. He said it wouldn't be very interesting because the Germans had run out of coke some days ago and had taken to dumping the bodies into a great hole nearby. Professor Richer said perhaps I would care to see the small courtyard. I said yes. He turned and told the children to stay behind. As we walked across the square I noticed that the professor had a hole in his left shoe and a toe sticking out of the right one. He followed my eyes and said, "I regret that I am so little presentable, but what can one do?" At that point another Frenchman came up to announce that three of his fellow countrymen outside had killed three S.S. men and taken one prisoner. We proceeded to the small courtyard. The wall was about eight feet high; it adjoined what had been a stable or garage. We entered. It was floored with concrete.

There were two rows of bodies stacked up like cordwood. They were thin and very white. Some of the bodies were terribly bruised, though there seemed to be little flesh to bruise. Some had been shot through the head, but they bled but little. All except two were naked. I tried to count them as best I could and arrived at the conclusion that all that was mortal of more than five hundred men and boys lay there in two neat piles.

There was a German trailer which must have contained another fifty, but it wasn't possible to count them. The clothing was piled in a heap against the wall. It appeared that most of the men and boys had died of starvation; they had not been executed. But the manner of death seemed unimportant. Murder had been done at Buchenwald. God alone knows how many men and boys have died there during the last twelve years. Thursday I was told that there were more than twenty thousand in the camp. There had been as many as sixty thousand. Where are they now?

As I left that camp, a Frenchman who used to work for Havas in Paris came up to me and said, "You will write something about this, perhaps?" And he added, "To write about this you must have been here at least two years, and after that—you don't want to write any more."

I pray you to believe what I have said about Buchenwald. I have reported what I saw and heard, but only part of it. For most of it I have no words. Dead men are plentiful in war, but the living dead, more than twenty thousand of them in one camp. And the country round about was pleasing to the eye, and the Germans were well fed and well dressed. American trucks were rolling toward the rear filled with prisoners. Soon they would be eating American rations, as much for a meal as the men at Buchenwald received in four days.

If I've offended you by this rather mild account of Buchenwald, I'm not in the least sorry. I was there on Thursday, and many men in many tongues blessed the name of Roosevelt. For long years his name had meant the full measure of their hope. These men who had kept close company with death for many years did not know that Mr. Roosevelt would, within hours, join their comrades who had laid their lives on the scales of freedom.

Back in 1941, Mr. Churchill said to me with tears in his eyes, "One day the world and history will recognize and acknowledge what it owes to your President." I saw and heard the first installment of that at Buchenwald on Thursday. It came from men from all over Europe. Their faces, with more flesh on them, might have been found anywhere at home. To them the name "Roosevelt" was a symbol, the code word for a lot of guys named "Joe" who are somewhere out in the blue with the armor heading east. At Buchenwald they spoke of the President just before he died. If there be a better epitaph, history does not record it.

—From Edward Bliss, Jr. ed., In Search of Light: The Broadcasts of Edward R. Murrow, 1938–1961 (New York: Alfred A. Knopf, 1967), 91–95. Copyright © 1967 by the Estate of Edward R. Murrow. Reprinted by permission of Alfred A. Knopf Inc.

CAMPS

Auschwitz

DELOUSING

Primo Levi, an Italian chemist, was arrested by the Germans for resistance activities, deported to the AUSCHWITZ concentration camp complex in early 1944, and eventually put to work at the Monowitz-Buna subcamp. When the Auschwitz complex was evacuated, he and 800 other ill prisoners were left behind, where they were liberated by units of the Soviet Army on January 27, 1945. In one of the universal rituals of liberation, he was deloused by the Russian army.

Here too, as at every turn of our long itinerary, we were surprised to be greeted with a bath, when we had need of so many other things. But this was no bath of humiliation, no grotesque-devilish-sacral bath, no black-mass bath like the first one which had marked our descent into the concentration-camp universe, nor was it a functional, antiseptic, highly automatized bath, like that of our passage into American hands many months later: it was a bath in the Russian manner, to human measure, extemporaneous and crude.

I am not questioning that a bath was opportune for us in our condition: in fact it was necessary, and not unwelcome. But in that bath, and at each of those three memorable christenings, it was easy to perceive behind the concrete and literal aspect a great symbolic shadow, the unconscious desire of the new authorities, who absorbed us in turn within their own sphere, to strip us of the vestiges of our former life, to make of us new men consistent with their own models, to impose their brand upon us.

The robust arms of two Soviet nurses lifted us down from the cart: *"Po malu!"* ("gently, gently!"); these were the first Russian words I heard. They were two energetic and experienced girls. They led us to one of the installations of the Lager, which had been summarily restored, undressed us, made us lie down on the wooden laths that covered the floor, and with tender hands, but without too much regard, soaped, rubbed, massaged and dried us from head to foot.

The operation went smoothly and quickly for all of us, except for some moralistic-jacobin protests from Arthur, who proclaimed himself *libre citoyen*, and in whose subconscious the contact of those feminine hands upon his bare skin conflicted with ancestral taboos. But a serious obstacle intervened when it came to the turn of the last of our group.

None of us knew who he was, because he was in no condition to speak. He was a shadow, a bald little figure, twisted like a root, skeleton-like, knotted up by a horrible contraction of all his muscles; they had lifted him out of the cart bodily, like an inanimate block, and now he lay on the ground on his side, curled up and stiff, in a desperate position of defence, with his knees pressed up against his forehead, his elbows squeezed against his sides, and his hands like wedges, with the fingers pressing against his shoulders. The Russian sisters, perplexed, sought in vain to stretch him on his back, at which he let out shrill mouse-like squeaks: it was in any case a useless effort; his limbs yielded elastically under pressure, but as soon as they were released, they shot back to their initial position. Then the nurses came to a decision and carried him under the shower as he was; and because they had definite orders, they washed him as best they could, forcing the sponge and soap into the entangled knots of his body; finally, they rinsed him conscientiously, throwing a couple of buckets of tepid water over him.

Charles and I, naked and steaming, watched the scene with compassion and horror. When one of the arms was stretched out, we saw the tattooed number for a moment: he was a 200,000, one from the Vosges: *"Bon dieu, c'est un français!"* exclaimed Charles, and turned in silence towards the wall.

— From Primo Levi, If This Is A Man: Remembering Auschwitz *(New York: Summit Books, 1986), 140–41. First published in translation in* The Reawakening, © *The Bodley Head, 1967.*

Bergen-Belsen

THE BRITISH ENTER

Derek Sington was the first British army officer to arrive in BERGEN-BELSEN concentration camp after the Germans surrendered it under the terms of a limited German-British truce. In this excerpt he vividly describes that experience.

Back at Brigade headquarters a staff officer stopped us as we were pulling into the field where the caravans were standing.

"A message has just come through from division. They want you to go forward with your loud-speaker into this place, Belsen."

Col. Taylor, commanding the 63rd Anti-Tank Regt. had got the job of camp commandant of Belsen Camp. He was understandably pre-occupied when I called on him on April 15 at his headquarters in a wood fringing the Schwarmstedt-

Winsen road. Sixty thousand "political prisoners," some SS personnel and a raging epidemic of typhus. The responsibility was a daunting one.

He showed me a copy of the truce concluded between the General commanding 8th British Corps and the German Army Commander at Bergen-Belsen. Under its terms an area round Belsen was to be treated as "neutral," i.e., no shots would be fired into or out of this zone. A battalion of German infantry and a Hungarian regiment would remain at Belsen to guard the perimeter of the camp and prevent any mass break-out. And about 50 SS men, acting in a purely administrative capacity, would await the British commandant, to hand over the camp.

Colonel Taylor's instructions to me were to drive forward with the leading British tanks, enter Belsen Camp and make an announcement by loud-speaker.

This announcement was to tell the inmates of the camp that, although they were liberated from the Germans they must not leave the camp because of the danger of spreading typhus. They were to be told that the Hungarian regiment, which had been assisting the SS to guard the camp, would pass under British command, and continue to stop anyone from trying to leave. But they were to be assured that food and medical aid were being rushed up with all possible speed.

We arranged to meet Col. Taylor in the afternoon at Bergen where he was going to seek out the German Army colonel responsible for the Belsen area, and at mid-day we drove away.

We passed through Winsen and took the main road northeast. Here we caught up with the long cavalcade of tanks, scout cars and Bren carriers of the 23rd Hussars. After speaking to the Intelligence Officer, who leaned dust-covered from the turret of his tank to shout through the din of clanking tracks and roaring exhausts, we fell into line. The open country outside Winsen gave place to thick fragrant-smelling fir woods on either side of the road. The infantry were firing the thickets, in case of snipers, and the undergrowth blazed and crackled on each side of the long armoured convoy. Suddenly the Intelligence Officer shouted back to me:

"Two Germans from the concentration camp are coming down the road. See what you can find out from them."

We stopped the two figures, dressed in civilian suits, each carrying a small bundle. I asked them who they were.

"I am an Alsatian. I was arrested in 1943 for refusing to join the German Army."

"I come from Guben. My father had a pub which was closed down by the Party because former Social Democrats used to meet there."

Neither of the men had been long in Belsen. Both had been taken out of the camp, together with the other 600 German prisoners there, and shepherded away on foot by the outgoing SS. They had straggled and then darted into a wood. When the British troops who were clearing the woods had come to their hiding-place they had given themselves up.

They told me that the edge of the Belsen neutral zone was clearly marked with white notices, "Danger Typhus," and in five minutes we reached the first of these boards. Two unimpressive lance-corporals, one German, the other Hungarian—distinguishable by his greenish khaki uniform—stepped forward from the roadside. The German handed me a note. It was headed: "Allied Commander, do pay attention!" and was an invitation in rather bad English to the British commandant to meet the German Army commandant at Bergen. The Shermans roared past and we too drove on. Turning the next bend in the road we saw the camp entrance—a single pole across the roadway with wooden huts on either side. A group of smartly dressed officers stood waiting in front of it. We pulled off the road. Glancing at the uniforms we picked out the forked lightning badge of the SS, the khaki of a Hungarian captain wearing three rows of medals, and the field-grey of the Wehrmacht.

The group of soldiers saluted as I got out, and I asked one of them, an SS Hauptsturmführer, what was the state of the camp. He was a powerfully-built man, fat-faced, with a scar across one cheek, and he answered simply:

"They are calm at present."

"I propose to go in and make a loud-speaker announcement," I said.

The Hungarian captain stepped forward and said in a voice of extreme solicitude:

"I shouldn't. Seven people a day are dying here of 'fleck typhus'."

The powerfully-built, fat-faced SS officer, who was Josef Kramer [the camp commandant], added quickly:

"They're calm now. It would be unwise to risk a tumult."

I remembered the purpose of the "truce," which was to prevent the spread of typhus in the rear of the advancing British forces. And we waited for the arrival of Colonel Taylor.

A desultory conversation started with the SS, Hungarian and Wehrmacht officers.

"What type of prisoners have you got in here?" I asked Kramer.

"Homosexuals and professional criminals," he said, "as well as some Bibel Forscher [Jehovah's Witnesses]." He watched me carefully as he said this.

"And political prisoners?"

"Oh yes, there are the Häftlinge [prisoners]," he said in a friendly confiding sort of way.

"What's the total?"

"Forty thousand in this camp and fifteen thousand more in the overflow camp in the barracks up the road."

The British tanks were still roaring past the gates and a bull-like German Army officer with a red moustache said:

"I've got two nephews in England. Perhaps I shall meet them." He laughed genially.

A few minutes later Colonel Taylor pulled his jeep up in front of us. I asked for confirmation of my orders to enter the camp.

"Go in and make the announcement," he said, and drove on up the road towards Bergen.

Bergen-Belsen concentration camp was shown in graphic photographs by the weekly magazine the *Illustrated London News* on April 28, 1945.
(Illustrated London News)

LIKE A DORÉ DRAWING OF DAN
THE CAMP WITH THOUSANDS DEAD OR DY

THE CHARNEL HOUSE OF BELSEN'S CONCENTRATION CAMP, NEAR BREMEN, WHERE 30,000 DIED IN RECENT MONTHS, MAINLY THROUGH STARVATION : ONE OF THE COMMUNAL GRAVES.

ANOTHER OF THE COMMUNAL GRAVES AT BELSEN, FILLED MOSTLY BY UNCLOTHED BODIES LARGELY OF WOMEN WHO DIED OF STARVATION. MANY HAD BEEN MUTILATED.

THE WEAK AND DYING EVEN WERE MADE TO CARRY THE DEAD TO A PILE OF CORPSES, ALL WITHIN THE SIGHT OF SEVERAL HUNDRED CHILDREN. THOSE WHO WERE TOO SICK OR UNABLE TO GET TO THE COMPOUND FOR FOOD OR WATER DIED.

MORE TERRIBLE THAN EVEN THE IMAGINATION OF OF THE GHASTLY COMMUNAL GRA

A COMMON SIGHT AT BELSEN WERE DEAD MEN AND WOMEN WHO DIED OF EXHAUSTION. THERE WERE 60,000 HERDED IN THIS CAMP, WITH SOME 500 CHILDREN.

THE SCIENTIFIC DEHUMANISATION OF ENSLAVED VICTIMS AT BELSEN : A CLOSE-UP OF ONE EMACIATED BUT YET SURVIVING PERSON OVERHAULING RAGS OF DEAD PRISONERS.

Nothing that Dante could conceive of the Inferno we term Hell can exceed in agony the ghastly scenes at Belsen concentration camp, near Bremen, which was taken over on April 17 by General Dempsey's Second Army. This huge camp, which had contained some 60,000 civilians, was little more than a mass of dead and dying, mainly from starvation, typhus, and typhoid. The camp was declared a neutral area before we arrived and the Allied military authorities stood by to reach it at the earliest possible moment, for it was known that the living had been without food and water for over six days. It was found to be littered with dead and dying, and huts capable of housing only thirty persons were in many cases crowded with as many as 500. It was impossible to estimate the number of the dead among them: while frequently being too weak to move, they had been suffocated, while those still living were also too feeble to remove them. There were communal graves into which the dead were pitched, making the camp a charnel house of terrible sights. There was a pile between 60 and 80 yards long, 30 yards wide and 4 ft. high, of the naked bodies of women in full view of the living,

…E'S INFERNO: SCENES IN BELSEN.
…G OF STARVATION, TORTURE AND DISEASE.

THIS ODIOUS CAMP WAS LITTERED WITH DEAD AND DYING, AND WAS OCCUPIED BY SOME 60,000 CIVILIANS, WHO DIED IN HUNDREDS DAILY FROM DELIBERATE NEGLECT.

BLACKENED CORPSES LEFT TO ROT. GENERAL DEMPSEY'S SENIOR MEDICAL OFFICER, A BRIGADIER, DESCRIBED BELSEN AS "THE MOST HORRIBLE, FRIGHTFUL PLACE."

…NTE COULD CONCEIVE IN HIS "INFERNO": ANOTHER …OF GERMANY'S HELPLESS VICTIMS.

A HEAP OF THE RECENT DEAD LYING OUTSIDE A HUT: WOMEN ARE STRIPPING THE CORPSES OF THEIR CLOTHING FOR FUEL. THE HUTS WERE CAPABLE OF HOUSING ABOUT THIRTY PEOPLE, BUT IN MANY CASES AS MANY AS 500 WERE SQUEEZED IN.

THESE FEMALE FIENDS, WELL-NOURISHED, AT BELSEN, WIELDED THE LASH WITH EQUAL VIOLENCE AS S.S. MEN. THEY SHOWED ABSOLUTELY NO REMORSE WHEN ARRESTED.

HERE IS THE COMMANDANT OF THE CAMP, S.S. HAUPTSTURM JOSEF KRAMER, NOW UNDER CLOSE ARREST. HE WAS QUITE UNASHAMED OF HIS GHOULISH DEEDS.

including some 500 children, whose crime, like most of the others, was that they were Jewish-born. There was bunk accommodation for only 474 women out of 1704 acute typhus, typhoid, dysentery and tuberculosis cases, and 18,600 women who should have been in hospital were lying on hard, bare, bug-ridden boards. The men's situation was little better. Women in the so-called hospital, lying on bare boards, were so feeble they could scarcely raise themselves on their arms to cheer their rescuers. Mostly they died directly or indirectly of starvation. Food was distributed by block leaders supposed to organise matters and get food from the cook-house to the compounds. Those too weak to move died of starvation. So terrible was the situation that the prison doctors told General Dempsey's senior medical officer that cannibalism was going on. The commandant, said the doctor, "was a typical German brute—a sadistical, heavy-featured Nazi. He was quite unashamed." He was subsequently arrested. Food sent by the Red Cross to Jewish inmates had not been distributed. The revelations of Belsen and the other camps have horrified the entire civilised world.

I told Kramer to open the gate. He looked taken aback. "I can't do that without authority from the Wehrmacht commandant."

I waved to him with my hand to lift the barrier. The barrier went up.

"Stand on the running-board," I said, and he mounted it.

"You have to guide us round the camp, stopping at suitable points to make loud-speaker announcements."

We swung through the almost deserted front compound of the camp (it was, we afterwards learned, used only by the SS), and two hundred yards further we reached a high wooden gate with criss-cross wiring. It reminded me of the entrance to a zoo.

Once through the gate this resemblance was strengthened. On the left of the thoroughfare stood row upon row of green wooden huts, and we came into a smell of ordure —like the smell of a monkey-house. A sad blue smoke floated like a ground mist between the low buildings.

I had tried to visualise the interior of a concentration camp, but I had not imagined it like this. Nor had I imagined the strange simian throng, who crowded to the barbed wire fences surrounding the compounds, with their shaven heads and their obscene penitentiary suits, which were so dehumanising.

We had experienced gratitude and welcome in France, Belgium and Holland. We had been surrounded in Paris, embraced and thanked. In a Flemish village our truck had been loaded with tomatoes and ripe pears, and jugs of cool beer had been handed to us by joyful people.

But the half-credulous cheers of these almost lost men, of these clowns in their terrible motley, who had once been Polish officers, land-workers in the Ukraine, Budapest doctors and students in France, impelled a stronger emotion, and I had to fight back my tears.

One man standing in the gateway to a compound wore a normal blue suit and smiled a greeting. While our loud-speakers were calling out the announcement I went and shook hands with him.

"I am a Dutchman," he said, "I used to work for the *Nieure Rottendamsche Courant.*"

He was tall and red-haired. He had fought in the International Brigade and was, we discovered afterwards, one of the great figures of the German concentration camps.

As we rolled on through the camp, crowds of prisoners began to surge through the barbed wire into the thoroughfare. Kramer leaned towards me:

"Now the tumult is beginning," he said.

Suddenly a German soldier began firing his rifle into the air. Gradually he lowered the muzzle until it was firing only just over the heads of the prisoners. I ran across to him and covered him with my revolver.

"Stop shooting," I said.

He stopped firing. But suddenly a dozen striped figures jumped into the crowd hitting again and again with sticks and packing-case strips.

No leaps in a ballet could have astonished me as did these kangaroo jumps. They were like prancing zebras, these creatures in broad-striped garments, careering here and there, smiting to left and to right, bending double with the impetus of the blows they struck. Or was it a cattle-drive, this onrush of scores of creatures running the gauntlet of fearful blows? And why did they not strike back, defend themselves, instead of dodging, surging on or falling down?

Half-way across the road I saw a thin creature on his back trying to ward off blow after blow from a thick stick.

I tried to understand what I saw. Could these 'policemen' be the political prisoners suppressing criminals among the inmates by the only possible means?

I did not know that they were hut-leaders 'keeping order' for the SS, nor that the stampeding mob was making for the kitchen beyond the highway. I did not understand that mortal starvation conditioned all happenings in the camp.

Passing the big kitchen we came out through a second wire gate opposite the smaller of the two women's camps. Crowds of women, all in the hideous penitentiary garb, lined the roadside. One of them called out in French:

"You must deliver us. It is *frightful*, this camp."

I went to her and she said: "We are 400 French-women here—all political prisoners. You *must* deliver us."

We turned and came up the main thoroughfare. The men were still cheering, and one wraith-like figure, with a crutch, threw it down and fell on his knees as our car passed, clasping his hands in thanksgiving. We turned left through a barbed wire gateway, entered the larger women's camp, halted and began our announcement.

In a few seconds the car was surrounded by hundreds of women. They cried and wailed hysterically, uncontrolledly, and no word from the loud-speakers could be heard. The compounds of the camp were planted with young birch trees, and the women plucked leafy sprigs and small branches and hurled them on to the car. One branch fell on Kramer's shoulder. He brushed it away.

We drove back to the main entrance. Kramer jumped off the running board and I said to him:

"You've made a fine hell here."

"It has become one in the last few days," he replied.

Half a mile up the road we saw the first concrete buildings of the Panzer Training School. A dozen or so of these formed an overflow concentration camp, housing 15,000 men who had been brought from the Dora Camp near Nordhausen, five days before. Kramer had turned them away, and the German Army commandant had accommodated them, together with their SS gaolers, in these buildings.

Our announcement here was again drowned by the cheering, and we left immediately for the Wehrmacht Kommandantur [commander's headquarters].

Ceremony and an attempt at an 'official front' were being staged at the Kommandantur. Colonel Harries, commander of the Wehrmacht battalion left behind to help guard the concentration camp, and Colonel Schmidt, whom I had seen in the farmyard at Schwarmstedt three days before, were talking to Colonel Taylor. The two German colonels were dapper and immaculate, and very conscious of their role as trustees of the 'Belsen truce.' Soon after I joined them a British medical officer came in.

"There have been some casualties down at the concentration camp."

Immediately afterwards the telephone rang. A German captain answered it, then turned to us, and said:

"It appears that a loud-speaker went into the camp and that it has started a disturbance."

Colonel Taylor said to Colonel Schmidt: "Who is causing casualties in the camp? Under the agreement only SS *administrative* personnel may be in the camp and they should be unarmed."

"They may have pistols," said Colonel Schmidt with a shrug of his shoulders.

Colonel Taylor ordered the German colonels to go down with us immediately to the camp.

Kramer came up and saluted as we alighted from our cars at the gate.

"Tell him that all SS must hand in their arms within half-an-hour," said Colonel Taylor to me.

I did so.

"Without arms I can't be responsible for the camp," answered Kramer.

"No, but you can show the British officers how it's administered."

"I can't enter the camp unarmed."

"In that case tell him," said Colonel Taylor, "he can keep his arms for the present but that for every inmate of the camp who is shot one SS man will be executed."

I asked Kramer why he needed to carry arms in the camp. He answered: "To protect the food-stores." "What reserve of food was there in the camp?" "For two days." "What meals did the inmates get?" "Turnip soup in the morning and turnip soup in the evening. Bread as often as possible." "What was the water supply?" "The main depended on Hanover and had been cut by bombing. Four basins of static water were now the only source."

Colonel Taylor ordered Kramer to show us his office. He took us to one of the huts. When we were seated he seemed more at his ease. He was once more "the camp commandant" and threw a leg nonchalantly over the side of his arm-chair.

Colonel Taylor demanded the personal documents of the 40,000 prisoners in the camp.

"They have all been destroyed."

"On whose authority?"

"That of the Hauptwirtschaftsamt in Berlin."

"Are there none left?"

"Perhaps 2,000."

"Get the 2,000 at once."

Kramer left the room and returned in a few moments with an SS Unterscharführer, who stood rigidly to attention, his thumbs glued to the seams of his trousers. Kramer gave him an order.

"Jawohl, Herr Hauptsturmführer!"

And the minion clicked to the salute and departed. In a few minutes he came back to report that no documents could be found.

The Chief Medical Officer of 2nd British Army, Brigadier Glyn Hughes, joined us, and we all walked out of the camp office into the compound.

At this moment a German Army captain, who had been much in evidence in the camp earlier in the afternoon, hurried up from the direction of the inmates' huts.

"The kitchens are being stormed," he said.

"Come on, let's see for ourselves," said a British officer.

The British party, consisting of about six officers and a few NCO's, walked towards the huts, Kramer and the German Army officer walking in front.

After we had passed through the tall wire gate the cheering began again. Hundreds of pyjama-clad figures were milling about on the highway. There were cries of "How do you do?" and "God Save the King." But the cheering and cries of welcome sounded unexpectedly timid and uncertain, which was understandable in the midst of violence and death. The sound of shots rang out from the far end of the camp.

Half-way down the main highway stood the kitchen, a long wooden shed equipped with thirty large cauldrons. This was the kitchen which "had been stormed." When we walked into it only the SS supervisor was there.

"I see no storming going on," I said.

The SS supervisor lifted the lid of one of the cauldrons and pointed to the level of the soup in it. This was about a foot below the top.

"All that has been taken," he said.

"And you call that 'storming the kitchen'?"

I noted down this SS man's name as a trouble-maker and went out to Kramer.

"Is this the extent of your 'riot'?" I asked.

"No, there's also been an attack on the potato-patch."

"Take us there," I said.

Kramer led us through the tall wire gate at the end of the camp.

In front stood the dismal little crematorium of brick, with its thin chimney. On our left was the small women's camp; on our right an undulating straw patch. Dusk was falling, but there was movement on the patch of straw. The emaciated figure of a woman, clad in black, her face yellow, her eyes shining like coals, was kneeling there. With her hands she was pulling up the straw, striving to uncover the potatoes underneath.

Kramer turned to me: "You see what I mean," he said. Just then the Chief Medical Officer pointed to something on the ground. "That fellow's in a bad way," he said.

I looked in the direction indicated and saw a man lying there with blood running over his face.

"He ought to be got on to a stretcher."

I turned to the nearest SS man.

"Go and get a stretcher—at the double!" He trotted away.

Suddenly we heard screaming coming from the potato

AS DORÉ MIGHT HAVE CONCEIVED IT: BELSEN DEATH CAMP,

DRAWN BY OUR WAR ARTIST, CAPTAIN BRYAN DE GRINEAU

THE PATHETIC PLIGHT OF THOSE YET LIVING AMID THE DEAD: A SCENE IN A WOMAN'S SECTION OF

In our last issue we said that the photographs published were reminiscent of a Doré drawing of Dante's Inferno. These pages and the preceding one show how the scene affected our Artist as compared with the camera-men, and give some idea as to the way Doré, were he living, would have treated the subject. Not the least ghastly aspect of the Belsen Camp, in which the scientific extermination of tens of thousands of unfortunate victims of various nations was deliberately practised by means of starvation, thirst, and disease, is here depicted by our Special Artist on the spot. Corpses of the, as yet, unburied victims lie grotesquely before a large tent filled with bodies of the dead, mingled with those yet living but too enfeebled to move. The dead at least are freed from the agonies of this bestial camp and

WHERE PRISONERS WERE SCIENTIFICALLY EXTERMINATED.

ON A SPECIAL VISIT TO BELSEN INTERNMENT CAMP.

BELSEN CAMP, WHERE SUFFERING SURVIVORS BECAME OBLIVIOUS TO THEIR GHASTLY SURROUNDINGS.

its sadistic cruelties, but the drawing especially stresses the pitiful plight of those who yet breathe but can scarcely be described as living. Here, in one of the women's sections, were those who, if survivors, were existing among the dead of this charnel house, and so inured to horror that they had become indifferent to their surroundings. The fearful stench—as our War Artist describes the scene—the

clouds of disease-infected dust, the complete cessation of all civilised decency, had reduced them to mere animals, and even, horrible to relate, to cannibalism. This terrible degradation of humanity is the worst crime civilisation can record throughout the ages and no punishment devised can offer sufficient retribution for these infamies.

patch. Lying on the straw was a man in great agony. He was jerking the upper part of his body up and down. Soon he became still and his screaming stopped.

As we walked on we came to another body, then to another, then to another. . . .

Sergeant C. came over to me.

"Why shouldn't Kramer carry one of these people away?" he asked.

I looked at Kramer.

"Pick up that man and take him to hospital!"

Kramer flushed, threw back his head, and stepped a pace back. He still felt himself "the commandant of the camp."

"Pick up that man!" I covered him with my revolver. Kramer came forward and stooped. I pushed my revolver into his back. He hoisted the body over his shoulder and ambled away.

It was pitiable to think of these men shot like rats on the very day of liberation. At first I thought: Could they not have restrained themselves and waited just three hours for the camp to be taken over? But such reflections were unimaginative and childlike. In their delirium of hunger they had lost the power to reason. Words like 'liberation,' 'tomorrow,' 'wait' had lost all meaning for them. They were consumed by the famine which was burning them up, possessed only by the wild urge to eat and survive.

It was not only the 'plunderers' who had been massacred that afternoon. Days afterwards a Hungarian Jewess told me how her Slovak friend (in captivity for fighting in the Slovak revolt of 1944) had been shot through the eye in the women's camp, while they were walking together near the kitchen.

"She was such a splendid girl. It was so terrible."

The Slovak girl had died in the night inside their hut. She had said: "If only this had happened a week ago; today it is sad. But it is good to know that all of you are free."

When Kramer returned to the potato-patch near the crematorium it was swarming with women. The British soldiers urged them with gestures to go back to their huts. Three white-faced, bright-eyed women called out: "Goodnight, boys!" It was like some fantastic closing-time.

Between two of the huts on the women's camp a grey cloud of smoke was rising. Little fires were burning in the compounds, and women were squatting by them throwing sticks into the flames.

"What are they burning?" I asked.

"Their huts," Kramer answered.

"And why?"

"Freedom," he replied, "soon the whole camp will be ablaze."

— *From* Belsen *(Tel Aviv: Irgun Sheerit Hapleita Me'haezor Habriti, 1957), 69–79.*

FROM THE GRAVE TO A NEW LIFE

While serving with the Yugoslavian army, Rabbi Zwi Azaria (Helfgott) was captured by the Germans. In 1945 he and several comrades escaped from the forced EVACUATION of their (unidentified) camp and were liberated by the British. After a short time in a DISPLACED PERSONS center, he managed to reach BERGEN-BELSEN soon after its liberation. He stayed at Belsen until 1948, when he was able to emigrate to Israel.

Long columns of prisoners-of-war were still being dragged from place to place across Germany in 1945. In April of that year four of us escaped from a German-driven column of four hundred-and-fifty Yugoslav-Jewish officers. We marched through the night, without knowing where we were going, and arrived at dawn in a wood near the town of Celle. It was there that we were liberated by the British some days later. The war was not yet over, and we had to stay in a British camp until things could sort themselves out. This is how I came to be in Nienburg on the Weser. As a Rabbi I was given a room in a private house.

One morning I switched on the wireless and I picked up the following announcement:

"The notorious Bergen-Belsen concentration camp was liberated this morning by Allied troops. Over fifty thousand Jews were found in the camp."

It was for the first time that I heard the name of Belsen. Perhaps some of my family were there? . . . I do not know how long I was in a trance. A knock on the door brought me back to reality. A captain and two lieutenants entered the room and asked whether I had heard the announcement about Belsen.

We decided to try and get there at once. The British officer in charge of our camp hesitated. The war was still on, he said. It took some time to make him change his mind. After all, I was a Rabbi, and there were liberated Jews at Belsen. They might need me. And how could he expect us to remain calm while there was a hope of finding a relative in Belsen?

At last the British officer gave me a jeep and an escort of three Jewish officers. We left for Belsen. . . .

It was a long journey. Bridges were demolished and roads blocked. But we got there. First we spotted those signs of warning against typhus, and then the gates of Belsen. But the writ of our camp commander was not valid at Belsen, and we could not enter the camp. I asked the guard whether I could see an army chaplain, explaining that I was a Rabbi. It did not take long and a British captain with a Magen David on his cap stood before us. He told me that I could come with him, as they needed a Rabbi, but my comrades could not go in.

Soon we came to a small barracks. Upon entering it I saw at a table another Jewish chaplain, a major, and next to him a Catholic chaplain. The Major was a picture of dejection; the Catholic chaplain wept unashamedly. They made a sign to me to go and see for myself.

I soon saw what they meant. I shall never forget the mass of human beings and corpses in the barracks I entered. Suddenly a weak voice spoke unto me: "Help me, Zwi, please." . . . It was an old friend. . . .

I ran out to look for a doctor. I shouted hysterically: "Doctor, doctor; is there a doctor here?" . . . As I came back I found my friend completely still. His eyes seemed to say "thank you." He was at peace. . . .

When I came back to the other chaplains, they told me that they were helpless in this sea of misery. I rushed back to Nienburg and told the officers at the camp what I saw. We managed to organise some sort of relief by collecting food in the town, and we went back to Belsen. This time there was another Rabbi with me, a chaplain of the Polish forces. He and I took over the macabre task of giving the numerous dead in the camp a decent burial.

There were countless corpses. We had not only to perform the burial rites but to carry them to the mass graves. Former Hungarian guards helped to dig the graves on British orders.

People were still dying after liberation. They had gone too far to be saved. I was running from barracks to barracks and from hut to hut making notes of the new dead. There were still about 200 a day.

At night I used to sleep in the attic of one of the hospital huts. I could find no other place. It was Dr. Hadassa Bimko, at the time in charge of that hospital, who took pity on me and let me sleep there.

After several days of burying the dead and reciting the Kaddish all day long my feelings were numb. I was longing to be dead and buried myself. I had a nightmarish idea that these dead were the last Jews upon earth, and I was performing my last mission before joining them. . . .

One day I was called to one of the barracks. A woman was waiting for me there, and she said: "Rabbi, my daughter died this morning. Could you, please, bury her in a grave of her own?" I tried to explain to her that this was against orders, but she repeated her plea, and I gave in. Two men helped me to bring the body to the cemetery and to dig a grave. The mother was there. I had to hurry so as not to be caught ignoring strict military orders. I said Kaddish quickly and began to fill the grave. As I was about to finish the mother stopped me and said in a clear voice: "God Almighty, I thank Thee for thy mercy to have given me the opportunity to give my child a decent burial." I led the lady back to her barracks, and have never seen her again. . . . But I shall never forget her.

— From Belsen *(Tel Aviv: Irgun Sheerit Hapleita Me'haezor Habriti, 1957), 117–20.*

Buchenwald

BUCHENWALD REVOLT

As the Allies approached the BUCHENWALD concentration camp in April 1945, a highly organized group of communist prisoners revolted on April 11, the day the Americans entered the camp. Czech, Polish, Yugoslav, and French internees, as well as a contingent of Russian prisoners of war, participated in this revolt, taking prisoner a number of SS men before the Americans arrived. Here Ivan Smirnov, one of Russian prisoners, describes the revolt as well as the events of the few days leading to it

The first signs of open resistance appeared early in April 1945. The SS *Kommandantur* [commander's Headquarters] radioed an order for all prisoners to report to the *Appellplatz* [parade ground] for evacuation. The political centres met and decided to resist evacuation and ignore the SS order. This act of open disobedience virtually marked the beginning of the rising. Everyone understood that evacuation meant extermination. It was only too evident that the SS men would stop at nothing realizing their diabolical plans.

On the evening of April 3, the camp radio carried the SS *Lagerführer*'s [camp commandant] new order: "All Jews in the blocks and in the *Revier* [camp infirmary] will immediately assemble on the *Appellplatz* for evacuation." The sinister purport of this order was obvious. The organization mobilized all its forces to save our Jewish comrades. Bibik, Motrich, and Tereshchuk, all three of the Soviet underground, together with Tingänger, a German Communist from Frankfurt, were able to save the lives of 370 Jewish prisoners on that day of terror by hiding them under the barracks floors, in the piggery, in demolished cellars, and garrets. We supplied many others with triangular red patches with the letter "R" which all Russian prisoners wore on their jacket fronts.

On April 4, the *Lagerführer* summoned forty-six political prisoners, veterans of Buchenwald, the majority of whom were German Communists and active members of the underground, to the camp gates. The SS had decided to behead the organization by killing off our bravest fighters. The International Centre unanimously resolved to oppose this. The forty-six disappeared. The *Lagerführer* made a new move: he ordered the chiefs of every block in which the forty-six had been registered to appear at the gates. Once again the centre gave instructions to ignore the Nazi order. The camp was openly defiant.

We expected the SS to enforce its orders and were prepared to rise up in arms according to our plan. But the Nazis had not made up their minds yet. On April 6, they ordered 6,000 prisoners to be sent on jobs outside the camp. A medical commission examined the prisoners near the gates. The old and the weak were turned down. This

BUCHENWALD AND LANGENSTEIN: RECORDED HORRORS OF TWO TORTURE CAMPS.

HUMAN WRECKS IN THE PRISON HOSPITAL AT LANGENSTEIN, ONE OF THE GERMAN TORTURE CAMPS OVER-RUN BY THE ALLIED ADVANCE. THIS CAMP, WHERE THE DYING SHARED BUNKS WITH THE DEAD, WAS FREED BY ADVANCE TROOPS OF THE U.S. NINTH ARMY.

THE WASTED BODY OF THIS WRETCHED HUMAN BEING, WHO ONCE WEIGHED 190 LBS., IS TYPICAL OF THE CONDITION OF PRISONERS IN THE LANGENSTEIN CAMP, WHOSE STARVED INMATES WERE FORCED TO WORK TWELVE HOURS A DAY.

CIVILIANS OF WEIMAR BEING FORCED TO GAZE ON ONE OF THE VICTIMS OF GERMAN BESTIALITY IN THE NOTORIOUS BUCHENWALD TORTURE CAMP. THE BODY, CLAD IN THE STRIPED RAGS WHICH CLOTHED THE INMATES, IS DANGLING FROM A HOOK.

ANOTHER SCENE WHICH THE CITIZENS OF WEIMAR WERE FORCED TO WITNESS— A TRUCKLOAD OF TORTURED AND MURDERED PRISONERS IN THE BUCHENWALD CAMP, WHOSE HORRORS THE CITIZENS MADE NO ATTEMPTS TO PREVENT.

THIS PITIFUL HEAP OF ASHES AND BONES IS ONE DAY'S HARVEST OF THE BESTIALITY OF THE BUCHENWALD CONCENTRATION CAMP, WHERE THOUSANDS OF HUMAN BEINGS WERE TORTURED TO DEATH AND THEIR SHRUNKEN CORPSES BURNED.

THESE VICTIMS OF GERMAN SADISM AT BUCHENWALD COULD NOT BE BURNED TO ASH AND BONE, BECAUSE THEIR S.S. TORTURERS HAD RUN OUT OF FUEL FOR THEIR FURNACES JUST BEFORE THE ARRIVAL OF U.S. THIRD ARMY TROOPS.

These final photographic records of German bestiality and sadism come from the notorious torture camp of Buchenwald, on the outskirts of Weimar, and from another torture camp at Langenstein, captured by the U.S. Ninth Army. Some of the pitiful human wreckage found in these centres of horror was still living; the rest was shrunken corpses and mountains of ash and charred bones. Their only crime was a dislike of Hitler and his ways. For this they had been tortured, starved, and beaten to death in cold blood. Their screams, and the evidence of their sufferings as lorry-loads of corpses and human ashes passed daily from the camps, were heard and seen by the German citizens of neighbouring towns, who did nothing to alleviate their lot. These German civilians have thus shown themselves to be willing accessories of a crime against humanity, and must share the collective responsibility of their nation for the cruelties practised by their chosen Government. The pictures here, and on preceding pages, carry the lesson to be taught to future generations of the free nations of the world that never again must the German race be allowed to regain a position in which it can systematically torture and exterminate defenceless peoples.

The horrors of Buchenwald were graphically portrayed in a special supplement to the April 28, 1945 issue of *Illustrated London News*, the British illustrated weekly. (Illustrated London News) prompted all the political centres to gain time by sending their old and weak to the gates.

The commission rejected these men and sent them back into the camp. But, on request of the underground, they trudged back to the gates along other streets. These tactics helped the camp to survive yet another day and successfully sabotage the evacuation of 6,000 men.

The crisis came to a head on April 8. After the *Lagerführer* thrice repeated a hysterical order for all prisoners to line up on the *Appellplatz* and no one obeyed, he sent some 800 furious SS men armed with submachine-guns, hand-grenades and automatics into the camp. There was much firing and many prisoners were killed or wounded. Though backed up by arms, the SS men were only able to drag out a small group of prisoners.

Despite our losses, we regarded our resistance on that day as a new victory.

On April 10, the Russian military and political centre agreed to evacuate a group of prisoners from Buchenwald, instructing them to scatter on the way. This plan was fulfilled.

On April 11, the struggle against evacuation finally erupted into open revolt. On the morning of that day we heard the booming of heavy guns in the west. We realized that the impending climax beyond the camp walls might very well hasten our own end. Indeed, our agents advised us that the Nazis were planning a blood-bath that night. At an emergency meeting of the united camp centre we set 3:15 P.M. as the hour of armed revolt. Immediately before the storming of the Buchenwald stronghold, meetings were held in every barracks. The commissars read the appeal of the Russian military and political centre. The text follows.

"Comrades! Nazi Germany, which has shaken the world by its monstrous atrocities, is crumbling under the blows of the Soviet Army, the Allied troops, and the weight of its own crimes. Vienna is surrounded, the troops of the Soviet Army are pressing towards Berlin, the Allies are 25 miles west of Hannover; Suhl and Gotha have fallen and the battle is on for Erfurt.

"Bloody Nazism, sensing its own doom, has reached the final stage of brutality and, already in its death throes, is trying to destroy us. But its last hour has struck. The time of reckoning has come. The military and political leadership of the camp has ordered us to launch our last and ruthless battle at 3:15 P.M. Rise like one man and win your liberation! Death to the Nazi beasts! And may he be damned for ever who forgets his duty and flinches in the last and merciless battle! Heroic is our path. In our heroic struggle victory will be ours!

"Like one man, faithful to military discipline, to the orders and instructions of the commanders and commissars, defying death and burning with hatred for our enemies— forward along our difficult but heroic path to liberty!

"Long live freedom!"

Apart from the massacre of April 8, dead silence had reigned in the camp during the period it had defied evacua-

tion orders. Suddenly, the silence was rent with jubilant, excited shouting. Men openly brandished their arms. The hatred that had grown during years of imprisonment turned into unbridled fury. But each man knew his place in the fighting ranks. The platoons, companies, and battalions began the assault.

The first to plunge into battle was the shock battalion of the Stone Brigade, led by Valentin Logunov. Almost at once the Wooden Brigade's shock battalion, led by Chorny, Tsatsura, and Khazanov, launched its attack. The reserve battalions could wait no longer and joined in. They tore the barbed wire down with spades, picks, crow-bars, and battering-rams made of logs.

In the Pathology Block an assault group waited for its chance to seize the gates, which were considered inaccessible, since several machine-guns were installed on a two-storied veranda above the gates. The SS men who manned the towers scattered after some firing: the number of the attackers and their organized tactics proved too much for them.

Other units encountered little resistance during the capture of the SS quarters and its arsenal. Inside an hour every prisoner was armed.

Georgy Ostapchuk from Barracks No. 30 displayed exceptional valour at this decisive hour. There were many courageous Soviet men in the same barracks. Unfortunately, it is impossible to recall their names after all these years.

The Russian attack was supported in their own sectors by detachments of Germans, Czechs, Poles, Yugoslavs, and Frenchmen. On April 11, we took about 150 Nazi prisoners.

— From F. Solasko, ed., War Behind Barbed Wire: Reminiscences of Buchenwald Ex-Prisoners of War *(Moscow: Foreign Languages Publishing House, 1959), 92–96.*

GENERAL PATTON'S REACTION

Gen. George S. PATTON, Commander of the U.S. 3rd Army and one of the most colorful American generals, made public and private statements on the horrors he saw in both OHRDRUF and BUCHENWALD during an inspection visit soon after the two camps were liberated.

GSP, Jr., Press Conference, Herzfeld, Germany, April 13, 1945

Patton: If any of you haven't visited the charnel house near here, you should go. It is the most horrible sight I have ever seen. We had as many soldiers as possible . . . visit it so as to know that kind of people they are fighting. I think they were duly impressed, and I told them to tell their friends . . .

Question: What is holding the Germans together?

Patton: Fear of "They." Everybody is afraid of everybody else. They say if we surrender they will raise hell with Willie or Charlie. I do not believe there will be much underground stuff.

We have found at a place four miles north of Weimar a similar camp only much worse . . .

I told the press to go up and . . . build up another page of the necessary evidence as to the brutality of the Germans.

Diary, April 15

The political prisoners who were sent here to die were fed 800 calories a day and died on the average—so it is said—of 100 a night.

I went through two of the buildings. On each side were four tiers of bunks in which the inmates lay at right angles to the wall. They looked exactly like animated mummies and seemed to me on about the same level of intelligence. When we went through they attempted to cheer but were too feeble.

We then went to the place where they had apparently put the finishing touches on those who had died or were about to die. In a basement which was entered by a chute, they had a number of iron hooks on the wall like those you hang the side of a beef on. To these hooks they had a short piece of stout cord with a loop spliced on each end. This was put around a man's neck. Two men then lifted him and the loops were placed over the hook. If anyone showed signs of life, they had a club like a potato masher with which they bashed in the brains.

Upstairs there were six furnaces much like a baker's oven, connected with the basement by an elevator. Apparently they put six bodies on the elevator at a time, hoisted them up to the furnaces, and put them in.

— *From Martin Blumenson,* The Patton Papers, 1940–1945 *(Boston: Houghton Mifflin Co., 1974), 685–87. Copyright © 1974 by Martin Blumenson. Reprinted by permission of Houghten-Mifflin Co. All rights reserved.*

Dachau

THE CAPTURE OF DACHAU

Felix Sparks was a lieutenant colonel commanding a battalion of the 157th Infantry Regiment (45th Division) as it advanced deep into Germany in April 1945. When driving toward Munich on April 29, he and his men encountered DACHAU *concentration camp, just north of that city. Although briefed about the location of the camp, Sparks received no orders to liberate it.*

By the late evening of April 28, 1945, we were less than thirty miles from Munich. Shortly after midnight, I received the regimental attack order for the next day. I was ordered to resume the attack at 0730 the next morning, with the mission of entering Munich. The order stated that, if my task force encountered any delay because of German oppo-

sition, the following first and second battalions of our regiment would continue the attack into Munich by bypassing the resistance area. I was also informed that the concentration camp near the city of Dachau would be in my attack area, but my orders did not include the taking of the camp. At that time, I knew virtually nothing about Dachau, except that it was a concentration camp near the city of Dachau. . . .

Soldiers of the 157th Infantry Regiment first set foot [in Dachau] on the morning of April 29, 1945. The initial shock was experienced even before entering the camp. The first evidence of the horror to come was a string of about forty railway cars on a siding near the camp entrance. Each car was loaded with emaciated human corpses, both men and women. A hasty search by the stunned infantrymen revealed no signs of life among the hundreds of still bodies. Few words were spoken as the grim-faced soldiers deployed in battle formation towards the camp itself.

At 0730 on the morning of April 29, the task force had resumed the attack with companies L and K and the tank battalion as the assault force. The attack zone assigned to Company L was through the city of Dachau, but did not include the concentration camp, a short distance outside of the city. Company I was designated as the reserve unit, with the mission of mopping up any resistance bypassed by the assault forces. Shortly after the attack began, I received a radio message from the regimental commander ordering me to proceed immediately to take the Dachau concentration camp. The order also stated: "Upon capture, post an airtight guard and allow no one to enter or leave."

At the time I received the order, it was not feasible to extract the two assault companies from the attack. I therefore directed the commander of Company I, the reserve company, to attack the camp. Dachau was not included in the original operations order for the day, but from my map I determined that it was only a mile or so off to my left flank. I advised the company commander that I would accompany him and would attach a section of machine guns from Company M to his command. A forward observer team from the 158th Field Artillery was already with the company. A small motorized patrol from the regimental I&R [intelligence and reconnaissance] Platoon was also dispatched to the Dachau area.

As the main gate to the camp was closed and locked, we scaled the brick wall surrounding the camp. As I climbed over the wall following the advancing soldiers, I heard rifle fire to my right front. The lead elements of the company had reached the confinement area and were disposing of the SS troops manning the guard towers, along with a number of vicious guard dogs. By the time I neared the confinement area, the brief battle was almost over.

After I entered the camp over the wall, I was not able to see the confinement area and had no idea where it was. My vision was obscured by the many buildings and barracks which were outside the confinement area. The confinement area itself occupied only a small portion of the total camp area. As I went further into the camp, I saw some men from

Company I collecting German prisoners. Next to the camp hospital, there was an L-shaped masonry wall, about eight feet high, which had been used as a coal bin. The ground was covered with coal dust, and a narrow gauge railroad track, laid on top of the ground, led into the area. The prisoners were being collected in this semi-enclosed area.

As I watched, about fifty German troops were brought in from various directions. A machine gun squad from Company I was guarding the prisoners. After watching for a few minutes, I started for the confinement area, after taking directions from one of my soldiers. After I had walked away for a short distance, I heard the machine gun guarding the prisoners open fire. I immediately ran back to the gun and kicked the gunner off the gun with my boot. I then grabbed him by the collar and said: "What the hell are you doing?" He was a young private about 19 years old and was crying hysterically. His reply to me was: "Colonel, they were trying to get away." I doubt that they were, but in any event he killed about twelve of the prisoners and wounded several more. I placed a noncom on the gun and headed towards the confinement area.

It was the foregoing incident which has given rise to wild claims in various publications that most or all of the German prisoners captured at Dachau were executed. Nothing could be further from the truth. The total number of German guards killed at Dachau during that day most certainly did not exceed fifty, with thirty probably being a more accurate figure. The regimental records for that date indicate that over a thousand German prisoners were brought to the regimental collecting point. Since my task force was leading the regimental attack, almost all of the prisoners were taken by the task force, including several hundred from Dachau.

The scene near the entrance to the confinement area numbed my senses. Dante's Inferno seemed pale compared to the real hell of Dachau. A row of small cement structures near the prison entrance contained a coal-fired crematorium, a gas chamber, and rooms piled high with naked and emaciated human corpses. As I turned to look over the prison yard with unbelieving eyes, I saw a large number of dead inmates lying where they had fallen in the last few hours or days before our arrival. Since all the many bodies were in various stages of decomposition, the stench of death was overpowering.

During the early period of our entry into the camp, a number of Company I men, all battle hardened veterans, became extremely distraught. Some cried, while others raged. Some thirty minutes passed before I could restore order and discipline. During that time, the over thirty thousand camp prisoners still alive began to grasp the significance of the events taking place. They streamed from their crowded barracks by the hundreds and were soon pressing at the confining barbed wire fence. They began to shout in unison, which soon became a chilling roar. At the same time, several bodies were being tossed about and torn apart by hundreds of hands. I was told later that those being killed at

that time were "informers." After about ten minutes of screaming and shouting, the prisoners quieted down. At that point, a man came forward at the gate and identified himself as an American soldier. We immediately let him out. He turned out to be Major Rene Guiraud of our OSS. He informed me that he had been captured earlier while on an intelligence mission and sentenced to death, but the sentence was never carried out. I sent him back to regimental headquarters.

Within about an hour of our entry, events were under control. Guard posts were set up, and communications were established with the inmates. We informed them that we could not release them immediately but that food and medical assistance would arrive soon. The dead, numbering about nine thousand, were later buried with the forced assistance of the good citizens of the city of Dachau.

Fearful that the inmates would tear down the gate to their prison area, I posted a number of soldiers at that point. While I was standing near the gate, three jeeps from the 42nd Infantry Division approached the gate area. Apparently someone, without my knowledge, had opened the main gate to the camp area. The first jeep contained Brigadier General Linden and a woman reporter, by the name of Margaret Higgins. The general informed me that the reporter wished to enter the compound to interview the inmates.

At that time, a sea of inmates was pressed against the gate, awaiting an opportunity to get out. I advised the general that my specific orders were to prevent anyone from entering or leaving the compound, until otherwise advised by my regimental commander. While I was explaining this to the general, the woman reporter ran forward to the gate and removed the restraining crossbar. The prisoners immediately surged forward, creating a brief period of pandemonium. I ordered my men to open fire over the heads of the prisoners and rush the gate. After a brief struggle, the men closed and secured the gate.

It had already been a most trying day. I therefore requested the general and his party to leave and directed one of my men to escort them from the camp. The good general was a dandy who carried a riding crop as his badge of authority. As my man approached the jeep, the general laid a blow on the man's helmet with his riding crop. I then made some intemperate remarks about the general's ancestry and threatened to remove him and his party from the camp by force. He then said I was relieved of my command and that he was taking charge. I then drew my pistol and repeated my request that he leave. He left, but only after advising me that I would face a general court-martial for my actions.

In the meantime, the men of Company I had rounded up a number of SS troops who were dispersed throughout the camp area. From these prisoners we learned that most of the Dachau garrison, including almost all of the officers, had fled the scene the day before our arrival. Only about two hundred were left to guard the camp. We captured most of those, but some were killed. The regimental history book contains a picture of these captives, accompanied by

Lt. Walsh, the Company I commander, and Chaplain Loy. Fate was much kinder to these captured SS men than they were to the inmates of Dachau.

—From Felix L. Sparks, "Dachau and Its Liberation," 157th Infantry Association Records Relating to the Liberation of Dachau, Record Group 09.020.01, United States Holocaust Memorial Museum Archives.

A DOCTOR'S ACCOUNT

Marcus Smith was a physician with a U.S. Army Displaced Persons Team when it reached DACHAU on April 30, the day after its liberation by American troops. He remained in the camp for several weeks helping to care for the survivors. His recollections of his encounter with Dachau are reproduced here.

We brake to a stop at a railroad unloading point.

An unbelievable sight. Flatcars and open boxcars contain hundreds of emaciated bodies piled on top of each other, bodies of men, women, and children, lying in grotesque positions. Their cadaverous arms and legs seem disproportionately long compared to their sunken abdomens, narrowed bony chests, visible ribs, protruding shoulder blades, and withered necks—all signs of starvation.

Some of the bodies are covered by pajamalike cotton uniforms with vertical blue and white stripes, the official clothing of concentration camp prisoners. Some are covered with coats. Many are naked. Because of the intense cold, the bodies and cars are now lightly coated with white frost, Nature's shroud.

Refuse and excrement are spread over the cars and grounds. More of the dead lie near piles of clothing, shoes, and trash. Apparently some had crawled or fallen out of the cars when the doors were opened, and died on the grounds.

One of our men counts the boxcars and says that there are thirty-nine. Later I hear that there were fifty, that the train had arrived at the camp during the evening of April 27, by which time all of the passengers were supposed to be dead so that the bodies could be disposed of in the camp crematorium. But this could not be done because there was no more coal to stoke the furnaces.

Mutilated bodies of German soldiers are also on the ground, and occasionally we see an inmate scream at the body of his former tormentor and kick it.

Retribution!

An incredible sight, a stench that is beyond experience. Horror-stricken, outraged, we react with disbelief. "Oh God!" says Rosenbloom. Ferris is silent, and so is Howcroft, his vocabulary inadequate to describe this circle of evil. I hear Hollis, our car-counting driver, say that even primitive, savage people give a decent burial to their own dead and the dead of their enemies. I shut my eyes. This cannot be the twentieth century, I think. I try to remember the redeeming attributes of man. None comes to mind.

"Lieutenant," says Private Eastman, our young driver who has never voiced his feelings before. "Maybe we should occupy this country for fifty years.". . .

Not as many inmates are standing at the fence as I had thought, probably because it is too cold. A few walk slowly over to us, and I see from their gait and then from their pinched features that they have been starved. They crowd around us, finger our insignia. One of them, listening to the distant cannon fire, asks if they are safe. Yes, I reply. The Nazis are gone; they will never come back; we have driven them away; soon the war will be over. They try to smile.

Yesterday, the day of liberation, must have been a great day for these men, I think. I wish I had been here. How they must have rejoiced!

The inmates volunteer to be our guides, to show us the sights. We head toward the barracks and reach them before our guides because they cannot walk as fast as we do. We detour around more bodies in their blue-white striped uniforms; there are bodies in front of and between these buildings.

There are thirty-two one-story, low-ceilinged wooden barracks, or blocks, arranged in two rows separated by a wide dirt street. Most of them have eight rooms filled with triple-tiered wooden beds, some of which have rags or filthy straw ticks thrown over them. Now, lying head to foot, as many as three men are crowded onto each narrow bed. Each building holds from 1,000 to 1,900 men; if each person had his own space in which to sleep there would be room for only 650 men in each block.

These are not really beds, but shelves measuring thirty-two inches wide and seven feet long. There are no places for the inmates to sit, so most of them lie on these slabs. As they look at us, their bald, shaven, or partly shaven heads jut out, and we can see part of their shoulders and chests. The rest of their bodies are hidden by the bedsteads. Some try to smile, but emaciated, sallow faces do not convey emotions.

The feelings are there, however. Some of the inmates come over and touch us; others, too weak to stand, wave their hands feebly; others weep.

Here are healthy prisoners, others who are sick, and some who are dying—too weak to get up for the biologic necessities: to eat, urinate, or defecate. When they are in an upper berth, the excreta drip down over the men below. They are dying of starvation, or are afflicted with a disease or combination of diseases made more serious by the starvation. There are no opportunities here for diagnosis and treatment, obviously. Why are they here? I ask some of the healthier men. Because there is no room in the hospital for them. In some of the berths are the recent dead. The well, the sick, the dying, and the dead lie next to each other in these poorly ventilated, unheated, dark, stinking buildings.

The washrooms have too few troughs, the water mains are inoperative, and the number of foul, deep-pit latrines are inadequate. There are no clothes closets but this is no deprivation because the only clothes the internees possess are the ones they wear; all other items were checked into

SS troops slain by liberating American troops at Dachau concentration camp on April 19, 1945. They had been defending one of the guard towers. (NARA)

the camp on admission and stored. Some of the barracks have lockers.

What do these people need? Everything. They have only their prison uniforms, inadequate, torn shoes, some have coats and caps. I should start making notes, and I pull out of my pocket a small German diary, a *Taschenkalender* for the year 1940, that I found somewhere. As I look for a blank page I find a list of important German dates, and I read that tomorrow, May 1, is a legal holiday for the German people. I wonder if it will be celebrated here? Richard Wagner was born on May 22, 1813. Hitler became the leader of the Nazi Party on May 29, 1921.

I find an empty page and start my list; these people will need underclothes, overclothes, shoes, socks, towels, bedding, beds, soap, toilet paper, more latrines, new quarters.

How have they survived? The human body has a greater capacity for endurance than I thought. Of course, my experience has been with the weak and the sick, people under attack by their natural and synthetic enemies: bacteria, cancer, faulty chromosomes, the aging process, battering automobiles, penetrating bullets, extremes of temperature, excesses of food, liquor, and drugs, arteriosclerosis, viruses, allergens, psychoses, malnutrition, accidents—deputies of death by the million, their pernicious intent to injure or destroy the marvelously intricate protoplasmic labyrinth we call the human body. My training and background have taught me that people are vulnerable and fragile, but they must be tougher than I have suspected in order to have survived this camp, these conditions.

But the survivors don't look tough. Some are skeletal in appearance, like the corpses outside—the walking dead. Others, in better condition, are still pale, lean, and unhealthy looking. I ask them questions and receive different responses. Some cannot understand my German, some talk about their gnawing hunger, some stare vacantly with a deathlike indifference, some clutch my hand.

How long have these men been in the camp? Are the best nourished prisoners those who have been here the shortest time? I find out that this is not necessarily true. Some without the strength to hold their heads up are recent arrivals from other concentration camps. I write more words in my notebook. But how am I to describe the dark shadows of disease, starvation, and imminent death?

I am escorted to the prison hospital, consisting of eleven converted barracks, some quarantined by the prisoners themselves, others open. I can see little difference between them and the ordinary barracks except for the presence of medical equipment. The sick lie in the same kind of triple-tiered beds, but they are more comfortable than the "healthy" inmates because there are only three patients for every two beds. Again, the sick, the dying, and the dead share space with each other, not only on the slabs but on the floors and in the latrines. Everywhere is the stench of decomposition and excrement. Some of the patients are too weak to reach the latrines, or, if they do, too feeble to crawl back to their beds.

Here are thousands of patients ranging in age from 12 to 65, all malnourished and emaciated, their diseases in all stages of development: early, late, and terminal. There are patients with typhus fever, dysentery, erysipelas, pneumonia, scabies, and a host of other infections. A great many inmates have infections of their skin, or of the tissues beneath their skin: abscesses, furuncles, sinuses, and ulcers. These are probably caused by many factors, among them the lack of cleanliness, the thinness and fragility of their skin, and the pressure exerted on the skin by the unpadded wooden slabs on which they were forced to sleep.

Diarrhea is ubiquitous.

Tuberculosis, the great killer, must be widespread.

There are many surgical patients, some with fractured limbs in makeshift slings, others with gunshot injuries. There are many instances of infected wounds and bones. There are cases of gangrene.

The injuries were accidentally or deliberately incurred.

There is supposed to be a castrated Jewish boy here.

It has been impossible to separate those with communicable diseases from those with ordinary disorders. . . .

What am I going to write in my notebook? Everyone is touched. One of my men weeps. Even my callous, death-hardened county-hospital exterior begins to crack. We would like to give these people something to indicate our concern. We were so emotionally moved when our inspection began that we have already given away whatever we had in our pockets that was edible or smokable. Our loose rations, candy, and cigarettes went to the first group of ambulatory inmates; now we have nothing left. We can do nothing for these half-dead people except find out what is going on, let them know we care, and then look for help.

I find it difficult to sort out my thoughts. A primitive instinct warns: Be careful. This place is loaded with dangerous epidemic diseases. Remember—handwashing, face masks. Instruct the members of the Team. Begin disinfection. Another mental relay says: Get the figures, the number of patients, the morbid statistics, and get out. Another thought: How these men have suffered! I cannot believe this is possible in this enlightened age. The gaunt faces and trembling, supplicating, dirt-impregnated hands. Is there any future for them?

I think incoherently, shocked by the insignificance of the human being in this mad Nazi world. But then I remember that the Nazis did not consider the prisoners to be members of the human race. I am appalled by the extent of the physical and mental suffering and anguish in these blocks. I cannot understand why our inexperienced Team was selected for this job. I feel sorry for our men, for myself. What is happening in this camp is beyond anything I have ever read about, imagined, or anticipated, and suggests to me that I was sheltered in my training by the scientific medical school I attended, by the sophisticated, departmentalized, specialized hospital where I interned, and by the modern, expense-is-no-object Army Medical Corps. The tools and brains of the medical profession have always been nearby, available for consultation and guidance, and with these one could face Death down for a while. But here there is not only the smell of Death, but his actual presence, and there are no weapons with which to fight. . . .

The grand tour must include the crematorium and the gas chamber, and our escorts lead us to the large concrete and brick building with the high smokestack. [*See Glossary: There was no systematic gassing program at Dachau.*] The smell here is stronger even than in the quarantined barracks. Outside is a small hill of bodies. In storerooms within, the corpses are piled high. Deaths have exceeded storage space.

The technique used by the Nazis is explained.

Prisoners scheduled for liquidation were marched to a point near the gas chamber and processed in the same way as those who were to serve prison terms. Then those to be executed were ordered into the building, told to undress, handed soap and towels, and directed into the *Brause Bad* (shower bath). That is what the black letters say on the sign that hangs over the door, and the prisoners believed it. The door through which they passed is made of smoothly fitting steel; when it closed, the victims were sealed in. They stood beneath innocent-looking shower heads, evenly spaced on the ceiling; from them the invisible lethal gas (carbon monoxide and hydrogen cyanide) flowed for ten to twenty minutes. I notice a thick glass window in the rear of the chamber: I am told that through this window a supervisor witnessed the executions so that he could decontaminate when they were over.

After the gas had dissipated, special inmates wearing protective clothing entered the chamber after opening another airtight door, then, using grappling hooks, dragged the bodies into storerooms. Other workers cleaned and hosed the chamber. Our guide calls attention to the floor, gently sloped for proper drainage.

From the storerooms, the bodies were moved into the crematorium, whose four furnaces were capable of consuming 150 corpses a day. The metal doors to the furnace are narrow, about two feet wide. They did not need to be larger. Coffins were not used.

In the rear of the crematorium is another sign, depicting a man riding a monstrous pig. "Wash your hands," says the caption. "It is your duty to remain clean."

The inspection has taken a long time. Emotionally exhausted, Mace, Hollis, and I return to the entrance, show our permits, and pass through the gate. I feel like Ulysses leaving the house of Hades.

Outside, we sit and talk with members of the guard unit. What was it like yesterday? asks Mace. Was it rough getting in?

Not bad, says a sergeant who has seen action in Africa, Sicily, and Italy. We were mad; we got those bastards. . . .

The sergeant participated in part of the action, which began about the time I was searching for quarters for DPs sixty miles away. Was that only yesterday? It seems a hundred light years away.

— From Marcus Smith, The Harrowing of Hell: Dachau *(Albuquerque: University of New Mexico Press, 1972), 79–80, 88–92, and 94–95.* The Harrowing of Hell *will be reprinted in the spring of 1995 by the State University of New York Press, in Albany.*

AN AMERICAN ARMY NURSE

U.S. Army Nurse Ann Franklin served with an evacuation hospital in Europe during the latter part of the war. During hostilities she had tended wounded soldiers, Allied and enemy, close to the fighting front. But several days after Dachau was liberated, her hospital was sent to the camp to help provide the medical care so badly needed by surviving prisoners.

As the war's ending drew closer and closer and we knew it could be only a matter of days before it was finished, we were becoming quite keyed up for "the day." For an evacuation hospital, out in the field with our troops, it would mean that no more boys would be brought to us in all stages of physical disability. Our work for the time would be finished and we would no doubt get a rest before our new assignment—we hadn't had any rest since we had joined the Seventh Army last fall.

But the "powers that be" had other plans. A stupendous situation had arisen and must be met. Our Army had conquered a concentration camp, one of the largest yet liberated, with 32,000 political prisoners. After this first report, the real picture came to the surface. The number was correct but it didn't tell what those prisoners were like. The Army that went in to liberate them knew. They couldn't be liberated. What they needed was medical care, lots of it and as

soon as possible. So a couple of days after our Army took over, two evacuation hospitals were sent down to get started. We of the 116th Evacuation Hospital won this assignment, and what a one it was.

Our problem was to nurse the living, and those we could keep living, back to a decent living; and for those we couldn't to make dying a little easier. Before we went to the living we accosted the dead. I doubt if any person can portray to another what it was really like. There has never before in the history of the world been anything like it and "Please God, there must never be a repetition."

Lifeless, emaciated, tortured human beings thrown together in huge stacks like so much kindling wood—the various causes of their departure evidenced by their conditions. Those the "supermen" had put in the gas chambers were stripped for it was more painful that way—a shower first to open the pores and make the torture a little more delicate. [*See Glossary: There was no systematic gassing program at Dachau.*] Even now our patients fight like mad men when we take them to the shower unit before admitting them on the ward. There were those in the stacks with their clothes on and their brains spilled on them. Not all the bullet holes were neat. Guns held close to the object tend to cause more splashing. Then the ones whose eyes bulge out and whose head seems to hang at a peculiar angle gave mute evidence of the row of ropes on pulleys still hanging in the crematory. The ashes and remnants of bones still lying in the huge ovens were all that was left of what was an ordinary human being, just as you or I, when that door was last closed.

Two or three hundred stacked in this room, two or three hundred more in that room over there, another equally large stack outside this door. Those freight cars over there loaded with the same human freight. It doesn't make you sick to look at it. It is too stupendous for that. Your mind can't assimilate it that rapidly. You know your eyes are recording it for your brain but because you have never known anything like this could be, you can't understand how it can be, nor why it could be done. That will all come later, in dreams and during waking hours, pictures of the young Russian girl with her face battered in and a bullet hole in her temple, the petite red-headed girl with her arms thrown over the aged naked man next to her—the confusion of arms and leg and heads, each belonging to someone who lived as you and me, who had a home and family, dreamed of things they would do, and worked to make these dreams come true. And each had a soul.

Let's leave the "land of the dead." There is no work for us here, nothing we can do to help them save utter, "Lord be merciful to these your servants." You know who did it and how it was done, but the why has not been able to penetrate your overtaxed mental powers. You haven't had time to learn to hate yet and to know what you must do about it. It will come though, and soon.

There is much for you to learn in the "land of the living." You yourself will work and sweat and much of your

Freed inmates of Ebensee concentration camp, a subcamp
of Mauthausen, leave for repatriation to their homelands
several days after the camp's liberation on May 4–5, 1945.
They pass under a sign raised by prisoners which reads
"We Greet Our Liberators." (NARA)

efforts will be in vain. You will be constantly with the results
of this horror for twelve and fourteen hours a day. Then
your mind will begin to understand and, with understanding, experience an entirely new emotion. You may have
been angry many times before and spoken of hate lightly,
but you have never really known hate. There is nothing
light about this; it is heavy, very heavy on your mind, and it
is as though it weighs your body down. You know you cannot let that be because much is required of you and you
want to be able to do it and do it well. Many times it is difficult to carry on and you try fervently to squelch the feeling of revulsion that arises in you. Then you remember,
"Verily I say unto you, Inasmuch as ye have done it unto
one of the least of these my brethren, ye have done it unto
me." And so you go on.

> — *From Ann Franklin, R.N., "An Army Nurse at Dachau," The*
> *American Journal of Nursing 45 (November 1945): 901–2. Copy-*
> *right American Journal of Nursing Co. Used with permission.*

A LIBERATED ROMA

*Wilna Leyakovitch, a Roma (GYPSY), was arrested by Italian
Carabineri near Mortegliano, a town south of Udine in
northeastern Italy. After imprisonment in Udine, she was
then deported to RAVENSBRÜCK, then transferred to DACHAU,
where she was liberated by the U.S. Army.*

When a woman died, they threw her, if you will pardon
the expression, in the toilets. Carts pulled by horses passed
for three days. The bodies were collected, piled, sprinkled
with gasoline, and then set on fire. Prisoners died en masse.
The guards ordered us to carry the bodies, but we did not
have the courage to do it. Thus they whipped the women
they found at the head of the line. I knew when it was
going to come and, as I did not have the courage to obey, I
remained behind so as not to be hit. In the face of our stub-
bornness, they finally made the men accomplish this task.
We were desperate, asking ourselves what they would want
to do to us. One day one was alive, the next day one was
dead. We must know nothing, not even the day of the week

or the month. Misfortune to whoever asked a question. The guards responded, "You must know nothing. You ought to be dead" (some of the prisoners spoke German well).

Spring arrived. The Americans were not far away but we did not know this. Three days before their arrival, we had a little more freedom. Behind the fence of the camp, there were two holes: one filled with potatoes. A friend succeeded in slipping through to collect some. I did the same. A German saw me and fired. I began to run and my leg was entangled in the barbed wire. Not having the time to lift it up, I got a gash 25 centimeters long. I returned to the barracks and concealed my wound to avoid a beating. I recovered without treating myself. That day, they shut us in the barracks. I said to my friends, "If they shut us in, it is certainly because they are going to kill us."

My friend [another gypsy woman] felt bad. Behind the barracks there was a trench, and I left by the window to go find water. I saw that the guards wore white brassards, signifying that they had surrendered. I also understood that the Americans had arrived. Returning, I said to my friend, "Have no fear; the Red Cross has arrived." In the afternoon, they brought us tea. The Americans who had arrived threw us packets of food. When the Americans arrived, prisoners of all nationalities came out to play the music of their countries. On that day more women died from joy than during captivity. In order to live out in the countryside we went to the stores to find canvas so as not to remain in the camp. American airplanes dropped packages containing food, clothing, and other things. We lit a fire to prepare food. They [the Americans] began to take away the sickest from the barracks. They gave us packets of food, tins, bread etc. When we prepared a meal we went to find potatoes and lettuce in the homes of peasants. They were unkind, but they were afraid of us. They were obliged to give us something, even if they had no desire to do so.

They [the Americans] finally took us to the barracks where they found the soldiers called "Magyars [Hungarians]." The rooms were large and four of us lived in ours. The prisoners were grouped by nationality. They put me with the Slavs. There were people from Posthumia and Buje [in Istria, Italy]. They brought us a pan and casserole to prepare our meals to our taste if we wished, but we could also eat at the kitchen if we wanted. At the end of six days, I fell gravely ill with typhus. I spent three days in the barracks infirmary, then, since my condition did not improve, they took me to a hospital. At the end of fifteen days, I was cured. The Germans had already shaved my hair in Ravensbrück. When leaving the hospital, I could not recognize the barracks where my friends were to be found because I didn't know how they had brought me there [to the hospital].

An American took some trouble with me. We spoke with each other but did not understand each other. I told him that I wanted to rejoin my friends. If they didn't see me return, the poor things would believe me dead. Afterwards a woman who came from the barracks arrived at the hospital, and she explained to me where she could be found. But I was not able to explain this to the others. Another woman explained to my friends where I was. One of them came to find me at the hospital and we left on foot, about 600 meters. In the barracks I asked where my package and clothing were. Believing me dead, my friends had burned everything; they gave me some of their own clothes.

We were not able to return to our homes because there wasn't any transportation and because we were still too weak. The Americans had discovered a great number of bodies thrown into trenches. They made the Germans collect them and bury them one by one as in a cemetery. They covered the bottom of the trench with branches, wrapping the dead in a cover and laying them in the trench. It was necessary for each of the dead to have his cross. No one knew their names. If a German mistreated the dead, the Americans struck him. The prisoners in the camp had died like flies. Who was able to know how many there were there? The Americans treated us well. They supported us and held us by the hand like children. They made the Germans clean all the rooms, all of the barracks. If they [the Germans] had insulted us, we could have killed them; the Americans would have said nothing. We would insult them, but we never killed anyone. They asked us for something to eat, but we had been ordered to give them nothing.

—From Christian Bernadac, L'Holocauste Oublie: Le massacre des tsiganes (Editions France-Empire: Paris, 1979), 275–77. Translated from the French by Kevin Mahoney. Previously published in Tzigari, vie d'un bohemian, by G. Leyakovitch and G. Ausenda, Hachette, 1977.

Dora

AN ARMY HISTORIAN AT DORA-MITTELBAU

On April 11, 1945, units of the U.S. 3rd Armored and 104th Infantry Divisions liberated DORA-MITTELBAU concentration camp. This eyewitness report, which mistakenly identifies the camp as Nordhausen because of its proximity to the town of that name, was written by Lt. George Moise, an army historian attached to VII Corps, the parent unit of these two divisions. He was accompanied by Lt. Col. D. B. Hardin, a Civil Affairs officer also attached to VII Corps. The original of this report was typed on the reverse of stationary obtained from a local German business firm.

—From the Adjutant General's History Files, "Concentration Camp at Nordhausen," 3 July 1946, Record Group 407, box 24204, file 1028, entry 427, National Archives, Washington, D.C.

CONCENTRATION CAMP AT NORDHAUSEN

Interview with:*

    Col D B Hardin, G-5, VII Corps

                          3 Jul 46   HSD
                           Date   Initials

By: 1st Lt George E Moise, 2d Info & Hist Sv (VII Corps Team),
Nordhausen, Germany, 14 April 1944.

     When the 3rd Armored Division overran Nordhausen (D1227) on
11 April 1945, a large concentration camp, housed in a group of
barracks buildings, was found on the southern edge of the town. Due
to the rapidity of the armor's movement, the division was unable to
do MUCH more than report the presence of the camp to Military
Government officials and to the 104th Division, which was following
the armor. The 3rd Armored division did, however, start the evacuation
to hospitals of 250 of the living prisoners.

     The 104th Division, occupying Nordhausen, found itself with
a concentration camp on its hands and proceeded to evacuate it as
much as possible, before the camp was taken over by the VII Corps
military government under the direction of Col D B Hardin, Corps G-5.
According to Col Hardin, a total of approximately 750 living inmates
of the camp have been evacuated to army hospitals.

     The living, however, constituted a comparatively small problem.
It was the approximately 3,000 dead in the camp that made work for
the G-5 section. The camp was literally a charnel house, with the
distinction that a small proportion of the bodies therein were not
quite dead. As the camp was cleaned out the living and the dead
were found intermingled indiscriminately, and in some
cases bodies had to be carefully examined by medical personnel to
ascertain whether they contained life or not. Those that were

*Col Hardin was interviewed more for background, statistics and factual
data than for the narrative itself, which is, in effect an "eyewitness
story" by the writer, who inspected the concentration camp and the
graves and who witnessed the process of mass burial. Any material herein
not definitely credited to a source is based, therefore, on the
observations of the writer.

living were in such advanced stages of starvation, and frequently
tuberculosis, that there was little hope for them.

A small percentage of the dead were killed by American bombing. The
section of Nordhausen in which the camp is located is close to the railroad
yards and other legitimate military objectives, and it had been heavily
bombed; some buildings were leveled and none escaped entirely. The bomb
casualties, however, were few in comparison to those caused by starvation
and disease.

When the camp was first found the great majority of the inmates,
living and dead, were in two large ~~barrackxxhe~~ two-story barracks buildings
that had been damaged but not wrecked by the bombing. Many lay on piles
of excelsior and straw on the floor and others were in double-decker
wooden bunks, with as many as three persons in a bunk. (Col Hardin
personally removed one of the starvation cases from his position in a
bunk between two corpses. "The man could speak," Col Hardin said,"And
that was about all.")

It was necessary, of course, to remove both the living and dead from
the camp, and this was done under the direction of the 104th Division
and Corps G-5. Mass for the dead was said by Lt Col Paul Mussel, Division
Chaplain of the 104th on 12 April.

On Col Hardin's orders all the able-bodied men in Nordhausen, about
2,000 in all, were rounded up and set to clearing the camp and burying
the dead. First all the bodies were removed from the buildings and laid
out in the area in front of the buildings, an area of about two acres.
Then the civilians were broken up into two groups. One group was set to
work digging graves on a hill overlooking the camp, and the other group
was employed in carrying the bodies to the graves.

The graves themselves were a series of trenches, roughly ~~xxxxxxxx~~
~~xxxxxx~~ 150 feet by three and one-half feet deep and five feet wide.
Between 50 and 100 bodies were placed in each grave, and as each was filled
with bodies it was immediately filled in and graded over. The carrying
parties used improvised ~~xxxxxx~~ litters made of poles and blankets or

2

doors or wall panels, and four men were needed to carry each body. The
half-mile ROAD between the burying ground and the camp was taken up by a
continuous procession of men carrying the litters on their shoulders,
taking the bodies to the graves and returning to the camp for more.

Although the camp and the great number of bodies, some partially
burned, was unpleasant in the extreme, there was not the stench of death
that might be expected, largely because there was not enough flesh on
most of the bodies to rot. They were literally skin and bones. The
parts of the body that would normally be rounded, such as the buttocks,
were nothing but skin stretched over bone.

The inmates of the camp were starved to death, it not deliberately,
at least callously. Their ration per day was 450 grams of black bread,
a 3/4-liter bowl of thin potato soup and one cup of ersatz coffee,
according to Col Hardin. The inmates also were allowed three cigarettes
per month.

Col Hardin said that this camp was a class 3 concentration camp. In
class one camps are housed the slave laborers who can be counted upon for
useful, hard labor. In class two camps are those who cannot do heavy work,
and in class three, such as this, are those who are no longer able to work
at all and are only a burden to the state. These, of course, get practically
no rations and no consideration.

"When a horse can no longer work," Col Hardin said, "He is started
down the road to the reduction plant. That, in effect, was what this camp
was for slave laborers."

In addition to obvious starvation, many of the prisoners were
suffering from advanced stages of tuberculosis, which is probably the
reason they were placed in the Nordhausen camp to die, Col Hardin said.

The prisoners were of all nationalities, according to G-5. Some were
German Jews; some were French, Dutch, Polish, Russian and Belgian. There
were even some German criminals in the camp. All, however, were
worn out slave laborers.

obviously the bodies had not been removed for some time. When the
camp was operating NORMALLY the bodies were removed to a crematorium
in another part of Nordhausen and burned, but the crematorium did not
have the capacity to take care of all of the dead, and as a result
they were allowed to lie where they died, even before the
operations ceased with the bombing and the approach of American troops.

Some of the bodies showed signs of mutilation such as broken legs
and feet, but, said Col Hardin "I would not say that there was any
torture there." The mutilations may have been the result of the bombings,
as were, probably, the burned bodies.

The civilian population of Nordhausen, Col Hardin stated, maintained
that they did not know of conditions in the camp. They do now, with
their men removing and burying the bodies. The camp is also to be used
as an object lesson. First Army asked permission of VII Corps to bring
Burgomeisters from surrounding towns to Nordhausen to show them the camp
and the graves, and, if any remain unburied, the bodies.

The total population of the camp. living and dead, was estimated
at slightly less than 4,000. Seven hundred and fifty were evacuated to
hospitals, and the dead were estimated at 3,000.

gem

GERMAN ATROCITIES IN PRISON CAMPS: GHASTLY SCENES AT NORDHAUSEN.

NORDHAUSEN CAMP, WITH EVIDENCE OF COLD-BLOODED ATROCITY: DEAD BODIES EVERY-WHERE, WHILE IN THE FOREGROUND ARE THE PITIFUL CORPSES OF A CHILD AND A BABY.

MORE VICTIMS AT NORDHAUSEN, HUDDLED TOGETHER IN DEATH. THE CONDITIONS HERE WERE TORTURE AND STARVATION. SEVEN THOUSAND DIED IN THIS CAMP.

A GRIM ROW OF THE DEAD ALMOST LIKE SKELETONS: GERMAN CIVILIANS UNDER ALLIED MILITARY ORDERS WERE FORCED TO CONVEY THE BODIES FOR DECENT BURIAL.

LIVING YET! AN EMACIATED FOREIGN WORKER, TOO WEAK TO STAND, STARES WITH FRIGHTENED EYES AS HE SITS AMID THE FILTH AT NORDHAUSEN.

AN AMERICAN RED CROSS WORKER AMONG THE VICTIMS, MANY DEAD AND OTHERS DYING, AT NORDHAUSEN CAMP, WHERE THEY SLAVED AND STARVED.

THE sadistic brutalities of Nordhausen are as harrowing and terrible as any, and its grisly secrets now revealed comprise crimes in which the entire German nation must share, and not the Nazis merely, as some undiscriminating persons argue. At this devilish murder camp there was a series of long sheds with wooden racks reaching to the ceiling. On these were laid hundreds of men, shrunken with starvation, only waiting to die. Most were naked, some had typhus, others dysentery, and still others had great gaping wounds from S.S. torture. Their bones showed through the skin—as seen in one of our photographs of those who had succumbed. The death-rate at Nordhausen at one recent period was 900 a day. The camp was designed to hold 8000, but 59,000 were thrown in there. Germans living near these camps said they had no idea such cruelties were being done, but at Nordhausen civilians, out walking with their girls, cracked jokes at the "extermination centre." The wife of one S.S. official used to spur her horse into kicking or trampling the slaves. Poles, Russians, Frenchmen and Belgians, including women, were forced to work and starve till they died, as witness the pathetic sight of a baby and a little child.

N.B.—This four-page detachable supplement contains photographic evidence of the sadistic brutalities practised by the Germans at various internment camps now in Allied hands. These revelations of coldly-calculated massacre and torture are given as a record for all time of German crimes, and are intended for our adult readers only. Our subscribers with young families whom they would not desire to see the photographs, can remove these pages, which are easily detachable, by a sharp pull, from the remainder of our issue.

The horrors depicted on this page of the special April 28, 1945, issue of the *Illustrated London News* were photographed at Dora-Mittelbau concentration camp, located near Nordhausen, Germany, and often mistakenly identified by the town's name in contemporary news accounts. (Illustrated London News)

Gestapo Headquarters

CAPTURE BY THE SOVIET ARMY

Late April and early May 1945 saw the culmination of the war in Europe with the battle for Berlin: Soviet forces first encircled, then captured the Nazi capital. The CENTRAL OFFICE FOR REICH SECURITY and its prison, located on Prinz-Albrecht-Strasse in the city's center, was the scene of heavy fighting during the battle, as the following two documents reveal. The first is a report on the conquest of the security office by the Red Army at the end of April 1945; the second is an excerpt from a 1947 letter from one former prisoner to another about the last days in the Gestapo prison.

On April 27 Red Army soldiers succeeded in reaching Hallesches Tor and even getting beyond it. One could already hear the firing of machine pistols and machine guns, and the artillery hammered away ceaselessly. The air was full of blazes and smoke. The *Gestapo* building had been included in the main line of resistance. Combat SS units had taken up positions in Prinz-Albrecht-Park and the adjoining ruins and piles of rubble. Now we were fired upon point-blank. The deafening noise rose at times to the roar of a hurricane. Through the windows of our cells we could see how hit after hit battered the Europahaus, which had been on fire for quite some time. Hit after hit struck our building as well, as we were lying helpless in our cells directly below the small barred cell windows. The building trembled and shook. It was impossible to get any sleep with all this excitement going on.

During the night of April 27/28: After a lull in the fighting, *Gestapo* officials raged and stormed through the cell block. They unlocked all the doors and rounded up us prisoners. Only ten of us were left. In a split-second the thought went through my head they are going to bump you off yet, after all—and the Russians are over on Hedemann-strasse already, perhaps even at Anhalter Bahnhof. The six people of the 20th of July were taken back again into one of the cells and locked up.

After the prison was emptied—you probably do not know yet that a massacre took place during the night from April 23 to 24; the mass grave has been discovered; very valuable people, including clerics, perished—about ten people were retained; ultimately there were but seven of us, during the last few hours only six people. What I experienced by way of sadism during those last one and a half weeks I can hardly describe. It was horrible. The guard who behaved most vilely was Otto Runge of the Security Service. Very decent and, in fact, helpful proved to be little Eduard Koth. I still got hit by three shell fragments, one very close below the eye. For 44 hours they locked us into a communal cell

that was under point-blank gun fire; we got neither food nor buckets as toilets, and all seven of us had stomach trouble, with nasty consequences. That's the way we were living, and under constant threats of being shot.

Suddenly, in the evening of May 1, we were taken—now only six of us—to a very secure cell where we found bread, jam, drinking water and buckets. They left us to our fate, whatever that might turn out to be. The Security Service then retreated. In the morning of May 2 the Russians arrived and liberated us. While we were in the kitchen, where we found marvelous things and began to supply ourselves, the man standing only a few centimeters away from me was accidently shot (the former *Gauleiter* Joseph Wagner, from Breslau).

> —*From Reinhard Rürup, ed.,* Topography of Terror *(Berlin: Berliner Festspiele GmbH, 1989), 184–85.*

Ohrdruf

GENERAL EISENHOWER'S INSPECTION

OHRDRUF concentration camp was the first such camp that General Dwight D. EISENHOWER visited. In a letter written several days afterwards to General George C. Marshall, Chief of Staff of all American armed forces, he described his motivation for the journey and his reaction to what he saw there.

DDE/nmr
15 April 1945
Dear General:

. . . On a recent tour of the forward areas in First and Third Armies, I stopped momentarily at the salt mines to take a look at the German treasure. There is a lot of it. But the most interesting—although horrible—sight that I encountered during the trip was a visit to a German internment camp near Gotha. The things I saw beggar description. While I was touring the camp I encountered three men who had been inmates and by one ruse or another had made their escape. I interviewed them through an interpreter. The visual evidence and the verbal testimony of starvation, cruelty and bestiality were so overpowering as to leave me a bit sick. In one room, where they were piled up twenty or thirty naked men, killed by starvation, George Patton would not even enter. He said he would get sick if he did so. I made the visit deliberately, in order to be in position to give *first-hand* evidence of these things if ever, in the future, there develops a tendency to charge these allegations merely to "propaganda."

> —*From Alfred D. Chandler, Jr., ed.,* The Papers of Dwight David Eisenhower: The War Years, *vol. 4 (Baltimore: Johns Hopkins Press, 1970), 2615–16.*

THE ILLUSTRATED LONDON NEWS

The World Copyright of all the Editorial Matter, both Illustrations and Letterpress, is Strictly Reserved in Great Britain, the British Dominions and Colonies, Europe, and the United States of America.

SATURDAY, APRIL 28, 1945.

THE USUALLY GENIAL GENERAL EISENHOWER SHOWS BY HIS GRIM ASPECT HIS HORROR OF GERMAN BRUTALITY: THE MACABRE SCENE OF VICTIMS MURDERED BY S.S. GUARDS AT OHRDRUF CAMP.

The scene of the appalling massacre at Ohrdruf camp, about 10 miles south of Gotha, was visited recently by General Eisenhower, with Generals Bradley and Patton. The General, standing in the centre of the group, square-jawed and grim, indicates by his pose how he regards this grisly atrocity. Here, the partly-clad bodies of thirty-one men lay huddled grotesquely together where they had been murdered by S.S. guards because they were too ill to be moved. In a wooden shed near by, many more bodies were found, which had been sprinkled with quicklime. Those in the hut had died either from starvation, torture or disease, or they had been beaten to death. Those in front of the hut had been shot in the back of the head excepting for one American shot in the throat. According to one prisoner who hid, some 2000 others died, and were taken in trucks to adjoining woods and burnt. U.S. Army authorities have compelled civilians at Ohrdruf to witness the horrors.

The April 28, 1945, issue of the *Illustrated London News* featured a special supplement on liberated concentration camps. This weekly magazine, founded in 1842, as the first illustrated weekly ever published has specialized in photographs of excellent quality and is still published today. (Illustrated London News)

AN AIDE'S DIARY

Col. Charles Codman was the aide-de-camp to Gen. George S. PATTON, commander of the U.S. 3rd Army. He accompanied the general on his visit to OHRDRUF concentration camp on April 12, 1945, and recorded his observations in his diary entry the next day.

If the morning visit to the salt mines seemed to have about it a quality of unreality, the afternoon was stark and terrible. After lunching at XII Corps we flew to XX Corps at Gotha, and from there proceeded to the recently overrun German concentration camp at Ohrdruf. In the midst of this lovely spring countryside, a festering wound. Rows of hideous wooden barracks surrounded by a double enclosure of barbed wire. Even before reaching the entrance, the smell of death and corruption was almost overpowering. An officer from XX Corps, still pale and shaken, received us. "They tried to eliminate the evidence before we arrived," he said, "but as you see, they were not very successful."

Lying individually and in piles throughout the area, the bodies of recently murdered inmates, in most cases shot at close range through the base of the skull. An ex-guard acted as guide. We were spared nothing. The building piled to the roof with emaciated naked bodies. The gallows—contrived to effect death as slowly and painfully as possible. The whipping racks, the butcher's block for the cleaving of jaws and smashing out of gold fillings. The half-filled and still-smoking ovens in the crematories.

The General officers present all are men who have seen much of life; in the raw, yet never on any human faces have I witnessed such horror and disgust. At one point General Patton frankly disappeared behind the corner of a building and was violently sick to his stomach.

As we stood by the entrance waiting for our transportation to draw up, one of our enlisted men accidentally bumped into the Nazi ex-guard, and from sheer nerves began to giggle.

General Eisenhower fixed him with a cold eye and when he spoke, each word was like the drop off an icicle.

"Still having trouble hating them?" he said.

Before leaving, General Eisenhower addressed the others.

"I want every American unit not actually in the front lines to see this place," he said. "We are told that the American soldier does not know what he is fighting for. Now, at least, he will know what he is fighting *against.*"

— From Charles R. Codman, Drive *(Boston: Little, Brown and Co., 1957), 282–83. Copyright © 1957 by Charles R. Codman; renewed 1985 by Russell S. Codman, Jr. By permission Little Brown and Company.*

Salzwedel

FREEDOM AT SALZWEDEL

On April 14, 1945, the U.S. Army's 84th Infantry Division liberated Salzwedel concentration camp, a subcamp of NEUENGAMME. Like most American divisions during World War II, the 84th had its own newspaper, called The Railsplitter *after the division's nickname, in which appeared a few weeks later the following report about the camp. Geneviève de Gaulle, mentioned in the piece, survived the war and later served as president of a French survivors organization, l'Association Nationale des Anciennes Déportées et Internées de la Résistance.*

—From The Railsplitter, *May 1, 1945.*

Salzwedel Concentration Camp Razed

The concentration camp at Salzwedel which the Railsplitters passed on their drive to the Elbe has been burned to the ground and its 3,000 women transferred to the Luftwaffe airfield at the edge of the town. Some women wept as they gazed at the fire which wiped out the scene of their recent suffering.

Many of the former prisoners were reluctant to talk about the Salzwedel camp because they considered it a country club compared with other camps where they had been held previously. At Salzwedel, they were merely starved and beaten and forced to work twelve hours a day making shell cases at the local munitions factory.

Of the 2,700 Jewish women at Salzwedel, a large number had been transferred from the notorious „death camp" at Oswiecim, Poland, where mass murder was performed in four giant crematoriums. There were also 300 non-Jewish, political prisoners from the Ravensbruck camp near Berlin where they drained marshes and built roads on Gestapo chief Heinrich Himmler's property.

The Salzwedel prisoners were beaten by the 60 SS men and women in charge of the camp almost until the moment American tanks charged down the main street to liberate them. Then most of the SS guards changed into civilian clothes and the former prisoners believe that a number of the SS women are still hiding out in the immediate vicinity.

Here are a few of the women freed by the Railsplitters at Salzwedel. Talking things over with them is Miss Helen Bolling (no kin to the general), Red Cross clubmobile girl from High Point, N. C.　　　　　　　　　**Staff Photo**

Claim Ignorance

Although the prisoners were marched to the munitions factory in broad daylight, townspeople have innocently claimed that they did not even know they had a concentration camp in their back yard. Visitors to the camp have commented that the smell should have given them some hint of the camp even if they saw nothing, heard nothing and said nothing.

One of the French women was Mme. Marie-Louise Bernanos, niece of the famous French Catholic writer, Georges Bernanos. At Ravensbruck, Mme. Bernanos slept next to Geneviève de Gaulle, niece of General Charles de Gaulle, whose fate has long been a mystery.

Screamed with Pain

A frail young woman of 25, Mlle. de Gaulle suffered so much from malnutrition and overwork at sand piles that she lost her sight for several weeks, Mme. Bernanos related. She used to scream with pain because the sores which soon appeared on her body were not bandaged and her clothes clung to the open wounds.

After the Allied breakthrough last September, however, General de Gaulle's niece was removed from the Ravensbruck camp and none of her former companions knew of her whereabouts at present.

The four crematoriums at Oswiecim operated on a 24-hour schedule for the three months she was there except for three days, Mrs. Blanka Konig said. Mrs. Konig was seized in a small Hungarian town the day after the Germans took over the country last April. As she told the story, other Jewish women in the room also from Oswiecim would break into uncontrollable weeping as memories of their experiences came back.

Since their liberation, all the women have received new clothes, eaten three meals a day and slowly accustomed themselves to the thought that they are slaves no longer. But, as Mrs. Konig said, „I cannot understand how I came out alive."

84th Div. Destroyed — German 84th Div.

„The 84th Division has been destroyed on the Western Front," blared the radio, and friends and relatives of the Railsplitters all over the States had a few anxious moments.

There were no further details until the next hourly broadcast when the announcement was clarified. „The 84th Division — the German 84th Division — has been destroyed on the Western Front."

Friends in the States report that a virtual nationwide sigh of relief could be heard.

Captors Get Jitters, Free Four Americans

Four Americans, prisoners of the Germans more than two years, found freedom with the 84th when their captors got the jitters about the onrushing Russians.

The Germans put the Americans on a small steamer, crawled on themselves and then floated down the Elbe River and surrendered to Railsplitter doughboys.

The Americans were Pvt. James Henry Walls of Wasco, Calif., and Pvt. Carl L. Williams of Sycamore, Ca., both formerly with the 168th Infantry; Pfc. Wallace K. Clifton of Blountsville, Ala., once an infantryman with the 45th Division, and Pvt. Richard Earl Haff of 827 W. 17th, Lorraine, Ohio, whose unit was the 701st Tank Destroyers.

They said they were patients in a hospital near Brandenburg when a medical officer anxiously told them:

„We're getting out of here. The Russians are coming."

Phony Burgomeister Frolics in Rathaus

The would-be Burgomeister turned out to be a nut with more interest in his pretty secretaries than in civic affairs.

The artillerymen from the 327th Field Artillery first suspected that something was wrong when they noticed a profusion of official passes all purportedly issued by the Burgomeister of Bomengien.

When several of the Railsplitters went down to the Rathaus, they found the pseudo-mayor in a most unprofessional position, petting his pretty blonde stenographer.

While thoroughly understandable, especially in view of the blonde, it did seem a little brazen and they asked for an investigation.

When the investigators descended upon the Burgomeister, a large sixfooter with popping blue eyes, they found him again attending to the affairs of the city with another woman. In the adjoining offices there was a virtual harem of secretaries blonde, brunette, all types and sizes.

Continuing the investigation, five policemen were found locked up in the jail, along with a man who claimed to be the real Burgomeister. He said that the man with the battery of stenographers was an usurper who had escaped from an insane asylum. A careful investigation proved that this was true.

At first the „great lover" was indignant, but as he was taken in custody and sent back to the asylum, he was heard to say, „It was fun while it lasted."

THE RAILSPLITTER

Published weekly or thereabouts by and for the men of the 84th Infantry Division. Contributions may be sent to The Railsplitter, Public Relations Office, through message center.

Theresienstadt

LIBERATION AT THERESIENSTADT

On May 8, 1945, the Soviet Red Army liberated the Czech town of Terezin—known in German as THERESIENSTADT—the site of a Jewish GHETTO and a Gestapo prison. Here Käthe Starke describes the liberation of Theresienstadt: the looting of supplies by both former prisoners and Red Army soldiers, the numerous deaths caused by the typhus epidemic, the reawakening of new hope and new life as well as the simple joys long forgotten

On the first of May it was said that the Americans were outside Pilsen. They should have come if they were in fact there. We believed only what we saw. We knew nothing of the Conference in Yalta where it had been decided at the green table to let Slavs liberate Slavic territory. Therefore, we didn't know that we had to wait for the Russians.

Then our prison guards left us without a stir, of which we were completely unaware. In the post office where my sister worked as Henschel's secretary, one thought it could be the 5th of May. From the country estate I observed two horses without riders, one sorrel, the other a bay. They were gathered together and wandered along the fortress wall. They came closer and closer to the narrow moats which during the reign of Joseph II were used to drive the enemy away. But in this warm spring there was no water in them.

On the evening of May 8, the last day of the Second World War, the people ran past the library windows to where the Dresden-Prague thoroughfare cut through the camp behind our prison block. The barbed-wire was already torn away from the wooden fence. During the excitement we got the strength to pull ourselves up. The wood broke under grabbing hands and trampling feet. Crates were turned upside down in order to climb up on them so we could see the conquering troops—the Russian vanguard—our liberators. Suddenly, red banners were hung across the street where it is perpendicular to the Eger bridge and turns toward Prague, and the deafening sound of *nazdar, nazdar*—hail, hail from the excited prisoners at the moment of their liberation. The Chetniks [guards] watch idly as the fence is trampled down. Now they join in the roaring cry of jubilation for their countrymen: *Nazdar, nazdar*—Hail to the victorious Red Army! we shouted.

The Russians are quiet. They came on their dust-covered artillery from the Leitmeritz battlefield and were headed for a new battle at Prague. The troops were on the trucks—men and women next to one another; their rifles in their arms. Officers drove requisitioned cars from Dresden; you could tell from the license plates. Some stop and hand out cigarettes, which are sold in the camp that same evening. A practical joker smashes the sign on the cafe, so that only the last three letters *AUS* (over) remained visible from

the square. Now it's finally happened, we are liberated. This evening we slept without fear. The first time after twelve frightening years without fear.

The next day the Russians took over the administration of the camp. Their first act was to "liberate" the sick who had spotted typhus because no one behind the German barbed wire cared for them. As soon as they were taken care of, they set up a medical service—they themselves lost doctors and interns to the epidemic—and put the city under quarantine. Nevertheless, that did not change our lives too much. Instead of Chetniks and SS, now Russian guards stood double-post by the camp gates. Troop units incessantly thronged the road to Prague. The tractors made a deep track in the sandy ground where they crossed the bridge; and the guns roared from afar, still audible even after they have disappeared over the Eger.

The squares and knolls were bivouacked. The soldiers lay on inflatable rubber mattresses and listen to music on a record player they had looted. They have children with them, small boys with crew cuts like the men, their necks shaved and in authentic uniforms that were cut to fit them. They are allowed to drive the large motorcycles carefully up and down the street.

The forbidden city opens itself to us, but not the gates. The Czechs from our camp were undeterred from leaving despite the barrier. With or without authorization they found a way to return home. Then they return and migrate little by little with their families.

The Hungarians quickly organized a commuter service. In trucks they transported furniture, typewriters, sewing machines, and other household and office materials taken from the SS headquarters. The trucks drove to the border, unloaded, and returned to be loaded again. Their boys slipped out with tied-up shoe boxes and bundles smiling modestly as they walk by the children-loving guards and make the area unsecured. In the evening one could see from the square Dresden's campfires burning, on which chicken and geese from the Sudeten region were being roasted. The mayor of Leitmeritz complained about losing the pups of his Saint Bernard. Not even the camp's own institutions were safe from their thieving grasp. They broke more than once into the courtyard of the Hebrew room; they weren't interested in the books, but rather the casks which Slonitz and others before their transport had deposited there, and they helped themselves to mine and my sister's property. There is a protocol regarding that.

The difference between a defeated and liberated country was not easy for the Russians to understand. There were different incidents and they were very suspicious. On the street before Magdeburg, a soldier searched a woman's suitcase and took from it what he liked. As she screamed bloody-murder, a patrol rushed over and roughly dragged their comrade away.

A young soldier climbed through the ground floor window in the prominent house on 26 Lake Street. A woman lived there who moved into the recently vacated room and was completely alone. For the first time in three years she was once again able to do what she had regularly done before, lay undressed on her bed in the warm summer night. Whether the open window or something else lured him in was never proven. The commotion in the house caught people's attention. It started and continued in the front stairwell that led to the Sea Street entrance which was never used. When the neighbors appeared, the culprit, finding the house door locked after Theresienstadt custom, shot the lock and fled. He was gone. In addition to the shocked woman, he left behind his pistol holster, which was later used to identify him.

A few days later Fanny, David's cousin, Elsa Meier, went in to the cellar of the house at 20 Lake Street to investigate some groans she heard and found a young soldier locked up, crouched on the dirt floor in a corner, without enough food to eat.

The Russians had set up quarters at 20 Lake Street. Elsa Meier helped in the kitchen. For this she received the leftovers from the pots she washed. It was good and nourishing food which she occasionally shared with her friends. Thus she was able to provide the poor soldier locked up in the dark with food and drink and give him some blankets through the slats of his shed. After fourteen days he was dismissed and had learned his lesson about subservience and brotherhood. The Russians who occupied Theresienstadt were nothing as we imagined them to be. They were tall, blonde, and very friendly. The women pulled their hair back tightly and tied it in a knot. Instead of wearing pants when they tended to their war duties, they wore dark blue pleated skirts, which reminded one of the Kiel uniforms the patriotic German youth wore at the turn of the century during the buildup of the navy under Kaiser Wilhelm II.

Also in the first days there was a roll call in Magdeburg, at which one of our liberators gave a long speech. It sounded propagandistic and was so poorly translated that we could simply infer that, as long as we did as we were told, things would go well for us. Doing as we were told was something we had practiced a great deal, so things went well for us. The rations were systematically and carefully increased. The kitchens had Russian officers who made sure that the contents of the canned meat found its way into the pots. The Russians knew their stuff. Eggs were distributed. They knew where to find flour and sausage, and in the store on the corner of Main Street and Bath Alley, where they sold spices and once in a while pickled vegetables, one could find a piece of meat.

The scene on the street was as sad as before. Instead of the elderly, now one would see young men being carried out of the houses dead. Typhus had overtaken the city. It would have taken a large cart pulled by strong horses to remove this feather-light load. It was heart-wrenching to see them writhe on the hard planks. Sometimes a transport of recovered patients arrived at the youth home near the church. While they were sick, ringlets of hair had grown on their shorn heads which framed their faces of moving, an-

gelic purity. Now one finally realized how many children and youths were among those on the transports.

Shortly after the liberation, one occurrence caused quite a sensation. Troops of blonde young women were put to work cleaning the streets, and they worked very flippantly. At first they stood out on account of their unusual clothes: newly made blue and white striped pajamas. They were hardly pajamas, but rather prisoner uniforms, and the women came from the SS retinue and were quickly pulled again from the traffic and put to work in the typhus stations.

Their male colleagues were allowed to keep their uniforms, but they were distinguished by a razor-wide strip shaved from their forehead to the nape of their necks.

In the commandant's headquarters in the town hall sat a Russian military staffer, Jiri Vogel, who was in charge of the self-government. He was a wiry young Czech who looked after the city's civilian concerns. During the quarantine he enlisted a part of the work force with various salary levels to handle and maintain the supplies.

Then there were the first passes, and the country opened up in all its early summer magnificence. Fields full of ripe tomatoes. Fields full of blooming poppies decked in delicate violet. The faded fruit capsules with ribbed coverings appeared like precious vessels covered with a copper patina. In abandoned gardens of the abandoned hamlets, the sun cooked the tall currants to their full sweetness; spread across the field in the gold of the sunflowers. And we were allowed to pick the meadow flowers: star heads in pink and purple, blue summer geraniums, sweet peas and little cuckoo flowers.

Suddenly, the population could no longer speak or understand German.

—From Käthe Stark, Der Führer schenkt den Juden eine Stadt *(Berlin: Haude & Spenersche, 1975), 162–66. Translated from the German by Neal Guthrie.*

Westerbork

LIBERATION BY THE CANADIANS

WESTERBORK, a transit camp in Holland for Jewish deportees, was liberated by units of the 2nd Canadian Division on April 12, 1945. In May 1945 Anne de Vries, a Dutch journalist, reported on the liberation in a series of articles for the Dutch newspaper Nieuwe Drentsche Courant. *The excerpt below describes the surviving prisoners' reaction to the news that the camp commandant had fled.*

Suddenly everyone is on their feet, screaming, laughing, cheering, crying and moaning. All of those 800 people storm the exit, pushing and shoving their way outside, race through the camp and through the gate up the road which runs along the barbed wire fence to the camp farm. Young men and women up front, hair streaming in the wind; behind them, the others, portly, panting gentlemen, old women —everybody is running in the wild exodus . . . towards the liberators, shouting and screaming with joy. . . .

Zielke [former head of External Service] rides back to the camp on top of the first tank. And soon Captain Morris, perched atop the tank, takes out his camera to record this unique event, the liberation of this ubiquitously notorious camp for Jews, for all time.

The tanks are practically being stormed by the Jews. Girls are being hoisted on top so that in no time at all the tanks are no longer visible.

Cheering, they ride back to the main gate of the camp. There the Canadians are dragged from the tanks, hugged and kissed and carried around the camp on shoulders. Suddenly a flag appears, the national tricolor, as well as an orange flag made out of parachute silk and carefully hidden from the Germans until this moment. They are taken to the flagpoles where only a few days ago the swastika flew and raised as the Wilhelmus is being sung.

One hour later the first German prisoners of war pass by the camp, shuffling, ill-clad, shifty-eyed creatures who glance stealthily at the exuberant camp population.

In the evening there is a party in the Big Barrack. . . . There are Canadian cigarettes and English cakes. German wine also appears. Signatures are being collected, also souvenirs. The Jewish girls go around with the insignia from the caps of the Canadian soldiers; all the Canadians have donned the Jewish star. There is singing and dancing, smoke billows from the open doors and the sounds of joyful voices echo across the dark moor.

— *From Jacob Boas,* Boulevard des Misères: The Story of Transit Camp Westerbork *(Hamden CT: Archon Books, 1985), 155–56.*

JOURNALISTS AND POLITICIANS VIEW THE CAMPS

AN INVITATION

General EISENHOWER was appalled and outraged by what he saw at OHRDRUF concentration camp. He sent the following cable to Gen. George C. Marshall, Chief of Staff of the Army in Washington D.C., in which he recommends that Congressional leaders and journalists make official visits to concentration camps in his command area [see pp. 149–156].

— From "Eisenhower to Marshall," April 19, 1945, Eisenhower's Pre-presidential Papers, box 134, item 5, The Dwight D. Eisenhower Library, Abilene, Kansas.

THE BRITISH PARLIAMENTARY DELEGATION INSPECTS BUCHENWALD

Members of Britain's Parliament visited Buchenwald at General Eisenhower's invitation on April 21, 1945. This was one of a number of such official visits planned by the SUPREME HEADQUARTERS ALLIED EXPEDITIONARY FORCE (SHAEF) to aid in documenting and publicizing Nazi atrocities. Upon their return to the United Kingdom they presented the following report to Parliament that was subsequently printed for public distribution.

[...] 4. Buchenwald Camp is set in hilly, well-wooded country about 15 minutes' drive from Weimar. It dates from 1934. It is badly laid out, on sloping uneven ground. The walls and paths are ill kept; at the time of our visit they were covered with dust, which blew about in the wind, and in wet weather the camp must be deep in mud. The ordinary huts of the camp are roughly constructed of wood, with earth floors, without windows or sanitation. (Latrines consist of poles suspended over trenches.) There are also some more solidly built brick blocks, of two storeys. Over the main gate of the camp is the inscription *"Recht oder unrecht—mein Vaterland"* (My country right or wrong).

5. The size of the camp is indicated by the fact that its maximum capacity was said to have been 120,000. On 1st April last the number in camp was 80,813. A few days before the arrival of the American forces (11th April), the Nazis removed a large number of prisoners, variously estimated at from 18,000 to 22,000. Some of those whom they wished to remove (because "they knew too much") were able to hide from them. It was impossible to form any accurate estimate of the percentages of various nationalities still remaining in the camp; we met many Jews and non-Jewish Germans, Poles, Hungarians, Czechs, French, Belgians, Russians and others. A detailed report presented to us by representatives of an anti-Fascist committee stated that, up to 1st April, the total number of those who had died or been killed at Buchenwald, or immediately on removal therefrom to subsidiary "extermination-camps," was 51,572—at least 17,000 of them since 1st January, 1945. The camp has now been thrown open, and a certain number of its inmates must have left independently. Detailed camp records, including nominal rolls, were left behind by the Nazis, but, at the time of our visit, it had not been possible to start drawing up rolls of those still in the camp, the American medical and sanitary authorities being naturally preoccupied with the cleaning of the camp (a task performed partly by German civilians from the neighbourhood, parties of whom are also brought daily to see what had been done in their name and in their midst), and with problems of feeding and medical attention.

6. Although the inmates of the camp are commonly referred to as "prisoners," they should not be confused with military Prisoners of War. They were in three main categories: (a) political internees and Jews from Germany itself, (b) as the Third Reich expanded, political internees and Jews from Austria, Czechoslovakia, Poland, etc.; (c) from 1940 onwards, men and youths imported for forced labour from the various occupied countries. There were few Britons at any time in the camp; one estimate was "a few dozen." Almost all of these were civilians. We were told of one French parachutist, Lieutenant Maurice Pertschuk, who was taken prisoner in 1943, transferred in civilian clothes from Compiégne to Buchenwald, and there hanged, shortly before the United States troops arrived. We also obtained a document, signed by Squadron-Leader F. Yeo-Thomas, Captain Harry Poole, and Lieut. Stephane Hessel (of the French War Ministry), testifying to the fact that they were saved from execution "by amazingly clever planning, under perilous circumstances," by Heinz Baumeister of Dortmund and Dr. Eugen Kogon of Vienna, who are still inmates of the camp.

7. Although the work of cleaning the camp had gone on busily for over a week before our visit, and conditions must therefore have been improved considerably, our immediate and continuing impression was of intense general squalor, the odour of dissolution and disease still pervaded the entire place. One of the first of a number of huts that we entered was one of the best: it was divided into small rooms with cement floor and windows, four of which had been used, the American authorities informed us, as a brothel to which the higher-grade prisoners—those employed in various supervisory jobs, with extra rations and other privileges—were allowed to resort for twenty minutes at a time. (In general, Buchenwald Camp was for men and boys only; the women in this brothel were prisoners from other camps, induced by threats and promises of better treatment, to become prostitutes, but subsequently killed. When the Americans arrived, fifteen women were found in this brothel. They were transferred to the care of the Bürgermeister of Weimar.) This hut was one of those now used as transit hospitals for some of the worst cases of malnutrition. Many were unable to speak: they lay in a semi-coma, or following us with their eyes. Others spoke freely, displaying sores and severe scars and bruises which could have been caused by kicks and blows. They lay on the floor on and under quilts. All of them were in a state of extreme emaciation. We were told by the U.S. authorities that, since their arrival, the number of deaths had been reduced from about a hundred per day to 35 on the day before our visit. The usual clothing was a ragged shirt, vest or cotton jacket, beneath which protruded thighs no thicker than normal wrists. One half-naked skeleton, tottering painfully along the passage as though on stilts, drew himself up when he saw our party, smiled, and saluted. The medical members of our Delegation expressed the opinion that a percentage of them could not be expected to survive, even with the treatment they were now receiving, and that a larger percentage, though they might survive, would probably suffer sickness and disablement for the rest of their lives. Among those in this hut were several writers and students, and one

member of the French *Deuxième Bureau* [French intelligence] captured in Warsaw.

8. The ordinary huts that we saw were lined on each side with four tiers of wooden shelves, supported and divided by upright struts. In each of the small open cubicles thus formed, about six feet in depth, four feet in width, and two feet in height, five or six men had to sleep. Even in their wasted condition, there was room for them to lie in one position only, on their sides. Several of them demonstrated to us how this had been done. For bedclothes they had such rags as they could collect. Heaps of these rags were being burned in various parts of the camp; the huts were still verminous.

9. There had been similar overcrowding in Block 61, which had been used as a rough hospital, chiefly for those suffering from tuberculosis or dysentery. This hut was about 80 ft. long by 24 ft. wide; estimates of its normal sick population varied from 700 to 1,300. Four, five, or six men, including those who had undergone operations (performed without anaesthetics by prisoner doctors on a crude operating-table at one end of the hut, in full view of the other patients), had regularly to lie in each of the small shelf cubicles. Here, too, there were no mattresses. The excreta of the dysentery patients dripped down from tier to tier. If the living were strong enough, they pushed the dead out into the gangway. Each night the dead were thrown into a small annexe at one end of the hut, and each morning collected and taken in carts to the crematorium or, if required as specimens, to the pathological laboratory of the Nazi doctors.

10. Many of the ordinary prisoners worked in a large munition factory near the camp or in the quarries; these were able to obtain more than the basic ration of a bowl of watery soup and a chunk of dry bread each day. Only those possessing the oblong metal disc marked "Essmarke KLB" were entitled to draw rations. We saw paper camp money which prisoners could earn by work and spend in the canteen. Some whom we spoke to paid tribute to the precision with which the Royal Air Force had bombed the factory (killing, it was said, about 200 Nazis, 400 forced workers, and 150 Nazi women resident near the camp, including the Camp Commandant's wife and daughter). Children, like adults, were made to work eight or more hours a day, seven days a week. We were told that there were some 800 children still in the camp. One 14-year-old boy, Abraham Kirchenblat, originally of Radom, Poland, impressed members of our party as an intelligent and reliable witness; he stated that he had seen his 18-year-old brother shot dead and his parents taken away, he believed for cremation: he never saw them again.

11. The mortuary block consisted of two floors, ground floor and basement. Access to the basement was by a steep stone staircase or by a vertical chute below a trap-door, down either of which, we were told, refractory or useless prisoners would be precipitated for execution. Hanging appears to have been the regular method of killing. In the yard, near a pile of white ashes, there was a gibbet; in the basement we saw strong hooks, at a height of about 8 ft. from the floor, and another gibbet. We were informed that there had been more than forty hooks, most of which Nazis had removed hurriedly before leaving. We were shown a heavy wooden club, about 2 ft. long, which was said to have been used for knocking out any who died slowly; it was stained with blood. The bodies were transported from this basement to the ground-floor crematorium in a large electric lift (similar to those used for stretcher-cases in hospitals). To the yard outside the crematorium came the carts, packed closely with the ordinary corpses from the dysentery and other huts, mostly stripped even of the meagre striped blue-and-white suits which were the normal camp clothing. We examined the last of these cart-loads that remained, awaiting the reverent individual burial which, on General Eisenhower's personal order, the American authorities have obliged the inhabitants of the neighbourhood to provide with their own hands. The bodies were beginning to decompose, but none that we could see bore the marks of violent death; all appeared, from their state of extreme emaciation, to have died of hunger or of disease. In the crematorium was a row of capacious arched ovens, each still containing calcined ribs, skulls, and spinal columns. The prisoner in charge of putting the bodies into the ovens had one of the privileged jobs, since it carried with it the advantage of a private room, with furniture and lace curtains, adjoining the crematorium. He told us that he was a Communist from Berlin, aged 30, named Kurt Faulhaber. He had been in the camp for ten years, but had obtained this job only last January. He stated that two other German prisoners had been mainly engaged in hanging the condemned. Their names were Heinrode (of Hamburg) and Josef Müller (of Dortmund). They had been taken away by the Nazis when they left. No Jews, we were told, would ever have been allotted these special tasks.

12. We were told of scientific experiments, such as the infecting of prisoners with typhus in order to obtain serum from them, by the camp's Nazi doctors; but obtained no direct and unchallengeable evidence of this. We saw a laboratory with a large number of glass jars containing preserved specimens of human organs. The walls of the laboratory and other medical rooms were decorated with death-masks of, we were told, the "more interesting" prisoners—many with features of remarkable nobility and refinement. It was alleged that various experiments in sterilisation had been practised on Jews. Two of our number were taken to the bed (in the improvised American hospital) of a Polish Jew, Number 23397, aged 29, who had been operated on in this way; they saw the scars of the operation, and confirm that the left testicle had been removed. Other subjects of the operation were said to have died; and we were assured that the policy of exterminating Jews had long superseded that of castrating them. We were told that Frau Koch, the wife of the German Commandant, collected articles made of human skin. We obtained pieces of hide which have since been identified by Sir Bernard Spilsbury

as being human skin. One of these pieces clearly formed part of a lampshade.

13. One of the statements made to us most frequently by prisoners was that conditions in other camps, particularly those in Eastern Europe, were far worse than at Buchenwald. The worst camp of all was said by many to be at Auschwitz, these men all insisted on showing us their Auschwitz camp numbers, tattooed in blue on their left forearms. One 19-year-old youth, Joseph Berman, Latvian-born but English-educated, had been in several camps; in one, he had suffered the loss of a forefinger when a Nazi, annoyed by his indolence at work, had pushed his hand into a machine.

14. Despite the desperate physical condition of many of the prisoners, and their long years of incarceration, there were signs of mental as well as physical recovery. Vivid slogans of greeting to the liberating Armies, in English and many other languages, were being painted on the outside of the huts. New notice-boards bore news-sheets and well-designed instructional and democratic propaganda messages, mostly in German. Near the entrance to the camp was a life-size effigy of Hitler hanging from a gibbet, with the superscription in German:—"Hitler must die that Germany may live!"

It would be impossible to praise too highly the selfless exertions of the 120th Evacuation Hospital Unit, under the command of Colonel William E. Williams (in charge of medical services), assisted by Major L. C. Schmuhl (in charge of sanitary services). We saw blood transfusion in process, and learned that glucose injections were being given and that carefully chosen diets were supplied to prisoners incapable of digesting normal food.

15. In preparing this report, we have endeavoured to write with restraint and objectivity, and to avoid obtruding personal reactions or emotional comments. We would conclude, however, by stating that it is our considered and unanimous opinion, on the evidence available to us, that a policy of steady starvation and inhuman brutality was carried out at Buchenwald for a long period of time; and that such camps as this mark the lowest point of degradation to which humanity has yet descended. The memory of what we saw and heard at Buchenwald will haunt us ineffaceably for many years.

(Signed) Stanhope.
Addison.
Tom Wickham.
Archibald R. J. Southby.
Mavis Tate.
Ness Edwards.
S. Sydney Silverman.
Graham White.
Henry Morris-Jones.
Tom Driberg.

— *From* Buchenwald Camp: The Report of a Parliamentary Delegation *(London: Her Majesty's Stationery Office, 1945), 3–7. Crown copyright is reproduced with the permission of the Controller of HMSO.*

REPORT ON GERMAN MURDER MILLS

Joseph Pulitzer, the editor of the St. Louis Post Dispatch, *was one of a number of journalists who traveled to several liberated concentration camps in Germany after Allied troops had arrived. His report on Buchenwald and Dachau— like stories by other prominent civilian journalists—was featured in* Army Talks, *the weekly publication from the Education Division of the European Theater of Operations, United States Army, that informed American soldiers in Europe in depth about important issues.*

— *From Joseph Pulitzer, "Report on German Murder Mills,"* Army Talks *4 (July 10, 1945): 7–11.*

"Abandon Hope All Ye Who Enter Here"
...the main entrance to Dachau

Report on German murder mills

by JOSEPH PULITZER

I WAS DISMAYED within an hour after getting home from my European trip to learn that there are still Americans who are saying, in effect, "this talk of atrocities is all propaganda. There may have been something wrong here and there but the German people would not stand for such things. It is outrageous to have these atrocity pictures forced upon us by the newspapers and the movie houses."

All I can say in reply is that persons who talk this way are tragically mistaken. They should visit their family doctors and have their heads and perhaps their hearts examined. I should say that 99 percent of what has appeared in the American press has been understatement. I urge the skeptics who because of prejudice or other reasons refuse to believe the truth of the atrocity stories and the many good people of America who have difficulty in believing them, not to take my word for it but to see the Signal Corps moving pictures which I trust will be shown. No honest person can refuse to believe the evidence they portray from a dozen or more different concentration camps, all of them telling the same unbelievable story.

What It Would Be Like in the US

These camps, there were about 100 of them in all of Europe, as the reader knows, were filled with "political enemies." I think there is significance in that word "enemies." Perhaps the easiest way to bring it home to the American reader is to remind him that if the Nazi system were in effect in St. Louis, where there happens to be a Republican administration in office, every Democrat and every independent voter and every member of a labor union and every Jew and every person of Russian or Polish extraction and many ministers would find himself or herself rotting to death down at Jefferson Barracks. There would be some six to sixteen of them—the women in separate barracks—sleeping in a bunk the size of a large American double bed. The great majority of them would die

10 JULY

7

of starvation. American surgeons stated that the adult corpses weighed only 60 to 80 pounds, having in practically all cases, lost 50 per cent to 60 per cent of their normal weight, and also having shrunk in height.

Some people are just naturally tough and a very few would survive in spite of starvation, dysentery and raging typhus epidemics. Some 125 of them would have died last night. If the picture of Dachau were repeated there would be standing on the Missouri Pacific spur which runs through the camp some 39 box cars recently arrived from another prison camp. Upon being opened, the contents would consist of the cadavers lying three or four tiers deep, with a few still alive among them, of prisoners who had been on the road without food or water for 20 days. It was the sight of this train which we newspaper men all saw, which, we were told, so enraged our troops when they overran the camp that they showed no mercy whatever for the German guards and troops who were still to be found .

Watch "The Hook"

At these same Jefferson Barracks there would be found, as we found it at Buchenwald, the much-pictured and much-described strangling chamber, with some 40 hooks protruding from the walls of a room perhaps 30 feet square. It was here that those, who for one reason or another had incurred the displeasure of the camp authorities, would not be hanged, for hanging breaks the neck and brings death comparatively quickly, but literally choked to death. When the bodies were lowered, if there was any life left in them, the victims were clubbed to death with that much pictured club resembling a large rolling pin. The bodies were raised in an elevator and cremated. In this crematory appeared this typically sadistic German expression, inscribed on an artistic bronze tablet high on the wall and seemingly addressing itself to the victims in the ovens. Translated it read: "Let not worms eat my body. Let it be consumed by fire flame. I love always warmth and light. Therefore burn, do not bury me."

Again, at these same Jefferson Barracks there would be found a well - designed, well - built brick building containing in its center section a number of efficiently designed gas - operated crematory ovens. The reader may say to himself, as I at first did, why not a crematory in a large camp built to contain some 32,000 prisoners? The visitor to the barracks, however, would soon change his mind.

Reception for Death

At one end of this rather handsome building and adjoining the crematory he would find a small ante-room containing a desk and a chair. At this desk sat a reception clerk. Usually the desk was decorated with a small vase of flowers—those flowers that grow so beautifully in beautiful Germany. The reception clerk would record the names and numbers of a group of prisoners. My estimate is—and it is only an estimate—that the group would consist of not more than 20 or 30 persons. Probably the first thing that would catch their eye after noticing the flowers on the desk would be a neat gilt sign over a door reading "Spritz Bad," or, in English, "shower bath."

Mass Production Murder·

The new arrivals would each be given a piece of soap and a towel and, after disrobing, would be directed to enter the shower bath. The door through which they entered the shower room, a room perhaps 20 feet square, would then be closed behind them. They may or may not have noticed that the door—I did not measure it exactly—was some 10 or 12 inches thick. Certainly they would not have noticed the pipes overhead connected with the pipes leading to the crematory ovens, nor would they have noticed that on one side of their shower room was a round glass circular peephole, some five inches in diameter, with a sliding metal plate to block off vision when that seemed desirable. This shower bath was, of course, the much-described gas chamber. The nozzles overhead discharged not water but gas. Indeed, there were

Inmates were packed into low, cramped, unlighted hovels; bunks the size of an American double bed " accomodated" six.

It was the sight of boxcars filled with the bodies of starved prisoners that enraged American troops and drained them of mercy for the SS.

no water pipes that we could see. It did not take long to dispose of the bodies in the adjoining crematory. Crematory and shower baths don't mix, and there is not the slightest doubt in my mind but that it was a well-designed plan to "liquidate" the undesirables and to leave no tell-tale evidence behind.

The Persistent "Why"

Why, I am often asked, did the Nazis take the trouble to starve, strangle and gas their prisoners to death? Why did they not shoot them? I do not know the answer to that question. I can only guess and my guess is that, having confined the undesirables within the limits of a concentration camp, they felt that they had better get what work they could out of them on adjoining farms or in nearby factories, and that when they were too weak to work, they merely let them die, with the strangling and gassing processes used on the obstreperous and on the Jews.

Is all this unbelievable? Perhaps it is. To a normal American these facts are very difficult to believe. I can only say that the groups of newspaper and magazine editors, whom I accompanied to Europe, made the most painstaking and scrupulous effort to sift the true from the false, to dismiss exaggerations or unprovable assertions of the prisoners and to present the true value of the evidence disclosed. I can only say that inspecting these two prisoners' camps at Buchenwald and Dachau I leaned over backwards in using my four senses—those of seeing, hearing, touching and smelling.

I have seen the bodies and the crematories and the gas chamber and many other things with my own eyes. I have seen the sinister appearance of one black barracks after another at Buchenwald, with the intervening streets or side-walks paved with small cobblestones, without a blade of grass or a tree to be seen anywhere. I have seen the pathetically sick lying on the floor on clean mattresses and with clean bedclothes and wearing clean clothing, all recently supplied by the United States Army. They were lying on the floor because cots were not yet available.

We were told that the great majority of them would die. When we entered the room, all but one of them were too sick even to raise their heads. All they could do was to roll their eyes in our direction.

"Because I am a Jew"

There was one exception. He was a Polish lad of perhaps 17. His hair was closely cropped; his face thin and very grey, his black eyes blazed as he told us his story. He spoke pretty good English. He was strong enough to be able to sit up, but from time to time he would bring the back of his hand up to his forehead to wipe off the sweat of extreme fatigue. Pathetically enough, the Signal Corps men were taking flashlight photographs, as they did wherever we went, and whenever a flashlight would go off, the boy's entire body would shiver.

We asked him why he was in this camp. He replied: "Because I am a Jew. You understand that? Because I am a Jew."

I have seen a half-acre of the dead, the crop of the previous night who perished at Dachau. I have seen and I took intense satisfaction in seeing lying near this field of dead, but separated from them, as though to avoid contamination of these helpless victims of the SS, eight bodies of SS prison guards. They were dressed in camouflaged coats and pants with brown and green spots on them, not unlike the camouflage outfit of our Army. There were various explanations of how they happened to be there. Some said they had been killed when our troops overran the camp four days before. Others said that the inmates had killed them, I shall always remember with intense satisfaction looking down at one hideous wretch.

"How Could This Have Happened to Me?"

He must have been even more hideous in life than in death. He had curly red hair and very blue eyes which seemed to stare up at me and to say, "How on earth could this thing have happened to

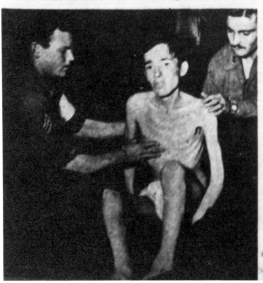

Pvt James L. Watkins of the 106th Infantry lost 60 pounds, was too weak to walk when rescued by 90th Div. troops

US newsmen touring the camps reported seeing "acres" of shrunken, shriveled corpses, "literally down to skin and bones," like those pictured above at Dachau.

me, a member of the SS?" We shall not have to trouble about trying those particular rats.

At Dachau it was a common sight to see bodies, two or three of them at a time, lying out in the street. They were still dying off so fast that as they died the surviving inmates would throw them outside to await the arrival of a pushcart which would take them away.

Joke—SS Variety

In demonstration of one of the SS's little jokes I have seen a prisoner lie on his stomach with his hands theoretically tied behind his back wriggling along on the ground. I have seen another demonstrating how they would tie a man's wrists together behind his back and then hang him up by his wrists for perhaps an hour, letting all his weight fall on his shoulders. Try it yourself and imagine what it would do to your shoulders. I have heard the testimony of many prisoners and of honorable American officers who had preceded us into Dachau by about four days.

I have heard a glorious and sublime sound, one which I shall never forget. As our group walked into a hospital ward of post-operative patients lying in double deck bunks and with everything, thanks to our Army doctors, spick and span, the patients observed the uniforms of the officers who preceded us and perhaps recognized the appearance of ourselves as American civilians. They tried to applaud and they tried to cheer, but they were so weak that the sound they made was almost plaintive. They were cheering the Americans. Hearing that sound made me proud to be an American.

The Unforgettable Smell

I have touched the emaciated hands of a considerable number of prisoners and of several hospital patients who insisted on shaking hands with the Americans, and I have smelt the unforgettable stench of the scores of bodies piled up in two rooms of the Dachau crematory which the Army had not yet had an opportunity to dispose of. On another nice, spring day I smelt the stench, too, that came out of an open window of a bunk house at

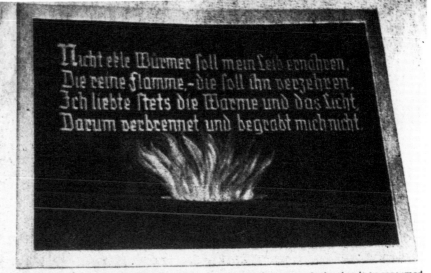

Bronze tablet on wall of crematorium reads: " Let not worms eat my body. Let it be consumed by fire flame. I love always warmth and light. Therefore burn, do not bury me."

Above, Weimar citizens view furnaces. Below, Congressmen inspect gas chamber

"Trophy Table" at Buchenwald. Below, SS guard lifted from Dachau moat.

Buchenwald which the Army had evacuated, had not yet had an opportunity to disinfect and which they had locked up. I believe that peering into that dark, filthy pesthouse, with its very few windows and its bunks still filled with the bedding of the inmates and smelling that smell, shocked me worse than anything else. Curiously enough, the bodies I was to see later shocked me comparatively little, for these poor creatures were so emaciated, literally down to skin and bones, that they appeared unreal. It was difficult to believe that they were corpses of human beings. They rather resembled caricatures of human beings.

Overwhelming Evidence

I have found exaggeration in previously published reports to be absolutely negligible. The evidence of the atrocities is so overwhelming that I feel, as we newspaper men all did, that it would weaken the case to report anything that was not obviously the truth. I will cite one such example. The wife of the commandant at Buchenwald had herself made a lamp shade and other objects of tanned human skin, much of it bearing tattoo marks. Photographs proving this have been published in the newspapers and should appear in the forthcoming Signal Corps film. The report was published in the United States that these pieces of skin were removed, probably under local anesthetic by the grafting process familiar to all surgeons, from living victims. I found no evidence to indicate the victims were alive.

Gen. Eisenhower gave us, the assignment to come to Europe and to report the existence of atrocities in Germany. I have met Gen. Eisenhower and I know that he is not a revengeful man. His purpose in giving us this assignment was to make the American people realize the incredible extent of the Nazi crimes so that those who were guilty would be justly punished—and here I repeat and emphasize the words "justly punished," not by Gestapo-like lynchings but by fair trials where a guilty man is found guilty and an innocent man has a fair opportunity to prove his innocence. If this report will help to bring about that result, I shall feel that my trip to Europe was justified.

A GERMAN JOURNALIST

German journalist Dr. Wolfgang Kraus visited the BUCHEN-WALD *concentration camp after it was liberated by the Americans in mid-April 1945. The sights at the camp disturbed and shocked Kraus: like many other German civilians, he claimed not to know about the details of persecution and genocide.*

The idylls faded. Behind sparkling foliage and brilliant blossoms Altenberg was hiding with its towers and nooks, its face spared the scars of war, an oasis within a field of ruin that National Socialism had made of Germany. Our journey goes westward. We pass the mass migrations of stateless people, walking along the sides of the road back to their homes with carts and baby carriages loaded down with beds and meager household belongings. Going through Gera and Jena, both heavily bombarded from air attacks, we reach Weimar. Piles of debris still fill the streets through which Goethe once walked. Cracks have split open the walls of the National Theater, the ostentation of the Party Buildings stretch their unfinished arms into the summer sky.

Out of the sun, we enter into darkness. The cold dread grasps at your heart. It is only a short way to Buchenwald. But the distance between the summit of German intellectual culture and the fall into the depths of spiritual night is worlds apart.

A beech forest in which the axe cuts bleeding wounds. In the middle of it all a small city. A city of terror. The ruins of the armaments factories destroyed by air attacks where the prisoners had to work open the entrance to the concentration camp Buchenwald with their demolished walls. The large, spacious grounds resemble a construction site. These low, flat halls and barracks would never have been completely finished. One had continually worked on their construction. Bricks and boards are lying around. Today everything has essentially been cleaned up. But an impression of uncompletedness still lingers over it all.

The former prisoners move about freely and unobstructed among the American guards. With the help of the occupying forces, they took control of their newly won lives in their own hands. Many of them seemed already to have recovered somewhat from the suffering they had gone through. Only their clothing betrayed who they were. Their blue-and-white-striped prisoner pants they wear mostly with simple shirts and jackets with the white-bordered red patches stating "Buchenwald." There are also various other insignia in red for Communism, in Polish white and red, or other national colors. On their heads there is often a black-dyed military cap, set off center, [and] some are in sandals, Among them are many pronounced, intelligent faces. Even in the streets and restaurants of Weimar they move about freely, still, quiet guests who do not obtrusively tell the world of their suffering. Their stories are also passionless and factual. Their reports almost sound as though all the horror were part of an unknown observation. They have separated themselves from the horror.

Only deep within the heart does the flame still burn; flickering now and then, it breaks through the eyes with a startled look. The first who come to greet us are a young German communist whose bright eyes reflect an unbroken will to live, and an eighteen-year-old Pole from Cracow who speaks German. Soon others encircle us, accompany us, explain, tell us stories. From their stories and the statements of official numbers, a shocking picture begins to unfold. . . .

When the accommodations in Buchenwald were no longer enough to fulfill their purpose, mass transports were sent to Auschwitz, the extermination center on the Upper Silesian border. Twenty thousand prisoners were still alive in Buchenwald when the Americans arrived so unexpectedly that the slave drivers had no time to clear them away. The attempt to transport the camp was ruined. Twenty thousand people, despite all their differences, were united through brotherly camaraderie hardened by a common terrible experience. They are the verbal witnesses and accusers of a terror which goes beyond all human comprehension. Crimes occur wherever people live; laws were therefore created to hinder them. However, here an organization of systematic murder was built up that was able to carry out its task unhampered because it was under the protection of federal legislation. That is the most atrocious aspect, which one cannot comprehend: the terror of the death factory that everyone who escaped it can relate.

When the German people learn the full truth about the hell of the concentration camps, they will turn away from every memory of this terrible time with a shudder of horror, a time that invented such a frightful desecration of humanity. This barbarity, an insult to every culture, is fundamentally so ungerman that only degenerate, spiritually homeless criminals could be responsible for it. It was a school of sadism, a brutality for beasts who have distanced themselves from every thought of humanity, that the connection between human society and them had long been broken before they were unmasked. Except for the accident of birth, these outsiders of humanity have nothing in common with the people in whose roots their heritage also lies. There can be only one voice in Germany as well as in the entire world: the way of thinking that gave rise to the establishment of concentration camps must be eradicated for the misdeeds it committed and never again be allowed the opportunity to make use of political power.

— From Miscellaneous Detachments, Detachment H7H2, General Records, Vicht Germany, European Civil Affairs Division 1944–45, Record Group 492, National Archives and Records Administration. Translated from German by Neal Guthrie.

Victims and Germans

GERMANS AND JEWISH DEAD

As the Allies entered Germany, they uncovered evidence of atrocities in many locations other than concentration camps [see pp. 69–77]. SHAEF ordered that German civilians dig new graves for the victims of these murders. As the following re-

port asserts, however, not all survivors agreed with this policy.

— From the Los Angeles Times, *April 30, 1945, © 1945, Los Angeles Times. Reprinted with permission.*

POLISH JEWS REFUSE TO LET NAZIS TOUCH DEAD

BY ROBERT RICHARDS

NEUNBURG, April 29. (U.P.)— Chuna Grunbaum and his fellow Jews from Poland, who had made the long march and survived, stood in the woods near this little town today and told Neunburg's Germans:

"Do not touch our dead. We will pick them up ourselves."

All the men of Neunburg gathered this morning with their women, and most of their children, and marched to a woodland where the bodies of 161 Polish Jews lay scattered carelessly in three shallow graves. The S.S. men who murdered them were in such a rush to escape approaching American columns that they hardly took time to spread earth over the pitiful heaps of what once were humans.

The Jewish victims were inmates of the Flossenberg concentration camp. They had been herded along the roads in a forced march as the Nazis attempted to remove as much evidence as possible of their own black record as jailers.

Those who were too weak to carry on, or who halted seeking food and water, were shot through the head or knocked down with clubs. Every one of the bodies bore evidence of violence, either a bullet hole or a smashed skull which nearly always had a wound that nearly obliterated the right eye.

After these bodies were found, Americans in this area decided it would be good for the Germans of Neunburg to see what has been going on in the Reich while German families lived a normal life. So, they marched the town's populace a half mile from the town to the woods, with parties of four German men carrying caskets.

Hated Nazi Touch

Their job was to take the bodies back to a tiny cemetery nearer town for decent burial. But when the time came to lift the bodies into the coffins, the few Jews who still survived cried:

"No Germans will touch our dead!"

So, tenderly and quietly, they lifted each body into its wooden box.

Then, with four Germans carrying each coffin, now filled, and with a Jewish refugee marching at the head of each coffin praying in Hebrew, the procession turned toward the cemetery.

2200 File Past

At least 2200 German men and women filed past the bodies in the woods, and it was difficult to say how they felt. Most seemed to have the attitude of:

"Why do this to me? I didn't do it. I didn't know about it." The very old appeared bewildered and not quite sure why they had come.

The procession of Germans past the dead lasted from 8 a.m. to well past noon.

An American soldier hands out oranges to hungry
and wide-eyed inmates at Wöbbelin concentration
camp on May 5, 1945, shortly after the camp's
liberation. (NARA)

THE LIBERATION OF WÖBBELIN

Wöbbelin concentration camp, a sub-camp of Neuengamme, was liberated by the US 8th Infantry and 82nd Airborne Divisions on May 3, 1945. The camp held about 4,000 prisoners of various nationalities, including some women who had been transferred from other camps in the last weeks.

Fortunately, U.S. Army photographers accompanied some of the first units to enter Wöbbelin and took many of the photos shown here. Others were taken shortly after the liberation by Major Alfred Sundquist, an army doctor who treated the inmates after liberation and became the first commandant of the displaced persons camp set up in Wöbbelin.

From Ludwigslust, the town next to Wöbbelin, the U.S. military ordered German civilians to walk through the camp and to see firsthand the atrocities committed there. Male Germans of all classes were forced to disinter many of the hastily buried victims or move the unburied corpses from the camp to another spot for reburial. The American military authorities ordered the local populace to attend the burials.

This was one of three funeral ceremonies for the dead of Wöbbelin arranged by the Americans on May 7–9, 1945, in towns surrounding the camp. At a service for one hundred forty-four victims buried in Hagenow, an American military government officer, Colonel Harry Cain, delivered the following address.

In these open graves lie the emaciated, brutalized bodies of some 144 citizens of many lands. Before they were dragged away from their homes, their livelihoods, to satisfy the insatiable greed and malice ambition and savagery of the German nation, they were happy and healthy and contented human beings. They were brought to this German soil from Poland, Russia, Czechoslovakia, Holland, Belgium, France. They were driven and starved and beaten to slake that unholy thirst of the German war machine. When possessed no longer of the will or ability to work or fight back or live, they were either tortured to death or permitted to slowly die. What you witness and are a part of in Haganow today is but a single small example of what can be seen thruout the length and depth of your German Fatherland. Untold numbers of other Allied soldiers and German citizens shudder before similar burial services as you shudder now. The Allies shudder because they never dreamed or visualized that human leadership supported by the masses could so debase itself as to be responsible for results like those who lie in these open graves. You Germans shudder from reasons of your own. Some of you, having been a party to this degradation of mankind, shudder for fear that your guilt will be determined, as in fact it will. Others among you shudder because you let depravity of this character develop while you stood still. The civilized world shudders on finding that a part of its society has fallen so low. That world isn't content to believe that what we are horrified about was

the work of any small group of German gangsters; maniacs and fanatics. That world must, as it does, hold the German people responsible for what has taken place within the confines of this nation. Time will prove to what extent the German people recognize the enormity of their crimes and to what extent they will shoulder a full national responsibility for making amends. That any future conduct can eradicate the knowledge and memories of a service like this is a matter of high dispute. If there be a soul within the German nation, it will rise now to make impossible the doing of such future wrongs. If there be not a soul in this German nation, its future is forlorn and totally lacking in hope.

The bodies in these graves came yesterday from Wöbbelin. They were buried there in a common grave or lying piled high on the open earth. Bodies from Wöbbelin will be buried in Ludwigslust and Schwerin as they are being buried here under the sight of God and true words consecrated by the Protestant, Catholic and Jewish faiths. In death these bodies are receiving from Allied, Christian hands the decent, humanitarian and spiritual treatment they didn't receive in life from German hands. As we listen, Allies and Germans alike, let us ask an understanding which Germany must find if there is to be a future life for her.

In a service last Sunday, held in the German Cathedral in Wismar two thousand Allied soldiers—the same, who had helped beat down and crush your military machine—spoke a prayer aloud that drifted into your German skies—God's skies. "Pray", they said, "for the German people, that they may be rid of the burden of false teaching and one day take their place again among honorable peoples."

—Reproduced from Statement Delivered at Hagenow, Germany on May 8, 1945, Papers of Meyer Gilden, United States Holocaust Memorial Museum Archives, Washington, D.C.

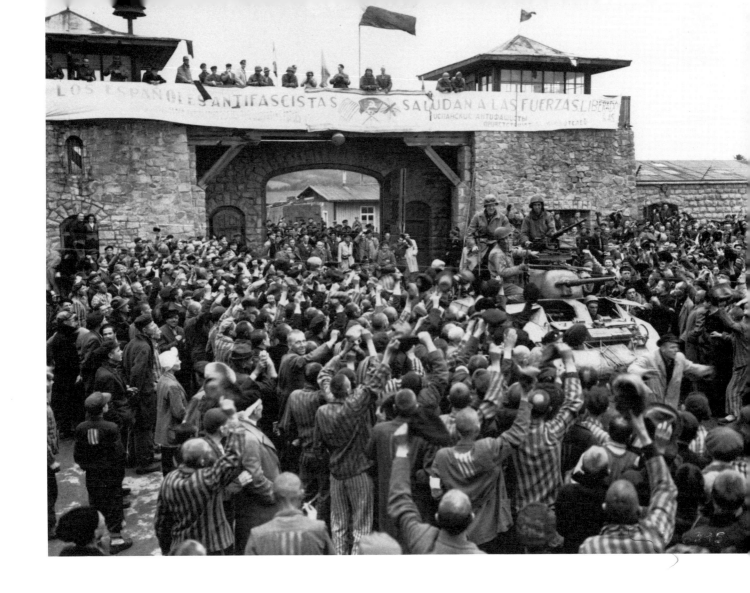

Mauthausen prisoners cheer U.S. troops as an armored car of the 11th Armored Division enters the camp on May 5, 1945. The banner was made by Spanish Republican prisoners. They had been deported to Mauthausen from France, where they had fled in 1939 after the Spanish Civil War. Such scenes were repeated at many liberated camps, including Wöbbelin. (NARA)

U.S. soldiers guard Wöbbelin concentration camp near Ludwigslust, Germany, after the camp's liberation. The Allies considered such guards a necessity to prevent the spread of diseases epidemic in most liberated concentration camps. (NARA)

A scene typical of those that the liberators of Wöbbelin beheld when they entered the camp; exhausted inmates huddled together with the corpses of recently dead inmates. (NARA)

The townsfolk of Ludwigslust, some visibly appalled, forced by the Allies to stare at the grisly handiwork of their regime. (NARA)

Local German civilians are compelled to load the
bodies of dead prisoners from Wöbbelin concentration camp into trucks, while U.S. soldiers watch.
The bodies were taken for re-burial in the town
square of Ludwigslust on May 7, 1945. (NARA)

The citizens of Ludwigslust forced to view bodies
prepared for the burial ceremony on May 7, 1945.
Similar viewings for the German populace were
ordered all over the former Reich. (NARA)

Crosses mark the graves of Wöbbelin's dead,
including the Star of David on the cross at
the right. (NARA)

The burial ceremony on May 7 for the dead of Wöbbelin concentration camp in the town square of Ludwigslust. The entire citizenry of the town was present to hear the eulogies castigating them for their complicity in such barbarism. (USHMM)

The graves of the Wöbbelin victims are covered with spruce boughs, a widespread German burial tradition. The U.S. military ordered the graves to be decorated by the populace. (USHMM)

DISPLACED PERSONS

- At war's end, the victorious Allies divided defeated Germany into four zones of occupation, governed respectively by the United States, the Soviet Union, Great Britain, and France. The CONTROL COUNCIL FOR GERMANY was the supreme governmental authority.

- Among the Allies' chief tasks was the REPATRIATION of millions of former concentration and labor camp prisoners, called DISPLACED PERSONS (DPs), from Germany and Austria.

- The UNITED NATIONS RELIEF AND REHABILITATION ADMINISTRATION (UNRRA) was to care for the displaced persons, but only in 1946 did it have sufficient personnel to do so. For the remainder of 1945, the Allied militaries took on the task.

- The Allies wanted to avoid any semblance of duplicating Nazi segregation and discrimination against Jews and grouped all displaced persons, Jews and non-Jews, by country of origin. This policy failed to recognize that continuing racial persecution demanded additional consideration for the Jews.

- President Truman appointed a committee headed by Earl G. HARRISON to investigate conditions in displaced persons camps. Though some camps were better than others, the "Harrison Report" criticized the Allied treatment of DPs, particularly of Jewish DPs.

- Many of the Jewish displaced persons living in DP camps in Germany by late 1945 were fleeing anti-Jewish POGROMS in eastern Europe.

- In addition to the Allies' efforts, Jewish survivors formed their own organizations to aid their return to normal life and to seek surviving family members dispersed by the Holocaust.

- Permanent post-war resettlement for Jewish survivors became a prominent issue. Jews hoped to establish an independent state in PALESTINE, but Britain, which controlled the territory, faced Arab opposition to increased Jewish immigration.

- An order from President Truman in December 1945 eased immigration of displaced persons to the United States.

DPs, some still wearing their prisoner uniforms, fixing a meal and living on the street in Dachau on May 1, 1945, soon after the camp was liberated. (NARA)

BROTHERS REUNITED

George Vida was a Jew who spent his youth in Budapest, Hungary; as an adult he lived in Czechoslovakia. After the German occupation of that country in 1939, he escaped with his wife and eventually reached the United States, joining the army as a Jewish chaplain in 1943. Serving in Europe he aided Jewish DPs in Germany during 1945. That fall he journeyed to Hungary to visit the country of his youth, and he wrote the following letter to his wife about the trip.

November 11, 1945

Amy dearest:

Yesterday, I used the excuse that it was getting late. It was late—I don't dare tell you what time it was, but that was not the reason why I interrupted my letter. The real reason was that I was about to describe experiences that defy description.

Actually, it all started at the Office of the American Joint Distribution Committee in Budapest, where I found long lists of survivors. These were mostly people who were sent into Slave Labor Battalions. I don't know if those words mean anything to you. There are some people who feel that any kind of Military service is a sort of slavery. You get up; you go to sleep; you do your work—everything by the numbers. To each number there is a prescribed motion and each motion has to be executed precisely. Can you imagine an Army in which the private soldier has no rights; no time at all on his own and no weapons with which to defend himself? With Companies and Battalions of men in uniforms sent far into the front lines without a rifle to hide behind. The few officers who commanded them had every right to kill any man without trial and without even listening to him for any infraction of the rule. They were working fifteen or sixteen hours—sometimes even more until they could not move. When they were sick, the only medical attention they could get was from fellow privates—slaves like themselves who had some medical training. They had no pills, drugs or anything else to kill pain.

Among the thousands of names of those who came back from such slave battalions, I found one I recognized, Kalmar Andor. You know who that is? My cousin Bandi! Just a few months younger than myself. We grew up together. We were just like brothers. For two years we went to school together. He spent many a summer in our house. You remember him? He was that handsome boy whose brother became a Rabbi. He went to medical school in

Vienna and he flunked out. He used to say it was intentional, because his parents needed his help in the business. He was the oldest son of my father's only sister. According to the list, he went home to the house in which he grew up. He was even born in that house. I was quite excited about it. So I organized myself some gasoline and took my jeep to that town with the name which you could never pronounce. You remember all the jokes we used to make about Kiskunfelegyhaza? The trip down there was uneventful. I drove my jeep directly to his front gate, got out of the jeep and opened the big heavy doors. I saw a couple of women run like scared rabbits from the yard into the house but I drove my jeep right into the yard and closed the gates behind me.

Then I saw Bandi. Hobbling, he came out to see what happened. He supported himself on two walking canes. I could see on his face he was walking with great pain but when he recognized me, he threw away one cane and literally jumped on my neck. We embraced one another and we both cried a little. Then he took me into the house leaning heavily on my arm as we walked. His wife, or whoever the young woman was he brought home after the war, put some milk and bread on the table. They didn't have much food nor any money to buy some on the black market. There we sat and talked. There was so much he wanted to tell me but I couldn't hear much; my eyes and my ears were clouded. I found somebody alive. Then, suddenly with a start, I awoke to his question. "Did you see your brother yet?"

"Who? Which one? Where?" This is how I found out that my brother, Imre, was alive and in Csongrad. When I heard that, I invited Bandi to drive with me in my jeep to Csongrad. He smiled sadly. "With this leg of mine? I would faint before we got out of town." He showed me a five-inch long and about one-inch wide open wound on his right thigh—a wound that was neglected, festering. "Medical attention? They can't do anything for me anymore. I got some morphine to kill the pain and my wife gives me an injection twice a day. I can't go anywhere." I promised him that I would come back from Csongrad to see him again but I couldn't wait to get into my jeep again and go "home." What a trip it was. Home. You remember our house in Csongrad? The huge dining room where we used to entertain fifty or sixty people; the beautiful living room with the needle-point pictures my mother made. The house was empty. Not one single piece of furniture anywhere. The beautiful garden with the fountain in the middle—totally neglected and in ruins. In the bedroom of my parents, there were two sacks of some grain. The mice or the rats must have eaten through the sacks because the grain spilled out over the parquet floors. Where my father's law office used to be, I saw horse manure on the floor. I ran out of the house and stopped the first person I could find and asked him where my brother was. He directed me to City Hall. Imre is now the City Clerk of Csongrad.

How can I describe the reunion with my brother? I was afraid to shock him with a sudden and unexpected appearance. So I sent a little boy to his office and asked him to come out. "His brother wants to see him."

Actually, he didn't change much. He was always taller than I, but he must have lost a lot of weight. He was now very thin. His six foot frame was bent; his eyes were full of tears from the first moment I embraced him until I left. He lives in a furnished room in the house of some friends. Of course, his wife was gone and his son was four years old when they killed him. We couldn't talk about it. We drove out to the cemetery to the graves of our mother and grandparents. There, the weeds had overgrown the wilderness of neglected graves and it was perhaps the most cheerful place in Csongrad.

I begged him. "Come with me. I will take you to America. I will take you to Germany. Go to Budapest and live among people." He smiled resignedly. "How can I? Who knows, somebody may still come back." I knew he didn't believe it. I stayed with him one day. I slept with him in his furnished room. I showed him snapshots of you and our children and this I think did give him more happiness than he has seen in five years.

He took me to visit the Farago girls. You remember the friends of my parents who had five daughters? They had a fine store on Main Street and their grandfather used to have a vineyard. Oh, what fun we once had in that vineyard. They used to have one of the biggest, most spacious homes in town. Four of the five girls returned home after the war. Now they are living in one room in back of the house. The rest of the house looked just like ours—empty, neglected and full of sadness. They told me stories I'll never forget.

Scores of non-Jewish farmers offered to hide my father. But his answer was the same to all of them. "I couldn't permit you to risk your life to save mine." Imre came home in his striped pajamas (that's what they used to call the Concentration Camp uniform). Somebody told him that a farmer, well known to him, hid a couple of suitcases of his clothing: shirts, underwear, all the things he needed now so badly. He took a bicycle and went to visit the farmer. He was told, "Yes, it is correct. Your father gave me two suitcases to hide in case someone from the family would return home alive. But the Russians came and found the suitcases and confiscated everything." While the farmer was telling him this, my brother noticed that he had a shirt on with the initials of my brother monogrammed on it. "What did you do? What did you say to him?" I asked. "What could I say? It was only a shirt! I lost so much more." Another time, he went to talk

to somebody. It was raining yet they would not invite him into the house. Of course, they apologized. "The living room wasn't clean; it was disordered, not fit to receive such an honored visitor." Imre just waved them aside and walked into a very clean and orderly living room. The first thing he saw there was a Grandfather clock which used to stand in our living room. "How can you stand it? Come away from here." He answered sadly, "Not yet. Perhaps in a little while I'll be ready to leave here and start life anew. Give me time." We were walking through the streets. We went down to the river where we used to go swimming every summer. We remembered the boat father gave us when we could prove to him that we could swim well enough. A thousand stories out of the past and every memory caused unbearable pain because in every one of those incidents, there was somebody who was no more—whose life ended brutally, violently! Even some of our relatives and friends who were lucky enough to survive the Concentration Camps and the Slave Labor Camps died after the war, either of malnutrition or of T.B. Wherever we went, we were walking in a cemetery. Whatever we talked about, we were surrounded by the dead.

I told Imre that I had five more days of leave. I begged him to come with me to Budapest and spend the remaining days together, but I couldn't budge him. He pleaded, "I have duties, responsibilities." But I think he's afraid of life. He's afraid of people. In Budapest, there are families that remained intact. He wanted to stay where there was no house without the sign of mourning on the door.

I feel very guilty about it, but I must confess that I felt actually relieved when I said goodbye to Imre and left Csongrad. If it were not for him, I couldn't have stayed there for one hour but even with him there, I could not stand it more than one day.

I only stayed in Budapest overnight to organize my return to Frankfurt. My return trip was not quite as uneventful and easy as my trip there. On the Czech border, the Russian guard stopped me and I had to wait about three hours before he could find his commanding officer who then gave me permission to continue on my way. I drove 1,667 miles and two blocks before I reached my office, I had a flat tire. Don't laugh! To repair a flat tire is not an easy matter in Germany today. But I was glad, for all the forms that I had to fill out and all the explanations which I had to make gave me time not to remember Bandi and Imre and all the others in Hungary.

Thanks for the many packages which I found here. They make it possible for me to repay a small part of a great debt. You have no idea what a comfort it is to help someone, anyone. Whoever comes to me will not leave empty-handed.

I love you. Kiss Ruth and Henry for me. How much I miss you all!

As ever,
GEORGE

—*From George Vida,* From Doom to Dawn *(New York: Jonathan David, 1967), 37–42.*

LIFE IN DP CAMPS

REPORT ON DACHAU

The chaotic conditions in Germany at war's end necessitated that a number of concentration camps be used to hold some of the flood of Germany's DISPLACED PERSONS. DACHAU was one camp used in this way. Assigned the task of administering occupied Germany, the G-5 Section of SHAEF, the Civil Affairs Division, made periodic inspections of all DP camps, including Dachau. A report of such an inspection is reproduced here. The WEHRMACHT personnel mentioned in the report had been members of the armed forces of the defeated THIRD REICH.

— From "Report on Conditions in Dachau Concentration Camp," July 9, 1945, SHAEF/G-5/DP/2748/6, Record Group 331, box 50, entry 47, National Archives and Records Administration.

SHAEF/G5/DP/2748/6   9 July 1945

SUBJECT: REPORT ON CONDITIONS IN DACHAU CONCENTRATION CAMP, 2 JULY 1945.

TO   :   EXECUTIVE, DISPLACED PERSONS BRANCH, G-5.

1. General Comments

The DACHAU Concentration Camp was visited on the 2 July, 1945. Contact was established with the Commanding Officer, Colonel PAUL A. ROY, Field Artillery, 34th Anti-Aircraft Group, 45th Division, 3rd US Army. Since several reports, fully covering conditions at this Camp at the time of its liberation, have already been made, the report given below will treat only with present conditions.

2. Staff

Colonel Roy is assisted by 42 officers and 68 EM. The 10th Field Hospital supervises all medical activities at the Camp. The staff of the 10th Field Hospital consists of 9 medical officers, 16 officer nurses and 171 enlisted personnel. This US Army medical personnel supervises the following additional medical staff, which has direct contact with the patients in the four hospital units at the Concentration Camp; 87 Wehrmacht medical officers, 2 Wehrmacht dentists, 214 Wehrmacht nurses, 322 Wehrmacht medical orderlies; 10 Belgian nurses; 13 Dutch nurses; 6 Polish doctors, 28 Polish medical orderlies, 1 Polish laboratory technician and 1 Polish dentist. 1,040 Wehrmacht prisoners of war are billeted in the Dachau Compound and are employed on an extensive program of cleaning up the premises.

3. Residents

The following tabular summary indicates the numbers by nationality of the residents in the DACHAU Concentration Camp on the 2 July, 1945:

Nationality	Total	Hospitalized	Balance
Polish	2,301	1,394	907
Russian	169	169	-
Yugoslav	173	173	-
Italian	116	27	89
Czechoslovak	33	26	7
German	100	67	33
Belgian	1	1	-
Hungarian	1,078	276	802
Austrian	141	30	111
Spanish	2	2	-
Greek	214	18	196
British	1	0	1

47   654

Esthonians	5	1	4
Lithuanians	47	24	23
Latvians	3	2	1
Norwegians	1	1	-
Rumanians	541	94	447
Americans	4	2	2
Bulgarians	1	1	-
Stateless	2	2	0
Irish	1	-	1
Argentinians	1	-	1
	4,935	2,310	2,625

Of the former residents, the following nationalities have been evacuated entirely from the Camp: French, Dutch, Luxembourgeois, Slovak, Albanian, Armenian, Turkish, Sudeten German, Corsican, Danish, Egyptian, San Salvadoran.

4. Living Accommodations

All of the residents of the DACHAU Concentration Camp not hospitalized are accommodated in SS barracks and other buildings formerly used for storage and light manufacturing purposes. Since the population of Dachau has been substantially decreased from a total of 32,000 at the time of liberation to a present population of 4,935, there is ample available in the way of beds, mattresses, blankets, and other equipment and facilities. Inspection of various quarters revealed that they were clean, uncrowded and comfortable. The compound area in which all of the residents were required to live under the German regime now accommodates the prisoners of war who work on the premises.

5. Feeding

The food supply at DACHAU is ample. The present ration for the well residents is 2,600 calories a day, and those who are recovering from malnutrition in the various hospitals are being given graded rations - depending on their condition - up to 4,100 calories daily. The kitchens and bakery were inspected, and the food appeared to be not only more than adequate but well-prepared. A copy of the July 2 menu, taken from the door of the kitchen, is appended. Virtually all food supplied at the Camp is obtained from local German resources and warehouses on the premises.

6. Clothing

Large supplies of cloth and prison garments were found on the premises when the DACHAU Concentration Camp was liberated. Prison garments are being dyed blue-black, and the cloth is being made into garments by resident tailors. At the time of departure, each resident is equipped by Colonel Roy with two shirts, two undergarments, two socks, a pair of shoes and a good suit.

7. UNRRA

One UNRRA team is operative at the DACHAU Concentration Camp. Two others had been requested, but got side-tracked. The UNRRA personnel is working on the problem of resettlement of Stateless persons and that of re-uniting family units.

47 655

- 2 -

8. **Future Plans**

Colonel Roy intends to have the premises completely cleaned; they were littered in some places to a depth of 3 - 4 ft. He further intends to clean out and burn the buildings in the compound. The hospitals, SS barracks and warehouses probably will be turned into a semi-permanent military installation.

Colonel Roy is anxious to repatriate or otherwise dispose of all the residents at the Camp. He stated, however, that the Army must make certain that the lot of the persons sent from the Camp is improved before they are shipped.

※　※　※　※　※　※　※　※

Subsidiary Camp at ALLACH

This Camp was entirely evacuated on the 18 June. It still represents a considerable hazard to health, in view of the filth and vermin remaining on the premises. It was recommended on 18 June that the Camp be destroyed as soon as all salvageable material had been removed.

M. J. PROUDFOOT,
Lt. Colonel, A.U.S.,
Chief, Operational Analysis Section.

47   656

A GI RUNS A DP CAMP

Major Irving Heymont was an infantry officer in the 5th Infantry Regiment of the 71st Infantry Division that liberated GUNSKIRCHEN concentration camp, a subcamp of MAUTHAUSEN. He was awarded the Silver Star for gallantry in action. As a battalion commander when the war ended, he found himself running a DISPLACED PERSONS camp in Landsberg, Germany. Selections from letters he wrote to his wife about this experience are reproduced here.

20 September 1945

It is 0530 hours, and I am up and dressed. No one else is awake yet. So much has happened in so short a time that I can't sleep. It seems as though years have passed since I was in London. My letter written last night must leave you as confused as I am. There is little that can be done now before the big inspection later this morning—might as well use this opportunity to describe the camp in more detail. It is located in a former Wehrmacht artillery *kaserne*, or permanent military post. The dwellings, known as blocks, are three-story brick barracks typical of any permanent Army dwellings. The rooms are very large and afford no privacy. Wash-rooms and latrines have long rows of the usual tile fixtures. From a military viewpoint, the barracks are modern and well designed. For housing families, they could not be worse.

The DPs sleep in bunks of rough, unfinished lumber that are often double and even triple decked. Mattresses are straw-filled sacks. Bedding consists of shoddy gray Wehrmacht blankets or U.S. Army blankets. Sheets seem to be unknown except in the camp hospital and among a few enterprising persons who must have black market resources. The people are provided with tall, narrow wooden wall lockers. In these lockers (or occasionally in a wooden box, a battered suitcase, or a rucksack), they keep their worldly possessions, food supply, and utensils.

To afford some privacy, the wall lockers are placed so as to form partitions. Blankets, hung over cords, and scrap boards and panels are also used in a usually unsuccessful effort to get away from the ever-present view of the neighbors. I was immediately struck by the intense desire of the people to gain a little privacy—to be individuals and not part of an ordered mass.

In the *kaserne*, there are a large number of two-story masonry stables and garages. Some of the stables are partly filled with abandoned Wehrmacht equipment—especially spare parts for half-track vehicles. Oddly enough, one stable is filled with glass bed urinals. Wonder how they got here. A few of the garages and stables have been converted into classrooms and poorly equipped workshops. Most of them, in the upper stories, are used to house people. One of the riding halls in the *kaserne* area is being converted into a recreational hall and camp theater. The other riding halls are just enormous barns with dirt floors.

The only organized kitchen facilities are in the two buildings that had been built as central kitchens. The equipment is fairly complete—but badly run down. Part of the kitchen equipment, I was told, was lost during the looting and confusion at the immediate end of the war. Both kitchens have very limited serving space. I would guess that, during the Wehrmacht days, only the officers actually ate in the kitchen buildings. I can't figure out where the enlisted men ate. One kitchen building is being used for a kosher (in accordance with Jewish dietary laws) kitchen and the other, slightly larger, is in use for the non-kosher people.

I received my first shock at the gates of the camp. The iron fence around the *kaserne* had been increased in height by the liberal use of barbed wire. The outside perimeter is patrolled by armed soldiers from the battalion. A soldier and a member of the camp police are stationed at the entrance gate. I learned that the people of the camp are permitted to leave only when they have a written pass. The passes are issued on a day-to-day basis—and only to a small number each day. I saw large numbers of DPs lolling along the fence and watching the Germans walking freely along the opposite street. The battalion took over the guard system they found, but I am going to make changes just as soon as I can catch my breath.

Once inside the camp, I found the streets littered, but no more so than some of the streets in the poorer sections of New York City. There were signs that efforts, none too strenuous, had been made to clean the streets.

In the makeshift cubicles of the living quarters, groups are trying to revive family life. Eating together, it was explained to me, had come to be the high point of the day for the family group. Tables and chairs had been improvised from scraps of lumber and boxes. Almost every family group has an electric hot plate. With such an overload, it does not seem possible that the electrical circuits can still function. The wall lockers are littered with clothing, food, and eating utensils. The latter are generally quite filthy. I soon learned that there were no real facilities for washing them. While the bunk beds were fairly neatly made up, little or no sweeping had been done. Here and there, a very few family groups had spotless areas.

The number of idle people is surprising. Many of the beds were occupied by people either dozing or just lying there listlessly. One could sense an air of resignation.

The hallways are littered with trash and scraps of old food. Behind a number of the staircases, I saw signs of human excrement that obviously had been there for some time. In a few instances, I even saw some human excrement in the corridors!

The toilets beg description. About half the bowls were inoperative but full of excrement. Toilet seats, while not entirely lacking, were smeared with excrement or wet with urine. No toilet paper was in sight. I was informed that toilet attendants had been designated—but not one could be seen on duty. In explanation of the deplorable state of affairs, I was told that the water pressure was low because of war damage to the water mains. However, the water pressure seemed more than adequate for at least the first two

DPs line up at one of the "human laundries" established to disinfect liberated prisoners near the Bergen-Belsen concentration camp in April 1945. (NARA)

floors of each barracks building. What appeared to be low was the general sense of responsibility for communal sanitary facilities.

In the washrooms, most of the sinks were out of order. As we inspected, people came to wash dishes and pans. The remains of the food were just washed into the sinks. The utensils were dried with dirty rags or old paper and the paper often just dropped on the floor. The washrooms and toilets had an intense acrid odor that almost caused me to vomit.

The visit to the two central kitchens was another shock. We inspected the non-kosher kitchen first. The kitchen was so steamy that it was difficult to see. The tile floor was greasy, making walking difficult. Bags of potatoes were lying on the floor. The stoves and cauldrons looked as though they had not been cleaned for weeks. They were heavily encrusted with black grease and food debris. The knives and forks, spatulas, and other utensils were filthy. I picked up a basting spoon only to have it drop from my grasp—it

was so greasy. The cooks were obviously as dirty as their filthy aprons. I asked one cook, who was kneading dough, to extend his hands. His fingernails were encrusted with dirt, and his hands looked as if he had been greasing a wheel bearing. In the walk-in refrigerator, a meat carcass was lying on the floor. All meat hooks were rusty and dirty. The meat block, near the refrigerator, was improvised from a tree trunk and had a layer of old caked blood.

The little dining room (called a *Kasino*), where the camp committee and functionaries ate, was a welcome contrast. The tables and chairs were neat and clean, and the room was nicely decorated. Pictures of Theodore Herzl, Ben-Gurion, F. D. Roosevelt, Harry Truman, the flag of America, and the blue and white Star of David flag adorned the walls.

The kosher kitchen was even worse. I was amazed—to my mind, the word kosher had always had a connotation of cleanliness. The utter filth of this kitchen and its cooks and workers had to be seen to be believed. In a corner of the kitchen store room, I saw human excrement on the floor. I could not understand how it would be possible to eat food prepared in that kitchen and not suffer from diarrhea or dysentery. I instructed the man in charge that, unless the kitchen was cleaned up within 24 hours, I would close it as a menace to the health of the camp. As I spoke to him, my fingers were crossed. General Rolfe had left instructions that we were to lean over backwards and make certain that nothing was done that could be interpreted as interference with religious practices.

The two bright spots of the inspection were the camp hospital and the camp schools. The few faults in sanitation that I saw at the hospital were very minor. The hospital, except for one UNRRA public health nurse and a few German nurses, is completely staffed and operated by personnel of the camp. Dr. Nabriskie, in charge of the hospital, has done a remarkable job. He has built up a nearly complete 200-bed hospital and nursing school. Starting with an empty barracks building and enthusiasm, he and his helpers have begged, borrowed, and even stolen equipment and supplies to bring their facilities to the point where they could care for almost all of the medical needs of the camp personnel. UNRRA and the Army have been helping with supplies, but it seems that it is a constant struggle to secure enough. The Army apparently makes available only items from captured German stocks. It appears that these stocks are quite adequate, but it is virtually legerdemain to get anything because of the tremendous red tape involved. This will take some looking into.

I was amazed to learn from Dr. Nabriskie that the overall health rate of the camp is quite good. It does not seem possible. He read the look of disbelief on my face and wryly commented. "Remember, we are the survivors. Only the strong ones survived."

The schools of the camp were impressive. Under the leadership of a Dr. J. Oleiski, a graduate of a concentration camp, Landsberg has developed a remarkable school system. Despite the paucity of equipment and trained personnel, he had a number of garages converted into classrooms and vocational schools. Children are now learning to read and write. Adolescents, for the first time, are learning trades. Instruction is being offered in a great variety of skills, including garment making, all phases of shop working, auto mechanics, radio and repair and construction, and many others. Nor were the adults neglected. Former shopkeepers and salesmen are learning to work with their hands. A variety of evening courses in cultural subjects is also offered.

Everywhere in the school and cultural life of Landsberg, the influence of Dr. Oleiski is obvious. Before Hitler, this remarkable man had been a trained agronomist in Lithuania, working for the ORT organization. (ORT is the Jewish philanthropic organization that sponsors training in production skills.) Now, he is preaching and putting into practice his credo of salvation through work. His problems are tremendous. The schools are short of every essential:

paper, pencils, tools, and raw materials of every description. I think the camp can best be helped by helping Dr. Oleiski—that is, after the camp has been cleaned up.

Time for breakfast now and later the big inspection. . .

28 September 1945

It is almost midnight but instead of going to bed right now as I should, I must write the longer letter I promised yesterday. Writing to you helps me to relax and then I sleep better.

After a quick inspection of Landsberg this morning, General Rolfe and I drove 45 miles over some abominable roads to inspect the Fohrenwald camp near Wolfratshausen. It was supper time before we got back to Landsberg.

Fohrenwald is a beautiful camp—well set up and apparently well run. It is located near a former German munitions factory. When the factory was built, the Germans also put up housing for the workers. These houses are semi-detached affairs containing apartments of four or five rooms. The houses are built along concentric circular streets with the inner circle containing administration and community recreation buildings. While a few of the buildings need minor repairs—mostly window panes—the general condition of the buildings is excellent. The whole community cannot be more than a few years old.

Fohrenwald is ideal for a DP camp with fine housing for families. Being a compact separate community, it is well suited for maintaining control and keeping the Germans at a distance. The town of Wolfratshausen is actually a few kilometers away. When the Jews and Germans are very close, there is tension and the possibility of clashes.

The camp is not filled to capacity and can easily absorb the excess Landsberg population. At the moment, the camp population is about half Jewish. The plan is to move out the non-Jews and make the camp completely Jewish, as at Landsberg. Incidentally, the non-Jews are being moved out of Landsberg fairly rapidly. This morning General Rolfe said that the 800 non-Jewish Hungarians at Landsberg will be moved next week—probably back to Hungary.

The status of the Fohrenwald camp is uncertain. At the moment, it is not known whether Third Army Headquarters or the Division will assume responsibility. In any case, I have been ordered to get the camp supplied with its winter wood. This will require more scavenging to round up additional power saws and trucks. Rolfe promised to help get us more saws and trucks. I can't count on him because things are so chaotic that getting unusual requirements filled through regular supply channels is difficult and very slow. . .

The meeting at the camp last night was quite an experience. After the ordeal of addressing the DPs I am ready for anything. The interpreting was done by Rabbi Alexander Rosenberg of Yonkers, N.Y. He is an orthodox rabbi who is here with the American Joint Distribution Committee people. This morning, the Jewish soldiers on duty at the camp told me that the speech was well received. I am glad.

Before the meeting, I discussed the comments I planned

to make with the officers of the Battalion who were familiar with the camp. After the discussion, I made rough notes to guide me because I planned to speak extemporaneously. This evening, I reconstructed my speech from these rough notes and the notes taken, while I was talking, by Lt. Harold Bell, the Battalion Intelligence Officer. This is about what I said:

"I am Major Irving Heymont. I am a professional soldier in the U. S. Army. By order of my higher headquarters, I have been placed in charge of the Landsberg Camp.

"As I speak to you tonight, I can also be called a sort of DP. I, too, am far away from my native land where I would like to be. I travelled from America to Europe to fight fascism. My Regiment fought in France, Germany, and Austria until the Nazis were defeated.

"We know what you suffered in the Nazi concentration camps—and not just through newspaper reports. My Regiment liberated a concentration camp in Austria, the Gunskirchen Lager (sub-camp) of the infamous Mauthausen camp. Because I know what you have suffered, I want to assure you that I do not intend to see Landsberg another prison camp. We did not conquer the Nazis so we could have the hollow honor of standing armed guard over the victims of Hitler.

"Effective tomorrow morning at 6:00 AM, the pass system is abolished. Every resident of the Landsberg camp is free to come and go as he sees fit, subject to current curfew regulations applicable to all civilians.

"Effective tomorrow morning, all American guards will be withdrawn from this camp. Americans do not run concentration camps, even humane ones, for the victims of political and religious persecution. We will, however, maintain one guard at the main gate. The duty of this guard will be to aid your own camp police and to keep out unauthorized Germans—not to keep you in.

"Tomorrow morning, I will ask your camp leaders to furnish men to tear down the barbed wire that now surrounds the camp. The barbed wire is a symbol of ignominy and shame that more properly belongs to the people of the town of Landsberg rather than to you.

"The important thing is that you should all feel that you are free human beings. As long as you have to live in the Landsberg camp, you should have autonomy over your camp life. But—and there always is a but—certain factors must be explained. The Army and UNRRA, who give me my orders, are responsible for the camp. Because of this responsibility, we must also retain control. However, I am ready and anxious to grant a part of this responsibility and control to your representatives. When your representatives, and I accept the camp committee as your representatives, prove that they can handle this control and responsibility, I shall gladly increase the amount of autonomy until we of the Army will only be here to furnish you with help. I have already requested your committee to submit a plan to bring about this administrative camp autonomy. Their recommendations have been submitted, and I have accepted them with some minor exceptions. Very shortly, when the camp is in good running order, I plan to hold an election so that you can, by democratic means, choose your representatives.

"I must stress that no plan for autonomy will succeed without self-discipline and good organization. If the Allied armies had not possessed these two qualities, you would all no doubt still be languishing in concentration camps.

"I must strongly call your attention to the question of sanitation and cleanliness. Last week, I inspected the camp for the first time. To say the least, I was shocked. To say more, I could add that I almost retched. Those are harsh words, but you know them to be the truth. I was astounded when Dr. Nabriskie told me that the sick rate was low. It was incredible, considering the utterly filthy state of the camp.

"Habits and attitudes do not change overnight. I understand that the *SS Totenkopf* (Concentration Camp Guard Units) and the concentration camp administrations did not employ methods that fostered your pride or enabled you to keep clean. Now, I dread to think that you who survived the horrors of Dachau and its sub-camps like Landsberg may fall victims to disease and germs caused by your own filth. I know that the Army and UNRRA can be accused of being lax in supplying adequate amounts of toilet paper, soap, mops, brooms, and brushes. Those things are in short supply all over Europe. I can only promise that within a week you have more of those items. If I can't get them through regular sources of supply, I believe I can persuade the Burgermeister of Landsberg to make a levy on the town— or on the whole *kreis* (county), if necessary.

"I cannot overestimate this danger of epidemic. It is not only a danger to you, but it is also a danger to the U. S. troops stationed here in the town. Don't be victims of disease. Keep yourself and your quarters clean. Don't finish what the SS failed to do. Since my first inspection, you have done much to clean the camp. While you have worked hard, the camp is still not as clean as it should be. There is a great deal of more work to be done, and I know that you can, and will, do it. Tomorrow General Rolfe, whom most of you already know, will be here again to inspect the camp. I have told him that you can and will get your camp clean. It is up to you now to prove to him whether I am correct or a liar.

"Cleanliness only comes with work. Your camp leaders tell me of the difficulties in getting the people of the camp to work. I know better than to accuse you of laziness. As I said before, the habits of years are not shaken off in a few weeks or months. Under the Germans, work meant death for you. The harder you worked, the weaker you got on the few hundred calories you were fed. Every bit of work you did only strengthened your oppressors. Even now you are reluctant to do any work in the camp. You think—'why work in the camp. We will not be here forever. The day will come soon when we will get to Palestine or some other country.' You feel that you have already enriched Germany enough with your blood.

"All of that is true. But now is the time to relearn the habits of work and industry. Now is the time to relearn how to be self-respecting civilized persons. No man can ask you to forget what you and your families have been through. However, you can't live in the shadow of the past forever.

"Right now we are faced with the prospect of winter. Preparations must be made now so that all the blocks will be warm this winter and that the camp will have an adequate wood supply. The Army has already provided ample equipment to cut the wood in the forests. I have also detailed a number of my men to help in this work. The main burden, however, falls upon you. It is for you that the wood is intended. The wood is to warm you during the cold winter months. You are the ones to be vitally concerned about getting the wood as soon as possible. Of course, it is not an easy job. It will take at least several weeks. You must organize to complete this job in the proper time.

"No doubt you have many grievances. They cannot all be adjusted immediately. I can only promise that we will solve all within our powers. I don't doubt that you have heard many promises. I can assure you that we do not intend to make any promises that we can't keep. Earlier this week we promised to do something about the terrible overcrowding in the camp. You all know that we moved out American soldiers so that decent lodgings could be provided for the women and children of the camp. We are willing and anxious to be judged by our acts and not by our words.

"I only wish to God that tomorrow the Landsberg camp and the others like it would close their gates forever. I only wish to God that tomorrow I could speed you all on your way to the countries of your choice. That time will come soon—I hope. In the meanwhile, we are still here at Landsberg.

"This is the time for relearning habits of work and smiling, to live again as a proud people, unashamed and unafraid before the world. You will have autonomy in the camp if you want it. You have only to prove that you are capable of handling it. Let no one again be shocked or want to retch when he sees how the liberated victims of the Nazis live as free people. If there are faults to be found, let them be only among those who are supposed to help you and not with yourselves. Let this be an active beginning and not a passive, unchanging interlude."

The speech must have had some effect. General Rolfe and I were pleasantly surprised, during our quick inspection this morning, at the marked improvement in the cleanliness of the camp. We hope it continues to improve. It was an impressive sight to watch them pull down the barbed wire surrounding the camp. At least I have accomplished something that I can see. . .

— *From Irving Heymont,* Among the Survivors of the Holocaust—1945, *ed. Abraham Peck (Cincinnati: American Jewish Archives, 1982), 8–12, 24–29.*

A REASON FOR LIVING

Jacob Biber and his wife Eva successfully avoided Nazi manhunts for Jews in the western Ukraine, eventually joining a PARTISAN *band. After the war, anti-Jewish sentiments among the local population forced them to leave the Ukraine for Poland. They eventually reached the U.S. occupation zone in Germany and lived in the* DISPLACED PERSONS *camp at* FÖHRENWALD.

Slowly, the city of Munich receded from our view. The truck carrying twelve of us, ten survivors and two English/ Israeli soldiers, on the open platform, gained speed on the highway. Our driver, an American soldier, whisked past pick-up trucks, motorcycles, and bicycle riders on both sides of the road. The rackety noise of the truck, along with our driver's frequent horn blowing, kept us silent but observing.

We were exhausted from walking all night up and down the hills which stretched through the length of the forest where we had illegally crossed the Czechoslovakian and West German borders, and from the subsequent train ride which took us to Munich. The clinking of the wheels and the frequent blowing of the whistle kept us tense and unable to rest. The German passengers wore fine clothing, talked and laughed, and were, seemingly, untouched by the war. The elderly men had long gold chains hanging from their vests; the women wore diamond rings, gold bracelets, diamond earrings, and diamond hair ornaments in their elegant hairdos.

We were glad to be free of the bombed-out ruins of Munich, glad to reach the quiet countryside. From our seats on the open platform, we watched the spread of ripening fields, pine forests, and ponds. This beautiful summer day in July took my thoughts back home to my childhood. The blue sky, the aroma of fresh cut hay and wild flowers, reminded me of working in the fields before the war. . . .

Throughout the years of running and hiding, of hunger and stress, Eva and I had lived like brother and sister. After the liberation, we longed for a child, but we grew doubtful as to whether Eva could bear any children. Despite our unsettled present and future, we welcomed the discovery of her pregnancy with joy. This pleasant surprise was a sign of the continuity of life.

Now we were passing by beautiful farm buildings, large brick houses, ripening orchards, and yellow corn fields stretching for miles. The trees cast long shadows over the highway. In the hot, early July afternoon, we welcomed the breeze from the speeding vehicle. After a half-hour ride on a straight level road, we suddenly came to a very steep decline. The valley below seemed far away and very deep. We caught a glimpse of a small town of tiny red and white houses sheltered among the trees.

We felt we were in a different world. We glanced at each other, our eyes registering each new sight: "look at that." Coming from the West Ukraine, where flat land stretches to the end of the horizon, this was a wonderful surprise to us. Later I learned from a German that Russian prisoners from the first World War had paved the roads around the hills.

The road turned downward, narrowed and cramped in spots where vehicles came up across from the valley. Our truck screeched and rolled as we circled lower. At every turn on the steep slope we passed demolished vehicles which lay scattered at the edges of the drops. A feeling of panic gripped me, and I sensed the same from the faces of the others.

Coming down into the valley, the panorama opened in front of us. A small town of one- and two-story houses appeared, surrounded by small pine tree forests, orchards, and straight, roomy streets. As we approached the town boundaries, we sighted a gigantic sign on a post, whose black-and-white letters loudly proclaimed Wolfratshausen. Several elderly men wearing leather shorts and hats with long, colorful feathers greeted us by lifting their hats in the air. The beauty and modernity of this German village made my little Ukrainian village of Matzeev seem centuries behind by comparison. . . .

Wolfratshausen, although about the same size as Matzeev, was a world apart, with its beautiful red brick houses with shingled roofs, modern restaurants, and posh shops. The serene houses blended with the unfettered sunshine, green gardens, and colorful flowers to create an illusion of a place unaffected by the destruction of war.

The smell of cooking and flowers accompanied us as we passed through the town. Soon we were rolling again, on a smooth, straight highway, with endless fields of rye and wheat on both sides. In about ten minutes, our truck slowed down and turned to the left. "This is Camp Föhrenwald," shouted Abraham, one of our two escorting soldiers.

I had thought that this might be a place of quick transit, a chance briefly to recoup our energies and spirits, but the word "camp" started my heart pounding in fear again. We had met survivors in Gleiwitz (Poland) who had escaped the gas chambers of Auschwitz and Treblinka. At a small gathering, they had sung a tragic Yiddish song from the latter: "Treblinka, there, there is a place for every Jew. *No one comes out of Treblinka.*"

Our truck slowly passed through a gate with the huge sign "CAMP FÖHRENWALD" above it. After a few hundred yards, we stopped on the right side of the street near a long, one-story brick building with signs on the wall saying "OFFICE" and "REGISTRATION." We jumped down from the truck. A voice shouted from the window facing the street: "Form a line!"

Within minutes the line started to grow. More trucks came through the gates. Passengers disembarked and joined the line. Some of the newcomers, emaciated and pale survivors from the camps, wore thin, black-and-white striped clothing. From other trucks, children of different ages jumped down. These were survivors from all over Europe. The registration line got longer and noisier. The new arrivals looked over the others for any surviving friends.

From the office window we received cards with street, house, and room numbers, and also a suggestion to stop on our way at the theater building—"there's a public kitchen there which has meals ready for you." We were all hungry and so went out to eat.

There we found another line, but the soup tasted delicious anyway. . . .

But we had survived. Later that evening we all stretched out on the floor of the room, using our bundles as pillows. The words of one of the DPs upstairs, who had been in Föhrenwald the longest, ever since the liberation, injected a huge dose of pessimism into our group: "The gates of Palestine are shut: The English are patrolling the shores heavily. They are stopping all incoming ships with survivors and placing them on Cyprus under arrest, in camps surrounded by barbed wire. So far the *Bricha* have only managed to sneak a few hundred survivors into Palestine."

Another survivor asked: "And what about other countries?"

"Nobody wants us. Nobody needs us, we are homeless," replied the pessimist.

"America?"

"The American immigration office in Munich is going by the old quota system. You have to have an affidavit from an uncle or a wealthy cousin and then wait for the next opening. Who knows when the next will come? The quota is exhausted. The world is quite cold to our suffering. We already had realized that when the slaughter of our people was going on, the free world was quiet and cold to our suffering. Through years of devastation one gets used to bad news."

That first night our group, plus a few from another group, slept on the floor in our middle-sized room. We were very tired after a long, hot, and active day and evening. Through the open windows came the sound of frogs and crickets, and the aroma of pine trees mixed with the smell of freshly cut hay. All of this contributed to our tiredness; and we collapsed into a sound sleep.

For us, sleep was not a respite, but a reliving of tragedy in our nightmares. As soon as I fell asleep, the horrible tales of the skinny concentration camp survivors tormented my rest. In my dream I suddenly saw a desert of gray ashes blowing; and there was Camp Föhrenwald with its enormous theater hall. From the waves of ashes, skinny men, women, and small children were jumping out, wearing torn clothes the color of a giraffe's skin. They were filling the vast theater hall with loud screams of "Help! Help!" I was unable to sleep for night after night. In my visions, I continued to see the sad faces of concentration camp survivors and the huge theater hall. Suddenly a thought came to me: "Yakov," I told myself, "you have duties. You are like a soldier whose officers have perished in combat. The Germans killed the Jewish intellectuals at the beginning of the slaughter, and we, the survivors, must maintain our cultural heritage."

So I asked myself, "What can I contribute?" lying with my head on the bundle of rags. I thought: "Why can't I

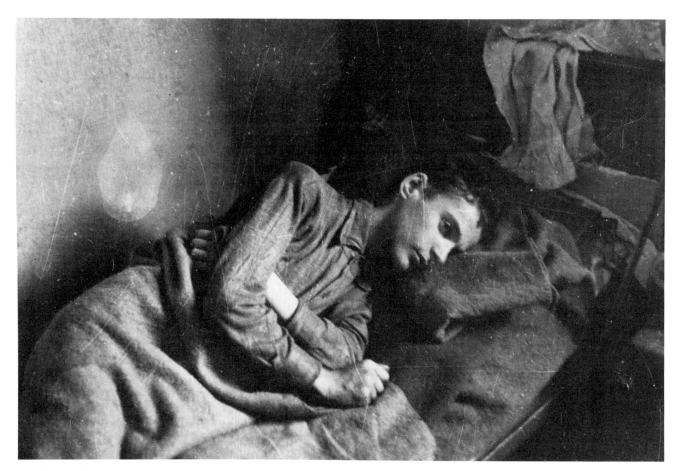

An ailing man lies in a hospital bed at the Bergen-Belsen DP camp located at the site of the former concentration camp. He was one of the thousands who survived the camps but later died from the effects of prolonged starvation, cruelty, and illness. (American Field Service Archive, New York City)

teach the surviving children, if we have to remain here for a while?" I knew I could at least organize theatrical performances.

The next morning a block counselor pounded on every door, ordering everyone to line up in front of the houses. A military truck stopped near the sidewalk. The servicemen stepped out and rolled down a long rubber pipe from a huge tank mounted on the platform of the vehicle. On its side were huge black letters, "D.D.T." From the pipe, a white powder was blown onto our bodies. We had to unbutton our shirts and pants in order to receive the treatment. After they had disinfected us and disinfected all the rooms, the counselor instructed us to go to the theater hall for soup, and from there to our permanent quarters.

Eva, Herschel, and I got a room on Roosevelt Street. Most of the streets carried names of American states or presidents, altered from their previous names of Nazi leaders. The rest of the group received quarters in the same neighborhood.

Once again we experienced a queasy feeling over our apparent luck—we had permanent quarters. But no one could shake the question, "For how long?" We felt as if we been stranded on an oasis; soon, everyone was calling our camp *"Bamdibart"* ("in the desert").

The caged-in environment forced a constant reliving of scenes from our horrible pasts. Even when I wasn't thinking of my own family, of our own painful sufferings, I recalled the others who lived in our town. . . .

The school opened a few days after my visit to the camp office. Posters were hung all over the camp and on the billboard of the theater hall in front of the public kitchen. The posters called for children and volunteer teachers to register at the *Tarbut* School (*Tarbut* is Hebrew for "culture").

I also hung a sign above the middle entrance of the schoolhouse building. I was determined to teach the children in Hebrew, hoping for a future for all of us in Israel, and knowing the need for some common language they could use to communicate with each other. The DPs had come from many different countries in Europe, each speaking the language of his native land, making the camp a veritable Tower of Babel.

Most of the children came immediately to register, but only two women responded to the call for teachers. I myself needed to work on my facility with Hebrew, but the two volunteers needed even more. So we taught classes in the daytime, and studied Hebrew in the evenings. The main problem was the difficulty in finding Hebrew books from which to learn and teach. The Nazis had managed not only to destroy the Jews in Europe, but also our books and our entire cultural heritage as well.

The school building was located on the north side of the camp. I liked the building from the first day I saw it. It was originally a twelve-room house, divided into four apartments, with bathrooms, washrooms, and a basement, running the width and length of the building. Across from the school, on the other side of a wide paved road, was a young, thick pine tree forest basking in the sunlight.

The camp was directed by UNRRA (The United Nations Relief and Rehabilitation Administration). The first person to lead the camp was a thin blond woman in a military uniform, Miss Blanchette, who habitually looked down on us with this little sarcastic smile pasted on her face, as if we were some kind of vermin or pests. At the meetings of the camp committee over which she presided, she used to put her legs on top of her desk.

The committee appointed me as cultural director shortly after I met Bekshtanski. In addition to the latter, Herman, Shparber, and myself, the committee included one of the finest men I ever met in my life, Rabbi Friedman, a tall, thin Hungarian in his early forties. His large brown eyes expressed a goodness and wisdom I have seen in few others, before or since. His short, reddish beard gave him a special charm. I felt embarrassed more for Rabbi Friedman than for myself by Blanchette's inconsiderate behavior.

Blanchette was not the only American who seemingly disdained us. The American Military Police raided the camp many times searching for gold and diamonds. There were some displaced persons who sold part of their weekly packages on the black market—we received these from UNRRA and JOINT, a Jewish welfare organization in the United States. The DPs needed the money to purchase medicine or clothing outside the camp. . . .

Miss Katel, a UNRRA worker from the U.S., gave her love, and was a great spiritual influence on all of us. She came often to the *Tarbut* School, and helped us in every way. In the beginning, she used another UNRRA worker for interpretation—a Jewish woman from Brooklyn, New York, who could speak very good Yiddish. But she also began teaching English to an eighteen-year-old DP girl, and within a short time was bringing this girl to the meetings as an additional interpreter. The latter, with the help of a fat dictionary which she always carried with her, and a quick and instinctive feel for languages, performed wonders. These two women became mother and daughter to each other, with a love that was noticeable to everyone. A few months later, when Miss Katel returned to the United States, she adopted the orphan girl, and took her back to America.

For us, however, a general *malaise* was growing as we realized how indifferent the world was to our tragedy. Soon we began seeing men and women who had survived the worst tragedies imaginable during the war years suddenly killing themselves, often by hanging. Such events, added to the news that Palestine remained closed to us, guarded by British soldiers who were turning away DPs by the thousands, only added to our gloom. In London the British Foreign Secretary stated: "Let America settle one hundred thousand DPs in New York." We felt like so much surplus junk, human garbage which the governments of the world wished would somehow go away.

At the same time, black markets flourished among the survivors. The long lines at the camp's distributing center prompted constant cries of complaint: "I'm not going to wait any longer, I'll protest!"—"That's exactly what the British want us to do!" Or: "I'm going to start a little business on the side"—"You'll be arrested by the MPs!"—"It's better to wind up in jail than live like dogs!"

Those DPs who were not interested in social activities sometimes turned their talents to buying and selling all kinds of goods, either from the Germans or from the American military guards. These included food, clothing, and cigarettes, and they did help relieve some of the tedium of camp life. But the careless or unlucky paid dearly for their "business."

A neighbor of ours confessed to me the story of his partner, a young Jew, who had been killed by the Germans in Munich in a smuggling deal gone bad:

> Mietik and I made a little money selling small items. Then, as business increased, we started trading in jewelry, our profession back home. My father had been in the jewelry business all of his life. There were no lack of buyers and sellers, believe me! We did our business mostly in Munich. Then Mietik fell in love with a German girl. I had never met her, but Mietik used to tell me of her beauty and intelligence. He stayed over at her apartment many nights, and every time he returned to the camp, he praised that girl to the Lord.
>
> One day he came to me, late in the morning, and said: "We're going to make a fortune. My girlfriend's Aunt Teresa has a lot of jewelry she wants to sell, including a five-carat diamond ring. Teresa wants twenty thousand marks in return, and I know we can sell the stuff for more than that."
>
> "Mietik," I responded, "Twenty thousand marks is a thousand American dollars. We don't have that kind of money."
>
> "So we borrow it from the other dealers," Mietik replied.
>
> "When does she need it?" I asked him.
>
> "Tonight," Mietik said.
>
> So we scurried about all day, going from dealer to dealer, borrowing a few marks from each. Some of these men we had helped in the past, and they owed us favors. Before evening we took the Postwagon to Munich. I walked him to his girlfriend's house, where he was supposed to meet her Aunt Teresa that night. Mietik smiled and then turned into the alley leading to his girlfriend's apartment.
>
> Just before we parted we arranged that I would come to meet him at the same place in front of her house, at nine

in the morning. After a half an hour of waiting, I got very nervous. Mietik was always on time. I walked back and forth on the sidewalk, perspiring under a hot sun till noon. By then I was convinced that something was wrong.

I went down the alley, knocked on the door to the girl's apartment. She opened the door. She was beautiful, tall and blonde with charming large blue eyes. I did not blame Mietik for falling in love with her. But my appreciation for her beauty quickly changed to anger when she said sweetly, "I was waiting up for Mietik till midnight. He never showed up." I could easily sense that she was lying.

I went straight to the nearest police station. I told them everything that had happened. Late that afternoon, Mietik's girlfriend and two of her brothers were brought in to the police station for interrogation. The commandant was suspicious as well, but after questioning them for two days, had to let them go, saying there was no evidence that they were guilty of any wrongdoing.

The three of them went home, unaware that the policeman had tricked them. Detectives were hiding in their yard and around their house. Upon returning home, the trio ran to a bombed-out building at the back of their house. In one of the partly demolished rooms, they pulled the corpse of Mietik from out of the rubble. They were arrested on the spot. Later they confessed that it was a set-up, that there was no aunt with jewelry waiting there for Mietik. The girl's brothers had hid on opposite sides of the alley, had fashioned a rope into a noose, and then had tossed it around Mietik's neck, choking him to death by pulling the rope from the two directions.

Not all Germans, of course, were like Mietik's girlfriend. A young man from our hometown of Matzeev, who had returned from service in the Red Army, and visited with us often in the camp, kept telling us that he was in love with a pretty German girl, and that she loved him as well. After four months of such happy tales, he came to us one day sad and pale, with tears running own his face. When we asked him what was wrong, he said:

> My girl died. She was pregnant. I wanted to marry her, but she was afraid that I was doing it out of a sense of responsibility only. She passed away in the hospital a week after the abortion. On her dying bed she asked her parents to love me, to help me in any way. I feel like killing myself. I loved her so much!

In the midst of all the turbulence, a German girl and a Jewish boy were dying of love for each other.

> —From Jacob Biber, Risen From the Ashes (San Bernardino: The Borgo Press, 1990), 9–11, 15–16, 20–24.

EVOLVING CONDITIONS FOR JEWISH DISPLACED PERSONS

The Harrison Report and Its Effect

SUMMARY OF THE HARRISON REPORT

Earl HARRISON, dean of the Law School at the University of Pennsylvania and a former Commissioner of Immigration, was selected by Henry MORGENTHAU, Secretary of the Treasury, to head a delegation investigating conditions in DISPLACED PERSONS camps in Europe during the summer of 1945. The group visited over thirty DP camps during July. Although the official copy of the delegation's final report reached President Truman on August 24, its contents were known several weeks earlier. Immediate action was deemed necessary, and a summary of the report's conclusions was cabled to General EISENHOWER on August 3.

> —*From "Harrison Report on Jews in Germany," August 3, 1945, Eisenhower's Pre-Presidential Papers 1916–1952, box 50, file Harrison-O to Harrison-Misc., Dwight D. Eisenhower Library, Abilene, Kansas.*

STAFF MESSAGE CONTROL

INCOMING ~~RESTRICTED~~ MESSAGE

CAD

WAR	USFET MAIN 228/04
TOO 032353Z AUG	TOR 040504B AUG

~~R E S T R I C T E D~~

R O U T I N E

FROM : AGWAR SIGNED WARCOS

TO FOR ACTION : USFET MAIN

REF NO : W-43716, 03 AUGUST 1945

Subject: HARRISON Report on Jews in GERMANY.

1. EARL G HARRISON report upon completion survey stateless and non-repatriables GERMANY on behalf State Dept contains following conclusions:

    A. Mil authorities refuse to recognize Jews as separate category or as stateless despite admitted greater suffering. Apparent policy is to treat all groups by nationality alone and to force repatriation by unpleasantness of surroundings and conditions.

    B. Immediate improvement in billeting is considered essential, if necessary by requisitioning from German civ population particularily in rural areas, a step which Mil Govt personnel have been reluctant to take despite authorization to do so.

    C. In addition, program of separate camps for Jews should be pushed more vigorously on model of FELDAFING Camp.

    D. Highly important UNRRA assume management camps especially non-repatriables earliest possible date. Despite military's professed eagerness to have UNRRA assume such responsibility, RHATIGAN not

SMC IN 2134

~~RESTRICTED~~
~~R E S T R I C T E D~~
THE MAKING OF AN EXACT COPY OF THIS MESSAGE IS FORBIDDEN

COPY NO 11

Civil Affairs 817

REF NO: W-43716, 03 AUG 1945   USFET MAIN 228/04

receiving adequate assistance in such matters as hq and
transport.
                    E. Official recognition and assistance
in communications and tracing of relatives sorely needed
to prevent complete breakdown of morale among Jewish families
separated for years.

                    2. Request you verify accuracy HARRISON's
conclusions and furnish the War Dept the results of your
investigation.

          ON   : G-5

     INFORMATION   : SGS
                        G-1
                        G-4
                        MR MURPHY
                        USGCC
                        SUSPENSE
                        **
                        AG RECORDS

     SMC IN 2134   4 August 45   1406B   FBH/al   REF NO: W-43716

EISENHOWER'S ANSWER TO THE HARRISON REPORT

After receiving President TRUMAN's letter of August 31 [see p. 190], General EISENHOWER cabled his response on September 14 that he was beginning a personal inspection of Jewish DIS-PLACED PERSONS centers to investigate their conditions first-hand. On September 18, when he had returned from this tour, he reported his findings in this letter to President Truman.

— From "Eisenhower to Truman," September 18, 1945, Eisenhower's Prepresidential Papers 1916–1952, box 116, file Truman-4, item 10, Dwight D. Eisenhower Library, Abilene, Kansas.

DDE/mgc

18 September 1945

Dear Mr. President:

During my absence from this Headquarters, receipt of your letter concerning the problem of displaced persons was acknowledged. I was then on a trip during which I made an inspection of a number of the installations in which we have displaced persons. This letter deals primarily with my own observations and will be supplemented, either immediately or in the near future, by a more extensive report comprehending the findings of subordinate commanders and staffs and of a special Jewish investigator.

As to the seriousness of the problem, there is not the slightest doubt. The hopelessness of the ordinary displaced person comes about from fear of the future, which involves questions, always of international politics, and from the practical impossibility of participating, at this time, in any useful occupation.

To speak very briefly about the psychological attitude of these people, I give you a few impressions gained by direct conversations with them. A very large percentage of the persons from the Baltic States, as well as from Poland and Rumania, definitely do not want to return to their own countries at this time. Although such a re-turn represents the height of their ultimate ambitions, they con-stantly state, "We cannot go back until there is a change in the political situation - otherwise we will all be killed." They state that the governments of all these states will persecute them to the point of death, although they insist that they bitterly opposed German domination of their respective states just as they opposed domination by any other government.

With respect to the Jews, I found that most want to go to Palestine. I note in your letter that you have already instituted action in the hope of making this possible. All of these matters are, of course, distinctly outside any military responsibility or authority and there is nothing whatsoever that I or my subordinates would be justified in promising or intimating in regard to them. However, the matter draws practical importance for us out of the possibility that caring for displaced persons may be a long-time job. Since I assume that most countries would be unwilling to absorb masses of these people as citizens in their respective countries, the only

- 1 -

alternative is that of hoping they will gradually voluntarily disperse in the areas of Western Europe and try to establish them in a self-sustaining life. To this end we encourage everybody to go out and get a job if he possibly can, and have been trying to explore the possibilities of agriculture and small business in the hopes of establishing small colonies of these people near their present locations. One great difficulty is that they do not desire to look upon their present location as any form of permanent home. They prefer to sit and wait rather than to attempt, as they say, "forcing themselves into a population where they would never be welcome".

With regard to actual living conditions; I personally visited five camps, two of which were exclusively Jewish and a third largely so. Two of the camps were villages taken from the Germans. Two others were city suburbs which had been taken over and occupied, one by the Jews, one by the Poles. In one camp, which was Jewish I found conditions less than satisfactory, but found also that the camp and local authorities were taking over additional houses in the immediate vicinity, throwing the Germans out of these houses in order to provide more and better accommodations for the displaced persons. You will understand that to provision these people adequately they must be housed in the same general vicinity; an impossible administrative problem would be presented if they were scattered indiscriminately throughout the German population. All feeding of displaced persons is under military or UNRRA control, whereas, with few exceptions, the German population has to look out for itself. You will understand, also, that when we speak of "camp" we do not mean either a tent camp or one made of huts. Speaking generally, every displaced person is in a permanent building of some sort, either an ordinary dwelling or building that was once used for other purposes. In the camp where I found conditions unsatisfactory, there were still guards on the entrance and passes were required for visits to any distant spot. This practice is stopped, but the Jewish leaders within the camp itself insisted that some form of control was necessary in order, as they said, that "all of us do not get a bad name." I found no instances of displaced persons still living in the old "horror" camps.

In one camp we have experienced, on the part of a considerable minority of the displaced persons, a distinct lack of cooperation. I am still reporting on evidence given me by these people themselves. The most simple of sanitary regulations were constantly violated to a degree that in some instances could be termed nothing less than revolting, although this has much improved.

- 2 -

The voluntary police begged me to permit them to have arms.
Upon my flat refusal to entertain such an idea I received the
reply, "We have some very mean men here and they can get us all
in trouble". However, I am certain that since these people are
completely dependent upon us for food, the necessary standard
of conduct can be maintained without any resort to harsh methods

At no place did I find any timidity on the part of any officer
to throw a German out of a house in order to give better accommodations to displaced persons, but as before mentioned, problems
of feeding, distribution and medical care for this completely
helpless group, make it imperative that they be sufficiently concentrated in order tthat these services can be performed. In those
instances where I believe officers have over-emphasized the administrative difficulties, vigorous steps are being taken and improvement will be prompt.

When it is realized that the Army in this area has been faced with
the most difficult types of redeployment problems; has had to preserve law and order; furnish a multitude of services for itself
and for the thousands of people it employs, and on top of this
has had this question of displaced persons with unusual demands
upon transportation, housing, fuel, food, medical care and security, you can well understand that there have been undeniable instances of inefficiency. Commanders of all grades are engaged in
seeking these out and I am confident that if you could compare
conditions now with what they were three months ago, you would
realize that your Army here has done an admirable and almost unbelievable job in this respect.

Respectfully,

The Hon. Harry S. Truman
The White House
Washington, D. C.

TRUMAN'S DIRECTIVE TO EISENHOWER

President TRUMAN attached this letter to the Harrison Report when it was officially sent to General EISENHOWER on August 31, 1945. By this date Allied authorities were addressing some of the criticisms found in the report, as can be seen in the general's order on Jewish DPs of August 22, 1945 [see p. 191].

My dear General Eisenhower:

I have received and considered the report of Mr. Earl G. Harrison, our representative on the Intergovernmental Committee on Refugees, upon his mission to inquire into the condition and needs of displaced persons in Germany who may be stateless or non-repatriable, particularly Jews. I am sending you a copy of that report. I have also had a long conference with him on the same subject matter.

While Mr. Harrison makes due allowance for the fact that during the early days of liberation the huge task of mass repatriation required main attention, he reports conditions which now exist and which require prompt remedy. These conditions, I know, are not in conformity with policies promulgated by SHAEF, now Combined Displaced Persons Executive. But they are what actually exists in the field. In other words, the policies are not being carried out by some of your subordinate officers.

For example, military government officers have been authorized and even directed to requisition billeting facilities from the German population for the benefit of displaced persons. Yet, from this report, this has not been done on any wide scale. Apparently it is being taken for granted that all displaced persons, irrespective of their former persecution or the likelihood that their repatriation or resettlement will be delayed, must remain in camps—many of which are overcrowded and heavily guarded. Some of these camps are the very ones where these people were herded together, starved, tortured and made to witness the death of their fellow-inmates and friends and relatives. The announced policy has been to give such persons preference over the German civilian population in housing. But the practice seems to be quite another thing.

We must intensify our efforts to get these people out of camps and into decent houses until they can be repatriated or evacuated. These houses should be requisitioned from the German civilian population. That is one way to implement the Potsdam policy that the German people "cannot escape responsibility for what they have brought upon themselves."

I quote this paragraph with particular reference to the Jews among the displaced persons:

"As matters now stand, we appear to be treating the Jews as the Nazis treated them except that we do not exterminate them. They are in concentration camps in large numbers under our military guard instead of S.S. troops. One is led to wonder whether the German people, seeing this, are not supposing that we are following or at least condoning Nazi policy."

You will find in the report other illustrations of what I mean.

I hope you will adopt the suggestion that a more extensive plan of field visitation by appropriate Army Group Headquarters be instituted, so that the humane policies which have been enunciated are not permitted to be ignored in the field. Most of the conditions now existing in displaced persons camps would quickly be remedied if through inspection tours they came to your attention or to the attention of your supervisory officers.

I know you will agree with me that we have a particular responsibility toward these victims of persecution and tyranny who are in our zone. We must make clear to the German people that we thoroughly abhor the Nazi policies of hatred and persecution. We have no better opportunity to demonstrate this than by the manner in which we ourselves actually treat the survivors remaining in Germany.

I hope you will report to me as soon as possible the steps you have been able to take to clean up the conditions mentioned in the report.

I am communicating directly with the British Government in an effort to have the doors of Palestine opened to such of these displaced persons as wish to go there.

Very sincerely yours,
Harry S Truman

— From Public Papers of the Presidents of the United States. Harry S. Truman, 1945 *(Washington, DC: Government Printing Office, 1961), 355–57.*

THE CREATION OF JEWISH DP CAMPS

Although an entirely Jewish DISPLACED PERSONS *center had been created as early as July at* FELDAFING, *Allied authorities did not officially recognize such facilities. One of the immediate effects of the Harrison Report was the following order "officially" creating such camps.*

— From "Special Camps for Stateless and Non-repatriables," August 22, 1945, Papers of George S. Patton, box 39, Policy File, Manuscript Division, Library of Congress.

C
O
P
Y

R E S T R I C T E D

HEADQUARTERS
U.S. FORCES, EUROPEAN THEATER   LW/MCB/smy

AG 354.1 GEC-AGO

(Main) APO 757
22 August 1945

SUBJECT: Special Camps for Stateless and Non-repatriables

TO   : Commanding Generals:
   Eastern Military District
   Western Military District

  1. It is the established policy of this headquarters that stateless and non-repatriable persons shall be granted the same assistance as United Nations displaced persons. This includes ex-enemy nations persecuted because of their race, religion or activities in favor of the United Nations. Persons discharged from concentration camps, if their loyalty to the Allied cause has been determined will receive all of the benefits granted United Nations displaced persons even if they were originally of enemy origin, such as German and Hungarian Jews, labor leaders or others put into concentration camps because of political activities or racial or religious persecution.

  2. While persons of Jewish faith who desire to be repatriated to the country of which they are nationals will be treated as citizens of that nationality and placed in the same centers as other displaced persons of that nationality, those Jews who are without nationality or those not Soviet citizens who do not desire to return to their country of origin will be treated as stateless and non-repatriable.

  3. In accordance with the policy of this headquarters, such persons will be segregated as rapidly as possible into special assembly centers. Those who are Jews will be cared for in special Jewish centers.

  4. In establishing these special centers, particular attention will be paid to a high standard of accommodation. Wherever necessary, suitable accommodation will be requisitioned from the German population. Military commanders' powers of requisitioning will be fully utilized in order to insure that those persons are accorded priority of treatment over the German population.

  5. In accordance with the policy of this headquarters, special UNRRA teams will be requested for these special centers without delay and those teams will be given maximum operating responsibility and all necessary assistance by military commanders.

BY COMMAND OF GENERAL EISENHOWER:

/s/ H. H. Newman
/t/ H. H. NEWMAN
Colonel, AGD
Acting Adjutant General

DISTRIBUTION:
(See reverse side)

RESTRICTED CLASSIFICATION
Removed per E.O. 10501

R E S T R I C T E D

-1-

BRIGADIER GENERAL ADCOCK'S REPORT

Brigadier General Clarence L. Adcock, Assistant Chief of Staff of the Civil Affairs Division, UNITED STATES FORCES, EUROPEAN THEATER (USFET), wrote the following report in October to President TRUMAN (for General EISENHOWER's signature) to explain the changes made in the disposition of Jewish DPs since the summer. In general, the conditions under which the "average" Jewish DP now lived had improved.

8 October 1945

Dear Mr. President:

This is my full report on matters pertaining to the care and welfare of the Jewish victims of Nazi persecution within the United States Zone of Germany. It deals with conditions reported by Mr. Earl G. Harrison, U.S. Representative on the Inter-Governmental Committee on Refugees, which was forwarded to me under cover of your letter of 31 August 1945.

Since Mr. Harrison's visit in July many changes have taken place with respect to the condition of Jewish and other displaced persons. Except for temporarily crowded conditions, the result of shifts between established centers and an influx of persons into centers as winter approaches, housing is on a reasonable basis. Nevertheless, efforts to improve their condition continue unabated. Subordinate commanders are under orders to requisition German houses, grounds, and other facilities without hesitation for this purpose.

The housing problem must be seen in full perspective. This winter the villages and towns in the U.S. Zone of Germany will be required to house more than twice their normal population. One million and a half German air raid refugees who were evacuated into Southwestern Germany, together with some 500,000 Germans, Volksdeutsche [ethnic Germans] and Sudetens who fled from Poland, New Poland, Czechoslovakia and Yugoslavia before the advancing Red Armies have created a condition of congestion in the U.S. Zone which forces the most careful conservation of housing space. At this moment the U.S. Zone is under orders to absorb 152,000 more Germans from Austria. Added to this influx of population, there is the loss of housing in bombed-out cities, averaging well over 50 percent; the necessity for billeting large numbers of our troops; and the accommodation required for prisoners of war. The resulting housing shortage is not merely acute, but desperate. Notwithstanding this situation, in my recent inspections and those made by my staff of Jewish centers, although crowded conditions were found, in nearly every instance more than the 30 square feet per person of floor space required for our soldiers was available.

Displaced persons have absolute preference over Germans for housing, but the requirements of the distribution of supplies, the provision of medical care, and the need for welfare activities make it desirable that displaced persons be sufficiently concentrated so that these services may be performed efficiently by the limited supervisory personnel and transport at our disposal. Thus, considerable use has been made of large installations such as brick barracks, apartment blocks and other public buildings in preference to scattered individual billets.

Special centers have been established for Jewish displaced persons. In the latter part of June, the armies were directed to collect into special assembly centers displaced person who did not wish to or who could not be repatriated. On 25 July 1945, Dr. Rabbi Israel Golstein, President of the United Jewish Appeal, recommended that non-repatriable Jews be separated from other stateless people, and placed in exclusively Jewish centers. As a result, the American Joint Distribution Committee was called upon to supervise the establishment of these centers. This policy was reiterated and expanded on 22 August. Special Jewish centers were established for "those Jews who are without nationality or those not Soviet citizens who do not desire to return to their country of origin."

At the time of Mr. Harrison's report there were perhaps 1,000 Jews still in their former concentration camps. These were too sick to be moved at that time. No Jewish or other displaced persons have been housed in these places longer than was absolutely necessary for medical quarantine and recovery from acute illness. It has always been our practice, not just our policy, to remove these victims with the utmost speed from concentration camps.

The assertion that our military guards are now substituting for SS troops is definitely misleading. One reason for limiting the numbers permitted to leave our assembly centers was depredation and banditry by displaced persons themselves. Despite all precautions, more than 2,000 of them died from drinking methylated alcohol and other types of poisonous liquor. Many others died by violence or were injured while circulating outside our assembly centers. Perhaps then we were over-zealous in our surveillance. However, my present policy is expressed in a letter to subordinate commanders wherein I said:

> Necessary guarding should be done by displaced persons themselves on the volunteer system and without arms. Military supervisors may be employed, but will not be used as sentries except in emergency. Everything should be done to encourage displaced persons to understand that they have been freed from tyranny, and that the supervision exercised over them is merely that necessary for their own protection and well-being, and to facilitate essential maintenance.

I feel that we have problems of shelter and surveillance in hand. Of equal importance is the provision of sufficient and appetizing food. In the past, a 2,000-calorie minimum diet was prescribed for all displaced persons in approved centers. Our field inspections have shown that in many places this scale was consistently exceeded, but there have also been sporadic instances where it was not met. Three or four thousand persons of the persecuted categories, including German Jews, in the American Zone have returned to their home communities. Many are there making a genuine effort to re-establish themselves. Until recently, there has been no clear-cut system of assuring adequate food for this group, although in most cases they have been given double rations.

I have recently raised the daily caloric food value per person for ordinary displaced persons in approved centers to 2,300, and for racial, religious and political persecutees to a minimum of 2,500. Feeding standards have also been prescribed and sufficient Red Cross food parcels and imported Civil Affairs/Military Government foodstuffs are on hand to supplement indigenous supplies and meet requisitions to maintain these standards. We are now issuing a directive that those Jews and other persecuted persons who choose and are able to return to their communities will receive a minimum ration of 2,500 calories per day, as well as clothing and shoes, the same as those in centers.

Clothing and shoes are available in adequate amounts and of suitable types. Uniformly excellent medical attention is available to all Jewish people in our centers where they have generally adequate sanitary facilities. UNRRA and AJDC staffs, which are administering an increasing number of our centers, are becoming efficient, and are making it possible for these people to enjoy spiritually uplifting religious programs as well as schooling for children.

It is freely admitted that there is need for improvement. The schools need more books; leisure-time and welfare activities must be further developed; paid employment outside the centers needs to be fostered; additional quantities of furniture, bedding and fuel must be obtained. We have made progress in re-uniting families, but postal communications between displaced persons and their relatives and friends cannot yet be inaugurated; roads and walks must be improved in anticipation of continuing wet weather. We are conscious of these problems, we are working on them, and we have expert advice of UNRRA, of Jewish Agencies, and of our Chaplains.

In certain instances we have fallen below standard, but I should like to point out that a whole army has been faced with the intricate problems of readjusting from combat to mass repatriation, and then to the present static phase with its unique welfare problems. Anticipating this phase, I have fostered since before D-Day the development of UNRRA so that persons of professional competence in that organization might take over greater responsibilities, and release our combat men and officers from this most difficult work.

You can expect our continued activity to meet the needs of persecuted people. Perfection never will be attained, Mr. President, but real and honest efforts are being made to provide suitable living conditions for these persecuted people until they can be permanently resettled in other areas.

Mr. Harrison's report gives little regard to the problems faced, the real success attained in saving the lives of thousands of Jewish and other concentration camp victims and repatriating those who could and wished to be repatriated, and the progress made in two months to bring these unfortunates who remained under our jurisdiction from the depths of physical degeneration to a condition of health and essential comfort. I have personally been witness to the expressed gratitude of many of these people for these things.

Respectfully,

— From "General Eisenhower to President Truman," October 8, 1945, Eisenhower's Pre-presidential Papers 1916–1952, box 116, file Truman-4, item 10, Dwight D. Eisenhower Library, Abilene, Kansas.

PATTON AND JEWISH DPS

The U.S. Third Army controlled part of the American occupation zone of Germany. Its commanding officer, General George S. PATTON, whose reactions to the concentration camps have been shown earlier [see pp. 127–28], held strong opinions about Jewish DISPLACED PERSONS which were, no doubt, shared by other Americans at this time. His attitudes toward DPs in general, regardless of their religion or nationality, were reflected in his orders to retain military guards at DP camps in the 3rd Army's area long after fear of the spread of epidemic disease had passed and to clear the city of Munich of all DPs not housed in camps in July.

Diary, September 15

Late yesterday afternoon I was notified that General Eisenhower would arrive . . . near Munich at 0930 this morning, having flown from the Riviera. . . .

I later found out that the purpose of his visit was to inspect the DP camps, particularly at least one occupied by Jews, to determine the condition of these Jews in order that he may write a letter to Mr. Truman.

Harkins and I went there to greet him in spite of the fact he had suggested that I not put myself out. I have always felt that an officer should be present to meet in person an officer of the next higher grade and in this case, General Eisenhower was also my friend.

Harkins and I waited until 12:00 o'clock, at which time we heard that General Eisenhower had been unable to land and had had to go to Paris to get down, using the beam at the field there.

While waiting, I talked to Brigadier General Mickelsen who is G-5 for Eisenhower's headquarters [in charge of DP affairs], and he showed me a letter from President Truman to General Eisenhower which was unnecessarily harsh and in much less considerate language than I would have used in cussing out a 2nd Lieutenant.

Mickelsen also showed me the report of a man named Harrison (which report was inclosed in the President's letter) on the condition of Displaced Persons in Europe, particularly Jews. Harrison is a member of the State Department [sic]. The report contained many allegations against General Eisenhower, the Army, and the various commanders.

One of the chief complaints is that the DP's are kept in camps under guard. Of course, Harrison is ignorant of the fact that if they were not kept under guard they would not stay in the camps, would spread over the country like locusts, and would eventually have to be rounded up after quite a few of them had been shot and quite a few Germans murdered and pillaged.

The brilliant Mr. Harrison further objected to the sanitary conditions, again being ignorant of the fact that we frequently have to use force in order to prevent the inmates, Germans, Jews, and other people, from defecating on the floor when ample facilities are provided outside.

Evidently the virus started by Morgenthau and Baruch of a Semitic revenge against all Germans is still working. Harrison and his associates indicate that they feel German civilians should be removed from houses for the purpose of housing Displaced Persons.

There are two errors in this assumption. First, when we remove an individual German, we punish an individual German while the punishment is not intended for the individual but for the race. Furthermore, it is against my Anglo-Saxon conscience to remove a person from a house, which is a punishment, without due process of law. In the second place, Harrison and his ilk believe that the Displaced Person is a human being, which he is not, and this applies particularly to the Jews who are lower than animals. I remember once at Troina in Sicily, General Gay said that it wasn't a question

of the people living with the dirty animals but of the animals living with the dirty people. At that time he had never seen a Displaced Jew.

Furthermore, I do not see why Jews should be treated any better or any worse than Catholics, Protestants, Mohammedans, or Mormons. However, it seems apparent that we will have to do this, and I am going to do it as painlessly as possible by taking a certain group of buildings in several cities and placing the Jews, who do not exceed 20,000, in sort of improved ghettos.

To put the Jews on farms would be disastrous because it would break up the agricultural economy of Bavaria on which we depend for providing what food is provided which is not paid for by American taxpayers.

We arranged a good itinerary for General Eisenhower which we will put into effect when he comes. Unquestionably he is just as much under fire as is anyone else and in this particular case, very unjustly so.

If the people in Washington would stop trying to find fault with others and wake up to the extent of making the Russians take back the Poles and other people whom they have not permitted to return, the situation in Displaced Persons would be much ameliorated. . .

It seems to be quite a hell of a mess.

A view of Feldafing DP camp, the first
entirely Jewish DP camp in the U.S. zone,
which was established in July 1945.
(Bund Archives, New York City)

Diary, September 17

Eisenhower and I drove to Munich where we inspected a Baltic Displaced Persons camp. The Baltic people are the best of the Displaced Persons and the camp was extremely clean in all respects. . . We were both, I think, very much pleased with the conditions here. . .

We drove for about 45 minutes to a Jewish camp . . . established in what had been a German hospital. The buildings were therefore in a good state of repair when the Jews arrived but were in a bad state of repair when we arrived, because these Jewish DP's, or at least a majority of them, have no sense of human relationships. They decline, where practicable, to use latrines, preferring to relieve themselves on the floor. . .

This happened to be the feast of Yom Kippur, so they were all collected in a large wooden building which they called a synagogue. It behooved General Eisenhower to make a speech to them. We entered the synagogue which was packed with the greatest stinking bunch of humanity I have ever seen. When we got about half way up, the head rabbi, who was dressed in a fur hat similar to that worn by Henry VIII of England and in a surplice heavily embroidered and very filthy, came down and met the General. Also a copy of the Talmud, I think it is called, written on a sheet and rolled around a stick, was carried by one of the attending physicians.

First, a Jewish civilian made a very long speech which nobody seemed inclined to translate. Then General Eisenhower mounted the platform and I went up behind him, and he made a short and excellent speech, which was translated paragraph by paragraph.

However, the smell was so terrible that I almost fainted and actually about three hours later lost my lunch as the result of remembering it.

From here we went to the Headquarters of the XX Corps, where General Craig gave us an excellent lunch which I, however, was unable to partake of owing to my nausea.

After lunch we visited a . . . model German workers' village. . . It was my purpose to turn this over into a Jewish concentration camp. Here we met the most talkative Jewish female, an American who was running the UNRRA part of the camp. . .

After inspecting this and making another speech, which I avoided, General Eisenhower directed that sufficient Germans be evicted from houses contiguous to the concentration camp so that the density per capita of DP's and Germans should be approximately the same. Also that the American guards be removed from the camp except for a standby guard in case of a riot, and that guards composed of unarmed inmates take over the police of the camp proper. . .

After this we returned home and went for a fishing trip on the lake which, while not successful, at least removed from our minds the nauseous odors and aspects of the camps we had inspected.

We then took as long and as hot a bath as we could stand to remove from our persons the germs which must have accumulated during the day.

I believe this was the first time General Eisenhower had inspected or seen much of Displaced Persons. Of course, I have seen them since the beginning and marvelled that beings alleged to be made in the form of God can look the way they do or act the way they act.

Diary, September 21

General Louis Craig came in to see me this morning to explain how he had arranged for taking care of the Jews. It has been necessary for him, against his and my instincts, to move twenty-two rich German families from their houses in order to put the animals in them. I told Craig to take pictures of the houses before they were occupied by the Jews and then subsequently. I also told him to move the Germans with as much consideration as possible and to give them transportation to move as much of their decent property out as they could.

Craig . . . told me he had inspected another Jewish camp yesterday in which he found men and women using adjacent toilets which were not covered in any way although screens were available to make the toilets individually isolated, which the Jews were too lazy to put up.

He said the conditions and filth were unspeakable. In one room he found ten people, six men and four women, occupying four double beds. Either the Displaced Persons never had any sense of decency or else they lost it all during their period of internment by the Germans. My personal opinion is that no people could have sunk to the level of degradation these have reached in the short space of four years.

— From Martin Blumenson, The Patton Papers *(Boston: Houghton Mifflin, 1974), 750–52, 753–55, 759. Copyright © 1974 by Martin Blumenson. Reprinted by permission of Houghton Mifflin Co. All rights reserved.*

Contrasting Conditions

A RESIGNATION OVER DP CAMP CONDITIONS

Toward the end of 1945, despite the impact of the Harrison Report, conditions in some DP camps had not substantially improved. This situation was partly because DP camp populations swelled as substantial numbers of Jews entered the western occupation zones of Germany to escape the rising tide of anti-Jewish sentiment and POGROMS in eastern Europe. Dr. Lee Srole, an UNRRA DP Team leader at the Landsberg displaced persons camp, resigned his position in early December to protest the poor conditions which he claimed were still prevalent in the camp. His resignation immediately brought an inspection by General Bedell Smith, Chief of Staff of the USFET, after which the army changed its mission regarding DPs from one of rescue to rehabilitation.

— *From* The New York Times, *December 6, 1945. Copyright © 1945 by the New York Times Company. Reprinted by permission.*

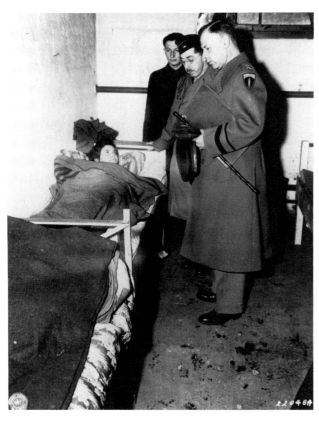

Lieutenant General Walter Bedell Smith, Chief of Staff of U.S. Forces, European Theater, and Judge Simon Rifkin, Theater Advisor on Jewish Affairs, inspect living quarters of Jewish DPs at the Landsberg DP camp on December 6, 1945. (NARA)

UNRRA AIDE QUITS; SEES JEWS ABUSED

Dr. Srole Charges Refugees in Germany Are Ill-Fed, Housed —Army Speeds Inquiry

By Wireless to THE NEW YORK TIMES.

FRANKFORT-ON-THE - MAIN, Germany, Dec. 5—United States headquarters here acted with unprecedented speed today to investigate a bitter protest against the treatment of Jewish displaced persons in the "D. P." center at Landsberg, made public by Dr. Lee Srole, sociologist of Hobart College, Geneva, N. Y. Within a few hours after receipt of the particulars on which Dr. Srole had based his resignation as principal welfare officer of Team 311 of the United Nations Relief and Rehabilitation Administration, a special train carrying Lieut. Gen. Walter Bedell Smith, Chief of Staff of the United States theatre, and newspaper correspondents was en route to the scene for an inspection of conditions there.

Headlining his accusations of overcrowding, underfeeding, lack of adequate clothing and of housing so bad it had been rejected as unfit for German prisoners of war, was the statement by Dr. Srole that "disastrous epidemics are expected to strike here at any hour." He added the claim that the United States Army Command had refused to face the problem of the "thousands of refugees fleeing for their lives from pogroms in Poland to the safe haven of displaced persons' centers in the American zone in Germany."

The population of 6,200 at the Landsberg center constitutes about 16 per cent of all the Jews of Central and Eastern Europe who had survived annihilation in Germany, Dr. Srole declared.

Resigns Against His Will

"I am resigning against my will," his vigorously worded communication reads, "as the only means of effective protest on the eve of a disastrous epidemic expected to strike here at any hour. Such an epidemic will almost certainly decimate this physically broken, tiny remnant of the millions of Europe's pre-war Jews."

Eight specific points are listed in his denunciation of the Army's supervision of the Landsberg community. They include charges of crowding three persons into a single bed, and twelve to fifteen in a "space no larger than the entrance to the average American house"; of housing "weak and sick women and children in dark and damp cellars, cold corridors and wooden shacks condemned as unfit for German prisoners of war"; of providing a "completely unbalanced diet of 1,800 to 2,000 calories daily for people still suffering the effects of six years of malnutrition and starvation at the hands of the Germans."

Says UNRRA Is Hobbled

After mentioning the issuance of summer-weight clothing for wear in a season of winter cold and snow, Dr. Srole makes his charge that the Army refused to cope with the problem of Polish refugees. Then he adds: "I protest against the policy of the American Military Government on local levels, which, contrary to the spirit and letter of General Eisenhower's directives, on the one hand tends to protect and often coddle the Germans, and, on the other, callously neglects the elementary human needs of those who were first declared the enemies of Nazism, and occasionally actively inflicts indignities upon them. Who, I ask, is America's enemy?"

"I protest," he goes on, "against the weak position in which UNRRA has been placed for the performance of its displaced-persons' mission in Germany and the resulting unrealistic lack-action or half-measure policies of UNRRA district headquarters in the face of urgent field reports from UNRRA team directors administering the displaced-persons' centers.

"In all, I protest against head-in-sand blindness or indifference or ineffectiveness in resolving the appalling conditions which at any moment may bring epidemic, disease and death to the thousands liberated a few months ago from outrageous Nazi extermination camps, and for whose care responsibility has been assumed by the United Nations and the United States Army."

He appended a footnote that if conditions were changed with the speed dictated by the emergency, he would gladly withdraw his resignation as a matter of professional conscience.

Inmates of the Landsberg center, which is one of the largest in Germany, are 90 per cent Jewish.

AN EXCEPTION TO HARRISON'S FINDINGS

FELDAFING was the first entirely Jewish DP camp, established in early July 1945. As this newspaper account suggests, conditions in DP camps varied widely. The circumstances of DISPLACED PERSONS *in any camp depended on the ability and concern of the military and UNRRA authorities who administered them as well as the organizational skills of survivors.*

— From The New York Times, *October 2, 1945. Reprinted with the permission of United Press International, Inc.*

Jews in One U. S. Camp Ridicule Charges of Abuse by Americans

By The United Press.

FELDAFING CAMP, Bavaria, Germany, Oct. 1—The ragged inmates of this sprawling home for Jewish displaced persons ridiculed today the Harrison report to the White House that Jews in American-occupied Germany were treated almost as badly as they had been under the Nazis.

They said that until two weeks ago their camp had been crowded and unpleasant, but that the conditions could not be put in the same category as the filthy Nazi concentration camps, where they had been beaten and tortured.

Gen. Dwight D. Eisenhower visited this and other Bavarian camps two weeks ago and immediately ordered Gen. George S. Patton Jr., American commander in Bavaria, to seize many neighboring German residences to relieve the congested condition at the camp.

"Things have been better for Jews since our liberation," red-bearded Rabbi Ezekial Ruttner told correspondents who flew here on an inspection trip.

"Now today it seems even more things are being done to make things better."

Until General Eisenhower's visit, however, it appeared that General Patton had taken little interest in Jewish welfare. The camp commander, Col. James H. Polk of El Paso, Tex., admitted that "the heat has been turned on" in the last fourteen days.

"I have been getting orders fired at me so fast since then that I have been unable to keep up with

Continued on Page 8, Column 6

JEWS IN U. S. CAMP RIDICULE CHARGES

Continued From Page 1

them," he said. He was unable to recall having received specific directives from General Patton's headquarters ordering improvements in camp conditions until after General Eisenhower's visit.

Colonel Polk said that General Patton had visited the camp earlier today and had seemed to be pleased with results that had been accomplished in the last two weeks.

Here is the situation found during a brief inspection of the rain-soaked camp this afternoon:

The Jews are unhappy, but they are not being victimized.

They are living in crowded quarters, but they are not dangerously overcrowded.

Every effort is being made to improve their living conditions before winter.

They perhaps are not getting the best food, but their diet of 2,600 calories daily is twice that of the average German.

They are well cared for medically and hundreds are being nursed back to the health they lost in concentration camps.

About 20 per cent of the camp's total of 4,300 inmates have some form of tuberculosis. A Jewish doctor said they were being well cared for and that most were recovering.

The majority of the Jews here live in bleak apartments, but they are well protected from the cold. Some rooms are occupied by twelve persons sleeping in bunks. Other large rooms have been turned into dormitories that hold forty persons —admittedly crowded but still livable.

They are relatively free people. There is no barbed wire and no Gestapo-type guards confining them. They have their own synagogue.

They appear to be living better than many Americans in slum areas, and the conditions here are similar to every other displaced-persons camp throughout Germany.

This camp was chosen at random for inspection only two hours ago and there has been no time to change things to make a false showing for the inspection.

It was chosen by a group of correspondents interviewing Lieut. Gen. Walter B. Smith, General Eisenhower's Chief of Staff, at his headquarters in Frankfort on the Main. General Smith offered his personal plane to the newsmen for an immediate inspection tour of the "worst-known camps" in the American zone.

General Smith had nothing to say on the report by Earl G. Harrison, American representative on the Inter-Governmental Committee on Refugees, which said conditions were appalling among Jews in American camps, but he offered to let the newsmen "visit the camps

REPATRIATION

Voluntary Repatriation

HOMEWARDS FROM THERESIENSTADT

Most of the millions of DISPLACED PERSONS found in Germany at the end of the war, including many Jewish survivors, desperately wanted to return home. Terezin in Czechoslovakia —which the Germans called THERESIENSTADT—was one of the major concentration camps from which survivors returned home after Soviet troops reached it on May 8.

— From The New York Times, *June 12, 1945. Copyright © 1945 by the New York Times Company. Reprinted by permission.*

TEREZIN EMPTIED OF 30,000 CAPTIVES

Concentration Camp's Inmates Being Repatriated at Rate of Thousands Daily

By DANIEL T. BRIGHAM
By Telephone to THE NEW YORK TIMES.

TEREZIN, Czechoslovakia (Delayed)—I have just spent two days and nights in this ghetto, described as the showplace of the Germans.

Its occupants, less than five weeks ago, were saved from extermination by a last-minute frustration of the Germans' plans. Russian armor, in a phenomenal drive southwestward as it by-passed Dresden, surrounded the camp, called Theresienstadt by the Germans.

Today only bullet scars on some buildings and a few scared faces remain to bear witness to the horrors that all expected to undergo. In the center of the town, hundreds of children, most of them born in the camp, play joyfully in a de-loused playground.

The exact official figures of the population inside the camp are still a closely guarded Russian military secret. Unofficial estimates by those who should know, including the camp commandant, place the number in the neighborhood of 30,000. These are being repatriated in batches of 1,000 several times a day, and present indications are that by the end of this month the camp will be deserted by all but a few quarantine cases of spotted typhus and maybe 100 or so of the hopelessly wrecked human beings now undergoing treatment in the ghetto's emergency hospital.

During my stay, I personally saw just out of the camp a convoy of Netherland Jews numbering more than 300 and a convoy of French deportees, some of them political prisoners, which must have been in the neighborhood of some 800. Both parties were moved with the participation of the International Red Cross, which, during my stay, made its first appearance behind the Russian lines with a convoy of trucks taking food and medicine as well as a delegate inspector who was expected to take up permanent residence to superintend the final evacuation.

Food has been relatively plentiful since the Russians moved in less than three weeks ago in the wake of a special corps of disinfection squads which in forty-eight hours had virtually eliminated vermin from the camp—including the 240 Elite Guards who had remained behind after their escape was cut off.

Train That Never Left

A tour around the town—before the Germans took over, Terezin was a health resort—brings out one surprise. There is only one door by which one enters the camp; during the German occupation the only exit was into that pitiful little cemetery standing well back behind the old fort. And in the middle of the ghetto to the south stands a monument to mechanized transport; a line of box cars standing incongruously high on their wheels, waiting for a re-loading that never came—3,000 Jewish designates for the crematories in Oswiecim, Poland.

Their departure was forever postponed when a Russian pursuit plane swooped down on a locomotive as it was standing at the gate waiting for the engineer to couple up the train. Its burned-out woodwork and shattered boiler still lie there and the cars now stand on rusted rails rotting under the hot sun.

When I first saw that train I jumped into one of the box cars "just to see what it was like." In the brief moment I was inside I saw why people died—and though possibly their death was merciful, I cannot help wondering whether the crematorium might not have been a less horrible fate.

The Russians are using that train today for an extremely useful purpose. Recalcitrant German prisoners working around Terezin are being locked inside for sentences up to six hours without food or water. I saw a few that came out, sobered individuals with all the fight gone out of them, welcoming the sight of a human face "even if it was only that of a Jew"—which phrase, incidentally, was more often than not the cause of their incarceration.

Terezin may return to the world in the not too distant future to fulfill the role that it once enjoyed, but the inmates today have a suggestion that might well bear consideration: turn it over to the War Crimes Commission with its train and put the "less guilty" war criminals inside under Jewish guards. They would come out with different ideas if they did not come out rehabilitated.

Forced Repatriation

SOVIET CITIZENS

By the terms of an agreement reached by the Allies at the YALTA CONFERENCE *in February 1945, all citizens from territories incorporated into the Soviet Union prior to August 1939 were required to return there regardless of their personal wishes. Thousands of Soviet citizens had fought in German uniform; hundreds of thousands had been deported to Germany as forced labor. Many had no desire to return to the tyranny of Stalin's Russia and resisted* REPATRIATION.

At war's end, American soldiers were given the task of escorting groups of Russian citizens who were being forcibly repatriated to the Soviet Union. One such soldier was William Sloane Coffin, Jr., who wrote of the experience in his memoirs. After the war Coffin worked with the Central Intelligence Agency, was ordained as a minister, and during the 1960s became prominent in the civil rights movement and active against U.S. involvement in Vietnam.

I tried to talk to some of the American colonels who I could see were finding the operation more and more distasteful. But their doubts were only increasing their desire to get the job over and done with. They had their orders and they were going to obey them. They told me the screening would soon be completed. Across the demarcation line the Soviets had been alerted. In nearby Landshut a train of boxcars was ready. The American first division was training secretly for a predawn "attack." When each deserter and traitor woke up he would find himself surrounded by enough GI's to prevent his escape or suicide. Those not to be repatriated would be herded off into a far corner of the camp to prevent their helping their comrades.

As it happened, the very night before this attack was to take place, the Russians in the camp organized an elaborate evening of entertainment—poetry reading, singing, dancing, skits. All nine colonels were invited. The evening was to be in their honor. I could understand the colonels' reluctance to attend. But I was incensed when I was told to make up some excuse for them and alone to represent them all, while they spent the evening drinking in the hotel where they were quartered.

Arriving at the door of the main hall of the camp, I was met by the commandant and escorted to a chair in the front row. There were no empty seats. Hundreds of Russians stood against the wall, while other hundreds sat on the floor, filling every aisle. A chorus started to sing a song I knew well, Lermontov's patriotic verses describing the battle of Borodino against Napoleon. Soon the entire audience was singing —three thousand voices. This was followed by balalaikas, dances and poetry reading, some men reading their own verses. They were all about Russia.

For a while I thought I was going to be physically ill. Several times I turned to the commandant sitting next to me. It would have been so easy to tip him off. There was still time. The camp was minimally guarded. Once outside the men could tear up their identity cards, get other clothes. It was doubtful that the Americans would try hard to round them up. Yet I couldn't bring myself to do it. It was not that I was afraid of being court-martialed; the commandant probably wouldn't give me away. But I too had my orders. It was one thing to let individual deserters escape in the woods. It was something else again to blow a Top Secret operation ordered by Washington itself with the Soviet government ready to make a terrible row if it failed. The closest I came was at the door, when the commandant said good night. In Russian it's "peaceful" night. When he said it I almost blurted out, "There's nothing peaceful about this place. Get out and quick." But I didn't. Instead I drove off cursing the commandant for being so trusting.

At 5:45 the next morning, the first division moved in as planned. Despite the fact that there were three GI's to every returning Russian, I saw several men commit suicide. Two rammed their heads through windows sawing their necks on the broken glass until they cut their jugular veins. Another took his leather bootstraps, tied a loop to the top of his triple-decker bunk, put his head through the noose and did a back flip over the edge which broke his neck. Others, less successful, were bandaged up and carried on stretchers to the boxcars into which the rest of the men had been herded. They were peering out through barred windows.

At the demarcation line, the Soviets were ready, only with passenger cars. There were nurses too, solicitous of the men's health, and officers inquiring gently where they came from and the names of relatives who should be notified of their forthcoming return. Suddenly I realized the men were being deceived all over again, deceived into believing that all was forgiven so that their families would be involved in their own punishment. As once they had trusted us, now they were trusting the Soviets.

I walked away as fast as I could. As I passed the baggage car I couldn't help noticing two Red Army sergeants looting the men's belongings. Beside myself with frustration, I jumped in and knocked them both out. But it was a futile, stupid act. If I hadn't had the courage to fight for the lives of these men, why fight for their belongings?

—From William Sloane Coffin, Jr., Once To Every Man: A Memoir *(New York: Atheneum, 1977), 76–77. Reprinted by permission of Frances Collins, Literary Agent. Copyright © 1977 by William Sloane Coffin, Jr.*

The Magnitude of the DP Experience

MILLIONS ON THE MOVE

Most of the millions of DISPLACED PERSONS *in Germany at war's end had returned home by the end of September 1945. The map reproduced here from the U.S. Army information weekly* Army Talks *gives some idea of the scale of this migration.*

— From Army Talks *4 (June 5, 1945): 7.*

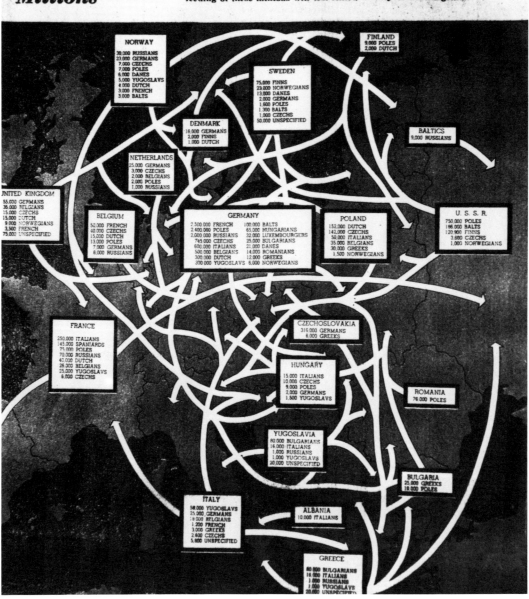

THE NATIONALITIES INVOLVED

The Office of Military Government, U.S. (OMGUS) was the occupation government in the U.S. zone of Germany. Its Weekly Information Bulletin *included stories on* DISPLACED PERSONS *in practically every issue during the summer and fall of 1945. This selection illustrates the change in U.S. policy in the fall of 1945 when Jewish displaced persons were*

treated as a special category by the occupation authorities rather than as nationals of their respective countries.

— From Office of Military Government, United States, Weekly Information Bulletin *18 (November 24, 1945): 20–21.*

General

Guide for Clarifying

NATIONALITY OF DPs

In order to clarify the question of nationality, a USFET letter has been issued listing countries and political entities. This furnishes a guide for military personnel concerned with care and repatriation of displaced persons, UNRRA teams in the determination of nationalities of displaced persons and summarizes standing policies and procedures for dealing with various categories.

There has been a tendency, in many cases, to identify persons by reference to their religion, geographical regions, national sub-divisions, ethnological groupings and to other unrecognized categories, rather than by reference to the political state of which they are citizens or nationals.

The list of countries and political entities is as follows:

UNITED NATIONS

Albania	Ecuador
Argentina	Egypt
Australia	El Salvador
Belgium	Ethiopia
Bolivia	France
Brazil	Greece
Canada	Guatemala
Chile	Haiti
China	Honduras
Colombia	Iceland
Costa Rica	India
Cuba	Iraq
Czechoslovakia	Iran
Denmark	Lebanon
Dominican Republic	Liberia

Standing policies and procedures for dealing with various categories of DPs summarized in USFET Letter.

Luxembourg	Syria
Mexico	Turkey
Netherlands	Union of South
New Zealand	Africa
Nicaragua	United Kingdom &
Norway	North Ireland
Panama	United States of
Paraguay	America
Peru	USSR
Philippine Islands	Uruguay
Poland	Venezuela
Saudi Arabia	Yugoslavia

Persons living in the mandated areas are to be reported in the category of the United Nation responsible for the mandate.

"Great Britain", as referred to in the above list, does not include British Dominions or India, but does cover the United Kingdom, the British Crown Colonies (e.g. Gibraltar, Cyprus, Burma), the Colonies (e.g. Malta, Newfoundland) and British mandated territories (e.g. Palestine). Persons from these areas should be classified and reported as "British".

The category "USSR" includes all Soviet Republics. The incorporation of Estonia, Latvia and Lithuania into the Soviet Union as republics has not been recognized by the United States government.

PREFERED TREATMENT FOR ITALIANS

While Italy is regarded as an ex-enemy nation, its nationals, under standing SHAEF and USFET directives, are to receive priority treatment over other ex-enemy nationals.

Persons of Jewish faith who desire to be repatriated to the country of which they are nationals will be classified as citizens of that country. Those Jews who are without nationality, or those Jews (not Soviet citizens) who do not desire to return to their country of origin, will be reported as "Jews".

Ex-enemy nationals (other than Jews) persecuted because of their race, religion or activities in favor of the United Nations, should be classified and reported separately from other ex-enemy displaced persons.

NEUTRAL NATIONS

Afghanistan	Spain
Eire	Sweden
Finland	Switzerland
Portugal	

POLITICAL ENTITIES

Estonia	Lithuania
Latvia	

EX-ENEMY NATIONS

Austria	Japan
Bulgaria	Roumania
Germany	Siam
Italy	

SPECIAL CATEGORIES

Jews (non-repatriable)
Other persecuted persons of ex-enemy nationality.
Stateless

20

JEWISH DISPLACED PERSONS IN EUROPE

The Special Circumstances of Jewish DPs

SETTING THE STAGE FOR JEWISH EMIGRATION

Before the ALLIES entered Germany, the Civil Affairs Division of the U.S. Army planned for both the governing of a conquered Germany and the handling of DISPLACED PERSONS. The plight of Jews in Europe was partially anticipated in a Civil Affairs Guide printed in 1944. While correctly forecasting the emigration of Jews from eastern Europe that would follow the POGROMS there in 1945–46,

the "desire to return to Germany" stated here was unrealistic since that country was only one point on their journey to PALESTINE.

> *—From United States War Department,* Civil Affairs Guide: Military Government and Problems with Respect to the Jews in Germany *(Washington, DC: Government Printing Office, 1944), 8.*

H. Return of Jews From Occupied Europe to Germany

Many Jews in occupied Europe will desire to return to Germany. Their number may increase if anti-Semitism should develop or increase in countries of deportation. On the other hand, many will be reluctant to go back to the scene of their former persecution. Having been forced to sever all personal ties and with poor economic prospects confronting them, they may wish to live in lands where they may reasonably expect the right to live and work on terms of equality.

In view of the fact that the countries of deportation and refuge may be either unable or unwilling to absorb the uprooted German Jews, the only remaining solution for many of them would seem to be emigration. This problem, however, clearly transcends the limits and resources of Military Government and cannot be solved by the individual governments acting independently. An intergovernmental machinery will be necessary to deal with the problem of the uprooted and also to assume responsibility for post-war migration and resettlement.

Pending such permanent solution, Military Government, in conjunction with UNRRA (which will be serving areas containing many German Jews) should permit jews (as well as other refugees) to return to Germany from German-occupied Europe if they so desire, and to provide necessary facilities in collaboration with intergovernmental and private agencies. This action, in all cases, should be purely voluntary. Refugees should be granted the documents necessary to legalize their stay. An intergovernmental committee might issue such certificates as would authorize persons to remain and to work in the locality until final arrangements are made.

German Jews who have acquired other citizenship (French, Belgian, Dutch) and were subsequently deported to the East should be given the right of option as to citizenship.

UNRRA'S SPECIAL JEWISH PROBLEMS

The special care required for Jewish DISPLACED PERSONS is detailed in this article by Leo Hermann, here reprinted from Rescue, *the journal of the Hebrew Sheltering and Immigration Aid Society. It originally appeared in the magazine* The New Judaea, *published in London.*

In addition to UNRRA's general functions and the problems which emerge in connection with the liberation of Europe from the Nazi yoke, the Jewish tragedy poses its own peculiar problems. Among other matters, the liberated nations are engaged in considering the return and repatriation of millions of their nationals. Both the Yishuv and the Zionist Organization are wondering whether and how UNRRA could be used as an instrument to facilitate the immigration and settlement of Jews in Palestine.

The word UNRRA is composed of the initials of its official title: UNITED NATIONS RELIEF AND REHABILITATION ADMINISTRATION. Each one of these words calls for an explanation, for each signifies at one and the same time the scope and limitations of UNRRA's activities.

UNRRA has been created by and for the "United Nations." It is an "Administration" on a State foundation. Forty-four States convened in Atlantic City in November, 1943, and established UNRRA.

Not to Repair Wrongs

The third letter of the word UNRRA stands for "Relief." UNRRA was founded to bring First Aid. It was never meant to repair all wrongs, or permanently to rehabilitate nations and lead them towards a happier future. UNRRA is not an instrument for building up the New Order; rather it is an organization of the kind established after World War I, which brought food supplies to Germany and Austria for the benefit of women and children during the blockade, under Mr. Hoover's direction. It was widely supported at the time, more especially by the Quakers, who went to Germany to organize soup kitchens, etc., immediately after the cessation of hostilities. This time UNRRA has planned help on a larger scale.

The fourth letter stands for Rehabilitation, another conception of UNRRA's activities. UNRRA is to aid the most miserable among the millions of miserable beings—the refugees, and people in and from the destroyed localities. The refugees are to be provided with a roof over their heads and essential foodstuffs. Further, they are to be returned to their former habitations, or transplanted to some spot where they can start a new life—in other words, to be provided with hutments, clothing and medical help. UNRRA will have to go to districts destroyed in the German retreat and, despite heroic efforts, unable to reestablish normal conditions without outside help. The foremost principle is to help those who wish to help themselves. That is why the provision of drugs, food, clothing, seed, manure, etc., looms so large in UNRRA's program.

Far Worse Off

The Jews do not quite fit into this general program. We are far worse off than the others. Practically nowhere in Europe can a Jew be found in his old house or profession under decent or halfway decent conditions. All Jews are refugees who have been robbed and deported. There can hardly be even a small group of Jews on the European Continent with any justified hope to return to, or be reinstated in, its former circumstances.

In hardly any country in Europe will a *restitutio integra* be possible for the Jews. You cannot expect anyone to start a new life among people who have more or less taken part in torture and murder, as has been the case in the Ukraine in the Baltic states, and in many Balkan countries. We have not forgotten that the Roumanians behaved as cruelly to the Jews in their midst as did the Germans.

Are these perhaps only sentimental or moral prejudices to which we should shut our eyes? Quite apart from any such, this war has awakened and nurtured instincts which cannot be eliminated easily. In France and Belgium, for example—with the exception of the collaborationists—the population did not persecute or oppress the Jews. On the contrary, it protected them against the Gestapo at the risk of their own lives. They have also saved countless Jewish children. That these children are growing up under Christian influence is another story. They have no deep recollections of Jews and Jewish ways, and it may be hard to bring them back to the fold. But not from missionary zeal did those Frenchmen and Belgians save our children, it was pure and unadulterated humanitarianism. But these selfsame people refused point blank to restore their houses and other property to the exiled Jews. They even had recourse to organized resistance, for they want to be rid of these competitors once and for all.

Did Not Share Weapons

We also know what happened in Eastern Europe. I quote from a report of two Ministers of the Free Slovakian Government who arrived recently in London. The Slovakian Partisans had fought the Germans with weapons supplied by the Allies. But they did not share them with the Jews who wanted to fight at their side. For they had learned from the Nazis that a weapon is a symbol of equality. These two Ministers, one a member of the Hodza Party, the other a Communist, declared that their Government could not act otherwise because the Slovakian people would neither have understood nor tolerated an equal status of the Jews.

It will be the same, or even worse, in other countries, from which it transpires that—apart from abstract insistence on equal rights—the remaining Jews in Europe cannot return to their former homes. For we cannot change the

At the house of the town mayor near the former
concentration camp at Bergen-Belsen, Germans
sort clothing for the camp's former prisoners in
June 1945. (NARA)

conditions that will prevail there. That is, no organization
which confines its activities to repatriating Jews to the
countries of their domicile in 1939, 1938 and 1933 is of practical value to us. We have to forge an instrument to find a
new home for these Jews.

I need not elaborate this point, nor try to prove that no
other country than Palestine offers any prospect, however
remote. True, a certain number of individuals will be able
to migrate overseas. People will be allowed to bring over
their parents and children. But what may succeed in the
case of five Jews does not affect the fundamental problem,
and if 500 Jews were to make the attempt it would be regarded in the light of a political move and provoke political
counter measures. Statistics are cruel. The Jewish problem
is a collective problem and always speedily recognized as
such. But no attempt to find a solution for this collective
problem has yet succeeded. The latest example in this
chapter of our sufferings has just occurred in Australia.
Government has pronounced a resounding "No" to the oft-
debated Kimberley proposal for the settlement of Jews,
even in the face of a positive resolution of the Australian
Labor Party.

Not UNRRA's Function

In order to complete the picture, it must be said again that, according to the Constitution, it is not UNRRA's function to help Jews from ex-enemy countries, even if they should now be in liberated countries. That is why last year the Jewish organizations concentrated their efforts on bringing about a modification in that Constitution. In point of fact, at Montreal, the Council actually decided to authorize help to nationals of ex-enemy countries, even if resident there, provided their status was that of refugees.

In the same way nationals of those countries who have fled abroad and reside in liberated countries may apply to UNRRA. Finally, still another demand was put forward—a cardinal one—that UNRRA should not merely facilitate the "repatriation" of Jews to their former home, but, in addition to helping to transport them to new homes, should contribute to their settling there.

This demand was rejected on the grounds that it went beyond UNRRA's competency. It was supposed to lie in that of the Intergovernmental Committee for Refugees, founded in Evian in 1938. In that way so vital a function was to be shelved. In view of the very limited resources of the Evian Committee, efforts to induce UNRRA to shoulder this responsibility will obviously have to continue.

Jewish Children Naked

In the meantime the actual situation has deteriorated. And the Greek tragedy continues. A recent visitor from Athens said that E.A.M. and ELAS had helped the Jews. Starvation is ripest among them. Jewish children roam the streets naked, looking for food in the gutter. Our unit is anxious to be among the first to go to Greece. Its members are familiar with the language and conditions. From all sides we are being offered money, clothing and shoes, but have had to refuse them for the time being. We are trying hard to be sent to Greece as a unit.

We have always maintained that Palestine could not be regarded in the light of a country unaffected by the war. Our immigrants are genuine victims of Nazi persecution. If Palestine did not exist, UNRRA would have to look after them wherever found. The people saved through Palestine are, therefore, legitimate objects of UNRRA's care. Certain subsidiary objects, such as the attempt to utilize Palestine industries for executing orders for the Balkan countries fall into the same category.

In conclusion, let me say that our immigrants who have found their feet here and are helping forward the progress of normalization of our people, are prepared to act like any normal unit of the family of nations in contributing their share to the general relief work without any thought of material gain. Let us hope that the present chaos will soon be mitigated through the instrumentality of UNRRA. Within UNRRA, Palestine should then be able to help others as well as itself.

— From Rescue *(September 1945): 3–4.*

THE BROADER DILEMMA

The New York newspaper PM Daily *featured stories about the plight of Europe's Jews soon after the Harrison Report appeared. The question of where the hundreds of thousands of the continent's dispossessed Jews would become increasingly important. Max Lerner, the author of the following report, was a prominent American journalist who wrote on many contemporary topics of the day. In 1945 he was editorial director of* PM Daily; *he later was a professor of American civilization and an editor at* The New York Times.

— From PM Daily, *October 2, 1945.*

◁CONTINUED▷ The Jew and the Western Conscience

problem of western humanity, and it goes to the roots of the survival of that humanity.

In this shrunken world of ours where we have all perforce become members one of another, no people can become the victims of injustice and fascist terror and democratic cowardice without dragging all other peoples along with it in its fall. That was proved true by what happened in Spain. It was proved true by what happened in China. It has proved abundantly true by what has happened to the Jews.

It goes deepest of all in the case of the Jews. That's why the pity of those who pity the Jews is as dangerous as the indifference of those who find the whole business too wearisome to think about. This is not a case for pity of a defenseless minority. It is not a case for the broad-mindedness of "tolerance." It is not a case for making a generous gesture—political or otherwise—toward a hapless people that has suffered so much. The suffering of the Jews has been—and still is—of such a staggering magnitude and intensity that it reaches farther and deeper than tolerance can ever go, and it makes pity seem a puny emotion.

Let me explain what I mean when I say that pity is not enough, and that the real problem is not a Jewish problem, but the problem of the survival of the western world.

Think back to the early 1930s, when Nazism first came into the open in its systematic slaughter of the Jews. Oh, how broad-minded the western world was at that time—with the Nazis. How judicious it was in weighing a few hundred thousand Jewish lives, a few million even, against the danger that Hitler might be offended, that his military force might be unloosed against western Europe. How prudent, oh how terribly prudent we were, how "realistic," as we wondered whether action to stop Hitler might not upset the delicate power balance in Europe.

The plain and simple fact that was staring us in the face all the time was that Hitler's assault on the Jews went far beyond the Jews, and was an assault on the whole western civilization. The western democracies waited and waited, hoping somehow to disentangle their own fate from the fate of the Jews. They could not. They waited until it was terribly late, almost too late. Then they acted.

We have passed through that first phase, and the war against fascism is won. Now we are in the second phase of the same continuing historical process. It is a different phase, because we are no longer dealing with an active fascist terrorism. Jews are no longer being slugged with truncheons, dragged naked through the streets, flung into mass graves, burned in furnaces.

But the same forces are still at work, passively but no less really. The Jews are still the despised, the rejected, the homeless. Even if they are let out of the concentration camps, and tents or attics are found for them in the German villages, it is unthinkable that they should want to remain for good in the Germany that tortured and killed their children, their wives, their parents. And not only Germany. Everywhere in Europe the fascism of Hitler and Goebbels has left behind a monstrous residue of anti-Jewish feeling and practice. That is why President Truman is so profoundly right in insisting that for these homeless Jews who want to go to Palestine the gates of Palestine must be thrown open.

But once again the old familiar voices are heard. It would not be prudent, say the British, to admit more than 1500 Jews a month to Palestine. It would be better, we hear, not to inflame the terrorism of the Arab League. It might possibly happen, we are told, that the delicate balance of power will be upset in the Near East. This is, they say, a problem not for Britain and Palestine, but a problem for the United Nations. There must be conferences, agenda, memoranda. And meanwhile the homeless wait.

Nor are the British alone in this guilt. The Americans too must share it. We have not shown any tendency to open our doors to those refugees who may wish to come to this land of freedom. No one pushes the idea because it might stir up the primitive Rankins in Congress, just as Clement Attlee fears to stir up the Arabs, just as Neville Chamberlain once feared to stir up Hitler.

What we do not see is that the big question is not the suffering of the homeless Jews, big as that is. The bigger question is the paralysis of the western conscience when faced with the plight of a people who have borne the brunt of

the struggle against fascism longer and more brutally than any other—a people who have become in the deepest sense the symbols of that struggle.

Palestine is not the only issue in Jewish survival. It is the emergency issue now, because no other country will admit the homeless Jews in large numbers, no other people will welcome and care for those who have borne the most terrible battle in world history. There are other Jews, millions of them, in Britain and America and elsewhere, who want to stay where they are in the countries they love, and whose fate will depend on the battle for democracy and liberty in those countries. But if the western peoples do not face up to the meaning of Palestine for the world today, the same forces of apathy that will doom the homeless Jews of Europe will also doom the western democracies, and the Jews and Christians in them alike.

Victor Gollancz, the British Laborite, has written a brilliant pamphlet about the Jews of Europe. He takes as his text the parable of Jesus: "The foxes have holes, and the birds of the air have nests; but the Son of man hath not where to lay his head." That parable has a tragic truth today that applies to millions of the sons of man. As long as it remains true the western peoples will not find a moral base on which to build their world after battle. The fate and survival of the Jews have become the crucial index of the fate and survival of western civilization.   —MAX LERNER

(Copyright, 1945, by The Newspaper PM, Inc.)

DP CAMP RESIDENTS

Beginning in the fall of 1945, Jews were registered as a separate category by U.S. occupation and UNRRA authorities. At the same time they were also housed in special camps authorized for Jewish DPs. Each UNRRA Displaced Persons Team was given a number and administered several camps. First District—Stuttgart was one of four administrative units that comprised the U.S. occupation zone; each was controlled by a U.S. Army division.

— *From UNRRA,* Summary of D.P. Population: UNRRA Assembly Centers in United States Zone *(Washington, DC: United Nations Relief and Rehabilitation Administration, 1946), 2.*

DATE: 24 August 1946
1st DISTRICT - STUTTGART, continued
9th Infantry Division Area

SUMMARY OF D.P. POPULATION
UNRRA ASSEMBLY CENTERS IN UNITED STATES ZONE
PAGE NO. 2

TEAM NO.	LOCATION	A.C. NO.	CAMP NAME / CAMP LOCATION	CAPACITY	DATE	POLES	POLISH UKR.	RUSS.	LITH.	ESTH.	LATV.	YUGO.	STATELESS	OTHERS	TOTAL A.C.	TOTAL TEAM	JEWS
67	HEIDENHEIM	627	Police School Heidenheim	550	17.8									493	493		493
"	"	632	Voth Settlement Heidenheim	1550	"	10				11	8		9	1640	1678	2171	1640
69	GMUND	650	Bad Mergentheim Bad Mergentheim	1650	3.8	2			348	11	877	202	11	1	1452	1452	1
91	LUDWIGSBURG	643	Jägerhof Ludwigsburg	1047	17.8	1026									1026		
"	"	644	Luitpold Kaserne Ludwigsburg	1000	"	1063							56		1119		
"	"	646	Karls Kaserne Ludwigsburg	426	"	432								1	433		
"	"	-	Aldingen Camp Ludwigsburg	1200	"	1031									1031	3609	
93	GMUND	616	Artillerie Kaserne Gmund	1400	10.8	1536				5	3		2		1546		
"	"	617	Bismark Kaserne Gmund	1900	"	2012		10		1		1	2	56	2082	3628	
94	ETTLINGEN	690	D.P. Camp Ettlingen	2000	"	1822		3		9	2			3	1839	1839	
126	WASSERALFINGEN	603	Siedlung Wasseralfingen	1850	17.8	1748				12		8			1768	1768	
149	ULM	677	Donau Bastian Ulm	550	"	14				7	4			401	426		399
"	"	678	Boelke Kaserne Ulm	1545	"	1781				3					1784		
"	"	-	Bleiborn Kaserne Ulm	325	"									246	246	2456	246
180	WEINSBERG	626	D.P. Camp Weinsberg	1730	10.8	1658				6				7	1671	1671	
190	GEISLINGEN	615	Private Houses Geislingen	4250	"	18				4463	1				4482	4482	

Revival of Life

A SURVIVORS' REGISTER

Immediately after the Holocaust ended, several Jewish groups set up registries to trace the whereabouts of Jewish survivors. Lists were prepared and disseminated in Germany as early as the summer of 1945. The Jewish Agency for Palestine opened a Search Bureau for Missing Relatives that year for the purpose of reestablishing contact between Jewish survivors in Europe and their relatives both in PALESTINE and around the world. The Search Bureau first published a list of CONCENTRATION CAMP survivors in 1945; one page is reproduced here.

—From Jewish Agency for Palestine/Search Bureau for Missing Relatives, Register of Jewish Survivors *(Jerusalem: Jewish Agency for Palestine, 1945), 1.*

שמות של נשים יהודיות במחנה בֶּרגֶן־בֶּלזֶן
(כפי שנמסרו ע"י הקונגרס היהודי העולמי, בסוף חודש מאי 1945)

JEWISH WOMEN LIBERATED IN THE BERGEN-BELSEN CAMP
(Submitted by the American Jewish Congress, May, 1945)

Abraham Erzsébet, 23, Ordon Csepel
Abris Erzsébet, 28, Kohon
Ackermann Hana, 25, Budapest
Adler Magda, 16, M. Sziget
Adler Ewa, 27, Nagyvárad Kolozsvar
Alter Aranka, 26, Gyergyo
Amszel Etel, 20, Szatmár
Amszel Regina, 22, Szatmár
Amszel Szeren, 20, Szatmár
Amsel Berta, 12, Kolozsvár
Aron Erzsi, 27, Nyirbátor
Aron Eva, 22, Nyirbátor
Aron Klara, 24, Nyirbátor
Arvay Erzsebet, 04, Budapest
Asztalos Liszi, 26, ?
Abelesz Ani, 22, Budapest
Abramowicz Rachela, 28, Lodz
Abraham Haja, 26, Budapest
Abraham Ilona, 06, Budapest
Abramowits Renja, 27, Suraggoni
Abramowitz Rusia, 19, Miechow
Abramowicz Ida, 15, Warszawa
Abramowicz Witka, 21, Sosnowiec
Abramowicz Bronia, 19, Sosnowiec
Acs Margit, 02, Budapest
Adler Bluma, 12, Tarnow
Agnes Rozia, 14, Chelm?
Ajzenberg Fela, 25, Kielce
Ajzer Jochwat, 23, Piautz
Ajzer Sara, 21, Piouki
Ackerman Gitta, 08, Radom
Albarlif Berta, 26, Saloniki
Albere Karoline, 25, Saloniki
Albere Rosela, 27, Saloniki
Albere Mathilde, 28, Saloniki
Alta Nadel, 20, Krakow
Altman Anka, 22, Lodz
Alter Aranka, 26, Gyergyoditro
Ancsel Berta, 12, Klausenburg
Angyal Eta, 17, Tiszapolgar
Anjel Ida, 04, Saloniki
Aron Eva, 27, Kolozsvár
Arner Ella, 21, Kolozsvár
Atela Klara, 22, Nagyvárad
Auzer Eszterjuw, 18, Saloniki
Asztalos Lili, 26, Aknaszlatina
Atteslonder Jewa, 25, Krakow
Amlaender Kato, 24, Kisvárda
Azysko Wladyslawa, 28,

Abisch Szeren, 28, Nyiregyháza
Abbe Estera, 26, Lodz
Abdellak Ester, 22, Korfu
Abraham Ibolya, 20, Budapest
Abraham Klara, 28, Aknaszlatina
Abraham Vera, 22, Ovaszifalva
Abrahamer Ruchela, 12, Krakow
Abrahamowicz Berta, 23, N. Mihály
Abrohamowics Zsofi, 11, Mikadapdlak
Abrohamowicz Giza, 22, Felsöapsa
Abrohamowicz Helena, 22, Felsökeresztica
Abroham Julia, 23, M. Sziget
Abramczyk Frida, 26, Sosnowiec
Abramoviz Diba, 23, Miechow
Abramowicz Rachela, 26, Olszany
Abramska Ania, 27, Bialystok
Abrawane Susanna, 26, Saloniki
Ackerfeld Sara, 20, Siewice
Ackerman Rozsi, 25, Zyska
Adla Erna, 21, Szatmar
Adler Ewa, 24, Szydlowiec
Adler Ida, 20, Budapest
Adler Jochewed, 28, Szydlowiec
Adler L, Lenke, 28, Budapest
Adler Klara, 13, M. Sziget
Adler Magda, 23, Szatmar
Adler Maria, 17, Lodz
Adler Rezsi, 14, Gabaldri Weresmenti
Aronowicz Hela, Lodz
Adroja Lili, 24, Saloniki
Afenstanen Anpi, 17, Kozienice
Afman Roza, 25, Częstochowa
Aftgang Regina, 24, Tomaszow
Ago Ewa, 23, Budapest
Ajas Mary, 25, Saloniki
Ajka Mechla, 23, Klodawa
Ajsenberg Chana, 27, Pionki
Ajsenstein Sisla, 10, Lodz
Ajzowicz Sala, 13, Miechow
Ajsikovicz Szlama, 21, M.Sziget
Alboher Stella, 23, Saloniki
Almalek Bonika, 26, Saloniki
Almalek Riketa, 26, Saloniki
Almelech Rachel, 26, Rodi
Almelech Dora, 24, Saloniki
Almoslino Stella, 26, Saloniki
Altalouv Bella, 25, Saloniki

Altman Jadzia, Będzin
Alszud Cesia, 25, Dabia n/Newem (?)
Ambolat Viktoria, 23, Saloniki
Amsel Erzsebet, 23, Kiswarda
Andzey Korina, 27, Saloniki
Angiosy Roza, 04, Budapest
Apel Hana, 22, Krynica
Apel Helen, 07, M. Sziget
Apelbaum, 18, Tarnow
Apelweiss Regina, 17, Lodz
Aplezer Anna, 25, Tarnow
Arditti Monika, 24, Paris
Arnstein Miriam, 27, Győr
Artman Roziska, 24, Sosnowiec
Arway Elisabet, 04,
Abraham Leopoldine, 32,
Abrahamowitz Berta, 23, Nagymihaly
Abramowicz Hana, 17, Wilno
Abramowicz Mania, 20, Czestochowa
Alaluf Alegra, 28, Saloniki
Adler Jochweta, 15, Ostrowiec
Adler Magda, 12, Budapest
Aeitkelo Laja, 26, Krzemieniec
Ajzenberg Fajga, 05, Olkusz
Ajzenberg Estera, 20, Radom
Ajzenberg Gitla, 11, Olkusz
Alter Naftali, 19, Köln
Amsterdam Lola, 09, Krakow
Anaton Chasia, 23, Lodz
Anstrafan Cela, 08, Radom
Asages Bella, 21, Athen
Asatonawier Rozia, 27 Ostrowiec
Aspis Sala, 15, Kazimierz
Ataj Estera, 20, Janina
Auer Anni, 10, Wien
Auerbach Hela, 16, Bedzin
Auswitzer Anna, 15, Krakow
Arenstejn Sara, 22, Kozienice
Asi Elwira, 24, Saloniki
Asi Rebeka, 17, Saloniki
Azieraka Chana, 04, Grodno

Badower Lodzia, 24, Lodz
Backenroth Rosa, 04, Drohobycz
Balaban Dora, 15, Bielsko
Balazs Iren, 02, Budapest
Balazs Margit, 09, Nagyvarad
Bloch Klara, 17, Budapest
Balter Hanka, 24, Lodz

Abraham   — 1 —   Balter

SABBATH IN DACHAU

David Max Eichhorn was an American Jewish army chaplain who arrived in DACHAU soon after liberation. He presided over the first camp-wide Sabbath service ever held in the camp, an event he recounts here.

On Friday afternoon, May 4, I held a service in the women's barracks. It was, of course, a very touching experience, as were all such services which I was to hold during the months to come in many DP camps in Germany and Austria. At the end of the service, a lieutenant colonel who had been standing at the rear of the room approached me with tears streaming from his eyes. He introduced himself. "My name is George Stevens. I am in charge of the Signal Corps unit which is taking the official Army pictures of Dachau. When will you hold another such service? I want to get a film of it for the historical record." I told him that a camp-wide Sabbath service was planned for the next morning, Saturday morning, and that he certainly could make a film of it if he wished.

The service was to be held at 10 A.M. in the main square of the Dachau compound. The International Committee had promised to have the platform in the square decorated with the flag of every nation represented in the camp (I think there were twenty-eight in all) and, in addition, every nationality would send a delegation to the service as an indication of its brotherly sympathy for the Jewish people. I arrived at the square at 9 A.M. to make sure that everything was in readiness for the service. To my amazement, no preparation of any kind had been made. I sent for Charles Baum, a young Belgian, the Jewish representative on the International Committee, and asked for an explanation. Greatly embarrassed. Mr. Baum informed me that the service would not be held in the main square. The Polish non-Jewish inmates had threatened that, if a Jewish service were held in the square, they would break it up by force. (This was only one of a number of ways in which the Poles of Dachau showed hostility for their fellow Jewish sufferers. I was informed that, when the Polish Red Cross distributed food packages to the Poles in Dachau, the packages were given out on the basis of one to every Polish Christian and one to every two Polish Jews.) Rather than cause a disturbance, the Jews had decided

The children and their teachers at a school at the Zeils-heim DP camp in 1945. Zeilsheim was one of the Jewish DP camps organized in the fall of 1945 at the order of General Dwight D. Eisenhower, commander of the U.S. forces in Europe. (Alice Robinson Lev Collection, USHMM)

to cancel the service in the square and to hold the service, instead, in the camp laundry, which was only big enough to accommodate about 80 people and could, therefore, hold only a very small percentage of the Jews who would want to be present. While I was not pleased with the decision, I raised no strong objection as I felt that the Jewish inmates were more knowledgeable in this particular situation than was I and should be allowed to do what they considered proper. So I set up an altar in the laundry and prepared for the limited service.

While the service was in progress, in a jam-packed room with hundreds of others outside crowded around the open doors and windows, Colonel Stevens came in, elbowed his way to my side and demanded to know why the service was not being held in the square. His cameras and crews were ready for action and he wanted the event to go on as scheduled. I stopped the "davaning" long enough to tell him that I would explain, after the service, what had happened. He waited outside until the end of the service to hear the explanation. After hearing the "inside story," he exploded in anger. "I did not give up a good job in the movie business in Hollywood," he bellowed, "to risk my life in combat for months and months in order to free the world from the threat of Fascism and then stand idly by while the very victims of Fascism seek to perpetuate its evils. I am going to do something about this." And do something about it he did. He took me to the Camp Commandant, a fine gentleman of Irish extraction who had formerly been Police Commissioner of Boston and, with loudness of voice and much banging of the table, George Stevens repeated his anti-Fascistic sentiments. The Commandant readily agreed with Colonel Stevens. It was decided that the service would be held next morning, Sunday, May 6, at 10 A.M. under the protection of an American military "guard of honor." As an added "movie" touch, Colonel Stevens requested that I teach some of the girls in the women's barracks to sing "God Bless America" at the service. I did as he asked. That Saturday night I spent about two hours teaching a choir of fifteen Hungarian Jewish girls to sing the Irving Berlin composition; and they learned to sing it quite well, even though they knew not one word of English.

And so, thanks to the decent instincts of an American movie director, the camp-wide service was held in the main square. It was attended by every Jewish male and female whose health permitted. As promised, every nationality was represented by flag and by delegation. There were an estimated two thousand Jews and non-Jews at the service. And ringing the outer rim of the service with faces turned away from the platform and with loaded rifles and fixed bayonets was the American military "guard of honor." They were prepared to deal with a situation which did not develop. No untoward incident of any kind marred the service. (Meyer Levin, who was present at the service, described it in an article in the American press. It is quite likely that the incident with which Irwin Shaw concluded his novel, "The Young Lions," is based on Levin's account of the Dachau happening.)

The program of the day was as follows: The opening remarks were made by Mr. Kuci, formerly Albanian Minister of Propaganda, chairman of the inmates' International Committee, who said that all the inmates of Dachau were very much aware of the exceptional intensity of Jewish suffering there and elsewhere under the Nazi yoke and that all freemen rejoiced that the Jews of Dachau were, at long last, able to resume their religious life without hindrance. Then the Ark was opened and I recited Shehecheyanu and benshed Gomel and went through a brief Torah service. After being formally introduced by Mr. Charles Baum, I gave a short talk. When I finished, one of the loveliest of the Dachau girls presented me with a bouquet of flowers on behalf of Dachau Jewry. Then a Palestinian "Chalutsa" came up to the platform bearing a Zionist flag and made an impromptu speech in beautiful Sephardic Hebrew to me and the assembly. Little American and Zionist flags made by the girls from their precious store of remnant materials were presented to me as priceless "souvenirs" of this never-to-be-forgotten occasion. My talk, given in English, was then translated into German by one of the inmates. He must have made what I said sound good because the crowd's response was very generous. Then my girls' choir sang "God Bless America" sweetly and enthusiastically. Then Mr. Baum spoke in French and German, thanking all the non-Jewish delegations for coming to the service and also expressing the hopes and aspirations of the Jews of Dachau. The latter part of his speech was so moving that it gave everyone a chance to have a good cry. The assembly joined in the singing of "Ha-tikva," after which I ended the program with a benediction. The entire service, about forty-five minutes in length, was filmed with sound by Colonel Stevens and his crew. While the service was in progress, a wagon-load of naked dead came past the assembly on the way to the crematorium. Colonel Stevens ordered the cameras turned on the wagon and a filmed record made of this weird though temporary addition to the audience. (Several years later I was invited to the Army Pictorial Center at Astoria, L.I., to witness a showing of the film of the Dachau service. The "staged" singing of "God Bless America" was retained in the film. The dead-wagon scene was eliminated. "We had to take it out," the movie people explained to me. "It seemed too improbable that a viewing audience would suspect that the scene had been 'staged'.")

For an hour after the service, I was mobbed, kissed, photographed and signed so many "autograms" that I vowed then and there to give up completely and absolutely whatever chance I had of becoming a movie star. It was a tiring and, as mentioned before, highly embarrassing experience.

The next morning I attended two Polish Catholic masses also held in the main square at Dachau as memorial services for the Polish dead of Dachau. I did so for two reasons: to express my gratitude by this act to the small number of Christian Poles who had attended the Jewish service and to show their less brotherly brethren that we have greater respect for their religion than they have for ours.

On Monday afternoon, May 7, I returned to HQ XV Corps, which, in my absence, had moved with the battle-line about seventy-five miles eastward from Munich, Germany, to Salzburg, Austria. Here, on May 8, the war in Europe officially ended; but die-hard Nazi units of the German forces did not cease fighting with our units until May 11. On that date, XV Corps was placed in charge of the Austrian Occupation Zone, a mission which it fulfilled until September 1. During this period, I travelled constantly between Innsbruck on the west and Linz on the east, holding services for our widely scattered troops and trying to be of some help to the DPs in the many camps throughout Austria.

The text of the speech which I delivered at Dachau on May 6, 1945 follows:

My Jewish brethren of Dachau,

In the portion which we read yesterday in our holy Torah, we found these words: "Ukrawsem d'ror baw-awretz l'chawl yoshvehaw; yovel hee ti'ye lawchem; v'shavtem ish el achuzawso v'ish el mishpachto tawshuvu" which mean "Proclaim freedom throughout the world to all the inhabitants thereof; a day of celebration shall this be for you, a day when every man shall return to his family and to his rightful place in society."

In the United States of America, in the city of Philadelphia, upon the exact spot where 169 years ago a group of brave Americans met and decided to fight for American independence, there stands a marker upon which is written these very same words: "Proclaim freedom throughout the world to all the inhabitants thereof." From the beginning of their existence as a liberty-loving and independent people, the citizens of America understood that not until all the peoples of the world were free the hearts of all men and all nations would there be lasting peace and happiness for themselves. Thus it has been that, throughout our entire history,

Jewish DPs read the camp newspaper posted on a board at the Landsberg DP camp in September 1945.
(American Jewish Archive, Cincinnati)

whenever and wherever dictators have endeavored to destroy democracy and justice and truth, Americans have not rested content until these despots have been overthrown.

Today I come to you in a dual capacity—as a soldier in the American Army and as a representative of the Jewish community of America. As an American soldier, I say to you that we are proud, very proud, to be here, to know that we have had a share in the destruction of the most cruel tyranny of all time. As an American soldier, I say to you that we are proud, very proud, to be with you as comrades-in-arms, to greet you and salute you as the bravest of the brave. We know your tragedy. We know your sorrows. We know that upon you was centered the venomous hatred of power-crazed madmen, that your annihilation was decreed and planned systematically and ruthlessly. We know, too, that you refused to be destroyed, that you fought back with every weapon at your command, that you fought with your bodies, your minds and your spirit. Your faith and our faith in God and in humanity have been sustained. Our enemies lie prostrate before us. The way of life which together we have defended still lives and it will live so that all men everywhere may have freedom and happiness and peace.

I speak to you also as a Jew, as a rabbi in Israel, as a teacher of that religious philosophy which is dearer to all of us than life itself. What message of comfort and strength can I bring to you from your fellow-Jews? What can I say that will compare in depth or in intensity to that which you have suffered and overcome? Full well do I know and humbly do I confess the emptiness of mere words in this hour of mingled sadness and joy. Words will not bring the dead back to life nor right the wrongs of the past ten years. This is no time for words, you will say, and rightfully so. This is a time for deeds, deeds of justice, deeds of love. . . Justice will be done. We have seen with our own eyes and we have heard with our own ears and we shall not forget. As long as there are Jews in the world, "Dachau" will be a term of horror and shame. Those who labored here for their evil master must be hunted down and destroyed as systematically and as ruthlessly as they sought your destruction. . . And there will be deeds of love. It is the recognized duty of all truly religious people to bestir themselves immediately to assist you to regain health, comfort and some measure of happiness as speedily as is humanly possible. This must be done. This can be done. This will be done. You are not and you will not be forgotten men, my brothers. In every country where the lamps of religion and decency and kindness still burn, Jews and non-Jews alike will expend as much time and energy and money as is needful to make good the pledge which is written in our holy Torah and inscribed on that marker in Philadelphia, the city of Brotherly Love.

We know that abstractions embodied in proclamations and celebrations must be followed by more concrete, more helpful fulfillments. We do not intend to brush aside the second part of the Divine promise: "V'shavtem ish el achuzawso v'ish el mishpachto tawshuvu." Every man who has been oppressed must and will be restored to his family and to his rightful place in society. This is a promise and a pledge which I bring to you from your American comrades-in-arms and your Jewish brethren across the seas.

"You shall go out with joy, and be led forth in peace;
The mountains and the hills shall break forth before you
    into singing;
And all the trees of the field shall clap their hands.
Instead of the thorn shall come up the cypress,
And instead of brambles myrtles shall spring forth;
And God's name will be glorified;
This will be remembered forever,
This will never be forgotten."

Amen

— *From David Max Eichhorn, "Report on the First Week in May 1945 by an US Military Rabbi," in* Dachau Review: History of Nazi Concentration Camps. Studies, Reports, Documents, *ed. Wolfgang Benz and Barbara Distel, vol. 1 (Dachau, Germany: Verlag Dachauer Hefte, 1988): 101–5. Originally published as "Dachau," in Louis Barish,* Rabbis in Uniform *(New York: Jonathan David, 1962).*

Restoration of Rights

HUNGARIAN REPEAL OF ANTI-JEWISH LAWS

The Hungarian government, formerly allied with Germany, signed an armistice with the ALLIES *in January 1945. The terms included the repeal of all discriminatory legislation—mostly anti-Jewish laws—which had been passed before and during the war. This was accomplished by March of that year.*

— *From* The New York Times, *March 28, 1945. Copyright © 1945 by the New York Times Company. Reprinted by permission.*

MIKLOS BANS JEWISH CURB

Hungary Lifts Discriminatory Laws, Stresses Equality

The Hungarian National Provisional Government of Col. Gen. Bela Miklos has issued a special order repealing all anti-Jewish laws passed by the former Hungarian Governments, the Moscow radio reported yesterday.

In this special order, according to the broadcast, the Government "wishes to emphasize that these laws and regulations are contrary to the sentiments of the Hungarian people and it thereby wishes once again solemnly to proclaim complete equality of all citizens."

As reported by the Federal Communications Commission, the Moscow radio quoted the order as declaring void all sentences passed under the anti-Jewish laws and demanding that "all persons sentenced or arrested under these laws must be freed."

Postwar Pogroms

POLISH POGROMS IN 1945

Dr. Jacob Wilf, a lawyer in Katowice, Poland, before the war, fled Soviet-occupied Poland in 1941 to the as-yet un-occupied Soviet Union and was subsequently drafted into the Soviet Army. Discharged because of his Polish nationality, he then worked as a lawyer in a Central Asian republic of the U.S.S.R. until 1945, when he returned to Poland with his wife. That July he experienced one of the first anti-Jewish POGROMS that occurred in Poland after the war and would continue into the next year.

Wilf's interviewer, David Boder, a psychologist, went to Europe in 1945 for the Illinois Institute of Technology and Psychological Museum in Chicago. Working through voluntary agencies such as UNRRA, he interviewed displaced persons using a recently developed wire recording device. The interviews gathered were intended for future anthropological and psychological study. In the following transcript, the comments inserted in brackets are Boder's.

Q-n: Tell me about the pogrom with all the details that you know. . .

Wilf: The pogrom, as revealed by the investigation of the various official agencies which have then taken place, was inspired by foreign agents.

Q-n: Polish. . . ?

Wilf: Polish foreign agents.

Q-n: Yes. . .

Wilf: The direct immediate provocation was the creation of a calumny [frameup]—that the Jews had snatched a Polish child for the purpose of taking blood from him, but they had managed to rescue the child.

Q-n: Yes. But tell me, what did they say that the Jews needed the blood for:

Wilf: Well, that is the old calumny that the Jews are using blood of Christian children for ritual purposes.

Q-n : Was there not another calumny?

Wilf: No, in this case that was the only calumny.

Q-n: The old calumny. Well, I have heard a different story. But if you are reporting it this way. . . That is interesting. How could they need blood. . . ? It happened in July, the pogrom. . .

Wilf: Yes.

Q-n: So how does that tie up with the Passover?

Wilf: No. That comes from the allegation that Jews use [blood] for various other. . .

Q-n: Oh. . .

Wilf: . . . ritual needs the blood of Christian children.

Q-n: Not only for mazos?

Wilf: Not only for mazos. And the child was going around. It was instigated by some 'agents,' and the child was going around; and it was said [alleged] that it was hidden by the Jews in a cellar for two days. . .

Q-n: Yes. . .

Wilf: . . . and only after that he managed to escape. . .

Q-n: Did he say that there were other children [with him], or not. . . ?

Wilf: No, only about himself.

Q-n: Yes. . .

Wilf: Afterwards, when the investigation got under way, it was established that the child was instigated, that his own father had hidden the child and had talked him into creating such a calumny. The population, the Poles seized upon the calumny—the masses were instigated by specially sent-in agents. One started already in the morning. . .

Q-n: Agent sent in?

Wilf: Agents sent in from abroad. . .

Q-n: Yes. . .

Wilf: And already from the early morning crowds began to conglomerate. The word about the calumny spread from mouth to mouth; and so they started to drag out the Jews from the building in which the Jewish Committee of Kielce was located.

Q-n: Yes. . .

Wilf: And besides, they also grabbed Jews from the street. This pogrom lasted nearly a full day. [Two words in between]. It was also revealed that a part of the officials of the militia. . .

Q-n: Hm. . .

Wilf: . . . have also participated in the 'action.'

Q-n: Yes. . .

Wilf: Only at the end of the day, thanks to the intervention of the Security Authorities and of the Polish Army, was the liquidation of the pogrom accomplished.

Q-n: What was the name of the Chairman . . . president of the Jewish . . .

Wilf: The chairman of the Jewish Committee, who was also killed that day in a most disgraceful manner, was Doctor Kahane.

Q-n: Kahane . . . ?

Wilf: Kahane.

Q-n: Hm . . .

Wilf: Only after that, when an investigation got under way—a special commission arrived from Warsaw and all measures were taken in order to bring about security for those Jews who still remained. They were transported in special automobiles to Lodz.

Q-n: The ones from Kielce?

Wilf: The ones from Kielce. And already in a few days, in order to convince [to silence?] the Polish masses, the strong hand of the Polish government, in a strong reaction against the events [?] in Kielce, revealed itself in the fact that the trial of the main instigators of the pogrom took place in only a few days, and within only ten days nine Poles were sentenced to death, and four days afterwards the death penalty was executed.

Q-n: So you think that the events of the pogrom will help to quieten things down, that the population will be pacified?

Wilf: The situation already now is such that thanks to the strong hand of the Polish government, which has responded so sharply to the pogrom of Kielce, a firm order [calm] has emerged [all] over the country; more so, since the working masses—the Polish working masses have held special meetings in all cities, and have mobilized the Polish masses for a struggle against the Fascists—the Polish Fascists. The workers—the Polish workers, have demonstrated at the meetings that they have proved to the Polish people that these pogroms are not only directed against the Jews, but that the hand that beats and kills the...the Polish 'democrats' [democratic people], the hand of intervention which fights against the Polish government, is provoking such pogroms in order to harm [the prestige, to prejudice against] the Polish people in [the eyes of] foreign countries; and in order to evoke unrest at home. And the effect is that during recent times order [calm] was established at all levels—more so, that the government takes all possible measures toward the aim that such events should not repeat themselves anymore. One of the measures is that the Polish government has released special pieces of armament to all Jewish committees—to all Jewish institutions; and they are specially guarded by the agencies of security. And so we hope that . . . that there shall not be repetitions of that what has happened.

Q-n: Well, did they permit the Jews to possess arms?

Wilf: All Jews who work in the Jewish committees, who occupy positions of responsibility . . .

Q-n: Yes . . .

Wilf: . . . have the right, and have received arms, and permission to bear arms on their person.

Q-n: Now tell me, one sees presently in Paris a lot of Jews who fled from Poland during the last few weeks.

Wilf: Yes. It is clear that in connection with the pogroms of Kielce a psychosis has come about within the Jewish masses. . . . There was a time, a few weeks after the Kielce pogroms, that substantial groups of Jews from various regions of Poland have departed, for the sole purpose of saving their bare lives. But we must say that besides the objective conditions which have created the alarmed [?] mood among the Jews in Poland, there were different, additional factors which have created the mood of alarm [despair (?)]. A number of irresponsible community [last word in Hebrew] workers have taken advantage. . . .

Q-n: . . . irresponsible what . . . ? [The corresponding words did not sound clear in the actual interview, although they are understandable in part from context on the wire.]

Wilf: . . . community [same word in Hebrew] workers . . . [repeats in German] community workers have taken advantage of the conditions; the objective factors, the alarmed mood which was brought about by the occurrence of the Kielce pogroms [he often uses the plural for this word], and started to call a special . . . to use a special propaganda—reinforcing the mood of alarm [unrest], so that the Jews should get away. In fact . . .

Q-n: . . . so that the Jews should flee.?

Wilf: . . . so that the Jews should flee; notwithstanding that at this time no real possibilities for emigration of the Jew are available. It is clear that for every Jew who has chances for emigration, it is proper and timely to . . . to leave [the country]. This view is also shared by the representatives of the Polish government, who have announced that they shall support the aspirations of the Jews to emigrate by legal methods. On the other hand, the Polish government in the interests of the Polish . . . the Jewish masses are against the moods of unrest and against the fact that the Jews should emigrate chaotically without an aim and without legal facilities of emigration. We deal here with a situation that would enhance the sufferings, the deprivations which are being undergone at present, by our brother refugees [?] from Poland, in the German lagers of the English and American occupation [zones]. That is how the situation in Poland has recently quieted down. . . .

— *From David Boder,* Typical Autobiographies of Displaced People, *(Psychology Department, University of California at Los Angeles, 1955, Mimeographed), 1484–90.*

The "Joint"

THE AJJDC IN AUSTRIA

DISPLACED PERSONS in Europe received aid from a number of charitable and welfare organizations as well as from the Allied military and UNRRA. The AMERICAN JEWISH JOINT DISTRIBUTION COMMITTEE (AJJDC), or "Joint," an overseas relief and rehabilitation agency, had representatives in sev- *eral DP camps; the military, however, forestalled extensive aid from them or similar civilian organizations during 1945.*

— From The New York Times, *July 29, 1945. Copyright © 1945 by the New York Times Company. Reprinted by permission.*

JEWS IN AUSTRIA GET ASSISTANCE

Relief Is Organized by Joint Distribution Committee— 3,000 Sent to Italy

Through efforts of the Joint Distribution Committee, approximately 3,000 Jews have been transferred from Austria to various cities in Italy, and will be helped to emigrate to Palestine, it was revealed in a first-hand report on conditions of Jewish people in the Allied zone of occupation in Austria, made public yesterday at the committee headquarters, 270 Madison Avenue.

The report from the Rome representative, Reuben Resnik, to Dr. Joseph C. Hyman, executive vice chairman of the committee, said 5,000 Jews are living in and outside Austria's liberated concentration camps in American, British and French zones.

A majority of the Jews, Mr. Resnik said, are living in Linz, Salzburg, Innsbruck and Hochst, with their number in Austria constantly changing, owing to the movement, both organized and unorganized, of masses of people migrating through the country.

2,000 Go to Hungary

"On July 12," he cabled, "2,000 Hungarian Jews left Wels on their way to Hungary, a few days before, hundreds of Jews, especially from upper Austria, moved toward Italy, many of them destined for refugee camps set up by the UNRRA."

Mr. Resnik's cable said that "many hundreds of Jews were heading for Italy." They were reported moving in from Bavaria, Northern Germany, Hungary and other eastern areas. The cable emphasized that although the basic essentials are being provided for the refugees in the Austrian camps, supplementary foodstuffs and medicinals are urgently needed. It said that supplies sent from Switzerland by the committee have been gratefully received by the Jews in Austria.

"One cannot describe these poverty-stricken, stunned, half-clad people as displaced persons or even refugees," Mr. Resnick said. "They are a pitiful lot who have for five years, and in some cases even longer, half lived and half hoped in the foul camps. It will take a great deal of courage, understanding and hard work to bring these people back to themselves."

Two Offices in Austria

The cable revealed that the committee had established offices in Linz and Salzburg in Austria and, as soon as military authorities move into Vienna, one will be opened there. A supplementary feeding program for those in need of special treatment, was set up in the Austrian camps, and steps taken to distribute clothing, establish a vocational retraining program and a location service, so that war-dispersed families might be reunited.

Arrangements for shipping additional food, clothing and medicaments into Austria from Switzerland have been made, Mr. Resnik reported, and these supplies should be coming through very soon.

Headquarters of the Joint Distribution Committee here disclosed that to meet the increased costs of relief operations in Italy, it has increased the allocation for that country from $70,000 in July to $95,000 for August and September. In addition, a special one-time grant of $75,000 was made for needy persons in Austria.

The committee receives its income from the campaign collections of the United Jewish Appeal for Refugees, Overseas Needs and Palestine.

THE ALLIES OCCUPY A DEFEATED GERMANY

THE REPEAL OF NAZI LAWS

The CONTROL COUNCIL FOR GERMANY was the supreme governing authority of the Allied occupation government. It was composed of representatives from the four victorious powers, the United States, the Soviet Union, Great Britain, and France. Among its major tasks was the dismantling of the Nazi political regime. As one of its first acts during the occupation, the Council repealed Nazi laws, including anti-Jewish legislation.

> — *From Control Council for Germany,* The Official Gazette of the Control Council for Germany *1 (October 29, 1945), 3–4.*

3

LAW N° 1
Repealing of Nazi Laws

The Control Council enacts as follows:

Article I

1. The following laws of a political or discriminatory nature upon which the Nazi regime rested are hereby expressly repealed, together with all supplementary and explanatory laws, ordinances and decrees:

   a) Law concerning the Relief of Distress of the Nation and the Reich (Gesetz zur Behebung der Not von Volk und Reich) of 24 March, 1933, RGBl. I/41,

   b) Law for the Reconstitution of Officialdom (Gesetz zur Wiederherstellung des Berufsbeamtentums) of 7 April, 1933, RGBl. I/175,

   c) Law for the amendment of the Provisions of Criminal Law and Procedure (Gesetz zur Änderung von Vorschriften des Strafrechts und des Strafverfahrens) of 24 April, 1934, RGBl. I/341,

   d) Law for the Protection of National Symbols (Gesetz zum Schutze der nationalen Symbole) of 19 May, 1933, RGBl. I/285,

   e) Law against the creation of Political Parties (Gesetz gegen die Neubildung von Parteien) of 14 July, 1933, RGBl. I/479,

   f) Law on Plebiscites (Gesetz über Volksabstimmung) of 14 July, 1933, RGBl. I/479,

   g) Law for securing the Unity of Party and State (Gesetz zur Sicherung der Einheit von Partei und Staat) of 1 December, 1933, RGBl. I/1016,

   h) Law concerning insidious attacks against the State and the Party and for the protection of the Party Uniform and insignia (Gesetz gegen heimtückische Angriffe auf Staat und Partei und zum Schutz der Parteiuniform) of 20 December, 1934, RGBl. I/1269,

   j) Reich Flag Law (Reichsflaggengesetz) of 15 September, 1935, RGBl. I/1145,

   k) Law for the protection of German Blood and German Honour (Gesetz zum Schutze des deutschen Blutes und der deutschen Ehre), of 15 September, 1935, RGBl. I/1146,

   l) Reich Citizenship Law (Reichsbürgergesetz) of 15 September, 1935, RGBl. I/1146,

   m) Prussian Law concerning the Gestapo (Preußisches Gesetz über die Geheime Staatspolizei) of 10 February, 1936, G.S. 21,

   n) Hitler Youth Law (Gesetz über die Hitler-Jugend) of 1 December, 1936, RGBl. I/993,

   o) Ordinance against support for the camouflaging of Jewish Businesses (Verordnung gegen die Unterstützung der Tarnung jüdischer Gewerbebetriebe) of 22 April, 1938, RGBl. I/404,

   p) Ordinance for the reporting of Property of Jews (Vor... dnung über die Anmeld...

GESETZ Nr. 1
Aufhebung von Nazi-Gesetzen

Der Kontrollrat verordnet wie folgt

Artikel I

1. Folgende Gesetze politischer Natur oder Ausnahmegesetze, auf welchen das Nazi-Regime beruhte, werden hierdurch ausdrücklich aufgehoben, einschließlich aller zusätzlichen Gesetze, Durchführungsbestimmungen, Verordnungen und Erlasse:

   a) Gesetz zur Behebung der Not von Volk und Reich vom 24. März 1933 RGBl I/41,

   b) Gesetz zur Wiederherstellung des Berufsbeamtentums vom 7. April 1933 RGBl I/175,

   c) Gesetz zur Änderung von Vorschrifen des Strafrechts und des Strafverfahrens vom 24. April 1934 RGBl I/341,

   d) Gesetz zum Schutze der nationalen Symbole vom 19. Mai 1933, RGBl I/285,

   e) Gesetz gegen die Neubildung von Parteien vom 14. Juli 1933 RGBl I/479,

   f) Gesetz über Volksabstimmung vom 14. Juli 1933 RGBl I/479,

   g) Gesetz zur Sicherung der Einheit von Partei und Staat vom 1. Dezember 1933 RGBl I/101...,

   h) Gesetz gegen heimtückische Angriffe auf Staat und Partei und zum Schutz der Parteiuniformen vom 20. Dezember 1934 RGBl I/1269,

   j) Reichsflaggengesetz vom 15. September 1935 RGBl I/1145,

   k) Gesetz zum Schutze des Deutschen Blutes und der Deutschen Ehre vom 15. September 1935 RGBl I/1146,

   l) Reichsbürgergesetz vom 15. September 1935 RGBl I/1146,

   m) Preußisches Gesetz über die Geheime Staatspolizei vom 10. Februar 1936 G. S. 21,

   n) Gesetz über die Hitler-Jugend vom 1. Dezember 1936 RGBl I/993,

   o) Verordnung gegen die Unterstützung der Tarnung jüdischer Gewerbebetriebe vom 22. April 1938 RGBl I/404,

   p) Verordnung über die Anmeldung des V... mögens von Juden vom 2...

Vermögens von Juden) of 26 April, 1938,
RGBl. I/414,

q) Law concerning the alteration of the trade regulations for the Reich (Gesetz zur Änderung der Gewerbeordnung für das Deutsche Reich) of 6 July, 1938, RGBl. I/823,

r) Second Carrying out Ordinance of the Law concerning the changing of Family Names and Christian Names (Zweite Verordnung zur Durchführung des Gesetzes über die Änderung von Familiennamen und Vornamen) of 17 August, 1938, RGBl. I/1044,

s) Ordinance concerning the Passports of Jews (Verordnung über Reisepässe von Juden) of 5 October, 1938, RGBl. I/1342,

t) Ordinance for the elimination of Jews from economic life (Verordnung zur Ausschaltung der Juden aus dem deutschen Wirtschaftsleben) of 12 November, 1938, RGBl. I/1580,

u) Police Ordinance concering the appearance of Jews in Public (Polizeiverordnung über das Auftreten der Juden in der Öffentlichkeit) of 28 November, 1938, RGBl. I/1676,

v) Ordinance concerning proof of German descent (Verordnung über den Nachweis deutschblütiger Abstammung) of 1 August, 1940, RGBl. I/1063,

w) Police Ordinance concerning the marking of Jews (Polizeiverordnung über die Kennzeichnung der Juden) of 1 September, 1941, RGBl. I/547,

x) Ordinance concerning the employment of Jews (Verordnung über die Beschäftigung von Juden) of 3 October, 1941 RGBl. I/675,

y) Decree of the Führer concerning the legal status of the NSDAP (Erlaß des Führers über die Rechtsstellung der NSDAP) of 12 December, 1942, RGBl. I/733,

z) Police Ordinance concerning the identification of male and female workers from the East on Reich Territory (Polizeiverordnung über die Kenntlichmachung der im Reich befindlichen Ostarbeiter und -arbeiterinnen) of 19 June, 1944, RGBl. I/147.

2. The abrogation of the above mentioned laws does not revive any law enacted subsequent to 30 January, 1933, which was thereby repealed.

Article II

No German enactment, however or whenever enacted, shall be applied judicially or administratively in any instance where such application would cause injustice or inequality, either a) by favouring any person because of his connection with the National Socialist German Labour Party, its formations, affiliated associations, or supervised organisations, or b) by discriminating against any person by reason of his race, nationality, religious beliefs, or opposition to the National Socialist German Labour Party or its doctrines.

q) Gesetz zur Änderung der Gewerbeordnung für das Deutsche Reich vom 6. Juli 1938 RGBl I/823,

r) Zweite Verordnung zur Durchführung des Gesetzes über die Änderung von Familiennamen und Vornamen vom 17. August 1938 RGBl I/1044,

s) Verordnung über Reisepässe von Juden vom 5. Oktober 1938 RGBl I/1342

t) Verordnung zur Ausschaltung der Jude aus dem deutschen Wirtschaftsleben vo 12. November 1938 RGBl I/1580,

u) Polizeiverordnung über das Auftreten de Juden in der Öffentlichkeit vom 28. November 1938 RGBl I/1676,

v) Verordnung über den Nachweis deutsch blütiger Abstammung vom 1. August 194 RGBl I/1063,

w) Polizeiverordnung über die Kennzeichnun der Juden vom 1. September 194 RGBl I/547,

x) Verordnung über die Beschäftigung v Juden vom 3. Oktober 1941 RGBl I/675,

y) Erlaß des Führers über die Rechtsstell der NSDAP vom 12. Dezember 1 RGBl I/733,

z) Polizeiverordnung über die Kenntli machung der im Reich befindlichen O arbeiter und -arbeiterinnen vom 19 J 1944 RGBl I/147.

2. Die Aufhebung der oben erwähnten Gesetze setzt kein Gesetz in Kraft, das nach dem 30. Januar 1933 erlassen, und das durch die oben erwähnten Gesetze aufgehoben worden ist.

Artikel II

Keine deutsche Gesetzesverfügung, gleichgültig wie oder zu welcher Zeit erlassen, darf gerichtlich oder verwaltungsmäßig zur Anwendung gebracht werden in irgendwelchen Fällen, in denen ihre Anwendung Ungerechtigkeit oder ungleiche Behandlung verursachen würde, entweder dadurch, daß a) irgend jemand auf Grund seiner Verbindung mit der Nationalsozialistischen Deutschen Arbeiterpartei, ihren Formationen, angegliederten Verbindungen oder Organisationen, Vorteile g würde; oder b) irgend jemand auf Grun Rasse, Staatsangehörigkeit, seines Glaub seiner Opposition zu der Nationalsozial Deutschen Arbeiterpartei oder ihren Lehrs teile erleiden würde.

U.S. OCCUPATION POLICY

A directive from the U.S. Joint Chiefs of Staff entitled JCS 1067 and the protocols developed by the Allies at the POTSDAM CONFERENCE held from late July to early August 1945 provided the policy bases for governing Germany by U.S. military government.

OUR BASIC AIMS

The United States is determined that Germany shall not again disturb the peace of the world. That is the underlying purpose of our occupation. Our policies for attaining this aim in governing the U.S. Zone of Occupation and in the quadripartite government of Germany are well defined in the basic directive from the Joint Chiefs of Staff to the Theater Commander, JCS 1067, and in the Protocol of the Potsdam Conference.

These documents lay out six major objectives for our occupation.

1. De-nazification of Germany

Nazism must be completely and finally eradicated from all aspects of German life. The Nazi Party and its affiliated agencies must be utterly destroyed. Active Nazis and militarists and their ardent supporters must be removed from positions of influence in any part of the German community. Nazi teachings and doctrines must be wiped out. War criminals must be tried and punished as they deserve.

2. Demilitarization of Germany

Germany must be deprived of her power to make war. Her armed forces, weapons and fortifications must be destroyed; all military and para-military organizations must be broken up. The military spirit and its traditions and customs must be rooted out, and the general staff must be completely dissolved and punished. The industrial capacity of Germany to wage war must be removed or controlled, and its large combines and cartels must be broken up.

3. Reparations

To make up for the devastation she has caused, Germany must furnish reparations to the countries against which she waged aggressive war. In large measure, these reparations will be paid by removals of industrial plants and equipment, especially from industries needed to make war. But Germany will be left enough capacity to provide a standard of living equal to the average of those of other European countries (excluding the U.S.S.R. and U.K.).

4. Re-education of German People

The Germans must learn to want a peaceful way of life and standards of decency and humanity. Nazi textbooks and teachers must be removed from all the schools and replaced by liberal textbooks and teachers. Their press, motion pictures and radio must provide factual news and other information to show the falsity of the Nazi doctrines and to build a foundation for democratic thought and action.

5. Restoration of Democratic Processes in Germany

The Germans must reconstruct their social life on a democratic basis. To disperse political power, Germany must be converted to a federal union by restoring substantial political autonomy to the states and lower units, and by confining the central government to activities essential to economic unity. As far as possible, local communities will govern themselves under officials elected by popular vote and responsible to the people for the conduct of their office. Free trade unions will be revived to enable workers to cooperate to improve their condition. A free press and a free radio are essential to these developments.

6. Rehabilitation of the German Economy

The Germans will be permitted to rebuild for themselves a peaceful economy providing tolerable living conditions. For the present, food, shelter and fuel available to Germany must be distributed equitably among the people. For the future, the Germans must produce more food and develop light industry to provide the permitted standard of living and exports sufficient to finance their essential imports.

Together, these major policies form a closely woven pattern for the treatment of Germany; a brief summary must oversimplify them and the reasons behind them. But, in general terms, this is our program for preventing Germany from again waging aggressive war.

— *From Office of Military Government,* The United States Program for the Occupation of Germany *(Berlin: Office of Military Government, United States, 1945), 3–5.*

THE EMIGRATION ISSUE AND PALESTINE

Where Will the Stateless Jews of Europe Go?

AMERICAN OPINION

The question of immigration to the United States has been a major issue throughout this century. In January 1945 the magazine Free World, *which began publishing in 1937 and later called itself "a monthly magazine for the United Nations," published the following results of a poll conducted by the magazine in collaboration with the National Opinion Research Center in the United States.* Free World *included among its editorial writers William S. Shirer, foreign correspondent; Orson Welles, film director; and Norman Angell, Nobel Prize-winning economist.*

— From Free World *9 (January 1945): 23.*

SOLVING THE JEWISH PROBLEM

Free World, *a monthly magazine for the United Nations, published the following article by Dr. Nahum* GOLDMANN, *chairman of the Executive of the* WORLD JEWISH CONGRESS *and Political Representative of the Executive of the Jewish Agency for Palestine. At the time of its publication, the issue of Jewish immigration to Palestine had already grown in importance.*

In the last few weeks the Jewish problem, one of the most urgent and tragic of our times, has again claimed headlines in the daily press. And yet it is not a new problem. The reason for its immediacy is that with war's end the extent of the Jewish tragedy has become known. Facts so horrible and fantastic that millions refuse to believe them, have become so evident that the conscience of even this not too sensitive generation feels obligated to find a solution to the problem.

That which we see today is the result of two historical facts: The age-old Jewish homelessness, and its aggravation by the nazi extermination policy. It is only because of the homelessness of the Jewish people, dispersed all over the world, persecuted and discriminated against in many parts of it, that Hitler's policy of annihilation could have been undertaken at all. As a result, the world now faces a Jewish problem so urgent there can be no further delay in solving it. There are two aspects involved: (1) the immediate problem of placing Jews surviving in the formerly Hitler-dominated countries of Europe, the remnant of over seven million, and (2) the fundamental problem of normalizing the status of the Jewish people.

Let us first analyze the immediate problem. Approximately six million Jews were killed or starved to death by the nazis during the war. Today there are one and one-half million Jews in Europe.

The position of these surviving Jews is one of indescribable misery and poverty. They have lost everything— not only their capital and property, but their most essential possessions. They have neither clothing nor dwelling places. Everything was taken by the nazis or the collaborationists to whom the nazis turned over Jewish property. One might think that with the physical extermination of 80 per cent of European Jewry, there would be no problem for those who survived. But it is one of the most glaring and tragic manifestations of the deeply rooted character of anti-semitism and of the anomaly of the Jewish position, that, although six million have been exterminated, the problem of the one and one-half million survivors is greater and more acute than it was before nazi liquidation.

Three Reasons

There are many reasons for this, all largely bound up with the situation prevailing in Europe generally. Ten years of nazi propaganda, organized and conducted with the devil-ish thoroughness so characteristic of the Germans, have left a tremendous mark on the European continent. As every observer of Europe today knows, the defeat of the nazi armies is not synonymous with the elimination of nazism. No part of nazi philosophy made a deeper impression on occupied countries than their anti-semitic ideology—added proof, if this is necessary, of the inherent existence of a Jewish problem in countries where anti-semitism had not been manifest for decades.

Another reason for the present extreme anti-semitism is that in the present European civil war between the forces of reaction and those of progress and revolution, the Jewish problem is used for their purposes by the reactionary forces, as it always has been. This technique of using the Jews as scapegoats is a classic method of fascism and yet it is gaining momentum for another reason—the looting of Jewish property. Jewish property was not confiscated only by the nazis themselves. Their collaborationists shared the spoils with the nazis, and they and many others acquired "legally" or illegally, the property of Jews. Surviving Jews naturally claim the return of their property, thus clashing with the vested interests of those who now have it. For that reason, many governments, though well-intentioned in principle, are reluctant to hasten the process of the restoration of Jewish property, fearing to antagonize those who benefited from the nazis. The amount of Jewish property in Europe, which had been owned by the millions who were massacred, leaving no heirs, runs into very high figures. Some governments are using this property for their own purposes, violating their moral obligation to use part of it at least for the rehabilitation of surviving Jews. And all this is going on in a Europe where each group and each individual finds the fight for survival much more brutal than it was before the war. There is fanaticism on the one hand, and immoral cynicism on the other. In a continent which has witnessed the extermination of more than twenty million people, there is callousness regarding the misery and death of another million. In such an atmosphere, there is no chance for the million and a half surviving Jews to rehabilitate themselves or to start a new, decent life.

Jews Can't Go Back

These are only the bare facts, and do not take into consideration the psychological factors which cannot be overlooked —the refusal of many Jews to start their lives anew in old surroundings. To give one example—60,000 Polish Jews are in camps in the American and British occupation zones. Earl Harrison's report, a product of American humanitarianism at its best, has drawn public attention to this aspect of the European Jewish problem. Polish Jews could legally return to Poland. The Polish government is eager to have them back. They refuse to go, not only because of conditions in Poland, but because they do not want to continue to live in countries where their children were gassed and their parents and relatives exterminated—where memories would haunt them and ruin their lives forever.

Among the majority of surviving European Jews, no feeling is stronger or more passionate than the desire to make a new start in a community where they can live as Jews, and where a repetition of the horrible experiences through which they have lived will be impossible either for themselves or their children, or their children's children.

This means that in order to solve the problem of European Jewry at least half of them will have to emigrate. Not all of them want to leave Europe. Many prefer to remain to make their contributions to the rebuilding of Europe. But on the basis of all reports, one is entitled to state that at least half of European Jewry want to leave and most of these want to go to Palestine.

Palestine the Solution

Palestine is the only place for them. This is not only because after five years of nazi persecution they have become more passionate Jews than ever before, and want to escape discrimination and persecution, but it is also because of the objective conditions. Realistically speaking, there is no other refuge for them. It is easy to take a map of the world and find empty spots, but these are meaningless in the light of realities. Does anyone seriously believe that countries like the United States, Canada, or England would open their gates to Jewish mass immigration? Only a year ago, a prominent Canadian liberal leader and statesman told me that, while in principle he favored Jewish immigration to Canada, 10,000 Jewish immigrants would become the paramount internal political issue of Canada. Latin America? In the last ten years a few thousand Jews going to one or another Latin American country created Jewish problems in each of them.

Is the world interested in creating new Jewish problems, which must follow if Jewish emigration from Europe is dispersed and decentralized? Or should not this generation, after the terrible lesson Hitler has taught of what Jewish homelessness means, discharge its moral responsibility of solving the Jewish problem once and for all?

Palestine opened to European Jews solves the question of a Jewish home. There but remains to normalize their status by recognizing Palestine as a Jewish state.

I know there is strong Arab opposition to this solution. I don't believe it can be brushed aside as meaningless, though its importance is greatly exaggerated. There is a legitimate Arab nationalism justified in its demand for the independence of Arab states. But Arab nationalism of today is directed and represented by some of the most reactionary oligarchies and cliques in the world. An investigation of the internal policies and development, or rather lack of development, in the Arab states, would result in a great many surprises. And in any case the Arabs are the spoiled children of the two World Wars. They contributed very little to victory in the last war and nothing to the defeat of Hitler in this one. But, because of the strategic importance of the Middle East and the natural inclination of colonial adminis-

trations and imperialistic policies to play along with such reactionary, oligarchic groups, the importance of the Arab world has been inflated into ridiculous proportions.

To think that the Arab world could checkmate a decision of the major powers to solve the Jewish problem by giving Palestine to the Jews, is pure nonsense. None of the Arab states has an army in the modern sense of the word, and all the threats of the Arab League in this respect should be taken for what they are: empty threats without the stature of serious arguments.

The Jewish problem must be primarily decided on a moral level. And the tragedy is that it has become a game of power politics. I do not deny that there is some moral justification to the claim of the Arabs to retain their majority status in Palestine. But there is greater justification of the Jewish claim for a real solution to their 2,000 year old tragedy.

For the Arab world as a whole, Palestine is of no decisive importance. It was never their cultural center. As for land area, Palestine is the size of New Hampshire plus half of Delaware, and represents only 1 per cent of the total area of the Arab states. The nations of the world, in addition to the Jews, have the full right, in the light of what has happened in the last decade, to ask the Arabs to make this contribution to the solution of this most tragic problem of our day. And if the Arabs refuse it, impose such a solution, as other solutions of territorial conflicts, boundaries, etc., will have to be imposed upon peoples and countries which will never settle these problems by themselves. All peoples must today accept the decisions of a higher tribunal, supported by force, if necessary, because otherwise there will never be a lasting peace.

Warning to the World

The solution of the Jewish problem cannot be postponed. Jews have waited for many years; have seen hundreds of thousands of their people massacred because Palestine was not opened to them. The survivors in camps and in other countries in Europe cannot be asked to wait until conflicts of interests among the great powers have been settled. If foreign offices and colonial offices make so much fuss about Arab feelings and Arab threats, they should start to take into consideration the mood and feeling of Jews all over the world, and of 600,000 in Palestine. The Jewish people have not much more to lose and a people fighting with its back to the wall has the courage of despair.

Let there be no mistake. Jews will go to Palestine with British entry certificates or without them. And this generation of European Jews, which has survived five years of Hitler and Gestapo agents, will not be afraid of the agents of the British Government who may try to prevent their entry into Palestine.

Goodwill and firmness are necessary on the part of leading powers. It is not only a British problem. America must share the responsibility, and so must Soviet Russia. The Jewish problem is an international one. It burdens the conscience of the world and is a political liability to the world. A firm decision on the part of the major powers, endorsed by the United Nations, will end the tension. The Arabs will protest. But when they know the decision is final, they will be ready to work out good neighborly relations which are of equal interest to Palestine Jews and the Arab world. Only a speedy decision will eliminate the current situation where threats and counter-threats, propaganda and counter-propaganda, muddy the waters. A Jewish state in Palestine is the solution to the Jewish problem. That problem must be solved as a whole, and it must be solved now.

— *From "The Jewish Problem Must Be Solved Now,"* Free World *9 (November 1945). 41–43.*

AN ALTERNATIVE VIEW

The magazine Commentary *was a publication of the American Jewish Committee. This article was written by Zachariah Shuster, a well-known Jewish journalist who was also a staff writer and columnist for the Jewish newspaper* The Day.

About the basic facts of the situation of the surviving Jews of Europe there can be little debate. The situation is extremely bad. No less than six out of every ten Jews in Europe are in need of assistance. In every liberated country the remaining and returning Jews have to start from scratch. They have to find homes; they have to fight to get back their property; they have to adjust themselves to following new occupations. Large numbers of them want to get away from the places where their nearest and dearest were slaughtered and from which they were violently uprooted. Emigration is certainly a vital necessity for many of the Jews who have survived Nazism. The discussion, however, is not about emigration; nor is it about Palestine as a destination for substantial numbers of Europe's Jews. No other country received so many Jews immediately after liberation from the German concentration camps. The Jewish community in Palestine eagerly awaits the survivors from Europe and gives them all physical and moral support. The crucial question remains whether all this must imply the total evacuation of Jews from Europe. . . .

The scope and importance of all this should not be exaggerated. Jews remaining in Europe face tremendous difficulties. Anti-Semitism has not vanished with the disappearance of the Hitler regime, and pogroms are still on the order of the day in the new Poland. The Jews of Europe will need all the help of all democratic forces, as well as of their fellow-Jews in the United States, to lay new foundations for their future. Yet rebuilding is going on and will continue to go on, in the words of Sommerstein, in accordance with the law of life itself.

This is admitted even by those who preach exodus. In July Dr. Arieh Tartakower, one of the leaders of the World Jewish Congress and of the Labor Zionist movement, said:

"The Jews of Europe do not want the bliss of the 'new democratic' Europe; they want to leave that continent, and almost all want to go to Palestine" (*Jewish Frontier,* July, 1945). But only a few weeks later, writing from London after the conference of the World Jewish Congress, which was attended by delegates from Poland, Bulgaria, Greece, Czechoslovakia, Finland and all Western European countries, Dr. Tartakower stated that, besides the immediate questions of restoration of rights, the struggle against anti-Semitism and restitution of property, there was also discussion of the future "and primarily of rebuilding a new Jewish life in Europe for those who desire and are able to remain. . . . It was rightly underscored," he stated, "by a number of speakers that there are no ideologies of emigration among us today—Jewish migration to Palestine cannot be considered emigration in the usual sense of the word. We are not ready to give up any single position in the countries of the Diaspora and as long as there are Jews there we shall fight for their rights and for a dignified life for them. This was the principle of reconstruction conceived and adopted by the conference. . . . If any evidence was needed that, despite the hell through which European Jewry has passed, it is alive and determined to continue to live and to fight and create, this conference produced the evidence" (*The Day,* September 6, 1945).

Dr. Leon Kubowitzki, another leader of the World Jewish Congress, recently returning from a visit to Western Europe, stated definitely that anti-Semitism there is on the wane and that "much of the reported anti-Semitism is the work of small groups or individuals who acquired confiscated Jewish property and want to hold on to it, rather than spontaneous mass reaction."

There is still another aspect of the new Europe that should give pause to the exodus adherents. Most of the remaining Jews of Europe today live in countries in the so-called Soviet sphere of influence. Dominating these countries are regimes that follow anti-emigrationist policies. Hungary, with its nearly 400,000 Jews, has now the largest Jewish community of Europe. Next comes Rumania, with its more than 300,000 Jews. Poland, Yugoslavia, and Bulgaria have between them another 200,000 Jews.

Most of these countries have already made known their opposition to mass emigration by any group of their population, including Jews. Rumania has forbidden young Jews of military age to leave for Palestine. The premier of Bulgaria, Kimon Gheorghieff, while expressing sympathy for a Jewish national home in Palestine, stated that the attitude of the Bulgarian government would have to be defined in accordance with the "general policy of the country" and that it was not desirable for "young and healthy Jews to leave Bulgaria for Palestine, because the new government is based on a program which practices equal treatment of all citizens." The Rumanian propaganda minister, Professor Constantinescu, declared that "for all democrats, the Jewish problem has never existed." They know only of a "so-called anti-Semitic problem and a Zionist problem; for they have never regarded the Jews as separate from the population at large." It has been known that the Rumanian government looked with disfavor on plans for Jewish emigration to Palestine. The new Polish government, it is presumed, will not put any obstacles in the way of Jewish immigration, while not encouraging it.

These countries in Southeastern Europe, in their passive or active opposition to emigration of any large group of their citizens, are following in the footsteps of the U.S.S.R., which has always prohibited any group of its citizens from leaving its territory.

All this adds up to the fact that among the European countries that have most of the Jewish population and where Jewish misery is the greatest, governmental policy will strongly oppose mass exodus. This is a matter not to be taken lightly.

At the same time there is an apparently contradictory tendency in some of these countries to eliminate their minorities, presumably as a result of experiences with their German minorities. Transfers of populations are now taking place on a vast scale. The Czechs are determined to get rid of their three million Sudeten Germans and seven hundred thousand Magyars, and the mass expulsion of these unfortunate minorities has been going on since the liberation of Czechoslovakia. The Poles are expelling the twelve million Germans living in the territories ceded to them after the Nazi surrender. The U.S.S.R. and the new Poland are exchanging populations as a result of the establishment of new boundaries between them. All these states seem determined to make nationality and religion synonymous with citizenship.

Edward Benes, president of Czechoslovakia, has even applied this principle to the Jewish minority. In a recent statement he declared that those Jews "who would not leave for Palestine ought to get assimilated completely into the people of the country in which they want to live, or reside there as citizens of a foreign state." Some of the exodus adherents point out that if this policy were to become general Jews would be confronted with three choices—to leave those countries, to disappear as Jews, or to be in the anomalous position of being the lone and single minority in a large section of Europe. None of these possible choices augurs well for the future, they assert. . . .

A sober evaluation of all the arguments on both sides and of the actual Jewish situation in the contemporary world must, in this writer's opinion, lead to the conclusion that no either-or proposition can solve the Jewish problem. Jews cannot and must not escape from the modern world. They are part of it; they helped create it; and their destiny is interwoven with it. In this atomic age, to envisage the future and safety of Jews as a thing completely separated and isolated from the rest of the world is an illusion that flies in the face of reality. We live in One World. Jews in Western civilization are here to stay, not as guests and tolerated exiles, but as permanent and equal members of a society which is struggling to evolve a way of life based on individual liberty and social justice.

What is urgently needed in Jewish life today is a recognition of the full compatibility of Palestine with Jewish life elsewhere. Such a balanced view is certainly not easy to achieve. The simple formula of the extremist always sounds more logical and consistent. But Jewish life cannot be imprisoned in any single viewpoint or slogan. Jews will live in Europe. Jews will live in Palestine. Jews will live in the United States. Each Jewish group in the world will have its own opportunities. Each will suffer, in one degree or another, from limitations and disabilities. From the interplay of complex and various factors, each may hope to evolve its own pattern combining Jewish distinctiveness with full participation in the life of the surrounding peoples. In each, Jewish group life and the Jewish heritage will continue and be carried forward.

—From "Must the Jews Quit Europe?" Commentary 1 (December, 1945): 13–16.

THE TRUMAN-ATTLEE CORRESPONDENCE

The Harrison Report [see pp. 184–86] revealed to President Truman *the intensity of Jewish hopes for immigration to* Palestine. *On August 31 he wrote to Clement* Attlee, *recently elected prime minister of the United Kingdom, requesting the British—who controlled Palestine—to fulfill these hopes. Attlee declined and continued the British policy not to declare Jews a special category of* displaced persons.

President Truman to the British Prime Minister (Attlee)

Washington, August 31, 1945

My Dear Mr. Prime Minister: Because of the natural interest of this Government in the present condition and future fate of those displaced persons in Germany who may prove to be stateless or non-repatriable, we recently sent Mr. Earl G. Harrison to inquire into the situation.

Mr. Harrison was formerly the United States Commissioner of Immigration and Naturalization, and is now the Representative of this Government on the Intergovernmental Committee on Refugees. The United Kingdom and the United States, as you know, have taken an active interest in the work of this Committee.

Instructions were given to Mr. Harrison to inquire particularly into the problems and needs of the Jewish refugees among the displaced persons.

Mr. Harrison visited not only the American zone in Germany, but spent some time also in the British zone where he was extended every courtesy by the 21st Army Headquarters.

I have now received his report. In view of our conversations at Potsdam I am sure that you will find certain portions of the report interesting. I am, therefore, sending you a copy.

I should like to call your attention to the conclusions and recommendations appearing on page 8 and the following pages—especially the references to Palestine. It appears that the available certificates for immigration to Palestine will be exhausted in the near future. It is suggested that the granting of an additional one hundred thousand of such certificates would contribute greatly to a sound solution for the future of Jews still in Germany and Austria, and for other Jewish refugees who do not wish to remain where they are or who for understandable reasons do not desire to return to their countries of origin.

On the basis of this and other information which has come to me I concur in the belief that no other single matter is so important for those who have known the horrors of concentration camps for over a decade as is the future of immigration possibilities into Palestine. The number of such persons who wish immigration to Palestine or who would qualify for admission there is, unfortunately, no longer as large as it was before the Nazis began their extermination program. As I said to you in Potsdam, the American people, as a whole, firmly believe that immigration into Palestine should not be closed and that a reasonable number of Europe's persecuted Jews should, in accordance with their wishes, be permitted to resettle there.

I know you are in agreement on the proposition that future peace in Europe depends in large measure upon our finding sound solutions of problems confronting the displaced and formerly persecuted groups of people. No claim is more meritorious than that of the groups who for so many years have known persecution and enslavement.

The main solution appears to lie in the quick evacuation of as many as possible of the non-repatriable Jews, who wish it, to Palestine. If it is to be effective, such action should not be long delayed.

Very sincerely yours,   Harry S Truman

The British Prime Minister (Attlee) to President Truman

[London,] 16 September, 1945

. . . I am now in a position to give you a considered reply, which I am telegraphing in order to save time, to your letter of August 31 enclosing a copy of Mr. Harrison's report.

I am sure you will appreciate the very grave difficulties that have confronted our representatives on the Control Commission and from my own investigation of the matter it is quite clear that they have endeavoured to avoid treating people on a racial basis. Had they done this then there would have been violent reactions on the part of other people who had been confined to these concentration camps. One must remember that within these camps were people from almost every race in Europe and there appears to have been very little difference in the amount of torture and treatment they had to undergo. Now, if our officers had placed the Jews in a special racial category at the head of the queue, my strong view is that the effect of this would have

been disastrous for the Jews and therefore their attempt to treat them alike was a right one. After all, the situation in Central Europe is appalling. The number of displaced persons, refugees from concentration camps, the violent driving of people from one territory to another, is one of the most horrible events in human history. So concerned are we about the starvation generally in that area that we have been taking steps to try and prevent epidemics arising and spreading to other countries. On this matter we shall be communicating with the State Department as soon as possible.

With reference to immediate relief there is a camp at Philippeville, North Africa, capable of taking 30,000 and another one at Fedala with a capacity of 5,000. I suggest that, in order to relieve immediate suffering, these two places be used. I understand that UNRRA have it under their control. It would of course involve our commanders in the task of sorting them out. This, however, should relieve the situation.

In case of Palestine we have the Arabs to consider as well as the Jews and there have been solemn undertakings, I understand, given by your predecessor, yourself and by Mr. Churchill, that before we come to a final decision and operate it, there would be consultation with the Arabs. It would be very unwise to break these solemn pledges and so set aflame the whole Middle East. I know you realize that as things are, the responsibility of preserving order with all the consequences involved rests entirely on this country.

As I mentioned in my earlier telegram the Jews are not now using the numbers of certificates available and up to the present have not taken up the 1,500 available for this month which was offered them. Apparently they are insisting upon the complete repudiation of the White Paper and the immediate granting of 100,000 certificates quite regardless of the effect on the situation in the Middle East which this would have.

In addition to this problem we are engaged upon another related one and that is India. The fact that there are ninety million Moslems, who are easily inflamed, in that country compels us to consider the problem from this aspect also. Therefore, while sympathising with the views of Mr. Harrison and weighing them very carefully, we believe that the suggestion which he has made raises very far-reaching implications, which would have to be most carefully balanced against the considerations which I have set out above. We have got the matter under urgent examination, with a view to the formulation of a long-term policy which we propose to refer to the World Organization as soon as practicable. Meanwhile we are considering how to deal with the immigration problem in interval and I shall be very happy to let you know as soon as I can what our intentions are in this matter.

—From U.S. Department of State, Foreign Relations of the United States: Diplomatic Papers, 1945, The Near East and Africa, *vol. 8 (Washington, DC: Government Printing Office, 1969), 737–39, 740–41.*

Immigration to Palestine

ATHLIT INTERNMENT CAMP

Most Jewish immigration to PALESTINE was illegal in 1945 because of British policy established in the WHITE PAPER OF 1939. Nevertheless, Jews tried to reach Palestine, and many were intercepted and detained in ATHLIT Internment camp. Located just south of Haifa, the camp had been set up by the British in 1939 to house illegal immigrants.

Somewhere in America there is an island, Ellis Island––the Island of Tears, some call it. It is a place which in former times served as a disembarkation center; for immigrants, a place of heart-sickness and uncertainty. Onward to America or back again? I thought of this island as I stood before the fence at the Athlit clearance Camp in Palestine. How many scenes it has witnessed, how many sighs it has heard, how many tears it has absorbed, this Fence of Tears, as I would call it. Over this fence greetings are borne from without and bitter tidings from within. Here eager hopes and joys, tragedies and disappointments meet together. If this fence could speak it would have much to recount. It would tell of a Jewish infant, 15 months old, which was smuggled over the borders of Europe and was brought to Palestine under one of the last remaining immigration certificates under the White Paper. It would tell how this Jewish mite was handed over the fence from the arms of a children's attendant to some sort of aunt.

A Heartbreaking Sight

As the train drew into the station the police cordon was unable to hold back the waiting crowds. At the doors of the cattle and freight coaches the children could be seen, filthy, ragged, emaciated, barefoot, some wearing clothing of a sort, others wrapped in sacking. The sight of them was harrowing. Everything about the children was dusty and dirty; only their eyes shone brilliantly, limpid eyes, lighting up at the sight of hands stretched out to them in greeting. They were the eyes of an afflicted people.

Even the British policemen, so still and phlegmatic, were touched, and some innate courtesy impelled them to walk at the side of the strange procession. I thought to myself: "Heavens above! If only the great ones of the world were here now, perhaps they could understand now what they have been unable to grasp from innumerable petitions, protests, resolutions, articles. Perhaps a mere photograph of this coachload would open their hearts."

Here Too?

The reactions of the children upon arrival at their camp varied widely. Some of them drew back in alarm and asked astonished: "Here too? A camp? A wire fence? Again?" Another smiled impishly: "This sort of camp doesn't frighten me. Only tell me, pal, is this a camp with soap or without soap?" I asked him what he meant, and he replied: "You see, I spent two years in a camp without soap or water. . . ."

At Ahuza on Mount Carmel I saw the children again. They were receiving treatment and getting well. One of the social workers from the Women's Welfare Society held a little girl in her arms. She hugged and kissed her. A boy of seven looked on jealously, then he approached her and said: "Auntie, give me a kiss too. I haven't been kissed for such a long time." And Auntie wipes her eyes with her handkerchief and distributes kisses right and left.

A few days later I came to the agricultural school at Magdiel. I saw clean, shining children, playing merrily in the nursery, or working in the storeroom or kitchen. I could hardly believe my eyes.

"We are glad you came. We are so happy here!" a little girl said.

"You like it here, don't you?" I asked her.

"Yes, but it would be still better if I had some news of mamma. . . ."

They Know It by Heart

Rescued children from Poland, 5, 7, 11, 14 years of age, chattering in Polish Yiddish, Rumania, Slovakian, Hungarian, Turkish. Now they are sitting under a shady tree outside the camp. They are waiting for a bus to take them away. Some Jewish soldiers sit down beside them and offer them chocolates and grapes. The children tell their story of the thousand and one nights. They know the history of the Jewish people very well, they know it by heart.

One child tells: "In Beirut when I saw a military bus full of Jewish soldiers, with the Magen Davod (Shield of David), I cried. I knew that emblem so well from Poland." And he turns to the military camp near by and points with his finger at the Shield of David emblem on the lorry, and he cannot stop trembling. Tears gather in his eyes and flow down his cheeks.

The children clamber and climb over the soldiers' knees. They cannot settle down. They ask thousands of questions, and suddenly they learn that one of the soldiers is a "sabra," a native of Palestine. The children cannot understand this.

"Where do you come from?" asks one child.

"From here. I was born here."

"But where did you come from?"

"I didn't come. I was born right here in Palestine."

"Really not from anywhere? Nowhere at all?"

And his eyes fill with wonder as he looks at this strange soldier.

—From "The Ellis Island of Palestine," Rescue *(June 1945): 6, 9.*

ILLEGAL VOYAGE

The Mossad l'Aliyeh Bet *(Institute for Illegal Immigration) was a Jewish group that arranged much of the illegal immigration to* PALESTINE *after the late 1930s. Beginning in the summer of 1945, the group organized voyages of Jewish immigrants to Palestine with the assistance of the naval branch (Palyam) of the* HAGANAH *military (Palmach). In November 1945 the group bought a Greek cargo ship, the* SS Dimitrios, *and renamed her the* Berl Katznelson. *She left a Greek port for Palestine with 211 immigrants on November 22, 1945, and attempted a landing on the coast of Palestine shortly thereafter. Intercepted by the Royal Navy, most of the immigrants safely reached shore; the remainder were interned by the British. Here the Palyam commander on the voyage recounts the experience.*

I let the passengers take turns on deck for some fresh air, though there was enough space below. They were in high spirits, because they were finally moving toward their goal. Our radio silence, imposed on all illegal ships nearing the coast, was interrupted only once, and even then just for a flash. That was when our radio-operator, anxiously waiting for a signal, finally heard what he had been waiting for: a coded message of barely two words. He rushed to me with a slip of paper; it was our landing instructions: "At Shefayim." [About 15 kilometres north of Tel Aviv, Shefayim was in 1945 little more than a secluded bay, with a kibbutz about 1 kilometre inland.] I knew that by the time we approached the spot a Palyam landing unit would already have arrived from its base in Caesarea, farther up the coast. It would include about 200 people, most trained in disembarking passengers, but also men to repair possible damage and a first aid team.

The landing area was enclosed by Palmach men who had taken up positions on the dunes overlooking the bay, ready to obstruct British police, army or patrols, and to prevent them from coming into the area while the operation was in progress. The Palyam people lit two fairly large gas-lamps. I spotted their familiar light from the command bridge and ordered the captain to take course accordingly. The *Berl Katznelson* proceeded for another few minutes, and then the captain threw anchor. The ship had arrived.

As usual, disembarkment began at great speed in row-boats standing by for this purpose. Just as we were starting, three Arab fishing-boats were sighted in the immediate vicinity by the observation patrol. They were taken into custody to keep them out of the way and to prevent them from making trouble while the operation was progressing. But there had been a fourth fishing boat—as we were to discover later—that got away. And the Arab fishermen did their civic duty: they reported to the nearby British police-station that something was going on in the little bay near Kibbutz Shefayim.

The British warship *Ajax* arrived as half of the passengers had safely disembarked. One hundred men, women and children had already reached land, were taken to Kibbutz Shefayim, served a hot drink, received a welcome hug and were already on their way by lorry to their next destination: a kibbutz farther inland, or perhaps a flat in Tel Aviv.

The *Ajax* drew near the *Berl Katznelson* and lowered several lifeboats with a detachment of sailors in each. By the time the first British sailors reached the rope-ladder of the *Berl Katznelson* and began to board her, all but eleven persons had disembarked and vanished in the dark of the night in the little row-boats of the landing team. The eleven remaining passengers were a fairly mixed group—some elderly people who had been kept waiting to last and seven youngsters. Three of them, including myself, were Palestinians and four—the captain and his mates—were Greeks, but nobody could have told them apart from me and my Palyam friends.

The British boarding-party approached us awkwardly and with hesitation, while the captain was ordered to float the *Berl Katznelson*. The rest of the prisoners were told to stand in line, surrounded by British sailors with submachine-guns on the ready, and wait for further orders. At that point, I felt the game was lost. They were going to arrest us sooner or later; I decided to get away before they took us on board the *Ajax* and into detention.

I was wearing my heavy winter clothing, a sweater and heavy boots, and I began to get out of them, as carefully and unobtrusively as possible under the watchful eyes of the British soldiers. I suggested that the rest try to get away with me, but they thought I was mad even to think of escaping—so closely were we being watched by the British soldiers, who outnumbered us about four to one. A soldier with a submachine-gun was following me as I walked towards the back of the ship, but I tried to show him that all I was doing was trying to help the Greek captain in complying with the British order to get the ship moving. I kept glancing sideways at my armed escort, and when he suddenly turned his head to hear an order shouted from the other end of the ship, I realized that my chance had come.

I jumped overboard, grabbed the anchor chain, and let myself down as fast as I dared. Just as I touched the water, the anchor came up out of the sea and the ship began to move. I felt the propellers of the boat dangerously close, but I began to swim towards the shore, blissfully aware of the fact that the foam of the propellers which had just about killed me had also hidden me from view. Against my skin I felt the heavy belt filled with gold coins that the Mossad had provided. They and the trousers of my uniform were so heavy that I had to get rid of them both.

The *Berl Katznelson* moved north, and I swam towards shore. Just as I reached shallow waters, I recognized Sara Jaffe of the Palmach landing team. She had remained to watch the departing ship as all the Palmach soldiers disappeared from the scene, and she looked at me now without recognizing who I was. But just seeing me standing there in my undershorts, shivering in the bitter cold of the autumn dawn, prompted her to take off her fur jacket and throw it at me. I am sorry to report that it was not long enough to cover my undershorts.

Sara took me to Davidka Nameri's command post, where I was received with no hint of surprise or emotion. I reported briefly to Davidka, and I remember being astonished that no one took the initiative to bring me any clothing. In my excitement I proposed to Davidka that the ship be attacked and taken as she passed near the Palyam base of Caesarea on her way to Haifa. Davidka brushed my suggestion aside without so much as a comment.

The remaining passengers, the few Greeks and the captain, were detained when they reached Haifa port and taken to the Athlit detention camp.

— *From Ehud Avriel,* Open the Gates! *(London: Weidenfeld and Nicolson, 1975), 225–28.*

The U.S. Congress Takes a Stand

RESOLUTION ON PALESTINE

Throughout 1945 members of both houses of the U.S. Congress introduced resolutions concerning the establishment of a Jewish homeland in PALESTINE. Although these were non-binding resolutions with no direct effect on U.S. policy, they did signify the growing American support for a Jewish state. This joint resolution of both Democrats and Republicans was introduced by Congressman Joseph Martin, a Republican from Massachusetts.

— *From* Joint Resolution Favoring Action by the United States looking to the Restoration of Palestine as a Homeland for the Jewish People, *70th Cong., 1st sess., 1945, H.J.R. 264.*

79TH CONGRESS
1ST SESSION

H. J. RES. 264

THE LIBRARY OF

NO 6

IN THE HOUSE OF REPRESENTATIVES

OCTOBER 29, 1945

Mr. MARTIN of Massachusetts introduced the following joint resolution; which was referred to the Committee on Foreign Affairs

---

JOINT RESOLUTION

Favoring action by the United States looking to the restoration of Palestine as a homeland for the Jewish people.

Whereas the Sixty-seventh Congress of the United States on June 30, 1922, unanimously resolved "that the United States of America favors the establishment in Palestine of a national home for the Jewish people, it being clearly understood that nothing shall be done which may prejudice the civil and religious rights of Christian and all other non-Jewish communities in Palestine, and that the holy places and religious buildings and sites in Palestine shall be adequately protected"; and

Whereas the ruthless persecution of the Jewish people in Europe has clearly demonstrated the need for a Jewish homeland as a haven for the large numbers who have become homeless as a result of this persecution; and

2

Whereas these urgent necessities are evidenced by the President's request for the immediate right of entry of one hundred thousand Jewish refugees: Therefore be it

1 *Resolved by the Senate and House of Representatives*
2 *of the United States of America in Congress assembled,*
3 That the United States shall use its good offices to the end
4 that the doors of Palestine shall be opened for free entry of
5 Jews into that country, and that there shall be full oppor-
6 tunity for colonization, so that they may reconstitute Pales-
7 tine as a free and democratic commonwealth in which all
8 men, regardless of race or creed, shall enjoy equal rights.

SURVIVORS IN TRANSITION

Most displaced persons (DPs) in Germany returned home when the war ended. Some were unable or unwilling to return to their homelands, and these included some Jewish survivors. Many Jews who did return to their homelands found their families missing or dead, their property stolen, and the lives they had known gone forever. A rising tide of anti-Jewish pogroms in the summer and fall of 1945 in Poland and other East European countries compounded their plight. They returned surreptitiously to Germany, where they were considered stateless. Many hoped to emigrate, especially to Palestine and North America. Palestine, however, was then under British rule, and the number of Jewish immigrants had been limited by the British White Paper of 1939.

While living in the DP camps, Jewish displaced persons recovered from their ordeal. Rehabilitation and retraining helped them resume their lives.

The two photos of the Zeilsheim DP camp, near Frankfurt, were taken by Ephraim Mayer Robinson. Trained as an agronomist, he and his family went to Germany from the Soviet Union after the war. He worked as a freelance photographer at Zeilsheim until he emigrated to the United States in 1948.

Soviet officers and others bid farewell to survivors of
the Theresienstadt concentration camp in May 1945.
Note the *Deutsche Reichsbahn* markings on the freight
cars: identical boxcars had earlier carried prisoners to
concentration camps and ghettos. May, 1945.
(Terezin Memorial Museum)

At Bergen-Belsen concentration camp, the inmates and their clothing and possessions were all deloused to help eradicate the raging typhus epidemic. One woman is wearing an SS tunic since adequate clothing was hard to find. April 15, 1945. (NARA)

This woman, who had been barefoot for a year or two, discovers that her feet are no longer their former size or shape. In June 1945 a British volunteer helps her to find a pair of shoes of the proper size. (USHMM)

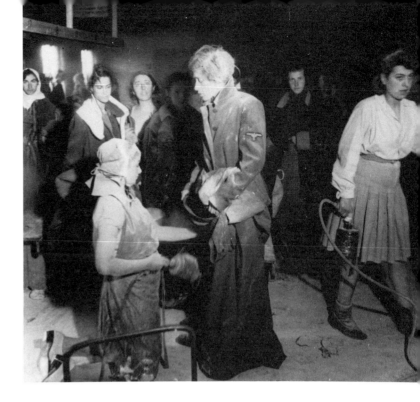

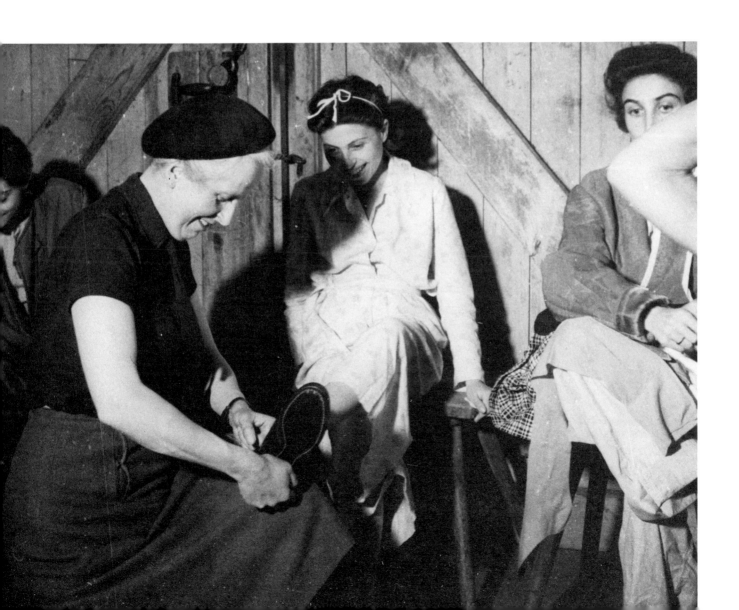

A former inmate of Bergen-Belsen concentration
camp is examined at a hospital set up in the
liberated camp. (USHMM)

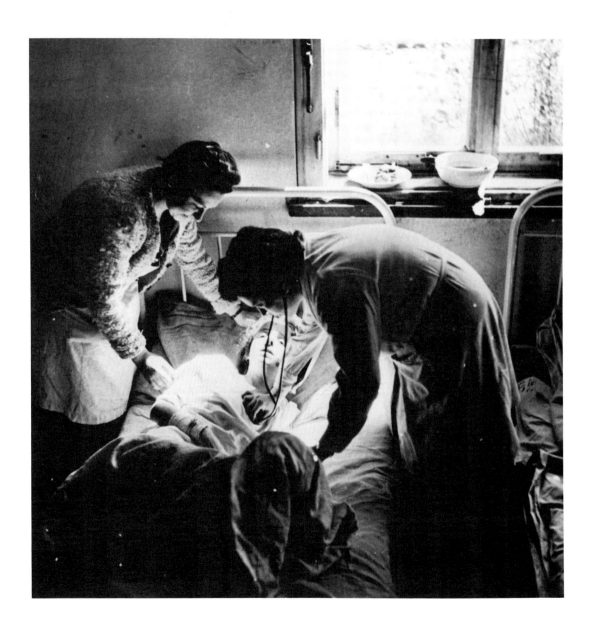

Apprentice seamstresses in the Organization
for Rehabilitation through Training (ORT) at
the Landsberg DP camp. A portrait of Theodor
Herzl, founder of Zionism, hangs inside the
Star of David on the wall. (USHMM)

Jewish DP policemen apprehend a former *Kapo* who was recognized on the street in Zeilsheim DP camp. 1945. (Alice Robinson Lev Collection, USHMM)

German women being forced from their homes in Landsberg to make room for Jewish DPs. 1945. (USHMM)

A Hebrew lesson at the Zeilsheim DP camp.
The child is writing "The Jews will immigrate
to the land of Israel." 1945.
(Alice Robinson Lev Collection, USHMM)

Three Jewish youths from Buchenwald concentration camp on a train, beginning their journey to Palestine in June 1945. From left to right are a Polish girl, a boy from Latvia, and a Hungarian girl holding a Star of David flag. (NARA)

WAR CRIMES

- As evidence of Nazi atrocities against civilians and prisoners of war mounted, the Allies decided to prosecute perpetrators of war crimes at war's end. Chiefly through the efforts of Great Britain and the U.S., a UNITED NATIONS WAR CRIMES COMMISSION was established in London in October 1943 to compile lists of possible war criminals and to collect data submitted by commissions of participating governments.

- Three months after the German surrender, the United States, Great Britain, France, and the Soviet Union signed the "London Agreement" that established the INTERNATIONAL MILITARY TRIBUNAL (IMT) the court of justice for "major" war criminals whose offenses had no specific geographical location.

- From October 18, 1945, through October 1, 1946, magistrates from the four Allied powers presided over the IMT at Nuremberg. Twenty-two defendants stood accused of war crimes, crimes against peace and humanity, and conspiracy to wage aggressive war.

- Though publicized most widely, the postwar "Nuremberg Trials" represented only one small facet of the war crimes prosecution. Hundreds of such proceedings, adjudicated by military commissions and tribunals in the British, American, French, and Soviet zones of Germany and Austria from 1945 to 1948, tried "minor" war criminals whose alleged crimes were against Allied nationals in specific geographic locations.

- The efforts to try war criminals was part of the Western military authorities' commitment to denazification and "democratization." In December 1945, the CONTROL COUNCIL FOR GERMANY promulgated Control Council Law No. 10 that laid a uniform basis in all zones of occupation for prosecuting war criminals, for the subsequent trials of criminal organizations at Nuremberg, and for the adjudication in German and Austrian courts of crimes against German and Austrian nationals.

The courtroom of the Dachau trial (see p. 265), December 4, 1945. The American military judges sit beneath the U.S. flag; the defendants are at the right rear. (NARA)

THE MEANING OF BUCHENWALD

by Ernst Reuter

A fugitive from Hitler's Germany, former Magdeburg mayor Ernst Reuter (1889–1953) emerged as one of the leaders of the German Social Democratic Party (SPD) after World War II. Reuter served as West Berlin's first mayor from 1948 until 1953 and is best remembered as Berlin's champion during the 1948–49 Soviet blockade and its early years of isolation and division. Reuter wrote the following essay in response to a pamphlet by Victor Gollancz, a British publisher well known for his stance against fascism and for his relief efforts in Germany following the war.

Sir,—Friends in London sent me a pamphlet entitled "What Buchenwald Really Means," by V. Gollancz. I have been in a German concentration camp twice personally, and I have been freed the second time, in 1934, only by the efforts of an English Quaker-woman, Miss Howard, who stayed in Berlin till she had succeeded in causing my release.

I do not think it is of great use to discuss whether the people who tasted life in one of Hitler's concentration camps were heroes or not. I think they were only people who did what decent people did in every country at all times; they did not deny their convictions and stood to all that had been for years of long and selfless work the scope of life for them. I will never forget the cries of my beaten comrades during the nights; but I will also never forget that these, my comrades, have stood erect and unbroken before their tormentors and that, though they were defenceless, they never failed to inspire them with respect.

I very well remember my visit to England in 1935. I have not met anybody who was not ready to give me all help he was able to give. But I do also know that very few people wanted to know anything of concentration camps at that time.

I had met this "Not-Want-to-Know" in Germany too, of course; and this confirmed me in my opinion that peoples are not so very different in their reactions towards such occurrences. I met every shade of personal behaviour in Germany; I saw low people, I saw cowards, I saw brave men and I saw decent people. I do not know if the percentage of these people in Germany was so much different from that in other countries under similar conditions, and I would rather like to abstain from such a decision, for it would suit a German badly to make it in such a deitic way. But only a man who never really lived under these conditions can say that there were never hundreds of thousands of brave, selfless and upright men who faced every cruelty in order to hold to their convictions, and who were not only ready to give their lives for them but really gave them.

We Germans surely have to take the responsibility for all that the Hitler regime has done to the world on our shoulders, and it must be a debt of honour for us to repair all that is repairable. But nobody will be able to force us to acknowledge that we are all responsible for the Hitler regime. The Hitler regime was for most people a terrible fate which swept over them, many times more terrible for the innocent than the guilty.

Those who have looked into the eyes of Hitler's Gestapo and S.S. men, those who know what it meant to remain true and faithful, these men will never take part in judging others wantonly; they will leave this judgment to those who are not fit to pass it because they are not able to imagine under what conditions Germans had to live.

The brave words of Mr. Gollancz's booklet strengthened my hope that it will be possible to attain our aim, namely, a real and true understanding between the peoples of Europe, faster than it seemed to be possible in the first days.

Ernst Reuter
Former Mayor of Magdeburg
Former Member of the German Reichstag

—From The New Statesman and Nation *30 (October 6, 1945): 228–29.*

INTERNATIONAL MILITARY TRIBUNAL

Preparations for the Trial

THE LONDON AGREEMENT AND IMT CHARTER

On August 8, 1945, the United States, the Soviet Union, Great Britain, and France signed an agreement in London to form the International Military Tribunal (IMT) to try major war criminals. The charter governing the operation of this International Military Tribunal, signed at the same time, covered the makeup of the IMT and its jurisdiction, the composition and duties of the international committee which would investigate and then prosecute the major war criminals, the procedures used to ensure a fair trial for the defendants, the powers of the IMT and rules for conduct of the trial, and the procedure for judgment and passing sentence. Sections of the agreement and the charter are reproduced here.

Agreement for the Prosecution and Punishment of the Major War Criminals of the European Axis

Whereas the United Nations have from time to time made declarations of their intention that war criminals shall be brought to justice;

And whereas the Moscow Declaration of the 30th October 1943 on German atrocities in occupied Europe stated that those German officers and men and members of the Nazi party who have been responsible for or have taken a consenting part in atrocities and crimes will be sent back to the countries in which their abominable deeds were done in order that they may be judged and punished according to the laws of these liberated countries and of the free governments that will be created therein;

And whereas this declaration was stated to be without prejudice to the case of major criminals whose offenses have no particular geographic location and who will be punished by the joint decision of the Governments of the Allies;

Now, therefore, the Government of the United States of America, the Provisional Government of the French Republic, the Government of the United Kingdom of Great Britain and Northern Ireland, and the Government of the Union of Soviet Socialist Republics (hereinafter called "the signatories") acting in the interests of all the United Nations and by their representatives duly authorized thereto have concluded this agreement.

Article 1. There shall be established, after consultation with the Control Council for Germany, an International Military Tribunal for the trial of war criminals whose offenses have no particular geographical location, whether they be accused individually or in their capacity as members of organizations or groups or in both capacities.

Article 2. The constitution, jurisdiction, and functions of the International Military Tribunal shall be those set out in the charter annexed to this agreement, which Charter shall form an integral part of this agreement.

Article 3. Each of the signatories shall take the necessary steps to make available for the investigation of the charges and trial the major war criminals detained by them who are to be tried by the International Military Tribunal. The signatories shall also use their best endeavors to make available for investigation of the charges against, and the trial before the International Military Tribunal, such of the major war criminals as are not in the territories of any of the signatories.

Article 4. Nothing in this agreement shall prejudice the provisions established by the Moscow Declaration concerning the return of war criminals to the countries where they committed their crimes.

Article 5. Any Government of the United Nations may adhere to this agreement by notice given through the diplomatic channel to the Government of the United Kingdom, who shall inform the other signatory and adhering Governments of each such adherence.

Article 6. Nothing in this agreement shall prejudice the jurisdiction or the powers of any national or occupation court established or to be established in any Allied territory or in Germany for the trial of war criminals.

Article 7. This agreement shall come into force on the day of signature and shall remain in force for the period of one year and shall continue thereafter, subject to the right of any signatory to give, through the diplomatic channel, one month's notice of intention to terminate it. Such termination shall not prejudice any proceedings already taken or any findings already made in pursuance of this agreement.

In witness whereof the undersigned have signed the present agreement.

Done in quadruplicate in London this eighth day of August, 1945, each in English, French, and Russian and each text to have equal authenticity.

For the Government of the United States of America: *Robert H. Jackson.*

For the Provisional Government of the French Republic: *Robert Falco.*

For the Government of the United Kingdom of Great Britain and Northern Ireland: *Jowitt.*

For the Government of the Union of Soviet Socialist Republics: *I. T. Nikitchenko, A. N. Trainin.*

Charter of the International Military Tribunal

II. Jurisdiction and General Principles

Article 6. The Tribunal established by the agreement referred to in article 1 hereof for the trial and punishment of the major war criminals of the European Axis countries shall have the power to try and punish persons who, acting in the interests of the European Axis countries, whether as individuals or as members of organizations committed any of the following crimes.

The following acts, or any of them, are crimes coming within the jurisdiction of the Tribunal for which there shall be individual responsibility:

(a) Crimes against peace. Namely, planning, preparation, initiation, or waging of a war of aggression or a war in violation of international treaties, agreements, or assurances, or participation in a common plan or conspiracy for the accomplishment of any of the foregoing.

(b) War crimes. Namely, violations of the laws or customs of war. Such violations shall include, but not be limited to, murder, ill treatment, or deportation to slave labor or for any other purpose of civilian population of or in occupied territory, murder or ill treatment of prisoners of war or persons on the seas, killing of hostages, plunder of public or private property, wanton destruction of cities, towns, or villages, or devastation not justified by military necessity.

(c) Crimes against humanity. Namely, murder, extermination, enslavement, deportation, and other inhumane acts committed against any civilian population before or during the war or persecutions on political, racial, or religious grounds in execution of or in connection with any crime within the jurisdiction of the Tribunal, whether or not in violation of the domestic law of the country where perpetrated,

Leaders, organizers, instigators, and accomplices participating in the formulation or execution of a common plan or conspiracy to commit any of the foregoing crimes are responsible for all acts performed by any persons in execution of such plan.

Article 7. The official position of defendants, whether as heads of state or responsible officials in government departments, shall not be considered as freeing them from responsibility or mitigating punishment.

Article 8. The fact that the defendant acted pursuant to order of his government or of a superior shall not free him from responsibility but may be considered in mitigation of punishment if the Tribunal determines that justice so requires.

Article 9. At the trial of any individual member of any group or organization the Tribunal may declare (in connection with any act of which the individual may be convicted) that the group or organization of which the individual was a member was a criminal organization.

After receipt of the indictment the Tribunal shall give such notice as it thinks fit that the prosecution intends to ask the Tribunal to make such declaration and any member of the organization will be entitled to apply to the Tribunal for leave to be heard by the Tribunal upon the question of the criminal character of the organization. The Tribunal shall have power to allow or reject the application. If the application is allowed, the Tribunal may direct in what manner the applicants shall be represented and heard.

Article 10. In cases where a group or organization is declared criminal by the Tribunal, the competent national authority of any signatory shall have the right to bring individuals to trial for membership therein before national, military, or occupation courts. In any such case the criminal nature of the group or organization is considered proved and shall not be questioned.

Article 11. Any person convicted by the Tribunal may be charged before a national, military, or occupation court, referred to in article 10 of this Charter, with a crime other than of membership in a criminal group or organization, and such court may after convicting him impose upon him punishment independent of and additional to the punishment imposed by the Tribunal for participation in the criminal activities of such group or organization.

Article 12. The Tribunal shall have the right to take proceedings against a person charged with crimes set out in article 6 of this Charter in his absence if he has not been found or if the Tribunal for any reason finds it necessary in the interests of justice to conduct the hearing in his absence.

Article 13. The Tribunal shall draw up rules for its procedure. These rules shall not be inconsistent with the provisions of this Charter. . . .

V. Powers of the Tribunal and Conduct of the Trial

Article 17. The Tribunal shall have the power:

(a) To summon witnesses to the trial and to require their attendance and testimony and to put questions to them.

(b) To interrogate any defendant.

(c) To require the production of documents and other evidentiary material.

(d) To administer oaths to witnesses.

(e) To appoint officers for the carrying out of any task designated by the Tribunal, including the power to have evidence taken on commission.

Article 18. The Tribunal shall:

(a) Confine the trial strictly to an expeditious hearing of the issues raised by the charges.

(b) Take strict measures to prevent any action which will cause unreasonable delay and rule out irrelevant issues and statements of any kind whatsoever.

(c) Deal summarily with any contumacy, imposing appropriate punishment, including exclusion of any defendant or his counsel from some or all further proceedings but without prejudice to the determination of the charges.

Article 19. The Tribunal shall not be bound by technical rules of evidence. It shall adopt and apply to the greatest possible extent expeditious and non-technical procedure and shall admit any evidence which it deems to have probative value.

Article 20. The Tribunal may require to be informed of the nature of any evidence before it is offered so that it may rule upon the relevance thereof.

Article 21. The Tribunal shall not require proof of facts of common knowledge but shall take judicial notice thereof. It shall also take judicial notice of official governmental documents and reports of the United Nations, including the acts and documents of the committees set up in the various Allied countries for the investigation of war crimes, and the records and findings of military or other tribunals of any of the United Nations.

Article 22. The permanent seat of the Tribunal shall be Berlin. The first meetings of the members of the Tribunal and of the Chief Prosecutor shall be held at Berlin in a place to be designated by the Control Council for Germany. The first trial shall be held at Nuremberg and any subsequent trials shall be held at such places as the Tribunal may decide.

Article 23. One or more of the chief prosecutors may take part in the prosecution at each trial. The function of any chief prosecutor may be discharged by him personally or by any person or persons authorized by him.

The function of counsel for a defendant may be discharged at the defendant's request by any counsel professionally qualified to conduct cases before the courts of his own country or by any other person who may be specially authorized thereto by the Tribunal.

Article 24. The proceedings at the trial shall take the following course:

(a) The indictment shall be read in court.

(b) The Tribunal shall ask each defendant whether he pleads "guilty" or "not guilty."

(c) The prosecution shall make an opening statement.

(d) The Tribunal shall ask the prosecution and the defense what evidence (if any) they wish to submit to the Tribunal, and the Tribunal shall rule upon the admissibility of any such evidence.

(e) The witnesses for the prosecution shall be examined and after that the witnesses for the defense. Thereafter such rebutting evidence as may be held by the Tribunal to be admissible shall be called by either the prosecution or the defense.

(f) The Tribunal may put any question to any witness and to any defendant at any time.

(g) The prosecution and the defense shall interrogate and may cross examine any witnesses and any defendant who gives testimony.

(h) The defense shall address the court.

(i) The prosecution shall address the court.

(j) Each defendant may make a statement to the Tribunal.

(k) The Tribunal shall deliver judgment and pronounce sentence.

Article 25. All official documents shall be produced, and all court proceedings conducted, in English, French, and Russian and in the language of the defendant. So much of the record and of the proceedings may also be translated into the language of any country in which the Tribunal is sitting as the Tribunal considers desirable in the interests of justice and public opinion.

— *Reprinted with permission from 39* AJIL *(Supplement) 257–64 (1945), © The American Society of International Law.*

IMT INDICTMENT

The International Military Tribunal *indicted the major war criminals on October 19, 1945. The four counts of the indictment included (1) conspiracy to commit crimes against peace, war crimes, and crimes against humanity, (2) crimes against peace, (3) war crimes, and (4) crimes against humanity. The indictment was served individually on each of the defendants in their cells at the Palace of Justice in Nuremberg.*

— *From Record Group 238, box 1, entry 22, National Archives and Records Administration. It has also been published in International Military Tribunal,* Trial of the Major War Criminals Before the International Military Tribunal, *vol. 1:* Official Text in the English Language, Official Documents *(Frankfurt, 1947), v.*

INTERNATIONAL MILITARY TRIBUNAL

No. 1

THE UNITED STATES OF AMERICA, THE FRENCH REPUBLIC, THE UNITED KINGDOM OF GREAT BRITAIN AND NORTHERN IRELAND, AND THE UNION OF SOVIET SOCIALIST REPUBLICS

— AGAINST —

HERMANN WILHELM GÖRING, RUDOLF HESS, JOACHIM VON RIBBENTROP, ROBERT LEY, WILHELM KEITEL, ERNST KALTENBRUNNER, ALFRED ROSENBERG, HANS FRANK, WILHELM FRICK, JULIUS STREICHER, WALTER FUNK, HJALMAR SCHACHT, GUSTAV KRUPP VON BOHLEN UND HALBACH, KARL DÖNITZ, ERICH RAEDER, BALDUR VON SCHIRACH, FRITZ SAUCKEL, ALFRED JODL, MARTIN BORMANN, FRANZ VON PAPEN, ARTUR SEYSS-INQUART, ALBERT SPEER, CONSTANTIN VON NEURATH, AND HANS FRITZSCHE, INDIVIDUALLY AND AS MEMBERS OF ANY OF THE FOLLOWING GROUPS OR ORGANISATIONS TO WHICH THEY RESPECTIVELY BELONGED, NAMELY: DIE REICHSREGIERUNG (REICH CABINET); DAS KORPS DER POLITISCHEN LEITER DER NATIONALSOZIALISTISCHEN DEUTSCHEN ARBEITERPARTEI (LEADERSHIP CORPS OF THE NAZI PARTY); DIE SCHUTZSTAFFELN DER NATIONALSOZIALISTISCHEN DEUTSCHEN ARBEITERPARTEI (COMMONLY KNOWN AS THE "SS") AND INCLUDING DIE SICHERHEITSDIENST (COMMONLY KNOWN AS THE "SD"); DIE GEHEIME STAATSPOLIZEI (SECRET STATE POLICE, COMMONLY KNOWN AS THE "GESTAPO"); DIE STURMABTEILUNGEN DER N.S.D.A.P. (COMMONLY KNOWN AS THE "SA") AND THE GENERAL STAFF AND HIGH COMMAND OF THE GERMAN ARMED FORCES ALL AS DEFINED IN APPENDIX B.

Defendants

PRESS COVERAGE

The indictment against the major war criminals tried at Nuremberg was formally issued on October 19, 1945. It carried the four counts described below. The persecution of Jews and Roma (Gypsies) by the Germans and their partners

was recognized in the indictment, as well as the suffering of the Poles.

— From PM Daily, *October 19, 1945.*

Top Nazis Indicted in Murder of 10,000,000

Sweeping Charges Handed to 24; 'Non-Party' Warmakers Like Schacht, Krupp, Papen Named

By R. H. SHACKFORD
United Press Correspondent

WASHINGTON, Oct. 19.—The Big Four powers have formally accused 24 top Nazi war criminals of plotting and starting World War II, of murdering more than 10,000,000 civilians and prisoners of war by barbaric methods, and of plundering Europe on a scale unprecedented in history.

Exclusive of battle damage, they were charged with looting and destroying nearly $160,000,000,000 of property in Russia, France and Czechoslovakia.

In the killing of more than 10,000,000 innocent persons, including 5,700,000 Jews, they were charged with practicing systematic exterminations outside regular military operations.

The formal charges were made by the joint international war crimes prosecutors of the United States, Britain, France and Russia in a 30,000-word indictment. The document was made public in Washington, London, Paris, Moscow and Berlin, and was handed to the Nazi criminals at Nuremberg today.

It was handed up by the four representatives at a one-hour session in Berlin of the special tribunal which will try the accused men, possibly starting by Thanksgiving at Nuremberg.

The indictment is the first complete official record of Adolf Hitler's mad conspiracy to rule the world and of the horrible era of Nazi terrorism he created.

It was divided into four counts. Twelve of the criminals, including Hermann Wilhelm Goering, Rudolph Hess and Joachim von Ribbentrop were accused on each count.

The four counts are:

1. **CONSPIRACY** — Formulation or execution of a common plan or conspiracy to commit crimes against peace, war crimes and crimes against humanity.

2. **CRIMES AGAINST PEACE** — Planning, preparing, initiating and waging wars of aggression in violation of international treaties, agreements and assurances.

3. **WAR CRIMES** — The practice of "Total War" which includes methods and practices in direct conflict with the laws and customs of war.

4. **CRIMES AGAINST HUMANITY** — The murder and persecution of all who were or were suspected of being hostile to the Nazi Party and to the Nazi Party's grand conspiracy to rule the world. This included a plan to exterminate the Jews, the Poles and the Gypsies.

The indictment and the trials to follow are more than an attempt to punish these particular 24 men.

The four powers seek to indict the Nazi master plan of world conquest and establish as a precedent in international law that the men who start wars must die for their crimes, as well as the common soldiers who have to fight the battles.

The defendants were indicted individually and as members of 13 organizations "which should be declared criminal by reason of their aims and the means used for the accomplishment thereof." These organizations included the entire General Staff and High Command of the German armed forces, as well as the Gestapo and the SS.

Conviction of the 24 leaders and a decision that the indicted Nazi organizations are criminal in nature would doom thousands of Nazi small fry.

All but one of the 24 defendants are held in Allied custody near Nuremberg. Martin Bormann, Hitler's deputy, is at large but was indicted with the rest to make sure he does not escape eventual justice.

The other 23 have been given 30 days to prepare their cases. Then they will go on trial before a four-power tribunal of which Francis Biddle, former Attorney General, is the U. S. member. Robert H. Jackson, Supreme Court Justice and also former Attorney General, is the prosecutor for the U. S. and signed the indictment for this country.

The indictment traces the history of the "master race" from the origin of the Nazi Party in 1919 to its doom last June. It is a story of barbarous atrocities, inhuman persecutions and slavery, large-scale plunder, and wanton devastation unmatched on such a scale in the history of mankind.

Many of the details of Nazi terrorism have been known for a long time. The indictment is the first official attempt to set down the entire sordid story of the Nazi bid to rule the world.

Each of the defendants is charged with responsibility for plotting and helping execute seven wars of aggression which are now known as World War II. They face almost certain execution.

Adolf Hitler, who is believed dead but whose body has not been found, and two other top Nazis—Paul Joseph Goebbels and Heinrich Himmler, who committed suicide—are missing from the list.

The scope of the criminal activities of these men is only indicated in the indictment.

For example, it lists only "samples" of the number of murders known to have been committed at specified places. But those total 9,381,988—for which each of

the criminals must atone—and do not include numerous references in the indictment to the "hundreds," "thousands," and "tens of thousands" of other murders.

In one concentration camp alone—Auschwitz, Poland—4,000,000 persons were "exterminated."

France alone was plundered of materials, equipment, produce and money worth 1,265,013,260,000 (trillion) francs ($200,000,000,000) in prewar value and $25,300,255,000 at the present value of the franc.

The material loss in Soviet Russia—which bore the brunt of Nazi savagery—was placed at 679,000,000,000 rubles ($27,652,000,000 at the official, but unused, exchange rate.)

The Nazi conspirators' economic spoilation of Czechoslovakia from 1939 to 1945 was estimated at 200,000,000,000 Czech crowns (about $6,000,000,000.)

Nazi persecutions left "only remnants" of Europe's Jewish population. Of the 9,600,000 Jews under Nazi domination, it is "conservatively estimated" that 5,700,000 have disappeared.

Nearly 100,000,000 persons were deported from their homelands by the Nazis for forced labor battalions.

The methods of torture devised by the fanatical Nazis ranged from their much-publicized poison gas chambers and wagons, some of which "broke down from overwork," to the "iron helmet," a medieval torture instrument.

Other methods included freezing to death in icy water, hanging, shooting, starvation, kickings, beatings, the use of hot irons, pulling out of finger nails, deliberate exposure of concentration camp victims to typhus and other deadly diseases, disembowelling, sterilization of women, and the use of victims as guinea pigs in experimental operations.

The main fact that stands out throughout the indictment is that the Jews and Russia bore the brunt of Nazi savagery and terrorism. Of the 9,381,988 specific cases of murder, nearly 9,000,000 occurred in Russian territory.

Hitler planned to "erase from the face of the earth" Russia's second city—Leningrad. Similar plans were indicated for other Russian cities.

The Nazis also tried to "erase" the Jewish race in Europe. Defendant Robert Ley, Nazi labor leader, was quoted as having said:

"The second German secret weapon is anti-Semitism, because if it is consistently pursued by Germany, it will become a universal problem which all nations will be forced to consider."

His equally anti-Semitic colleague Julius Streicher contended:

"The sun will not shine on the nations of the earth until the last Jew is dead."

In addition to Goering, the fat, drug-addicted Nazi Air Marshal who established the first concentration camps as far back as 1933, Hess, who as Hitler's deputy, flew to Britain in search of a "phony" peace, and Ribbentrop, the double-crossing former champagne salesman turned Nazi diplomat, the defendants include:

Ernst Kaltenbrunner, Austrian terrorist and SS leader; Alfred Rosenberg, Nazi editor and Jew-baiter; Hans Frank, Governor-General of Poland; Bormann, successor to Hess and still at large; Wilhelm Frick, interior minister and director of lands seized by the Nazis; Ley, labor leader; Fritz Sauckel, head of the slave labor organization; Albert Speer, abuser and exploiter of human beings in the slave labor program; Walther Funk, minister of economics; Hjalmar Schacht, finance wizard; Franz von Papen, diplomat and master of duplicity; Gustav Krupp von Bohlen und Halbach, head of Krupp munitions industry; Constantin von Neurath, former foreign minister; Baldur von Schirach, youth leader; Arthur Seyss-Inquart, Austrian "quisling;" Streicher, Jew-baiter; Field Marshal Wilhelm Keitel, chief of the High Command; Col. Gen. Alfred Jodl, member of the General Staff who signed the surrender at Reims; Grand Admiral Erich Raeder of the Navy; Grand Admiral Karl Doenitz, submarine corps commander; Hans Fritsche, propaganda chief and head of DNB news agency.

Germany and the Nazi Party violated virtually every law and custom of the civilized world, and the indictment named the Nazi Party as "the central core of the common plan or conspiracy" for world domination.

In the course of that conspiracy—put down at such terrific loss of life and wealth—the indictment charged that:

1. The Nazis "exhorted" Japan to attack the U. S. A. to weaken the Allies.

2. Germany was guilty of 64 violations of 26 international treaties she signed, dating back to the Hague Convention of 1899 and including the Versailles and Locarno Treaties as well as the Munich agreement.

3. American prisoners of war were murdered in Normandy and in the Ardennes in 1944, and were starved, beaten and otherwise mistreated in prisoner of war camps in 1943, 1944 and 1945.

4. Annihilation of the Jews became "an official state policy" soon after the Nazis gained control of Germany.

5. Hitler and his gang recognized after the bloodless conquests of Austria and Czechoslovakia that further "successes" could not be achieved without war.

The indictment painted a vivid picture of what the Nazis did to Soviet Russia:

"On the territory of the Soviet Union, the Nazi conspirators destroyed or severely damaged 1710 cities and more than 70,000 villages and hamlets, more than 6,000,000 buildings and made homeless about 25,000,000 persons . . .

"The Germans destroyed 427 Russian museums. . . . The losses suffered by the coal mining industry alone in the Stalingrad region amount to 2,000,000,000 rubles ($376,000,000 at the official rate.) Stealing of huge dimensions and the destruction of industrial, cultural and other property was typified in Kiev. More than 4,000,000 books, magazines and manuscripts and a large number of artistic productions and valuables were stolen and carried away."

The Germans destroyed 1670 Greek Orthodox churches, 237 Roman Catholic churches, 67 chapels, and 532 synagogues in Russia, and "destroyed the estate and museum of Leo Tolstoy and desecrated the grave of the great writer."

(In Sunday's PM . . . Further reports and a comprehensive map on the war crimes.)

The Tribunal's Proceedings

JACKSON'S OPENING ADDRESS

Supreme Court Justice Robert H. Jackson, Chief U.S. Counsel to the International Military Tribunal, made the opening address to the Tribunal on November 21, 1945. His speech, lasting into the next day's morning session, laid the groundwork for the prosecution's case. Excerpts from this speech are reproduced here.

The privilege of opening the first trial in history for crimes against the peace of the world imposes a grave responsibility. The wrongs which we seek to condemn and punish have been so calculated, so malignant, and so devastating, that civilization cannot tolerate their being ignored, because it cannot survive their being repeated. That four great nations, flushed with victory and stung with injury stay the hand of vengeance and voluntarily submit their captive enemies to the judgment of the law is one of the most significant tributes that Power has ever paid to Reason.

This Tribunal, while it is novel and experimental, is not the product of abstract speculations nor is it created to vindicate legalistic theories. This inquest represents the practical effort of four of the most mighty of nations, with the support of 17 more, to utilize international law to meet the greatest menace of our times—aggressive war. The common sense of mankind demands that law shall not stop with the punishment of petty crimes by little people. It must also reach men who possess themselves of great power and make deliberate and concerted use of it to set in motion evils which leave no home in the world untouched. It is a cause of that magnitude that the United Nations will lay before Your Honors.

In the prisoners' dock sit twenty-odd broken men. Reproached by the humiliation of those they have led almost as bitterly as by the desolation of those they have attacked, their personal capacity for evil is forever past. It is hard now to perceive in these men as captives the power by which as Nazi leaders they once dominated much of the world and terrified most of it. Merely as individuals their fate is of little consequence to the world.

What makes this inquest significant is that these prisoners represent sinister influences that will lurk in the world long after their bodies have returned to dust. We will show them to be living symbols of racial hatreds, of terrorism and violence, and of the arrogance and cruelty of power. They are symbols of fierce nationalisms and of militarism, of intrigue and war-making which have embroiled Europe generation after generation, crushing its manhood, destroying its homes, and impoverishing its life. They have so identified themselves with the philosophies they conceived and with the forces they directed that any tenderness to them is a victory and an encouragement to all the evils which are attached to their names. Civilization can afford no compromise with the social forces which would gain renewed strength if we deal ambiguously or indecisively with the men in whom those forces now precariously survive. . . .

3. Crimes against the Jews:

The most savage and numerous crimes planned and committed by the Nazis were those against the Jews. Those in Germany in 1933 numbered about 500,000. In the aggregate, they had made for themselves positions which excited envy, and had accumulated properties which excited the avarice of the Nazis. They were few enough to be helpless and numerous enough to be held up as a menace.

Let there be no misunderstanding about the charge of persecuting Jews. What we charge against these defendants is not those arrogances and pretensions which frequently accompany the intermingling of different peoples and which are likely, despite the honest efforts of government, to produce regrettable crimes and convulsions. It is my purpose to show a plan and design, to which all Nazis were fanatically committed, to annihilate all Jewish people. These crimes were organized and promoted by the Party leadership, executed and protected by the Nazi officials, as we shall convince you by written orders of the Secret State Police itself.

The persecution of the Jews was a continuous and deliberate policy. It was a policy directed against other nations as well as against the Jews themselves. Anti-Semitism was promoted to divide and embitter the democratic peoples and to soften their resistance to the Nazi aggression. As Robert Ley declared in *Der Angriff* on 14 May 1944: "The second German secret weapon is Anti-Semitism because if it is constantly pursued by Germany, it will become a universal problem which all nations will be forced to consider."

Anti-Semitism also has been aptly credited with being a "spearhead of terror." The ghetto was the laboratory for testing repressive measures. Jewish property was the first to be expropriated, but the custom grew and included similar measures against anti-Nazi Germans, Poles, Czechs, Frenchmen, and Belgians. Extermination of the Jews enabled the Nazis to bring a practiced hand to similar measures against Poles, Serbs, and Greeks. The plight of the Jew was a constant threat to opposition or discontent among other elements of Europe's population—pacifists, conservatives, Communists, Catholics, Protestants, Socialists. It was in fact, a threat to every dissenting opinion and to every non-Nazi's life.

The persecution policy against the Jews commenced with nonviolent measures, such as disfranchisement and discriminations against their religion, and the placing of impediments in the way of success in economic life. It moved rapidly to organized mass violence against them, physical isolation in ghettos, deportation, forced labor, mass starvation, and extermination. The Government, the Party formations indicted before you as criminal organizations, the Secret State Police, the Army, private and semi-public associations, and "spontaneous" mobs that were carefully inspired from official sources, were all agencies that

U.S. Chief Justice Robert Jackson, the American prosecutor, delivers his opening statement at the IMT in Nuremberg. November 22, 1945. (NARA)

were concerned in this persecution. Nor was it directed against individual Jews for personal bad citizenship or unpopularity. The avowed purpose was the destruction of the Jewish people as a whole, as an end in itself, as a measure of preparation for war, and as a discipline of conquered peoples.

The conspiracy or common plan to exterminate the Jew was so methodically and thoroughly pursued, that despite the German defeat and Nazi prostration this Nazi aim largely has succeeded. Only remnants of the European Jewish population remain in Germany, in the countries which Germany occupied, and in those which were her satellites or collaborators. Of the 9,600,000 Jews who lived in Nazi-dominated Europe, 60 percent are authoritatively estimated to have perished. Five million seven hundred thousand Jews are missing from the countries in which they formerly lived, and over 4,500,000 cannot be accounted for by the normal death rate nor by immigration; nor are they included among displaced persons. History does not record a crime ever perpetrated against so many victims or one ever carried out with such calculated cruelty.

You will have difficulty, as I have, to look into the faces of these defendants and believe that in this twentieth century human beings could inflict such sufferings as will be proved here on their own countrymen as well as upon their so-called "inferior" enemies. Particular crimes, and the responsibility of defendants for them, are to be dealt with by the Soviet Government's counsel, when committed in the East, and by counsel for the Republic of France when committed in the West. I advert to them only to show their magnitude as evidence of a purpose and a knowledge common to all defendants, of an official plan rather than of a capricious policy of some individual commander, and to show such a continuity of Jewish persecution from the rise of the Nazi conspiracy to its collapse as forbids us to believe that any person could be identified with any part of

Nazi action without approving this most conspicuous item in their program. . . .

The responsibility of this Tribunal:

To apply the sanctions of the law to those whose conduct is found criminal by the standards I have outlined, is the responsibility committed to this Tribunal. It is the first court ever to undertake the difficult task of overcoming the confusion of many tongues and the conflicting concepts of just procedure among divers systems of law, so as to reach a common judgment. The tasks of all of us are such as to make heavy demands on patience and good will. Although the need for prompt action has admittedly resulted in imperfect work on the part of the Prosecution, four great nations bring you their hurriedly assembled contributions of evidence. What remains undiscovered we can only guess. We could, with witnesses' testimony, prolong the recitals of crime for years—but to what avail. We shall rest the case when we have offered what seems convincing and adequate proof of the crimes charged without unnecessary cumulation of evidence. We doubt very much whether it will be seriously denied that the crimes I have outlined took place. The effort will undoubtedly be to mitigate or escape personal responsibility. . . .

While the defendants and the prosecutors stand before you as individuals, it is not the triumph of either group alone that is committed to your judgment. Above all personalities there are anonymous and impersonal forces whose conflict makes up much of human history. It is yours to throw the strength of the law back of either the one or the other of these forces for at least another generation. What are the real forces that are contending before you?

No charity can disguise the fact that the forces which these defendants represent, the forces that would advantage and delight in their acquittal, are the darkest and most sinister forces in society—dictatorship and oppression, malevolence and passion, militarism and lawlessness. By their fruits we best know them. Their acts have bathed the world in blood and set civilization back a century. They have subjected their European neighbors to every outrage and torture, every spoliation and deprivation that insolence, cruelty, and greed could inflict. They have brought the German people to the lowest pitch of wretchedness, from which they can entertain no hope of early deliverance. They have stirred hatreds and incited domestic violence on every continent. These are the things that stand in the dock shoulder to shoulder with these prisoners.

The real complaining party at your bar is Civilization. In all our countries it is still a struggling and imperfect thing. It does not plead that the United States, or any other country, has been blameless of the conditions which made the German people easy victims to the blandishments and intimidations of the Nazi conspirators.

But it points to the dreadful sequence of aggressions and crimes I have recited, it points to the weariness of flesh, the exhaustion of resources, and the destruction of all that was beautiful or useful in so much of the world, and to

greater potentialities for destruction in the days to come. It is not necessary among the ruins of this ancient and beautiful city with untold members of its civilian inhabitants still buried in its rubble, to argue the proposition that to start or wage an aggressive war has the moral qualities of the worst of crimes. The refuge of the defendants can be only their hope that international law will lag so far behind the moral sense of mankind that conduct which is crime in the moral sense must be regarded as innocent in law.

Civilization asks whether law is so laggard as to be utterly helpless to deal with crimes of this magnitude by criminals of this order of importance. It does not expect that you can make war impossible. It does expect that your juridical action will put the forces of international law, its precepts, its prohibitions and, most of all, its sanctions, on the side of peace, so that men and women of good will, in all countries, may have "leave to live by no man's leave, underneath the law."

> —*From International Military Tribunal,* Trial of the Major War Criminals Before the International Military Tribunal, Official Text in the English Language, *vol. 2:* Proceedings 14–30 November 1945 *(Frankfurt, 1947), 98–99, 118–19, 152, 155.*

A JUDGE'S MEMOIR

U. S. Attorney General Francis Biddle was appointed the senior American judge to serve on the International Military Tribunal. *His memoirs contain some observations concerning the preparation for the trial.*

In this excerpt, Biddle writes of the Soviet prosecution and the Katyn Woods Massacre: the murder of more than 4,000 Polish officers in the spring of 1940. Almost 15,000 Polish officers and non-commissioned officers were killed at three different massacre sites at this time. Though the Soviet secret police had actually committed these mass murders, the Soviet government falsely accused the Germans of the atrocity and tried to include it in the indictment against the Germans at the IMT. (In 1990, the Soviet government of Mikhail Gorbachev formally acknowledged Soviet responsibility for the massacre.)

The Katyn Woods incident was typical of the Russian attitude.

The inclusion in the indictment of the allegation that the Germans had massacred 11,000 Polish officers and civilians in the Katyn Forest, on the banks of the Dnieper near Smolensk, was dictated by political considerations. Since there was no evidence that any defendant was remotely connected with the killings, the charge was irrelevant. Although he had not seen the reports indicating that the Russians might be guilty, Jackson sensed trouble, and did his best to persuade them to omit the charge. But Rudenko insisted on including it. The matter was at that time highly controversial, and the evidence inconclusive. In addition to spreading in detail on the record the report made in 1944 by the Special Soviet Commission, he produced three witnesses to establish German guilt. This took a week. When he had concluded Dr. Otto Stahmer, counsel for Göring, against whom the charges had been leveled in the indictment, since he was considered the highest-ranking officer among the defendants, petitioned the Tribunal for leave to produce three witnesses to show that the Russians had killed the Polish prisoners. Rudenko indignantly opposed the motion.

When we came to consider it in chambers, General Nikitchenko threw all his weight behind the Soviet prosecutor. It was obvious that he attached great importance to our decision. I do not think that many things were expected of him by his superiors in Moscow, but there can be little doubt that they were eager to have the Tribunal brand the Germans as the perpetrators of these systematic and sordid killings.

To the rest of us it seemed trifling to argue that, having permitted the Russians to introduce the hearsay evidence of their own self-serving report, and to support it with eye-witnesses, we should not allow the Germans direct evidence in their defense. The general's argument—and he spoke with conviction for a solid hour—was based on a phrase in the Charter which provided that the Tribunal need not require "proof of facts of common knowledge, and might take judicial notice of official governmental documents . . . including the acts and documents of the committees set up . . . for the investigation of war crimes." Under this language the Russian report was obviously admissible. But the phrasing was unfortunate. "Facts of common knowledge" were coupled with "Government documents"; and in the Russian translation the two phrases might have interlocked. "Judicial notice" must have been hard to translate.

Not however for the Russian member. Since, he insisted, governmental documents had been given special treatment, and recognized for what they were—statements of the true facts—how could their contents and conclusions be denied? We had no right to disregard the Charter, to flaunt its provisions.

He was as emphatic as he had been on the former occasion when I had pleaded with my brethren to go along with him lest he withdraw from the Tribunal. And this issue must have been more important to him than a postponement to correct an error in the indictment. And yet I thought he would not; he was too far committed, and such an action would appear like an admission of guilt. But whether he bolted or not we must let the Germans call their witnesses, who had examined the corpses on behalf of an International Medical Commission formed by the Germans on April 30, 1943, two weeks after they had discovered the bodies of four thousand Polish officers, in uniform, in some cases shackled, with pistol bullets in the back of the neck.

We announced our decision the next morning. The Russian prosecutor immediately filed a petition for a rehearing of the question. It was the only petition for reargu-

ment we received. Its language was intemperate: the court, Rudenko claimed, had misconstrued the Charter, violated its duty, and was grossly in error. The petition followed Nikitchenko's argument and indicated his co-operation.

The occasion warranted action. At our conference the next afternoon I asked my confrères to permit me to speak on a matter of personal privilege not on the agenda, but of the most vital importance to all of us. For it concerned the integrity of the members of the Tribunal, their honor, and their competence.

The brethren were by now giving me their attention.

One of the prosecutors—I looked at General Nikitchenko —had filed a slanderous, arrogant, and unwarranted attack on the Tribunal, a body that would go down to history as the most important court in the world. I did not know what the practice would be in other countries. In mine the author of such an outrage would be cited for contempt. Perhaps in this very extreme case we should send him to prison immediately—there could be no defense.

"What do you think, General? Have you read General Rudenko's petition? What do you propose should be done?"

General Nikitchenko was taken off base. He mumbled that he had read the petition, but rather hurriedly. He had nothing to propose. The French were amused—they guessed what I was up to. The British were surprised—they had not been consulted.

I produced an opinion, which Herbert Wechsler and I had drafted with a good deal of care the night before. With their permission I would read it. It could be read in open court immediately before General Rudenko was arrested.

I read the opinion. It denied the contention that government reports should be accepted as "irrefutable evidence of the facts found"—a contention "unsupported by the Charter and intrinsically unreasonable in itself." The Soviet prosecutor was in gross error in his construction of the Charter.

After a good deal of discussion, it was agreed that the opinion should be filed but not made public—with the Soviet member's dissent. The president would simply announce in court that the petition was dismissed. Nikitchenko no longer argued that German witnesses should not be called. His whole energy was directed to keeping the opinion from the press. He took seriously my suggestion that Rudenko be held in contempt; and as part of the "compromise" it was understood that no such action would be taken. He was pleased with the result. Two hours after we had adjourned I got a pleasant note from him indicating that we understood each other—would I pay his country a visit after the trial? He evidently had grasped the purpose of my tactic after he had time to think a little about it.

The doctors called by the Germans were vigorously (though without damage to their position) cross-examined by the Soviets. But from that day on we heard nothing more about Katyn Woods. The Soviet prosecutor failed to mention these atrocities when he summed up the case against Göring. The evidence before us was inconclusive, and, as I have said, was unrelated to any defendant. Any mention of

The U.S. representatives to the Nuremberg Trial,
1945: Francis Biddle, senior judge, and John Parker,
alternate judge. (USHMM)

Katyn Woods was omitted when the judgment was under consideration.

But an investigation conducted by a House committee in 1952 left little doubt that the Soviet N.K.V.D. had been guilty of the killings, as a step in the "extermination of Poland's intellectual leadership . . . to eliminate all Polish leaders who subsequently would have opposed the Soviet's plan for communizing Poland."

The officers, lawyers, doctors, clergymen, government officials, and intellectuals who had been taken prisoner when Russia invaded Poland were separated from the other prisoners and placed in three special camps, 15,000 men in all, where they remained from the fall of 1939 until the following spring. During this period they were exhaustively examined to determine whether they could be converted to communism. A few hundred were. The rest were killed before the Russian evacuation in the spring of 1940, when the Katyn area was still under Soviet control—4143 were

"identified in the mass graves of Katyn." Testimony of doctors who had performed autopsies on the bodies indicated that in some cases wounds had been inflicted by bayonets "of the four-bladed type which are used exclusively by the Soviets." The Germans had supported an investigation by an international committee of the Red Cross in 1943, but the Russians had refused to permit one. It was testified that Stalin's son, when asked about the disappearance of the Polish officers, said, "Why those were the intelligentsia, the most dangerous element to us, and they had to be eliminated."

— From Francis Biddle, In Brief Authority (Garden City, NY:
Doubleday and Co., Inc., 1962), 413–17.

The Evidence

TESTIMONY ABOUT GASSINGS

Engineer Kurt Gerstein (1905–1945) worked as an assessor for the Mining Bureau in Saarbrücken and was an active member of the Confessing Church *(Bekennende Kirche), a Protestant religious movement deeply critical of Nazi policy. In 1936, Gerstein was dismissed from state service for his religious affiliation; in 1938 he was discharged from the Nazi party, of which he had been a member since 1933, and he was briefly interned in a concentration camp. Upon learning that his sister-in-law had been gassed at the* Hadamar "euthanasia" *facility, Gerstein resolved to discover the truth about Nazi crimes. Voluntarily joining the Waffen-SS, Gerstein was assigned to the German Hygiene Institute as a disinfection expert, where he worked with* Zyklon *B. Gerstein's efforts to inform the outside world of the Nazi extermination camps via Swedish and Dutch contacts met with limited success. Arrested by the French for SS membership, Gerstein penned this report in May 1945. Shortly afterward, he was found hanged in his cell; his death was ruled a suicide, but many suspect he was murdered by fellow SS men confined in the same jail.*

OFFICE OF U.S. CHIEF OF COUNSEL
FOR THE PROSECUTION OF AXIS CRIMINALITY

Doc. No. 2170 PS   Date 26 October 1945

STAFF EVIDENCE ANALYSIS

DESCRIPTION OF ATTACHED DOCUMENT (Under following headings):

    Title and Nature: Statements by Engineer Kurt Gerstein re:
                       Gassings in Concentration Camps.

    Date: 13 August 45 Original ( ) Copy (X) Language: German

LOCATION OF ORIGINAL (also WITNESS if applicable) as of 26 Oct 1945:

    SI Branch, OSSI Germany; copy in OCC files Nurnberg

SOURCE OF ORIGINAL: OSS USFET

PERSONS IMPLICATED: GLUECKS, Richard; MUELLER, Heinrich; HIMMLER,
                     Heinrich; KALTENBRUNNER, Ernst

KEY TO INDEX HEADINGS (Key to Par. nos. of Summary below):
ATROCITIES:against civilians--CONCENTRATION CAMPS--CHURCHES, PERSECU-
TION OF--SS--POLICE:SD:Sipo:Gestapo

NECESSARY PROCESSING TO PUT IN EVIDENTIARY FORM; LEADS: Pohl,
Loerner, Pastor Niemoeller, Doc. 1553 PS

SUMMARY OF RELEVANT POINTS (with page references):

1. This is a sworn statement by Dr. Kurt Gerstein, German engineer,
    who himself has spent some time in the concentration camp.

2. He claims to have been a close friend of Pastor Niemoeller.

3. In the report he gives detailed descriptions of the gassing of
    prisoners in his presence. He himself has constructed a new
    diesel engine which was used by the SS in connection with the
    gassing.

4. There are reports of his in French, English and German available
    for more detailed analysis, see document 1553 PS.

Analyst: Schafer   Doc. No. 2170 PS

Political activities:

Active adherent of Stresemann and Brüning. Since 1933 under constant persecution by Gestapo because of anti-state activity in favor of the church of Christian resistance (Bekennende Kirche, Pastor Niemöller) and because of continuation of the suppressed Protestant youth organizations. Beaten and injured on 30 January 1935 because of protest against presentation of anti-Christian play "Wittekind" on the occasion of a party-dedication festival at the municipal theater Hagen/Westphalia. 27 November 1935: mining-assessor examinations at the Ministry of Economics; thereafter, official with Saar Mines administration at Saarbrücken. Was arrested out of office on 27 September 1936 by Gestapo because of mailing 8500 anti-National Socialist pamphlets to all state and ministerial councils, and to all higher justice officials. Excerpt from accusation document: "is being arrested because of anti-State activity in spite of repeated warning and because of a concentrated, systematic and organized literary mass-attack against the National Socialist state, and is taken into protective custody. . . ."

In consequence of my favorite wish did I then, after my removal from state service, study medicine at the "Evangelisches Deutsches Institut für ärztliche Mission" (Protestant German Institute for Medical Mission) at Tübingen. Being a partner in the firm De Limon Fluhme & Co., and drawing an annual income of ca. 18,000 (Reichsmark) I was economically free and independent. One-third of my income I spent, since 1931, to the benefit of my religious ideals. I ordered, at my expense, the printing and mailing of 230,000 anti-National Socialist pamphlets of religious character. That was on 14 July 1938. On 14 July 1938 I was arrested for the second time by the Secret State Police [Gestapo] and SD (Security Service) Stuttgart and was brought to prison and subsequently into the concentration camp Welzheim because of anti-state activity. Previously I had been questioned and forewarned by the Gestapo and the SD a total of two dozen times. I was forbidden to speak publicly anywhere within the Reich; the prohibition lasted until the end of the system (until the end of the Nazi regime—Translator).

When I learned of the mass-murder of mentally disabled at Hadamar, Grafeneck, and elsewhere, I had only one desire: "You must look into the cauldron and must spread what is happening there among the people, at the risk of your life." I did not have [to feel guilty about] such an undertaking, for had I myself not twice the victim of SD agents, who had gained admittance into the innermost circle of the Brothers of the Bekennende Kirche (Niemöller), even the most intimate prayer circles, and had there kneeled with everybody else and had prayed? I thought: "What you can do, I can do anytime." And I reported voluntarily to be admitted in the SS. I was urged on by the fact

Some of the thousands of German documents that were collected in 1945 from the former Third Reich and the areas it occupied as evidence for the International Military Tribunal. These documents were also used in other war crimes trials during 1945 and in later trials. (NARA)

that my sister-in-law, Bertha Ebeling from Saarbrücken, had been killed at Hadamar. On the basis of recommendation by two Gestapo officials who worked on my case, I had no difficulty to be accepted into the SS (Waffen-SS). The gentlemen were convinced that an idealism such as mine had to be utilized for the benefit of the NSDAP [Nazi Party]. Thus they showed me the road that I had to follow.

I received my basic training together with 40 other physicians in Hamburg-Langenhoorn, then in Arnheim [Arnhem], Holland, and then in Oranienburg. In Arnheim, through the services of a university colleague of mine, the manufacturer Ubbink from Diesburg, a certified engineer, I contacted immediately the Dutch resistance movement. Because of my double study in medicine and technology I was soon called to the SS Führungshauptamt, Amtsgruppe D, Sanitätswesen der Waffen-SS, Abteilung Hygiene (SS Main Office, Dept. D, Medical Affairs, of the Waffen SS, Hygienics Section). Admittedly, this outfit was remarkably generous. Thus, it was left up to me to seek my own field of activity. In order to alleviate a most urgent necessity, I constructed installations for disinfection, mobile and stationary units, in large numbers, for prisoner of-war camps, concentration camps, and for the fighting troops. Without my doing, I had extraordinary successes and was from then on considered a remarkable technical genius. For that reason I was also employed in the same capacity by the Ostministerium (Ministry for Eastern Affairs) and by the Reich Labor Ministry. Anyway, the horrible wave of typhus (1941) that called, at times daily, for tens of thousands of victims in the POW camps and concentration camps, was considerably reduced. Because of that I became soon lieutenant, then first lieutenant. Once again my undertaking was endangered when the party court, which had decreed my expulsion from the party, learned of my admittance to a leading office of the SS. Because of my successes and because of my general esteem, however, I was protected [by] my office and retained. In February 1942, I became *Chief of the Dept. of Health Technology,* at the same time in charge of drinking-water affairs and [of] all technical disinfection, including that [employing] highly poisonous gasses.

On the 8 June 1942, I was visited in my office by the SS Sturmbahnführer Guenther, RSHA, Kurfürstenstrasse. G. came in mufti. I had not known him until then. He instructed me, under most secretive indications, to obtain a quantity of prussic acid [the active ingredient in Zyklon B] (260 kg). He ordered me further to deliver that poison, by means of an SD truck, to a spot known only to the driver. The affair was supposed to be, at that time, a Top Secret matter. (Geheimste Reichssache). A short time thereafter, I drove with that truck to Kollin, near Prague. I had an idea about the character of that order. I accepted it though because fortune permitted me thus to gain admission into the machinery. I did not have the slightest scruples. Would I have rejected the order, someone else would have carried it out in the desired sense. As an authority in the field, however, I was able to declare the poison as decomposed, dan-

gerous, or spoiled, and could have it disposed of. Thus it was only I who could prevent the use of prussic acid for the killing of human beings.

Because of a vacancy in the car, I took SS-Obersturm-bahnführer Prof. Dr. med. Pfannenstiel along. He was Ordinarius (Instructor and head of a class) for hygiene at the University Marburg/Lahn. In Kollin, at the factory, I wanted to [personally establish] that the prussic acid was to be used in the killing of human beings. I did that by asking seemingly unskillful questions. I used that method later on, considering it as most appropriate to spread the affair among the people. As a result, the truck was carefully observed in Kollin. General SS Obergruppenführer Globocnik received us in Lublin and said: "This affair is Top Secret, in fact it is at present the most top secret [thing] of all. Everyone who gossips about it will be shot at once. It just so happened that yesterday we silenced two gossipers." At this moment —that was on 17 August—we have three installations:

1. Belzec, on the Lublin-Lemberg road . . . exactly at the spot where the line of demarcation with the Russians cuts across the highway. Daily achievement ca. 15,000 killings. Average utilization since April: 11,000 per day.

2. Sobibor, near Lublin in Poland, I don't know exactly where. 20,000 killings per day.

3. Treblinka, 120 km . . . from Warsaw, 25,000 killings per day. Average utilization ca. 13,500 killings per day since June 1942.

4. Majdanek, near Lublin, was at that time still under construction. I inspected Belzec, Treblinka and Majdanek in the company of Police Captain Wirth and viewed these killing-installations at work. Wirth is the one, who, by order of Hitler and Himmler, had murdered the mentally disabled at Hadamar, Grafeneck, and elsewhere.

Globocnik said to us, that is, he said to me only: "It will be your task to disinfect great quantities of fabrics, laundry, clothing, and shoes that turn up in these installations. The quantities amount to the ten- to twentyfold of the result in the fabric collections. (Author is probably referring to national fabric collections—Translator.) All those collections are merely carried on in order to explain to the foreign workers and to the German people the origin of all those clothes. Your other task will be, and that is the more important, to induce different, faster methods in these death installations. The affair is now being done by an old Russian diesel motor, i.e., exhaust gases. In order to accelerate this procedure, I am thinking of prussic acid. Day before yesterday, on 15 August, the Führer and Himmler himself were here. I am not permitted to issue those people who visit the installations any admittance tickets. For purposes of secrecy, I have to deliver them personally." Pfannenstiehl inquired: "What did the Führer say to all of this?" Globocnik: "The entire action must be carried out at greatest speed." In his company was also ministerial councillor Dr. Herbert Linden of the Reichsministerium. He opined that it may be better to cremate the corpses instead of burying them. It could happen that a generation would follow us that would not comprehend the whole affair. Whereupon I told Globocnik: "Gentlemen, should ever a generation come after us that would not comprehend our so grateful and necessary task, then indeed our whole National Socialist movement will have been in vain. I am of the opinion, to the contrary, that we bury bronze tablets along with [the bodies], on which we relate that it has been we who had the courage to carry out this so necessary and important work." (It appears that the author erred when he ascribed the above quotation to himself; judging from the following it should rather read: "Whereupon replied Globocnik"—Translator.) Whereupon Hitler [said]: "Good, Globocnik, this is also my opinion."

After a while, however, the other view won out, the bodies were burned with benzine and diesel oil. Furthermore, I had to visit the plant office of the extensive installation at Lublin, the so-called "Julius Schreck-Kaserne." The next day, we travelled with the car of Captain Wirth to Belzec. A small railroad station had been created on the slope of a yellow hill. South of the highway there were several buildings with the inscription "Sonderkommando Belzec der Waffen-SS [Special Unit Belzec of the Waffen SS]." Globocnik turned me over to SS Hauptsturmführer Obermayer who permitted me only reluctantly to view the installation. Behind thick bushes, close to the RR station was a large barrack with the inscription *Garderobe* [wardrobe closet]. There was a window [with a sign that read] "Money and Valuables." Then a room with ca. 100 stools, the barber's room. Then a birch alley for ca. 150 meters with barbed wire strung on both sides and signs: "To the inhaling rooms and bathrooms." Then loomed before us a building resembling a bathhouse, with a small stairway which was flanked by pots of geraniums. On the roof, the Star of David as a weathervane. In front of the building a sign: "Heckenholt Stiftung [Heckenholt Foundation]." More I did not see that afternoon. But the air was full of millions of flies and the odor of pestilence and death lay over the highway. In the bathroom itself, to the left and to the right on each floor, were 3 chambers, somewhat like garages, 5 x 5 meters wide and 1.9 meters high. On the next morning I was told, shortly before 0700 [7:00 a.m.]: "The first transport will arrive at once." So it was. At 0700 sharp, the first transport arrived. A train with 45 cars came from Lemberg. Behind the windows, "protected" by barbed wire, one saw children, horribly pale, also some men and women, their faces distorted by fright. The train disappears behind the hedge. 200 Ukrainians tear the doors open and whip the people out of the cars with cat-o'-nine-tails. 6700 persons [were told to] undress completely, to discard artificial limbs and glasses (a guard tells a girl: "Take your glasses off; you will get new ones in there."), to surrender valuables at the window, without receipts. A small Jewish kid gets a bundle of short strings under his arm, which he distributes among the people, not knowing what this is about. It is to tie the shoes together, for in the pile of 20-40 meters high, no one would be able to find the matching shoes again. Then the

women and children (young girls) [go] to the barber who rips the hair down [i.e., cuts the hair off] and makes it disappear in a potato sack. That is supposed to go to the submarines, for insulation.

As the poor creatures proceeded to the death chamber, a husky SS man announces, "Nothing will happen to you. All you have to do is to inhale deeply, that will widen your lungs. It is necessary to combat diseases and epidemics." When he is asked what is going to happen to the people, he replies: "Of course, the men will have to work. They will have to build homes and roads. But the women do not have to work, unless they wish to." That is a ray of hope to some of the creatures and they go willingly into the chambers. Most of them knew what is up—the odor tells them all about it. Thus they mount the little staircase and then they see everything. Mothers with infants clinging to their breasts, small nude children, grown ups, men and women, all in the nude and jumbled—they hesitate—but enter the chamber of death, partly pushed by those who follow, partly driven by the leather whips of the SS. . . .

A Jewess, 40 years of age, cries out with flaming eyes: "The blood that is being shed here, in the most outlandish murder, will come over the heads of the murderers." Captain Wirth personally strikes her 5 to 6 times with his riding rod—then she too disappears in the chamber. Many turn to me: "Oh sir, please help us, help us, please." I turn away and pray to my God, to their God. Shall I enter the chamber with them? . . . That would not do, I must live to see and publicize what I see. No one else sees what I see and is an opponent of those murder-gangs at the same time. . . . Of course, it is the more difficult road, but I must continue. . . . The chambers are filling up. "Pack them well and full," thus Captain Wirth had ordered. . . .

Now I understand why they call the installations "Heckenholt Foundation." Heckenholt [devised] the diesel engine [mechanism], a small technician, a tireless worker. Already with the killing of the mentally disabled, he, according to Wirth, earned extraordinary praise; he is the constructor of the installation. The exhaust fumes of his diesel are to kill these people. But the machine does not function. That is a rare occurrence, I am told. Captain Wirth comes. He is embarrassed that this has happened just when I am here. Yes, I observe everything. My stopwatch has everything well registered. 50 minutes, 70 minutes, the diesel does not start. The people are waiting in their gas chambers. In vain. One hears sobbing, crying. "Like in the synagogue," remarks Prof. Pfannenstiehl, his ear at the wooden door. After 2 hours, 49 minutes—the stopwatch has it well registered—the diesel starts. Until that moment, there are living people, 4 [times] 750 people in 4 [times] 45 cubic meters. Again 25 minutes pass. Surely some of them are dead already. One can see that through the window as the chamber is momentarily lit by the electric light. Wirth had interviewed me as to the right way: should the people die in lit or unlit chambers? He asked that in a manner as though he asked whether I'd prefer to sleep with or without a pillow.

After 28 minutes pass, only a few are still alive. Finally, after 32 minutes, everybody is dead. From the other side, men of the labor-commandos are opening the wooden doors. They were promised, even Jews, that they were to obtain their freedom and one-thousandth of the gained [valuables] for their horrible work. Three accountants are calculating the figures. The dead stand up as though they have been cast. . . .

Dentists open the mouths, looking for gold: "Gold, left; without gold, [to the] right." Other dentists rip the gold fillings out of the mouths with iron hooks. Captain Wirth is everywhere. Some of the workers seek valuables in private parts. Wirth calls me over: "Lift this can with gold teeth; this is the result of yesterday's and the day before yesterday's production." And he adds, "You have no idea what amounts of gold and jewels we find everyday. . . ." On the day of my visit, there arrived in Belzec only two transports, with a total of ca. 12,000 persons.

This installation was in working condition since April 1942 and achieved an average, per day, of 1,000 killings. Then my friends, or I, listened to London broadcasts or to one of the voices from America; we were amazed over those unsuspecting angels who counted in hundreds of thousands, while in fact millions had been killed. . . . The Dutch resistance movements let me know, through [the engineer] Ubbink from Diesburg that I should stick to the truth and should not crowd my reports with atrocity stories. In spite of my transmission of the facts to the Swedish Embassy in Berlin in August 1942, no one believed me.

And yet it is the truth, unfortunately, I swear that upon my oath. I estimate the total of those that have been murdered, on orders of Hitler and Himmler, who have been lured into those death traps without the slightest chance of opposition, at least 20,000,000 people. For the murder was not at all restricted to the 5 or 6 million Jews in Europe.

— From "Statements by Engineer Kurt Gerstein," October 26, 1945, Office of U.S. Chief of Counsel for the Prosecution of Axis Criminality, Record Group 238, document 2170 PS, National Archives and Records Administration, 2–6. The original translation has been edited for clarity.

ATROCITY FILMS

Among the more graphic evidence presented by the American prosecution team at the Nuremberg Trial in December 1945 was a film showing atrocities in concentration camps. As can be seen from this article, the defendants reacted to the film in different ways.

— From News of Germany, *December 1, 1945.*

Defendants Silent After Showing of Atrocity Pictures

BY JOHANNES HAAS-HEYE
DANA Staff Correspondent

NUREMBERG, Nov. 30 (GNS)—A documentary film on the horrors of the concentration camps of Nazi Germany, shown Thursday afternoon on the eighth day of the war crimes trial before the International Military Tribunal, did not miss its effect on those responsible for these atrocities — the men in the defendants' dock. When the lights in the courtroom came on again, the defendants were silent — in contrast to their usual animated conversation after the close of a trial day.

SCHACHT TURNS HEAD AWAY

While the graphic film was being shown, the defendants' dock had been kept lighted dimly. Schacht ostentatiously had turned his head away from the screen and did not look at it even once during the hour it took to show the film. On the other hand, Hess, who normally does not show any interest in the proceedings, attentively watched the screen.

Dönitz, his chin buried in his hand, repeatedly turned away from the screen for extended periods of time, and Funk repeatedly shook his head. The massive silhouette of Göring who was leaning on the dock's railing seemed, however, to be immovable.

When the film was finished, Schacht immediately jumped to his feet. He exchanged a few excited words with his attorney. The other defendants kept their seats, and only Neurath and Speer still had their normal, healthy color. Göring did not move until Ribbentrop addressed a few words to him. Papen got up and then was emptily staring into the air. There was not a single one of them who did not appear to be deep in thought. Frank, still sitting, tightly grasped the railing and did not move. When it was his turn to leave the courtroom he got up shaking and — this may have been intentionally overdone by him — seemed to be unable to walk unaided.

VIOLATION OF AUSTRIA RELATED

Before the film was shown, the American prosecution had closed its case relating to the violation of Austria, with Prosecutor Sydney S. Alderman naming Papen, Seyss-Inquart, Neurath and Göring as those principally responsible. Alderman called them "dexterous and brutal. They wore a faked mask of saintliness to camouflage their two-facedness."

Alderman cited the record of a telephone call exchanged between Göring in Berlin and Ribbentrop in London on March 13, 1938, two days after the events which destroyed Austrian independence. In this conversation Göring said, "The weather here (in Berlin) is wonderful. The sky is blue, and I'm sitting on the porch all wrapped in blankets, getting some fresh air and drinking coffee. Later on I shall have to drive downtown, as I have to make a speech. The birds are singing, and now and then I can hear on the radio the enthusiasm there (in Vienna) which appears to be wonderful."

Göring was laughing unrestrainedly when these words of his were read—words spoken on the day when Austria became the first victim of Nazism.

THE TRIALS

In the months following the war's end, the Allies began a long series of war crimes trials that addressed, but was not restricted to, the countless atrocities committed in the Nazi concentration camps and killing centers.

The Bergen-Belsen trial, held by a British Military Court from September 17 to November 17, 1945, in Lüneberg, Germany, tried 45 members of the camp's staff, including commandant Josef Kramer; Kramer and nine others— including two women—were sentenced to be hanged; 21 received prison sentences ranging from a few years to life, while the remaining 14 defendants were acquitted.

A U.S. Military Tribunal tried seven staff members of the Hadamar euthanasia institution from October 8–15, 1945, for killing more than 400 Russians and Poles. All seven defendants were convicted.

The U.S. held its first concentration camp trial at the infamous Dachau concentration camp. Charging 40 camp officials with war crimes against Allied nationals, the trial, which lasted from November 15 to December 14, 1945, found 36 defendants guilty, 23 of whom were hanged.

The four Allied powers—the United States, the Soviet Union, the United Kingdom, and France—formed the International Military Tribunal and tried 22 principal Nazi state and party chiefs (including one in absentia) on four counts: crimes against peace; war crimes; crimes against humanity, and conspiracy to commit these crimes. The trial was held in Nuremberg and formally opened on November 20, 1945, and lasted 10 months, until October 1946. Twelve of the defendants were sentenced to death, seven were imprisoned, and three were acquitted.

These proceedings were all officially photographed by the victorious Allies as part of the documentary record of their attempts to mete out justice to the perpetrators of the "Final Solution."

Twenty of the Nuremburg defendants in the dock on November 23, 1945, soon after the trial had begun. Front row, left to right: Hermann Göring, Rudolf Hess, Joachim von Ribbentrop, Wilhelm Keitel, Alfred Rosenberg, Hans Frank, Wilhelm Frick, Julius Streicher, Walter Funk, and Hjalmar Schacht. Rear row: Karl Dönitz, Erich Raeder, Baldur von Schirach, Fritz Sauckel, Alfred Jodl, Franz von Papen, Arthur Seyss-Inquart, Albert Speer, Constantin von Neurath, and Hans Fritzsche. Ernest Kaltenbrunner was ill and is missing from the photo. (NARA)

Sir Geoffrey Lawrence of Great Britain, President of the International Military Tribunal, reads the opening statement of the court at Nuremberg on November 20, 1945. Judges, rear row, left to right: Lt. Col. A. F. Volchkov, U.S.S.R.; Maj. Gen. I. T. Nikitchenko, U.S.S.R.; Justice William Norman Birkett, Great Britain; Lord Justice Lawrence, Great Britain; Francis Biddle, U.S.; Judge John J. Parker, U.S.; Prof. Henri Donnedieu de Vabre, France; Robert Falco, France. (NARA)

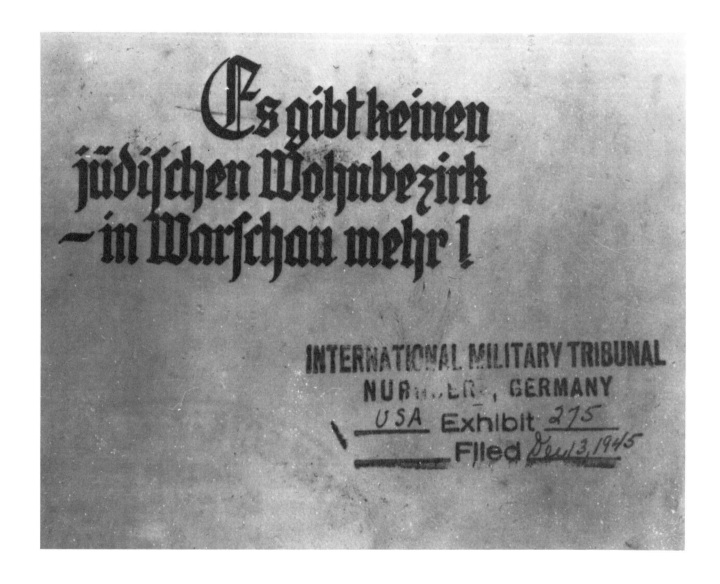

Dr. Adolf Wahlmann and Karl Willig, defendants
in the Hadamar Trial, shown soon after their
capture in April 1945. Col. Leon Jaworski was the
chief U.S. prosecutor. (NARA)

Hadamar nurse Philomine Ingart being interrogated by U.S. officers about the murder of Russians
and Poles. (NARA)

THE TRIAL AT LUNEBERG OF KRAMER AND 44 GAOLERS O[

HAROLD LE DRUILLENEG, A BRITISH SUBJECT WHO SUFFERED THE TERRORS OF BELSEN CAMP. HE GAVE HARROWING EVIDENCE OF THE GHASTLY HORRORS PRACTISED.

SOME OF THE ACCUSED IN THE DOCK AT LUNEBERG COURT TRIAL. IN FRONT ARE (LEFT TO RIGHT) HERBA EHLERT (8), IRMA GRESE (9), AND ELSE LOTHE (10).

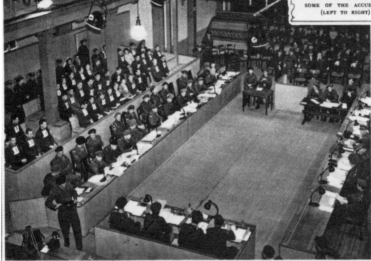

THE COURT SCENE AT LUNEBERG, WHERE (LEFT) FORTY-FIVE GERMAN OFFICIALS, WEARING NUMBERS, ARE ON TRIAL BY COURT-MARTIAL. UNDER THEM ARE BRITISH OFFICERS, DEFENDING COUNSEL. JUDGES ARE SEATED ON RIGHT.

THE PRESIDENT OF THE COURT, MAJOR-GENERAL H. P. ADVOCATE-GENERAL, MR. C. L. STIRLING. DURING THE TRI[

DR. ADA BIMKO, A JEWISH WOMAN DOCTOR, WHO GAVE EVIDENCE OF ATROCITIES AT AUSCHWITZ AND BELSEN.

GERHARD SCHIEDLAUSKY, CHIEF SURGEON OF BUCHENWALD CAMP. HE STOOD ACCUSED OF PERFORMING OBSCENE OPERATIONS.

HELEN KLEIN, A POLISH JEW WITNESS, SIX MONTHS IN BELSEN, PREVIOUSLY IN AUSCHWITZ.

The trial of Kramer, commandant at Belsen, and forty-four others, charged with the most ghastly crimes at Belsen and previously at Auschwitz, opened at Luneberg on September 17. Colonel Backhouse, chief prosecuting officer, in his outline declared that 13,000 corpses were found when British troops occupied the camp. Another 13,000 died within six weeks after that. The average life of a man in Block 18, he said, was twelve days from the time of his arrival.

Some of the twenty accused women, previously at Auschwitz, were said to hav[regularly amused themselves by setting hounds on women prisoners, who wer[torn to pieces. The Jewish witness, Dr. Ada Bimko, whose father, mothe[brother, and little son were murdered at Auschwitz, picked out Johanna Borma[as in the habit of setting her great hound on helpless prisoners. She walke[down the well of the Court and picked out one after another, and gave damnin[

Photos from *The Illustrated London News* of September 29, 1945, showing the proceedings at the Bergen-Belsen Trial. (Illustrated London News)

THE GHASTLY MURDER CAMPS OF BELSEN AND AUSCHWITZ.

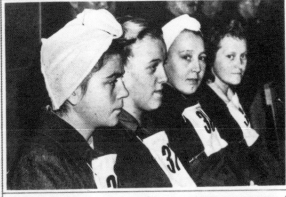

OTHER GERMAN WOMEN ON TRIAL ; (L. TO R.) CHARLOTTE KLEIN, HERTHA BOTHE, FRIEDA WALTER, AND IRENE HASCHE, SOME OF WHOM WERE DENOUNCED BY DR. ADA BIMKO.

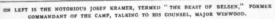

ON LEFT IS THE NOTORIOUS JOSEF KRAMER, TERMED "THE BEAST OF BELSEN," FORMER COMMANDANT OF THE CAMP, TALKING TO HIS COUNSEL, MAJOR WINWOOD.

...ERNEY-FICKLIN, AND (LEFT) THE DEPUTY JUDGE ... FILM OF THE ATROCITIES AT THE CAMP WAS SHOWN.

THE PRISONERS, NUMBERED, ALL OF WHOM SELECTED BRITISH LEGAL AID EXCEPT FOR ONE MAN, WITH THEIR DEFENDING COUNSEL IN FRONT. MANY HAD BEEN AT AUSCHWITZ CAMP PREVIOUSLY, INCLUDING WOMEN.

BRIGADIER H. L. GLYN-HUGHES, R.A.M.C., THE FIRST MEDICAL OFFICER TO ENTER BELSEN.

THE PROSECUTING COUNSEL AT LUNEBERG : (L. TO R.) COLONEL T. M. BACKHOUSE, MAJOR H. C. MORTON-BEALE, CAPTAIN S. M. STEWART, AND LT.-COLONEL L. CONN. COLONEL BACKHOUSE DETAILED ATROCITIES UNPARALLELED IN HISTORY.

...evidence against Kramer, both at Belsen and Auschwitz, at which latter camp, Colonel Backhouse contended, was "quite deliberate extermination of millions." She accused Dr. Klein of sending persons into the incinerating chamber, giving revolting details. Terrible details at Belsen were revealed by Le Druilleneg, a Jersey man, who was, fortunately for himself, only nine days at Belsen, but in those nine days he was beaten, ill-treated, and starved, and when released he weighed only 7 stone, against a normal thirteen. He still limps from ill-treatment, and led the Court to the foulest portions at Belsen when they visited it for inspection. Dr. Bimko, telling of Auschwitz, alleged that she saw healthy persons lined up for the gas chamber. One girl she knew, who cut a blanket to put around her shoulders one cold day, was sent promptly to the gas chamber. Even Germans listening to the trial have called Kramer a "schweinhund."

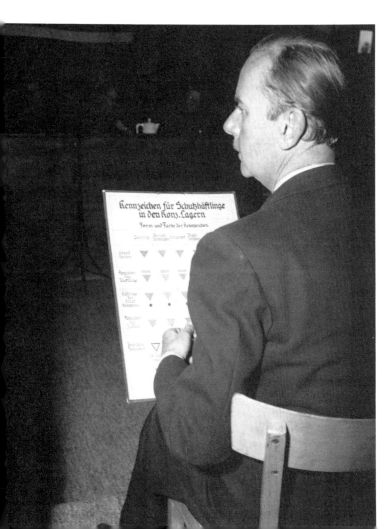

Dachau doctor Klaus-Karl Schilling appeals to the court for permission to conclude his report on his malaria experiments, saying, "It would be an enormous help for science, for my colleagues. . . ." December 7, 1945. (NARA)

Prince Leopold of Prussia, nephew of the last German emperor and a prosecution witness, explains the symbols used to identify various categories of prisoners in concentration camps during the Dachau Trial in November 1945. (NARA)

OTHER WAR CRIMES TRIALS

Justice in the Occupied Zones

THE BERGEN-BELSEN TRIAL

The Bergen-Belsen Trial of September–November 1945 was the first major war crimes trial in the British occupation zone of Germany. Forty-five men and women who had served on the staff of BERGEN-BELSEN concentration camp, including some who had also served in the AUSCHWITZ concentration camp, were tried by a British military court. Thirty-one were convicted, fourteen acquitted.

— *From* News of Germany, *September 22, 1945.*

Democratic Process Amazes Germans at Belsen Camp Trial

LÜNEBURG, Sept. 21. (GNS). — Graphic eyewitness accounts of the horrors of Belsen, supported by grim and revolting moving pictures, forged new links in the chain of evidence closing around Josef Krämer and his co-defendants in the fifth day of Britain's war criminal trials in the Lüneburg gymnasium.

Maj. Adolphus Berney, British Liaison officer, declared tons of food and large stores of medical supplies were within close proximity of the miserable huts where thousands were starving and dying of hunger and neglect.

Harold Osman Druillenec, a British subject, testified that internees threw the dead on to stacks of grotesque corpses where they dangled like marionettes suddenly freed from their controlling strings.

In closeups filmed when the camp was liberated, Krämer showed no sign of concern over the fate of his charges.

NEW EXPERIENCE FOR GERMANS

It was a new experience for German spectators unfamiliar with democratic court procedure. They heard men and women already depicted as arch criminals, defended ably by eleven British and one Polish officer, who little more than four months ago were fighting the German armed forces in the field.

In contrast to the summary judgment by Nazi "justice", they heard the defense counsel for Krämer and his co-defendants battle point by point in an attempt to break the story of Brigadier H. L. Glyn Hughes, former deputy medical director of the British Second Army, and the testimony of Captain Derek Sington, Intelligence Corps officer and the prosecution's chief witness.

139 AFFIDAVITS WILL BE ENTERED

Captain Sington's story of the Belsen camp horrors was unshaken in lengthy cross-examination. The testimony and cross-examinations reiterated many allegations previously made in the world press.

Brigadier Hughes' testimony and re-examination offered an affidavit of Col. James A. F. Johnson, medical officer with troops that entered Belsen April 15. It was the first of 139 affidavits which are expected to be entered during the trial.

SAW EVIDENCE OF SYSTEMATIC STARVATION

The medical officer added that everywhere was evidence of systematic starvation. "All of those responsible must have known these conditions would result in death on a gigantic scale, in short, mass murder," the officer stated.

Captain Sington termed Krämer's attitude as "confident, fully content and completely unemotional." Krämer took full advantage of benefits given him by democratic legal processes. He spent much time in whispered consultation with his counsel and smiled broadly whenever the defense made the slightest dent in the prosecution's case.

The galleries where packed with German civilians, most of whom had denied knowledge of the camp's brutalities and murders. During recess several girls, former inmates at Auschwitz camp, bearing numbers branded on their arms, paced up an down outside the gymnasium. Later the girls will testify when the trial moves on to the horrors at Auschwitz.

THE HADAMAR TRIAL

In October 1945, seven staff members of the HADAMAR "EUTHANASIA" facility faced trial before an American military commission in the U.S. occupation zone of Germany. Six men and one woman were tried for the murders of 460 Allied nationals—Polish and Russian forced laborers who had been diagnosed with tuberculosis. The U.S. prosecution team, headed by Col. Leon JAWORSKI, had initially hoped to try the staff members for the murders of some 15,000 German mental patients killed at Hadamar but could not, since military commissions of the occupying armed forces were empowered solely to try cases involving crimes against Allied nationals under international law. Jaworski won convictions for all seven defendants; three were sentenced to death and executed.

— From News of Germany, *October 16, 1945.*

Hadamar Prosecutor Cites Confessions In Summing Up Case

WIESBADEN, Oct. 15 (GNS)—The defendants' own confessions were cited by Prosecutor Leon Jaworski in summation this morning as the most damaging evidence in support of the War Crimes Branch contention that seven officials of the Hadamar Insane Asylum brutally killed over 400 Russians and Poles by injections of morphine and other drugs. Now in the seventh day, the trial is expected to go to the Commission for judgment tonight or early tomorrow.

Jaworski said, "Hadamar was a machine of death which called on many persons to perform the whole operation. These persons are being tried because they held key positions. Accessories who aided or countenanced such crimes are equally guilty with those who did the killing."

EVERYONE CONTRIBUTED IN WORK

"Each defendant performed some essential function that resulted in the deaths of the Russians and Poles," Jaworski declared.

The defendants are Alfons Klein, superintendent; Heinrich Ruoff, chief nurse, and his assistant, Karl Willig, office manager; Irmgard Huber, chief female nurse; Philip Blum, undertaker, and Adolf Wahlmann, physician at Hadamar.

The evidence against Klein, Jaworski said, showed that he was a Nazi since 1930 and was by his own admission chief of the asylum. Wahlmann admitted being at the initial conference where Nazi leaders decided to kill foreign workers, to sign false death certificates, and devise the death injections.

Ruoff was called the only defendant who admitted his part honestly. Jaworski repeated Ruoff's testimony on the technical aspects of the proper needles and drugs for the most efficient killing, and cited the defendant's admissions that he had killed little children.

Jaworski said that denying knowledge of the crimes was typical of Nazi arrogance, because even the laundress testified that she knew about the murders.

In the courtroom packed with German spectators, Jaworski ended his sumation with the declaration that, "Even in this land where sin and horror were rampant, it was shocking to find men and women who thrived on the killing of others in their daily walk of life."

LETTERS ASK TRIAL FOR MURDER OF GERMANS

Letters naming friends who died in the Hadamar Insane Asylum have been received by the Military War Crimes Commission.

Col. Leon Jaworski said the letters addressed to him and the judges offered testimony about thousands of Germans killed there. Some of the letters asked that the defendants be prosecuted also for deaths of Germans.

"We are trying the defendants only for war crimes against citizens of United Nations who are entitled to protection of international law," Jaworski said. "It's up to German courts to prosecute for the other deaths."

THE DACHAU TRIAL

The Dachau Trial involved forty defendants who had served at DACHAU concentration camp and who were charged with killing Allied nationals and prisoners of war from 1942 to 1945. All but one were SS guards; two others were indicted but neither arraigned nor tried. The U.S. Military Tribunal, enjoined to try only crimes against Allied nation-

als and not crimes against citizens of countries of the former Axis, convicted all forty defendants; thirty-six were sentenced to death. The killing of Jews—a crime against humanity—was not included in the indictment.

42 MEN INDICTED IN DACHAU CRIMES

Doctor Who Used Prisoners for Tests Among Accused— Trials to Open Nov. 15

By KATHLEEN McLAUGHLIN
By Wireless to THE NEW YORK TIMES.

NUREMBERG, Germany, Nov. 2 (Delayed)—Forty-two members of the staff of the Dachau concentration camp were indicted here this afternoon. All, except one, were S S men. They will be brought to trial Nov. 15.

Decapitation will be the sentence for any found guilty on two counts cited.

Lieut. Col. William D. Denson of the United States Third Army, chief prosecutor, read the indictments in English as the accused stood rigidly at attention in one of the court rooms now functioning on the site that they and their associates made infamous. The document was then interpreted in German, and Colonel Denson instructed the Germans as to their rights in selecting their own attorneys, in addition to the four American officers already appointed to handle the defense.

Doctor Among Those Accused

The single civilian arraigned was Dr. Klaus Karl Schilling, who planned and supervised the inhuman medical experiments on the Dachau prisoners in a futile attempt to find an antidote for malaria. He will be one of the major figures in the forthcoming trial.

Freshly shaven for the first time in weeks and wearing belts and neckties, which have not been permitted since Robert Ley committed suicide at Nuremberg, the Germans not only were shabby but also were markedly dirty, despite the adequate sanitation facilities in their barracks.

They were ignorant of the purpose for which they had been summoned and apprehension was visible in every expression until the Army translator gave them the context of Colonel Denson's statement.

All were charged in the first count with having participated in the subjection of civilian nationals of nations at war with Germany to "cruelties and mistreatment, including killings, beatings, tortures, starvation, abuses and indignities" between Jan. 1, 1942, and April 19, 1945.

The second count referred to prisoners captured by the members of the armies then fighting Germany and accused them of having violated the rules of war.

No. 1 on the list of defendants was Martin Gottfried Weiss, last commandant of Dachau. No. 2 was Friedrich Wilhelm Ruppert, who operated the gas chamber at Lublin, although those crimes are irrelevant in the present instance. Third on the list was Joseph Jarolin, deputy camp commandant at Dachau and one of the most vicious now in custody.

Others who will get special attention in the presentation of evidence were Christof Ludwig Knoll, who repeatedly bragged that he had hanged ninety-eight Jews as well as many Russians, Poles, etc.; Franz Xavier Trenkle, sergeant who was particularly abusive to Dachau victims; Engelbert Valentin Niedermeyer, who liked to attend to the various tortures imposed on inmates; Johann Kick, head of the political department who selected the punishments to be visited on groups of unfortunates under his command, and Franz Boettger who, like Niedermeyer, delighted in witnessing hangings.

Another of defendants, Vinzenz Schoettl, a tall, robust youth characteristic of the SS bullies, found himself being interrogated in the preparation for the prosecution of the case by a former victim he had often beaten but who is now wearing the uniform of a lieutenant in the United States Army.

Lieut. Col. Douglas A. Bates of Centerville, Tenn., will head a panel of four Army defense attorneys. His associates to date are Maj. Maurice J. McKeown of Maplewood, N. J., and Capt. Dalwin J. Niles of Johnstown, N. Y.

Gen. John M. Lentz will preside over the military court that will try the Germans. His associates are Cols. George E. Bruner, George R. Schithers, Wendell Blanchard, John R. Jeter, Lester J. Abele, Peter O. Ward and Laird A. Richards.

Friends and relatives of the 36 convicted Dachau
defendants, including 23 sentenced to hang,
watch a truck carrying the prisoners leave Dachau.
December 13, 1945. (NARA)

At the Dachau trial, Father Theodore Korcz, a
Polish priest, reads evidence that Catholic priests
were used as "human guinea pigs" in malaria
experiments conducted at the Dachau concentration camp. November 22, 1945. (NARA)

Basis for Future Trials

CONTROL COUNCIL LAW NUMBER 10

The CONTROL COUNCIL FOR GERMANY promulgated Law No. 10 on December 20, 1945. Based on the Moscow Declaration of 1943 and the London Agreement of 1945 [see p. 241], the law provided for the apprehension, extradition, and trial of war criminals in all four occupation zones of Germany. It became the basis for all subsequent war crimes trials in occupied Germany.

Punishment of Persons Guilty of War Crimes,
Crimes against Peace and against Humanity

In order to give effect to the Moscow Declaration of 30 October 1943 and the London Agreement of 8 August 1945, and the Charter issued pursuant thereto and in order to establish a uniform legal basis in Germany for the prosecution of war criminals and other similar offenders, other than those dealt with by the International Military Tribunal, the Control Council enacts as follows:

Article I

The Moscow Declaration of 30 October 1943 "Concerning Responsibility of Hitlerites for Committed Atrocities" and the London Agreement of 8 August 1945 "Concerning Prosecution and Punishment of Major War Criminals of the European Axis" are made integral parts of this Law. Adherence to the provisions of the London Agreement by any of the United Nations, as provided for in Article V of that Agreement, shall not entitle such Nation to participate or interfere in the operation of this Law within the Control Council area of authority in Germany.

Article II

1. Each of the following acts is recognized as a crime:
    (a) *Crimes against Peace.* Initiation of invasions of other countries and wars of aggression in violation of international laws and treaties, including but not limited to planning, preparation, initiation or waging a war of aggression, or a war of violation of international treaties, agreements or assurances, or participation in a common plan or conspiracy for the accomplishment of any of the foregoing.
    (b) *War Crimes.* Atrocities or offenses against persons or property constituting violations of the laws or customs of war, including but not limited to, murder, ill treatment or deportation to slave labour or for any other purpose, of civilian population from occupied territory, murder or ill treatment of prisoners of war or persons on the seas, killing of hostages, plunder of public or private property, wanton destruction of cities, towns or villages, or devastation not justified by military necessity.

    (c) *Crimes against Humanity.* Atrocities and offenses, including but not limited to murder, extermination, enslavement, deportation, imprisonment, torture, rape, or other inhumane acts committed against any civilian population, or persecutions on political, racial or religious grounds whether or not in violation of the domestic laws of the country where perpetrated.
    (d) Membership in categories of a criminal group or organization declared criminal by the International Military Tribunal.

2. Any person without regard to nationality or the capacity in which he acted, is deemed to have committed a crime as defined in paragraph 1 of this Article, if he was (a) a principal or (b) was an accessory to the commission of any such crime or ordered or abetted the same or (c) took a consenting part therein or (d) was connected with plans or enterprises involving its commission or (e) was a member of any organization or group connected with the commission of any such crime or (f) with reference to paragraph 1 (a), if he held a high political, civil or military (including General Staff) position in Germany or in one of its Allies, co-belligerents or satellites or held high position in the financial, industrial or economic life of any such country.

3. Any person found guilty of any of the Crimes above mentioned may upon conviction be punished as shall be determined by the tribunal to be just. Such punishment may consist of one or more of the following:
    (a) Death
    (b) Imprisonment for life or a term of years, with or without hard labour
    (c) Fine, and imprisonment with or without hard labour, in lieu thereof.
    (d) Forfeiture of property
    (e) Restitution of property wrongfully acquired.
    (f) Deprivation of some or all civil rights.
    Any property declared to be forfeited or the restitution of which is ordered by the Tribunal shall be delivered to the Control Council for Germany, which shall decide on its disposal.

4. (a) The official position of any person, whether as Head of State or as a responsible official in a Government Department, does not free him from responsibility for a crime or entitle him to mitigation of punishment.
    (b) The fact that any person acted pursuant to the order of his Government or of a superior does not free him from responsibility for a crime, but may be considered in mitigation.

5. In any trial or prosecution for a crime herein referred to, the accused shall not be entitled to the benefits or any statute of limitation in respect of the period from 30 January 1933 to 1 July 1945, nor shall any immunity, pardon or amnesty granted under the Nazi regime be admitted as a bar to trial or punishment.

— From Correspondence, Office of the Chief Counsel, Record Group 238, Reports and Other Records 1945–49, box 1, National Archives and Records Administration.

ATTITUDES

Of the Perpetrators

THEIR GUILT

The U.S. Army information weekly Army Talks *reprinted this article, "German Bigwigs Prepare Their Alibis." Its author, Edgar Snow, was world correspondent for the* Saturday Evening Post *from 1941 to 1953. A prolific author, Snow wrote many books dealing with the Far East.*

In a stone-walled jail in Salzburg, Austria, a rich bag of SS, Gestapo and high Nazi war criminals were taken by our troops combing the snow-fringed valleys leading down to Italy and Yugoslavia. Here I thought I might collect some "last-minute revelations." Instead, what I attended was a clinic of the Nazi mind, and a preview of the defense which war criminals will make when they come up for trial before the bar of the United Nations . . .

Among other distinguished villains in the jail was Fritz Sauckel, who had more slaves at his disposal than the Pharaohs of ancient Egypt. When I visited him he was all alone in the cell, a dark little man wearing a blue suit, who rose when we entered and glared, sullen and suspicious.

Until a few days before, Sauckel had been governor of the state of Thuringia and head of manpower mobilization. He had some 8,000,000 forced laborers under him in the thousands of barbed wire enclosures surrounding Nazi war factories.

Our information was that Sauckel carried party card No. 1395 and was one of the most ruthless and hated Nazis.

"What do you want of me?" the prisoner demanded in halting English.

"We thought maybe you had something to say to the world."

"I am an Innocent Man!"

The little man braced himself, took a Hitleresque pose with his hand in his coat, and thrust out his chin. "Yes, I am glad to speak at last."

An expression of indignation blackened his face. "For two days now," he began, dramatically sweeping the narrow cell with his arm, "I have been kept here, and again and again I have asked myself, Why? Why? I swear by God that I am an innocent man who wronged no one! My only crime is that I loved Germany." Tears flooded his eyes. He paused before continuing. "I love the German working people. Do you understand? I married a working woman—a good woman. She's a good woman, she served me well. She gave me ten children—a good German wife. . ."

No Sense of Guilt

This man's sense of blood guilt seemed nil, his fanaticism remained just below the surface, his conviction that Nazism alone could save Germany—and hence the world—absolute. He was originally elected governor of Thuringia by a huge majority, he said, and the majority had been with him almost to the end.

"It was only when the collapse came that people began to lose faith," said he. "Only a few trouble makers opposed us."

"You mean the millions of Jews, Poles, Russians, French, Belgians, Dutch—the nationals of all Europe that you starved and gassed in concentration camps?"

But Sauckel said it couldn't have been; only a few had to be punished—only the bad elements. And the camps themselves were models of cleanliness and health; he had personally inspected them. "But some enemies of the state had to be eliminated, of course."

"Then suppose we operated on the same principle. We would shoot you and put your wife and ten children to work behind barbed wire. Wouldn't it be justice according to your code?"

Sauckel denied such a policy had ever been carried out; foreign workers in Germany were volunteers, better off here than at home. He professed incredulity when shown photographs of Dachau and Buchenwald. The Führer couldn't have known it.

"But Goering himself told me only a couple of days ago," I said, "that Hitler had personally ordered and authorized all the measures and atrocities perpetrated against victims in the concentration camps. How do you explain that?"

He was nonplused for a moment, but then he answered that if Goering had actually said that, he must have lost faith. But the majority of the German people had not lost faith.

Germans Did Not Lose Faith

"Then, if a free election were held in Germany tomorrow, you think the Nazis would be returned to power?" I asked.

"There is no hope for Germany except along the road of National Socialism. The German people will eventually go back to some such system—I know it."

"That's just what we are afraid of. That's why so many think Germany cannot be allowed to exist again, except as a colony under foreign rule. . ."

In subsequent interviews here and at other CIC interrogation centers, I talked to Nazis high on our list of unsavory dishes, among them Hermann Goering's brother Albert, who ran the Skoda Works for the Reich; Hans Frank, former governor-general of Poland, where about 3,000,000 people were obliterated in ghettos, and at Maidanek and in other *Lagers;* Otto Skorzeny, the SS colonel who captured Mussolini; Joachim Von Richter, *Standartenführer* of the Viking SS division and former headman at Dachau; Col. Wilhelm Führer, Himmler's secretary; Paul Schmidt, Nazi Foreign Office spokesman; and to many lesser accomplices.

Pattern of the Answers

Most of them were slicker, more ingratiating, more subtle, than Herr Sauckel. But he was typical in other respects. All denied any personal guilt; there was no repentance in them, and—with the exception of the Goerings and Paul Schmidt —no criticism of Hitler; they were married men with children for whom they showed great tenderness and concern; and their expressed differences with Nazis were over tactical matters, not basic ideology or philosophy.

All these men had fled to our territory in terror of the Russians, who got few Nazi hierarchs. They seemed to think we did not intend them much harm. They gave you their lies and their hypocrisies with such blank faces that you could not often be sure that they were not convinced of their own honesty. The value of such testimony on any subject is highly dubious, yet it was interesting that, questioned separately and in different places, some made the same answers to certain questions.

Everybody from Hermann Goering down agreed, for example, that Pearl Harbor came as a complete and unwelcome surprise to Hitler. He had wanted and expected Japan to attack—but Russia, not the United States. Goering and Paul Schmidt both said Hitler made the decision to invade Russia against his best military advice; Adolf was convinced the war would be won before the end of 1941 and would have no general near him who disagreed.

Hitler changed Party

Like Von Rundstedt and Kesselring and most of the General Staff officers, Goering explained the loss of the war in terms of mechanical and technological inferiority and ranked American air power high in the causes of defeat. Only the suave, English-speaking Paul Schmidt carried his analysis farther into the realm of politics.

Schmidt claimed membership in the "Nazi intellectuals," who have always stood for the original, the "pure," principles of National Socialism, and had kept hoping to dissuade the fanatics away from the reckless course that led first to the *Blitz* on England, then the invasion of Russia.

"Three fatal political mistakes brought about our downfall," Schmidt said. "First, the Socialist aims of the party were abandoned after the purge of Röhm and his followers in 1934. Secondly, the annexation of Prague meant the party had abandoned its original territorial principle— namely, not to incorporate non-German territory into the Reich. Finally, Hitler threw aside the last party principle, the principle of nationalism, when he tried to colonize the Ukraine . . ."

Germany's Moral Position

Like Goering, Schmidt took for granted the truth about the concentration camps, and both placed the primary blame on Hitler. Hermann for the moment seemed to have forgotten his own words on record, such as "I am not here to administer, but to destroy, to exterminate . . . Kill! Kill! Kill! Not you shall answer for this, but I."

"The concentration camps and atrocities will determine the moral position of Germany in the world for the next hundred years," volunteered Schmidt.

Neither Schmidt nor Goering claimed to have made any protest against the death factories, however. Only the self-pitying Nazi governor general of Poland, Hans Frank, pleaded for his life on the ground that he had "exposed" himself and angered Himmler by once lecturing against persecution of political prisoners. I saw Frank lying on a cot under an OD blanket in our 193rd Evacuation Hospital outside Munich. His neck and wrists were ringed with jagged, festering sores where he had scratched himself with his fingernails. He groaned and twisted, avoiding my eyes.

Frank admitted he had not intended to destroy himself. His self-inflicted cuts, he said, were a protest against the Americans' refusal to let him pay a farewell visit to Munich to see his wife and their children, whom he dearly loved.

Something made me ask him if he knew his name was high on the Polish list of war criminals.

"I didn't know it—no—and it can't be so. I am a man of culture, not a gangster. I opened the first museum for Chopin that Cracow ever had."

The Warsaw ghetto massacres? Maidanek? Oswiecim? These crimes were the work of Himmler!

"All Poles know how I loved their country. They are fine people. It is my greatest tragedy now to know they are falling under the influence of the Bolsheviks, in spite of all we could do. How many of them came to me on bended knee to ask me to save them from the Russians!"

All—but one—Blame Himmler

So, just as all the wretched underling guards I had questioned in camps in Poland and Germany had invariably excused themselves with the magic words "orders from above," now the men who gave those orders sought a way out by blaming Himmler. All, that is, except Himmler's secretary, Col.—and Doctor of Science—Wilhelm Führer. Our dossier showed that Führer had been in the SS since 1922, although he asserted that he had been peacefully teaching astronomy at Munich University till 1942. In fact, he looked the part of a man of science—tall, blue eyed, obviously Aryan, soft-spoken, and with a diffident, sincere manner. He had, of course, become Himmler's secretary against his will. One of his duties was to look after important visitors—and among them he mentioned Hans Frank as a favored guest. He used to edify these elite with lectures on the planets, as observed through a telescope that Himmler liked to carry around with him.

Himmler was Kind!

"Would you say that Himmler was a kind man?"

"He always treated his staff very considerately," answered Führer. He had, for instance, given Führer a car of his own from his l,000-car garage. "He even remembered birthdays and wedding anniversaries of his servants and there was always a little gift for each one."

"He loved his family?"

"They were very affectionate. He had a daughter of his own and one adopted son. He was fond of them and he was kind to all children. . ."

"On my word," said Führer, looking me directly in the eye. "I never heard Himmler say anything against the Americans. He liked the English too. He and Hitler used to go personally to visit the British and American prisoners of war, to see if there was anything they needed. . ."

Then at last something pricked Führer's aplomb. I had been looking through his papers and I came upon some photographs of three beautiful children, fat and robustly healthy. I showed them to the prisoner and asked if they were his. He nodded.

"Didn't ever occur to you, when you played with these lovely children, how they might look in a gas chamber or beside the skeletons of the women and children thrown into a furnace? Didn't you ever think they might have to pay the same penalty?"

"The Children are Innocent!"

Under his even coat of tan, Colonel Führer blanched and his knuckles turned white as he grabbed the arms of his chair. For a minute he said nothing. Finally, barely whispering, "They are innocent. You won't harm innocent children. . ."

Yet indictment and punishment of the fathers alone will not rid the children, nor Germany itself, of its schizophrenic mind. You can't talk to people here without noticing how the answers and excuses of the war criminals themselves are parroted by much of the population. Our men are not in town a week before, after getting acquainted with local people, they come back to camp reporting how German girls, once given the confidence to speak their minds, say that Hitler was a great man; he saved Germany from Bolshevism and the Jews, banished unemployment and tried to avoid war. On the whole, there seems little reason to doubt that Sauckel was right when he said, "It was only when the collapse came that people began to lose faith. . ."

Hitler "Wound Up" Germany

What independent testimony one can gather from neutrals who lived in Germany suggests that as long as Hitler was winning or seemed to have a chance, the German people were with him. I remember especially a conversation I had with Arent Waggener, a clever young Dutchman who worked in a German chemical plant at Stuttgart during the war and was also in the employ of our counter-intelligence service. He said there was no criticism of Hitler's methods and no noticeable objection to concentration camps and forced labor: "As long as the Wehrmacht was victorious, people applauded, and it was only when the American bombing became worse and worse that you heard people grumbling—not because they disagreed with the Nazis, but because they were not stronger than the Americans. The Germans continually reminded me of those little mechanical toys they used to make so well at Nuremberg. They run perfectly, once they are wound up. Hitler had the key, and until he began to lose heavily he never had any trouble keeping most of them wound up and running the way he wanted them to."

Depressing confirmation that Nazism suits the mentality of the German people came from Pastor Martin Niemöller, when he was interviewed after his release from a concentration camp. Even his own opposition, he emphasized, was based purely on religious doctrinal grounds and not against the Nazi political ideology.

"The German people are incapable of democracy as it is known in America," he said, "and even if they had it, they would not like it."

Not One Thousand Rebels

In Italy, at least, the people in the end assassinated Mussolini. In defeated Germany, when the worst war criminals hid among the people for protection, none was harmed. Nowhere was there a popular rising; even the brief flurry at Munich was abortive. . . No mutinies; no fights between SS and the Wehrmacht, for all their vaunted rivalries; no assassinations of officers by men. Millions of Germans had been led to crime and punishment by these officers; millions had died or lost everything. But not even a thousand of them rebelled to show the world they repudiated them.

So nothing has really happened to convince the Hitlerized populace that their defeat was the consequence of their own wrongdoing or the depravity of their methods and ends . . .

At first all Germans were so cowed by their defeat that there was little they wouldn't do to curry favor. Now they do not fear their conquerors. They are certain of lenient treatment. And they become arrogant.

Their former leaders, awaiting trial for the most terrible crimes in history, reflect this attitude more and more. The Allies are still "decadent"—meaning that they will hold a fair trial.

—*From* Army Talks *4 (August 26, 1945): 9–12.*

Toward the Holocaust

GERMAN PUBLIC OPINION

The Office of Public Opinion Research was established in 1940 to gather an archive of survey data from twenty-three organizations and sixteen countries. The surveys reprinted here were taken by the American Military Government in Germany from October 1945 to December 1946, during the INTERNATIONAL MILITARY TRIBUNAL'S proceedings when Nazi crimes were receiving wide publicity.

28. (Germany Oct 26 '45) The Allies have indicted some German organizations in their entirety; for example, the SS, SA, the general staff of the armed forces, the Gestapo, as well as the cabinet of the Reich, and the entire leadership of the Nazi Party. In your opinion, is the prosecution of these organizations justified? (OMGUS)

Yes 56%   No 27%   No opinion 15%   No answer 2%

Are there any organizations against which you think an indictment should be drawn up? Asked of 27% of the sample who thought the prosecution of some German organizations was not justified.

SS	10 %
SA	5
General staff of the armed forces	8
Gestapo	13
Cabinet of the Reich	10
Leadership of the Nazi party	14
None of these	1
No opinion	1
No answer	3
	65 %

* Percentages add to more than 27 as some respondents gave more than one answer.

(Dec 27 '45) The four Allies have laid charges against entire German organizations; for example, the SS, SA, the general staff, and the whole party leadership. In your opinion, is the prosecution of these organizations justified?

Yes	60 %
No	25
No opinion	13
Partly yes, partly no	1
No answer	1

29. (Germany Oct 26 '45) Do you think that the press reports of the Nuremberg trials are complete and authentic? (OMGUS)

	Yes	No	No opinion	No answer	Don't know	Other
	79 %	6 %	3 %	6 %	5 %	1 %
(Nov 19 '45)	75	4	20	1	—	—
(Nov 26 '45)	77	5	17	1	—	—
(Dec 27 '45)	75	7	17	1	—	—
(Mar 15 '46)	69	15	16	—	—	—
(Aug 9 '46)	67	10	23	—	—	—
(Oct 4 '46)	68	6	26	—	—	—

30. (Germany Nov 26 '45) In your opinion, are (Do you think that) the trials in Nuremberg (against Nazi leaders) (are) being carried out fairly? (OMGUS)

	Yes	No	No opinion	No answer	Other
	83 %	2 %	14 %	—	1 %
(Dec 27 '45)	81	3	16	—	—
(Jan 14 '46)	82	2	15	1 %	—
(Feb 14 '46)	81	6	13	—	—
(Feb 21 '46)	75	7	17	1	—
(Aug 9 '46)	76	5	18	1	—
(Oct 4 '46)	78	6	16	1	—

31. (Germany Dec 27 '45) What do you think of the way in which the newspapers are handling the Nuremberg trials? (OMGUS)

Good, satisfactory; tells the truth; objective, reports fairly; like it; informative; glad to hear the truth; just	51%
Good in general but: insufficient or dubious details; bad pictures; should give more details	6
Incomplete; inadequate	3
Biased; much propaganda	3
Slow and tedious; dull; too much irrelevant material	3
Unjust; untrue; don't like it; can't believe it; humiliating	2
Don't (or rarely) read the papers; don't or can't get a newspaper	14
No interest in politics	1
Other	1
No opinion; can't say	14
No answer	1

—*From Hadley Cantril, ed.,* Public Opinion, 1935–1946 *(Princeton, NJ, 1951), 1035–36.*

The end at Mauthausen concentration camp,
May 6, 1945. (NARA)

CHRONOLOGY

Items found in the Glossary are indicated only at first reference.

January 1

The Lublin Committee is established by the Soviet Union as the provisional Polish government.

200 Polish men and women are shot at Crematorium V in BIRKENAU CONCENTRATION CAMP and KILLING CENTER. They had been sentenced by a German police court, held in Block 11 at AUSCHWITZ I, and then transferred to the Birkenau crematorium for execution.

The Hungarian ZIONIST leader of the Relief and Rescue Committee of Budapest, Otto KOMOLY, is arrested by the ARROW CROSS and later murdered.

January 3

House Resolution 16 is submitted to the U.S. House of Representatives urging President Franklin D. ROOSEVELT and Secretary of State Edward Stettinius to effect the establishment of an emergency shelter in PALESTINE for the persecuted Jews of Europe.

The U.S. House of Representatives' Committee on Un-American Activities is given permanent status by a House vote of 207 to 186; this Committee's concern with communist subversion subsequently causes the departure of many left-wing anti-Nazi refugees from the United States, for example, the authors Bertolt Brecht and Heinrich Mann.

SUPREME HEADQUARTERS ALLIED EXPEDITIONARY FORCE (hereafter SHAEF) issues an administrative memorandum about the transfer of DISPLACED PERSONS (DPs) to the authority of the UNITED NATIONS RELIEF AND REHABILITATION ADMINISTRATION (hereafter UNRRA). The SHAEF Memorandum elaborates the principles of the SHAEF-UNRRA agreement of November 25, 1944, the intent of which is to have UNRRA personnel assume as quickly as possible responsibility for the care of the many displaced persons expected when the Allies enter Germany.

January 4–7

Approximately 120 young GYPSY (Roma) girls, the youngest under eight years old, are sterilized at RAVENSBRÜCK concentration camp by injection into the uterus. The few who survive the procedure are gassed.

January 5

The last transport of 14 Jews departs Berlin for Auschwitz.

A group of 35 Polish prisoners escapes from Pampitz (Pampice), a subcamp of GROSS-ROSEN concentration camp located in Brieg (Lower Silesia). While working outside the camp, they disarm some German soldiers, steal a truck, and drive for some distance before fleeing into the forest. All but two are recaptured, sent to Gross-Rosen, and later transferred to DORA-MITTELBAU.

January 6

Four female Jewish prisoners—Roza Robota, Ella Gartner, Esther Wajsblum, and Regina Saphirstein—are hanged in the women's camp in Auschwitz. They had provided explosives for the *SONDERKOMMANDO* revolt of October 7, 1944, in which one crematorium was destroyed.

1,004 female inmates of Birkenau are transferred to BERGEN-BELSEN concentration camp.

January 7

The National Administrative Council of the ZIONIST ORGANIZATION OF AMERICA demands that President Roosevelt support the opening of Palestine to Jewish immigration.

January 10

The trial of the assassins of the British Minister Resident in the Middle East, Lord Moyne, begins in Cairo. Eliahu Betsoury and Eliahu Hakim, members of the STERN GANG, a Jewish terrorist group, had killed Moyne on November 6, 1944, in Egypt. The two are found guilty, sentenced to death, and executed on March 22, 1945.

The American-Jewish Conference and the WORLD JEWISH CONGRESS appeal to the Allies to rescue the estimated 550,000 Jews remaining in German-occupied territory and to provide relief for the estimated 650,000 Jews already liberated. They also state that of the 5,600,000 Jews who lived in Europe before the Holocaust (excluding the Soviet Union), only 1,200,000 survive.

The GESTAPO in Bad Kreuznach, Germany, orders the deportation to THERESIEN-STADT of Jews living there in mixed marriages. Exemptions are provided for those Jews unable to perform labor, Jews granted special exemptions from these measures, and spouses of non-Jewish civil servants or public sector employees of German or foreign citizenship. Persons under the age of 16 with partly Jewish ancestry, *MISCHLINGE*, are not to be deported and will be cared for by their relatives; *Mischlinge* who are minors and considered to be Jews, the so-called *Geltungsjuden*, are to be transferred to Theresienstadt.

January 11

The Board of Deputies of British Jews urges the Foreign Office to naturalize refugee Jews in their current country of domicile.

Members of the Arrow Cross sack the Maros Hospital of the Jewish Holy Society of Buda in Budapest, then under the protection of the International Red Cross, killing 92 patients and staff; only one nurse survives. Such attacks continue in Buda until its liberation in February [see January 19 entry].

January 12

The Russian winter offensive in Poland begins with an attack by the First Byelorussian and First Ukrainian Fronts [see January 17 entry].

125 female prisoners are transferred from Auschwitz to Gross-Rosen concentration camp.

Hungarian police are assigned to protect the ghetto in Budapest after continued Arrow Cross attacks.

January 13

The CENTRAL OFFICE FOR REICH SECURITY decrees that all stateless Jews and those in mixed marriages capable of labor are to be transported to Theresienstadt.

January 14

Members of the Arrow Cross massacre approximately 150 patients and staff at the Orthodox Jewish Hospital in Varosmajor, Hungary, including Jews recently transferred from a sanitorium.

January 15

German reports indicate that the prisoner population of Auschwitz-Birkenau is 15,325 men and 16,421 women.

January 16

Soviet troops liberate 800 Jews in Czestochowa, Poland, the remnant of the city's prewar Jewish population of 28,500. In liberated Lodz, only 870 Jews remain.

The ninth deportation convoy from Sered transit and LABOR CAMP in Slovakia transfers 681 persons to camps in the Reich.

January 17

Massive EVACUATIONS of the prisoners in the Auschwitz complex begin. The last roll call registers 66,020 prisoners at Auschwitz and its satellite camps. From the women's camp in Birkenau, 5,345 female prisoners leave for Auschwitz in columns of 500 to await the columns of prisoners being marched west to avoid the advancing Soviet Army.

Warsaw is captured by the 1st Byelorussian Front, including the Polish 1st Army.

The *New York Times* reports that Secretary of State Stettinius has reassured the Jewish Labor Committee that the U.S. will take all necessary steps to prevent the Jews of Belgium from being annihilated if that area is retaken by the Germans. This is in response to the German offensive in the Ardennes the previous month.

Swedish diplomat Raoul WALLENBERG disappears in Pest.

A group of 179 female prisoners sent to Auschwitz after the Warsaw Uprising are transferred from the women's camp in Birkenau to Berlin, where they are assigned to forced labor in the AEG (*Allgemeine Elektrizitäts-Gesellschaft*) plant in Henningsdorf.

860 prisoners from the Auschwitz subcamp Sosnowiec march for twelve days to Troppau, where they board a train bound for MAUTHAUSEN concentration camp. The approximately 600 surviving prisoners arrive there on February 4.

January 17–18

The CHELMNO killing center is liquidated during the night of January 17–18 and the SS attempt to kill all remaining Jewish prisoners; two Jews escape and survive. During the same night, 1,000 prisoners held in the Gestapo prison in the Radogoszcz section of Lodz are shot or killed when the prison is set on fire.

January 18

Columns of prisoners leave Birkenau all day following a selection of prisoners into categories of those who cannot travel, those who can travel only to nearby trains, and those able to march at least thirty miles. The last column contains 1,500 prisoners who are marched to Wodzislaw in Silesia. On one part of the route, between Kryry and Marklowice, 171 prisoners are buried.

The Gleiwitz subcamps of Auschwitz are used as temporary assembly centers for prisoners evacuated from the Auschwitz complex. Approximately 1,300 prisoners in Gleiwitz I are marched to the Blechhammer subcamp; sick and incapacitated prisoners are shot. On the same day, more than 9,000 prisoners from MONOWITZ (Auschwitz III) are marched in columns of a thousand to Gleiwitz.

January 19

The last large transport of approximately 2,500 prisoners leaves Auschwitz main camp early in the morning, joining columns of prisoners from other camps in the Auschwitz complex already on the march west. All of these columns head for Wodzislaw in Silesia. Some 2,500 prisoners board a train for the journey to Mauthausen concentration camp, where they arrive on January 26.

The Arrow Cross attacks an alms house maintained by the Orthodox Holy Society in Buda, massacring 90 residents.

January 20

In the armistice between Hungary and the Allies, the Hungarians agree to repeal all discriminatory legislation and release all Hungarians held for religious or racial reasons, beginning the process of restoring legal equality to Hungarian Jews.

SS Major Franz Xaver Kraus, head of the Auschwitz Liaison and Transport offices, receives the order to kill all prisoners in the Auschwitz camp complex who are unable to march.

January 21

Approximately 4,000 prisoners leave Blechhammer, an Auschwitz subcamp, as the camp is dissolved. The column marches to Gross-Rosen concentration camp, arriving there on February 2. Approximately 800 prisoners are killed during the march. On February 7, the prisoners are transported by train to BUCHENWALD. Some prisoners are killed by Allied air attacks before they arrive on February 9.

Prisoners collected at the Gleiwitz subcamps [see January 18 entry] are transported by train to Buchenwald, Gross-Rosen, SACHSENHAUSEN, and Mauthausen concentration camps. The prisoners sent to Gross-Rosen are refused because of overcrowding and sent on to DACHAU concentration camp. Before their arrival on January 28, 42 die, and 25 more die soon after. Almost one-quarter of the prisoners on the Sachsenhausen transport freeze to death before arriving at that camp. The Mauthausen transport is also not accepted because of overcrowding and is redirected to the Dora-Mittelbau camp complex in Nordhausen, arriving on January 28. Approximately 500 die en route; another 600 die within two days of arrival.

January 22

President Roosevelt receives a memorandum proposing that an Allied court be set up to try the major Nazi leaders and organizations. This proposal is brought to the YALTA CONFERENCE in February.

A transport of 2,223 prisoners from Auschwitz, mostly Polish and Hungarian Jews, arrive at Buchenwald concentration camp.

Some 3,500 prisoners are marched from Gross-Rosen; 500 are killed by the SS at the railroad station there. Some of the survivors travel by train to Leitmeritz (Litomerice) in Czechoslovakia while others march. Columns of prisoners from other camps join along the way. In early February, the prisoners arrive at Leitmeritz, where a subcamp of FLOSSENBÜRG concentration camp is located. A typhoid epidemic in Flossenbürg kills about 550 prisoners every week.

January 24

A transport from Auschwitz of female prisoners, including 166 Poles, arrives at Ravensbrück concentration camp.

January 25

The forced evacuation from STUTTHOF concentration camp begins.

January 26

At 1:00 A.M., the SS blows up Crematorium V, the last crematorium in Birkenau. On the same day, a transport of 3,987 Auschwitz prisoners arrives at Buchenwald concentration camp.

January 27

U.S. Army Brig. Gen. William O'Dwyer is appointed executive director of the WAR REFUGEE BOARD to replace John PEHLE, who had resigned to assume new duties as an assistant to the Secretary of the Treasury. General O'Dwyer had served on the Allied Control Commission for Italy.

The Soviet Army liberates Auschwitz-Birkenau. They find 1,200 ill prisoners in Auschwitz, 5,800 prisoners in Birkenau (4,000 of whom are women), and 600 sick prisoners in Monowitz.

The last transport destined for Mauthausen from Auschwitz-Birkenau arrives. Mauthausen concentration camp now holds 6,025 prisoners from Auschwitz.

A transport of approximately 2,000 female prisoners from Auschwitz reaches Ravensbrück. Another 2,000 arrive the next day. The last transport with 3,000 women from Auschwitz reaches Ravensbrück at the beginning of February.

January 30	Soviet Army General Georgi K. ZHUKOV's First Byelorussian Front crosses the German border near Posen (Poznan), reaching the Oder River at Küstrin the same day, thereby establishing a bridgehead on the west bank of the Oder within 40 miles of Berlin.
January 31	Lord Quincy Wright of Australia becomes the chairman of the UNITED NATIONS WAR CRIMES COMMISSION (hereafter UNWCC).
	Selected numbers of German Jews in mixed marriages are deported to Theresienstadt.
Also in January	The internment of Japanese-Americans in the United States ends.
February 1	In response to a request from the previous October, the German Ministry of Foreign Affairs informs the International RED CROSS that it is authorized to send both personal and general delivery parcels to Belgian and French prisoners in concentration camps.
February 2	The SS shoots 178 prisoners at Sachsenhausen concentration camp; among those killed are 19 Luxembourg citizens and 7 British and 60 Soviet officers.
	During the night of February 2–3, more than 570 prisoners, many of them Soviet prisoners of war under death sentence, revolt and escape from Block 20 at Mauthausen, a detention block for prisoners awaiting execution. They are fired upon by the SS guards inside the camp, but two groups manage to break through the barbed wire. All but seventeen are captured and killed.
February 2–22	At Station Z in Sachsenhausen, 4,000 prisoners are killed.
February 4–12	The Yalta Conference in the Crimea takes place. U.S. President Roosevelt, British Prime Minister Winston CHURCHILL, and Soviet Marshal Joseph STALIN also discuss the postwar "denazification" of Germany and procedures for the prosecution of German war criminals.
February 7	A transport of about 1,200 Jews released from Theresienstadt reaches Switzerland at Kreuzlingen.
February 10	The Swedish government authorizes Count Folke BERNADOTTE, then vice-chairman of the Swedish Red Cross, to negotiate with the Germans for the rescue of Scandinavian prisoners in concentration camps. On February 16, Bernadotte flies to Berlin to meet with Ernst KALTENBRUNNER, head of the Central Office for Reich Security, and German Foreign Minister Joachim von RIBBENTROP.
February 13	Gross-Rosen concentration camp is liberated by the Soviet Army. The Soviet Army also liberates the Pest section of Budapest.
February 14	Members of *EINSATZKOMMANDO* 13 shoot nine persons, apparently Jews and Roma (Gypsies), after discovering them hiding in a forest near L'utov in Slovakia.
February 16	The Reich Ministry of Economics issues a circular ordering that records of anti-Jewish activities are to be destroyed if they cannot be moved, to prevent their capture by the Allies.
February 18	Dr. Stephen WISE, president of the World Jewish Congress, announces that an official report from Moscow states that less than one percent of the Jewish population of thirty-eight liberated Russian and Polish cities remains alive.

Transports of persons with partly Jewish ancestry *(Mischlinge)* arrive in Theresienstadt, including 169 from Leipzig, 195 from Frankfurt, and 146 from Halle.

February 19	Swedish Count Bernadotte meets Heinrich HIMMLER at the SS hospital at Hohenlychen. Himmler agrees to place Scandinavian prisoners of all concentration camps under Red Cross control at NEUENGAMME concentration camp. By February 23, Bernadotte is to report to Swedish officials that men and vehicles of the Swedish Red Cross would be allowed into Germany for this purpose. [See February 10 entry.]

At Mauthausen concentration camp, 66 prisoners are gassed. |
| **February 23** | Turkey declares war on Germany and Japan.

Members of *Einsatzkommando* 13 remove 26 prisoners from Dubnica nad Vahom in Slovakia and murder them in a forest near Trnova. |
| **February 24** | The final deportation convoy leaves La Risiera di San Sabba concentration camp in Trieste for Bergen-Belsen.

The Blechhammer transport leaves Buchenwald, arriving on February 26 at the Berga subcamp of Buchenwald. The prisoners board trains headed toward Czechoslovakia. Many casualties are suffered on the journey from Berga. The survivors are liberated by the Soviet Army. [See January 21 entry.] |
| **February 26** | 390 Dutch and other Jews are transferred from Bergen-Belsen to Neuengamme concentration camp. |
| **February 28** | The prisoner population of Ravensbrück is registered as 46,473 men and women. |
| **Also in February** | In mid-February, the Hartheim EUTHANASIA institution is converted into a children's home.

A GAS CHAMBER is built in a subterranean passageway at Theresienstadt. |
| **March 1** | Sir George Rendel, Britain's Superintending Under Secretary of State for Prisoners-of-War and Refugees, proposes that Britain reject the naturalization of Jewish refugees from Germany residing in the United Kingdom or serving in the British armed forces. A Foreign Office memorandum entitled "Status of Ex-Enemy Refugees in View of Impending Repeal of Nazi Discriminatory Legislation," is distributed to appropriate British officials. The memorandum recommends that there be no forcible repatriation to post-Nazi Germany, but advises against "automatic naturalization or permanent settlement" for anti-Nazi and Jewish refugees residing in Great Britain.

The U.S. National Council for Jewish Women announces that the first refugee from the refugee center at FORT ONTARIO, New York, will be resettled outside the country: sixty-year-old Elsa Neumann, an Austrian, will go to Capetown, South Africa, where four of her children live. |
| **March 2** | Fifteen Dutch prisoners are executed at Neuengamme.

2,000 female prisoners are evacuated from Ravensbrück to Mauthausen concentration camp; only 740 survive to liberation.

480 prisoners are transferred from Bergen-Belsen to Neuengamme concentration camp. |

March 5	Since November 5, 1944, members of *Einsatzkommando* 14, with their fascist Slovak confederates of the Hlinka Guard, have killed 747 people, including 211 women and 58 children, in the vicinity of the town of Kremnicka. The victims were taken from a local prison, robbed, led to an anti-tank ditch, and shot.
	A fascist riot occurs in Bucharest, Romania, as bands including recently escaped criminals roam the city shooting into homes and attempting to create anti-Jewish disturbances among university students. The rioters are protected by the Ministry of the Interior.
March 7	Units of the U.S. 1st Army make the first crossing of the Rhine after capturing the Ludendorff Bridge at Remagen (Germany).
March 9	The SS deports 549 people from Sered labor camp to concentration camps in the German Reich.
March 12	General Zhukov's Soviet forces capture the city of Küstrin, near Berlin.
	The land convoy of the Swedish Red Cross rescue mission, commanded by Lt. Col. Gottfrid Bjorck, crosses the German border. Consisting of 298 men in four transport platoons of the Swedish Army in Red Cross uniforms, the group initially stops near Friedrichsruhe.
	The Swedish Red Cross transports approximately 300 Scandinavian prisoners from Sachsenhausen and its subcamp at Oranienburg to Neuengamme concentration camp.
March 14	A second Swedish Red Cross mission travels to Dachau, Mauthausen, and Schömberg, a subcamp of Natzweiler.
March 16	Ernst Kaltenbrunner, head of the Central Office for Reich Security, and Carl Burckhardt, president of the International Red Cross (IRC), conclude an agreement that permits the sending of Red Cross parcels to concentration camp prisoners. Red Cross representatives may also be placed in all concentration camps. An exchange of Belgian and French prisoners for Germans interned in France is anticipated; in the meantime the IRC is given the right to REPATRIATE women, children, and the aged, including Jews, particularly those in the Theresienstadt ghetto.
March 17	The Hungarian Provisional National government adopts decree No. 200/1945 ME that repeals all anti-Jewish laws enacted during the HORTHY and SZALASI regimes.
March 20	Felix Kersten, Himmler's masseuse, contacts the Swedish Legation in Berlin and reports that Himmler has agreed to release 5,000–10,000 Jews.
March 22	Egypt, Saudi Arabia, Iraq, Lebanon, Syria, and Transjordan agree to establish the Arab League at a meeting in Cairo. The agreement is ratified by May 10.
March 22–23	The Germans gas 95 Jewish Hungarian Labor servicemen in a sealed barracks because the Jewish forced laborers are too ill to be evacuated as the Germans abandon the city of Koszeg in Hungary. Approximately 2,500 other Jewish Labor servicemen are killed or die while building fortifications in the area. Those who survive are sent to Mauthausen concentration camp, and later to its subcamp GUNSKIRCHEN.

March 23	Some 1,000 prisoners of Aschersleben, a subcamp of Buchenwald, are marched through Magdeburg and Torgau to Delitzsch. They are liberated there on April 23.
	At Mauthausen, 76 prisoners, including seven Czech women, are gassed.
March 24	At Dora-Mittelbau, 30 Russian prisoners are hanged for sabotaging the production of V-2 rockets there.
March 26	American troops liberate the town of HADAMAR, Germany.
	465 prisoners die during a transport from Neuengamme to Ravensbrück concentration camp.
March 27	The Swedish Red Cross rescue mission reports to the Swedish government that 4,800 prisoners are under its care. On the same day, Count Bernadotte is summoned to Stockholm, where he is instructed by Eric von Post, the chief of the Political Department of the Swedish Foreign Ministry, to include an additional 800 Jews in his rescue efforts. Bernadotte later told the British minister in Stockholm that the scope of his rescue activities has broadened to include 50,000 Jews.
	About 800 prisoners are marched from Flossenbürg to Lengenfeld, a subcamp of Flossenbürg, arriving there on April 12.
March 29	A debate begins in the British House of Lords concerning the immigration of Jewish refugees from liberated areas of Europe to Palestine and the lifting of immigration quotas.
	Members of the U.S. 2d Infantry Division investigate the facilities of the Hadamar euthanasia killing institution after local inhabitants report the murder of thousands of people. The Americans find 550 patients still alive. Several members of the staff are arrested.
March 30	Count Bernadotte visits Neuengamme concentration camp.
March 31	Anne Frank dies at the age of 15 in Bergen-Belsen concentration camp.
	The last transport leaves Sered labor and transit camp with 370 people destined for Theresienstadt.
Also in March	Last transport of Jews from Berlin to Sachsenhausen concentration camp.
	Sick and incapacitated prisoners in Mauthausen are separated from the other inmates and housed in a special camp with the intent of gassing them. Organized resistance succeeds in smuggling over 2,000 of the sick prisoners out of the special camp and hiding them. Nevertheless, 1,000 prisoners are gassed.
April 1	The Soviet army liberates Sered labor camp in Slovakia.
	The first UNRRA teams enter Germany in the wake of the Allied armies to facilitate and assist in the relief of displaced persons.
April 1–2	A transport of Polish, Czech, French, Belgian, Russian, and Jewish prisoners leaves Kochendorf, a subcamp of Natzweiler, for Dachau. The column marches to Heilbronn and boards trains which are bombed on the journey to Crailsheim. Many prisoners are killed during the air raid; a number are also killed by the SS near Crailsheim on April 6 or 7. At Zobingen, 42 prisoners are killed; another 47 are "buried" at Hütten.

April 2	Count Bernadotte meets with Himmler and obtains permission to transfer women and the sick from the Red Cross shelter at Neuengamme to Sweden.
April 3	British Royal Air Force bombers attack the city of Nordhausen, where former military barracks are used to house prisoners of the Dora-Mittelbau concentration camp. More than 1,000 prisoners are killed in the raid.
April 4	Bratislava, the capital of Slovakia, is liberated by Soviet troops.
	A transport of prisoners is sent from Buchenwald to Bergen-Belsen, where the group arrives on April 12. While most of the trip is made by train, the last portion from Celle to Bergen-Belsen is completed on foot.
	350 prisoners are evacuated from Vienna. They are soon joined by a column of 400 prisoners from the Floridsdorf section of Vienna; 157 prisoners are killed during the trip. The survivors eventually reached Steyr, where a subcamp of Mauthausen is located.
April 4–5	OHRDRUF, a subcamp of Buchenwald, is liberated by advance units of the 4th Armored and 89th Infantry Divisions.
April 5	Franz ZIEREIS, commandant of Mauthausen, is present at the execution of 11 prisoners in that camp: 6 crematorium workers from Auschwitz, 2 Germans, 1 Englishman, and 2 American flyers.
April 6	An International Red Cross delegation headed by Paul Dunant inspects the Theresienstadt ghetto, accompanied by Adolf EICHMANN and SS officers. The Red Cross reports that Theresienstadt has 17,556 inmates. [See May 3 entry.]
	During the evacuation of prisoners from Buchenwald to Dachau, 450 prisoners escape; and another 400 prisoners, mostly Poles, escape on April 12.
April 6–10	Forced evacuations of the inmates of Buchenwald continue despite resistance and the refusal of the prisoners to assemble.
Second week of April	The Swedish rescue mission takes under its protection 425 prisoners from the Theresienstadt ghetto.
April 7	Kurt Bruns, a German army captain, is convicted in Düren, Germany, by the 1st Army Military Commission for murdering two Jewish-American prisoners of war in December 1944. This is the only war crimes trial of a German by a U.S. military tribunal before the end of the war.
	Several groups of prisoners are marched from Blankenburg, a subcamp of Dora-Mittelbau, to Magdeburg. Many of the prisoners die or are killed on this march. From Magdeburg the survivors are taken by ship to Lübeck; from there, they once again march, this time towards Sarau, where they are rescued by the Swedish Red Cross on April 29.
	Prisoners in the subcamps of Buchenwald at Wieda, Osterhagen, Nüxei, and Mackenrode are simply driven out of the camps.
	The train containing prisoners evacuated from Neuengamme towards Lübeck is bombed by the Allies in Lüneburg. The SS shoot 256 wounded prisoners and send 144 survivors to Bergen-Belsen.
April 7–8	Prisoners from a subcamp of Neuengamme in Watenstedt are evacuated to Ravensbrück, where they arrive on April 15. More than 700 die during the journey.

April 8	Rezso KASZTNER begins a visit to concentration camps in the company of Kurt Becher, newly appointed Special Reich Commissioner for Concentration Camps. By April 18 they visit Bergen-Belsen, Theresienstadt, Neuengamme, and other sites.

A transmitter secretly built by prisoners in Buchenwald begins broadcasting to approaching American troops. The prisoners appeal for help in both German and English in the face of the impending liquidation of the camp. The message is acknowledged.

At Mauthausen 37 Czech women are gassed.

Two groups of prisoners are evacuated from the subcamp Plauen and returned to the main camp of Flossenbürg. The first group, 600 men, travels by train, arriving in Flossenbürg on April 14. The second group leaves Plauen on foot, is bombed during the journey, and reaches Flossenbürg on April 20.

April 8–9

Prominent prisoners, including Kurt von Schuschnigg, Hjalmar SCHACHT, and Franz Halder, are evacuated from Flossenbürg to Dachau.

April 9

The British 8th Army begins its offensive in Italy.

Dietrich Bonhoeffer of the CONFESSING CHURCH is executed in Flossenbürg.

Approximately 2,500 prisoners are evacuated on foot from the subcamp Blumenthal, north of Bremen, towards the main camp Neuengamme.

April 10

A truck convoy of 300 French female prisoners from Ravensbrück reaches Switzerland. They are exchanged for German civilians held by the French under the terms of the French-German exchange agreement arranged by Carl Burckhardt [see March 16 entry].

The U.S. 84th Infantry Division liberates Hanover-Ahlem, a subcamp of Neuengamme.

Prisoners are evacuated from the Buchenwald subcamp Berga to the Flossenbürg subcamp Plauen. Their train is routed through Czechoslovakia via Marienbad and Karlsbad.

April 11

Prisoners in the Buchenwald concentration camp revolt to forestall the planned evacuation of the camp and take 150 Germans prisoner. The camp is liberated by the U.S. 4th Armored and 6th Armored Divisions.

The U.S. 83d Infantry Division liberates Langenstein, a subcamp of Buchenwald.

The U.S. 3d Armored and 104th Infantry Divisions liberate Dora-Mittelbau concentration camp.

April 12

Franklin Delano Roosevelt, 32d President of the United States, dies of a stroke in Warm Springs, Georgia; Vice President Harry S TRUMAN takes the oath of office as 33d President.

The British Cabinet unanimously decides against a full trial for the Nazi leadership, agreeing only to publish a formal statement detailing the case against them before their summary execution.

The Germans evacuate the WESTERBORK transit camp in Holland, leaving behind only 909 Jews who are that same day liberated by the 2d Canadian Division.

The prisoners evacuated on March 27 from Flossenbürg to the Lengenfeld subcamp leave Lengenfeld by truck for the Flossenbürg subcamp Johanngeorgenstadt, where all the sick are killed by the SS. The majority of the remaining prisoners continue on foot to the Flossenbürg subcamp Regensburg.

A train provided by the Romanian government to the *Oeuvre d'assistance*, an agency of the International Red Cross newly created to aid people made destitute during the war, leaves Hungary for Poland to retrieve Hungarian Jews who had survived deportation. It returns to Nagyvarad with 202 survivors.

April 13

Vienna is captured by Soviet forces.

The SS burns to death more than 1,000 prisoners evacuated from several camps to Mieste and Gardelegen. Soldiers of the U.S. 102d Infantry Division find only a few survivors among the dead the next day.

April 14

The Central Registry of War Criminals and Security Suspects, known by the acronym CROWCASS, is established by SHAEF in Paris.

The U.S. 2d Infantry Division liberates Leipzig-Hasag, a subcamp of Buchenwald concentration camp.

The U.S. 84th Infantry Division liberates Salzwedel, a subcamp of Neuengamme.

April 15

Bergen-Belsen concentration camp is liberated by British units. Approximately 40,000 mostly Jewish prisoners are freed.

General George S. PATTON, commander of the U.S. 3d Army, inspects Buchenwald.

Swedish Red Cross buses remove 413 Danish prisoners from Theresienstadt for transfer to Sweden.

A transport of prisoners evacuated from Neuengamme and destined for Bergen-Belsen is rerouted on April 15 to the Neuengamme subcamp Sandbostel because Bergen-Belsen had already been liberated. Another transport from Neuengamme is rerouted to the Neuengamme subcamp WÖBBELIN.

The Mauthausen subcamp Melk is evacuated. Sick and infirm prisoners are sent to Mauthausen, while the remainder arrive at the subcamp Ebensee on April 17.

April 16

Soviet Army General Zhukov begins the offensive to capture Berlin. The suburbs of the city are reached by April 21 and the city itself encircled by April 25.

A U.S. Army War Crimes Investigation Team reports to the commanding general of the 1st Army that a *prima facie* case for legal proceedings against the staff of the Hadamar euthanasia killing facility exists. The basis for indictment is the murder of Polish and Russian forced laborers in violation of the Geneva Convention.

SHAEF issues Administrative Memorandum No. 39, setting forth the policies and regulations of the United States, Great Britain, and France in dealing with displaced persons in Germany. SHAEF's Displaced Persons Executive expands the previous definition of any citizen of an Allied country outside their native country to include "stateless" persons, a category consisting mostly of Jews.

The Salo Republic, the fascist government in northern Italy, passes its last anti-Jewish law, which calls for the dissolution of the Union of Italian Jewish Communities and all Jewish charitable institutions, as well as the confiscation of all their property.

1,123 prisoners from subcamps of Flossenbürg in the vicinity of Johanngeorgenstadt are taken by train toward Theresienstadt. At Karlsbad they are forced to continue on foot. Near Buchau 60 are shot, and only 750 prisoners arrive at Theresienstadt.

| April 17 | Spergau concentration camp is liberated by the U.S. 2d Infantry Division. |
| | A convoy of ten trucks with relief supplies for Mauthausen leaves Geneva. Another convoy with supplies for Oranienburg and Ravensbrück concentration camps leaves the next day. |

April 18 The second trial before the French HIGH COURT OF JUSTICE begins. General Henri Dentz, VICHY high commissioner of Syria, is accused of aiding the Germans and fighting against Free-French and British forces in Syria during May 1941. He is convicted and sentenced to death. However, the head of the French Provisional Government, Gen. Charles DE GAULLE, commutes the sentence, and Dentz eventually dies in a prison hospital.

April 19 Prime Minister Churchill informs Parliament that eight members of the House of Commons and two members of the House of Lords will inspect conditions in the liberated concentration camps at the invitation of Gen. Dwight D. EISENHOWER. The official delegation, which left London on April 20, includes Lord Stanhope, Lord Addison, Lt. Col. Edward Thomas Wickham, Mavis Constance Tate, Comdr. Sir Archibald Southby, Henry Graham White, Sir Harry Morris-Jones, Thomas Driberg, Samuel Sidney Silverman, and Ness Edwards. Their report, *Buchenwald Camp: The Report of a Parliamentary Delegation*, is submitted in late April 1945.

Neuengamme is abandoned by the Swedish rescue mission as fighting approaches. Some of the inmates in Red Cross care are transferred directly to Sweden; the remainder are sent to two temporary camps in Denmark.

Joseph SCHWARTZ, director of the European Executive Council, AMERICAN JEWISH JOINT DISTRIBUTION COMMITTEE (AJJDC), reports from Athens that the prewar Jewish population of Greece has been reduced from 75,000 to only about 8,500.

Leipzig-Thelka, a Buchenwald subcamp, is liberated by the U.S. 69th Infantry Division.

The evacuation of the Neuengamme concentration camp is ordered.

April 19–20 The first Red Cross convoy leaves Mauthausen with French, Belgian, and Dutch prisoners.

During the nights of April 19–20 and April 22–23, between 650 and 800 sick and incapacitated prisoners are gassed at Mauthausen. During April approximately 1,400 prisoners are gassed at the camp.

April 20 U.S. troops enter the city of Nuremberg.

Walter Masur, a Swedish representative of the World Jewish Congress, meets with Himmler in Berlin. Himmler states that no harm will befall concentration camp inmates from this date but denies requests for any large-scale rescue operation.

Representatives of the International Red Cross arrive at Mauthausen. Permission for their vehicles to enter the camp is given the next day. Camp commandant Ziereis selects for repatriation 67 men and 740 women, most of whom had been transferred from Ravensbrück the previous month. The prisoners are loaded on trucks and driven out of the camp.

The evacuation of the Sachsenhausen concentration camp begins, as over 30,000 prisoners are marched out of the camp.

The evacuation of all Flossenbürg prisoners, except those unable to walk, is completed. Approximately 22,000 prisoners, including 1,700 Jews, are evacuated from the main camp.

The transfer of prisoners from Neuengamme to ships off Neustadt begins. Within the next ten days approximately 10,000 prisoners are transferred to three ships in the Bay of Lübeck: the *Athen*, *Cap Arcona*, and *Thielbek*.

At the Mauthausen subcamp Gusen I, the SS surround Block 30, seal the windows, and gas the ill prisoners inside.

20 Jewish children used in medical experiments at Neuengamme are hanged along with their inmate attendants in the basement of a school at Bullenhuser Damm in Hamburg. The murders were ordered by the commandant of Neuengamme on instructions from Berlin to remove evidence of the experiments.

The first transport of 2,000 prisoners evacuated from eastern camps arrives in Theresienstadt. Within the next two weeks, more than 13,000 prisoners arrive at Theresienstadt. A typhus epidemic begins.

April 20–21	The U.S. 65th Infantry Division liberates a subcamp of Flossenbürg concentration camp.
April 21	The British Parliamentary delegation [see April 19 entry] visits the recently liberated Buchenwald camp.
April 21–28	The last gassings of mostly sick inmates occurs in Ravensbrück and Mauthausen concentration camps.
April 22	Advance units of the 47th Soviet Army and infantry units of the Polish 1st Army liberate Sachsenhausen concentration camp and the town of Oranienburg in greater metropolitan Berlin. Evacuated Sachsenhausen prisoners who survived the forced marches are not freed by Soviet troops until the first days of May 1945.
	The Swedish rescue mission begins evacuating all "healthy" inmates, regardless of nationality, from Ravensbrück. The inmates are transferred by train to ports on the Baltic and then shipped to Sweden. The Swedes rescue more than 21,000 concentration camp prisoners by war's end.
April 22–May 7	At the invitation of General Eisenhower, a bipartisan congressional delegation tours the liberated concentration camps of Buchenwald (on April 24, about two weeks after liberation), Nordhausen (on May 1, about three weeks after liberation), and Dachau (on May 2, liberated 48 hours before their arrival). The delegation for this two-week trip consists of six senators: Alben W. Barkley (D-Ky, Senate majority leader, later U.S. vice-president 1949–53), C. Wayland Brooks (R-Ill), Walter F. George (D-Ga, acting chairman of the Committee on Foreign Relations), Leverett Saltonstall (R-Mass), Elbert D. Thomas (D-Utah, chairman of the Committee on Military Affairs), and Kenneth S. Wherry (R-Neb); and six members of the House of Representatives: Ed V. Izac (D-Calif), James W. Mott (R-Ore), James P. Richards (D-S.C.), Dewey Short (R-Mo), R. Ewing Thomason (D-Tex), and John M. Vorys (R-Ohio). Their report to Congress was presented by Senator Barkley on May 15, and was published as "Atrocities and Other Conditions in Concentration Camps in Germany."
April 23	Flossenbürg concentration camp is liberated by the U.S. 90th Infantry Divisions.

353 French prisoners, so-called "prominent deportees," are evacuated from Neuengamme in the direction of Flossenbürg. The transport is diverted and the prisoners eventually end up at Theresienstadt and Brezany, Czechoslovakia, the location of a subcamp of Flossenbürg called Jungfern Breschan.

Stara Gradiska in Slovenia, a subcamp of Croatian Jasenovac concentration camp, is liberated by units of the 28th Division of the Yugoslavian Army of National Liberation.

April 23–May 8

At General Eisenhower's invitation, 18 American editors and publishers tour the European Theater of Operations and inspect the liberated German concentration camps. The delegation on this fifteen-day trip consists of: Julius Ochs Adler, vice-president and general manager of the *New York Times*; Malcolm Bingay, editor of the *Detroit Free Press*; Amon G. Carter, publisher of the *Fort Worth Star-Telegram*; Norman Chandler, editor and publisher of the *Los Angeles Times*; William L. Chenery, publisher of *Collier's*; E. Z. Dimitman, executive editor of the *Chicago Sun*; John Randolph Hearst, assistant general manager of Hearst Publications; Ben Hibbs, editor of the *Saturday Evening Post*; Stanley High, associate editor of the *Reader's Digest*; Ben McKelway, editor of the *Washington Star*; William I. Nichols, editor of *This Week Magazine*; Leonard K. Nicholson, president and editor of the *New Orleans Times-Picayune*; Joseph Pulitzer, publisher of the *St. Louis Post Dispatch*; Gideon Seymour, executive editor of the *Minneapolis Star Journal*; Duke Shoop, Washington correspondent of the *Kansas City Star*; Beverly Smith, associate editor of the *American Magazine*; Walker Stone, editor of the Scripps Howard Newspaper Alliance; and M. E. Walter, managing editor of the *Houston Chronicle*. They visit and inspect conditions in Weimar and Buchenwald on April 25 (twelve days after liberation), Essen and Mannheim on May 2, and Munich and Dachau on May 3 (four days after liberation). The extensive coverage of their impressions of liberated Buchenwald and Dachau is published throughout May and June.

April 23–25

Three truck convoys arrive in Switzerland with a total of 781 French, Dutch, and Belgian prisoners released from Mauthausen.

April 25

American and Russian forces meet on the Elbe River at Torgau, effectively cutting the German Reich in half.

A convoy of the International Red Cross arrives at Mauthausen subcamp Gusen I and removes most of the French prisoners.

Count Bernadotte relays through the Swedish government a written peace request from Heinrich Himmler. The Allies refuse the request two days later. The BBC reports this as a separate peace offer on April 28.

April 26

Marshal Henri Philippe PÉTAIN and his entourage cross into France from Switzerland and surrender to French authorities. Three days earlier, Petain's indictment had been read to an examining board.

A delegation from the UNWCC visits Buchenwald and submits a report to the Commission upon its return.

The SS and the Italian fascist Nere Brigade shoot 6 foreign Jews in Cuneo, Italy.

April 27

LANDSBERG am Lech, a subcamp of Dachau, is liberated by the U.S. 10th and 12th Armored and the 103rd Infantry Divisions.

The final evacuation of Ravensbrück begins in the morning. About 15,000 are marched from the camp by April 28, while 3,000 ill prisoners remain behind.

	The Ravensbrück subcamp at Neubrandenburg is evacuated.
April 28	Benito MUSSOLINI is executed by Italian partisans.
April 28–29	The U.S. 4th Infantry Division liberates a subcamp of Dachau.
April 29	Dachau concentration camp is liberated by the U.S. 20th Armored Division and the 42d and 45th Infantry Divisions.
April 29–30	The Bolzano-Gries transit and concentration camp in northern Italy is liberated and then transferred to the International Red Cross.
April 30	Adolf HITLER and Eva Braun, whom he married the night before, commit suicide in their Berlin bunker. Admiral Karl DÖNITZ succeeds Hitler.
	Ravensbrück concentration camp is liberated by Soviet army units.
	Judge Samuel Rosenman, Counsel to the President of the United States, presents his report on the economic needs in Europe. In the report he addresses the plight of European Jews, helping to provide the groundwork for the Harrison Report [see August 3 and September 29 entries].
	The first of 96 British medical students from London arrive in Bergen-Belsen to help with relief work.
	A fourth truck convoy of about 300 French prisoners, mostly women, arrives in Switzerland from Mauthausen. About ten had died during the trip.
Also in April	Since the previous September, the French have arrested 126,000 people suspected of collaborating with the Germans. Of this total 55 percent were freed and 45 percent passed to the courts for trial.
May 1	The British evacuate 7,000 sick inmates from Bergen-Belsen.
May 2	President Truman issues Executive Order 9547 to appoint Justice Robert H. JACKSON of the U.S. Supreme Court as Chief Counsel for the United States to the UNWCC and as Chief Prosecutor to the projected international war crimes trial. He is authorized to represent the United States during negotiations to create such a tribunal.
	The German garrison in Berlin surrenders to the Soviet Army.
	German forces surrender in Italy.
	The Croatian concentration camp Jasenovac is liberated by units of the 21st Division of the Yugoslavian Army of National Liberation.
	A poll conducted by the American Institute of Public Opinion asks Americans if reports that the Germans have killed many people in concentration and prison camps are true or false; 84 percent reply that they believe the stories to be true.
May 2–3	Subcamps of Dachau concentration camp are liberated by the U.S. 14th Armored Division.
May 3	The Psychological Warfare Section of SHAEF issues a thirteen-volume report on atrocities committed in France during the occupation.
	Representative Clare Booth Luce (R-Conn) addresses the House of Representatives about conditions in Buchenwald she witnessed during her inspection visit of the concentration camp on April 21.

Commandant Ziereis hands his command of the Mauthausen concentration camp to the Police Commander of Vienna.

Theresienstadt is turned over to the International Red Cross.

In the early afternoon, British planes attack three ships holding concentration camp prisoners in the Bay of Lübeck. The prisoners had come from Neuengamme and its subcamps, but also from Dora-Mittelbau and Stutthof. The *Cap Arcona* and the *Thielbek* sank in the bay; the *Athen*, docked in Neustadt, escaped total destruction. Most of the prisoners on the *Cap Arcona* and *Thielbek* perish—burned or drowned on the ships, succumbed in the cold water, or shot by the SS—while many on the *Athen* survive. About 7,300 prisoners die, and some 3,100 are saved.

Wöbbelin, a subcamp of Neuengamme, is liberated by the U.S. 82d Airborne Division and 8th Infantry Division.

May 3–4	The U.S. 99th Infantry Division liberates a subcamp of Dachau concentration camp.
May 4	British troops liberate Neuengamme concentration camp.
	During the evacuation of Loibl-Pass, a subcamp of Mauthausen, the prisoners are freed by Yugoslav partisans who attack the Germans guarding the marching prisoner column.
May 4–5	Ebensee, a subcamp of Mauthausen, is liberated by the U.S. 80th Infantry Division.
May 5	A message from General Eisenhower is broadcast in a number of languages to displaced persons in Europe. It directs them to "wait for orders" from Allied military authorities in an attempt to forestall the movement of masses of displaced persons that would interfere with Allied military operations and adversely affect law and order in areas already occupied by the Allies.
	Gusen I, a subcamp of Mauthausen, is liberated by the U.S. 11th Armored Division.
	The International Red Cross reports more than 30,000 prisoners in Theresienstadt; no less than 12,000 of them are prisoners transferred from Dachau, Buchenwald, and Bergen-Belsen in the previous month.
May 5–6	Gunskirchen, a subcamp of Mauthausen, is liberated by the U.S. 71st Infantry Division, including African-American troops of the 761st Tank Battalion.
May 6	Mauthausen concentration camp is liberated by the U.S. 11th Armored Division.
May 7	General Alfred JODL signs Germany's unconditional surrender at Reims, France.
	The Soviet Extraordinary State Commission issues its report on Auschwitz, concluding that millions of people were killed in the camp.
	The U.S. 9th Armored Division and 1st Infantry Division liberate Falkenau a.d. Eger, a subcamp of Flossenbürg.
May 8	V-E Day.
	SHAEF's Displaced Persons Executive sends an order to all military units stating, in part, that the care of displaced persons is a principal Allied objective.
	The first Soviet Army tanks reach Theresienstadt en route to Prague.

May 10	Soviet troops liberate the Stutthof concentration camp.
May 14	President Truman sends to General Eisenhower the eighth revision of Joint Chiefs of Staff order JCS 1067 that is to serve as the basic policy tool of U.S. occupation in Germany. JCS 1067 ordered the dissolution of the Nazi party; the demilitarization of Germany; control of the press, education, and communications; the decentralization of the German government; and the payment of reparations. In its final form it excluded the total dismantling of German industry sought by Secretary of the Treasury Henry MORGENTHAU, Jr.
May 18	Having visited the sites of Nazi concentration camps, Joseph Pulitzer, publisher and editor of the *St. Louis Post Dispatch*, addresses the Missouri legislature.
May 19	Influential film critic, playwright, and screenwriter James Agee, writing in *The Nation*, attacks the release to the American public of details of Nazi atrocities, claiming that "such propaganda"—even if true—is designed to make Americans equate all Germans with the few who perpetrated the crimes.
May 20	Joseph Pulitzer publishes an illustrated, 125-page pamphlet, *A Report to the American People*, in which he describes evidence of the atrocities he witnessed at Buchenwald and Dachau. In it he expresses his dismay that there are still Americans who say "this talk of atrocities is all propaganda."
May 21	In order to prevent the spread of typhus epidemics, British soldiers burn all the barracks in the former concentration camp at Bergen-Belsen. The site will be transformed into a DP camp.
May 23	Heinrich Himmler, chief of the SS, commits suicide after his capture by British forces.
May 27	In Munich, Jewish survivors celebrate liberation with a concert at Saint Ottilien convent.
May 29	Thirty-three days after U.S. troops liberated the town of Kaufbeuren, one child is killed in the local state hospital, thus becoming the last victim of the Nazi euthanasia killing program.
May 30	After negotiations lasting over a month, the British Cabinet reverses itself and approves a U.S. draft proposal for a trial of the Nazi leadership. This follows French General de Gaulle's agreement to a trial the previous month. The United States and the Soviet Union had long supported such trial.
Also in May	General Eisenhower as Supreme Commander of Allied Forces issues Proclamation No. 1, stating that all persons in occupied territory (Germany) must obey all orders of the Allied military government.
June 1	A delegation of the JEWISH BRIGADE starts arriving at DP camps. This is the first group from Palestine to establish contact with Jewish survivors.
	The first volume of *Surviving Remnant (She'erit Ha-peletah)*, listing the names and locations of Jewish survivors, is published by Rabbi Abraham Klausner.
	The forced repatriation of about 20,000 Russian Cossacks who had fought with the WEHRMACHT begins in the Drau Valley region of Austria, an act based on an Allied agreement to repatriate all pre-1939 Soviet nationals without exception. By June 7, approximately 35,000 Cossacks and their families are turned over to the Soviets.

June 2	The first AJJDC staff arrive to organize educational and welfare activities in the DP camps in Europe.
	Zionist pioneers in Germany establish "Kibbutz Buchenwald," an agricultural training facility for survivors. The first group of trainees leaves Buchenwald for Palestine in August.
June 6	SHAEF complains that Allied field commanders have ignored previous instructions to equate the status of displaced persons with that of persecuted people. It also orders that all DP children are to be transferred from Germany immediately, and that any person holding a card showing release from a concentration camp is entitled to admittance to a displaced persons camp.
June 7	Justice Jackson, Chief of Counsel for the United States in the Prosecution of Axis War Criminals, submits his report to President Truman.
June 8	520 orphaned Jewish children from Buchenwald enter France to become charges of the French government.
June 19	The U.S. War Department grants General Eisenhower limited authority to try war criminals.
June 20	The first congress of Zionists is held in Bavaria, in the American zone of occupation. The bylaws of the newly created UNION OF JEWISH SURVIVORS in the American Zone of Bavaria are adopted. The Union's main task is to represent the interests of displaced persons. The bylaws call for cooperation with the World Zionist Organization.
	An unofficial delegation of five soldiers from the 2d Battalion of the Jewish Brigade, headed by Aharon Hoter-Yishai and Rabbi Y. Lifschitz, enters the U.S. zone of occupied Germany. Their ostensible mission is to locate surviving members of their own families. They travel to Dachau, St. Ottilien, Landsberg, and Feldafing in southern Germany and Salzburg and Traunstein in western Austria. They organize the transportation of Jewish displaced persons from Germany and Austria to Italy and provide food, money, and transport via *Bet Aliya* centers in Italy for emigration to Palestine.
June 21	The U.S. Government authorizes UNRRA to continue to work with displaced persons in the U.S. occupation zone of Germany under the auspices of the UNRRA-SHAEF Agreement of November 1944 [see January 3 entry]. The British follow suit on June 28.
June 22	Prompted by reports of poor conditions in DP camps, President Truman agrees that Earl G. HARRISON, dean of the University of Pennsylvania Law School, head a commission to investigate the plight of displaced persons in Germany, with particular attention to be given to the situation of Jewish displaced persons.
June 26	Representatives from 51 nations sign the United Nations Charter in San Francisco.
June 27	The Soviet government agrees to allow 300,000 Polish Jews currently living in the Soviet Central Asian republics to emigrate to Palestine, provided that Arab states are in agreement. This was the result of negotiations among the "Big Three" at the Yalta Conference.

June 30	The exhibition "LEST WE FORGET" opens at the Library of Congress, Washington, D.C.
Also in June	A Soviet judicial commission investigates crimes committed at Sachsenhausen concentration camp.
	The first conference of liberated Jews in the British zone of occupied Germany takes place at Bergen-Belsen.
July 1	The AJJDC announces that it has distributed goods and relief parcels valued at $3,000,000 in Poland during the previous year.
	The Central Committee of Liberated Jews for the U.S. zone of occupied Germany and Austria, one of the earliest Jewish DP organizations, is created during a meeting of survivors at the DP camp in Feldafing.
July 2	U.S. officers enter the Kaufbeuren state hospital to discover "a wholesale extermination plant," one part of the Nazi euthanasia killing program that had continued to operate even after Germany's unconditional surrender.
July 4	It is announced in Berlin that Gemma LaGuardia Gluck, sister of the mayor of New York, has been found safe with her daughter and grandson. After their transfer from Ravensbrück to Kaiserdamm prison in Berlin in April, they had been liberated by Soviet troops. Since then they had been living with a German family in the city.
July 5	The Central Committee of Liberated Jews in Bavaria is officially established in Munich.
July 15	1,164 Jewish refugees from Britain, France, and Italy arrive in Haifa as part of the official quota of Jewish immigrants allowed under the British MANDATE in Palestine. The group includes 500 children formerly held in concentration camps.
July 16	The press is invited to the Grand Hotel in Bad Mondorf, Luxembourg, where the major defendants destined for the International Military Tribunal are being held.
	UNITED STATES FORCES, EUROPEAN THEATER (hereafter USFET) sets up Military Government Tribunals for war crimes trials.
July 17–August 2	The "Big Three"—President Truman, Marshal Stalin, and Prime Minister Churchill (who is succeeded by newly-elected Prime Minister Clement ATTLEE on 28 July)—meet at Potsdam, near Berlin.
July 20	The World Jewish Congress, meeting in London, appeals to the "Big Three" at the Potsdam Conference to remedy the poor conditions under which Jewish displaced persons are being held in Germany.
July 23	The trial of Marshal Pétain before the French High Court of Justice begins.
July 25	A conference of 94 Jewish DP delegates representing 40,000 Jewish survivors in the American and British zones of Germany and Austria meets at St. Ottilien, Munich, under the sponsorship of members of the Jewish Brigade. The next day, the conference meets in the beer hall where Hitler had staged the 1923 putsch; there they read a proclamation demanding that all liberated Jews be allowed to emigrate to Palestine.

July 28	The first British war crimes trial begins with the arraignment of Italian General Bellomo. He is convicted of killing escaped British prisoners of war and is executed on September 11, 1945.
July 29	Approximately 3,000 Jewish displaced persons leave Austria for Italy with hopes of being transported to Palestine.
July 31	349 UNRRA teams and 36 voluntary agency teams are working in DP camps in the western occupation zones of Germany.
Also in July	The DP camp in Feldafing, near Munich, becomes the first such camp holding only Jews. Hungarian prisoners held there previously are replaced by Jews from Dachau.

The Yiddish Theater of Belsen puts on its first post-liberation performance. The staff of the Central Committee of Liberated Jews of Bavaria publishes volumes of lists of Jewish displaced persons in German DP camps. |
| August 3 | A summary of the Harrison Report is sent from the War Department to General Eisenhower with a request to verify its conclusions: that conditions in DP camps must be improved, efforts to trace survivors be increased, separate camps for Jewish displaced persons be established, and Jewish displaced persons not be categorized solely by their nationality.

By this date, about 65 percent of all displaced persons have been repatriated from the American, British, and French occupation zones of Germany. Of the 6,340,000 displaced persons in these areas at the end of the war, 2,074,182 remain; Poles compose the largest group. |
| August 6 | The atomic bomb is dropped on Hiroshima.

Upon the conclusion of the Potsdam Conference, General Eisenhower issues his "Message to the German People" in the U.S. zone that spells out Allied plans for the occupation.

About 100,000 Czech nationals—virtually all the Czech displaced persons in the Allied areas of Europe—have been repatriated as of this date; 8,000 remain in Norway and almost 6,000 in France and Belgium. |
| August 7 | Rabbi Wise of the AMERICAN JEWISH CONGRESS cables General Eisenhower from the WORLD ZIONIST CONGRESS in London to ask for the assignment of a Jewish officer to the Civil Affairs Division of USFET to coordinate aid for Jewish displaced persons. Maj. Judah Nadich, an Army rabbi, is appointed on August 29. |
| August 8 | The London Agreement, establishing the INTERNATIONAL MILITARY TRIBUNAL (hereafter IMT) at Nuremberg and the Tribunal's charter, is signed by the four Allied powers: the United States, the French Republic, the United Kingdom of Great Britain and Northern Ireland, and the Union of Soviet Socialist Republics.

The COMBINED DISPLACED PERSONS EXECUTIVE of USFET issues one of the first statistical reports on casualties during the Holocaust. Of 400,000 people deported to Germany from France, Belgium, the Netherlands, and Norway, 234,000 were Jews. Fewer than 10,000 had been repatriated as of July 20. No mention was made of those Jews who were not to be repatriated. |

August 9	The atomic bomb is dropped on Nagasaki.
	British military government authorities issue a denial of the charges made earlier by the World Jewish Congress of poor conditions in DP camps in Germany. An investigation resulting from the charges find that those in the camps "were getting the best accommodations under the circumstances."
August 11	The first postwar anti-Jewish disturbances occur in Poland: several Jews are killed in Cracow at the instigation of right wing Polish groups.
August 13	The World Zionist Congress demands the admission of one million Jews to Palestine.
	The Soviet Union suggests assigning each of the counts in the IMT indictments to one of the four prosecution staffs. Thus the United States addresses the conspiracy charges and criminal organizations, the British the crimes against peace, the French the war crimes, and the Soviets the crimes against humanity.
August 15	Japan surrenders: V-J Day.
	Marshal Pétain is convicted and sentenced to death by the High Court of Justice with the proviso that the sentence should not be carried out because of his age. France's Provisional Government head de Gaulle later commutes his sentence to life imprisonment.
August 16	President Truman calls for the free and open Jewish settlement of Palestine "consistent with the maintenance of peace," reaffirming the position the U.S. had taken on the issue at the Potsdam Conference.
August 19	Rabbi Israel Goldstein, president of the Zionist Organization of America, announces that an estimated 100,000 Jewish displaced persons in the Allied occupation zones of Germany are prepared to immigrate immediately to Palestine.
August 20	Dr. Joseph Tannenbaum, president of the World Federation of Polish Jews, announces that a wave of POGROMS against Jews, particularly against the few returning from concentration camps, has begun in Poland. The most recent outbreak occurred in Cracow, where 2,000 returning Jews were attacked; 500 were besieged in a Jewish community house in the city. Such actions help swell the large numbers of Jews who leave eastern Europe for Germany beginning in the fall of 1945.
August 21	The International Committee for Transient Ex-Concentration Camp Inmates and Refugees is formed in Vienna by Bronislaw Teich. By the end of the year, more than 8,500 Jewish refugees from eastern Europe are assisted by this Committee, using the facilities of a former Jewish hospital.
	The *Dalin*, the first Jewish immigrant ship to travel to Palestine since the end of the war, leaves Bari, Italy, with 35 Jewish immigrants. They successfully land at Caesarea a week later.
August 22	General Eisenhower issues an order establishing separate camps for Jewish displaced persons, stating that Jewish displaced persons from former enemy countries are to be treated equally with those displaced persons from Allied countries. The order is initially misinterpreted in some American occupation areas, and Jewish displaced persons living outside DP camps are rounded up and placed in the new camps.

August 24	Richard Lang, a German architect, is convicted of blowing up a Jewish synagogue in Forchheim during the infamous *KRISTALLNACHT* pogrom of November 1938. He is sentenced to five years hard labor by one of the newly organized German courts, the first person to be tried and convicted for participation in this pogrom.
	Four trainloads of Jews from Poland, assembled by BRICHAH, the Jewish group organizing emigration to Palestine, are turned away from the border of the U.S. occupation zone of Germany on the orders of General Patton. The official explanation given for the order is that the transport had not been announced beforehand and that there is no room for any more Jews in the U.S. zone. This is one of the last times the U.S. military attempts to use force to stop Jews from entering the U.S. zone.
August 28	53 Yugoslav refugees, part of the group held at Fort Ontario since August 1944, set sail for home. They are the first sizeable group of refugees to be repatriated from Fort Ontario.
August 29	The list of defendants to be tried by the International Military Tribunal is published.
August 31	President Truman writes Prime Minister Attlee to demand the immediate immigration of 100,000 Jews to Palestine. The British reject this demand.
Summer–Autumn	Jewish Hospital and five synagogues reopen in Berlin. The weekly newspaper *Der Weg* (today *Berliner Allgemeine jüdische Wochenzeitung*) is founded.
September 2	The *Nettuno* sails from Italy with Jewish immigrants, landing successfully at Caesarea in Palestine on September 4.
September 4	A special war crimes tribunal in the Netherlands passes its first death sentence: J. Breedvelt is condemned for having betrayed a number of Jews to the Germans.
September 6	The Institute of Jewish Affairs announces that a survey on Jewish civilian casualties during the war found 5,700,000 Jewish civilians had been killed. This number includes only persons regarded as Jewish by their own communities, not those who may also have been classified as Jews by Axis governments.
September 7	The Combined Displaced Persons Executive announces that the two-millionth Soviet citizen has been repatriated from the American, British, and French occupation zones. Fewer than 60,000 Soviet displaced persons remain in the western zones as of this date. A total of approximately 4,800,000 displaced persons of all nationalities located in the western occupation zones have been repatriated to date; some 1,520,000 remain.
September 12	U.S. Attorney General Biddle is appointed as the American judge on the International Military Tribunal; Judge John Parker is appointed as alternate.
September 13	U.S. Army Colonel Leon JAWORSKI, judge advocate in the Hadamar trial, informs the War Crimes Branch of the Judge Advocate General that the prosecution's case is ready. Charges are served against the seven defendants on September 25.

September 15	Gen. Bedell Smith, Eisenhower's Chief of Staff, orders General Patton's 3d Army to remove armed guards from DP camps and eliminate the pass system and travel restrictions previously imposed on displaced persons in 3d Army's area of occupation. The guards are removed immediately, but the restrictions are eliminated only several weeks later after personal intervention by Eisenhower.
September 16	Major Nadich, Special Advisor on Jewish Affairs to USFET, makes his first report on the condition of Jewish displaced persons in Germany and Austria. Among his recommendations is that the AJJDC be allowed to work more closely in DP camps.
September 17	The Belsen Trial of Josef Kramer and 44 other defendants begins in Lüneburg, Germany, before a British military court. Three defendants are dropped from the proceedings, which last until November 17. General Eisenhower makes his first inspection tour of Jewish DP camps, attending a Yom Kippur service at the DP camp in Feldafing.
September 18	SS Lieutenant General (*Obergruppenführer*) Walter Schmitt is sentenced to death by a People's Court in Prague, Czechoslovakia, for crimes committed in Mauthausen, Schlossenburg, Ravensbrück, and Sachsenhausen concentration camps.
September 19	UNRRA estimates that there are currently 1,675,000 displaced persons in western Germany: 850,000 in the British zone, 150,000 in the French zone, and 675,000 in the American zone. The SS *Pietro* successfully lands 168 Jewish immigrants from Italy at Shefayim in Palestine. The ship returns to Italy carrying representatives of the Jewish Agency and Histadrut to work in DP camps.
September 20	General Eisenhower issues a memorandum on the treatment of displaced persons in the U.S. zone of Germany. The memorandum directs that the Germans themselves must provide the bulk of the resources needed for the care of displaced persons, including the requisitioning of housing for displaced persons; that displaced persons should serve as guards at DP camps; and that displaced persons should be given priority over Germans in employment by the occupation authorities.
September 23	The British Cabinet rejects demands to abrogate the WHITE PAPER OF 1939 on Palestine, offering instead the immigration of 1,500 Jews each month. President Truman states that he supports the Jewish Agency proposal to grant 100,000 immigration certificates for Palestine.
September 24	An anti-Jewish pogrom occurs in Topoliciany, Slovakia, during which 49 Jews are injured. Attacks spread to other localities, despite government attempts to punish those responsible.
September 29	The Harrison Report is released to the public in the United States. USFET reports that there are 293,000 displaced persons living in the western occupation zones of Germany who are "probably non-repatriable."
October 1	UNRRA "unofficially" takes control of displaced persons camps in the U.S. occupation zone of Germany.

| October 4 | The trial of Pierre Laval, premier of the Vichy government, before the French High Court of Justice begins. The defense lawyers initially boycott the proceedings, complaining of insufficient pre-trial examination. |

| October 5 | A verdict is reached in the first war crimes trial held in the Soviet occupation zone of Germany. In this trial, which began on September 30, three SS guards are sentenced to death for murdering fifty concentration camp inmates. Two other guards are acquitted. |

| October 6 | The Berlin Protocol is signed, reconciling discrepancies between the English, Russian, and French texts of the London Agreement [see August 8 entry] concerning the interpretation of the concept of crimes against humanity. |

The final draft of the IMT indictment is agreed upon and signed by the four prosecutors, including Justice Jackson for the United States. The original draft had been proposed on September 18 but was rejected by the U.S.; negotiations continued to date. The Soviets insisted on placing the Katyn Massacre of Polish soldiers in the indictment against the resistance of the other prosecution staffs, even though the Soviets had perpetrated the massacre themselves in 1940.

| October 7 | Gen. Mark Clark, commander of the U.S. occupation zone in Austria, states his intention that President Truman's orders to improve conditions in DP camps, following the publication of the Harrison Report, would be carried out in his area and given top priority. |

| October 8 | Start of the Hadamar Trial against Alfons Klein and six other defendants before a U.S. Military Commission in Wiesbaden. Colonel Jaworski leads the prosecution as judge advocate. The defendants, who operated the Hadamar euthanasia killing center, are charged with the murder of Polish and Russian slave laborers during 1944–45. The charge of killing German handicapped patients at Hadamar is not included in the indictment because it did not fall under the jurisdiction of the court. The trial lasts from October 8 to October 15. |

| October 9 | Vichy Premier Laval is sentenced to death by the High Court of Justice. A request for a new trial by the defense several days later is denied by General de Gaulle. Laval is shot on October 15, following a suicide attempt. |

| October 10 | The Allied prosecution staff for the upcoming trial before the IMT at Nuremberg completes the forty-eight page indictment against the defendants. |

A HAGANAH raid on the detention camp at ATHLIT in Palestine frees 208 illegal immigrants held there.

| October 11 | In response to the publication of the Harrison Report, Assistant Secretary of War John J. McCloy reports, "It is fantastic for anyone to say that their [displaced persons'] condition is the same as it was under Hitler except for the extermination policy." |

| October 12 | Gen. Anton Doestler is found guilty of ordering the execution of fifteen U.S. servicemen of the OSS's Operational Groups who had been captured during a commando mission in March 1944. He is sentenced to death by a U.S. military tribunal in Rome and executed on December 1. |

A meeting between British representatives of the War, Admiralty, Foreign, and Colonial Offices results in an order to British forces in the Middle East to stop illegal immigration to Palestine at ports of embarkation, on the high seas, and inside Palestinian waters.

October 15	Colonel Jaworski, judge advocate trying the seven Hadamar defendants, describes in his summation the killing of more than four hundred Russian and Polish prisoners. He adds that thousands of Germans were also killed, but that "it's up to German courts to prosecute for the other deaths."
	The first AJJDC representative, Philip Skorneck, arrives in Berlin with the task of facilitating the movement of Jews leaving eastern Europe and dealing with the transient camps created to handle them.
October 16	General Eisenhower responds to the Harrison Report's criticism of conditions in DP camps, stating "it is freely admitted that there is need for improvement."
October 17	The "Peleus" Trial begins in Hamburg: a British military tribunal sits in judgment of *Kapitanleutnant* Heinz Eck, a German submarine commander, tried for killing the survivors of a merchant ship. He is subsequently convicted and sentenced to death on October 20, and executed on November 23.
	As part of the Allied plan to house a portion of displaced persons in better conditions outside DP camps, the Office of Military Government for the greater Hessen area in the U.S. zone of occupation announces that all members of the Nazi party and its affiliates must vacate their homes to provide winter housing for displaced persons and other victims of Nazi persecution.
October 18–19	The Evangelical Church in Germany meets in Stuttgart with a delegation from the World Council of Churches. The German church leaders issue a public statement of repentance and moral guilt on October 19, subsequently known as the "Stuttgart Declaration of Guilt."
October 19	The International Military Tribunal formally indicts the Nuremberg defendants on four counts: crimes against peace, war crimes, crimes against humanity, and conspiracy to commit these crimes.
	Lord Halifax, British ambassador to the United States, and James Byrnes, U.S. Secretary of State, meet to discuss a British proposal to form a committee to study the plight of Jews in Europe and the possibilities for their immigration outside Europe. U.S. terms for the committee are accepted on October 24, and the committee is officially created on November 13.
October 20	New York State District Judge Simon Rifkind arrives in Germany after being appointed by President Truman as the Civilian Advisor on Jewish Affairs to General Eisenhower. He replaces Major Nadich in this capacity.
October 21	David Ben Gurion, chairman of the Jewish Agency, visits Landsberg DP camp on election day at the camp.
October 25	Robert Ley, former head of the German Labor Service and under indictment by the IMT, hangs himself in his cell in the Palace of Justice at Nuremberg.
October 29	The U.S. House of Representatives issues House Joint Resolution 264 favoring action by the United States in "restoring" Palestine as a Jewish homeland.
October 30	The CONTROL COUNCIL FOR GERMANY enacts Control Council Law No. 4 that regulates the reopening of German courts. The law dissolves the People's Court, all special and party tribunals, and prevents the reopening of the Reich Supreme Court. It also specifically excludes the German courts from dealing with Nazi war crimes, prohibiting them from judging crimes committed against Allied nationals.

November 1	UNRRA "unofficially" takes control of DP camps in the British occupation zone of Germany. On November 27 UNRRA and the British military government in Germany sign an agreement governing the responsibilities for displaced persons in the zone.
November 2	Judge Rifkind, Eisenhower's special adviser on Jewish Affairs, states that the problem of Jewish displaced persons in Europe will be insoluble unless their free emigration to Palestine is assured. This follows the judge's tour of five DP camps in the Munich area, where he found an overwhelming desire for immigration to Palestine.
November 7	As part of the plan to transfer control of DP camps to UNRRA, 212 DP camps holding 248,179 people in the occupation area of U.S. 3d Army are placed under UNRRA control. German authorities are responsible for an additional 180,257 displaced persons living outside camps. To date, the 3d Army has handled 1,456,740 displaced persons.
	Order is restored in Tripoli, Libya, by British troops after several days of anti-Jewish rioting in which 74 Jews were killed. This follows several days of anti-Jewish rioting in Cairo over Jewish immigration to Palestine.
November 13	British Foreign Secretary Ernest Bevin and the White House announce the creation of a joint commission to study the plight of Jews in Europe and the number of those wishing to emigrate to Palestine or elsewhere. This follows President Truman's letter to Prime Minister Attlee of August 31 in which he asked the Prime Minister to open immigration to Palestine for the thousands of Jewish displaced persons still in Europe.
	A Polish special criminal court opens proceedings in Lublin against Paul Hoffman, supervisor of the crematorium at MAJDANEK concentration camp. He is convicted of the mass murder of camp inmates the next day and is sentenced to death on December 23.
November 14	The first preliminary session of the International Military Tribunal takes place. Two more sessions are held prior to the official opening of the trial on November 20. A number of procedural issues are addressed during these sessions, including an unsuccessful attempt by the United States to substitute as defendant Alfred Krupp for his senile and ailing father Gustav, and the question of the missing Martin BORMANN, who is tried *in absentia*.
November 15	The trial of 40 officials of the Dachau concentration camp begins: 36 are convicted on December 14, and 23 are executed in May 1946, including the camp commandant and a physician convicted of killing up to 3,000 people in medical experiments.
November 16	General Eisenhower publishes a letter clarifying the nationality of all displaced persons. Jewish displaced persons are placed in a special category as non-repatriables.
	UNRRA agrees to take responsibility for tracing missing persons in a Central Tracing Bureau, operating in Germany and Austria.
November 17	The Belsen Trial ends with the conviction of 31 defendants, including Josef Kramer, the commandant of Bergen-Belsen and earlier of Birkenau. Death sentences are handed down to nine of the defendants, including Kramer.

November 20	First public session of the trial of the major war criminals opens before the IMT at Nuremberg. The 24,000-word indictment is read in rotation for two days by junior members of the prosecution staff. An IBM simultaneous translation system is used to translate into the four languages used in the proceedings: English, French, Russian, and German.

November 21

After the defendants before the IMT make their pleas to the charges—not guilty in all cases—the chief U.S. prosecutor, Justice Jackson, opens the prosecution's case with a compelling and emotional address describing the scope and depths of the crimes of the THIRD REICH.

Capt. Robert Marcus, a U.S. Army Air Force chaplain in Europe, charges that conditions in Jewish DP camps in Germany have recently deteriorated, following a short period of improvement after the publication of the Harrison Report.

At a mass meeting held at the German Museum in Munich, members of the Bavarian Jewish Federation protest British plans to create a commission to study Jewish problems.

November 22

The Greek cargo ship SS *Dimitrios*, later renamed the *Berl Katznelson*, leaves a Greek port with 211 immigrants, mostly Greek Jews, destined for Palestine. Upon reaching Palestine the ship is intercepted by the British, but approximately 200 passengers manage to land successfully at Shefayim with the help of the Haganah; the remainder are seized with the ship by the British.

November 25

U.S. forces turn back 450 Jews attempting to enter the U.S. occupation zone of Austria near Linz. They are returned to Vienna by the Russians. A demonstration against the action follows in a DP camp near Linz. The result is an "unofficial" policy under which Jews would be allowed to enter the U.S. zone as transients on a regularized basis to avoid overcrowding in DP camps. A similar policy is instituted the same month in Germany.

November 26

Gen. Joseph McNarney succeeds General Eisenhower as commander of USFET.

November 27

British occupation authorities agree to transfer the administration of DP camps in the British zone of Germany to UNRRA. The transfer is to begin on January 1, 1946, and would take about one month.

December 5

British authorities in Germany and Austria issue an occupation order prohibiting additional Jewish refugees from entering their zones. This is part of their policy of restricting immigration to Palestine since it is believed that such refugees would eventually try to immigrate there.

Dr. Lee Srole, leader of an UNRRA team working at the DP center in Landsberg, resigns because of conditions in the camp. He charges that overcrowding, underfeeding, and lack of adequate clothing and housing make conditions intolerable and ripe for the outbreak of epidemics. He adds that the U.S. Army has refused to face the problem of the "thousands of refugees fleeing for their lives from pogroms in Poland to the safe haven of DP centers in the American Zone of Germany." The next day, Lieut. Gen. Walter Bedell Smith, USFET chief of staff, inspects the DP camp in Landsberg. Although he believes that Dr. Srole's charges are exaggerated, he states that the U.S. Army policy regarding Jewish displaced persons in the U.S. zone would change from rescue to rehabilitation, preparing them for resettlement.

December 11	Thomas J. Dodd, executive trial counsel for the United States before the IMT, opens the U.S. case concerning slave and forced labor.
	A documentary film made expressly for the IMT, entitled "The Nazi Plan," is shown at the trial of the major war criminals. Lasting four hours, it recounts the history of the Nazi regime up to 1944.
December 13	At the trial of the major war criminals, Maj. William F. Walsh opens the U.S. case about the persecution of the Jews as related to war crimes and crimes against humanity.
December 14	At Nuremberg, the U.S. prosecution team presents evidence that the Nazis killed 6,000,000 Jews: 4,000,000 in various extermination camps, and 2,000,000 by other means.
December 16	Speaking at a national conference of the UNITED JEWISH APPEAL, Earl Harrison, author of the Harrison Report, states that despite claims of action after the publication of his report, the Jewish minority in Europe is still in the worst condition: "The actual need is for food and clothes and medicines and everything else that goes into everyday life."
December 17	CROWCASS [see April 14 entry] delivers "Wanted List No. 7" to the War Crimes Group, Judge Advocate General, USFET. It is characterized as the first "usable" list of war criminals to aid in their apprehension.
	The United States appropriates about $2.5 billion for the work of UNRRA.
December 20	The Control Council for Germany enacts Control Council Law No. 10 "to establish a uniform legal basis in Germany for the prosecution of war criminals and other similar offenders." Based on the Moscow Declaration of 1943 and the London Agreement of August 1945, the law recognizes four crimes: crimes against peace, war crimes, crimes against humanity, and membership "in categories of a criminal group or organization declared criminal by the International Military Tribunal." It regulates the apprehension, extradition, and trial of war criminals in the four zones of occupation. It also permits German courts, at the discretion of each zone's military authority, to deal with cases involving crimes committed by German nationals against other German nationals or stateless persons.
December 22	President Truman issues a directive to the State Department, the War Department, and several other government agencies to send representatives to Europe to establish facilities for hastening the emigration of the most destitute displaced persons, especially children, to the United States. The move is made under the existing immigration quotas and does not allow for additional immigrants to be admitted to the United States, but gives preference to displaced persons. The same order allows those refugees held at Fort Ontario who desire to remain in the United States to do so.
December 24	The SS *Andarta*, later renamed the *Hannah Senesh*, successfully lands 250 illegal Jewish immigrants in Palestine off Nahariya. The ship runs aground and is abandoned after the immigrants are safely taken off.
December 26	Rabbi Leo Baeck, a Berlin Jewish leader who had served as the president of the Association of German Jews and had been deported to Theresienstadt during the war, announces that only 4,000 of the 200,000 German Jews alive in 1939 are currently alive in Germany. He adds that only 3,000 of the 150,000 prewar Jewish population living in Austria remain.

December 28	UNRRA adopts the doctrine of "internal displacement" to broaden its powers to aid those people, mostly Jews, who left their native countries *after* the war ended. Until this time UNRRA could only aid those people deported during the war. The "internal displacement" category includes all those forced to move within their own countries during the war because of Nazi persecution, a criteria met by all Jews.
December 29	Gen. Friedrich Bernhardt, late commander of the German Second Tank Army, is sentenced to death by a Soviet tribunal for atrocities committed in the Bryansk area of Russia during the war. He is hanged the same day.
December 31	As of this date, approximately 5,675,000 displaced persons have been repatriated from the western occupation zones.
	UNRRA teams in Germany have charge of 227 assembly centers for displaced persons and assist the military with twenty-five others.
	In the second half of 1945 more than 33,000 Polish Jews leave Poland for Germany, in part because of persistent antisemitism.

GLOSSARY

Allies: The nations joined in the war against Germany and the other AXIS nations; included the United States, Great Britain, the Soviet Union, as well as the Free French, Polish, and Czech governments-in-exile.

AJJDC: see AMERICAN JEWISH JOINT DISTRIBUTION COMMITTEE.

American Jewish Congress (AJC): An affiliate of the WORLD JEWISH CONGRESS (WJC), created in 1932 and active from 1936. Under the leadership of the American Rabbi Stephen S. WISE, both the AJC and WJC attempted to alert the Allied governments and publics of the atrocities against European Jews, to stimulate action to force the Germans into abandoning the "FINAL SOLUTION," and to secure asylum for those European Jews able to escape.

American Jewish Joint Distribution Committee (AJJDC, the "Joint"): Founded November 27, 1914, from three separate commissions representing the three major trends in American Jewish life. In 1939, the AJJDC and the United Palestine Appeal joined efforts with the UNITED JEWISH APPEAL and, from 1939 to 1945, spent more than $78 million on relief and rescue efforts in Europe. Between 1945 and 1953, the AJJDC spent $34 million for food, clothing, and the rehabilitation of DISPLACED PERSONS.

Arrow Cross Party: Party of the Hungarian fascist movement founded in 1937 by Ferenc SZALASI.

Aryan: Originally, peoples speaking Indo-European languages. The Nazis perverted the term and proclaimed the Aryan "race" superior to all other racial groups. They considered those of Teutonic, that is, Germanic, background to be prime examples of Aryan stock. For the Nazis, the typical Aryan was blond, blue-eyed, and tall.

Aryanization: The expropriation of Jewish businesses and property by the German authorities as well as similar measures by other AXIS nations, including Romania and Slovakia.

"Asocial" elements: An umbrella category including the "work-shy," migrants, GYPSIES, homosexuals, pimps, prostitutes, and any person the German police thought unfit for civilian society. Many of those considered "asocial" were arrested by the CRIMINAL POLICE rather than by the GESTAPO. They were sent to CONCENTRATION CAMPS after December 1937 under new laws creating "preventive arrest" for prisoners in this category.

Athlit: Detention camp established by the British in 1939 near Haifa, PALESTINE, for Jews captured while trying to enter Palestine in violation of the immigration quotas set by the British WHITE PAPER OF 1939.

Attlee, Clement (1883–1967): English Labor Party politician and leader of the Opposition in Parliament after 1935. In 1943, having served as Dominions Secretary for nearly a year, he was named deputy prime minister in the Conservative cabinet of Prime Minister Winston S. CHURCHILL. In the July 1945 election that turned out the Conservative Party and Churchill, Attlee became prime minister, a post he held until the conservatives returned to power in 1951. Attlee thereafter led the Opposition in Parliament until his retirement in 1955.

Auschwitz (in Polish, Oswiecim): A camp complex in Upper Silesia. *Auschwitz I,* the main camp, was established in 1940 as a CONCENTRATION CAMP. *Auschwitz II* (also known as BIRKENAU) was the KILLING CENTER built by 1942. *Auschwitz III* (Monowitz, also known as Buna) was a LABOR CAMP for the I. G. FARBEN industries. Auschwitz ultimately had some 40 subsidiary camps. Auschwitz was liberated by the Soviet Army on January 27, 1945.

Axis: Alliance of Germany, Italy, and Japan created by a pact signed in Berlin on September 27, 1940, that divided the world into spheres of political interest. The founding member-states were later joined by Bulgaria, Croatia, Hungary, Romania, and Slovakia.

Badge, Jewish: Insignia worn by Jews in Germany and German-occupied territories, on Nazi orders, to distinguish them from the rest of the population. Most commonly it was a yellow Star of David with or without the word "Jew" in the local language; it sometimes was an armband imprinted with a Star of David.

Bergen-Belsen: A camp complex in Lower Saxony, northern Germany. Opened in 1940 as a prisoner-of-war camp for Belgian and French prisoners, in 1941 it was renamed Stalag 311 for about 20,000 Soviet POWs, 16,000–18,000 of whom died of epidemics, malnutrition, and exposure by 1942. The camp was renamed Bergen-Belsen in April 1943, and it became a camp for male and female Jews with foreign passports or visas who might be exchanged for German nationals held abroad. Between March 1944 and early 1945, it received incapacitated prisoners for possible exchange, prisoners with foreign visas from other camps, and large numbers of prisoners evacuated from the east. In the last months of the war, rapidly deteriorating conditions led to large-scale epidemics, starvation, and the deaths of thousands.

Bernadotte, Count Folke (1895–1948): Diplomat and humanitarian, nephew of King Gustav V of Sweden. As vice chairman of the Swedish Red Cross Association, he headed efforts to gain the release of thousands of Scandinavian concentration camp prisoners in 1945. Acquainted with prominent Axis and Allied officials, he arranged for the exchange of disabled and sick Allied and German soldiers in 1943 and 1944. He also became the intermediary for last-minute peace overtures from Heinrich HIMMLER to the western Allies. Bernadotte was assassinated while serving as a United Nations mediator in PALESTINE, apparently by remnants of the STERN GANG.

Bet Aliya (Hebrew for "illegal immigration"): Unofficial entry into PALESTINE during the time of the British MANDATE, usually with the aid of a ZIONIST organization.

Birkenau: The second, much larger section of the AUSCHWITZ camp, also known as Auschwitz II. Birkenau held the most prisoners of the Auschwitz complex and was known to be the most severe. Birkenau was the site of the Auschwitz KILLING CENTER's GAS CHAMBERS and crematoria. Birkenau was liberated by the Soviet Army on January 27, 1945.

Blockältester (German for "block elder"): The senior prisoner functionary within a barracks in a concentration camp.

Bormann, Martin (1900–1945): Joined the Nazi Party and the Storm Detachment (SA) in 1925; chief of the Party Chancellery after 1941. Bormann exercised considerable influence as Adolf HITLER's official secretary and close adviser. As a defendant *in absentia* before the INTERNATIONAL MILITARY TRIBUNAL, Bormann was found guilty of war crimes and crimes against humanity and sentenced to death. In 1972 Bormann's skeleton, showing signs of suicide by cyanide poisoning, was found in Berlin; he was officially declared dead in 1973.

Brichah (Hebrew for "escape"): An organization that, assisted by soldiers of the JEWISH BRIGADE, helped Jews fleeing POGROMS in postwar eastern Europe into the western zones of occupied Germany and then on to PALESTINE.

Buchenwald: One of the first major CONCENTRATION CAMPS, opened in 1937 on the Ettersberg hillside overlooking Weimar, Germany. The first German and Austrian Jewish prisoners arrived in 1938; German and Austrian GYPSY prisoners were deported there after July 1938. During the war, some 65,000 of Buchenwald's quarter-million prisoners perished; others died in its more than 130 satellite LABOR CAMPS. Buchenwald was one of the few major camps whose prisoners rebelled in the days preceding liberation by units of the U.S. Army on April 11, 1945.

Bund: A Jewish, socialist, non-ZIONIST labor and educational organization founded in Vilna in 1897 and active mainly in Poland between the two world wars.

Byelorussia (also Belorussia or White Russia): A territory divided between Poland and the U.S.S.R. between the two world wars. On the eve of the German occupation in June 1941, the Jewish population was 1,075,000 (670,000 in western Byelorussia, 405,000 in eastern Byelorussia). Thousands of Byelorussian Jews, Gypsies, and disabled were killed by the EINSATZGRUPPEN in 1941–42. A second wave of mass murder began in spring 1942 and ended with the virtual annihilation of the Jews of western Byelorussia.

Central Office for Reich Security (*Reichssicherheitshauptamt*; RSHA): Nazi administrative office formed in September 1939 from the union of the SS and the SECURITY POLICE (the latter included the GESTAPO and the CRIMINAL POLICE).

Chelmno (in German, Kulmhof): KILLING CENTER in incorporated western Poland (the *Wartheland*) that operated from December 1941 to March 1943 and again after April 1944 when it reopened during the liquidation of the Lodz ghetto. At Chelmno, the SS—using special mobile gas vans—killed more than 320,000 Jews from Lodz and Poznan provinces as well as about 5,000 Austrian Gypsies incarcerated in the Lodz ghetto.

Churchill, Sir Winston (1874–1965): British prime minister during most of World War II (May 1940–July 1945) and again after the war (1951–1955).

Collaboration: Cooperation between citizens of an occupied country and its occupiers. There were Nazi collaborators in all occupied countries.

Combined Displaced Persons Executive (CDPX): Organization set up to coordinate policy concerning DISPLACED PERSONS in the American, British, and French zones of occupied Germany upon the dissolution of SHAEF on July 13, 1945. (The Soviets claimed to have no DP problems within their occupation zone). The CDPX was dissolved on October 1, 1945, when displaced persons became the concern of the military commanders in each occupation zone.

Concentration camp: Place of imprisonment to which political and religious dissidents and ethnic and racial undesirables are sent, usually without judicial process. Before the end of World War II, the Germans set up more than one hundred major concentration camps with several thousand satellite LABOR CAMPS.

Confessing Church (in German, *Bekennende Kirche*): Protestant church founded by Martin Niemöller, Dietrich Bonhoeffer, Karl Barth, and Eberhard Bethge that confronted the Nazi-organized "German Christian" movement with its declaration that Christianity was incompatible with the Nazi theory of the "total state."

Control Council for Germany: Governing body created after the AXIS surrender to deal with matters for the whole of Germany after Germany was divided into zones and its capital city, Berlin, divided into sectors under the jurisdiction of the four Allied powers. In practice, however, each occupying power administered its zone independently. Nevertheless, the Control Council did play a significant role in the denazification of Germany.

Criminal Police (*Kriminalpolizei; Kripo*): The German detective forces charged with investigating non-political crimes. Together with the GESTAPO, they formed the SECURITY POLICE. In 1939, the Criminal Police became Department V of the CENTRAL OFFICE FOR REICH SECURITY.

Croatia: Fascist puppet state in Yugoslavia established with German encouragement in April 1941 (see USTACHI). Among its population of 6.3 million were 40,000 Jews and 30,000 Gypsies; at least 80 percent of the Croatian Jews and the overwhelming majority of the Gypsies were killed.

Dachau: The first CONCENTRATION CAMP, opened on March 20, 1933, near Munich, Germany. Initially only known political opponents were interned at Dachau; gradually other groups were incarcerated there. Although a gas chamber was installed at the site in 1942, most historians agree it was never used to gas inmates; thousands of prisoners selected for execution at Dachau were transferred to Hartheim EUTHANASIA facility near Linz or to other camps for gassing. Even without a systematic extermination program, there were 31,591 registered deaths among its 206,206 registered prisoners. The total number of deaths at Dachau, including the victims of individual and mass executions and the final DEATH MARCHES, will never be known. Units of the U.S. Army liberated Dachau on April 29, 1945.

Death camps: see KILLING CENTERS.

Death marches: Forced EVACUATIONS of concentration camp prisoners who were capable of walking, conducted upon the approach of Allied forces to a camp.

de Gaulle, Charles (1890–1970): General in the French Army; leader of the Free French movement after refusing to accept the collaborationist government of VICHY and fleeing to London. Following the liberation of Paris in August 1944, de Gaulle became head of the Provisional Government. He returned as president of the Fifth Republic in May 1958, a post he retained until his resignation in 1969.

Deportation: The forced relocation of Jews, Gypsies, and other "undesirables" from their homes to different localities, usually to GHETTOS or Nazi CONCENTRATION CAMPS, LABOR CAMPS, or KILLING CENTERS.

Displaced Person (DP): A survivor of a CONCENTRATION or LABOR CAMP. Millions of displaced persons were encountered by the ALLIES when they entered the German Reich; most were REPATRIATED within the first four months of the war's end.

Dönitz, Karl (1891–1980): Supreme Commander of the German Navy whom Hitler named to be his successor. As a defendant at the INTERNATIONAL MILITARY TRIBUNAL, he was found guilty of crimes against peace and war crimes, and sentenced to 10 years in prison. Dönitz was released in 1956.

Dora-Mittelbau: Camp established near Nordhausen in the Harz Mountains in August 1943 as a subsidiary of the BUCHENWALD concentration camp. Originally named Dora, the camp for men provided labor for the production of V-2 rockets in underground factories. Dora became independent in November 1944 and was renamed Mittelbau. Dora-Mittelbau was liberated on April 11, 1945.

DP: See DISPLACED PERSON.

Eichmann, Adolf (1906–1962): SS lieutenant colonel and head of IVb4, the Jewish department of the CENTRAL OFFICE FOR REICH SECURITY. Eichmann was instrumental in implementing the "FINAL SOLUTION," organizing transports of Jews from all over Europe to the KILLING CENTERS. Arrested at the end of World War II in the American zone of Germany, Eichmann escaped to Latin America, where he went underground and disappeared.

In 1960, members of the Israeli Secret Service discovered and kidnapped him in Argentina and covertly took him to Israel for trial. He was tried in Jerusalem (April–December 1961), convicted, sentenced to death, and executed in 1962.

Einsatzgruppen: Mobile units of the SECURITY POLICE and SS SECURITY SERVICE that followed the German armies into the Soviet Union in June 1941. The four *Einsatzgruppen* (A,B,C, and D) in the U.S.S.R. and the Baltic, subdivided into *EINSATZKOMMANDOS*, were to kill all Jews as well as Soviet commissars, the handicapped, institutionalized psychiatric patients, and GYPSIES. They were supported by units of the uniformed German Order Police and often used local auxiliaries (Ukrainian, Latvian, Lithuanian, and Estonian volunteers) and occasionally German army troops. The victims, including at least one million Jews, were executed by mass shootings and buried in unmarked mass graves; the bodies were later dug up and burned to disguise all traces of what had occurred.

Einsatzkommando: Subunit of an *EINSATZGRUPPE*.

Eisenhower, Dwight D. (1890–1969): Military leader and 34th president of the United States. Eisenhower commanded the Allied forces in Europe (SHAEF) that liberated the CONCENTRATION and forced LABOR CAMPS, several of which he visited soon thereafter. After the war Eisenhower's command of U.S. forces in Europe in part addressed the REPATRIATION of the millions of DISPLACED PERSONS in Germany.

Euthanasia: Nazi euphemism for the deliberate killing of the institutionalized physically, mentally, and emotionally handicapped to "improve" the quality of the German "race." The euthanasia program began in 1939 with German nationals as the first victims; the program was extended to the eastern occupied territories in 1940.

Evacuation: Nazi euphemism for deportation.

Extermination camps: See KILLING CENTERS.

"Final Solution": In German, *"die Endlösung der Judenfrage in Europa,"* or "the final solution of the Jewish question in Europe." Nazi code name for the physical extermination of European Jews.

Flossenbürg: CONCENTRATION CAMP for men opened in May 1938 in northern Bavaria, Germany.

Föhrenwald: DISPLACED PERSONS camp located near Ingolstadt, Bavaria, created in the fall of 1945. One of the largest of Jewish DP camps housing a large population of orthodox Jews, Föhrenwald was the last DP camp in Germany, closing only in 1957.

Fort Ontario (Oswego, New York): The site of a Temporary Refugee Shelter used by the U.S. WAR REFUGEE BOARD after June 1944. Fort Ontario was a token action taken by President ROOSEVELT, at the time in the midst of a reelection, to bring refugees from Europe to safe havens in the United States. Only 1,000 refugees—many of whom were Jews from areas that had already been liberated—arrived in the United States, and they were to be returned after the war.

14f13: A continuation of OPERATION T4, the Nazi program to exterminate Germany's mentally and physically handicapped. In the spring of 1941, Heinrich HIMMLER gave orders to extend the so-called EUTHANASIA program to concentration camp inmates who were sick or unable to work. Selection for this extermination campaign was rarely discriminating; seemingly healthy criminals, political prisoners, and Jewish inmates were also killed by gassing or lethal injection at the Sonnenstein, Bernberg, and Hartheim euthanasia facilities.

Frank, Hans (1900–1946): Joined Nazi party and SA ("Storm Detachment") in 1923 and was the chief Nazi jurist, having founded the Reich Legal Office of the Nazi party in 1930. He served as administrative head of occupied Poland from 1939 to 1945. As a defendant at the INTERNATIONAL MILITARY TRIBUNAL, he was found guilty of war crimes and crimes against humanity, and sentenced to death by hanging.

Frick, Wilhelm (1877–1946): Former Minister of the Interior and Protector of occupied Bohemia and Moravia. As a defendant at the INTERNATIONAL MILITARY TRIBUNAL, he was found guilty of crimes against peace, war crimes, and crimes against humanity, and sentenced to death by hanging.

Fritzsche, Hans (1900–1953): Chief of the German Propaganda Ministry's Radio Division. As a defendant at the INTERNATIONAL MILITARY TRIBUNAL, he was found not guilty of any of the charges and released.

Führer: "Leader," Adolf Hitler's title as chancellor and head of state in Nazi Germany.

Funk, Walther (1890–1960): President of the Reichsbank. As a defendant at the INTERNATIONAL MILITARY TRIBUNAL, he was found guilty of crimes against peace, war crimes, and crimes against humanity, and sentenced to life imprisonment. He was released in 1957 due to illness.

Gas chamber: Sealed room at a KILLING CENTER into which Jewish and other prisoners were crowded and murdered by released poison gas (ZYKLON B at BIRKENAU and MAJDANEK) or by carbon monoxide (at the other killing centers).

Gauleiter: Nazi party head of a *Gau*, the principal territorial unit in the Reich during the Nazi period.

Genocide: The systematic killing of a nation or race of people. The term was devised and first applied to the goal of the Nazi's "FINAL SOLUTION."

Gestapo (abbreviation of *Geheime Staatspolizei*, German for "Secret State Police"): Established in Prussia in 1933; by 1936 its authority extended throughout Germany. The Gestapo and the CRIMINAL POLICE together constituted Nazi Germany's SECURITY POLICE.

Ghetto: Compulsory "Jewish Quarters" established mostly in occupied eastern Europe (Lodz, Warsaw, Vilna, Riga, Minsk, etc.), where all Jews from the city and its surrounding area were forced to reside. The Nazis revived the medieval term "ghetto" to describe these poor sections of a city that were enclosed by barbed wire or walls and sealed so that no one could leave. They were characterized by overcrowding, disease, starvation, and heavy labor. Several ghettos (Warsaw, Lodz, and Bialystok) also housed Gypsies deported from surrounding regions and from western Europe. All the ghettos were eventually dissolved and the Jews were deported and murdered.

Globocnik, Odilo (1904–45): SS major-general appointed by HIMMLER as SS and Police Leader in Lublin, occupied Poland, who established the KILLING CENTERS of Belzec, Sobibor, Treblinka, and Majdanek as chief of Operation Reinhard (1942–1943). He also established the San Sabba CONCENTRATION CAMP and KILLING CENTER in Trieste as HIGHER SS AND POLICE LEADER for the Adriatic Coast (1943–1945). Arrested by Allied troops in Austria, he committed suicide in May 1945.

Glücks, Richard (1889–?): Joined the SS in 1932 and the Nazi party in 1933; became Inspector of Concentration Camps and Commander of Death Head units in 1939; promoted to SS Major General in 1943. After 1944, Glücks headed the SS CENTRAL OFFICE FOR ECONOMY AND ADMINISTRATION. Glücks disappeared in 1945.

Goebbels, Josef (1897–1945): Minister of Propaganda in Nazi Germany and close associate of Hitler. On May 1, 1945, Goebbels and his wife took their own lives and those of their six children.

Goldmann, Nahum (1895–1982): Statesman and ZIONIST leader. Along with Stephen WISE, he was the moving spirit in the organization of the WORLD JEWISH CONGRESS and became chairman of its executive board in 1936. Goldmann took an active and sometimes decisive part in the diplomatic and public relations activities to bring about the establishment of the state of Israel. He was largely responsible for initiating negotiations with postwar Germany and Austria to pay reparations to Israel and indemnifications for Nazi victims.

Göring, Hermann (1893–1946): Early associate of Hitler; responsible for the Nazi rearmament program (which utilized forced conscript labor from the CONCENTRATION CAMPS), and the creation of the German air force (*LUFTWAFFE*). He was the virtual dictator of the Nazi German economy and was responsible for Germany's air war. On July 31, 1941, Göring directly authorized Reinhard Heydrich to organize the "FINAL SOLUTION." As a defendant at the INTERNATIONAL MILITARY TRIBUNAL, he was found guilty of conspiracy to commit and of committing crimes against peace, war crimes, and crimes against humanity. Sentenced to death, he committed suicide hours before his scheduled hanging.

Gross-Rosen: CONCENTRATION CAMP opened in August 1940 for Polish male prisoners in Lower Silesia. Initially a subsidiary of SACHSENHAUSEN, by May 1941 Gross-Rosen became an independent concentration camp. On February 13, 1945, Gross-Rosen was liberated by the Soviet Army.

Gunskirchen: An assembly camp near the town of Wels in Upper Austria for Jewish prisoners from MAUTHAUSEN concentration camp. Gunskirchen opened in March 1945; by the end of April 1945, 17,000–20,000 inmates were crowded into the tiny compound. Food and water were in appallingly low supply; as epidemics of typhus and dysentery ran rife, the mortality rate soared. Units of the U.S. Third Army liberated Gunskirchen on May 5, 1945.

Gypsies: Today considered a pejorative collective term for Roma and Sinti, a nomadic people believed to have come originally from northwest India, which they left for Persia in the first millennium A.D. They became divided into five main groups that are still extant. Traveling mostly in small caravans, Gypsies first appeared in western Europe in the fifteenth century; during the next century, they spread to every country of Europe. Alternately tolerated and persecuted since that time, they were defined by the Nazis because of their race as ASOCIALS or "work shy" and thus considered enemies of the state and relentlessly persecuted. Approximately 500,000 Gypsies are believed to have perished in Nazi CONCENTRATION CAMPS and KILLING CENTERS.

Hadamar: Site of a psychiatric hospital founded in 1906 and renamed as State Psychiatric Hospital and Sanitorium in 1933. From 1941 to 1945 the hospital served OPERATION T4 as a EUTHANASIA center, where more than 11,000 people were killed.

Haganah: Underground military organization founded in 1920 of the *Yishuv*, the Jewish community in PALESTINE.

Harrison, Earl G. (1899–1955): Former U.S. Commissioner for Immigration and U.S. representative to the Intergovernmental Committee on Refugees; dean of the law school at the University of Pennsylvania in 1945. President Truman appointed Harrison, at the request of U.S. Treasury Secretary Henry MORGENTHAU, to head a committee investigating the conditions of DISPLACED PERSONS in liberated Europe in the summer of 1945. The report of this committee, the Harrison Report, bears his name.

Hess, Rudolf (1894–1987): Deputy to Adolf HITLER, head of the Party Chancellory until 1941, and member of the Council for Reich Defense. As a defendant at the INTERNATIONAL MILITARY TRIBUNAL, he was found guilty of conspiracy to commit and of committing crimes against peace, and was sentenced to life imprisonment. He died in prison at age 93, reportedly hanging himself with an electrical cord.

High Court of Justice [France]: Court created by General Charles DE GAULLE by a decree of November 21, 1944, specifically to try Marshal Henri PÉTAIN, his ministers, and high officials of the VICHY government who ruled France during the German occupation. The court consisted of three judges and twenty-four jurors.

Higher SS and Police Leader (*Höherer SS- und Polizeiführer*): Heinrich HIMMLER's personal representative for the coordination of all SS and police offices and units in a region.

Himmler, Heinrich (1900–1945): Reich Leader of the (black-shirted) SS, the elite Nazi party paramilitary organization Himmler made independent of the brown-shirted SA (Storm Detachment). Himmler presided over a vast empire, including all SS formations, the *WAFFEN-SS*, all police forces, all CONCENTRATION and LABOR CAMPS and their Death Head guard units, the SS SECURITY SERVICE (SD), and the various offices for the resettlement of ethnic Germans. In 1943, he also became Minister of the Interior. He was the senior SS leader responsible for the implementation of the "FINAL SOLUTION" and told senior SS officers in 1943 that he was implementing Hitler's orders; in late 1944, he ordered an end to the gassings. Early in 1945, with the war turning against Germany, he attempted to negotiate with the Allies. Himmler was captured by British troops, but he committed suicide before trial and sentencing.

Hitler, Adolf (1889–1945): Nazi party leader, 1919–45, and German Chancellor, 1933–45. Hitler committed suicide in a Berlin bunker as the Soviet Army was conquering the city in April 1945.

Horthy, Miklos (1868–1957): Regent, that is, leader, of Hungary from 1920 to 1944. After the German occupation of Hungary in March 1944, Horthy appointed a Hungarian government which authorized the deportation of nearly 500,000 Hungarian Jews; in July 1944, Horthy halted the deportations. He was deposed by the Nazis on October 15, 1944.

Höss, Rudolf (1900–1947): Member of the Nazi party since 1922, served a prison sentence for a political murder from 1923–28, joined the SS in 1933 and was promoted in 1942 to SS Lieutenant Colonel. Höss was commandant of the AUSCHWITZ concentration camp (1940–43 and summer 1944) and chief of Department D, the Inspectorate for Concentration Camps, of the SS CENTRAL OFFICE FOR ECONOMY AND ADMINISTRATION (1943–45). Sentenced to death in Poland, Höss was hanged at Auschwitz in 1947.

Hull, Cordell (1871–1955): U.S. Secretary of State, 1933–44. Hull declined to get involved in Germany's "internal affairs" and opposed any relaxation of the United States' immigration laws and regulations, thus limiting U.S. ability to aid the Jews of Europe. Hull worked on establishing the postwar United Nations, for which he received the Nobel Prize in 1945.

I. G. Farben (IGF): Powerful German industrial conglomerate comprising eight leading German chemical manufacturers that benefitted enormously from Hitler's Four-Year Plan to revitalize Germany's economy for war. Farben established an installation near AUSCHWITZ known as Buna that took advantage of the cheap conscript labor there. ZYKLON-B gas, used in Auschwitz for the killing of Jews, was a product of DEGESCH, a firm in which IGF had a major share.

IMT: See INTERNATIONAL MILITARY TRIBUNAL.

International Military Tribunal (IMT): Court established by the London Agreement of August 8, 1945, signed by the four Allied powers: the United States (Justice Robert H. Jackson), the French Republic (Judge Robert Falco), the United Kingdom of Great Britain and Northern Ireland (Lord Chancellor Sir William Jowitt), and the Union of Soviet Socialist Republics (Major General I. T. Nikitchenko and Professor A. N. Trainin). Following the principles of the Moscow Declaration of 1943, the Tribunal, which opened in Berlin but subsequently sat at Nuremberg, tried 21 war criminals whose offenses had no specific geographical location: Karl DÖNITZ, Hans FRANK, Wilhelm FRICK, Hans FRITZSCHE, Walter FUNK, Hermann GÖRING, Rudolf HESS, Alfred JODL, Ernst KALTENBRUNNER, Wilhelm KEITEL, Constantin von NEURATH, Franz von PAPEN, Erich RAEDER, Joachim von RIBBENTROP, Alfred ROSENBERG, Fritz SAUCKEL, Hjalmar SCHACHT, Baldur von SCHIRACH, Arthur SEYSS-INQUART, Albert SPEER, Julius STREICHER. Martin BORMANN was tried *in absentia* as the twenty-second defendant. Two additional men never came to trial: Robert Ley, head of the German Labor Service, was indicted but committed suicide on the eve of the trial; and Gustav Krupp von Bohlen und Halbach, head of the Krupp industrial conglomerate, was found to be too senile to stand trial. The Tribunal also tried and ruled on the criminality of eight Nazi party and German government organizations: Reich Cabinet, Leadership Corps of Nazi Party, SS, SECURITY SERVICE (SD), SA, GESTAPO, General Staff, and the Armed Forces (WEHRMACHT) High Command.

IVb4: Jewish Office headed by Adolf EICHMANN within the CENTRAL REICH SECURITY OFFICE. IVb4 oversaw the deportation of Jews to the KILLING CENTERS as part of the "FINAL SOLUTION."

Jackson, Robert: (1892–1954), Pennsylvania-born jurist who became an assistant attorney general (1936), solicitor general (1938), and attorney general (1940) under President Franklin D. ROOSEVELT. In 1941, Roosevelt appointed Jackson to the U.S. Supreme Court. From 1945 to 1946, Jackson served as chief U.S. prosecutor at the INTERNATIONAL MILITARY TRIBUNAL (Nuremberg Trial), about which he reported in his book *The Nuremberg Case* (1947).

Jaworski, Leon (1905–82): American jurist and early war crimes trial prosecutor. A respected corporate lawyer in peacetime, Jaworski served during the war as chief of Investigations and Examinations Divisions of the U.S. War Crime Branch. Following the war, Jaworski became chief of the War Crimes Trial Section in the American zone of occupied Germany and prosecuted a number of early war crimes trials, including the HADAMAR trial. Jaworski would later gain fame in the 1970s as a Watergate Special Prosecutor.

Jehovah's Witnesses: American religious sect organized in Germany as the *Internationale Bibelforscher Vereinigung* (International Bible Student's Association). Although outlawed in several German states beginning in 1933, it was only when the Witnesses refused to use the *Heil Hitler* salute and, after 1935, to serve in the army that they were seen as enemies of the Nazi state. This led to the first wave of arrests and imprisonment in CONCENTRATION CAMPS in 1936 and 1937. At all times, the Witnesses in the concentration camps were a relatively small group of prisoners (not exceeding several hundred per camp), mostly of German nationality; after 1939, Witnesses from Austria, Belgium, Czechoslovakia, the Netherlands, Norway, and Poland were arrested and deported to various concentration camps. About 10,000 Witnesses were imprisoned by the Germans; of these about 2,500–5,000 died.

Jewish Brigade: British Army unit in which some 5,000 Jews from PALESTINE served between its formation on September 20, 1944, and its disbanding in July 1946. The Jewish Brigade fought in the final Allied offensive in Italy in April 1945. The World Zionist Organization offered the British government the full cooperation of the Jewish people in the war effort against Nazism. After reports of the fate of Jews in occupied Europe became known, it seemed unjustifiable to deny the Jews the right to fight their oppressors. As a result, some 30,000 Jews in Palestine volunteered to serve in the British army between 1939–46.

Jodl, Alfred (1890–1946): Chief of Operations Staff, German Armed Forces (WEHRMACHT). As a defendant at the INTERNATIONAL MILITARY TRIBUNAL, he was found guilty of conspiracy to commit and of committing crimes against peace, war crimes, and crimes against humanity, and sentenced to death by hanging.

Juden: German for "Jews."

Kaddish: A traditional Hebrew prayer for the dead recited by Jewish mourners.

Kaltenbrunner, Ernst (1903–46): Head of the CENTRAL OFFICE FOR REICH SECURITY after the 1942 death of Reinhard Heydrich. Kaltenbrunner played an important role in implementing the "FINAL SOLUTION" as well as the EUTHANASIA program. As a defendant at the INTERNATIONAL MILITARY TRIBUNAL, he was found guilty of war crimes and crimes against humanity, and sentenced to death by hanging.

Kapo: In popular language of the era, a generic term for all inmate functionaries. Although the origin of the term is not fully known, the word probably came from the Latin *capo*, meaning "head," and was probably introduced to DACHAU by Italian workers in the 1930s.

Kasztner, Rezso (Rudolf *or* Israel; 1906–57): Journalist, lawyer, and ZIONIST leader who worked under Otto KOMOLY in the aid and rescue of Jews in Hungary. After the war, Kasztner was brought to Nuremberg to help investigators in their work with Nazi criminals. Kasztner testified in favor of Nazis who had shown some mercy toward Jews near the end of the war. He was murdered by nationalist extremists.

Keitel, Wilhelm (1882–1946): Chief of the Armed Forces (WEHRMACHT) High Command (1938–45) and general field marshal. Keitel signed many orders which affected prisoners of war and civilians in occupied territories, including the infamous "Night and Fog Decree" (1941) under which "enemies" vanished without a trace. On May 8, 1945, Keitel signed Germany's unconditional surrender. As a defendant at the INTERNATIONAL MILITARY TRIBUNAL, he was found guilty of conspiracy to commit and of committing crimes against peace, war crimes, and crimes against humanity, and sentenced to death by hanging.

Killing centers: Camps built to kill Jews and other "enemies of the German nation." The killing centers included Belzec, Chelmno, Sobibor, and Treblinka, as well as killing sections of AUSCHWITZ and MAJDANEK concentration camps.

Komoly, Otto (also called Nathan Kahn; 1892–1945): Hungarian Jewish leader and active ZIONIST; elected deputy chairman of the Hungarian Zionist Federation in 1940. Komoly took part in the efforts to smuggle Jewish refugees into Hungary that continued until German occupation in March 1944. As head of Section A of the International RED CROSS in Hungary, the section assigned to assist Jewish children, Komoly set up children's houses under international protection. Shortly before the Red Army liberated Budapest in February 1945, Komoly was executed by the ARROW CROSS, apparently for his rescue activities.

Kristallnacht (German for "Crystal Night," also called "Night of Broken Glass"): The organized attack against synagogues and Jewish stores in Germany and Austria during the night of November 9–10, 1938, ordered by Reinhard Heydrich, chief of the SECURITY SERVICE (SD). The name comes from the smashed window glass that littered the streets.

Labor camp: A Nazi CONCENTRATION CAMP in which the prisoners were used as forced conscript labor.

Landsberg: One of the subcamps of DACHAU concentration camp whose prisoners were slave laborers for Albert SPEER's late-war program to build airplane factories underground, protected from Allied air attacks. American troops arrived at Landsberg on April 27, 1945; the prisoners had been evacuated to Dachau the previous week. After the war, Landsberg became a DISPLACED PERSONS camp for approximately 6,000 people, 5,000 of whom were Jews.

"Lest We Forget" (June 30–July 14, 1945): An exhibition containing "life size photo murals of German atrocity pictures" at the Library of Congress, Washington, D.C., sponsored by the Library of Congress, the *Washington Evening Star,* and the *St. Louis Post Dispatch.* More than 29,000 visitors viewed the exhibition during its first five days. The exhibition subsequently traveled to Boston, Cleveland, and twenty towns in Illinois and Missouri under the auspices of the Office of War Information (OWI) and the *St. Louis Post Dispatch.*

Luftwaffe: The German Air Force during World War II, headed by Hermann GÖRING.

Majdanek (also Maidanek): Nazi CONCENTRATION CAMP, LABOR CAMP, and KILLING CENTER built in October 1941 near Lublin, in eastern Poland. Majdanek was liberated by the Soviet Army in July 1944; one of the first war crimes trials was held there in October 1944.

Mandate: See PALESTINE, BRITISH MANDATE OF.

Mauthausen: A CONCENTRATION CAMP for men opened in August 1938 near Linz, Austria. Established to exploit the nearby stone quarries, it was classified by the SS as a camp of utmost severity, and conditions there were brutal even by concentration camp standards. Many prisoners were killed by being pushed from 300 foot cliffs into the quarries. Mauthausen was liberated on May 6, 1945.

Mengele, Josef (1911–77): Member of the Storm Detachment (SA; 1933–34), the Nazi party and SS (after 1938), and promoted to SS Captain in 1943. Wounded while serving in the *WAFFEN SS* medical corps, he was transferred to the AUSCHWITZ concentration camp in 1943. As senior SS physician at Auschwitz-Birkenau from 1943 to 1944, he conducted medical experiments on twins. In 1985, the corpse of a Wolfgang Gerhard who had died in Brazil in a swimming accident in 1979 was identified by forensic pathologists as Mengele's.

Mischlinge (German for "individuals of mixed race"): Nazi term for persons having one or two Jewish or Gypsy grandparents. In 1943, German policy proposed to deport or sterilize many Germans of mixed Jewish or Gypsy ancestry and to kill or sterilize part-Jewish and part-Gypsy children in Germany. Most *Mischlinge* survived the war because the "FINAL SOLUTION" was applied only to full Jews.

Monowitz (also known as Buna): A LABOR CAMP at AUSCHWITZ (Auschwitz III) for the I. G. FARBEN industries.

Morgenthau, Henry, Jr. (1891–1967): U.S. Secretary of the Treasury from 1934 to 1945, and the highest Jewish official in the Roosevelt administration. He used his influence to encourage rescue efforts by the United States. In January 1944 Morgenthau played a major role in the establishment of the WAR REFUGEE BOARD. His proposed policy for U.S. occupation in Germany called for the complete dismantling of German industry, thereby converting Germany into an agrarian and nonthreatening state. His plan, in its entirety, was rejected.

Mussolini, Benito (1883–1945): Fascist dictator of Italy (1922–43), and Hitler's ally. Mussolini was killed by Italian partisans in 1945.

Neuengamme: A CONCENTRATION CAMP opened northwest of Hamburg in December 1938 as a SACHSENHAUSEN satellite. Neuengamme became an independent concentration camp in June 1940. British troops liberated Neuengamme concentration camp on May 4, 1945.

Neurath, Constantin von (1873–1956): Former Minister of Foreign Affairs and former Protector of occupied Bohemia and Moravia. As a defendant at the INTERNATIONAL MILITARY TRIBUNAL, he was found guilty of conspiracy to commit and of committing crimes against peace, war crimes, and crimes against humanity, and sentenced to fifteen years in prison. He was released in 1954.

Nuremberg Trial: For the trial of 1945–46, see the INTERNATIONAL MILITARY TRIBUNAL. From 1946–49, the United States prosecuted a series of "successor" Nuremberg Trials against Nazi war criminals.

Office of Strategic Services (OSS): U.S. agency established June 13, 1942, by President ROOSEVELT for intelligence, sabotage, subversion, and research overseas, with General William J. Donovan as its head. It was the forerunner of the present-day Central Intelligence Agency.

Ohrdruf: Nazi LABOR CAMP near Gotha, Germany, established in late 1944 as a satellite camp of BUCHENWALD. Discovered quite by accident by units of the U.S. Army on April 4, 1945, Ohrdruf was the first Nazi concentration camp on German soil to be liberated by the western Allies. On April 12, 1945, U.S. Generals EISENHOWER, Bradley, and PATTON made an official visit to the camp; the horrible sights U.S troops encountered there steeled Eisenhower's determination to fully publicize Nazi atrocities.

Operation T4: The Nazi program to exterminate the institutionalized mentally and physically handicapped. Named for the address of its Berlin headquarters, Tiergartenstrasse 4, this EUTHANASIA program began in October 1939, with German and Austrian mental patients as its first victims. Protests from citizens and church circles halted T4 in August 1941; by this time at least 70,000 persons had died by gassing or lethal injection at the program's six KILLING CENTERS: Bernburg, Brandenburg, Grafeneck, Hartheim, HADAMAR, and Sonnenstein. Many members of the T4 staff subsequently provided the trained force of killers at the Nazi extermination camps in Poland.

Organization Todt: Semi-militarized construction agency established in 1933 and named for its first chief, Dr. Fritz Todt, at his death in 1942. Organization Todt provided forced labor for building the Atlantic Wall, highways, and other state-funded, military-related construction projects.

Palestine, British Mandate of: Middle Eastern territory acquired by Great Britain in World War I and commissioned ("mandated") to British authority by the League of Nations in 1920, effective in 1923. Although the British expressed support for the creation of a Jewish homeland in Palestine with the Balfour Declaration of 1917, the WHITE PAPER OF 1939 reversed that position. An increase in the number of Jewish immigrants into Palestine led to growing conflict between Jews and Arabs, both of whom opposed British control of the region. The mandate was abolished on May 15, 1948, and the territory was divided into the State of Israel and the Kingdom of Jordan.

Papen, Franz von (1879–1969): Former German Chancellor and ambassador to Vienna and Turkey. As a defendant at the INTERNATIONAL MILITARY TRIBUNAL, he was acquitted of all charges.

Partisans: Guerilla fighters against a territory's occupiers.

Patton, George S. (1885–1945): American commanding general of the U.S. Third Army in the drive across France and into Germany during 1944 and 1945. As post-war commander of the Third Army, he headed the eastern district of the U.S. occupation zone which contained many DP camps. He was later transferred to command the U.S. Fifteenth Army, a headquarters set up to interview captured German generals and prepare material for the official history of the war. He died as the result of an auto accident in December 1945.

Pehle, John: Head of the WAR REFUGEE BOARD, January 1944 to January 1945.

Pétain, Marshal Henri Philippe (1856–1951): French military leader and head of state for the VICHY government in the southern, unoccupied zone of France. Tried after the war by the HIGH COURT OF JUSTICE, Pétain was sentenced to death, but because of his advanced age the punishment was commuted to life imprisonment.

Pogrom: An organized and often officially encouraged persecution or massacre of a minority group, especially of Jews.

Pohl, Oswald (1892–1951): Member of the Nazi party after 1923, chief of the SS CENTRAL OFFICE FOR ECONOMY AND ADMINISTRATION from 1942 to 1945. At Pohl's disposal was a work force of more than 500,000 CONCENTRATION CAMP prisoners, some of whom were also "leased out" to industry. He also ensured that personal and bodily effects of the gassed Jews were reutilized by the German economy. Pohl was sentenced to death by the U.S. Military Tribunal at Nuremberg in 1947 and executed in 1951.

Potsdam Conference (July 17–August 2, 1945): A postwar conference of the "Big Three" attended by British Prime Ministers CHURCHILL and ATTLEE, U.S. President TRUMAN, Soviet Premier STALIN, and their respective foreign ministers. Held in the German city of Potsdam, some 16 miles outside Berlin, the conference confirmed initial Allied plans to demilitarize, denazify, and democratize Germany and to decentralize the existing German administration. The Potsdam Agreement, signed on August 4, provided a legal basis for U.S., British, French, and Soviet administration of occupied Germany and for the eventual restoration of a unified German state. Economic provisions of the agreement promoted the dismantling of German industrial cartels and set reparation terms, while territorial provisions ceded northern East Prussia (including Königsberg) to the Soviet Union, placed German lands east of the Oder River-Neisse River line under Polish administration pending a formal peace treaty, and provided for the expulsion of ethnic German populations from Eastern Europe.

Quisling: From the name of Vidkun Quisling, the pro-Nazi Norwegian leader, a generic, pejorative term used for a citizen of one of the conquered nations who collaborated with the Germans.

Raeder, Erich (1876–1960): Former Supreme Commander of the German Navy. As a defendant at the INTERNATIONAL MILITARY TRIBUNAL, he was found guilty of crimes against peace, war crimes, and crimes against humanity, and sentenced to life in prison. He was released in 1955 due to ill health.

Ravensbrück: CONCENTRATION CAMP for women built by male inmates from SACHSENHAUSEN during the winter of 1938–39 near Fürstenberg, north of Berlin, and opened in May 1939. Designed to hold 15,000 prisoners, Ravensbrück eventually housed more than 120,000 women from 23 nations, including political prisoners, Jews, Gypsies, and Jehovah's Witnesses. It later included a separate men's camp, a children's camp at Uckermark, and from January to April 1945 an extermination installation for women. Ravensbrück was liberated by the Soviet Army on April 30, 1945.

Red Cross, International Committee of (ICRC): Private humanitarian organization founded in 1863. Among its primary roles was the mediation between belligerents in time of war and monitoring the application of humanitarian law. During the war the Nazis often denied the Red Cross access to CONCENTRATION CAMPS and EXTERMINATION CAMPS. It was only near the end of the war that the Red Cross gained this access, when in 1944 the SS allowed a visit to THERESIENSTADT.

Reichsführer-SS ("Reich Leader of the SS"): Heinrich HIMMLER's primary title.

Reichssicherheitshauptamt (RSHA): see CENTRAL OFFICE FOR REICH SECURITY.

Repatriation: The process of returning to one's country of origin following a period of residence in a foreign country.

Resettlement: War-time German euphemism for deportation to KILLING CENTERS in Poland. After the war, the term was used to describe the solution to the problem of stateless DISPLACED PERSONS in Europe who did not want to return to their homelands. PALESTINE became the goal of much Jewish resettlement.

Ribbentrop, Joachim von: (1893–1946) German foreign minister. As a defendant at the INTERNATIONAL MILITARY TRIBUNAL, he was found guilty of conspiracy to commit and of committing crimes against peace, war crimes, and crimes against humanity, and sentenced to death by hanging.

Roosevelt, Franklin Delano (1882–1945): U.S. President from March 1933 until his death in April 1945, almost the entire period of Nazi rule in Germany.

Rosenberg, Alfred (1893–1946): Leading proponent of Nazi ideology and Minister for Occupied Eastern Territories. As a defendant at the INTERNATIONAL MILITARY TRIBUNAL, he was found guilty of conspiracy to commit and of committing crimes against peace, war crimes, and crimes against humanity, and sentenced to death by hanging.

RSHA (*Reichssicherheitshauptamt*): see CENTRAL OFFICE FOR REICH SECURITY.

Sachsenhausen: CONCENTRATION CAMP for men, opened in 1936 in Oranienburg, a suburb of Berlin, adjacent to the Inspectorate of the Concentration Camps. It held about 200,000 prisoners, 100,000 of whom perished. It was liberated by the Soviet army on April 22, 1945.

Sauckel, Fritz (1894–1946): Plenipotentiary-general for labor mobilization from 1942 to 1945. Sauckel's task was to supply the manpower for the German armaments and munitions production program. His exploitation of Jewish laborers resulted in the deaths of thousands of Jewish workers in Poland. As a defendant at the INTERNATIONAL MILITARY TRIBUNAL, he was found guilty of crimes against peace and crimes against humanity, and sentenced to death by hanging.

Schacht, Hjalmar (1877–1970): Former minister of economics and former president of the Reichsbank. As a defendant at the INTERNATIONAL MILITARY TRIBUNAL, he was acquitted of all charges.

Schirach, Baldur von (1907–74): Leader of the Hitler Youth, GAULEITER of Vienna. As a defendant at the INTERNATIONAL MILITARY TRIBUNAL, he was found guilty of crimes against humanity, and sentenced to twenty years in prison. He was released in 1966.

Schwartz, Joseph J. (1899–1975): European director of the AMERICAN JEWISH JOINT DISTRIBUTION COMMITTEE, 1940–42.

SD (*Sicherheitsdienst*): see SECURITY SERVICE.

Security Police (*Sicherheitspolizei*; *Sipo*): Nazi security police, composed of the GESTAPO and the CRIMINAL POLICE.

Security Service (*Sicherheitsdienst*, SD): The SS security and intelligence service, established in 1932 under Reinhard Heydrich and incorporated in 1939 into the SS CENTRAL OFFICE FOR REICH SECURITY.

Selection: The process of separating Jewish deportees immediately after arrival at an EXTERMINATION CAMP into those assigned to forced labor and those to be killed. The term also refers to the selection of Jews for deportation from ghettos.

Seyss-Inquart, Arthur (1892–1946): Reich Commissioner for the occupied Netherlands. As a defendant at the INTERNATIONAL MILITARY TRIBUNAL, he was found guilty of crimes against peace, war crimes, and crimes against humanity, and sentenced to death by hanging.

SHAEF: See SUPREME HEADQUARTERS ALLIED EXPEDITIONARY FORCE.

Sicherheitspolizei (*Sipo*): see SECURITY POLICE.

Sonderkommando (German for "special squad"): SS or *EINSATZGRUPPE* detachment; also refers to the Jewish forced labor units in extermination camps like Birkenau who moved the bodies of gassed prisoners for cremation, removing gold fillings and hair for recycling into the German war economy.

Speer, Albert (1905–81): Hitler's architect and later Reich Minister for Armaments (after 1942) and Reich Minister for Armaments and War Production (after 1943). Speer was responsible for forced labor allocation in the German war industry. As a defendant at the INTERNATIONAL MILITARY TRIBUNAL, he was sentenced to twenty years in prison for war crimes and crimes against humanity. He was released in 1966.

SS (*Schutzstaffel*, German for "Protection Squad"): Formed in 1925 as Hitler's personal body guard; became the elite units of the Nazi party after 1929 as Heinrich HIMMLER built the SS into a giant organization that, among other roles, provided staff for the police, camp guards, and fighting units (*WAFFEN-SS*). These paramilitary, black-shirted troops used a symbol copied from Teutonic runes, a parallel jagged double S, also used as a warning for high-tension wires or lightning.

SS Central Office for Economy and Administration (*Wirtschafts-Verwaltungshauptamt*; WVHA): Responsible for all SS economic enterprises and, after March 3, 1942, included the Inspectorate of the Concentration Camps that administered the CONCENTRATION and EXTERMINATION CAMPS.

Stalin, Joseph (1879–1953): General Secretary of the Communist Party of the Soviet Union and leader of the U.S.S.R. from 1927 to 1953.

Stern Gang: Armed underground group in PALESTINE formed by Avraham Stern (1907–42); also known as *Lohamei Herut Israel*. During World War II, the Stern Gang declared their own war against the British government and opposed any voluntary enlistment of Jews in the British Army [see JEWISH BRIGADE]. In retaliation, the British authorities actively searched out Stern Gang leaders. In 1942, they found Avraham Stern and shot him on the spot. In November 1944, the Stern Gang assassinated British Minister of State for the Middle East, Lord Moyne, in Cairo. The Stern Gang was also believed to have assassinated Count Folke BERNADOTTE, after which Israeli authorities enforced the final disbanding of the group.

Streicher, Julius (1885–1946): Owner and publisher of the antisemitic newspaper *Der Stürmer*, and former director of the Central Committee for the Defence against Jewish Atrocity and Boycott Propaganda. As a defendant at the INTERNATIONAL MILITARY TRIBUNAL, he was found guilty of crimes against humanity and sentenced to death by hanging.

Stutthof: Detention center for Polish men opened near Danzig in September 1939; became a CONCENTRATION CAMP in January 1942. Stutthof received a large number of Jewish women concentration camp prisoners deported from the Baltic, especially Riga. On May 10, 1945, Soviet troops liberated the Stutthof concentration camp.

Supreme Headquarters Allied Expeditionary Force (SHAEF): The combined Allied military force that fought in western Europe from the Normandy invasion until Germany's surrender. SHAEF did not include Soviet forces.

Szalasi, Ferenc (1897–1946): Leading figure of Nazism in Hungary. After Hungary's attempt to extricate itself from the Nazi empire on October 15, 1944, Szalasi, with support from the Germans, emerged as head of state. In power, Szalasi, a member of the secret, ultraright racist Hungarian Life League, subjected the Jews of Budapest to a reign of terror until the liberation of the city in February 1945. Szalasi fled with the retreating Nazis, was captured by the Americans, extradited to Hungary, tried, found guilty of crimes against humanity, and was executed on March 12, 1946.

Terezin: See THERESIENSTADT.

Theresienstadt (Terezin): Town in Bohemia near Prague; known as Theresienstadt before 1918, as Terezin after Czechoslovakia's creation, and renamed Theresienstadt under German occupation. The town's "Small Fortress" was a GESTAPO prison that held more than 32,000 political prisoners between 1940 and 1945. Theresienstadt was made into a GHETTO for Jewish deportees from the Protectorate of Bohemia and Moravia, Slovakia, Germany, Austria, the Netherlands, and Denmark. The SS used the ghetto to show various national and international RED CROSS investigators how well Jews were being treated. However, most Jews held there were deported and killed in the EXTERMINATION CAMPS in Poland between 1942–44. Barely 1,100 of the 15,000 children incarcerated in the ghetto survived. On May 8, 1945, the Soviet Army liberated Theresienstadt.

Third Reich: The official name of the Nazi German state. The first Reich was the Holy Roman Empire; the second was created by Otto von Bismarck and existed from 1871 to 1918. The Third Reich was proclaimed by Adolf Hitler in 1933 and lasted twelve years.

Truman, Harry S (1884–1972): United States vice-president under Franklin D. ROOSEVELT (1944–45) and, at Roosevelt's death, the 32d president (1945–53). Among the postwar problems Truman faced were the questions of Jewish DISPLACED PERSONS and the disposition of PALESTINE. Truman requested Congress to liberalize the immigration laws so that more displaced persons might enter the U.S. He also wished to see 100,000 Jewish refugees enter Palestine. But Truman was less certain regarding the establishment of a Jewish state and maintained that the United Nations was the proper agency for handling the long-range solution of the Middle East problem. When the State of Israel was proclaimed on May 14, 1948, Truman personally made certain that U.S. recognition was extended to it.

Union of Jewish Survivors: Formed on June 20, 1945, in Germany, with the goal of uniting all Jewish DISPLACED PERSONS under one organization. The union's main directive was to represent displaced persons and protect their interests.

United Jewish Appeal (UJA): U.S. organization founded in 1939 that has been the major means for providing American Jewish support for Jews overseas. Much of the money the UJA raised was used for Jews in DP camps in Europe and in the newly established state of Israel.

United Nations Relief and Rehabilitation Administration (UNRRA): Organization founded in 1943 to aid refugees and the citizens of the Allied nations in the liberated countries of Europe and the Far East. The United States held the principle executive post and was responsible for 40 percent of the agency's budget. This organization dealt with financing countries unable to provide basic commodities for their citizens as well as handling and repatriating thousands of displaced persons.

United Nations War Crimes Commission (UNWCC): Founded on December 17, 1942, by a joint declaration to punish Nazi war criminals at the war's end issued by the American, British, and Soviet governments and signed by all other Allied governments. The UNWCC investigated, recorded, and assisted in the preparation of indictments of Nazi crimes against peace and crimes against humanity, including the crime of genocide. Between 1944–48, UNWCC compiled 8,178 files relating to more than 36,000 individual criminals and criminal organizations. Due to the increasing tensions of the Cold War, various nations refused to extradite persons whom the UNWCC had listed as war criminals. In February 1948, UNWCC operations came to an end.

United States Forces, European Theater (USFET): Successor military command organization for the American component of the SUPREME HEADQUARTERS ALLIED EXPEDITIONARY FORCE, created in mid-July 1945.

UNRRA: See UNITED NATIONS RELIEF AND REHABILITATION ADMINISTRATION.

UNWCC: See UNITED NATIONS WAR CRIMES COMMISSION.

USFET: See UNITED STATES FORCES, EUROPEAN THEATER.

Ustachi (also Ustasha, Ustashi, Ustasi): Croatian fascist organization that came to power in April 1941 with the establishment of a Nazi puppet state in the Croatian region of conquered Yugoslavia. A militia formed under Ustachi auspices set out to rid Croatia of foreign elements, especially its Serbian minority. In collaboration with the Germans, they were responsible for the mass murder of Serbs, Jews, and Gypsies.

Vichy: Spa town in central France; became the capital of unoccupied France and headquarters of the pro-Nazi, nationalist regime headed by Marshal PÉTAIN. The Germans occupied Vichy France in November 1942.

Waffen-SS: Armed SS military units serving with the German armed forces.

Wallenberg, Raoul (1912–47): Swedish diplomat in Budapest who, in 1944, devoted himself to saving the Jews of occupied Europe. He organized a system of feeding and preserving the lives of Jews in the Budapest ghetto. He saved thousands by providing them with Swedish "passports of protection." In September 1944 he concealed himself to avoid the GESTAPO. After the Red Army liberated Hungary in January 1945, he made contact with Soviet authorities. On January 15, 1945, Wallenberg was called to the headquarters of Soviet army Marshal Rodion Malinovskii and disappeared without a trace. The Soviets claim he died after the war; in the 1970s, however, rumors that Wallenberg was still alive in a Soviet prison camp awoke an international movement for his release. His disappearance remains a mystery.

War Refugee Board (WRB): U.S. agency for rescuing and assisting World War II victims, established by President ROOSEVELT in January 1944, fourteen months after the U.S. had confirmed the systematic destruction of European Jewry. Under its executive director John PEHLE, the WRB's major project was the refugee camp at FORT ONTARIO, New York. The WRB's actions were limited because many U.S. government agencies lacked the desire to act.

Wehrmacht: The combined German army, navy, and air force.

Westerbork: Transit camp in northeast Holland, created by the Dutch Ministry of Interior in October 1939. Initially, Westerbork held 750 German Jews interned after arrest for illegal border crossings in 1939. From July 1942, when the Germans took command of the camp, to December 1943, more than 90 trains left Westerbork carrying 88,363 Dutch and German Jews and about 500 Dutch Gypsies to their deaths at AUSCHWITZ, Sobibor, BERGEN-BELSEN, and THERESIENSTADT. Westerbork was liberated by units of the 2d Canadian Division on April 12, 1945.

White Paper of 1939: The sixth and final policy statement on PALESTINE published by the British government between 1922–39. Stating that "His Majesty's Government now declares unequivocally that it is not part of their policy that Palestine should become a Jewish State," the British government severely restricted Jewish immigration to Palestine to 75,000 people during the subsequent five years. The announcement of the new policy coincided with the beginnings of Jewish emigration from Europe in 1939 and thus left many European Jews no escape from the imminent Holocaust.

***Wirtschafts- und Verwaltungshauptamt* (WVHA)**: see SS CENTRAL OFFICE FOR ECONOMY AND ADMINISTRATION.

Wise, Stephen S. (1874–1949): Noted Reform Jewish Rabbi based in New York and ZIONIST leader; founder and President of the AMERICAN JEWISH CONGRESS in 1920 and WORLD JEWISH CONGRESS in 1936. Wise led the effort to alert the American public to the German mass murders and to appeal to the U.S. and Allied governments for action to stop the killings.

Wöbbelin: A satellite camp of NEUENGAMME near Ludwigslust, Germany, that served as a LABOR CAMP and transit facility for prisoners evacuated from Nazi CONCENTRATION CAMPS threatened by the Allied advance. Units of the U.S. Army liberated the camp on May 2, 1945.

World Jewish Congress (WJC): A congress of representatives from Jewish communities worldwide formed to foster and ensure the survival and unity of Jewish peoples throughout the world, including defending the rights and interests of Jews, assisting the development of Jewish social and cultural life, and representing the Jewish people as a whole before governmental and international authorities. The WJC played an important role in the Jewish policies towards the trials of Nazi war criminals and reparations for Jewish victims of the Holocaust.

World Zionist Congress (WZC): Formed in 1897 to work primarily for the establishment of a Jewish state in Israel. The WZC was a staunch opponent of the British WHITE PAPER OF 1939. The WZC did not convene between 1939 and 1946.

WVHA (*Wirtschafts- und Verwaltungshauptamt*): see SS CENTRAL OFFICE FOR ECONOMY AND ADMINISTRATION.

Yalta Conference (February 4–12, 1945): A "Big Three" conference in the Crimea attended by U.S. President ROOSEVELT, British Prime Minister CHURCHILL, and Soviet Marshal STALIN. The conference reaffirmed the Allied policy of unconditional surrender in Germany, and planned the postwar occupation of Germany by the four major Allied powers, which now included France. The leaders also discussed the postwar "denazification" of Germany and procedures for the prosecution of German war criminals. Plans for the San Francisco Conference, which would establish the United Nations, were made as well.

Yellow Star: See Badge, Jewish.

Zeilsheim: A Nazi-built housing project for industrial workers within the city of Wiesbaden, near Frankfurt am Main, Germany. In the fall of 1945, Zeilsheim was taken over for use as a DISPLACED PERSONS camp for Jews liberated from the CONCENTRATION CAMPS. Because this camp was near the military headquarters in Frankfurt, it was visited often by newspaper correspondents, dignitaries, and military inspectors. Zeilsheim DP camp was closed in fall 1948.

Zhukov, Georgi Konstantinovich (1896–1974): Russian general and marshal of the Soviet Union who played an important part in the overall strategy of the war and in the U.S.S.R.'s repelling of the German offensive. He was personally involved in the defense of Leningrad and Moscow, the battles of Stalingrad and Kursk, and the Soviet capture of Berlin, where on May 8, 1945, he signed the document that formally concluded the war.

Ziereis, Franz (1905–45): Commandant of the MAUTHAUSEN concentration camp from August 1939 until its liberation in May 1945. A captain in the German Army when appointed commandant, he was promoted in 1941 to major, in 1943 to lieutenant colonel, and in 1944 to colonel. After the camp was liberated by U.S. troops, Ziereis hid in the camp but was shot several days later by a U.S. patrol when he tried to escape.

Zionism: Political and cultural movement calling for the return of the Jewish people to its Biblical home.

Zionist Organization of America (ZOA): U.S. organization of General Zionists formed in 1918 from a merger of various Zionist groups.

Zyklon B: Hydrogen cyanide, a pesticide used in crystalline form in the GAS CHAMBERS at the KILLING CENTERS of AUSCHWITZ and MAJDANEK.

BIBLIOGRAPHY

English Language Sources

Bauer, Yehuda. *Flight and Rescue: Brichah*. New York: Random House, 1970.

Berben, Paul. *Dachau 1933–45: The Official History.* London: Comité International de Dachau, 1968.

Bethel, Nicholas. *The Last Secret.* New York: Basic Books, 1974.

Braham, Randolph. *The Hungarian Labor Service System.* Boulder: East European Quarterly, 1977.

———. *The Politics of Genocide: The Holocaust in Hungary.* New York: Columbia University Press, 1981.

Cantril, Hadley. *Public Opinion.* Princeton: Princeton University Press, 1951

Cohen, Michael. *Palestine to Israel: From Mandate to Independence.* London: Frank Cass, 1988.

Czech, Danuta. *The Auschwitz Chronicles 1939–1945.* New York: Henry Holt & Co., 1990.

Dinnerstein, Leonard. *America and the Survivors of the Holocaust.* New York: Columbia University Press, 1982.

Draper, Paula, and Harold Troper, eds. *National Archives of Canada, Ottawa and Canadian Jewish Congress Archives*, Montreal. Vol. 15 of *Archives of the Holocaust.* Edited by Sybil Milton and Henry Friedlander, New York: Garland Publishing, 1991.

Dunin-Wasowicz, Krzysztof. *Resistance in the Nazi Concentration Camps, 1939–1945.* Warsaw: PWN-Polish Scientific Publishers, 1982.

Fargion, Liliana Picciotto. "The Anti-Jewish Policy of the Italian Social Republic, 1943–1945." *Yad Vashem Studies* 17 (1986).

Hadari, Ze'ev. *Second Exodus: The Full Story of Jewish Illegal Immigration to Palestine, 1945–1948.* London: Vallentine Mitchell, 1991.

Heberer, Patricia. "'If I Transgress My Oath': The Story of the 1945 Hadamar Trial." Master's thesis, University of Southern Illinois, 1989.

Helmreich, Ernst Christian. *The German Churches under Hitler: Background, Struggle, and Epilogue.* Detroit: Wayne State University Press, 1979.

Ilan, Amitzur, *Bernadotte in Palestine, 1948.* New York: St. Martin's Press, 1989.

International Military Tribunal. *Trial of the Major War Criminals Before the International Military Tribunal, Nuremberg, 14 November 1945–1 October 1946.* 42 vols. Nuremberg: International Military Tribunal, 1947–49.

Lottman, Herbert. *The Purge.* New York: Wm. Morrow and Co., Inc., 1986.

Maser, Werner, *Nuremberg: A Nation on Trial.* London: Allen Lane, 1979.

Middlebrook, Martin, and Chris Everitt. *The Bomber Command War Diaries.* London: Penguin, 1990.

Nadich, Judah. *Eisenhower and the Jews.* New York: Twayne Publishers, 1953.

Neave, Airey. *Nuremberg.* London: Grafton Books, 1989.

Peterson, Edward. *The American Occupation of Germany: Retreat to Victory.* Detroit: Wayne State University Press, 1977.

Podet, Allen H. *The Success and Failure of the Anglo-American Committee of Inquiry 1945–46.* Lewiston, NY: Edwin Mellon Press, 1986.

"Report to the President from Justice Robert H. Jackson, Chief of Counsel for the United States in the Prosecution of Axis War Criminals, June 7, 1945." *American Journal of International Law Supplement* 39 (1945): 178–90.

Rioux, Jean-Pierre. *The Fourth Republic.* Cambridge: Cambridge University Press, 1987.

Schwarberg, Guenther, *The Murders at Bullenhuser Damm: The SS Doctor and the Children.* Bloomington: Indiana University Press, 1984.

Smith, Bradley F. *Reaching Judgment at Nuremberg.* New York: Basic Books, 1977.

Stamps, T. Dodson, and Vincent J. Esposito, eds. *A Military History of World War II.* 2 vols. with atlas. West Point, NY: U.S. Military Academy, 1953.

Stanislav, Jan, and Micev Stanislav. "The Anti-Jewish Reprisals in Slovakia from September 1944 to April 1945." In *The Tragedy of Slovak Jews.* Edited by Dezider Toth. Banska Bystrica: Datei, 1992.

Phillips, Raymond, ed. *Trial of Josef Kramer and Forty-four Others (The Belsen Trial).* London: William Hodge and Co., Ltd., 1949.

Tusa, Ann, and John Tusa. *The Nuremberg Trial.* New York: Atheneum, 1984.

United Nations Relief and Rehabilitation Administration, Central Tracing Bureau, Documents Intelligence. *Death Marches.* 3 vols. Washington, DC: UNRRA, 1946.

United Nations War Crimes Commisssion. *History of the United Nations War Crimes Commission and the Development of the Laws of War.* London: H. M. Stationery Office, 1948.

Vilenskii, M. E., comp. *War Behind Barbed Wire: Reminiscences of Buchenwald Ex-prisoners of War.* Moscow: Foreign Languages Publishing House, 1959.

Wasserstein, Bernard. *Britain and the Jews of Europe, 1939–1945.* Oxford: Clarendon Press, 1979.

Woodbridge, George. *UNRRA: The History of the United Nations Relief and Rehabilitation Administration.* New York: Columbia University Press, 1950.

Wyman, David, ed. *War Refugee Board "Weekly Reports"*. Vol. 11 of *America and the Holocaust*. New York: Garland, 1989.

Ziemke, Earl F. *The U.S. Army in the Occupation of Germany, 1944–1946*. Washington, DC: Center of Military History, U.S. Army, 1975.

Foreign Language Sources

Aly, Götz. *Aktion T4, 1939–1945: Die "Euthanasie"-Zentrale in der Tiergartenstrasse 4*. Berlin: Hentrich, 1987.

Amicale de Neuengamme. *Le Camp de concentration de Neuengamme et ses Kommandos Exterieurs*. Paris: Amicale de Neuengamme, 1967.

Benz, Wolfgang, ed. *Dimension des Völkermords: Die Zahl der jüdischen Opfer des Nationalsozialismus*. Munich: Oldenbourg, 1991.

Bernadac, Christian. *Les 186 Marches*. Paris: Editions France Empire, 1974.

———. *Les Mannequins Nus*. 3 vols. Paris: Editions France-Empire, 1971–73.

———. *L'Holocauste Oublié: Le massacre des tsiganes*. Paris: Editions France-Empire, 1979.

———. *Le Neuvième Cercle*. Paris: Editions France-Empire, 1975.

Internationales Buchenwald-Komitee. *Buchenwald: Mahnung und Verpflichtung, Dokumente und Berichte*. 4th, expanded ed. Berlin: VEB Deutscher Verlag der Wissenschaften, 1983.

Chládková, Ludmilla. *Ghetto Theresienstadt*. Terezin: Verlag Nase Vojsko, 1991.

Choumoff, Pierre S. *Les Chambres à gaz de Mauthausen*. Paris: Amicale des Deportées de Mauthausen, 1972.

Denzler, Georg and Volker Fabricius, ed. *Die Kirchen im Dritten Reich*. Vol. 2, *Dokumente*. Frankfurt am Main: Fischer Taschenbuch Verlag, 1984.

Finn, Gerhard. *Sachsenhausen, 1936–1950: Geschichte eines Lagers*. Berlin: Westkreuz Verlag, 1988.

Fonteneau, Homère. *Le Long Chemin: Buchenwald, Maidanek, Auschwitz, Mauthausen*. Baignes, Cahrente: Imprimerie Poly-Imprim, 1979.

International Tracing Service. *Verzeichnis der Haftstätten unter dem Reichsführer SS (1933–1945)*. Arolsen: Der Suchdienst, 1979.

Miletic, Antun. *Koncentracioni Logor Jasenovac 1941–1945: Dokumenta*. 2 vols. Belgrade: Narodna Knijiga, 1986.

Mazaleyrat, Maurice. *Flossenbürg: Arbeit Macht Frei*. Brive: Chastrusse and Sons, 1984.

Sachsenhausen: Dokumente, Aussagen, Forschungsergebnisse und Erlebnisberichte über das ehemalige Konzentrationslager Sachsenhausen. 3d, expanded ed. Berlin: VEB Deutscher Verlag der Wissenschaften, 1981.

Velikaia Otechestvennaia Voina 1941–1945: Sobytiia, Liudi, Dokumenty. Moscow: Izdatel'stvo politicheskoi literatury, 1990.

Walk, Joseph, ed. *Das Sonderrecht für die Juden im NS-Staat: Eine Sammlung der gesetzlichen Massnahmen und Richtlinien, Inhalt und Bedeutung*. Heidelberg and Karlsruhe: Müller Juristischer Verlag, 1981.

Weinmann, Martin. *Das nationalsozialistische Lagersystem*. Frankfurt am Main: Zweitausendeins, 1990.

Wetzel, Juliane. "Die Polizeidurchgangslager Bozen." *Dachauer Hefte* 5 (1989).

Zörner, G., and others, ed. *Frauen-KZ Ravensbrück*. Berlin: VEB Deutscher Verlag der Wissenschaften, 1986.

Periodicals from 1945

Office of Military Government, U.S. Forces European Theater, Reports and Information Branch, *Weekly Information Bulletin,* 1945.

Rescue: Information Bulletin of the Hebrew Sheltering and Immigration Aid Society.

United Nations Relief and Rehabilitation Administration. *Monthly Review*. Washington, DC: UNRRA, 1945.

———. *Report of the Director General to the Council*. Washington, DC: UNRRA, 1945.

———. *Review of the Month*. London: UNRRA Information Division, European Regional Office, 1945.

Newspapers from 1945

News of Germany.

New York Times.

PM Daily.